UTOPIAN EPISODES

Utopianism and Communitarianism

UTOPIAN EPISODES

Daily Life *in* Experimental Colonies Dedicated *to* Changing *the* World

SEYMOUR R. KESTEN

SYRACUSE UNIVERSITY PRESS

First Edition 1993
93 94 95 96 97 98 99 6 5 4 3 2 1

The publication of this book was assisted by a generous grant from the William Fleming Educational Fund.

The paper used in this publication meets the minimum requirements of American National Standard for Information Sciences – Permanence of Paper for Printed Library Materials, ANSI Z39.48-1984. ∞™

Library of Congress Cataloging-in-Publication Data

Kesten, Seymour R.
Utopian episodes : daily life in experimental colonies dedicated to changing the world / Seymour R. Kesten.
p. cm. – (Utopianism and communitarianism)
Includes bibliographical references and index.
ISBN 0-8156-2593-6
1. Collective settlements – United States. I. Title. II. Series.
HX654.K46 1993
335'.12 – dc20 92-40186

Manufactured in the United States of America

I dedicate this book to my beloved wife,

Rose Edith Kesten.

Her advice, devotion, and sacrifices made it possible.

SEYMOUR R. KESTEN teaches undergraduate humanities, a field devoted to the accomplishments of the human spirit. A humanist in the everyday sense of the word, that is, someone concerned with people – how they live, what they do, and what they believe – his writing evolves in terms of the human condition. Dr. Kesten and his wife, Rose, make their home in Philadelphia, Pennsylvania.

Contents

Illustrations

TABLE

Acknowledgments

FIRST AND FOREMOST, I want to acknowledge the assistance of my wife, Rose, whose suggestions were indispensable at every step of this study. I want to thank my son Philip for creating a series of computer programs – in the days before off-the-shelf software – that made it possible for me to organize and keep track of the large number of diverse items of research from a wide variety of sources. My son Randy offered many invaluable and thoughtful recommendations, particularly on political theories, which helped me through some controversial thickets.

I want to express my gratitude to Professor David Tatham and to Professor Michael Barkun of Syracuse University for their valuable advice and criticisms. The librarians at the Ernest Stevenson Bird Library and the George Arents Research Library of Syracuse University were tireless helpers in virtually every aspect of my research, and I depended heavily on them. To mention a few names would be to slight many. To all of them I extend my most heartfelt thanks.

Many archivists helped make research easier and more productive, and I especially want to acknowledge the assistance of Jo Anne Pugh of Bentley Historical Library, University of Michigan; Mrs. N. Greene, Phyllis McLoughlin, and Virginia Dochterman of the State Historical Society of Iowa; F. Gerald Ham, Josephine Harper, Mrs. Joanne Hohler, and Katherine Thompson at the State Historical Society of Wisconsin; Mrs. Leona Alig and Miss Caroline Dunn of the Indiana Historical Society Library; Paul D. Spence and Roger Bridges, of the Illinois State Historical Library; Robert M. Sutton and Dennis F. Walle of the Illinois Historical Survey, University of Illinois; Robert Allison and Alice Eysenbach at the Joseph Regenstein Library, University of Chicago; Kent Keeth at the Texas Historical Collection, Baylor University; Mrs. J. Macdonald at the Indiana State Library in Indianapolis; Frank Paluka, University of Iowa Library; and David A. Randall and Miss H. Mauck at the Lily Library, Indiana University.

I also want to thank the fine staff at the Massachusetts Historical Society in Boston, not only for their help with their remarkable collection of manuscripts, but also for allowing me to examine in detail the painting of Brook Farm attributed to Josiah Wolcott. For their many courtesies and assistance with their collections, I want to thank the staff at Houghton Library, Harvard University; Seymour Library at Knox College, Galesburg, Illinois; Beinecke Library at Yale University; Olin Library at Cornell University; and Mrs. L. Mitchell of Brown University Library.

I express my appreciation to the following libraries for their courtesy in letting me use their collections of manuscripts and rare books: New York Public Library, Rochester Public Library, the Newberry Library, Chicago; Perth Amboy Public Library; and Boston Public Library. In addition, I want to thank the following historical societies for their many kindnesses: New Jersey Historical Society; Monmouth County Historical Association, Freehold, New Jersey; and Suffolk County Historical Society, Riverhead, New York.

Seymour R. Kesten

Philadelphia
October 1992

UTOPIAN EPISODES

Ivory-tower revolutionists dreamed up fantastic palaces for life in their ideal worlds . . .

1. "La Théorie sociétaire de Ch. Fourier," a lithograph by Charles Daubigny, Paris, ca. 1844. By permission of the Houghton Library, Harvard University.

. . . but real life reduced palaces to farmhouses, and even farmhouses to rude cabins.

2. Cabin drawn in pen and ink by a member of the ill-fated Community of Equality, Thomas Steel. By permission of the State Historical Society of Wisconsin.

Introduction

IN THE NINETEENTH CENTURY tens of thousands of Americans took a negative view of what they saw around them: an evil world. Then they took a positive step in response to its evils. They left traditional society and set out for a colony in an isolated area where they hoped to insulate themselves from its corrupt values. Even today countless people look for that same road, and as we know from stories that sometimes make headlines, some still travel down it.

Not all who chose that route in the last century responded to the same call. For most of them the sad state of the human condition provided the spur. They turned away in disgust from the values that had developed in society, the prevailing morality, the actions of pitiless fellow beings, and said the equivalent of "there's got to be a better way." They believed they could find a better way in a new kind of society that offered an alternative to the American mainstream.

Well over one hundred colonies based on such alternatives – life off the beaten path – appeared in the United States from the 1820s to late in the century. In each case the founders tried to create a little realm where they could control living conditions to perfection and so avoid the evils of a world run amok beyond their fences. They believed they could carve out a haven where life would be ideal – as they conceived of the ideal – for the goals they had in mind. In this sense all of these colonies, regardless of their differing beliefs and goals, can be described as utopian.

Within this host of little ideal worlds that once dotted our country's map, colony longevity varied widely. Some colonies lasted more than a century, but the vast majority survived only a short time, from a few months in the extreme cases to a handful of years in the typical. That aspect has occupied the attention of all writers on the subject. Most try to associate a group's lengthy existence with religion, maintaining that only "the glue of religion" could hold together such unconventional ways of living. In fact, you can usually find the long-lived utopian colonies listed in books about the subject under the heading "Religious Communities." Of course, that leaves a vague implication about the others, the short-lived variety, that has fostered a simplistic dismissal of their efforts.

However, if we take the pulse of those "others," if we listen to the words of their people and look into their souls, we find a unique aspect in our national experience too significant to be left moldering in dusty archives. First of all, we discover human endeavors eminently broader and more complex than can be covered by a simple explanation for their short life. Surprisingly, as we begin to appreciate their aspirations we understand our own better. Second, the utopian impulse that drove those efforts has continued to churn below the surface of our society like an undercurrent, and it tugs at feet even in our own troubled times. So these episodes have more than a passing, historical interest. Their story has a peculiar gift for illuminating the blessings and blunders of our century. And today's events share that knack in mirroring the blue skies and blind alleys of these episodes.

But to make sense out of the strange mixture of beliefs and goals that characterize the utopian episodes of America, we need to probe deeper than surface appearances. Since all of those groups, long or short-lived, represent a response to evil, we can gain a better understanding by asking some pointed questions of them through their documents and records: What is evil? What do you plan to do about evil? and What is your ultimate goal? In the answers, two major categories of utopians emerge.

In one category we find people who looked on sin as the great evil. They acted against it by founding colonies free from the temptations of the world, ideal places to work out the salvation of their souls. Their goal: eternal happiness in heaven. Two of the best-known groups in this category are the Shakers and Iowa's Amana colonies.

The other major category, the larger one, consists of groups who found evil in poverty, ignorance, and inequality. They saw these conditions as the inevitable products of our social system, which they called inherently defective. Its flaws led to exploitation, crime, war, alienation, and the degradation of the human spirit. As evidence of the failure of our social system, they pointed to the general unhappiness of humanity. Their plan of action: eradicate evil forever by completely reorganizing the social system. Their goal: happiness in this world.

So they too established utopian colonies. They tried to create little, ideal social systems where people could live free from the stress and corruption of the traditional society they saw as defective. Their new way of life, they believed, could satisfy all human needs through moderate, dignified work, and could allow everyone to enjoy the fruits of brotherhood and peace. They had a dream: the quality of life would be so excellent in their colonies that soon all the world would admire them and would rush to copy them. Two well-known groups in this category are New-Harmony in Indiana and Brook Farm in Massachusetts.

The distinctions between the two major categories stand out clearly. Those in the first sought eternal joy in the next world. To achieve that, each individual in the group had to work to save his or her own soul. I refer to these groups as the colonies of *individual salvation.* Those in the second wanted to secure universal happiness in this world. To do that they had to collectively reorganize society. I call their efforts the movement for *social reorganization.*

The colonies dedicated to individual salvation are the ones that histories have labeled *religious.* Religion played an important role in the colonies of social reorganization too, as we shall see, but with a key distinction. The colonies of individual salvation permitted only one religion. There church and state were one, and it controlled every thought and action of every individual. On the other hand, the colonies of social reorganization, with one exception, held to a basic tenet of democracy: separation of church and state. People in such colonies could follow the religious practices of their choice under the same guarantee of rights that all other Americans enjoyed.

Establishing environments for individual salvation where people could live so as to gain entrance to heaven was hardly new. In fact, monastic ideas of celibacy, self-denial, fencing off sin, rejecting worldly pleasures and the temptations of the flesh: these all go back into the shadows of the distant past. Such constraints governed life for the Amana people, the Shakers, and other colonies concerned with individual salvation.

But the nineteenth-century flowering of cooperative colonies organized for the express purpose of enhancing the quality of life for everyone here on earth through abundance, education, equality, and culture: that indeed was something new. Their mere presence in an era drifting toward insensitive materialism raised issues that elevated the humanistic spirit. And on the broad stream of democratic concepts that carried our nation forward, they set afloat some worthy ideas. Quietly, these ideas converged with values we now recognize as standards of a caring society. It is on these groups, the movement for social reorganization, that this book focuses.

Although this movement encompasses a variety of doctrines and tactics, all of its colonies had the same revolutionary idea in mind: eradicating our social system and establishing another based on different principles. As a revolutionary movement, however, it must be distinguished from others whose specters have haunted Europe and the rest of the world in the past 150 years. Unlike them, groups in the movement for social reorganization held no concepts of class antagonism, never considered seizing the means of production, and rejected violence of any kind. Their programs grew out of what they thought it would take to make people happy and went far beyond basic calls for bread and land. These gentle revolutionaries rested their hopes entirely on two assumptions: their radically new social systems would work; and sooner or later all the world, having seen the light, would democratically discard the old and adopt the new way of life.

The promise and potential of these colonies generate many questions: What can we learn from their experience that applies to our age? Did they make life better for their members? Did they bring them happiness, and if so, how? Where did pleasure stand in their values? Did they achieve equality? What can we tell about them from the books they read, the music they favored, the words they wrote? And finally, Why did they fall so quickly into the abyss of obscure footnotes?

Indeed, given their promise to make everyone's life better, why should they have fallen at all? That question defies simple answers. As we shall see, they fell not from a single fault but from the proverbial straw. The straws accumulated from minor details of life, from what people in the movement did and what they said. Those seemingly small points often combined in situations laced with irony, usually of the tragic type.

The movement for social reorganization went beyond idle speculation about ideal social systems, and in trying to satisfy hungers that asked for much more than our daily bread, it encompassed the widest spectrum of human aspirations. In a particularly egregious misreading of this phenomenon, one writer on the subject compiled a summary table with columns for the vital statistics on each group: dates, location, and membership. The table also includes an absurd column that attempts to explain in four words or fewer the reason each group ended, as if the deepest yearnings of the soul could be reduced to the terse efficiency of an Einstein formula.

A few studies mistakenly see this movement primarily through the narrow lens of either economics or politics. But its story cannot be grasped in those terms. Most people in its colonies opted for life under a new social system not as an end in itself – few understood the abstruse concepts – but because it promised them a means to an end: human happiness. We cannot evaluate the achievement of that goal by examining their economy. As many in our century have learned to their regret, happiness does not equate with production records. But it can be perceived through culture. Approaching this movement as the abstract working out of economic or political theory, rather than as the comprehensible efforts of human beings who think and feel, yields a warped impression of the past rather than a better understanding of it.

Real people created the colonies of social reorganization. Ordinary individuals of their time, they left no markers in history's graveyard. A few did become famous later, but most were unknown outside their small circle. Indeed, what impressed me early on in this research was the major role such people played in shaping these colonies, and the minor role of theoretical speculations and famous leaders. The most prolific mentor of the movement, Charles Fourier, whose detailed utopian schemes fill many dense volumes and whose name inspired most of the colonies of social reorganization, gets top billing in virtually every book about the subject. Yet, in reality, barely a wavelet from his sea of words washed the foundations that people, long since forgotten, chose for building those very colonies. You will meet many of those people in this book, and meeting them by name helps establish each one as a real human being. Their humanity makes it easier to understand what they did – and what they could not do. Appendix A has short notes about a few of the frequently mentioned names, and the Index also helps identify some.

To understand the utopian episodes, we need to visualize them through the eyes and souls of those individuals. Their world comes alive for us through their letters and other documents, through the words they published about their efforts, and through the observations of their friends – and their enemies. To the extent possible, I built this book around that material.

History has tended to focus on the foibles and stupidities of these utopians. But the story of this movement cries out for a more balanced account. As we shall see, its people were neither heroes nor great thinkers. Yet they had admirable courage: they sacrificed and lived through terrible hardships with the conviction that what they did would help you and me and the rest of the world. But in the end, that world salted their wounds with ridicule and then ignored the positive contributions they made to their time and to ours. Their story runs the human gamut: from people of principle and surprising achievements to fools, false prophets, and not-so-surprising tragedies. A fair appraisal, this book covers both sides of the ledger, the credits as well as the debits.

1

The Who, What, When, and Where of the Utopian Episodes

THIS BOOK IS NOT A TREATISE on utopian philosophy nor an economic or political history. It deals with the way people lived in the colonies of social reorganization and with what came out of their experiences. But the movement to reorganize society is hardly known today, and its goals are poorly understood. Therefore, before getting to the heart of the subject, it would be helpful to look at some background information and put some of the strange names and concepts into perspective. This chapter briefly surveys the basic ideas of the movement, the people who promoted those ideas, and the groups associated with them. The following sections are arranged so that you can refer back to this information later, as you wish.

The movement waxed and waned through three phases. It began in the 1820s, then a new phase peaked in the mid-1840s, another strain came on in the 1850s, and the movement faded away in the post–Civil War decades. During that span nearly one hundred of its colonies rose and fell.

Unfortunately, we have little information about most of them for the following reason. These groups set off on the utopian road with great hope and faith. But most ran into a dead end so quickly that it crushed dreams and left members frustrated and bitter. In that mood we would hardly expect them to think about preserving records and other documents for us, and few did. That creates blank spots in almost every case. Developing a clear idea of how people live requires details on many aspects. Memoirs and other first-hand accounts—when they pass the test of reliability—do help fill gaps. But few mention items we need to know about in order to assess the state of the human spirit: books, pictures, songs, and musical instruments. Perhaps their existence seemed self-evident, or people took them for granted. Compounding the problem, only a few such artifacts survive.

However, enough documents and records remain from about a dozen groups to piece together a picture of life in their colonies. A more bountiful supply of information exists for New-Harmony, established in Indiana in 1825; Brook Farm, near Boston, 1841; and Icaria [ee CARRY uh], in Illinois (later in Iowa), 1849. Because each of these three exemplifies a different phase of social reorganization and each has attributes that elucidate main trends in the movement, they yield insights into what took place elsewhere. Through them the links that join all into a single, significant phenomenon become clear. For these reasons, I made these three colonies the principal focus of this book. To help fill in the gaps, I have taken additional illustrations from several others, listed later in the chapter.

The Mentors of Social Reorganization

Most groups identified themselves with some particular set of utopian ideas. But in fact, these speculations – the word *theory* implies more science than they had – had little to do with the reality of life in their colonies. Most of the ideas, notably in the case of Charles Fourier, could almost be ignored without detracting from their stories. Still, most groups made a point of claiming to the world the strength and virtues of the plans worked out by their mentors. The vast gulf between those claims and what members actually knew stands out as one of the great ironies of the utopian episodes. Even a glance at the ideas of social reorganization's mentors makes that disparity clear each time it surfaces.

Three utopians developed a significant number of adherents in the United States during the first half of the last century: Robert Owen, Charles Fourier, and Etienne Cabet. Each inspired one of the three exemplary colonies listed here, and each fueled a principal phase of the movement. The Owenite phase came in the 1820s, and the Fourierist dominated the 1840s. Cabet's group peaked in the 1850s, and his followers in Iowa hung on until the 1890s, by which time the movement had long since flickered out except in the dim memories of a few old-timers.

ROBERT OWEN

A soft-spoken textile manufacturer, Robert Owen stepped across the threshold of the nineteenth century at thirty years of age and showed the world the possibilities of enlightened capitalism. At his mill in Scotland he provided his workers with good working conditions and benefits unheard-of in that era, including free schools for their children. During the following decade, wealthy and in his forties, he became an activist in behalf of England's poor and unemployed. He tried to get the government to set up agricultural cooperatives where these forgotten by-products of a cruelly competitive society could work and support themselves. That experience led Owen to the idea of founding a model colony, where he intended to prove that through education the evils of poverty and immorality could be eradicated forever. In his fifties, he took his wealth and ideas to Indiana and used them to found and sustain New-Harmony as a first step in reorganizing society. After the demise of that attempt he returned to England and became active in the emerging trade union movement.

Owen's utopian speculation flowed from his belief that people do not form their own characters; their characters are formed for them by the society in which they live. From this he concluded that human character can be better or worse depending on the character of society. Therefore, society should be organized so as to make people good.

Owen said society could make people better by, for example, providing work for everyone. In that way people would not need to compete against each other just to eat. With everyone working, antagonisms and conditions that foster crime would disappear.

Education, in Owen's scheme, was the key to a better society. Because humans can change, education could transform all people into hard-working, moral citizens. To be effective, Owenite education had to be carried out in a special way. Children had to start school as infants so that teachers could mold them into adults devoted to the *New Social System.* Schools had to be pleasant places without punishments, and there children would learn only practical things. Owenite teachers would inculcate emotional restraint and thereby eradicate individualism, the great enemy of the New Social System.

Owen's economics originally had capital and labor sharing in the fruits of production. In New-Harmony he completely reversed himself and denounced private property as a great evil. However, on one axiom he never varied: everything in society can be evaluated as good or bad according to its social utility.

CHARLES FOURIER

Unlike Owen, his contemporary, and unlike the younger Etienne Cabet, Charles Fourier remained aloof from the rough and tumble of politics and social strife except as a youth during the French Revolution. A solitary man known only to a handful of disciples, he died a few years before Americans began to take any notice of his ideas.

His works fill twelve hefty volumes and cover utopian life in minute detail. Hardly easy reading, his obscure ideas carry the added burden of lengthy arguments piled on to make each point. He mixed some noteworthy insights about the human condition with naïve solutions to complex problems and bizarre observations about the universe. While the latter can be dismissed as the ravings of a crackpot, his severe criticisms of social values, especially with respect to the status of women, and his assumptions about the psychology of work and the workplace can stand up under scrutiny.

Fourier classified human progress as a series of stages beginning with *Chaos,* then *Savagery.* Eventually it will reach *Harmony,* the highest stage. According to his scheme we now live in an intermediate stage he called *Civilization,* a term that fell from the lips of his followers with sneers of contempt. His speculations cover such a wide range that it is easy to oversimplify them in any summary.

Fourier's key axiom holds that pleasure and happiness are the supreme motivators. Nature, he said, gives each individual a complex of various sensitivities, or *passions,* and differing combinations of these passions determine an individual's personality type. There are many types, and each naturally finds certain kinds of work attractive. Doing work we find attractive leads to happiness, while unhappiness comes from doing work that is inharmonious with our personalities. Thus, a society that forces people to go against their natural instincts – that creates unhappiness – is evil.

But even attractive work can become boring, and boredom leads to faulty products. So people need to shift frequently from one appealing task to another, just as the butterfly (*le papillon*) does. A society that allows people to work according to this *papillon* concept would be much more efficient, could produce enough for everyone in less time, could end hunger, and could provide for the culture to bring happiness to newly found leisure hours.

Fourier's speculations about psychology made personality inherent. Thus, in effect, he believed that – as people now often say – "you can't change human nature." With that conviction as a basis, a good social system does not attempt to mold character. But it does provide a way to encourage natural instincts toward a positive goal, and that benefits everyone. Happy people do better work and produce more. Fourier imagined that even capitalists, who must cope with the stress of the competitive system daily, would be happier in the new system.

Fourier's view of society includes two crucial principles: nothing in society exists in a vacuum – all parts and all activities are organically linked in "Universal Unity" – and the extension of women's rights is a mark of social progress.

Association was Fourier's term for the advanced stages of society. Its basic unit, the *Phalanx,* requires about sixteen hundred people, and they must be carefully selected to balance personality types. Having the right people assures high productivity, and the right mix of personalities creates harmony. A Phalanx must have a variety of talents to create the musical and other cultural events that are absolutely essential to life.

Phalanx people live, work, and enjoy recreation and culture all under one roof in a huge building called the *Phalanstery* (see illustration 1, p. 2). An underground transportation system moves people quickly to distant locations within it, a necessity in a society where everyone, free as *le papillon,* switches to other work when a task becomes boring. The building's wings enclose an open, central area with gardens, fountains, and plazas large enough for parades and mass festivities. Outside the Phalanstery walls, farms and orchards recede into the distance. Owen had a similar but less elaborate utopian palace in mind for New-Harmony and showed a model to Congress in 1825.

Fourier's influence is deceptive. His name served as an impetus for most of the movement's colonies as disciples spread the word *Fourier* across the land in the 1840s. Yet, during the gush of enthusiasm that followed, few Americans who identified with him actually knew much about his ideas. Since none of his words had been translated, aside from some brief newspaper excerpts, what they did know came from propaganda. This material watered down his grandiose plan and tended to emphasize only economics. All of it carefully side-stepped his ideas on sexuality and sexual relations, topics that would have scandalized prudish Americans had they gotten wind of such things. By the time any of those ideas became known in the United States, the country had already lost interest in Fourier. Even today, his complete works remain closed to those who read only English.

ETIENNE CABET

Unlike placid Owen and reclusive Fourier, his seniors by a generation, Etienne Cabet developed and honed his ideas on the barricades. He took an active role in the 1830 revolution in France and won a seat in the Chamber of Deputies. A staunch, uncompromising ideologue, he soon found himself exiled and later threatened with death by counterrevolutionaries. In England he threw himself into the growing labor movement and its strikes. There he picked up ideas from Owen's union activities and, more significantly, read and was deeply influenced by Thomas More's *Utopia.*

Cabet's basic ideas can be found in his most important book, *Voyage en Icarie* (Voyage to Icaria), a novel that leans heavily on More's classic. In it Cabet tells the story of Icaria, a fictional land with an ideal society, and in effect we see his vision of life after social reorganization. He proceeds from the premise that humans are born good, but an evil society and its inequality corrupt them. Humans are perfectible, however, and Icaria, the land of his imagination, has made them perfect through education. Icaria reached its final form after a fifty-year transition. That period allowed for a gradual introduction of the new social system to everyone's benefit and no one's detriment.

Absolute equality is the fundamental rule in Icaria, and every aspect of society flows from it. Women are equal to men, and everyone gets the same education. To avoid hints of past inequality all men dress alike, and women do likewise.

In Cabet's economic system private property is abolished because the greed and other evils it brings lead to inequality. Everyone must be productively employed, and everyone must take a turn serving the demands of farm and industry. All receive as much as they need of whatever society produces. So effectively, all get equal remuneration regardless of work.

Cabet's political system gives everyone an equal vote. But, of course, everyone naturally agrees on what is best for Icaria, so factions and parties do not exist. And because equality has brought an end to war, militarism and its wasteful cost are gone forever.

Education is the main objective of government. Therefore, in Cabet's fictional land of Icaria teachers take first place among public functionaries.

Cabet's religious views have a gospel-like character because he designates the Icarians as the true followers of Christ. He called the Icarians the true Christians.

SOME COMPARISONS

Owen and Cabet shared an axiom: people can be changed by society. Placing great faith in the efficacy of education, they took it as the sure route to a better world just over the horizon. A closer look at their vision, however, shows that their idea of equality stifled individual differences and pointed to a homogenized, humdrum world.

Fourier's world has more verve, a more colorful texture. His axiom told him that society should not force people to conform to some uniform standard of personality when nature itself ordained differences. Although he may not have shouted "*vive la différence!*" his ideal world thrived on diversity. The heart of balanced, harmonious relationships, diversity encouraged individual interests as a stimulus to creativity. That promised to enhance every aspect of the Phalanx, from music to art to gourmet food, to all things that make life pleasurable. Without them, the Phalanx had no reason to exist. Compare that with Cabet's values. He put pleasure into a category he called the Agreeable, the lowest of his three priorities. In Icaria he wanted to tackle *the Necessary* first, then *the Useful*, and last *the Agreeable.* Owen saw pleasurable things as a loosening of the reins on feelings. They remained suspect, as an open door to individualism, the poison of his New Social System.

In Fourier's world, feelings and instincts – the passions – defined personality types and, coming from nature itself, held no greater dangers than physical characteristics. Within his variety of types some would have a natural inclination to own property. Fourier considered it a trait no more to be denied than any other. But to Owen and Cabet, who distrusted the passions, the acquisition of anything for private use represented the worst expression of individual interests. They made holding property in common – abolishing private property – a centerpiece of their utopian schemes.

The Movement and Its Colonies

The table, Divisions Within the Movement for Social Reorganization, shows the relationship between colonies in the movement and lists a representative sampling of them. As mentioned earlier, New-Harmony, Brook Farm, and Icaria are the primary focus of this book.

Notice that the question of private property creates the two principal divisions. The followers of Cabet and Owen make up the two subdivisions of those who abolished private property. However, New-Harmony holds a place there in only a nominal sense. Shortly after founding the colony, Owen raised his usually quiet voice in a strident attack on private property. He called it one of three great evils and tried to slay it with constitutions and speeches. Still, the colony continued to depend on his wealth and philanthropy for survival, and in that context ending private property remained nothing more than a hollow slogan. In reality, as opposed to mere speculation, holding property in common in this movement became a fact of life only for the Cabetists and for a handful of colonies that tried to keep Owenism alive. (It was, however, the absolute rule for the Shakers and for most of the colonies of individual salvation.)

NEW-HARMONY

Owen bought the New-Harmony property using his own capital. Located on the Wabash River near Evansville, Indiana, it had some twenty thousand acres of rich bottomland, a complete and functioning village with church, mills, and workshops. For a decade it had served as home for a large German colony of individual salvation called Harmonie, the congregation of a charismatic leader, George Rapp. When Owen came along, Father Rapp saw a rare opportunity to take his people out of this land of fevers, something we now know comes with bottomland. Owen knew nothing of that but saw the deal as a chance to hit the ground running, as some would now say, with housing and physical plant in place.

In May 1825 the Preliminary Society, Owen's name for the long transition to his New Social System, got under way. Barely a month later, when the fledgling colony needed all the leadership and experience it could get, Owen left for Europe on one of his trips to drum up support. At that crucial moment the critical start-up decisions fell to his son William, who was twenty-three years old. Robert Owen

Table

Divisions Within the Movement for Social Reorganization *(in approximate order of their establishment)*

	No Private Property		Private Property			
	OWENITES	CABETISTS	ETHICALISTS	ASSOCIATIONISTS ("FOURIERISTS")	INDIVIDUALISTS	PRACTICAL CHRISTIANS
1820s	New-Harmony Yellow Springs Macluria Feiba-Peveli Franklin					
1830s	Equity					
1840s	One-Mentians Equality Skaneateles Utilitarian	Icaria in Illinois	Brook Farm Institute of Agriculture and Education Northampton Fruitlands	Jefferson Phalanx North American Phalanx Sodus Bay Phalanx Bloomfield Association Ohio Phalanx Alphadelphia Association Sylvania Association Clermont Phalanx Trumbull Phalanx Wisconsin Phalanx Philadelphia Industrial Association Integral Phalanx Brook Farm Phalanx Spring Farm Phalanx Pigeon River Association	Utopia	Hopedale
After Mid-Century		Cheltenham Icaria in Iowa Jeune Icaria New Icaria Speranza		Raritan Bay Union La Réunion Silkville	Modern Times	Union Grove

returned seven months later to a colony disorganized and racked by dissension.

Inexplicably, Owen decided to cut the transition and move directly to the advanced phase of his plan, which called for an end to private property. He leaped into this great leap forward without looking at the serious, unsolved preliminary problems. Against a mountain of mismanagement he tried optimism and new constitutions. The mountain remained. In the meantime, he continued to pay the bills. The colony, which at its peak had close to a thousand people, sapped his fortune. In June 1827 Owen left the colony again, this time under clouds of complications so dark that they obscured the bitter end of this utopian episode.

ICARIA

In 1848 Cabet sent an avante-garde of his best, most dedicated followers from Europe to Texas to create a real Icaria like the one in his novel. When the brutal Southwest heat nearly wiped out these Northern Europeans, Cabet rushed to America to salvage the plan. With about three hundred men, women, and children who remained, he went up the Mississippi to Nauvoo, Illinois, from where the Mormons had recently been driven, and bought some of their former land and houses. With the expectation of moving to a better location when conditions permitted, Cabet began his attempt to change the world.

The Icarians expanded the farm and started manufacturing and mining. With the products of their shoe and clothing shops, the Icarians opened a retail store in St. Louis, 150 miles downriver. By the mid-1850s, the colony began to enjoy a moderate prosperity, and the membership reached nearly five hundred. At the same time, Cabet's penchant for wrangling and forcing members to side with him on every issue led to violent factionalism and finally to a split. The majority expelled Cabet in 1856. With a group who remained loyal he went to St. Louis hoping to find a site to start anew. But events in Nauvoo had been too much, and, broken-hearted, he died within a month.

A year later, the Icarians in Nauvoo, carrying out the original plan, moved to a permanent home, a tract purchased earlier near Corning, Iowa, about seventy-five miles from Des Moines. But they found life on the plains an uphill struggle. The remnants who held out – the number fluctuated between forty and eighty – suffered but somehow managed to survive on bare necessities for two decades before things began to look up.

Then, with the first taste of joy, a split developed in 1879. The "young faction" took control after a court fight and pushed the "old faction" into a remote corner of the property. The terrible Cabet legacy of polemics that had torn the group apart continued to haunt the Icarians, and soon it split the "young faction" too. This time the losers broke away and started a colony near San Francisco. That attempt foundered within five years. Meanwhile, back in Iowa the "old faction," many from the generation of pioneers who had left France with grand, heroic visions of their role in reshaping the world, managed to eke out another decade. They outlasted the "young faction," but attrition took its toll, and after forty-six years of dispute and hardship, they too finally gave up the ghost in 1895.

ETHICALISTS

The table lising colonies shows four subdivisions among the ones that retained private property. The one I call Ethicalists consists of groups who, unlike the Fourierists, for example, attached themselves to no particular set of utopian speculations. Guided only by ethical principles, they started down the utopian road to create a moral society that respected the worth and dignity of every human being. The Ethicalists includes the most famous of the movement's colonies, Brook Farm.

Brook Farm came out of discussions by a group of New England intellectuals and clergymen. Troubled by the excesses of unbridled competition that fostered dog-eat-dog values and by the reluctance of established churches to act in behalf of the poor and oppressed, some of them talked about creating an alternative to a society they saw as evil.

George Ripley, a former minister, and his wife Sophia, a teacher, decided to turn ethics into action. Leaving the talkers behind, they took a few doers to 175 meager acres in West Roxbury, about eight miles from downtown Boston, and in 1841 they turned to haying and milking. The core of the group consisted of well-educated people from the middle class, and several divinity graduates from Harvard who had served in the pulpit. Thus, they stood far removed from the day-to-day economic evils that society visited on the less fortunate. More than altruistic, they proceeded from a belief that ethics and morality rather than the expediency of the bottom line ought to govern human relationships. In Brook Farm they saw the possibility of creating at society of "brotherly cooperation" based on "simplicity, truthfulness, refinement, and moral dignity."[1]

The Brook Farm Institute of Agriculture and Education operated as a joint stock company and sold shares to raise cash. All members, men and women alike, shared equally in all work of the farm and the house. They lived by a rule that esteemed labor in the field or at a washtub no less honorable than at a desk. Still, with their wealth of teachers and their values, which elevated intellect and education, only the income from the school they established sustained them. In all the movement, no colony found an industry more appropriate to the available skills and the spirit of its goals. But the school could not cover Brook Farm's losses.

The Brook Farm Phalanx evolved from a growing interest by the leadership in the ideas of Fourier. In 1845 they reorganized the colony from one based simply on ethical principles into one with a doctrine. This change, unique in the movement, appears in the table listing colonies under the "Fourierists" subdivision. During this phase, Brook Farm became the flagship colony of the Associationists and the home of the movement's most remarkable newspaper, the *Harbinger.*

American misinterpreters of Fourier called for new Brook Farm goals: Bring in more working-class members! and Increase the production of goods for sale! became their slogans. But such goals had an alien tone in that pastoral retreat and a profoundly unsettling effect on the colony's middle-class intellectuals. Some of the early, devoted members left, and the colony began to flounder. Just then, religious zealots pushing their own agenda swayed this broadly tolerant colony, which had always prohibited any religious test of membership, into the establishment of religion. Each of these traumas left unresolvable tensions. Stressed in so many ways, reduced to meals of little more than bread and milk, even the strongest faltered. In 1847 this utopian episode, a humanistic vision of good and beauty, staggered to a bad and ugly end.

INDIVIDUALISTS

Modern Times, the best-known colony of the Individualists, started in 1851 on New York's Long Island near present-day Brentwood. It grew out of the many utopian experiences of Josiah Warren beginning in New-Harmony, where at age twenty-seven he was music director. During the next two decades he tried his hand at several other utopian ideas, including a colony called Utopia. At the same time he devoted himself to studying the causes for the collapse of New-Harmony and published a periodical, *Peaceful Revolutionist,* that contained his evolving ideas. Ultimately, he rejected Owenism as inherently flawed, and in his manuscript "Natural Liberty" he arrived at a position on the individual and society directly opposed to Owen's.

Warren's basic axiom holds that each human is by nature a distinct individual endowed with "natural liberty." Because of that endowment, society has no right to impose a collective will on anyone. From this grew other tenets. Each of us has the right to live as we please and do what we please, but at our own cost. That means that each of us has to bear individual responsibility for our actions. However, because individuals must coexist, we cannot do anything that injures others or interferes with their equal and natural liberty. Warren's *Individual Sovereignty,* as he called the concept, requires "new social arrangements" (read social reorganization) that would give labor "a just reward," establish peace, and bring "enjoyment for all."[2]

While Cabet and Owen considered individualism anathema, Modern Timers wore it proudly as a badge of honor. One of their celebrations included a march to the Long Island Railroad station at Thompson. There the children met the train from New York and held aloft their banner proclaiming "We Are Individuals!" Today some might call them "libertarians."

Because of the peculiar organization of Modern Times, it did not go through the loud, soul-wrenching discord that laid low most other colonies in the movement. Late in the 1850s it began to fade quietly, leaving behind few details about its end.

PRACTICAL CHRISTIANS

This group occupies a unique position at the fringe of a movement marked by a wide range of views. Hopedale, the principal colony, started in 1841 near Worcester, Massachusetts, under the inspiration of Adin Ballou, a New England clergyman. In his tracts and early books he condemned the greed and cruelty of society and argued for a *New Social State* based on the beneficent teachings of Jesus. A pragmatist, he rejected fixed economic systems, saying that production should be based on what proved efficient from year to year. Ballou stressed equality, brotherhood, and "Christian nonresistance," which today we call nonviolence. With the Sermon on the Mount as their guide, members could not hate, injure, or kill anyone, even an enemy, and even in self defense. They did not vote, serve in the military, or use any governmental agency, including the courts.

Ballou looked critically at society, and unlike all other proponents of social reorganization, he named sin as an evil. Among the hymns he wrote for his colony, one includes the following lines:

Not individual souls alone
Require the new and heavenly birth;
Society in sin up-grown
Needs Christianizing o'er the earth.

Thus, his efforts to correct the tangible economic and social injustices of the world through social reorganization also had as a component the intangible spirit of individual salvation. He called Hopedale "a Bethlehem of salvation," and alone among all the colonies of the movement, his made a religious test of faith a condition of membership.[3]

Ballou differed from the movement in other ways. For example, in response to the evil of poverty he urged charity. But others in the movement saw individual actions as a futile dissipation of the energies for change. The movement's mainstream had faith only in collective action, believing that it could remove the causes of poverty once and for all and end the demeaning effects of charity. Still, Ballou and the Practical Christians shared the movement's fundamental goal, the happiness of humanity, and identified themselves with its means, social reorganization. Indeed, Ballou believed that by the end of the century the Practical Christian Republic would be firmly established in America. Hopedale lasted until 1856, longer than any other group except the Icarians.

ASSOCIATIONISTS

The word *association* has several meanings, but as used here with a capital *A* it refers to a particular type of colony. Making up the largest subdivision of the movement, colonies of this type set out to establish the system of society Fourier called Association. The table listing colonies shows "Fourierists" in quotation marks to emphasize that, although groups identified their efforts with his name, no colony attempted to put any of his ideas into practice except in the most superficial sense. Indeed, as I pointed out earlier, very few had read his comprehensive speculations or understood what he had in mind for his basic social unit, the Phalanx. Although some Associationists called their colonies Phalanx, no true Fourier Phalanx or Phalanstery ever existed.

During the mid-1840s, when Fourierism spread across America like a prairie fire, new Associations withered so quickly that it may never be possible to know their story. The table of colonies lists six Associations that will be mentioned frequently in these pages. A complete list of the formal names, dates, and locations of the main colonies mentioned in this book appears in Appendix B.

A Few Words about Words

People in the movement called themselves reformers. But they had no faith in patching up the cracks in traditional society. In fact, when they used the word *reform* it meant total, not piecemeal, change. They assumed that issues of the day – voting rights or abolition, for example – would all be settled as part of the vast change they had in store for society. In 1825 William Owen predicted: "The world [is] about to experience the greatest revolution which it ever has seen, or ever can see." He added that no stone would be left unturned because it would "strike at the root of all evil and misery of every kind from the greatest to the least." His prediction echoed through the movement's next phase when two decades later George Ripley declared, "The times are ripe for a peaceful social revolution." Moreover, the movement made clear the universality of its goal. A disciple of Fourier stated the vision in its most expansive form: "Association, once established in the township would soon embrace the province, the continent, humanity."[4] The people in social reorganization saw reform in terms of that magnitude. They took *reform* in a literal sense: *re-form*, to *form again*, to remake society.

The movement encompassed a wide range, from aggressive programs demanded by Cabet and Owen on one side to the gentle moralizing of the Practical Christians on the other. Designations such as Left and Right appear tempting in this context, but they would obscure a simple truth: all of these groups stood far to the left of the American mainstream. The *Harbinger* (June 14, 1845) summed up the "the cause" this way: "radical, organic, social reform."

Actually, *radical* is an apt description for the people of the movement. That word, powerful and inflammatory, conjures up a certain stereotype in twentieth-century minds. Fiery Cabet, a rabble-rouser toughened on the streets of the class struggle in France, might fit its overworked image. But the word hardly seems appropriate for the bookish divinity graduates from Harvard teaching poetry and philosophy in Brook Farm; the soft-spoken Owen preaching restraint; the pacifists at Hopedale turning the other cheek; or the dozens of introspective, almost colorless leaders who sat quietly at the helm of social reorganization. Still, all of them dedicated their lives totally to a single purpose: removing every vestige of traditional society from the root on up. Therefore, radical (from the Latin for *root*) fits them perfectly.

Unfortunately, other terms often used in relation to this movement do not serve as well. Rather than speeding ideas down the highways of thought, as good words should, they force them into the slow lane. *Socialism, communism,* and words that look like *communism* create a special kind of confusion. It arises from the varying and changing ways in which people have interpreted these terms in the past and even today. The word *socialism,* for example, turned up on the doorstep of the last century with one identity, but by the 1830s and 1840s defenders of divergent doctrines began claiming it. Not stopping to make it legitimate with a definition, various groups picked it up, wrapped it in their own colors, brought it into their jargon, and adopted it as their own.

In the course of a century terms like *socialism* and *communism* have become like the words of Humpty Dumpty: they mean whatever someone chooses them to mean. Even now, politicians Left and Right who like to persuade with passion more than precision find this quality a handy tool. One need look no further than the evening news, where socialism may mean welfare programs, or farm subsidies, or government regulation of an industry, or government ownership of it, depending on who speaks.

Community and *communitarian* compound the problems because of the contradictory ways in which they have been used. Linked through their stems to *communism,* they encourage unwarranted assumptions about the society they describe. How should we interpret *community?* As a place where members hold all property in common? If you belonged to Icaria, where the colony owned everything and the individual nothing, you would say yes and agree with Cabet that "communism cannot be established by violence . . . community can only be established . . . by the consent of all."[5]

Community, of course, has a number of meanings, but in the context of fundamental social change the idea of property held in common carries the greatest weight. For example, people often used *community* in reference to Brook Farm although that word never appeared in any name it took as it evolved from Institute to Phalanx. It always stood firmly on a foundation of private property and dividend-paying shares. Yet, many members and sympathizers felt compelled to deny the implications of *community.* One close friend of the colony took exceptional pains to repudiate it: "Brook Farm was not a 'community.' . . . There was no element of socialism."[6]

Unfortunately, each additional explanation or definition tends to blow more smoke in the eyes of clarity. A Brook Farm leader declared, "We . . . take the name of socialist, . . . we believe in individual property. We are not communists!" Can we then at least conclude from this that socialism and communism are different? Adin Ballou, president of Hopedale, would say no. His list of socialists included: the "Primitive Christians," the Owenites, the Fourierists, and "the French and German Communists." Ballou defended private property, yet Cabet, an opponent of private property, also equated socialism and communism.[7]

An inexhaustible supply of such conflicting definitions of *socialism, communism, community,* and words with their stems fills volumes, and additional examples could surely bulk up this one. They show the hazards in the too-easy acceptance of terms in a field where a word, a mere word, can become a classical tool of obfuscation. Therefore, this book avoids the sidetracks that inevitably open up with imprecise but potentially charged terms. Its deals with a defined idea, *social reorganization:* a nineteenth-century movement that tried to bring about a fundamental change in society by creating ideal colonies as models for the world to emulate.

Three other words will be used in relation to the movement. To describe the place where these groups set up shop, this book adopts *colony.* The word conveys its meaning more clearly than *community* because it carries none of that ambiguous word's heavy connotative baggage. But it has a more important, positive attribute. *Colony* evokes the true qualities of the site: a place apart, unfinished, where emigrants come to build something new.

Second, those characteristics relate to another attribute of all the utopian colonies that tried to change the world. Despite claims made by the followers of various Utopian mentors, no blueprint existed for creating an ideal colony. Pragmatism directed most efforts. A few of the more candid and perceptive of the movement's leaders frankly acknowledged their undertakings as trials; and in fact, *experiment* turns up frequently in their documents. So *experiment* justifiably belongs among the words appropriate for these colonies.

Finally, people in the movement liked to think they would be establishing the Kingdom of Heaven on earth, and that promise generated other scriptural allusions. People in a western group called their domain "the promised land," and a leader referred to Brook Farm as "consecrated ground." A woman member there described it as "this Eden," a name that shows up often. For example, one visionary promised that his colony would be "a garden, . . . a veritable Eden." Hopedale's founder, Adin Ballou, converted the word into a process, calling his Social Christendom a world *Edenized.* One of the movement's newspapers published desirable names for new colonies, and of course Eden made the roster. The list also anticipated an Elysium and a Cythera (two places of ideal happiness in Greek myth) and, most important of all, a Utopia.[8]

Utopia? That name might seem a travesty to us today because everything about the word had been invested with pejorative implications by an age that cannot see the horizon, let alone look beyond it. But during the heyday of the movement, the word did not necessarily come with a sneer attached; for many people it simply represented in the most positive sense the ideal.[9] And on that great goal social reorganization had set its sights.

Therefore, I shall use *utopian* in that positive sense as appropriate for this movement, its people, and their attempts to solve the world's problems by creating an ideal society free of social evils. It is an ideal word for these episodes.

The Spur to a Utopian Life

ON A RAW NOVEMBER AFTERNOON in 1842, Amelia Russell, a single woman of forty-five, gave up her warm, comfortable home in the city for the uncertainties of Brook Farm, a rural colony dedicated to making a fundamental change in the way people live. Her resolve outweighed her apprehensions as she exchanged security for an unproven social idea. But she was hardly a rare phenomenon in that era. On the contrary, she did what countless thousands did from 1825 through the later decades of the century. Like Louisa Sheldon, age twenty-six, from Paris, Illinois, who "left a home of plenty and comfort and the very kindest relatives" to risk her future in a similar Wisconsin experiment, most of those people were not society's unfortunates desperately grasping at revolutionary straws.[1]

American interest in utopian colonies as solutions to our problems peaked in the 1840s. One year in the middle of that critical decade some four thousand people visited Brook Farm to see for themselves the utopian promise. For our present population that would translate into about a half a million, an impressive number for any attraction.

What did those crowds of curious want to know? And what hunger brought members into dozens of similar colonies, ready to commit their savings and futures to the unknown difficulties of creating a new society from the ground up in some out-of-the-way place?

As we begin to look into such questions we find people spurred on by causes, slogans, and programs that seem to step right out of late twentieth-century news stories. Justice for the exploited, the poor, and the disadvantaged motivated them, as we might guess. But they also had antiwar groups and a deep concern for the state of morality, religion, the environment, and education. We hear calls for protecting human rights, and particularly for women's equality. There were vegetarians, other groups promoting health foods, and even campaigns against smoking. Some, claiming that the stress of modern society would destroy us, hoped to find refuge by getting back to nature, to a simpler way of life.

Many of the problems they addressed have always been with us, and perhaps some will always remain. But social reorganization made its mark by first of all pointing to what it saw as their ultimate source. "It is impossible to survey the present condition of the world, . . . without perceiving [that] the great evils that afflict humanity, . . . [are] the direct consequences of existing social arrangements." A typical example, those words from Northampton's constitution show that the movement looked past single issues and patchwork social repairs to the essence of why people chose to live in a relationship we call society.

Though the emphasis on issues varied among groups, all partisans of social reorganization paid a big price for their commitment. First, many had difficulty just getting to a remote colony. Augustin Savardan, making the trek from New Orleans to La Réunion, put up with blisters caused by ticks, voracious mosquitoes, and other insects. But fear eats deeper than skin. A world he could never have imagined in France terrorized him: poisonous snakes, scorpions, and enormous, hideous tarantulas. Another La Réunion member, Kalikst Wolski, a Pole, told of his horrors along the trail across Louisiana and Texas created by dreaded rattlesnakes. He also endured a more poignant ailment common to the pioneers—American or European—who tried to make a life in such distant, isolated places: homesickness.[2]

En route, Wolski ran into Cabet's avant-garde on their way to found Icaria in Texas. He left us a keen observation about them that helps explain why certain utopian colonies had a short life. Exhausted from their three-month voyage from France and overland from New Orleans, the Cabetists had no money and spoke no English. Wolski foresaw their fate: they were intellectuals "unfit for the hard work of colonization. . . . They will experience terrible want." Sure enough, they wilted almost immediately under the searing Texas sun.[3]

Upon arriving at a colony, new members faced a second problem, the chronic housing shortage characteristic of these experiments. A typical situation comes from Frances Judd's recollections of life in Northampton. "Houses were scarce, and to accommodate all who wished to join us, part of the brick factory was fitted up as a boarding house. The quarters were rude and plain."[4] A movement newspaper, the *Phalanx,* reported (June 29, 1844) that the Trumbull experiment in Ohio had to crowd two hundred people into a farmhouse, a barn, and some "loose sheds." In most colonies, members found other basic necessities in short supply too, and under those conditions disease often took an expected but terrible toll.

Finally, hostile elements in all parts of the country brought enduring troubles to partisans of the movement. Even an outstanding public figure such as Horace Greeley, publisher of the *New York Tribune,* could not remain immune. In a letter to one of the Brook Farm leaders, he bemoaned the price he had to pay. "I have encountered much opposition and ridicule on account of what I have published and . . . written in favor of Association. . . . Worthy friends . . . have stopped my paper on account of this, and all [have] chilled in their friendship."[5] Greeley, of course, had big-city power and position to weather such things, but for others not so fortunately placed, social stigma could be much more destructive. In Preston, New York, a small upstate town, George Throop and his brother, a teacher, supported the local Fourier Club. Because of that support the townsfolk had his brother fired and ostracized George, as we learn from one of his letters of 1844. "I feel lost in this . . . community where all the better feelings of the human mind are denied . . . [by] those who profess to be the followers of Him who taught: do as you wish to be done to." Pupils could no longer talk to his brother, and George, called corrupt, an infidel, even by his uncle, found most doors in town closed to him.[6]

So in addition to the obstacles of the trip and the discomfort of the colonies, adherents of the movement endured personal abuse. With those three strikes waiting for them, it seems likely that few people would want to go to bat for social reorganization. Indeed, Frederick Douglass, the abolitionist leader and former slave who often visited Northampton, wondered why the the well-to-do people he saw there volunteered to "leave the smooth and pleasant paths of life to which they were accustomed for the rough and thorny ways they were now compelled to tread."[7] The answer, or rather answers, get to the heart of the movement's attraction. They show that the spur consisted of two components: a negative reaction to the evils of society and positive action based on the expectations and promises of social change.

The Evils of Society

Horace Greeley believed that severe economic conditions drove people into the movement, a commonly held opinion both then and now. In his autobiography he recalled the winter of 1837–38 as a time of great suffering. A paralysis seized the business world, most banks and factories closed, and an influx of agricultural workers into the cities swelled the already enormous ranks of the unemployed.

However, the worst effects of the 1837 crisis had abated long before the dormant interest in social reorganization reawakened in the 1840s. Only four colonies dedicated to changing society began operations during 1841 and 1842, and the movement did not begin to rattle windows until the years 1843 and 1844, when some two dozen experiments exploded on the American scene.

This does not mean that people in the movement remained aloof to the hardships that the economic system bred. It does show, however, that the movement did not simply reflect a direct response to a depression and that a broader view of society and its flaws generated impulses to fundamental change. In that context, the economic system simply became another defect to be eradicated under the totality of social reorganization.

The movement drew most of its membership from people who, because of their backgrounds, never knew the hunger and despair the poor faced even in good times. For example, Victor Considérant, founder of La Réunion, claimed that his followers were not "driven from Europe by misery" to join in a test of his social ideas but were people of affluence and worth. Similarly, Cabet said his people, solid citizens from Lyon, France, were not a mob "induced by misery" to cross the sea for an experiment in community of property. George Bradford recalled that many of his fellow Brook Farmers, tasting manual labor for the first time, had come from a background of books, comparative luxury, and "elegance of living." For these people, knowledge of economic hardships came secondhand, as we shall see.[8]

But the movement did, in fact, cry out against those hardships. In particular, the propaganda for social reorganization repeatedly held a magnifier to the plight of the poor and the downtrodden. New-Harmony's newspaper, the *Gazette* (October 15, 1825), tells of the appalling conditions in Ireland: women toiling on the roads for two pence a day; many dying of starvation or diseases caused by it; children laboring fourteen to sixteen hours a day and those who survive becoming wretches. Alphadelphia's paper, the *Tocsin* (December 6, 1844), features a gloomy picture of "civilization" in its "Social Evils" column: in France, 20 million people without shoes or suitable clothing, forced to get by on six cents a day; in England, millions starving; in Ireland, one-third of the people subsisting on substandard potatoes; in Boston, seamstresses compelled to work for one cent an hour; and in the slave states, "beings created in the image of God . . . held as merchantable commodities, and crushed down to the level of beasts."

Some traced these problems to the system that forced people to compete against each other just to secure necessities. For example, Raritan Bay Union's constitution established "cooperation" as a social principle to counter the "evils of competition."

The American disciples of Fourier stressed his economic criticism, which cataloged the wrongs against the poorer classes. These included commonly voiced grievances such as unhealthy and dangerous working conditions. But to his credit, and with an uncommon sensitivity by someone of the middle class to the way the less fortunate had to exist, he detailed other wrongs: the nagging fear of unemployment and old age, intimidation by the legal system, the shame that society visits on the poor.

Fourier identified the commercial system in Europe as a source of all kinds of vice and crime. And his followers in America recognized the emergence of a similar atmosphere of corruption emanating from commerce here. Brook Farm leader Charles A. Dana, writing in the colony's *Harbinger* (June 21, 1845), blamed its excesses on laissez-faire, the "magical words" that have "humbugged the world." He went far beyond that, concluding that "in commerce, absolute and complete honesty, integral Christian honesty, is impossible." John Allen, another Brook Farmer, took that even further. He said people could not live a truly Christian life within the prevailing system.

Others held similar views. Charles Lane and A. Bronson Alcott saw trade as "a nursery for many evil propensities." So in Fruitlands they grew or made everything they needed or they obtained necessities through "friendly exchanges" without the intervention of money.[9]

"The love of money is the root of all evils." That scriptural lesson (I Tim. 6:10) became a leitmotiv of the movement. It appears on the title page of the plan for an ideal city called Monodelphia, and with variations it turns up in the movement's newspapers, tracts, and books. But social reorganization treated it not as a warning but as the stepping-stone to a more elevated existence, beyond the economic concerns that represented only a small part of the spur to a utopian life. In that broader view of society, immorality, alienation, inequality, ignorance, and cultural disadvantages loomed large.

"Man is more than meat"; so said Fredrika Bremer, the Swedish writer, impressed by what she saw in her visit to North American Phalanx.[10] As a general motto for the movement her words come even closer to the underlying rationale of the movement than the biblical teaching on money. The circumstances implied by her observation counteracts the idea that this movement germinated in the loins of economics.

Clearly, much more than the economic system fueled the drive for social reorganization. The people in Northampton listed their concerns in their constitution, among them the meager education available to Americans, the perversion of religion into a tyranny over the human mind, sectarianism, war as a solution to disputes, and government corruption. They pointed out that society "has sprung out of these evils, is maintained by them, and has a direct tendency to reproduce them."

In a letter to the *Phalanx* (June 1, 1844), a member of a western colony emphasized the social evil that motivated his group. They found that "honest industry [and] frugality . . . are no longer guarantees of . . . independence, nor intellectual acquirements [and] moral virtues . . . a sure passport to places of trust and dignity." Henry Schetterly of Alphadelphia in a letter to the *Phalanx* (July 13, 1844) pointed out the consequences of that decline in integrity. "Men have lost all confidence in each other." George Throop of Preston, New York, whose brother had been fired by the town school, saw it leading to alienation.

A letter inquiring about membership in Alphadelphia indicates how the corruption of values functioned as a spur. John Bliss—his style and his fine penmanship suggest a well educated person—wrote that he was "heartily sick of the present state of things, and extremely anxious to unite myself with my brethren of a kindred faith."[11]

In the heyday of social reorganization, the great promise of equality embodied in our Declaration of Independence still remained unfulfilled for many people. The evil of inequality attracted many men to the cause. But no group except the slaves suffered from inequality more than women. Women had none of the rights we now take for granted; for example, they could not vote and could not own property. And when a woman married she remained subservient to a husband in every respect—by custom and by law. Fourier, again, to his credit in an age when few men even looked into the question, showed great sensitivity to the situation women faced. He included among the evils of society the position forced on woman by public ignorance, by cruel laws, and "by the prejudices that torment her from infancy."[12] The Associationists included this radical criticism in their propaganda. It opened the eyes of many Americans, men and women, to concepts of equality virtually unknown and to a gross defect in traditional society. That recognition became another driving force for social reorganization. Uncharacteristically for that era, women joined a movement, and in some colonies they actually became a majority.

Taxes, though universally unpopular, would not be considered a social evil by most people. But Adin Ballou of Hopedale found an ironic twist in them. He deplored the taxes his colony had to pay to support what he called "the old order." These taxes helped maintain the very evils Practical Christians opposed, evils inherent in the old order. He listed among them the army and navy, "the tools of war and killing." In addition, the old order, which created poverty and bred crime, taxed him to help its poor and to pay for its prisons.[13]

Last in this summary but by no means least, the movement attracted many who saw ignorance and cultural deprivation as social evils. The *Tocsin* (December 6, 1844) explained how these twin evils came to be the inescapable lot of the poor. Forced into long working hours to survive, they never had a chance to get the education and self-improvement they needed to lift themselves out of poverty.

Brook Farmers went beyond basics; they branded the stifling of humanity's aesthetic instincts by society as evil. George Bradford, one of the earliest members, recalled that the colony had come into existence because of disgust with New England values. In Boston, "the few" had access to the arts, music, books, and refined recreation. But in that Athens of America, "the many" could not escape wearisome drudgery and incessant toil and so had no opportunity for what Bradford called "the enjoyments of intellect and taste."[14]

Expectations and Promises

Cabet hung this slogan in the huge dining hall of Icaria in Nauvoo:

> From each according to his ability
> To each according to his needs.[15]

Those famous words held the economic promise of many utopian experiments despite their differences on the question of property. Cabet and Owen, of course, both stressed economics. Even Fourier's American disciples focused on it, although to the detriment of his sweeping social propositions.

But when we look into the motives that actually brought people to the movement and hear their expectations, we discover a different emphasis. Undoubtedly, some might have looked to a new society simply for an abundance of the necessities, but few mentioned that as a spur. However, judging from the record that remains, most people went past the assumption that efficiency would provide enough, and they demanded more out of life than just a better cut of the pie. They expected to see the evil that impelled them to join a colony replaced by a humane, social good. For example, in place of alienation they wanted brotherhood and sisterhood; in place of ignorance, education.

What would that ideal society be like? Conceptions varied, of course, but the following example, concise yet comprehensive, would have found favor with most people in the movement. Victor Considérant saw this vision of a Texas remade by La Réunion: "The arts, the sciences, pleasures, collective luxuries, the refinement of the population, a higher education: all these flowers of social life bloom upon the deep beds of public wealth in a sphere animated by the new faith in humanity."[16] It sounds like a digest of all the goals everyone looked for in the movement. But of course, all of these things did not motivate each individual with equal force, although a complex of reasons impelled most people to join the movement.

When Charles Lane visited Brook Farm, he found three motives that brought people there. Primarily they hoped that the colony would elevate human relationships through ethical living, fraternity, and a moral atmosphere. A smaller number expected to better their material condition, and the third category wanted the education that it offered. Amelia Russell, an early member, recalled the main reason people came to Brook Farm: to cultivate all that was good in every person so that a noble ambition would govern each one's moral and intellectual life. Some three decades later, when the Brook Farm idea had long since passed from the American scene, she looked around at post–Civil War radical movements and made an important comparison. The new era emphasized only material goals; Brook Farm had aimed for the intangible concerns of the human spirit. Georgiana Bruce, who taught in the Brook Farm School, said the members wanted to "spiritualize the dish-washing and scrubbing."[17]

That kind of environment went hand in hand with one of the great attractions of these colonies: an informal atmosphere stripped of artificialities. When it worked well, the informality helped inspire a sense of belonging in each member. The companionship it brought, hard to quantify but part of the mission of social reorganization, sometimes stood above ideology. Frédéric Olinet of Icaria, for example, confessed that he had less enthusiasm for meetings than for picnics.

At the latter they danced, and they had good fun that was "all the better since we had no harangues there." Companionship undoubtedly attracted George Throop as much as abstract social doctrines. In an 1843 letter to his brother he describes efforts to establish an Association near Preston, New York. "We [already] have a little Association here in feeling. . . . I do not believe that God ever designed we should make ourselves unhappy by separation and divisions to comply with the present aristocratic notions of the age. There are a few . . . congenial souls [here] so attached in their interest and feeling, so united, we cannot live and be happy [except] in Association."[18]

That deeply felt human need he expressed cannot not be underestimated. It became even more compelling in the rapidly expanding industrial and commercial centers, teeming with strangers forced into an increasingly depersonalized urban life. In the face of its indifference the movement's promise of brotherhood and sisterhood had a powerful appeal. It comes through clearly in "Reflections on Returning from a Funeral in Association," which a woman sent to the *Phalanx* (February 8, 1845).

> How blessed the privilege of dying in Association! How comfortable to realize that . . . the last sad rites shall be performed by true friends – brothers and sisters. How consoling to know that those whose hearts swell with the noblest sense of humanity, shall consign the body to its mother earth. Our sister has left us, . . . yet she did so with sweet serenity and calmness, conscious of a glorious immortality, and knowing well the deep-felt sympathy of those . . . with her in her last moments. Though our sister had no kindred near her, yet she knew . . . her memory would be cherished. . . . Though distant from her native country . . . without wealth to barter for that mockery of friendship which, in society as it is, is purchased by gold, she was not friendless or unprotected.

The writer goes on to say that she has feared death, mainly because of her concern for her children's upbringing. "But the consolations of Association quiet all my forebodings."

Obviously, for some a utopian colony promised a haven from a world that even in the nineteenth century could seem forbidding. Not surprisingly, the words *refuge* and *escape* appear often in the documents of the movement. For example, the people who gathered to organize Clermont Phalanx in Ohio explained in a report to the *Phalanx* (May 18, 1844) that social conditions forced them to "seek a refuge." And members in Northampton declared in their constitution:

"The vices of . . . civilization are so gross . . . that no apology is required for the honest attempt to escape from them."

Moncure Conway wrote a novel based on his Modern Times experience. In it he calls the members "refugees from a world inharmonious with their ideals." The novel's principal character explains why people choose life in a utopian colony. "It's not mere trouble that makes people leave the great world for a . . . place like [Modern Times]. The heart is born for an unbounded world, and if it turns away from it the motive is . . . something that renders life with mankind impossible."

Some eight months before Brook Farm started, Sophia Ripley, spending the summer on the property destined to become the home of the colony, mentioned this sense of refuge and escape. She wrote to John Sullivan Dwight about the location and praised the benefits of being nearly two miles from any other creature. "In this quiet retreat I have found that entire separation from worldly care." Rev. A. Bloomer Hart found in Brook Farm a place "to retire from the falsities of the world." And he admitted, "I could prescribe myself no better exorcism of 'the blues' than an hour, a day, or week of mingling in its ranks, and participation in its feeling."[19]

The idea of refuge as a spur implies an insular psychology among utopians. Confirmation comes in a frequently encountered concept: *the outside*. For example, a newspaper reporter asked a Modern Timer if he took an interest in politics. No, he replied, but "some of our folks get mixed up with the outside world."[20] Maria Marchand complained that Icaria's religion was misunderstood "outside." The concept took other forms. Elijah Grant promised that Ohio Phalanx would carry on a system of exchange with "external society," and Cabet too had a program of "external commerce" for Icaria.

Such phrases suggest the subtle nature of the spur to utopianism. But other, more obvious reasons also motivated people to join. The opportunity for education made a strong incentive, as Charles Lane found out when he visited Brook Farm. Its excellent school became the backbone of the colony, attracting members, students with cash, and outside support. Word of its achievements spread, and newspapers as far away as Wisconsin wrote about it. Although few utopian experiments could match the quality of the school's curriculum and its core of Harvard graduates, most included education as a main feature in their own programs. Robert Owen based the success of New-Harmony entirely on education, and Cabet said he would spare no expense for it.

We can see the importance people attached to education from the letters of Elijah Grant, president of Ohio Phalanx. He received a constant stream of inquiries from potential members, and his replies show that people who thought about joining wanted to know about the educational program more than anything else. In that era, free education, even the minimum, existed only in a few localities. Therefore, we need not be surprised by the fact that the movement attracted many who hungered for that rare commodity for their children.

Adults also yearned for education, and many groups developed "practical" courses and special educational activities for self-improvement. Victor Considérant promised adults that La Réunion would satisfy their three needs: the physical, the social, and the intellectual. The last included the study of English and French and "a higher class of enjoyments." Those who lacked these advantages before, would now feel "raised in dignity and incited by a noble ambition." Marcus Spring, a comfortably placed New York businessman and movement supporter, told of a workingman who had aspired to a "higher intellectual and spiritual culture." He joined Brook Farm and found himself elevated by "some of the finest minds in the country."[21]

Integral Phalanx convincingly promoted these cultural advantages in their newspaper, *Ploughshare and Pruninghook* (February 14, 1846). Situated on the lonesome prairie of central Illinois, it asked midwestern pioneers, "Would it not be better to be surrounded with the works of Art and Science, with every opportunity for cultivation and refinement, than be confined to the dull monotony and imperfect education in the isolated household?"

Strong feelings on certain moral issues impelled some toward social reorganization. For example, the Icarians hung the slogan No More War! in the Nauvoo dining hall. The Practical Christians of Hopedale, following the literal teaching of Jesus, took an exemplary pledge "never to kill, assault, [or] beat . . . any human being . . . [or] serve in the army or navy."[22] Charles Sears, of North American Phalanx, told Americans to expect a future in which soldiers would be replaced by industrial armies dedicated to reclaiming the environment.

Vegetarians who branded the killing of animals immoral wanted a world that respected the sanctity of life. One fervent group had to fend off the Kansa Tribe of Native Americans in an attempt to establish their experiment in the Kansas Territory. Closely related to the vegetarians, but not the same, believers in the importance of health foods looked to the spirit of the movement as a natural ally of their dietary beliefs. The Grahamites, followers of Sylvester Graham, remembered today in our graham crackers, found a home in several colonies. Brook Farm, for example, set aside a special table for them.

Women flocked to the movement because they saw an opportunity there to take their rightful places in society. New-Harmony's constitution promised "Equality of Rights uninfluenced by sex," and Northampton's guaranteed that "The rights of all are equal without distinction of sex, color or condition, sect or religion." The *Harbinger* (September 26, 1846) confirms what those promises had achieved; the movement's "most devoted advocates" are "intelligent and earnest-minded women who have been won to its principles by a perception of the benefits it would confer."

Finally, the ever-present back-to-nature urge played a role. Arcadian nostalgia for a simpler past rooted in the soil attracted city dwellers who longed for life in a rustic setting. A New Yorker in Raritan Bay Union listened to the "mournful song of the whippoorwill" through his open window and it reminded him of other days, "when life as well as the year was in its spring." And he wondered how "people could endure the brick walls and dust and noise of the city."[23]

Happiness

The evils of society led to unhappiness, and all the goals of social reorganization can be summarized under one heading: bring happiness to the world. Happiness, as a philosophical concept, has a long history. At least as early as the first century B.C., it was considered by some to be a supreme good, and by the seventeenth century a school of thought had come to regard it as a natural right. In America, a prerevolutionary pamphlet called it the first law of every government, and finally a government, through the Virginia Bill of Rights, recognized "pursuing and obtaining happiness" as an "inherent right." The pursuit of happiness became an inalienable right in the Declaration of Independence.

However, to the evolving concept of happiness as a right, people in social reorganization brought two qualitative changes: they made it society's responsibility, and they gave it concrete meaning.

First, while the trailblazing documents of the American Revolution spoke only of a right to *pursue* happiness, this movement set out to create a society specifically designed to *bring* happiness. That transferred the burden from the individual, the one with the least control over circumstances, to society, which had the power to create conditions conducive to happiness.

New-Harmony's constitution, which the *Gazette* published in its first printing (October 1, 1825), proclaimed to the world the colony's goal: to bring to its people "the greatest amount of happiness, to secure it to them, and to transmit it to their children to the latest posterity." Owen read the text at a town meeting when the experiment began and explained to the members how society forms human character, and how people could turn out "good or bad, and experience the extremes of happiness or misery through the circumstances that exist around [them]." Owen promised them that the New Social System would form character with happiness as its goal.

Owen's plan, therefore, went beyond a mere statement on natural rights and beyond a simple right to pursue happiness. He would remake, adjust, and control all the circumstances of society to guarantee happiness. He assured the meeting that it would soon be easy to create "good instead of evil, and happiness instead of misery." And Owen dedicated himself to that noble end. "I now live but to see this system fairly established in the world, well knowing that this alone is wanting to secure permanent happiness to all my fellow creatures."

The second change that social reorganization brought to the concept of happiness has to do with its meaning. Before the advent of the movement, happiness had been treated as an abstraction. But these colonies, through their promises and the programs they tried to institute, spelled out what it takes, or what they thought it would take, to make people happy. And the expectations of members and potential members reduced those things to everyday, human terms.

Many of the colonies of social reorganization set up programs and activities designed to bring happiness. For example, Owen established schools with a curriculum based on the premise that teaching should never include punishments. And he held a rationale for entertainments consistent with his ideas on character formation. He pointed out in the *Gazette* (October 29, 1825) that "well regulated amusements should be no less a part of the business of life than other occupations; but this important object has hitherto been mostly directed by chance." In accord with this principle he designated Friday night for concerts; Tuesday, dances; and Wednesday, lectures.

Such attitudes toward happiness existed throughout the movement. Hopedale published a pamphlet listing seven things the colony would do. First, the colony would be "a practical illustration of [how] all human beings . . . may become individually and socially happy." A founding member of Modern Times told a reporter, "We were born to be happy, we must have happiness, no matter how we get it."[24]

The people in social reorganization set quite a task for their movement. But, egged on by the evils of society and spurred on by their expectations of a better life, they generated a faith that stood ready to take on the world. Charles A. Dana, a Brook Farm stalwart, remembered that period as a time of great agitation unmatched in history. According to Octavius Frothingham, a friend to Brook Farmers, the spirit of the times rejected "Let us eat and drink for tomorrow we die" and instead espoused "I must work while it is day." He said that plans filled the air for "social regeneration," and "radical social reform." Recall that to the people in this movement *reform* meant re-form, that is, remake society. William Throop, in Preston, New York, wrote to his brother that "reform is the order of the day." And the editors of the *Tocsin* (December 6, 1844) exhorted readers not to give up in the face of an evil world. They sounded the rallying cry "Go and reform it!"[25]

Daily Life

The Necessities

THE STORY OF THE EXPERIMENTS in social reorganization begins with basics. Its leaders offered, and had to offer, the basic promise of abolishing concerns about the essentials of life. This included the opportunity to work reasonable hours at an acceptable job, to enjoy a satisfying diet, and to have a decent place to live. Social reorganization also stood for far more ennobling rewards: equality, intellectual enrichment, access to the arts, and the peace of mind that comes from living in a just and moral society. However, it is the basics that provide immediate insight into a fundamental weakness in utopian speculations. As we look into how they worked, what they ate, their houses, their clothing, and even their hairstyles, we can understand their efforts not in dry theoretical terms but in more compelling human terms. And here we come upon the first of the many bitter ironies that characterize the utopian episodes.

The Workday and Work

Utopian roosters crowed early, earlier perhaps than their brothers in traditional society. Victor Duclos recalled that schoolboys in New-Harmony began the day at 3:00 A.M., and Miner Kellogg remembered well the required eye-opener: a plunge in the Wabash River even in winter. In Northampton they awoke at four o'clock, and they too started off with a cold bath, but they used tubs. Of course, in winter they first had to break up the layer of ice that had formed overnight. In Fruitlands the day began at dawn. Charles Lane, the ideological mentor there, believed that a cold bath at that hour contributed to cheerfulness, and he won a convert in ten-year-old Louisa May Alcott. She noted in her diary, "I rose at 5 and had my bath. I love cold water!"[1] The typical utopian wake-up call came at 5:00 A.M., but the genteel Brook Farmers held off until six, when "the rising horn," a trumpet blast, drove away sleep. The sound of the trumpet also called the Icarians to the daily battle for the new way of life, but in New-Harmony the steeple clock did the job.

Utopian conjecture held out the promise that a four- or five-hour day of pleasant employments would suffice, but in reality the day that waited for most members as they opened their eyes turned out to be long and arduous. Life may have been just as hard for people in traditional society, of course, but social reorganization had pledged a better way of life. In La Réunion, the members put in only nine hours, which seems moderate compared with other colonies until we realize that the cruel Texas heat dictated the workday. In summer they began at 4:00 A.M. and worked until the breakfast bell at six. After eating, they worked until about ten o'clock, had a snack, and then went to sleep until the dinner bell woke them at 3:00 P.M. After this main meal they returned to work and finally quit for the day at about 9:00 P.M.

City-bred utopians endured considerable hardship in tackling an agrarian life, especially on the frontier. Thomas Steel, an English physician in Equality, a little-known experiment in southeastern Wisconsin, described life there in letters to his father in London. From them, a picture emerges of drudgery and fatigue. The members had to cut the native oak forest, clear the land, hew bulky logs for cabins, and scythe from sunup to sunset – the typical frontier life but with a critical difference. The hardy pioneers who settled our West wanted only to carve out a homestead for themselves, and most knew what it took to reach that familiar, tangible goal. Utopians sweated for a grander but much more remote prize, a new and ideal world, yet most came physically and mentally unprepared for the price nature asked.

From a letter Huldah Bayley wrote to her brother, Calvin, who had remained at home in Manlius, New York, we learn of the tragic toll such work extracted in an obscure experiment on the Pigeon River north of present-day Sheboygan, Wisconsin. Of the small group of families who started the colony early in 1846, half could not make it through the summer. Others, worn down and weakened, became victims of "the ague" and fever and had to "return to civilization" early in the fall. Dr. Cady, their leader and inspiration, toiled on only to succumb to disease before winter.[2]

Even in the larger, more highly developed experiments, the workday turned out to be long and taxing. From Owen's New-Harmony, Sarah Pears wrote her aunt that she could no longer face the prospect of twelve hours a day of scrubbing, sewing, cooking, and washing. In Wisconsin Phalanx, Harriet Haven recorded in her journal that she put in a good day's work: sewing by hand, she made twenty-four cotton sacks, the heavy kind the flour mill used. The Dining Room Group there worked nine hours. In Icaria, the standard workday ran from 6:00 A.M. to 6:00 P.M.

Often, hours varied according to the job. Alphadelphia's shoemakers and farmers worked eight hours a day, the teamsters ten. Female cooks put in twelve hours; female tailors, ten; and female spinners, sixteen. Fortunately for us, the labor record book of Hannibal Taylor has survived, and from it we can learn something of the working life at Alphadelphia. The book contains daily entries from March to September 1845. On a typical day he worked ten hours, but occasionally it might be eight or less, depending on the weather. When it rained all day he did not work. His most grueling labor came on April 12, when he toiled fifteen hours making sugar, and three days later, when he boiled soap for seventeen hours through the night.[3]

The workday in the eastern experiments appears to have been less rigorous; still it overwhelmed utopians, many of whom came from clerical or professional backgrounds. Elizabeth Curson wrote to her sister about a pleasant gentleman who wanted to join Brook Farm. "The difficulty is he is a lawyer, and not strong enough for what John calls spade work." The seemingly indefatigable Georgiana Bruce confessed that when evening came she often felt too tired to do anything except listen to music. Nathaniel Hawthorne, an early member of Brook Farm, planned to use his free time there to write, but after a week he discovered an unexpected barrier. Chopping wood all morning left its mark on fingers unused to anything more taxing than a pen. "What an abominable hand do I scribble," he complained to his notebook. Toiling in the field opened his eyes to a simple truth. "It is an endless surprise to me how much work there is to be done in the world." Then, a few weeks later, after a wrenching stint at cleaning the manure from the barn, he came to the realization that "this present life of mine gives me an antipathy to pen and ink. . . . In the midst of toil, or after a hard day's work . . . my soul obstinately refuses to be poured out on paper."[4]

Just as country work exhausted city-bred members physically, the tedium of rural life drained them psychologically. Country hours seemed longer, and some people could not adjust to that place. Kalikst

Wolski, the cosmopolitan Pole at La Réunion, told his diary why he had so few entries for it. "Life is monotonous, and there is nothing new to write about." And even at Brook Farm, where the members provided many diversions, Amelia Russell admitted she found the daily routines dull. But Fourier, thinking of the butterfly flitting from flower to flower, offered them a solution to boring work: switch from one job to another throughout the day. We get an idea of how that worked from a Marianne Dwight letter. In the following summary of her schedule abstracted from the letter, notice that she had to walk back and forth among three of the colony's buildings, situated around the perimeter of a large, hilly, open area the size of several football fields. That routine made New England weather, good and bad, a part of indoor work.

6:30	wait on breakfast table (the Hive)
7:00	clean up dining room and kitchen, 1½ hours
8:30	clean rooms for Dormitory Group, 1½ hours
11:00	change clothes; Sewing Group 1½ hours (the Aerie)
12:30	eat dinner (the Hive)
1:30	teach 2 drawing classes, 2 hours (Pilgrim Hall)
3:30	Sewing Group, 2 hours (the Aerie).
5:30	set tables for supper (the Hive)
6:00	eat supper
	after supper: wash dishes till about 7:30.

"A long day," she admitted, "but alternation of work and pleasant company and chats make it pleasant."[5]

A visitor to North American Phalanx in 1855 described the typical workday of a woman there. Although similar to Dwight's thirteen-hour day, her schedule has one significant difference: a period of free time in the course of the working day for recreation or study. Nothing, here or elsewhere, suggests that the movement's colonies had adopted this as general practice. Yet such an idea had indeed been part of the attraction of social reorganization.

Brook Farmer Elizabeth Curson often mentioned in her letters that she spent time drawing in the middle of the day. But that happened only on Sundays, or during time off. However, no other adult member ever mentioned anything like it. Ralph Waldo Emerson wrote that at Brook Farm, "One man ploughed all day and one looked out the window all day, and perhaps drew his picture, and both received at night the same wages." Emerson never saw this himself although he visited Brook Farm periodically. Rather, he said, he had it from the "country members," and in this way the Sage of Concord took idle gossip and placed it into history as fact.[6]

No evidence exists to support Emerson. On the contrary, the Brook Farm records show that members received labor credit only for producing necessities or commodities that could bring in income. For example, Marianne Dwight painted lamp shades and drew flowers as her job, and the money from their sale went into the colony's treasury. No entry in these records credits anyone for time spent in the colony's theatrical or musical performances, for writing a poem, or drawing for pleasure. Not even the cost of a platform for a play shows up in the ledgers. Yet Brook Farmers held such activities among the most important of life and participated in them more than any other group. But they could do so only at their own cost. Actually, that may be a much more serious debit against the utopian promise than any that an antagonist could invent.

John Sears, a youngster of the Phalanx period, wrote that they would take two afternoons a week for "diversions." That may have been true for the students, but the labor records do not show it for workers. For example, one of the surviving account books for that period lists daily labor credits for each member of the Printing Group. They worked Monday through Saturday, the full-time workers averaging almost nine hours per day. The daily hours did vary from more than thirteen to as low as five on a Saturday. But rather than any time-off plan, that schedule reflected the work of the shop: producing a weekly newspaper, the *Harbinger,* which came out on Saturday.[7]

Furthermore, those hours in the print shop do not indicate any application of the "butterfly" theory. They set type by hand in those days, and even if they had enough skilled typesetters and printers to switch jobs, such work requires continuity. That and the needs of timely production probably ruled out for them and for all similar work the kind of shifting around that Fourier visualized for gardening or domestic work.

Brook Farmers could choose their occupations, something few other colonies allowed. In North American Phalanx leaders posted the job assignments each night to meet the colony's needs for the following day; members had no choice. In Communia members had a constitutional obligation to do certain jobs. William Pelham, of New-Harmony, did not see any of his fellow members doing work they disliked. But anecdotes suggest otherwise. For example, a German nobleman, Duke Bernhard, who visited New-Harmony in 1826, told one about Virginia Dupalais, the cultivated niece of French artist Charles Lesueur. She had been entertaining the group with her fine voice and piano playing when her turn came to milk the cows. She had to leave, but she went out crying and, in the interpretation of the duke, an aristocrat, decrying equality.[8] Situations like that – not unusual – confirm that these experiments attracted many people who had only a foggy idea of the underlying principles.

Icaria's arbitrary work assignments led to charges of favoritism and to virtual mutiny. Leaders assigned workers to shops, and then reassigned them at will. Members called it "changing the harness." François Lacour found himself in nine different occupations in a three-month period.[9] A list of jobs in *Colonie Icarienne* (September 20, 1854) shows many people working at trades other than their regular one. This waste of skills helps explain the inefficiency of the colony. For example, they had two bakers by trade, Cit. Biey and Cit. Bacon, but the colony's managers reassigned one to work as a saddler and the other to the farm. Who baked the bread? Cit. Jalagers, a tailor, and Cit. Vannier, a coachman, got that assignment. The labor directors took Cit. Zwicker from his trade, shoemaker, and put him to work making barrels, and they sent Cit. Richard, a weaver, to a flatboat crew.

A small detail of Icaria's job assignment system confirms the leadership's cruel indifference to human feelings. They used the word *corvée* for colony work. That word had a hateful past in feudalism. For France's downtrodden it meant state-controlled forced labor, and its tyranny had long ago incited the masses to revolt. Cabet, who had written a history of that revolution and who had promised to erase the ugly past, showed his doctrinaire insensitivity in allowing a word stained by French blood to stand beside his slogans on equality. It could only serve to inflame passions in this colony already reeling from charges of corrupt labor practices.

Most utopian experiments suffered because the membership consisted of a select group and so lacked the full range of skills that makes a society function. To get things done, they had to disregard the axioms of social reorganization that had brought them together and resort to some of the very evils they abhorred in the old social order: expedience, coercion, and inefficiency. In La Réunion, for example, when they needed housing, the leadership handed out saws and hatchets to members who knew nothing heavier than a pen, and told them to be carpenters.

LEADERS AS WORKERS

To their credit, the leading people in many, but not all, of these experiments put in the same hours as the rank and file and stood ready to work as hard as they did. That fact impressed Marianne Finch, an English tourist who visited North American Phalanx. There she saw the democratic spirit in action: "Even the president forgets his high station, and becomes a worker. . . . He is at the head where he is fit, [but] where he does not excel, he is satisfied to work under the direction of others." Similarly, the board of directors of the Sodus Bay experiment, faced with the problem of an accumulation of dirty laundry too large for the regular Washing Group, formed themselves into an Auxiliary Group and rolled up their sleeves.[10]

Robert Owen brought several well-known people to New-Harmony when he returned to the colony in 1826, among them Thomas Say, the famous entomologist. A member of the Academy of Natural Sciences in Philadelphia, he stood out among the distinguished scholars who joined Owen's experiment. Yet, Say, a firm believer in the cause, took his turn at physical work there. Duke Bernhard noticed Say's hands, swollen and blistered from labor as a colony gardener and came away with the impression that he was "obliged" to do such work.[11]

Say's efforts have a parallel in the work John Dwight did in Brook Farm. A student there, Arthur Sumner, nephew of the famous senator, left this description for us. "Mr. John Dwight used to come in from his toil in the hot sun at noon to give me a lesson on the piano: and after faithfully doing that job, he would lie down on the lounge and go to sleep while I played to him. What a piece of nonsense it was to have a man like that hoeing corn and stiffening his eloquent fingers." But the Brook Farmers deemed all labor equally honorable, and as Sumner expressed it, the poet, painter, and philosopher had to take their turn "in the ditch." Dwight did indeed carry a heavy burden for a leader. Besides his other duties, he wrote for the *Harbinger* each week. In a letter to a friend, he complained that "all the world has claims upon me. . . . I am undertaking too many things."[12] In fact, during the last two years of Brook Farm, Dwight wrote fifty-one critical articles on music and performances, forty-seven book reviews, and numerous poems, translations, and essays interpreting Fourier.

George Ripley's position as a director of Brook Farm kept him busy. And in the Phalanx years his editorial work on the *Harbinger* took a slice of his day. All of that came on top of his farm responsibilities: milking and barn care. Sophia Ripley, his wife and partner in founding the experiment, taught in the school. She also had to entertain visitors, oversee the girl students, take care of fourteen rooms, and scrub the kitchen floor. In her spare time she wrote musical plays for the Amusement Group.

Some rejected the idea that leaders had to soil their hands. In Raritan Bay Union, Theodore Weld, the abolitionist, directed the school. He and his wife, Angelina Grimké, abolitionist and women's rights champion, took their turn at the regular labor requirements of the colony. But surprisingly, her sister Sarah Grimké, the noted activist in the cause of equality and the colony's bookkeeper, did not agree with them. She argued that Angelina "was no more designed to serve tables than Theodore to dig potatoes."[13]

Such a patrician attitude seems to contradict the essence of social reorganization, and other instances turn up elsewhere, as we shall see. But, whatever their errors and faults, in general these groups made it a practice to share, particularly when it came to food. When they violated this spirit the record shows disaster following close behind.

On the other hand, privilege typified the groups dedicated to individual salvation. In such colonies the congregation, with an abiding faith in their charismatic leader, accepted privilege as part of the divine order, and in those cloistered environments it had no destructive consequences.

Food and Food Beliefs

In the colonies of social reorganization, the hand of austerity generally doled out the meals. Therefore, luxuries such as coffee and sugar rarely appeared on the menu. And as in the case of work, the leading people, with a few exceptions, assumed no special food privileges. Slogans on equality aside, such inequities would have been difficult since in most colonies everyone ate together. In Brook Farm, to cite a typical situation, George Ripley, Charles Dana, and John Dwight sat at the tables in the colony dining room with all the other members and shared whatever they had. In Icaria, Cit. Cabet ate among *les citoyens* and *les citoyennes* in Nauvoo's seven-hundred-seat dining hall.

Most colonies served three meals a day. Breakfast generally came at about six o'clock, but some groups used the principle of work first, eat later. The Icarians, for example, had to stay their hunger until eight o'clock. However, Icarians who worked in the cold, those doing heavy labor, and washerwomen received a ration of corn whiskey first thing upon arising to tide them over until breakfast, and also between meals when necessary. In most colonies members ate their main meal around noon and they used the word *dinner* for it. They then had a light meal variously called supper or tea at about six o'clock. Some groups offered additional refreshment. Communia, for example, had bread, milk, and cheese available in the kitchen between meals.

Cabet recorded the food on the Icarian menu in 1855. If true, Icarians probably ate better than other experiments in social reorganization. Still located in Nauvoo on the Mississippi in that year, they benefited from easy access to trading centers along the river, especially St. Louis, where they operated a retail outlet for the clothing and shoes they made. Though Cabet filled their minds with radical ideas, such traditional economics undoubtedly help fill their stomachs. Their dinner included a thick soup, a meat dish such as fresh pork and sauerkraut in winter, and sometimes mutton, ham, chicken, or fresh fish in season. They had butter and cheese and plenty of vegetables: peas, carrots, turnips, spinach, potatoes, beans, and rice. That year peaches produced an abundant crop, enough to last ninety meals.[14]

Though plentiful, Icaria's diet came in for criticisms that have an important place in the history of utopianism. François Lacour, who had a basically negative reaction to his experience there, nevertheless confirmed everything Cabet said about the food. In 1855 he even had items considered luxuries elsewhere, for example, coffee and *kneips* (a kind of doughnut). Yet he left us a crucial observation on the quality of collective life when he pointed out that though pure and abundant, the food had little variety and lacked the taste and freshness of individual cuisine. Today we would call it institutional food. Frédéric Olinet reacted with greater intensity: he found the monotony of the cuisine "actually painful." Emile Vallet, who ate those meals for six years, showed how food affected the colony's viability. Keeping in mind the fact that the Icarians did not join up as losers or destitute unemployed, but as people with a vision, makes Vallet's point more convincing. He argued that the meals, lacking variety, with too much pork and beans, drove away people used to better things and people with limits to self-sacrifice.[15]

People in North American Phalanx during the early years ate food typical of the movement, dull and inconsistent in quality. When Fredrika Bremer, the Swedish novelist, visited in 1849, her dinner included meat, and a few good items: break, milk, and cheese. However, Marianne Finch stopped there two years later, and found the basic menu inadequate: hominy, buckwheat cakes, and cold meat for breakfast, and the same for supper. Potatoes distinguished the dinner menu.

Later, in an attempt to put into practice Fourier's ideas about attracting wealthy people and also to help cut losses, North American Phalanx tried a novel idea never before attempted in the movement, they replaced the egalitarian shared-food system with a restaurant. This new arrangement featured an elaborate, somewhat pretentious printed menu, with a wide choice of foods. The dinner menu differed from breakfast only in the addition of an item or two. As in traditional restaurants, a waiter took the order and brought the food. The check then became a charge against the member's labor account. Fortunately, about a dozen of these menus have survived, and on one of them someone wrote in the prices. That menu is reproduced in illustration 3. Notice that this is an à la carte menu; every item, no matter how small, had to be paid for.[16]

Soups, 1½¢.
Meats: roast beef, 4¢; veal, 5¢; ham, 8¢.
Vegetables: potatoes or beets, 1¢; tomatoes, 3¢.
Breads, biscuits, cakes, butter, cheese, 1¢.
Desserts: pies and fruits, 2¢ and 3¢.
Beverages: tea or coffee, 1¢; milk per quart, 2¢.

A writer for *Life Illustrated* spent a week there for a feature story (August 18, 1855) and enjoyed breakfasts of eggs, graham bread and butter, blueberries with milk, and "excellent coffee." He concluded that "the cooking is excellent, and the fare, . . . though far from luxurious, suits our simple tastes better than that of our first class hotels." In addition, he described the mealtime atmosphere as relaxed and congenial.

Congeniality, probably fostered by a spirit of cooperation for a noble cause, enlivened mealtimes throughout the movement except in Icaria, where Cabet required spartan silence at the table. But congeniality could not substitute for food. No mealtime in the movement matched that of Brook Farm, where a steady stream of brilliant wit and wisdom darted back and forth over the dishes. Gradually, how-

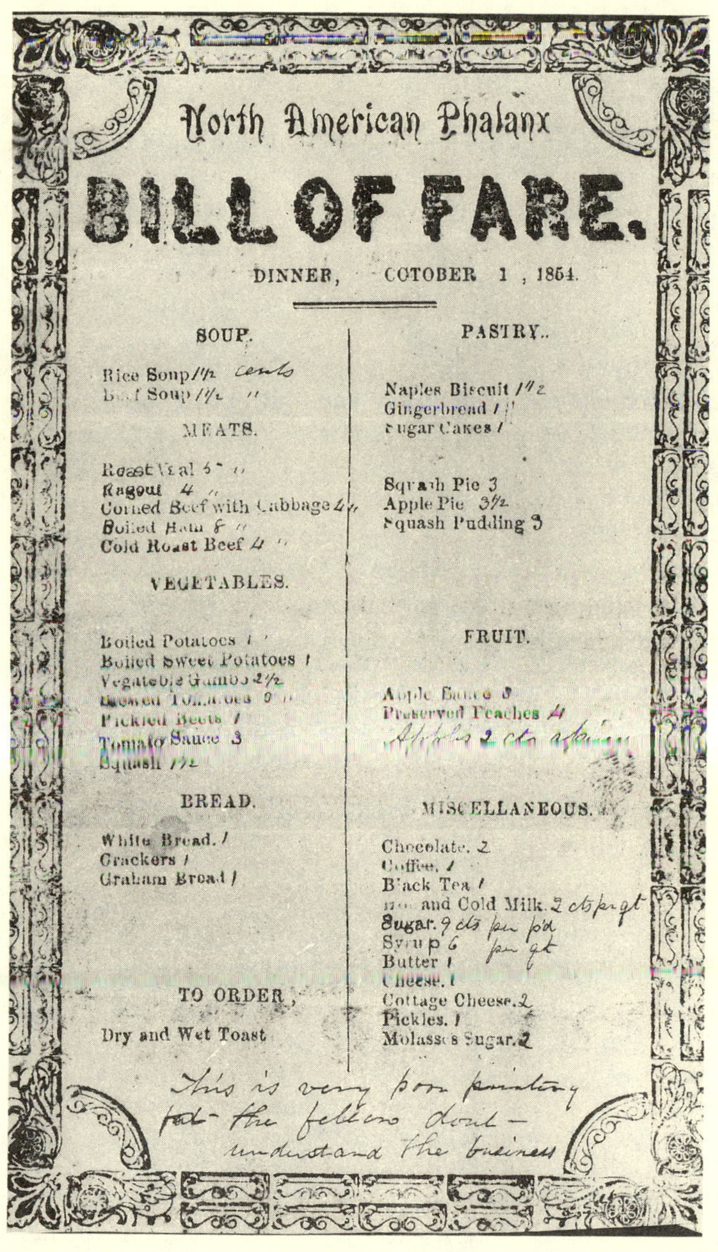

North American Phalanx

BILL OF FARE.

DINNER, OCTOBER 1, 1854.

SOUP.

Rice Soup 1½ cents
Beef Soup 1½ "

MEATS.

Roast Veal 5 "
Ragout 4 "
Corned Beef with Cabbage 4 "
Boiled Ham 8 "
Cold Roast Beef 4 "

VEGETABLES.

Boiled Potatoes 1
Boiled Sweet Potatoes 1
Vegetable Gumbo 2½
Stewed Tomatoes [illegible]
Pickled Beets 1
Tomato Sauce 3
Squash 1½

BREAD.

White Bread. 1
Crackers 1
Graham Bread 1

TO ORDER.

Dry and Wet Toast

PASTRY.

Naples Biscuit 1½
Gingerbread 1
Sugar Cakes 1

Squash Pie 3
Apple Pie 3½
Squash Pudding 3

FRUIT.

Apple Sauce 3
Preserved Peaches 4
Apples 2 cts a plate

MISCELLANEOUS.

Chocolate. 2
Coffee. 1
Black Tea 1
Hot and Cold Milk. 2 cts per qt
Sugar. 9 cts per p'd
Syrup 6 per qt
Butter 1
Cheese. 1
Cottage Cheese. 2
Pickles. 1
Molasses Sugar. 2

This is very poor printing but the fellows dont — understand the business

3. Menu from North American Phalanx's restaurant. By permission of the Houghton Library, Harvard University.

ever, the delightful conversations encountered less and less food on those dishes. Indeed, the alimentary history of almost all of these experiments can be summarized in one ironic phrase: progressive retrenchment.

Georgiana Bruce gives no hint of food shortages during her stay at Brook Farm in its early years. In fact, she mentions quite casually such dishes as steaming platters of corned beef and cabbage and on Fridays fresh fish for Roman Catholic members. So we can assume that Brook Farmers probably had enough to eat in that period. It certainly must have satisfied young George Curtis, who got too fat for the clothes he had brought.

But in Brook Farm's third year its situation began to change. Organizational minutes, formal, dry, and dull, usually seem remote from human feelings. However, Brook Farm's minutes from then on contain proposals that throb with the pain of an ideal slipping away. This sampling of five motions that carried suggests the fate in store for the experiment.

September 24	Discontinue coffee at breakfast.
December 10	Clear breakfast at 7:45 (cut meal to 45 mins.).
June 30	Charge member for a guest's food.
July 21	Children eat only at Children's Table (they used to arrive first and clean up everything in sight. That forced working adults to go hungry).
December 8	Clear breakfast at 7:30 (mealtime now 30 mins.).

Retrenchment had become the principal tactic in coping with financial difficulties. Meat, butter, and tea became special items, coffee a rarely encountered luxury. Still Marianne Dwight said she found enough for a meal with potatoes, turnips, squash, and pudding. She saw the bright side. "I trust that our people will find by and by that meat and tea have lost their relish. . . . Perhaps we shall have fewer headaches." Brook Farmers gave dispensations, though. Charles Newcomb, a special boarder who wanted to be a poet, got tea and butter. Two months later, the minutes show a motion carried to permit Hannah Colson to sit at the "meat table." Retrenchment continued, and the following spring Dwight wrote joyfully to her friend about a party Mr. and Mrs. Cheswell gave. "They offered us the tempting luxuries of hot coffee, cakes, crackers, and cheese."[17]

The colony set aside "Grahamite tables," where followers of Sylvester Graham's health food ideas and vegetarians ate. The financial report of 1844 noted the lower cost for these members, and agreed that an adjustment to benefit them should be made. Yet despite the reasonableness of the vegetarians' argument – the difference should be returned to them through larger portions – no equalizing appears in the records. Denying them added to potential discord, but increasing austerity probably left few choices.

Even if the Brook Farmers had options left, these went up in smoke when a fire destroyed their almost-finished new building in 1846. That tragedy forced them to hunt for new ways to cut back, but as Amelia Russell observed, "We had now reached a point at which it was impossible for us to retrench any further." Reduced to mush and milk for breakfast and for supper, and to vegetables flavored with salt pork for dinner – Grahamites had to forgo even that – she satisfied her hunger with bread and molasses. John Codman, who spent four years in the colony, claimed that "enthusiasm . . . sweetens many dull dishes."[18] But even enthusiasm reached its limit at empty dishes, and by the spring of 1847 Brook Farmers had virtually nothing left to sweeten.

Real sweetening, not the kind that comes from enthusiasm but from sugar, remained a rare treat in most of these colonies, particularly in the western experiments, where members called it a luxury. New Harmony, La Réunion, and Communia all reported sugar in short supply. In a most surprising development for a colony based on mutual trust and cooperation, Alphadelphia locked it up, and kept a precise record in the daybook of each use showing the exact weight taken. The Alphadelphians suffered from a scarcity in other foods too. Evidence for that comes from the fact that just a few months after getting organized, their board of directors voted to require new members to bring their own provisions for half a year. One old-timer recalled the following verse:

> And if perchance a luckless wight
> Should from his dinner bilk,
> His supper then was sure to be
> Cold buckwheat cakes and milk.[19]

Brook Farm's fire forced Charlotte Haven, Sophia Ripley's cousin, who was waiting for a room, to give up her application. Determined to try life in Association, she went west at the age of twenty-seven to join Wisconsin Phalanx. After a month she wrote back to her sister in New Hampshire describing the situation. Their diet for the first three weeks consisted of vegetables only. Then one evening "as I entered for supper, the atmosphere was most savory; my eyes glistened . . . I thought of stuffed turkey, but my countenance fell . . . when I perceived . . . [only] pitchers of sage tea and bowls of onions." Occasionally varied with cabbage, that menu lasted a week. Later new cooks improved the fare with pies, cakes, and "chicken fixen." Charlotte Haven's sister Harriet recorded the menu of a Wisconsin Phalanx Sunday dinner in her journal. The "feast," as she called it, lasted three hours and consisted of baked squash, toast, johnnycakes, squash pie, honey, and bread.[20]

Wisconsin Phalanx members, like those in Brook Farm, enjoyed a better life when they first started out. In their second year they had an abundance of potatoes, corn, cabbage, turnips, and carrots. They also had sheep, cattle, and four hundred acres of wheat. Otis Capron, referring to wild game – geese, duck, and deer – boasted in a letter to a friend, "We live on the fat of the land, no mistake." But by their fourth year conditions had changed. Charlotte Haven said that then she rarely tasted meat, and she labeled coffee and tea luxuries.[21]

Shortages plagued large groups like New-Harmony but brought greater misery to small groups such as little-known Philadelphia Industrial Association in northwest Indiana. A. E. Winter wrote his sister Sarah in Belchertown, Massachusetts, that during their eighteen months in the colony he and his wife, Cornelia, "suffered" from lack of proper food. Dr. Thomas Steel, a member of Equality, an obscure group in Wisconsin, tried to raise revenue to keep the experiment going by treating people from the surrounding area. Being mostly poor farmers, they paid in kind, and one baked some bread for the fee. That came at a desperate time for the colony, and as Dr. Steel put it in a letter to his father in London, "the payment in this manner was really a godsend."[22]

At La Réunion the Texas heat created the food shortages. Augustin Savardan found that meat quickly took on a sickening smell that made it repulsive. The sun parched their crops, but watering by hand with buckets simply wasted a precious luxury. In August 1855 their spring went dry, many members took sick, and many died of thirst.[23]

TABOOS

The movement tended to attract people with unconventional ideas, some sound, some eccentric, and both helped create dietary notions, fads, and taboos that blanketed the experiments. Many of these live on today.

Fruitlands – the name itself symbolized their diet – stood at the extreme. Members lived on fruits, vegetables, and grains, and they prohibited all animal foods: meats, eggs, cheese, and milk. In this ethic they remained admirably consistent, banning all animal products: fur, leather, wool, candles, even manure for fertilizer. They opposed stimulants such as tea and coffee, which were taboos in many other colonies, and drank only clear, cold water. Charles Lane, one of the founders of Fruitlands, had no concern about criteria for selecting members but preferred "open house to all comers." He knew that "if they come not in the right name and nature they will not long remain. Our dietetic system is a test quite sufficient for many." But they had to order Anna Page, Louisa May Alcott's teacher, to leave. She had eaten fish.[24]

Warren Chase, after four years at the helm of Wisconsin Phalanx, offered guidelines to help other experiments select members. A few of his criteria relate to food and exemplify the kind of beliefs that to varying degrees pervaded the movement. He classified coffee drinkers, tea drinkers, and pork eaters as the least desirable. Those who ate pork and used tobacco could be particularly harmful. Most of all, they should not even consider people who used "ardent spirits."[25]

Alcohol taboo. A major article on alcohol in the *Harbinger* (July 29, 1845) traced its use to the evils of traditional society. It saw hope only in "the radical cure," that is, social reorganization. The article also proclaimed a principle revolutionary for that time but one we consider perfectly acceptable today: society has a "duty" to prevent the sale of "any article of food or drink . . . which is injurious to health." The movement, going back to New-Harmony days considered that principle an essential characteristic of a caring society. Its colonies codified it into various prohibitions, and with a few exceptions, these included a constitutional ban on alcohol.

Although the *Harbinger* article came from Brook Farm, its own constitutions, brief and simple, with a minimum of restrictions and untold implied rights, say nothing on this topic. However, colony records tell the Brook Farmer's policy. Just ten days after the article appeared, their daybook has an entry – not unusual – showing the purchase of wine for member Charles Hosmer.

Sylvania Association's constitution, unlike all others in the movement, actually guaranteed the right of members to use alcohol. It said the Association could not exclude "the use of wines and spirits"; moreover, it had to "furnish the same to any member . . . according to the plan adopted with reference to wearing apparel or other articles." Nevertheless, grounds for expulsion included drunkenness. A more typical example of how the movement dealt with the question shows up in the constitution of Sodus Bay Phalanx. It simply said that no intoxicating liquor could be "made, sold, or used as a beverage by the members."

The land and village that Robert Owen bought from Father Rapp included a tavern and a distillery. When Owen took over Harmonie in 1825 and renamed it New-Harmony he prohibited alcohol there. But questions persist about the effectiveness of that rule and about the consistency of his leadership. The tavern remained, but William Pelham claimed that he and fellow members used it as a place for rational conversation, not for drinking and carousing. Because of that, he maintained, they had no drunken buffoons or brawls. However, they did expel three drunks who, he explained, got their whiskey from country neighbors. Duke Bernhard believed the drunkards got it from passing riverboats. But the New-Harmony ledgers show that drinkers did not have to go that far.

The tavern received a continuing supply of spirits. For example, in the colony ledgers the Tavern Account for July 1826 discloses the receipt of seventy-eight gallons of "New-Harmony Wine," five barrels of beer, and thirty-four gallons of brandy. Moreover, these records list such sales to accounts within the colony. The account of Robert Dale Owen, Robert Owen's son, has an entry for two gallons of wine on July 8. Surprisingly, both the Youth School Account, and the Education Society Account list wine purchases at various times. Later entries show whiskey charged to the Brickyard Account and others.

Owen's beliefs shine through the legal terms of a deed he signed conveying a parcel of land out of his New-Harmony holdings. He placed a restrictive covenant in the document banning liquor on that piece of real estate.[26] Yet, nothing in the records suggests that he tried to dismantle the distillery in New-Harmony although he said he would do so. And despite his principles, alcoholic beverages remained available in the colony. Wisconsin Phalanx members, in contrast, not only banned the use of alcoholic beverages on their own land but even succeeded in forcing a nearby distillery to move.

Alphadelphia, like most of these experiments, considered alcohol anathema. Therefore, the board of director's vote on July 30, 1844, to buy thirty-three gallons of whiskey "for pickling cucumbers" should have raised some eyebrows at the board meeting. But judging from the minutes all remained respectfully lowered. I could not find any such recipe, but even if one did exist, only muddled thinking would have risked violating a principle by choosing it over the old standards, brine or vinegar. Charges of duplicity appear throughout the colony's records, so that purchase adds yet another question mark between their beliefs and their practices. At the same meeting they also voted to buy some brandy, without any additional explanation. The colony usually recorded purchases of brandy under Miscellaneous Accounts with the explanation "for sickness" appended.

The Icarians considered whiskey a food for hard workers. But abuses crept in and forced Cabet to publicly condemn, with intemperate language, the growing intemperance. He listed the offenses: members lied; they used subterfuge to get additional whiskey – once sixteen liters seemed to evaporate in six days; they stole it; they even broke in through a window for it; they drank on the job; they became drunks. Cabet had rules of membership, and rule no. 25 emphasized: No Intoxicating Liquor! The Iowa colony had similar rules, but no greater success. One of the collections of Icarian manuscripts has a journal dating from the early Iowa period, when the experiment barely managed to survive. It contains the record of a buying trip to St. Louis. And there, among pencils, string, and chocolate, an entry for fifteen gallons of whiskey appears.[27] The group by then had dwindled to about forty adults and children.

Throughout the movement, the attempts to ban alcohol, whether misguided, inept, hypocritical, or any combination of these, end up as negatives on the utopian score sheet.

Tobacco taboo. Tobacco generally followed liquor as a taboo. Most groups banned it entirely or erected barriers to its use. Cabet despised tobacco and railed against it frequently. He tried to intimidate the smokers by displaying slogans across the walls of the large dining hall: No Tobacco! and War on Tobacco! and he extracted a promise from the Icarians never to plant it. For Icarians who smoked he had nothing but abuse; it disgusted Emile Vallet to hear Cabet call his comrades filthier than hogs for their habit. Yet the war against tobacco had the same effect as Cabet's campaigns against strong drink. The colony inventory for 1853 listed 450 liters of whiskey, and one hundred dollars' worth of tobacco.[28]

In the broadly tolerant atmosphere of Brook Farm, a few smoked. Based on entries in the colony's daybook, which lists items bought for members, tobacco use centered primarily among the working-class members newly recruited when Brook Farm became a Phalanx. It soon became a class distinction and encouraged a growing chill between these newer Brook Farmers and the ones they thought of as "aristocrats," that is, the remaining intellectuals, who tended toward vegetarianism and eschewed tobacco.

Modern Times seems like the one place that would taboo taboos. Their founding principle, "individual sovereignty," proclaimed that every human had a right to live free from the pressure of conforming with another's way of life. They took as their motto *Fais ce que voudras* (Do As You Wish). In Moncure Conway's novel based on his Modern Times experience, one character warns another, "Close questions about people are not asked [here]." Yet this tolerant group tolerated no tobacco and no liquor within its precincts. Charles Codman, a former Brook Farmer who became a Modern Timer, related the case of a New York City cigar maker who believed in the principles of Modern Times and wanted to live and operate his business there. The colony had financial difficulties, and new industry could have helped it survive. But the individualists would not have him.[29] In one of the great ironies of these utopian episodes, a society designed to serve the individual came up against the clash of two mutually exclusive principles, both laudable perhaps. And in this classical conflict between the individual and society, society won. It shows a fundamental error in utopian thinking: the belief that one ideal could serve the infinite variety of human urges.

Shelter

Before the colonies of social reorganization began to build, they needed to decide where to build and how to build. The speculations of Owen and Fourier captivated the movement with grandiose architectural visions. The basic social unit they saw in their imaginations consisted of a huge palacelike building big enough to incorporate within its center a vast tract of open land. This gigantic building would house living quarters, industrial shops, schools, and cultural facilities, all under one roof. Its generally square shape would enclose acres of gardens, fountains, parade grounds, recreational areas, and other, smaller buildings. In that carefully planned urban environment people would live, work, and enjoy themselves without going beyond the perimeter building except to reach the large farms and the forest. Fourier even envisioned a kind of nineteenth-century subway system to whisk people around the immense complex so that they could take advantage of the "butterfly" system of varied work or partake of its vast menu of recreations.

Fourier's ideas became widely known through large lithographs, one executed by a noted French artist and sold in Paris (see illustration 1 facing p. 1 for an example). American Associationists made these lithographs the center of attraction at public meetings in New York City and Boston and gave them prominent places in their colonies. Owen had a model constructed of his design, which he demonstrated to the U.S. Congress in 1825. Drawings appeared in the press.

Theory is one thing, and practice another. Yet these castles in air did touch a spirit deep within the utopian soul. In the real world that spirit dictated the places utopians selected for their homes, and it surfaced in their feelings about home. Their choices and feelings reflected the symbolism in the enormous building conjured up in speculation. Its perimeter can be seen as a wall that formed gigantic arms to enfold and protect the believers within. The whole construction is, after all, nothing other than a citadel. The walls did three things: they separated the enclave from evil; they created a barrier that encouraged isolation; and they helped turn the members' focus inward to their utopian refuge, away from the "outside world." These three functions took on a life of their own in the reality of the utopian experience. In word and deed all utopians tried first of all to distance themselves from the evils of society. Second, they welcomed isolation barriers. And third, as I showed in the previous chapter, they held a vision of the colony as a refuge, a place apart from the "outside world." A few brief examples clearly illustrate the first two points.

Separation from evils. The *New-Harmony Gazette* (July 21, 1826) published the classical argument against trying a utopian experiment within a city. "How shall the morals of youth be preserved . . . where evils and tempations are daily exhibited before their eyes, where gormandizing and drunkenness present themselves at every step?" Warren Chase expressed a similar idea when he referred to his experiment, Wisconsin Phalanx, as being "out of the reach of the corrupting influence of large cities" and "free from the vices of towns." He recalled that when his advance party first arrived at their new home on the prairie, they had to sleep in tents, "but not the 'tents of wickedness,' for they had no . . . drunkenness, profanity, or licentiousness, and no lawyering, doctoring, or Gospel-preaching, and therefore were nearly free from the wickedness of civilization."[30]

Isolation barriers. Fourier, thinking in terms of a crowded Europe, believed a new Phalanx would be forced into isolation to avoid contact with the sick morality of "Civilization." The name Phalanx itself has ironic symbolism through its link to ancient Greek wars, when soldiers formed a human wall. Fourier visualized his Phalanxes as walled cities surrounded by antagonistic neighbors. In fact, he fully expected that members would need to "lower the cannons on all who approached."[31]

Isolation came naturally in rural America. Bronson Alcott saw it in the property he selected for Fruitlands. "The place is quite remote from the busy haunts and thoroughfares of trade; it lies in a sequestered dell. . . . We are thus protected from the invasion of the ruder secular world." His associate Charles Lane described it more succinctly. "It is extremely retired, there being no road to it."[32] Modern Times was just three hours from Broadway via the Long Island Railroad tracks. But it stood in the midst of the island's desolate pine barrens, a place where trains rarely stopped.

Even a gate can create psychological isolation. Brook Farm suffered from a shortage of rooms, and as a stopgap the colony rented a cottage just across the road from the colony entrance. As they did for all their buildings, they gave it a fanciful name, the Nest, and at one time they filled it with members. Although technically not on Brook Farm property, it stood only a few steps away – but outside the gate. And an odd thing happened to the seemingly gregarious Brook Farmers who lived on the grounds – inside the gate. Amelia Russell reveals how they felt about the Nest. "Somehow those who lived there seemed in a degree separated from us . . . more like a separate family who visited us an neighbors. . . . It was as if the atmosphere which encircled us did not reach beyond our gates, and the moment we crossed the road we had left Brook Farm far in the distance."[33]

Not surprisingly, some colonies tried in a feeble way to ape the all-in-one building proposed by Owen and Fourier. Except to the credulous, however, it should have been clear that the resources of the movement in America simply did not share the same universe with the imagination of an Owen or a Fourier run riot in the hush of a study in London or Paris. The grand visions came out as modest dormitory-style buildings. Some groups even stuck to smaller units that accommodated only a few people.

Regardless of the type of housing, almost all suffered from overcrowding. Two causes lay at the root of the problem: inept management and visionary but short-sighted schemes. The best example of administrative blundering comes from New-Harmony. The winter of 1825–26 brought a flood of new people there after Robert Owen went east to publicize the colony's virtues. His son William, whom he had left in charge, tried to stop his father from encouraging additional recruits. In an urgent letter he warned, "It will be impossible to give them rooms here until we shall have built more houses." Almost worse than the housing shortage, the warehouse ran out of blankets as December's cold set in.[34] However, Robert Owen's eyes, which focused so well on fantastic architecture, simply glazed over when they fell on a laundry list of mundane necessities like blankets and beds. Ignoring his son's advice, he took no decisive measures to stem the influx or to mitigate the suffering it brought that winter. Only late in the spring did the *Gazette* print a small notice, buried on an inside page, warning people not to start out for New-Harmony without "previous . . . assurances of accommodations" (May 17, 1826). Too little and too late, the notice could do nothing about the discord this crisis bred, one of many in the experiment's turbulent history.

The second cause of the widespread housing shortages, less obvious but more basic, stemmed from a conceptual blind spot. It created a dilemma akin to the-chicken-or-the-egg conundrum. George and Lydia Arnold expressed the idea succinctly in a letter they wrote from Raritan Bay Union. "If we had all said we will not come till everything is ready . . . I should like to know when or who would make a beginning."[35] How to make a beginning hardly concerned visionaries who, in speculating on the wonders of life in a functioning ideal world, gave scant attention to the practical problems of actually constructing that world. Fourier does describe a trial Phalanx, but only in terms of operation and decoration. Thus, he implies that everything has to be in place before the residents arrive.[36]

The movement had two options:

1. *Build now, go later.* They could hire professionals to get everything done, ready, and working right. Then the members could move in, with nothing to do but test the untested utopian principles.

2. *Go now, build later.* They could let the members move to the chosen site, let them do the building, and let them get everything working while trying to test the untested utopian principles.

The experimenters in social reorganization always took the second option. Typically, they went out to some virgin tract with a maximum of vision and faith but a minimum in resources and the necessary special skills. There they tried to establish, all at once, housing, agriculture, industry, schools – in short, a complete and operating human environment. And at the same time they expected to thrive and raise children. Forced to the wall by the inevitable problems this impossible scheme generated, they grasped at impromptu solutions. And from such tactics, compromises in basic principles naturally flowed. Improvisation as a strategy reduced the grand utopian palaces of speculation to the farmhouses of reality and even farmhouses to log cabins.

When Kalikst Wolski got to La Réunion after the rough journey from New Orleans, he was dismayed to find that the "Large Building" was simply four bare rooms. He knew then that he faced "a continuation of the camping . . . only here it is not in tents but under a wooden roof." When Dr. Savardan arrived five weeks later, he got a straw mattress and a place on the floor of the "Large Building." To accommodate the newly arrived, the members built shelves on the walls to serve as bunks. Soon the council simply gave up on a Phalanstery, the Fourierist ideal of the palatial all-in-one building, and opted for smaller houses that could be finished quickly. The Integral Phalanx in Illinois had to consider a similar compromise in Fourierist doctrine when, according to a leader, William Pearse, they ran out of brick before finishing part of their large building. At least they had an announced and enforced policy of admitting no one unless there was a room for that person.[37]

The Ohio Phalanx apparently had no such policy and allowed overcrowding. That created discord and led directly to the crisis that forced a reorganization of the Phalanx. Moreover, contention for rooms fostered abuses such as favoritism, a common complaint. Substantiation for it turns up in a letter that Elijah Grant, president of the Phalanx, wrote to Robert Wheatly, a worker who had quit the colony. In it, Grant promised him a room that had been assigned to someone else if he would agree to return.[38]

The disparities inherent in makeshift or provisional lodgings inevitably generated competition for rooms that eroded the very ideals these groups professed. In Sodus Bay Phalanx a committee set the yearly rent for each room. From the list it compiled, the average rent works out to a little over eleven dollars. But consider the disproportions in the range: from a low of two dollars to a high of fifty dollars.

House	*Low*	*High*
Main	$6	$50
Small	2	20
Meeting	10	15

House	*Low*	*High*
South	$10	$14
Orchard	10	12
East Farm	2	12
Middle	5	8
Milk, all $5		

The rent and room assignments precipitated endless disputes. Charges of nepotism surfaced, and like greedy heirs fighting over an item in a will, members wrangled through tedious meetings after someone quit in order to get the vacated room. All of this spawned personal antagonisms that haunted Sodus Bay to the end.[39]

In many of these colonies certain locations had real disadvantages. In Brook Farm, walking from the three houses on the hill – the Pilgrim, the Cottage, and the Aerie – to the common dining room in the Hive must have made winter meals a hardship, especially in fresh snow and in the dark at breakfast time. In Icaria, Frédéric Olinet complained bitterly about the favoritism the bureaucrats showed in assigning lodgings. He made his criticisms widely known, and for his efforts he got the whistle-blower's reward. He ended up having to walk a longer distance to the dining hall, often against the intense cold of biting winds that swept across the frozen, mile-wide Mississippi.

The comfort of lodgings varied widely throughout the movement. Members of Equality had rough log cabins and had to sleep on the floor at the mercy of prairie winds that slithered through the chinks. The Icarians in Iowa made their log cabins more snug, but still they remained just log cabins, austere and dark. Raritan Bay Union stood at the other end of the spectrum with a rather elegant stone and brick building that suited both its interpretation of Fourier and the larger pocketbooks of its members and supporters. However, most of the experiments dedicated to changing the world settled for plain old farmhouses, large and small. A few tried the long, dormitory-style building and ended up with a parody of an imitation of the all-in-one edifice from Owen's and Fourier's fantasies.

Charlotte Haven left us a description of the Wisconsin Phalanx's original long building. It resembled in a rudimentary way a late twentieth-century motel. A 5-foot-wide center hall ran through the building with rooms along both sides of its 208 foot length. At each end of the hall a tiny window let in some light. The rooms, quite small at 10 feet square, had no closets, forcing residents to store all their belongings, including flour barrels, sacks of potatoes, even pans of milk, along the hall, making passage through its dim light a hazardous experience. Warren Chase, one of the founders of this experiment, looked back on the building as "a ridiculous plan."[40]

Too often these colonies that professed Fourierism overlooked his teaching on individual needs and on differences in tastes. Eugenia Mason lived in the long building and enjoyed the good social times the crowd generated. On the other hand, Charlotte Haven, who lived there at the same time, found the full house came with a serious drawback: lack of privacy. One evening she started a long letter to her sister, hoping for no interruptions. But as usual visitors just came dropping by, and as usual she had to put off writing to another time. She eventually got a small cottage with a fourteen-by-ten-foot room for herself and her sister Harriet. It had two hay-stuffed lounges for beds, trunks served for seats, and they bought a one-dollar pine table. Apparently, uniting in a noble cause fosters a warm gregariousness in certain people, and creates a social environment that they find attractive and satisfying. But not everybody wants that; Eugenia Mason's delight in sociability conflicted with Charlotte Haven's need for privacy. The effect would be more extreme on a Thoreau. No surprise, he suffered from the same problem while on a visit to the Raritan Bay Union and wrote to his sister, Sophia, that it is "hard to find solitude here."[41]

The Icarians had a long building that included the dining hall and workshops on the first floor and a dormitory surrounded by a balcony on the second. Emile Vallet recalled that couples got the standard sixteen-by-twenty room: one window, one bed, one mirror, one table, two chairs. Single members got the standard white pine bed, one chair, one small table with a basin, a shelf, a candlestick, a broom, and a bucket. Their trunks served for closets as well as for guest seats. But despite Cabet's stringent community-of-property rules, all members had to supply their own blankets. François Lacour suffered from the many defects of the thinly shingled building. It leaked cold drafts in winter and rain penetrated and often drove the members from their beds at night. The double-hung sashes brought a special misery because they opened only a bit and made the hot Illinois summers unbearable. Ironically, they could not be closed and so in winter they rattled all night as the prairie winds raced through the room.[42]

In almost all the colonies of social reorganization, the leadership lived in the same lodgings as the rank and file. For example, George and Sophia Ripley had an ordinary room in the large farmhouse at

Brook Farm called the Hive; Cabet had a room above Icaria's dining hall; and Warren Chase had a two-room duplex in Wisconsin Phalanx's long building.

The Sodus Bay Phalanx records show that some leaders paid rent in the highest bracket and a few paid below the average. We cannot, of course, make any judgments about the quality of their lodgings based on the rents but they did live alongside the rank and file. For example, the president, Benjamin Fish, had a room in the Main House at thirty dollars. Two members of the Rent Committee lived in the Meeting House at an above-average fourteen dollars per room, while the head of the Finance Committee was off in one of the farmhouses in a modest seven-dollar room.

Robert Owen undoubtedly could have chosen to move into Father Rapp's house when he bought and converted Harmonie to New-Harmony. It stood out from all the houses in the village. William Hebert, a visitor, called it a "mansion." Even Duke Bernhard admired it, from the two lightning rods to the ornate gardens, which he compared to those of a rich German landowner. Such perquisites may have seemed only right for a divine shepherd whose flock asked only eternal salvation. But unlike Rapp, Owen preached equality, and he therefore chose a small upstairs room in the tavern.

But Fourier did not preach equality. He believed that by providing luxurious accommodations the rich would rush to support their local Phalanx. Raritan Bay Union adopted this as policy, one of the few to try it. There Sarah Grimké had a suite of six rooms, and Marcus Spring, a wealthy New York merchant, and his wife, Rebecca, built a fine private house on the grounds. The North American Phalanx also permitted private homes so that sympathizers could observe the progress of the experiment without the work obligations of membership. For example, Marcus and Rebecca Spring had a nice vacation house there before the factional split took them to Raritan Bay Union.

Surprisingly, the Modern Times housing system, unique among all the utopian experiments, adhered to the practice of traditional society. The founders platted the village, and members had to buy lots and build their own private homes. Eventually they had nearly one hundred neat, cheerful cottages, all with pretty gardens, on well-laid-out streets planted with fruit trees.[43] Thus, they had no common living arrangements, no common dining halls, and no dormitories with their crowding and their frictions. Like the smoking and drinking taboos they had, their system of individually owned houses counters Modern Times' reputation as an outlandish group. Moreover, by its system of individually owned, private houses it serves to demonstrate to us in yet another way the hazards in applying such terms as socialist and communist to these experiments in social reorganization.

Dress and Personal Style

The people of social reorganization contributed to our culture in several ways. Most of their legacies came out of their critical response to the past, their refusal to accept tradition simply because it was there. In clothing, most of them looked beyond the ephemeral values of fashion and consciously attempted to create a style in keeping with human needs and to a lesser extent in keeping with their social views. Thus, their dress customs have practical as well as symbolic ramifications.

Members in most of the colonies of social reorganization tended to dress differently than people in traditional society. The name of Amelia Jenks Bloomer (1818–94), a champion of women's rights after midcentury and an activist in dress reform, has come to be associated with long pants as an acceptable garb for women. But women in New-Harmony adopted a similar mode of dress decades before she came on the scene. They wore a type of long pants tied at the ankles and a tunic or knee-length skirt. The basic concept of this style, which we take for granted today, created a radical breakthrough for women because it made it possible for them to take a more active part in the work world. Without the centuries-old burden of skirts dragging on the ground, they could move about farms and shops as freely as men, and could go up and down stairs more easily. Moreover, the concept opened new vistas for women by allowing them to participate more freely in recreational activities. Fredrika Bremer, who saw women wearing long pants when she later visited America, found them "well-calculated for walking in the woods." As we might expect, opinions about them differed. Duke Bernhard, the German aristocrat visiting New-Harmony, who called them *Pantalons,* liked them. Sarah Pears, a member, described them as undertrousers and "declared war against them for both my daughters and myself."[44]

Women in later social experiments took up the style. Marianne Finch, the English tourist who visited North American Phalanx, reported that women at work wore trousers with a short dress of the same material "on account of their convenience." The reporter for the *Life Illustrated* article (August 18, 1855) came away with the impression that women wore the "short dress or tunic . . . and loose pantaloons" only for working and taking walks. Julia Bucklin Giles, daughter of a Phalanx leader, recalled that women members used to change from this convenient style to the traditional long dress when going into town. Fredrika Bremer attended a festival there and noticed that many of the young women came to the ball in short dresses with pants. But even in utopia traditions can persist: she took special note of the fact that the president's daughter, Abbie Arnold, insisted on a long dress. The Arnolds later moved out with the splinter group Raritan Bay Union.

Modern Times women adopted the pants style, according to Charles Codman, an early member of the experiment. But when Moncure Conway visited, he noticed an emphasis on individual taste. He recorded that "as they came streaming into church they seemed at first like a party of masqueraders." On closer examination he saw that they had simply rejected convention, and only one or two dressed according to the style of American society then.[45]

The spirit of Brook Farm fostered independence of dress for women. John Codman (brother of Charles) recalled that some chose the pants and skirt because it helped them "walk well and work well." But others chose to dress differently. Nora Schelter, who came there as a student, remembered the women "in motley array" when she arrived. Sophia Ripley was wearing a dress of "checkered domestic," the kind that slaves wore. And others there continued to use starched lace and wear little lace night caps.[46]

For Icarian women, Cabet established well-defined style criteria, but these did not include personal comfort or suitability for work and recreation. Practical things to him meant dresses simple to make and repair, utilitarian, and versatile. Most of all, his rules prohibited any hint of adornment. "All which tends toward luxury and coquetry is contrary to our economic necessity."[47]

Cabet's conceptions of equality required a single style of clothing for each sex, in effect, a uniform. As the ship carrying the Icarian pioneers to America weighed anchor in Le Havre, he had them assemble on deck in real uniforms. But labor in Nauvoo soon made short work of the uniforms, which disappeared through attrition. Then members simply wore whatever they had, mending here and there and again and again with blue denim patches.

In the difficult days of Nauvoo, Cabet reiterated his ideal of conformity. He wrote an article, really a wish list, in which he said that if he had $500,000 he would buy uniforms for all Icarians. Even without uniforms, the Icarians had to put up with a sameness because they had access only to whatever the commissioner of clothing decided to buy and put in the warehouse for them. The detailed inventory of 1853 lists no individual items of clothing. But it does show a stock of 252 "wardrobes" for men and for women, clearly implying standardization. It also lists material for making clothing. But as with everything else, Icaria had restrictive rules. For example, a bride had to use material for her wedding dress that would also be serviceable for work in the years ahead.[48]

Maria Marchand recalled a Mr. Gaskin who visited the colony in Iowa during the 1870s and tried to introduce the idea of pants for women. But Cabet, long dead, lived on in their conservative approach to dress. The members rejected change and Icarian women continued to work about the colony in full-length dresses. Their dark, somber muslin "Amana Blues" came from the Amana colony 150 miles to the east.[49] In that colony a style rooted in the past dictated the kind of clothes permitted women. Of course, Amana aimed for individual salvation. Strange that the Icarians, who wanted to change the world, should hold to the same restrictive rule of dress.

People in the movement generally rejected the conventions of dress style. Owen for example, induced a young New-Harmony bride to give up her white wedding gown because of its association with traditions of the old social order. Others, recognizing an aspect of clothing design that stood above function and the transient vagaries of fashion, went to extremes. They reaffirmed the symbolic property in dress by believing – mistakenly as it turns out – that through their personal style they could make a political statement and win converts.

Undoubtedly that kind of thinking motivated the young men of Brook Farm to attend a Boston performance of Beethoven's Fifth Symphony dressed with deliberate disregard for accepted customs, which had the rigidity of New England granite. George Curtis, who spent his late teen years in Brook Farm, said he and his comrades repudiated stiff collars and ties and wore woolen blouses as "a mute protest against the body coats of a selfish and competitive civilization." John Codman agreed that the young men of Brook Farm used dress as a "protest" against the "unnatural life" in the cities, and mentioned the kinds of things they wore: a blue plaid tunic, a broad straw hat, and a full shirt with a broad rolling collar known then as a Byronic collar, a fitting symbol for the revolutionary spirits of Brook Farm. Such exotic garb shocked proper Bostonians at the concert. It startled Nora Schelter, too, when she arrived at Brook Farm as a student and saw these "curious belted blouses, something like the pictures of old English carters." She admitted that she had never seen such "eccentricities in dress and such absence of tonsorial effects."[50]

Tonsorial effects referred, of course, to hair. History on that topic can be summarized as an alternation of styles: beards during one period, then close shaven faces in the next. A similar cycle applies to hair length: long during one period, short in the next. As it turned out, the Brook Farm years coincided with the clean-shave/short-hair phase of the cycle. No surprise, the young men in the colony chose "tonsorial effects" of the opposite kind: beards and long hair. Significantly, they justified their appearance with a rationale we hear in our own times: letting hair grow is "natural"; shaving and cutting it is "unnatural."

Men elsewhere in the movement adopted the idea. The Fruitlands men let their hair grow. Those at Modern Times did the same, but the women there wore daringly short bobs without resorting to any justification. However, it may be significant that women in America then did not cut their hair but bound it up tight in "pugs" or buns, the "proper thing" to do. The young women of Brook Farm, not to be outdone by the young men, liberated their hair from those bindings of tradition and allowed it to flow out loosely – "naturally" – behind them.

In a few of the experiments in social reorganization, those doing hard work changed out of dirty work clothes for meals. Individually owned farms rarely practiced that custom, and industrial shops in the cities would have ruled it impractical. But those groups in the movement who adopted it saw it as an advance. Mealtime at most of these colonies turned into a gathering of large numbers of people in a crowded common dining room. At a place like Brook Farm, despite the spare menu, they sought convivial fellowship. And everyone there, according to John Codman, understood "the common rules of personal neatness." They left their soiled garments in a special dressing room and put on a "belted tunic, adopted as a convenient, easy, and comfortable dress, before going to meals." A bugle call half an hour before meals gave them time to wash up and change.[51]

The leader of North American Phalanx, Charles Sears, pointed to the symbolic importance of this practice before the evening meal. In traditional farm life the real burden, more harassing than a day's work in the field, came from the never-ending chores from arising to bedtime. But at North American the bathing and changing for supper marked the end of the workday. Then, clean and refreshed, members could make some use of the evening hours in social activities or activities related to self-improvement. Kalikst Wolski, who stayed there in 1852 before getting involved with La Réunion, confirmed both the practice of dressing for the evening meal and the social life afterward.

That has the quality of a utopian promise fulfilled. But there as in other aspects, when joy came despite shortages and crowding, the members paid a lot for a little fulfillment.

Civic Life

Freedom, Tolerance, Equality, and Fraternity

"THE AIR OF FREEDOM AND DEMOCRACY about the place was one of its principal attractions." So said Charles Dana, editor and publisher of the *New York Sun,* looking back half a century to his Brook Farm days. Georgiana Bruce found the atmosphere there more exhilarating than any she had breathed before. "Democracy and culture made the animus," she recalled. George Ripley had planned it that way. Exultant, he wrote Dana soon after the colony began that life there was "truly democratic and Christian." In a later letter to Dana he broadened that to: "We are the first to attempt the organization of a society on purely democratic, Christian principles." Other groups had that spirit too. Kalikst Wolski, newly arrived in America, visited the North American Phalanx in New Jersey and discovered an enchanting prospect: "Each person enjoys the greatest degree of personal freedom."[1]

But disputes and discord also marred civic life. Most of the dissension grew from four seeds: rules restricting freedom, bureaucratic thinking, ignorance of the experiment's principles, and, ironically, the democratic process itself.

Personal Freedom

The advocates of social reorganization promised to enhance individual freedom and extend social equality. But they differed on how to achieve these ideals, and few succeeded even in approaching them. Some tried to legislate them into existence, thinking that elaborate rules and constitutions covering the details of daily life would bring ideal individual conduct, ideal social relations – in short, an ideal society. When Integral Phalanx in Illinois published its "Rules and Pledges," the editors of the *Harbinger* (August 16, 1845) pointed out that the necessity for such codes depended on local circumstances. The editors asserted however, that in a perfectly organized Phalanx "few written laws would be necessary: everything would be regulated with spontaneous precision by the pervading common sense of the Phalanx." But that, they admitted, lay far off in the future.

Brook Farmers, exceptional in so many ways, wrote no such list of rules. Their various "Articles of Association" are the shortest of all, covering only general principles of organization. The articles of 1844 did require that meetings and activities end by ten o'clock. But they applied this with common sense; Marianne Dwight mentions certain parties and other functions that ran later. However, that hour did hold for students attending the Brook Farm School. One of them, Charles Codman, wrote his brother that as long as they followed the canons of "good breeding" they had no restrictions although the colony expected them to be in their rooms by ten o'clock.

Icaria stood at the other extreme: total regulation. Icarians left no ecstatic comments about freedom such as we have from Brook Farmers. Cabet's constitution contains 183 articles and requires some twenty pages of fine print. Another document spells out in detail the workings of the leadership and the general assembly. In addition, Cabet wrote regulations governing schools, workshops, and recreation that fill many more tedious pages. But none of these documents reveal Icarian values with such poignancy as his pamphlet *Icarian Community: Conditions of Admission.* Its name notwithstanding, this code for daily living actually molded colony life after admission by imposing forty-eight "conditions" on the members. Here is a sampling from its thirty-two dense pages (condition number in parentheses). As you can see, some of these promote freedom, some put a damper on it, but all place the needs of the colony above the individual.

Personal

- Keep yourself clean (31).
- Be able to read and write (2).
- No obscenities (32).

Social

- Adopt principles of equality and fraternity (6, 7).
- Avoid abuse and calumny (8).

Do not be envious, or excite envy (29, 30).

No unnecessary talk (35).

No recreational hunting or fishing (34).

You must marry; celibacy not permitted (38).

Labor

Do useful work; wherever and whenever required (15–17).

Economy

Adopt community of property (10).

Cede everything to the colony; keep nothing (12, 13).

Colony

Submit to discipline (37).

Love organization and order (36).

Religion

Adopt Cabet's *True Christianity.* No Catholicism, atheism, or materialism. No religious dissent.

A generation earlier the *New-Harmony Gazette* published nineteen "Considerations for Those Who Wish to Unite under the New System" (April 19, 1826). Although the second "Consideration" tells them to discard "vexatious and useless" regulations, the other eighteen clearly fulfill that role. Like Cabet's "Conditions," some serve a noble end, and all, even the inane ones, place society above the individual. Several attempt to codify Robert Owen's belief in nonviolence and his incessant homily that society forms a person's character.

Do not force others to agree with you (3).
No grumbling, carping or murmuring against the negligent (5).
Do not abuse the lazy or the intemperate (11, 9).

However, this code of behavior takes its primary aim at the individual. Indeed, Consideration 1 decrees that members must "sink completely, individual interests." And others spell that out.

No preferences in food or drink permitted (7).
Teach your children the extreme folly of competition (19).
No voting or party system: these are individualism's seed (18).
Since the strong or the expert had no hand in gaining their advantage, they must devote it to serving the community (6).

And then there are restrictions without any basis in social theory.

Absolutely no children in the Dining Hall during meals (8).

La Réunion's regulations generated deep resentment, and members fought back. Dr. Augustin Savardan, who bitterly opposed the autocratic attitude of Victor Considérant, the colony's founder, did agree with him on the need for "formulas concerning reciprocal rights and duties in society." Still, he recognized two sides to the question. "Ah the Regulations! We were repeatedly and sternly criticized for these, to our great surprise. But there are in our movement intelligent people who believe that a group of humans can and should live without regulation and legislation."[2] The two sides expose a dilemma along the road to utopia: should people who are ready to sacrifice all in the cause of liberty need to have rules imposed from above?

With that in mind, and considering the grand goals of these experiments, most regulations turn out to be petty, if not degrading. In Northampton, rule 1 commanded members in the Boarding House – all adults – to be in their rooms at nine-thirty, and lights out by ten. Hopedale's constitution "required" parents to see that the children "refrain from all profanity, from all vulgarism in word or action, and from all obscene utterances and writings." Wisconsin Phalanx had a long list of such rules, but unlike almost all other colonies in the movement, it also dealt with violations. The by-laws specified "misdemeanors" that could be grounds for expulsion. They included

> Using, keeping, or allowing others to use ardent spirits.
> Gambling, laziness, vulgar language, licentiousness.
> Hunting, fishing or "unnecessary labor" on Sunday.
> Faultfinding, personal abuse of members.
> Abuse of cattle and horses.

Vaguely defined offenses and little encroachments on personal freedom could have been a repressive tool, but nothing suggests that result. However, the recognition and elevation of trifles opened the door to petty wrangling, a plague that infected and weakened many of the experiments in social reorganization.

Indeed, Wisconsin Phalanx's council minutes read like a plot to encourage bickering. For example, the council held lengthy, formal discussions to place a value on some minor service a member had rendered, an open invitation to controversy. Warren Chase made it a point at various times to deny that they had this problem there. Boasting in print that "not once in a week" could a profanity be heard, he claimed that during five years of cramped living for 160 people, Wisconsin Phalanx had no lawsuits and no quarrels of any kind. Members there and in other colonies differed on that aspect of colony life. Reminiscences sometimes paint rosier pictures than the harsher images we get from contemporary documents. The reminiscences of Isabella Hunter, a member of Wisconsin Phalanx, for example, confirm Chase. "We were like brothers and sisters living together in the sweetest harmony." On the other hand Louisa Sheldon and her husband had a different experience in Wisconsin Phalanx. In her letter to a relative in Rochester, New York, Louisa discloses, "We have had considerable disputing in the Association this winter. It causes me a great deal of trouble to hear quarreling and then where they have associated together to live in peace and harmony." That terrible contradiction prodded the couple into the painful idea of quitting.[3]

Disputes in some colonies ended up being settled in the courts although most groups looked with disfavor on that solution and attempted to limit it. Northampton, for example, made such litigation grounds for expulsion.

William Pelham heard a diversity of opinion in New-Harmony, but no political or religious quarrels. Most of all, he discovered personal freedom there. "I did not expect to find everything regular, systematic, and convenient, nor have I found them so. . . . [But] I am at length free, my body is at my own command, and I enjoy mental liberty after having been deprived of it."

However, others did not find liberty there. Minor Kellogg, the American artist, kept a journal that he marked "Private," and there a different view surfaces. He often went into the woods on Sundays and sketched from nature. "I could sit with perfect contentment in sight of an old bridge . . . and hear the distant murmurings of the water . . . until the last glimmerings of . . . sunset would remind me that night approaches, and I must return to my *prison* [original emphasis]." Strange, but *prison* has a counterpart in an expression Sarah Pears used in a letter to her aunt. The letter, which discloses her feelings about life in New-Harmony, contains these words: "I feel like a bird in a cage shut up forever."[4] A similar idea turns up in one of the most bitter expressions of disappointment in all the movement, Frédéric Olinet's description of his life in Icaria. "The individual is imprisoned there, entangled in a way that is inescapable." If Olinet's judgment seems harsh, Cabet's own summation of the role of his government tends to explain why. "The Icarian State . . . regulates everything that concerns its people, what they do, their welfare, food, clothes, housing, education, work, and even their pleasures." Cabet boasted that his "government is a radical and pure Democracy." But his constitution ruled out the crucial benchmark of a democracy, the secret ballot. Article 113 decreed, "All voting is public. The written vote must be signed." Cabet called frequent meetings, and the rules required every member to attend. So Cabet could indeed force the individual to become "entangled."[5]

Meetings ultimately turned into a negative factor, not only in Icaria but throughout the movement. Critics charged that Associations needed too much discussion and too many managers to get things done. The *Harbinger* (July 11, 1846) admitted that that criticism could be true of small, poorly organized experiments but not in large, well-regulated ones. Because the latter had never existed, that response remained pure speculation. But the penchant for long and frequent meetings in the experiments that did exist clearly hindered their efforts. That fact shocked and perplexed democratic spirits who had proceeded on the basis of a noble principle: all action should derive from consensus.

Elijah Grant, president of the Ohio Phalanx, having just brought his colony through a crisis and reorganization, wrote to a friend about its problems. "There was too little subordination, too much 'self-government,' so-called, and too many planners and advisors." In another letter he explained the new plan. It would be more arbitrary because "the democratic principle . . . has been . . . the source of our worst troubles." In Brook Farm they called a special meeting for each problem. John Codman remembered that "the interminable number of meetings for consultation . . . held almost nightly" consumed many hours. David Mack, president of Northampton Association, wrestled with the requirement that department managers give daily explanations and reports. In New-Harmony, Thomas Pears dubbed the problem the "Reign of Reports."[6]

An unforeseen development came along with the flood of meetings and with attempts to make sure everything reflected the members' wishes precisely: growth of a bureaucratic mentality. Alphadelphia provides a clear example. From a reading of its record books, their meetings must have been wearisome affairs and the long-winded officers a deterrent to progress. The governing body and the committees held only open sessions. Perhaps to show fairness the leaders adopted an elaborate parliamentarianism. And from this they fell into a pretentious, legalistic language at meetings, totally out of keeping with the educational level of the rank and file. Not surprised, I found a handwritten copy of the "Rules of the House of Representatives" among the papers and books that remain from the colony.

The meetings of the board of directors took up minute details of daily life: permission to use a horse for plowing, or for a required trip to town, ratifying the trade of a chair and the purchase of insignificant items, a lock, for example. They also approved each new member and assigned people to various work groups.

The board had to list and appraise all possessions that new members brought into the Association. Each appraisal, a credit to the member's account, had to be sanctioned by vote. These lists, which include the humblest of items, incidentally offer a remarkable insight into the lives and values of the people attracted to Alphadelphia. The appraisals contain such minor items as a spoon, a dish, a horseshoe, an old hoe and even expendables such as a small quantity of pepper and a bit of tallow. The board and the new members arrived at prices through negotiation, a process loaded with irritants when dealing with someone's life possessions. For most items they settled at a few pennies. Then they had to repeat this petty, time-consuming process when a member left, haggling to the end.

One leaf from a typical appraisal, that of Henry D. Hall, who later became a director, is reproduced in illustration 4. Notice the kind of items he brought in. Tools such as an iron wedge, 67 cents, and scales, $3, could be useful. The 16¼ pounds of coffee, $2.34, would have certainly been welcome. But much of his credit came from a long list of small kitchen items, some of which you can see in the reproduction: a pint bottle, 6 cents; a funnel, 15; six bake tins, 6; and a coffee pot, 38. These family items would be useless in a large, efficient kitchen designed to serve an entire colony.

The meetings of the Committee on Arbitration bore the weight of trifles not taken up by the board of directors. James Thompson was said to have used profanity. Leonard Luscomb, later expelled, was thought to have hunted on Sunday. He denied it but admitted to card playing – a vice in most colonies. James Noyes, later elected president, was accused of a falsehood.[7]

Similar examples of an obsession with pettiness and parliamentary posturing can be found in other experiments. In Sodus Bay Phalanx, the board of directors ruled that "all matters" had to come before them. Within two months the records show meetings turning ugly with needless disputes that mocked everything the Phalanx stood for. The minutes of Wisconsin Phalanx's council meetings puff out with the stale air of tedious hours droning over the trivial details of daily life. The council members assigned rooms, dickered over the value of trifles, and busied themselves buying or selling inconsequen-

To amount brought up	239	88
To 1 lot of Knifes and forks	1	25
6 chairs	2	25
2 Patent pails		40
1 Axe		50
1 Glue Kettle	1	50
1 Beetle	1	00
2 Skimmers		13
1 Funnel		06
6 Bake Tins		50
1 dipper and Pepper box		12
4 Tin basins		63
16¼ lbs of Coffee	2	34
1 Coffee Pot		38
1 Colinder		25
1 Coffee Mill		38
1 Toaste pan		44
7, 10 quart tin Pans	2	62
3. 6 Do Do		25
1 [illegible] Dish		18
1 Tin pot cover		12
1 Box and cake emptings		38
1 quart cup		60
1 Oil Can		38
1 Pint Bottle		06
1 Bag and Hops		13
1 Tea Server		25
21¾ lbs Sal Eratis	1	30
1 Hog Hook		38
1 Iron wedge 3¾ lbs		47
1 Set of Scales and weights	3	00
1 bar and weights	1	25
2 Door bolts		18
Amount carried over	263	56

4. Alphadelphia's appraisal of Henry D. Hall's property. By permission of the Bentley Historical Library, University of Michigan.

tial items, most of which could have been entrusted with no loss to a volunteer.

In many experiments the various reports and minutes of administrative meetings bear witness to angry controversies among the members, who, of course, attended. The most damaging and shameful of these involved the basic philosophy of the experiment.

Thus, the meeting records confirm another crucial influence on civic life. They show that most members had little knowledge of the underlying concepts that had generated their experiment. In this respect the situation at Alphadelphia, a joint stock company, can be taken as typical. For example, when members short of money joined, they used property in lieu of cash to purchase shares. Those items then became colony property and should have been stripped of any previous identity. Nevertheless, in meetings and in official documents such as the list "Association Property," the leaders adopted a misleading practice of retaining that identity: "Wilson wagon," "Mcomber carriage," "Taylor wagon," and so forth. That led to unneeded confusion in the minds of members already deficient in the collective aspects of the experiment, not to mention the potential for creating ill will.

Isabella Hunter, a member of Wisconsin Phalanx, complained that Chase, in his zeal to expand, brought an influx of people ignorant of Associationist principles. How would such people come to join? A clue comes from a letter that Huldah Leavens wrote from Sheboygan Falls, Wisconsin, to her family back in Manlius, New York. In it she describes the excitement that some lectures on Fourier created in town. A visionary, Dr. Cady, impatient to start an experiment, wants to sign up volunteers. "What do you think?" she asks in her letter. "Should we join?" Shortly afterward, moved by altruism but knowing virtually nothing about Fourier's complex system, she becomes a founding member of the Pigeon River experiment in southeastern Wisconsin. No surprise, that utopian episode came to a tragic end within six months. Similarly, Thomas Steel wrote his father from Equality, the short-lived experiment in Wisconsin, that the members had no understanding of the principles of a collective society.[8]

At meetings in most of the movement's colonies, the uninformed members had the same power as the informed. Moreover, imbued with the democratic spirit, these unsophisticated experiments in changing the world readily gave the courtesy of the podium to visitors. As a result, partisans of various unrelated or even antagonistic causes materialized to take advantage of a cheap and unlimited forum. Their irrelevancies often derailed the immediate work of the colony. In addition, the antiestablishment reputation of these experiments seemed to attract faddists and eccentrics, and they too had a showcase at the meetings for their peculiar notions and manias. Some were innocuous; for example, the "water cure" invaded Brook Farm without changing the course of events. However, in Wisconsin Phalanx, spiritualists got a foot in the door and had a devastating effect on the colony's future. Thus, people who knew nothing of a colony's basic rationale or who had ideas in conflict with its founding principles could affect it in ways that armchair revolutionists never imagined.

Thomas Pears, who called the New-Harmony meetings "useless," witnessed such absurdities as quibbling over the meaning of *all.* This self-destructive policy extended into the colony's publications. The *Gazette,* in a democratic free-for-all, opened its columns to anyone with an opinion on anything. Sure enough, crackpots rushed to fill the space with bizarre philosophies, religious disputes, and even polemics against the experiment itself. There was an opponent of dancing, one objected to playtime for children, one urged free choice in clothing, while others supported gambling and evolution. A war of words on free will ran up and down *Gazette* columns for months. And all of this diverted the social experimenters from the serious and pressing problems they faced.

In the early years of North American Phalanx, differences developed among the members over fundamental social doctrine, so that "their days were spent in labor, and their nights in legislation."[9] In later years, zealots tried to impose their religion on this colony, which had always held separation of church and state as a sacred principle. The heated debates led to a schism that created the splinter group Raritan Bay Union.

Many experiments, particularly the dozens of Associationist disasters of 1844 and 1845, suffered from a membership who lacked a basic understanding of the colony's goals. During this time, when the crisis engulfed Ohio Phalanx, Elijah Grant wrote to Horace Greeley that they had people there who saw any deviation from "old Puritan standards" as evil. He admitted that he had never expected the movement to attract people "so encrusted with bigotry."[10]

Of course, all of these problems that could shorten the life of a utopian colony arose only where members insisted on free speech and free thought. Groups that tolerated no dissent, such as evangelical colonies concerned only with salvation, not with liberty and equality, had no such problems.

Here we come upon another irony of the utopian episodes. The proponents of social reorganization fostered democracy, one of their principal attractions, yet they allowed the democratic process itself to make colony life unattractive. They never learned how to balance its great strength against its weakness. Modern Timers, staunch champions of individual freedom, started their colony late in the history of the movement. Thus, they had lessons from a quarter of a century of utopian tragedies. Yet they dealt with problems just as their departed predecessors had. Charles Codman remembered the discussions well. "Each one wanted to propose his own solution, not accept someone else's." Everett Chamberlain, in looking back at Wisconsin Phalanx after it ended, pointed to a fault in that experiment that we could just as easily apply throughout the movement. He saw Wisconsin Phalanx "bickering over little questions of detail, and gradually losing sight of the stupendous plan."[11]

Freedom of Conscience

In the Introduction, I pointed out that writers on the utopian groups of the nineteenth century have generally used the term *religious communities* as a kind of category. It includes such groups as the Shakers, Amana, and the Harmonie Society of Father Rapp. But designating some as religious leaves a question about others not included in that category, such as Brook Farm, New-Harmony, or Icaria. Were they not religious? A better distinction can be made based on a colony's goals. The principal objective of groups traditionally categorized as religious was the salvation of their members. The others set out primarily to reorganize society, a secular goal, of course. But even a cursory glance at the religious life in this "other" category shows a people no less devout than their neighbors in surrounding towns. Moreover, in their religious life, most groups dedicated to social reorganization adopted a principle basic to the American democratic tradition: the wall between church and government. And that principle makes a world of difference between these two categories.

Among the motives that prodded people into social reorganization, one needs emphasis. Many who joined the movement had lost faith in the established churches as willing fighters against the evils of society and as a force for ameliorating the condition of humanity. And in the face of what they considered sanctimony from the pulpit, they raised their voices in disgust and began to look elsewhere for moral leadership. Their protests, as we might expect, aroused defenders of the status quo, who attacked the critics as atheists. In mudslinging, some mud always sticks. It has persisted as a stain on the histories of most colonies in the movement. But when we scrape it away, we discover that among all of these experiments atheism had significance in only a handful.

In fact, as we look into the religious life of the movement, a picture emerges of devout leaders, members, and sympathizers and of sacred observances and services in the colonies typical of their time and place. First of all, we find a movement intent on putting into practice the teachings of Jesus. Elizabeth Peabody, who knew Brook Farm and its members, called the colony "Christ's idea of society." Indeed, the leaders in most of these experiments believed that Christ had ordained the way of life they adopted and proposed for the world and that they simply followed in Christ's footsteps. Even in that putative den of atheism, New-Harmony, the members saw it stated in their *Gazette* (October 29, 1825) that "it was for the introduction of this system [New-Harmony] that Christ lived and died." Of course, merely invoking the name of Jesus, a centuries-old practice by saints and sinners soliciting support for every imaginable cause, does not constitute proof of godliness. However, more solid evidence testifies to the place of religion in this movement.

The leaders in almost every experiment included clergy. In Brook Farm both Rev. George Ripley, founder, and Rev. John Dwight held divinity degrees from Harvard and were ordained ministers. Their associates included Rev. John Allen, Rev. George Bradford, and Rev. Warren Burton, who had served many years in the pulpit. In fact, the key leadership only included one layperson, Charles Dana. Wisconsin Phalanx had among its founders Rev. George Stebbins, a Baptist minister, and the list of members shows two preachers. Ohio Phalanx's organizers included Rev. Charles Calkins and Rev. James P. Stuart. In Alphadelphia, Rev. James Billings took a leading role, and when the Universalist paper the *Primitive Expounder* began publishing there, the membership heard preaching by its editor, Rev. Richard Thornton, and by Rev. E. Wheeler.

Among the friends of the movement we find a preponderance of devout individuals. Some idea of their faith appears in a letter Almira Throop wrote when she heard that an Associationist experiment in central New York was about to get started. "I glory. I rejoice. I exult. I thank my God I live in the present age. . . . Have I any fears as to the outcome? . . . No. God Rules." John Bliss, checking on the progress of Alphadelphia, called Association "a plan under God for the amelioration of the condition of mankind." Marcus Spring, a New

York merchant, was an influential backer of the movement. For a Christmas gift one year he sent Brook Farm a daguerreotype (expensive in those early years of photography) of a sculpture of Christ. Rev. William Henry Channing supported utopian causes, and like an itinerant preacher, he would stop at various colonies and conduct services. In one of his letters he called the movement "the great cause of the Kingdom of Heaven upon Earth."[12]

Evidence of sacred observances abounds. When Wisconsin Phalanx's advance party made it through the wilderness to the site chosen for the experiment, they immediately held a prayer meeting to ask for divine blessing. In the early days, visiting clerics helped start a religious program there. Rev. William Sampson, presiding elder of the Green Bay District of the American Home Missionary Society, came and conducted services. Not long after that Rev. Miller from the Winnebago Lake Mission at Oshkosh arrived and started a Bible class. We even know the names of some of those in the class: Mrs. Morris Farmin, Mrs. Beckwith, George Limbert, and Uriel Farmin and his wife.

Soon, according to various reports, the colony began routine religious practices on its own. Jason Lathrop, on a visit, saw the Sabbath School; it had thirty students, and he described it as "very respectable." Otis Capron, a Wisconsin Phalanx member, wrote home that religion was "thriving." On the other hand, William Stillwell was not a member and because of that his observations would tend to be impartial. He worked for the colony one summer as a carpenter and wrote to his wife, Sarah, who had remained at home in Pleasant Valley, New York, about the Phalanx. In one letter he described both Methodist and Baptist services "on each Sabbath" as "excellent." He also told her that the members did not break the Sabbath by hunting or fishing on Sunday.[13]

Obviously, religion played an important role in Wisconsin Phalanx. And as in traditional society, it extended into secular celebrations. For example, the second anniversary celebration opened with a Bible reading (Deut. 25) and prayer. Ohio Phalanx members followed a similar practice. Their July Fourth celebration opened with prayer; there was a speech, another prayer, and the benediction by Rev. James P. Stuart. After-dinner toasts included one to the Bible, "[May] its precepts [be] practiced by the whole world."[14]

Brook Farm, on the outskirts of Boston, had a choice of churches in the neighborhood. Arthur Sumner, a student there, recalled that on Sunday mornings George Ripley would hitch up a couple of horses to a hay wagon and take members to Theodore Parker's meeting-house in nearby West Roxbury. Whenever William Henry Channing visited, he conducted services. John Codman said that in good weather they used a natural amphitheater in a pine grove where "like the Pilgrims . . . we raised our voices in hymns of praise, and listened to a sermon." Channing's services remained in Codman's memory as moments of great spiritual exaltation.[15]

New-Harmony had a reputation as a godless den that survives in histories. Its notoriety stemmed in part from lurid accounts given by hostile observers and in part from the ideological blundering of its leaders. For example, Robert Owen, in a famous infamous speech, outlined a "Trinity of Evils" that burdened humanity, and he named "Irrational Systems of Religion" as one of the three. It shocked Americans, and as we shall see, it inflicted a devastating wound on the experiment. Nevertheless, *Gazette* items and other documents do refer to religious practices there and in such a matter-of-fact way that they must have been considered commonplace, hardly noteworthy. For example, the *Gazette* (November 19, 1825) carried a story about a Masonic installation in the colony and mentioned purely in passing that the ceremony began with "an introductory prayer by the Rev. J. Meek." From a brief item (August 9, 1826) reporting the wedding of two members, M. R. Southard to Matilda Harshee, we learn that Rev. Burkitt performed the rites. Unlike Owenite partisans, Miner Kellogg, the American artist, would hardly want to polish the colony's image, because, as we have seen, he had such negative feelings about his experiences there. That enhances the credibility of his observations of its religious life. In his notes for an autobiography he tells us that the colony reserved the town hall on Sundays "for religious services by believers of every doctrine."[16]

Clearly, the colonies of social reorganization did not merit imputations about religion. Still, when all is said and done, devotion should hardly call for any notice in history. But the steadfast dedication to freedom of conscience in most of these social experiments does. It surely triggered the hostility of those who considered religion synonymous only with the rituals they knew, and they quickly fired off charges of atheism for anything else. Actually, any discussion of religion in the movement ought to be qualified by an evaluation such as the one that Rev. Octavius Frothingham made of Brook Farm. He knew its people very well and observed that their colony, "Though not 'religious' in the usual sense of the word was enthusiastically religious in spirit and purpose." With no established creed and no imposed ecclesiastical forms, members had the freedom to worship according to their own beliefs. Thus, an Episcopalian member who died in this colony of mostly Unitarians had a right to the Episcopal funeral he received there, a rite denied in the the so-called religious communities.[17] Willard Saxton recalled that some chose to go to church and some chose not to go. As we know today, neither choice necessarily speaks for the soul. Thus, the significance of a Brook Farm resides in the idea of choice itself, of the right of individuals to make a choice based on the dictates of their own consciences, not social pressure.

Tolerance

In New-Harmony, one of the few groups with agnostics and atheists in the leadership, the activities of the devout were accepted and respected. According to Miner Kellogg, Owen and his sons encouraged tolerance. Kellogg saw that the hall "was held sacred on Sunday for the uses of religious people, . . . [and] the square in front of it was not used for any species of amusement which might disturb worshipers within." In a letter from New-Harmony, William Pelham relates an anecdote that includes as incidental information the fact that clergy had use of the hall whenever they wanted it. A Baptist minister arrived on a Thursday and announced that he was going to speak that night. He got a large and "attentive congregation," according to Pelham. Then, on Friday evening, a leading member, Robert Jennings, who had been a Universalist clergyman, used the hall to take issue with the speech of the night before. When he finished, the Baptist minister got up and responded while the audience listened. Later in the evening the Baptist minister officiated at a wedding.[18]

Like New-Harmony, Wisconsin Phalanx had a reputation as antireligious. But Rev. Miller, an itinerant preacher from the Winnebago Lake Mission, reported that "they always received ministers gladly and treated them with consideration. They were specially gratified to have religious services held among them, and the ringing of the bell would generally insure a good audience." According to Warren Chase, a founder, many religions were represented among the membership, and one could find "divine services every Sabbath by different denominations."[19]

Brook Farm's encouragement of pluralism shows up in the effort the colony made to provide fish on Fridays for Roman Catholics and other minority members whose beliefs required it.

Most of the colonies dedicated to social reorganization had guarantees of tolerance in their constitutions. These covenants ranged from simple statements protecting religious freedom to complex clauses designed to encourage worship by providing members with the means to do so. Brook Farm simply prohibited any religious test or "any authority over individual opinion." The Trumbull Phalanx's constitution said religious or political opinion could be neither a bar to admission nor a ground for expulsion. The North American Phalanx recognized the right of every human being "to worship God under any form or in any manner agreeable to his convictions."

Many groups, wary of abuses in the establishment of a single creed, wrote constitutional safeguards to prevent it. Sylvania Association's bylaws, for example, prohibited the Association from hiring any minister or paying for the performance of any "religious duties." However, members had the right to do so at their own expense. The bylaws guaranteed them the use of the public room set aside for that purpose. Wisconsin Phalanx's "Articles of Incorporation" protected every member "in his or her religious belief," but at the same time banned taxes that would be used for the support of a minister or other religious teacher.

For a few colonies freedom of conscience had its limits. Alphadelphians began with guarantees that sounded good: first, the clauses in their constitution that dealt with religious freedom could never be repealed or amended; second, no member could be compelled to contribute to any aspect of worship; and finally, the colony would provide space so that members could build houses of worship for their own denominations. But consider the potential for intolerance in these two clauses: the provision for space applied to "professed Christians"; and they could use the space "as long as they did not disturb the peace and quiet."

The separation of religion and government and the tolerance it fosters were part of the attractiveness of social reorganization. In North American Phalanx religion remained neutral in colony affairs and as a consequence Christians, those of other faiths, and freethinkers lived together without pressure to conform to someone else's beliefs. But zealots in the colony, intent upon making religion integral to every aspect of life, formed a splinter group and founded Raritan Bay Union. The new colony's rules reveal its rejection of tolerance and clearly show how an establishment of religion narrowed the movement when its goals cried out for the widest possible appeal. The members declared in the bylaws that they had organized so that "Industry, Education, and Social life may in principle and practice, be arranged in conformity to the Christian Religion."

Icaria also had an establishment of religion, one of the few experiments in social reorganization to do so. Its constitution declared, "The Icarian Community adopts as its Religion the Religion of Christianity in its primitive purity." Primitive meant simple because Cabet conceived of his religion, which he called *vrai christianisme,* True Christianity, as a step forward, not a return to the past. "We replace the old world with a new world, the reign of Satan or Evil with the reign of God or Good, the Death of morality with the Resurrection." He proclaimed the Icarians the True Christians, "the disciples, imitators, and workers of Jesus Christ, taking up his Gospel and his Doctrine, working to bring about his Kingdom of God, his new City, and his Paradise on Earth."

Cabet described Icarian religious observances as simple, "without images, freed of all ceremony and superstitious practices, and devoted primarily to wonder at the Universe, to gratitude toward the Supreme Being."[20] Emile Vallet recalled that Cabet lectured on Sundays to large audiences about Christ. Without referring to the miracles or the supernatural, he emphasized the perfection of Christ's moral teaching. Cabet built these Sunday lectures on Christ around his religious treatise *Le Vrai christianisme . . .* (True Christianity). The copy I found among the items that survived the colony shows the wear and tear that many hands impart to a book. The collection also includes several dog-eared Bibles, and a copy of *Imitation or Following of Christ.* That book holds a message quite different from Cabet's. In its encouragement of values associated with monastic self-abnegation, it places its hope in a world infinitely far from Cabet's promised land. Frayed from obviously heavy use, the book indicates that members gave thought to religious ideas not necessarily in sympathy with Cabet's. In their excellent library (discussed in a later chapter), they had a small collection of other religious works.

Such books suggest a more complex religious life in Icaria than appears on the surface, but they also hint at additional causes for the factional strife that racked Icaria throughout its history. Recall that one of the forty-eight "Conditions of Admission" described earlier required all members to accept Cabet's True Christianity as their religion. Cabet stated clearly that he would not tolerate Catholicism, materialism, or atheism. Although the movement generally encouraged tolerance, he saw it as the seeds of discord. Like many of the utopian episodes, this one has its tragic irony: rather than creating the unity Cabet wanted, the intolerance he fostered led to the most destructive factional clashes within the entire movement. It drove him to his death, and kept Icaria on its knees, not in supplication, but in suffering until the bitter end.

Equality and Fraternity

In New-Harmony, Robert Owen hoped to bring about a reconciliation of classes and an end to class-oriented conventions. The "Nineteen Considerations" point in that direction. His son, Robert Dale Owen, then in his mid-twenties, later recalled the social relations there: informal and unaffected, people using first names and treating each other as brother and sister.

Of course, people often see what they want to see. That applies to Owen's son as well as to observers at the other extreme. From that end of the spectrum, a different story unfolds, told by Paul Brown, an exceptionally hostile disparager of all that Owen attempted. In his experience, members remained strangers "in spite of all their meetings, their balls, their concerts, and . . . pretense of cooperation." He could think of no other town where people would pass each other constantly yet take no interest in each other's feelings, views, or names.[21] Duke Bernhard, the German nobleman who spent a week in New-Harmony, noticed that the educated and aristocratic did not mingle with the common folk. Other first-hand accounts, more balanced, suggest something in between, an emerging equality marred by a small, clannish elite.

Class distinctions did appear in many of the utopian colonies. For those who called Fourier mentor, such distinctions should have been an acceptable part of their plan. Fourier saw the acquisitive spirit and the production of wealth as one of many human traits and designed the Phalanx on the premise that society, rather than suppressing natural tendencies, should allow people to do what they enjoyed. On the practical side, he saw wealthy members as an asset because they had what every Phalanx would need: cash. Most Fourier experiments missed the point of Fourier's inequality, or never knew it, and declared for equality. But a couple of Associations did try that element of Fourier. For example, Raritan Bay Union not only allowed people to bring servants, it actually made it attractive to do so by charging half-rate for servants, as it did for children. No surprise, the members soon formed cliques based on wealth.

These aspects brought forth strong criticism of Fourier from Adin Ballou, founder of Hopedale. Although he called Fourier's plans to avert poverty a step in the right direction, he abhorred the inequality that came with them. "Wealth, display, luxury and all the artificial creations of barbarism are merely passed through his polishing process and then adopted as permanent." Ballou compared Raritan Bay with his own experiment and pointed out a crucial difference. Hopedale "makes all members coequal in social and political suffrage, without distinction of sex, age, complexion, rank, wealth or any other peculiarity."[22]

As it turned out, however, in those Fourier experiments that did favor equality, the members had at best only a superficial knowledge of his writings. Even among those who could read French and cope with Fourier's verbiage, the results suggest that few saw the cosmic sweep of his ideas. Most dipped in only here and there, hoping to find a simple solution to some complex problem of everyday life.

For example, the Brook Farmers had no dining room system. With equality on their banner, they had set out to share all work and erase every vestige of the master-servant relationship. But their noble instincts led to confusion. Pancakes, which must be eaten hot, of course, presented a special dilemma. As the members satisfied their morning hunger, a few of the brothers and sisters had to stand over a hot stove making additional batches. Georgiana Bruce explained, "It seemed so selfish to eat while others as hungry stood to serve." What would you do? They did what these groups always did for every problem big or small: they called a meeting. One radical proposed dropping that popular dish entirely. At this time in the colony's history the ideas of Fourier had just begun to make their first inroads. Charles Dana searched the texts and came up with an ideological sanction: a "Servitors Group," in other words, people who would wait on tables.[23] Thereafter Brook Farmers got their food in the old way, the way of the society they had rebuked and left behind. Raritan Bay Union, North American Phalanx and Wisconsin Phalanx also used the waiter system.

But in any case and regardless of their underlying theories, if any, experiments of every stripe fell short of their declarations on equality.

Cabet made equality a central tenet of Icaria. However, class distinctions there show a perversion of his stated goals, and a situation reminiscent of the society he denounced as corrupt and hoped to replace. Frédéric Olinet watched as bureaucrats, shop heads, and administrators became a new class. In all things they took care of themselves first. Nevertheless, the aristocratic and bourgeois clans, as Olinet called them, got recognition and privileges. As a close friend of Cabet's secretary, he learned "the secrets of office." Then it became clear why certain people never had to struggle through the webs of red tape that ensnared most members, yet somehow managed to get the best rooms and adequate supplies of candles, firewood, shoes, and other necessities. Olinet thought that his complaints, heard from a distance, would be considered "childish." But on the spot they loomed as "a very gross affair" that kept life "in a state of bitterness and acrimony." Olinet told rank-and-file members what he had learned, and his account goes on to describe secret meetings where they flirted with overt action against the privileged class.[24]

Olinet's strong resentment may tend to devalue his observations, yet other first-hand accounts support him. For example, François Lacour described some of the disdainful attitudes that skilled workers held toward other Icarians. "The outdoor crews look down on the . . . shoemakers, the tailors, etc., as idlers hiding from the severe weather. . . . The tailors and shoemakers consider themselves more intelligent than the farmers, and want to boss them." Emile Vallet, recalling similar irritants he had suffered, cautioned against underestimating the effect of these "little incidents." And he added a point that we too might use to explain the death of many other colonies. "It looks most ridiculous to relate these small events. But they worked slowly and surely to the destruction of the society."[25]

Thomas Pears wrote from New-Harmony, "We are living under an aristocracy," referring to the arbitrary management of Owen's assistants. Apparently, a select few enjoyed perquisites. Robert Dale Owen inadvertently provided an illustration as he recalled his first efforts in the experiment. He had tried physical work for several weeks, but found that too tiring. So he decided to settle down to what he called "more congenial pursuits." In traditional society, the boss's son always has that prerogative.[26]

Another kind of nepotism surfaces in the council minutes of Wisconsin Phalanx. Stephen Bates wanted to get his nephew into the colony school. But under its strict policy, only members could attend, and his nephew did not meet that requirement. Yet Bates, influential director of the colony's all-important mill, managed to arrange an exception that others could not have.

In La Réunion Victor Considérant used favoritism as a tool of leadership. August Savardan watched him play off one faction against another and maintain his power through privilege like a corrupt politician. Such actions made a mockery of Considérant's noble words about equality. He called himself one of the "soldiers of humanity" and vowed to fight for "one great family," humanity. Yet when it came to real-world situations he remained an aristocrat. He referred to freedom for blacks as an abstract principle, and said that blacks were better off as slaves than as free people. Among the vast and varied leadership of this movement only Considérant supported the slave owners in the Civil War.[27]

Surprisingly, Modern Times, founded on the principle that each human should be free from the rule of others, had among its collection of odd characters a member who supported slavery, Thomas Nichols. Known for his writings on the "water cure" and other fads, he also published a book with an elaborate defense of the slave system. God sanctioned the holding of slaves, he pointed out, citing the instruction to Moses (Lev. 25:44). Besides, he argued, blacks were really better off as slaves. Racism in its purist sense shows up in the views of Warren Chase, well known in the movement as the founder of Wisconsin Phalanx. He divided humanity into three races, Indian, Negro, and Caucasian, and he characterized the first two as "inferior" and "moribund." Only the third had "the intellect" to master the earth.[28]

One colony in this movement actually had a formal bar to blacks. New-Harmony's first constitution banned from membership "persons of color." Later versions eliminated that phrase, but its spirit remained. In this movement that stood for brotherhood and sisterhood, most colonies never saw a black walk their grounds. An odd exception, Raritan Bay Union, which avidly sought wealthy members, had a core of Quakers and abolitionists who opened the colony doors and schoolroom to former slaves. Northampton Association stands out as the most consistent champion of equality. Sojourner Truth and the blind former slave David Ruggles found a home there, and the colony always kept the welcome mat out for Frederick Douglass.

Racist attitudes sometimes appeared in poems, "jokes," and other items in colony publications, but they generated no reaction from members who had said they believed in equality. These are covered in chapter 9.

Another aspect of this ambivalence on equality, anti-Semitic attitudes, surfaced occasionally. Fourier lent his voice to the common bigotry of Europe. He decried the usurers, "the hordes of Jews and vagabonds," who he said were taking away French property. Wilhelm Weitling, one of the leaders of Communia, held similar views. The *New-Harmony Gazette* (October 29, 1825) published an editorial on

Ararat, a little-known Jewish utopian attempt near Niagara. The editorial, remarkable for its sensitivity to the plight of the Jews, still repeats the old afflicting stereotype of Jews as a race of "plodding merchants" with "vast accumulations of wealth." Some groups had Jewish members, and I found no evidence of official bias. However, subtle prejudice does show up – and in surprising places. For example, John Codman's memoirs radiate the exalting spirit of brotherhood that ennobled Brook Farm. Still he wrote that one member was so taken with the idea of a society based on justice for all that she could no more resist it "than St. Paul could the heavenly influences that brought his Jewish heart to love all." Here is another example from a letter written by Christopher Cranch, a notable contributor to the cultural life at Brook Farm as well as to the poetry columns of the *Harbinger.* While visiting Richmond, Virginia, he befriended Julia and Catherine Meyers, and in his letter he described them. They were from "one of the finest families I ever saw. They are Jewish ladies, not young or handsome, but everything else: refined, educated, Christian in point of fact."[29]

Utopianism promised to clear away the venom of the past, but obviously, even with the most benevolent influence, old ideas do not die easily.

5

Life for Women

THE MOVEMENT FOR SOCIAL REORGANIZATION attracted women because it held out the hope of a better life for them. That promise takes on greater significance when we consider how much the world has changed since then. At that time the simple basics we now assume as essential in a decent society did not extend to women in traditional America. They did not have the right to vote, they had little or no rights in property, and they had virtually no support for improving their lot in a male-dominated world. Women trapped in a destructive marriage had no recourse because most states banned divorce or imposed impossible conditions. Indeed, almost all that women now take for granted, from law courts to long pants, did not exist for them except perhaps in the dreams of a few, female and male.

The acceptance of an inferior status for women was so entrenched that any questioning of it seemed like a challenge. At the 1826 National Jubilee in Ohio, the festivities included several formal toasts. In one of them the celebrants raised their glasses "To Woman" with these remarkable words: "May the experiment . . . being tried in New-Harmony, [with] the same intellectual cultivation of the sexes, prove that women's mental capabilities are equal to those of men." A generation later Thomas Steel, a member of the Equality experiment in southeastern Wisconsin, attended a debate in a nearby town. The question that evening was "Should Women Receive an Education Equal to Men?" The debaters and the audience consisted of intelligent, educated people, many of them recently arrived from New England, and to Steel's amazement, on this issue the negatives carried.[1]

Into that kind of milieu, the people working for social reorganization brought a noble and encouraging message. It raised the consciousness and confidence of women, and many embraced the utopian idea. In fact, among some groups in the movement, women actually constituted a majority of the membership. That message of hope, just the words alone, published and widely distributed, represents a historic achievement. But the movement's deeds did not match the words. Efforts varied over a broad range from positive to negative, and typical of this movement, these two extremes often appeared side by side.

Five Positive Aspects

Five aspects have great historical significance, and each represents an advance over a past that cared little for the plight of women. They apply to the movement in general, but glaring exceptions, listed later under "Negatives," mar the record.

1. Social reorganization held the promise for women of a good education, dignity, and full partnership in the operation of society.
2. People in the movement showed sensitivity to subtle as well as obvious prejudices against women.
3. People in the movement advocated economic independence for women as a key to social parity.
4. They wrote equal protection and equal opportunity clauses into their bylaws and constitutions.
5. They ignored arbitrary fashion by pioneering clothing that gave women greater freedom in work and recreation.

Some brief examples of each aspect follow. First, those who pondered utopian solutions to society's ills recognized, as few outside the movement had done, the disadvantages that society forced on women. And among that small group of social critics, none showed Fourier's understanding of the wrongs committed against women by the old way of life. None took a stauncher, more principled stance in assuring women equal opportunity in the new society. Fourier saw a clear historical relationship. "Social progress [occurs] in proportion to the progress of woman toward liberty, . . . the decline of society takes place in proportion to the diminution of woman's liberty." That led him to proclaim this principle, which he had set in italics for emphasis: "*The extension of woman's rights is the common foundation of all social progress.*"[2]

Few Americans could read French and therefore had no access to his words until an authentic English translation of one of his books appeared after midcentury. By then Association had all but passed from the scene. But at the beginning of the Associationist phase Americans did have a chance to glean some of his thoughts from an interpretation of Fourier by a Frenchwoman. Translated in 1841, the pamphlet came across the Atlantic and placed before the minds of the new world stunningly new ideas. "Fourier's system gives independence and opens a career to woman; it reconciles her household cares and the duties of maternity with intellectual development and artistic and scientific employments. . . . It gives her a high place in the general estimation, a dignified and pure position." Most important, it reformulated a key principle of Fourierism to emphasize the necessity for the reorganization of society. "All progress in the condition of woman depends upon a social renovation."[3]

Owen and his followers, though outrageously inconsistent at times, voiced support for the advancement of women, sometimes with surprising perception. The *New-Harmony Gazette* published a detailed review in two installments (November 19 and 23, 1825) of Mary Wollstonecraft's *Vindication of the Rights of Women,* a landmark work in the history of women's efforts to advance. Extended editorial commentary followed, and made an exceptional point about the great promise of Owen's experiment: equal education for men and women. "Knowledge is power," it said, and by keeping women ignorant in the past men had been able to "tyrannize over them with impunity." Moreover, it recognized that women needed access to government because the evils of society "fall more heavily on them." However, in an example of the mingling of positives and negatives, the *Gazette* editor then diluted the force of that understanding by recognizing only second-class citizenship for women: when a woman marries, "her husband becomes her political representative."

As for the second aspect, sensitivity to the plight of women, the disciples of Fourier clearly led the movement. Elijah Grant, president of Ohio Phalanx, succinctly expressed a view held by many Associationists. "The laws of civilization pay little attention to the rights of women, and none to their feelings."[4]

A practical example of how some thinkers reacted to the subtle bias against women comes from the *Harbinger.* In his review of George Sand's *Consuelo* (June 14, 1845), John Dwight took up a defense of her maligned reputation. Her unconventional way of living, he asserted, actually reflects her "resistance to . . . the soul-killing and enslaving bonds under which woman has especially pined." His review of a book by Elizabeth Oram (May 9, 1846) showed a similar awareness. He vacillated at first between principle and paternalism in his admitted reluctance to be critical of a faulty book when the author was a woman. That disinclination, he explained, "grows out of a keen sense of the wrongs suffered by woman from conventional prejudice." It prevents his discouraging authors who are trying to "shake-off that accumulated load of oppressions which so cruelly fetters the efforts of females." But the principle of honest criticism won out, and Dwight went on to itemize the book's defects in a thoroughly objective fashion.

The obvious aspects of women's status received trenchant publicity in a *Harbinger* series of twenty-six articles on labor in New York (beginning September 6, 1845). This most comprehensive effort in the movement's press exposed with a great deal of insight the distressing conditions of women workers. An early example of investigative journalism, the articles probed various trades, such as those of seamstresses, book folders, straw braiders, dressmakers, milliners, and domestics, with shocking conclusions. The series brought home to the basically middle-class male readership of the *Harbinger* the realities of life for women workers.

Many in the movement proposed economic independence for females as a key to the advancement of women, the third of the positive aspects. They found a parallel between slavery and the complete control that a husband exercised over his wife's money, property, and even her person. The most powerful statement in this respect also comes from the *Harbinger* (October 4, 1845). It appeared in a commentary on the work of women abolitionists and declared that women, even as they advocated freedom for the slaves, were themselves slaves. "Many do not bear their own names; they cannot dispose of anything that belongs to them; . . . they must submit and follow their masters to the ends of the earth."

The spirit of these ideas echoed through the movement. *Ploughshare and Pruninghook,* the newspaper of Integral Phalanx, ran an article, "Woman in Association" (February 15, 1846), that declared that Association elevates woman, "it places her in a state of pecuniary independence and consequent freedom in opinion and action." Some people saw the implications of this position reaching deep into the foundations of society. James Fisher, an important supporter of the movement, asked Charles Sears, president of North American Phalanx, about the nature of marriage in Association. Sears wrote back that "until woman is assured social position and pecuniary independence we cannot legislate on the question."[5] As we might expect, such ideas did not find universal acceptance in a movement that had its share of adherents to tradition when it came to women.

But some experiments began legislative steps to insure financial liberty for women members. Early in the 1840s Northampton included such a provision in its Articles of Association. "ART. 23. Every man, woman, and child . . . shall have a separate account with the Association, and shall have a separate and distinct interest." In other words, each member's remuneration and expenses would be credited and debited only to that member's name. The provision assured a married woman that whatever she earned belonged to her, and that whatever she spent of course came out of her earnings.

Such guarantees are closely related to the fourth of the positive aspects, constitutional provisions for equal opportunity and equal protection. Some colonies specified equal pay for equal work in their fundamental laws. That principle, radical in the nineteenth century and still in contention in some places today, stood out as a specific requirement in the earliest Brook Farm constitution.

Others covered such issues under general declarations of rights. The Northampton constitution said, "The rights of all are equal without distinction of sex, color, or condition." Its simplicity probably reflected the kind of life that from all indications the colony members had. Frances Judd, an early and steadfast member, recalled that "the question of the equality of the sexes was never discussed. It was accepted as one of our fundamental principles." And she added wryly, "A wife had been known to vote contrary to her husband, and the family remain intact."[6]

Similarly, the Brook Farm Phalanx constitution said that all rights, privileges, and guarantees "expressed or implied" belonged equally to men and women. The Hopedale bylaws assured political equality by making women and men equally eligible for office. And where the bylaws or constitution referred to members or officers, the writers of the documents carefully avoided assumptions by specifying "he or she." The Wisconsin Phalanx constitution took special care. "Each member shall be protected in his or her religious belief," it said, and "no member shall be taxed without his or her consent."

The final positive aspect, pioneering a style of clothing that met women's needs in work, though discussed in a previous chapter, merits emphasis here. In today's world of pants, jeans, and shorts, we completely accept the idea that women should be free to choose clothing that they find suitable for working or that makes shopping easy and recreation practicable. But in the nineteenth century, when floor-length skirts carrying the weight of centuries ruled how women could live, they had no choices. Many people today do not know that men and women in the movement for social reorganization promoted and suffered scorn for a once-radical idea: style should be responsive to function.

Four Negative Aspects

Every page in the historical ledger of social reorganization has debits as well as credits. And for women, the negative aspects weakened and even nullified the promises, the guarantees, and the hard-won gains. Most of the movement's colonies transgressed at least some of the noble declarations to a greater or lesser extent. Four offenses stand out.

1. Some utopians showed a callous insensitivity to the situation of women members.

2. Some colonies diluted the political rights of women members, and most kept the reins of leadership in the hands of men.

3. Most colonies limited job opportunities and kept women in the same work that had been their historical lot.

4. Most of the movement's publications perpetuated demeaning stereotypes and false images of women.

The first point, callous insensitivity, turns up in widely different guises. Consider the situation at Fruitlands, the Massachusetts experiment of Bronson Alcott and Charles Lane. They made ethics and morality a way of life, and these governed every aspect of colony life. They would harm no animal. But their ethical principles went beyond that: they refused to exploit animals or even to use animal products in any way: no draft horse or ox for plowing, no leather for shoes, and no tallow for candles. Their morality forbade the use of cotton, a product of slavery, one of the "fruits of oppression and blood."

Yet there seems to be no indication that the sensitivity to animals and slaves extended to Abigail May Alcott, Bronson Alcott's wife. She had to bear almost the entire domestic burden of Fruitlands. She did the cooking, the washing, and the cleaning. She had to take care of the children as well as the foibles of the inept, irresponsible Alcott, the ineffective and heedless Lane, and the strange coterie of eccentrics these impractical men attracted to the colony. She had to manage under extreme financial duress, and in fact, only her practical hand sustained the experiment for the time it existed. At the end of the Fruitlands debacle she unburdened her soul to her journal. Writing with a restraint that barely masked her emotion, she admitted disgust with the "arrangements" and her impatience to move on to "some more simple way of life. . . . My duties have been arduous, but my satisfaction small. . . . The care of Mr. Lane and [Lane's son] has been at times exceedingly arduous. My children have been too much bereft of their mother, and she has murmured at a lot which should deprive her of their society."[7]

A more obvious, more public example comes from New-Harmony's nineteen "Considerations For Those Who Wish to Unite under the New System," a document described in the previous chapter. "No. 17. No anger . . . ought to be felt toward female members when they . . . talk aloud, because they have been taught that . . . [it] is an effectual way of giving force to what they have to urge in their own favor. These are failings that will be laid aside as soon as they become acquainted with human nature."

Furthermore, the Owenites detracted from their positive efforts by publishing *Gazette* items that showed little sensitivity to the problems women faced. These articles not only violate principle but good taste as well. As we read them, we would like to think that we have merely come upon some clumsy parodies. But, sad to say, that is not the case. An early issue (November 25, 1825) contains a lengthy advice-to-wives article. Here a woman learns that if her husband is a drunkard she must look to herself for the cause. It reflects her failure to be mild, to submit to his intemperance. If she would just say nothing, the article advises, he would be sober. The article also recommends a similar tactic for wives with ill-natured husbands, angry ones, and jealous ones. It concludes by cautioning the wife with these problems not to complain to anyone. "If you cannot remedy your own misfortunes . . . suffer in private, and wait with a becoming fortitude for better times."

A later article offers "Hints on Conversation" because women's conversation needs to be "rescued from vapid commonplace" (March 7, 1827). In referring to women's conversation it uses words like *trite, hackneyed, frivolous, false,* and *of no moment.* "Let us not, however, be misunderstood," the writer cautions, "It is not meant to advise that women should affect to talk on lofty subjects," only that women bring "good sense" into those "common subjects" of conversation. The writer decides that the root of the problem lies in women's minds, which are too "relaxed" because of petty employments. That should have been an embarrassing slip for the *Gazette* because New-Harmony itself did not offer women anything better than petty opportunities. The article does stumble onto a manifest truth: men have systematically left women out of "instructive discourse." But it ends without exploring that crucial point.

We can easily imagine what such an environment would do for a woman's self-confidence. The experience of Sarah Pears shows how the male-dominated atmosphere could discourage women from "instructive discourse." She would have liked to have read a newspaper, possibly one from Pittsburgh, where she lived before joining Owen's experiment. "I hear little more of the old world than if I were an inhabitant of another planet," she wrote her aunt. New-Harmony did have a reading room that received many newspapers. But, the letter continued, "only the male part of the community has as yet assumed the privilege of reading them." So she did not go there and lost a cultural advantage that even women in traditional society had.[8]

The final example shows how positives and negatives can stand side by side. In the previous section on positive aspects, I mentioned an article, "Women in Association," from the newspaper *Ploughshare and Pruninghook* because it promoted financial independence for women as the way to assure their advancement. But the article also contains trite paternalism and even outright defamation: "Association elevates woman to her merited station, a station superior to man in morals and influence . . . though she may be in some degree inferior in intellect."

Most groups diluted women's rights, the second negative aspect. They did so by substituting symbol for substance, a classical fault of middle-class movements working for social change – then and now. A clear example of it shows up in the Wisconsin Phalanx bylaws quoted earlier. A careful reading shows that the nice-sounding "he or she" phrases do not carry as much weight as a first glance suggests. For example, when the bylaws get down to serious questions, such as the procedure for expelling a member, we discover that the "he or she" does not get to do the voting. "ART. 2, sec. 3. He or she shall be considered expelled if those voting in the affirmative be two-thirds of the resident male members over twenty-one." The Alphadelphia constitution did give women the right to vote on expulsions but denied them the vote on business matters.

Nothing exposes the dilution of women's rights as does their absence from the leadership. Nowhere in the movement can we find a woman in any of the top executive positions, none among the important decision makers. Perhaps we ought not be surprised to see that perversion of principle in groups with a limited understanding of the movement's goals, those who saw the effort only in terms of an efficient way to produce and profit. But Brook Farm certainly did not fall into that category; it grew out of a dedicated commitment to an ethical way of life. It had a solid core of steadfast, capable women with obvious leadership qualities and a group of earnest men who presumably understood the barriers facing women. Yet there, too, leadership remained, with one minor exception, a male dominion.

The Sylvania Association gave with one hand and took away with the other. Its constitution gave women the right to vote, but ARTICLE 10 limited women's wages to five-eighths the scale established for men.

And that lesser wage points up the essence of the third negative. Even where women had political rights, they usually suffered economic disadvantages by being forced into the same mold that traditional society has always reserved for them. The kinds of work a colony offered women tells us of its inclination to strive for the complete utopian promise. For example, when Kalikst Wolski visited North American Phalanx in its twelfth year of operation, he noticed that women there had full political rights. But in his account we can also discover the kind of work they did: washing, ironing, sewing, and gardening.[9]

The Alphadelphia records show how "women's work" could become institutionalized. The colony had a handwritten form, "Roll of Female Members reported ready to labor for the Association," for women to check their choice of jobs. The document, reproduced in illustration 5, seems to have a nice, democratic flavor, but notice the choices: cooking, housework, tailoring, common sewing, washing and ironing, dairy work, spinning, weaving, nursing, and "anything." No surprise, a committee of men compiled that list. And that committee provided Alphadelphia's women with no better opportunities than they had before they joined.

Moreover, the colony actually relegated women to an inferior status. A list from the "Report of the Committee to Organize and Equalize Labor," reproduced in illustration 6, defines Alphadelphia's standard working hours. Clearly, this committee of men went wide of the mark if they really wanted to "equalize." As you can see, the men's workday ranged from 6 to 10 hours for an average of 7.2 hours. Women had to put in from 8 to 16 hours, an average of 12 hours. In other words, women's workday was 40 percent longer than men's.

Alphadelphia Association. Roll of Female members reported ready to labor for the Association, with their choice of labor: what they are willing to do.

Names of Females	Cooking, Housework	Tailoring	Common Sewing	Washing & Ironing	Dairy Work	Spinning	Weaving	Nursing	Anything	
Susan Mead			.							Lodg
Susan T Mead	/		.						.	4
Betsey C Taylor	.		.					.	.	
C Flanders	.		.			.	.			
Mrs Starlie	.		.						.	
Selina D Deming		.	.							
Marion Wilcutt			.							
Mrs Wheeler		/	/							
Mrs Hunt	/		/			/				
Adaline Hunt									/	
Mrs Waldgen	/			.	.					
Mrs Whitcomb			/		/	/			/	2
[illegible] Whitcomb										
Mrs Robinson		/	/				/			5
Zipporah Liming	/					/				2
Fanny J. Hinkle	/					/				[illegible]
Mary Riedner	/					/				
Caroline L Miller			/							
Mrs Catharine Miller	/					/				
Alfleda Keith	/					/				
Hannah Low	/		/			.				
Phebe Curtis	/									2
Julia Etta Pierce	/									2
Jane Ball	/									
Sarah Curtis									/	
Mrs Hall			/							
Mary Berry				/				/	/	
Mary Camp	/	/	/						/	
Philena Arnold			/	/					/	
Mary Crookhurst			/	[illegible]		/			/	
Deborah Clinton	/								/	
Mrs Wolcott	/									
Mrs Earl	/								/	
Mrs Charlotte McOmber	/								/	

5. Work opportunities for Alphadelphia's women members. By permission of the Bentley Historical Library, University of Michigan.

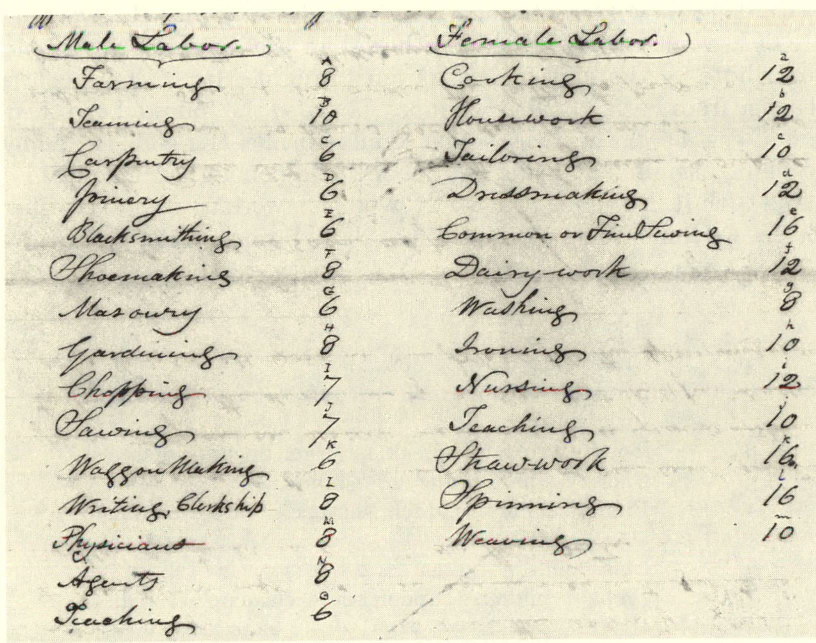

Male Labor.		Female Labor.	
Farming	8	Cooking	12
Teaming	10	Housework	12
Carpentry	6	Tailoring	10
Joinery	6	Dressmaking	12
Blacksmithing	6	Common or Fine Sewing	16
Shoemaking	8	Dairy-work	12
Masonry	6	Washing	8
Gardening	8	Ironing	10
Chopping	7	Nursing	12
Sawing	7	Teaching	10
Waggon Making	6	Strawwork	16
Writing, Clerkship	8	Spinning	16
Physicians	8	Weaving	10
Agents	8		
Teaching	6		

6. Standard working hours in Alphadelphia. From the Report of the Committee to Equalize Labor. By permission of the Bentley Historical Library, University of Michigan.

Notice that for teaching, the one occupation common to both sexes, the committee set the standard day for men at 6 hours, but they demanded 10 hours from the women.[10]

Robert Owen's scheme, regardless of its novelties, made no break with traditional prejudices. He wrote regulations for his model experiments, which the *Gazette* published (February 21, 1827). There the masses that Owen wanted to win over, the unconvinced of both sexes, could learn, perhaps for the first time, what the New Social System had in store. What would they say to this regulation? "33. The employments of the female part of the community consist in preparing food and clothing; in the care of the dwelling houses, dormitories and public buildings; in the management of the washing and drying houses; in the education (in part) of the children; in the lighter operations of gardening and other occupations suited to the female character."

Consider how that attitude could find its way into the working life of a women who had skills other than the domestic variety to contribute to the experiment. Owen brought Marie Fretageot, a teacher from Paris, to New-Harmony because she followed the theories of Pestalozzi, the Swiss educational reformer. Her New-Harmony teaching assignment would have been taxing enough if nothing else came with it. But something did: "women's work." From one of her letters we can develop a profile of her daily burden.[11] Her day began at 4:00 A.M.

4	Rise
4:30	Class: older boys, 2 hours
6:30	Straighten rooms; make breakfast (boys off to mandatory work)
8	(boys return) Serve breakfast; clean up, wash dishes etc.
9	Class: children under 12, 2 hours
11	Prepare children's lunch; serve; clean up; wash dishes etc.
2	Class: children under 12, 2 hours
4	Prepare children's supper; serve; clean up, wash dishes etc.
6	Class: teenagers, 2 hours
8	end of day

In this sixteen-hour day a teacher had eight hours of classes and still had to give seven and one-half hours more to housework, all without help. I found no evidence to indicate that New-Harmony women had any better opportunity to escape the timeworn ties to a domestic role.

In its fourth negative aspect, the movement perpetuated stereotypes of women through its publications. At first glance it might seem odd to find the old-fashioned attitudes of a narrow-minded milieu surfacing in this movement. But, in fact, women there had to put up with centuries-old demeaning literary images even from those who claimed to hold high moral and ethical principles. Such people allowed attitudes, sometimes subtly belittling, sometimes blatantly scornful, even vicious, to appear in poems, "jokes," and other printed items in the publications of social reorganization. A few examples show the diversity of that material and the surprising way in which otherwise sincere people never countered with "but . . ." when the butt of ridicule was Woman.

Hopedale published a weekly periodical called *Mammoth* devoted almost exclusively to stories, light verse, and so-called jokes. Each of these comes with a moral hidden not too far below its surface. Yet many of them transgress the spirit of the noble principles enshrined in Hopedale's constitution. The fact that these items attempt to teach a lesson in morality makes them all the more insidious when we think of what they inculcated. For example, one issue has a poem titled "Why Women Have No Beards" (May 12, 1847). It purports to explain that nature decreed no beards for women, for how could they be shaved, they never stop talking. A later issue had a column of "proverbs" (June 14, 1848), including items like these: "A woman that paints [uses cosmetics] puts up a bill that she is to let" and "Commend a wedded life, but keep thyself a bachelor."

Mammoth used stories as a favorite vehicle for its homilies passing as entertainment. "The Widow's Daughter" (August 8, 1847), a mawkish piece, tells about a poor girl who wears gold rings while her mother must labor over a washtub to provide them with a meager living. How a poor girl would come to have gold rings, we never learn, although we should hardly expect logic or consistency in such hack work. But the story includes the expected lesson, in this case wrapped in the words of a mother's wisdom. She advises the girl, "Take every ring from your fingers, and commence an apprenticeship to the trade of housewifery. . . . Learn to sew, to knit, to bake, to wash, to cook. . . . Become the wife of some honest mechanic." Before dismissing this as just a shallow story, notice the message. To the women of Hopedale, where the very name encouraged thoughts about overcoming the dismal past, it says something they could hear in any New England town: a woman's place is in the home.

Similarly, the Fourierist newspaper, *Phalanx* ("Dedicated to the Elevation of the Human Race"), carried an item, "Sketch of the Women," which makes a pretense of witty folk wisdom. It says that a woman's mind is always speculating on marriage, her own, her friends', and when she is older, "her darter's weddin' is uppermost. . . . Oh, it takes a great study to know women. How cunnin' they are!"

These attitudes ordained stereotyped roles for each sex and accepted certain human qualities as necessarily feminine or masculine. A case in point occurs in the poetry column of the *Gazette* (December 27, 1826), where the editors foster a generalization about the tastes and interests of all women. They apologize because recent selections had been serious. But this week they have a poem for "our female friends," which they describe as "something of a lighter nature," its subject "a favorite with the fair sex." The poem is titled "Love."

A poem called "Woman" in a later issue (August 27, 1827) seems at first to be an attack on the caricatures, on the very defamations that the *Gazette* itself published.

> There are, who lightly speak with scornful smiles,
> Of woman's faith, of woman's artful wiles;
> Who call her false in heart and weak in mind,
> The slave of fashion, and to reason blind.

But as you plod deeper into its nearly one hundred hackneyed lines, the message slowly emerges: woman's place is not in the affairs of state, not to legislate, nor is she meant to write or speak eloquent thoughts. But she can be the partner of man by staying home and raising the children.

Alphadelphia's *Tocsin* had a column called "Ladies Department." It offered poetry, trite and sentimental, along with other banalities in what is known as the genteel tradition. That emphasis reflected the attitude of the experiment's founders and supporters. One of them wrote to Henry Schetterly, secretary of the group, urging him to encourage Alphadelphia women to use "gentle language."[12] Sticklers for equal treatment may note that he urged no such thing for the men, although their language, judging from a reading of officious official reports and acrimonious minutes of the completely male leadership, could have used a little gentling.

John Dwight's musical criticism in the *Harbinger* perpetuates stereotypes in a more sophisticated way. He proceeds from an implicit concept: males and females have different, inherent, characteristic attributes. Furthermore, he makes the assumption that everyone knows the attributes of masculinity and of femininity and accepts their validity. In a review of Chopin's music (July 11, 1846), Dwight tries to increase our understanding of the composer's style by resorting to a time-worn epithet based on that assumption. "His sadness," Dwight asserts, "is most sweet to the soul. A feminine spirit his is, and pleasant as woman's spiritual smile." Dwight expands on this subtle bias in a review of poetry by Christopher Cranch (July 26, 1845). "There is an almost feminine grace and delicacy in his thoughts. . . . From this you would not expect great energy, strong determination of will, or the kind of eloquence which excites the will in others."

The *Harbinger* generally avoided the incongruous little jokes that other colony papers found acceptable. But that integrity began to falter in Brook Farm's desperate, waning days, and then we get an exceptional item: "Female Curiosity" (February 13, 1847). In it, the butler, a practical joker, entices the maid into opening a large, mysterious box that belongs to the master. She cannot resist her whetted temptation to look inside. When she does, a huge jack-in-the-box figure leaps out and frightens her out of her wits. We are then supposed to laugh at her weakness. The *Harbinger*, forgetting its strongly principled position on equality, universalizes her particular plight with the weight of a Shakespeare line, which Brook Farmers, being well-read, surely knew. "Frailty, thy name is woman," it jeers, and thus contradicts the empirical evidence about women's strength that Brook Farm itself provided.

Almost all of these negative aspects came together in Icaria. A clue to the way women counted in Cabet's scheme can be found in his specifications for the ideal social unit within the Icarian state. "The population should not exceed the number of citizens that can meet in a single assembly, about 1000 to 1200. With their wives and children [there would be] about 4000 to 5000 souls."[13] Obviously, when Cabet counted "citizens" he left women out.

The basic laws of Icaria contain many contradictions. In the 48 "Conditions of Admission," described in the previous chapter, no. 6 called for equality "without privilege for anyone." On the other hand, no. 5 promised women that Icaria would "neglect nothing to render them happy." Icaria's constitution in Nauvoo declared that "all are equal in rights and duties," and it also proclaimed the equality of husband and wife. But amazingly, Cabet modified equality for women by granting them "relative equality," which put him a century ahead of George Orwell's "Some . . . are more equal than others."[14]

Under scrutiny, however, Cabet's "relative equality" for women turns out to be merely a word game because Icaria's constitution barred women from both voting and holding elective office. Article 120 gave them a voice, an advisory one, limited to "questions which particularly concern them." Decades after Cabet's death his legacy of prejudice lived on in the Iowa colony, even after agitation by the younger generation forced some liberalization. Albert Shaw visited the colony in 1883, and his report says that Icarian women vote on certain questions such as admitting new members, amending the constitution, choosing the director of clothing and lodging, and on exceptionally important issues and matters "of more than usual concern to the women themselves." But we can read the true state of their progress in this line of his report, "On most current questions they do not vote."[15]

Cabet's paternalism should not be mistaken for equal opportunity. He maintained that "woman required by her nature to be more favorably treated than man." And he required that "everywhere and always the first place and the first share shall be hers, that the [legislators] shall regard the laws which interest her as the most important."[16] Cabet used such trite if not disingenuous sentiments, I believe, as a way of attracting young Frenchwomen to emigrate to Icaria, where a shortage of brides existed. That scarcity undoubtedly prompted Cabet to announce in *Colonie Icarienne* (July 19, 1854) that for unmarried young women he would waive the usual three-hundred-franc entrance fee required of all new members.

In any case, he did not intend his talk of "first shares" to give rise to thoughts of economic independence for women, as others in the movement proposed. The crucial question of jobs for women substantiates that. What kind of opportunities did women have in Icaria? Etienne Ravat, a satisfied Icarian and therefore one less inclined to disparage Cabet's effort, wrote home from Nauvoo describing conditions there in 1850. On labor he wrote, "Women are employed according to their abilities and their intelligence. Some do washing, some ironing, others do sewing, and some teach the young girls."[17]

Four years later *Colonie Icarienne* (September 20, 1854) published a list of the shops and trades for men and another for women. Men could find work under more than forty job titles, including baker, carpenter, cobbler, fisher, mechanic, and weaver. They made dozens of products, including barrels, mattresses, saddles, soap, suits, and wooden shoes. They worked in a variety of places indoors and out: on farms and in gardens, mills, distillery, and print shop, as well as on riverboats.

But Icaria kept the women in the one location traditional society had always reserved for them: the house. The women's list has only five job titles: seamstress, laundress, ironer, kitchen worker, and handler of linens. Therefore, this listing of jobs by sex shows at once that opportunities for women had not changed in the four years since Etienne Ravat's letter, even though Icaria had made great strides during that time and enjoyed prosperity.

The list of shops and trades also has a miscellaneous jobs category. It lists eight specialties for men: bookkeeper, chef, doctor, livestock buyer, musician, nurse, pharmacist, and secretary. Women had but three: midwife, head seamstress, and infirmary cook.

Among the tragic ironies that scar the utopian episodes, the last job has a special poignancy. Though the infirmary had a woman as cook, its resources, the only medical facilities in the town of Nauvoo, could be used only by men. *Colonie Icarienne* (July 19, 1854) tried to justify the policy by saying the colony could not afford to accept women in the infirmary. But that excuse exposed all the more the hollowness of Cabet's high-sounding promises.

Cabet's utopian novel, *Voyage en Icarie,* which he modeled after Thomas More's famous *Utopia,* lays out the basic premise and promise of the Nauvoo colony. He required every member to read it. In it Cabet takes us on a trip to an imaginary land called Icaria, where everything is perfect. There the children get vocational experience throughout their school years, the same for both boys and girls, so that each one can decide what kind of work to pursue as an adult. The women who came from France to take part in Cabet's attempt to recreate the imaginary Icaria on the banks of the Mississippi saw in it their dream of a better life. But Illinois is an infinite distance from imagination. In Illinois, in the real Icaria, boys got a wide range of job experiences, indoors and out, in agriculture, in transportation, and in the shops. But, from the earliest age, Cabet cast the die for the girls, intellectually and psychologically. He limited their vocational exploration to washing clothes, washing dishes, sewing, and folding the printed pages for the newspaper.

Cabet's violation of his own noble words went even further. In his imaginary Icaria all children study music. In the real world of Illinois boys got music lessons, but he closed off this enrichment and pleasure for girls, something that even the traditional society Cabet disparaged did not do.

Cabet had his own peculiar stereotypes of women, most with sexual overtones. He considered coquetry a most serious vice, and his paternalistic conception of women fathered such musty bromides as "Modesty and decency are the most beautiful ornaments of woman." He displayed that line on the wall of the colony's dining hall, alongside the large antiwar and other radical slogans there. Cabet had a restrictive dress code for women that ruled out fancy, stylish, and formal garments. He enforced that dictum personally. In one case, he severely and publicly rebuked and embarrassed Maria Marchand's mother on a Sunday promenade because she wore a satin dress, one brought from France and saved for special occasions.[18]

Cabet opposed what he called "absolute independence" for women because it might deter some from an Icarian requirement, marriage. We can get an idea of the quality of the marriage relationship Cabet had in mind from instructions he issued in *Colonie Icarienne* (July 19,

1854) for couples planning to come from France. On the subject of clothing he told them not to bring silks, luxuries, or "any item of coquetry." A women interested in attire will not become an Icarian, he warned. And for a man whose wife might hesitate because of those restrictions, he had a simple rule: leave her in France.

Guilt by Association

In addition to these four negative aspects that originated within the colonies of social reorganization, some outside sources also countered the utopian promise for women. Certain public figures, not members of any colony but associated in the popular mind with the movement, made known their intolerance, and that surely served to reinforce the negative aspects among interested but uncommitted people. As usual, prejudice ranged from subtle to blatant. One example of the subtle and one of the blatant follow. Each example represents the attitude of a well-known public figure, and both come from late years in the movement's history and therefore indicate solidly entrenched beliefs.

The first demonstrates the subtle bias of Ralph Waldo Emerson. Because of his friendship with many of the leaders at Brook Farm and because of his appearances there from time to time, the public linked him with that experiment. That association tended to add credibility to a little tale he told. "Of course, every visitor found that there was a comic side to this Paradise of shepherds and shepherdesses. . . . The ladies took cold on washing day; so it was ordained that the gentlemen-shepherds should wring and hang out the clothes. . . . And it would sometimes occur that when they danced in the evening, clothes-pins dropped plentifully from their pockets."[19]

The implication of this anecdote would clearly put Brook Farm into the same category as colonies that kept women in stereotyped jobs. However, the facts of life in Brook Farm discredit Emerson's story. Brook Farmers of both sexes shared in the colony's work, and that included washing clothes. The group who took on the laundry jobs consisted of both women *and* men. Therefore, the emergency that Emerson described could not have occurred. So this invention probably originated in his own sexist view of work roles in society. The yarn irked John Codman, who in his memoirs of Brook Farm wrote, "There was no dancing of clothes-pins from the pockets of the dancers, as Emerson has said, or if it once happened it was the intentional freak of a happy schoolboy, a bit of farcical fun, too unworthy even to be mentioned by the 'Sage of Concord' in his 'Historic Notes.' It was poor history and undignified in its connection."[20]

This anecdote is one of the many ways in which Emerson ridiculed the experiment. Much of what he said about it shows his distaste for Brook Farm and the principles that brought it into being. True, he lectured there, but he did that as a professional lecturer, and in that capacity he appeared at other colonies of Association too and charged a fee. In any case, the scorn he heaped on Brook Farm marks him as a hostile source for information about it. Still, the public mind thought of him as a Brook Farmer – some careless scholars even today do so – and the influence of his disparaging remarks needs to be taken into account.

The second example illustrates Horace Greeley's blatant disregard for the situation of women. An outspoken activist in many causes, publisher of the *New York Tribune,* and candidate for president of the United States, Greeley was far and away the best-known and most influential of the public figures supporting the movement. At about the time that interest and enthusiasm for Fourier began to peak, he offered the use of a column in the *Tribune* for the cause. But he obviously had little understanding of Fourier's philosophy in general, and particularly of Fourier's axiom that made women's independence the basis of social progress.

At a time when interest in Association was waning, Greeley wrote an editorial in the *Tribune* opposing any change in New York State's extremely rigid divorce law. The editorial provoked a letter to the *Tribune* from Robert Dale Owen, by then a leader in national politics, that not only attacked Greeley's position on divorce but also lashed out at his archaic attitude toward women. Greeley's instant, angry reply, which was followed by an Owen rebuttal letter, precipitated a continuing debate in the columns of the *Tribune.* It developed into what had to be the most remarkable series of exchanges on divorce and related questions of women's rights that Americans had seen in any major newspaper.

In a battle that raged back and forth for two months, Greeley's atavism remained unyielding to the point of viciousness. The law, according to him, says, "We rectify no mistakes: it rests with you not to make any. If you do, bear the penalty as you ought." And what of the woman who wants a divorce when the husband she had believed to be a decent man turns out to be a cruel brute or a drunkard? Greeley's answer, "The law says No, and we stand by it" shows his callous indifference. Greeley vilified Owen's home state, Indiana, which permitted divorce, calling it "the paradise of free-lovers." And unabashed, he claimed that easy divorce laws had led to the downfall of Rome, "blasted by the mildew of unchaste mothers and dissolute homes."[21]

What faith could American women who aspired to free themselves from the subservience of the past place in a movement symbolized by a national figure such as Greeley? The answer probably lies buried with the corpse of social reorganization. That is not to say that the demise of the movement can be attributed only to its forsaking the rights and dignity of women. Still, these negative aspects contributed their share of weight to the accumulating burden that ultimately crushed the movement.

A balanced account cannot, of course, end on that note. Most of all, and contradictions notwithstanding, if believers in social reorganization did nothing else, they pushed into the American mind ideas that had never entered that provincial precinct before.

For example, the same page of the *Gazette* that contains a negative poem about women has an article, "Female Artists" (August 29, 1827). It depicts in accurate terms the work of Joanna Koerten Block (Amsterdam, 1650–1715) and Mademoiselle Rozee (Leiden, 1632–82). In an age when few cared about women's achievements, especially those of women artists, this item represents a significant advance. Indeed, only recently, more than a century and a half later, has the world begun to remove the blinders that have shut out the contributions of women artists to our culture. Yet a *Gazette* article in 1827, out on the frontier, did bring a little information to America that could counter the stereotypes and the prejudice.

Furthermore, believers in social reorganization placed before the American consciousness a new principle that sooner or later we would have to deal with. In our history, the persistence of principles mattered most. And there it stood in 1846 on the pages of the *Harbinger* (July 18) for Americans to ponder and eventually to act on. "It is, of course, an established principle among us that Woman must finally determine upon her own sphere of duties, and limit and arrange her own modes of influence."

Life for the Future
Education

In our day, the teacher—not the warrior, worker, nor statesman—leads the vanguard of humanity.[1]

THE SPIRIT OF THIS SLOGAN resounded throughout the efforts in social reorganization, and it distinguishes this movement from all others dedicated to radical change. Education: people in the movement placed all their faith in it as a sure route to the goal.

Education would function both within the experiment and outside. Within the colony each child would learn the utopian principles from infancy and would grow up into a new kind of person dedicated to the new way of life. Civic-minded, refined, such people would not only make utopian society possible but would also make it a beautiful way to live. On the outside, education would be used to teach the masses the true source of the evils that beset them and to show them how the utopian solution would bring them happiness. The utopians believed that having seen the light, all the world, in a democratic upheaval, would enthusiastically flock to the new system.

Robert Owen based the success of his New Social System entirely on that premise. Fourier mixed education into the bricks and mortar of the Phalanx, making it the foundation as well as the superstructure. Cabet displayed powerful slogans on the walls of the Nauvoo dining hall where everyone could see them at each meal. They included:

Develop Intellect, Perfect Humanity!
The Present Should Learn From The Past!
Teach The Elements Of The Arts And Sciences!

In Cabet's list of what he needed to change the world, schools, teachers, books, and instruments took a prominent place. He would run his schools like miniature colonies, and they would develop a new breed of people, selfless and hardworking. He promised that Icarian children through "molding" would truly become beings in the "image of the Creator."[2]

Similarly, John Dwight, writing in the *Harbinger* (October 4, 1845), envisioned a new kind of human that would people the world of Association. He called that person "Collective Man," a name that foreshadowed visions held by social revolutionaries of a different breed in our century.

The kind of educational system we now take for granted did not exist when the colonies of social reorganization flourished. The poor who managed some education could find it only in the hand of charity. By midcentury a few states had begun to mandate grammar schools, but even then only the affluent could afford anything more than a rudimentary education. However, the programs of social reorganization held aloft a great promise: universal education, free to the highest level.

Few in the movement believed that traditional society could or would ever provide that kind of education. Charles Dana, who taught in the Brook Farm School, pointed out in a *Harbinger* article on education (July 25, 1846) that even if the state opened the doors of the universities and said, "Enter freely, the knowledge and the culture you long for is yours," the invitation would not help. How could the poor take advantage when they had all they could do just to feed and clothe themselves? He argued that only in Association, where the struggle for daily necessities no longer existed, would true mass education be possible. Dwight, the theoretical spirit of the school, defined education as more than lessons in a classroom. In a key *Harbinger* article (October 10, 1846), he recognized the collective influence of the sphere in which children developed, the child's world as teacher. He speculated that only Association could provide the sympathy and care children needed, and only Association could surround them with a "watchful and harmonious influence" and "the collective maternal sentiment."

With these concepts so basic to their programs, almost every colony in the movement promised education and enshrined the promise in a fundamental document. For example, the constitution of Sylvania Association mandated "a complete system of Education in all useful and elevating branches of physical, intellectual and moral science." Compulsory education, an idea rarely heard in traditional society then, became a requirement in the Communia constitution.

Several colonies incorporated the word *education* into their names. Of these, the Brook Farm Institute of Agriculture and Education had the best justification. The founders clearly stated their goals in the original Articles of Association: "to promote the great purposes of human culture," and "to secure our children . . . the benefit of the highest physical, intellectual, and moral education." *Education* remained in the colony's name and in its goals when the members recast the experiment as Brook Farm Association for Industry and Education in 1844. Although the word disappeared from the name when the colony reorganized as Brook Farm Phalanx in 1845, its spirit remained to counter the new industrial emphasis of the experiment.

The members of Northampton Association of Education and Industry took the most advanced step. A century or more ahead of their time, the members boldly elevated education from a privilege to a basic right. They wrote this noble principle into their constitution, "The opportunity for self-improvement in all knowledge is the right of every human being." A few years later, Dana expressed that principle more forcefully. Writing in the *Harbinger* (January 24, 1846), he called education the "undeniable right" of children, on a par with the right to air and light. He invoked the voice of Divine Justice: "Give to every child of every class and condition the best possible education . . . not as act of charity but as the debt you owe it."

At that time such words came across as though from another world. Radical then, generally accepted now, the championship of free, universal education as a basic human right ranks among the movement's most important contributions to the agitation for a better life. Unfortunately, those voices of the future have been filed away in quiet archives where their words in the noble message remain unheard.

The word *education* encompassed much more than classrooms and schoolhouses for this movement. It required four distinct programs.

1. Raise each child as a new kind of person, devoted to the principles of the new way of life and prepared morally and intellectually for it.

2. Teach every adult the colony's doctrines of social change to keep the experiment on track and to prevent it from being derailed by the uninformed or by misleaders.

3. Provide self-improvement opportunities to help adult members increase skills and intellectual satisfaction.

4. Educate the rest of the world to the excellence of the new system so as to win them over to the cause.

Without the first two – the subject of this chapter – the movement could not hope to reach the utopian goal. Later chapters will focus on the third program and on the movement's folly in tackling the fourth when its colonies had all they could do just to stay alive.

We have already seen how a membership ignorant of the guiding principles can mutilate an experiment. So the kind of effort leaders made in teaching their generation the founding principles and in raising the new generation as utopians provides yet another clue to the viability of the movement. It reveals the depth of their confidence in a key tenet of social reorganization – education can change the world – and their readiness to put that assumption to the acid test.

Raising the New Generation

Undoubtedly, a genuine desire existed among some leaders to breathe life into the words promising education. For example, Charles Sears, president of North American Phalanx, writing to Horace Greeley about plans for a school, called it one of the colony's "cherished life purposes." And to a key financial backer he confided that he had worked harder for education than for anything else. Undoubtedly, a great desire also existed among the rank and file to see the words that promised education brought to life. Charles Lane's visit to Brook Farm convinced him of the power of education to attract members. A similar interest shows up throughout the movement. From New-Harmony, Sarah Pears wrote her aunt that "Most of the individuals here assembled came principally on account of educating their children." Additional support for that idea comes from an entry Donald Macdonald made in his diary while traveling down the Ohio River to meet his friend Robert Owen in New-Harmony. At Steubenville, about six hundred miles to the east, a judge who had heard of the New-Harmony school, boarded the riverboat to ask Macdonald if he would enroll his ten-year-old son there. Macdonald agreed to arrange it, and accepted a twenty-five dollar advance for the tuition.[3]

Yet, as we have already seen, the movement's strength lay in words, its weakness in deeds. So despite the promises of leaders and the desires of the membership, education in these experiments, with one notable exception, bore no resemblance to the crucial role that Owen, Fourier, Cabet, and others had assigned to it. Efforts ranged from nothing at all to perfunctory programs inconsistent with the movement's goal.

REVOLUTION ON A SHOESTRING

Icaria, both in its original Illinois location and later in Iowa, provides a case study of the gulf that separated speculation and reality. Cabet required each member to own and study his utopian novel, *Voyage en Icarie.* He called it "a scientific and philosophic treatise on political and social organization."[4] The equivalent of More's *Utopia,* it shows us life in the fictional Republic of Icaria, an ideal state in every respect. When the real Icarians left France in 1849 with the hope of realizing the book's glories in Nauvoo, Illinois, its visions sailed with them. Thus, Icarians, more than any other group, knew the educational ideas at the heart of their experiment and could compare what the words promised with what they saw around them every day. And just as they could have done, we can let fantasy face up to fact.

Voyage en Icarie takes us to a far-off land, Icaria, where the society is created out of the perfectibility of humanity. Its history proves that education, "the base and foundation of our entire social and political system," made perfection possible. Therefore, these fictional people and their representatives give education "the most attention." Cabet's picture of their educational system, which he develops in the warmest tones, includes a visit to one of their schools. Situated in a broad open area bordered with beautiful trees, we see a monument of a building, its magnificent exterior festooned with inscriptions and surmounted with statues. Inside, splendor dazzles the eye. But wait, this is just a local school. Yet it tells the world that "the Republic of Icaria considers education the highest good," and it "inspires in the children a kind of religious respect for Education and for the Republic, which gives it to them."[5]

Possibly the newly built British Museum or reminiscences of Paris or Versailles influenced Cabet when, a decade before the Illinois experiment, he sat in exile in a lonely London room and dreamt up this romantic vision of an ideal school in an ideal world.

However, for Icarians in the real world such beautiful images could only have stood in stark contrast to the pale imitations they improvised. Cabet, it is true, emphasized the significance of education in Nauvoo by creating a directorship for it in the six-member governing body. But did he make education "the base and foundation"? And was it an object of "the most attention"? We can guess the answers from the fact that nearly four years passed before they even started building a school in Nauvoo. An undistinguished little schoolhouse made from the rubble of the temple the Mormons had abandoned when they went west, it gave no indication of the paramount place that education held in the Icarian value system. Even so, the building was certainly superior to the log cabin that the Iowa Icarians would have to put up with in the following decades.

In the fictional Icaria, Cabet emphasizes the quality of the educational system. It has the finest teachers and the most advanced methods to make learning easy and pleasant. Every lesson becomes a game, and every game a lesson. Love for their pupils motivates the teachers, each a master in the profession and a specialist in one of its subjects. Committees continually search for new, imaginative techniques and eagerly adopt them. In that happy land, they do everything possible for education. And it works. "The beauty and comfort of the schools, the patience, tenderness, and skill of the teachers, the simplicity of the methods, the clarity of the demonstrations, the mix of study and play, all harmonize to attain the goal."[6]

Alexander Holynski visited the real Icaria in 1855, and found only one teacher. Except for English, which required a special "professor," that one teacher had to cover everything, including drawing, arithmetic, history, and geography. Though mature, well-informed, and a loyal follower of Cabet, those attributes did not necessarily qualify him to be an Icarian educator. Did he have patience and tenderness, as teachers in Cabet's novel have? We can judge from the facts: the members threw him out when they discovered that his teaching methods included physical punishment. Early in the experiment's history Emile Vallet, listed on the census as a teacher, arrived there. Sixteen years old at the time, his qualifications to fill a role so crucial to Icaria's future remain unclear. His experiences during his years as an Icarian led him to call the education system cautious and rigid, characterized by maintenance of "perfect control." He eventually broke with Cabet, and so his reminiscences may have been biased.[7]

But, Vallet's charge finds convincing affirmation in a reading of the colony's school regulations. As we saw in the chapter dealing with personal freedom, parts of Icaria's constitution and some of the rules in Cabet's "Conditions of Admission" served a worthwhile end. Ultimately, however, Cabet's attempt to codify the details of daily life through such documents and through the school regulations led him toward state control of the individual. In the fictional Icaria the students enjoy gentle freedom based on love and understanding that allows for their unfettered self-expression. There, the students themselves make the regulations for the schools. In Nauvoo, Cabet wrote the rules.

Every society, it goes without saying, has values and social conventions that it teaches its children. But only a legalistic mentality such as Cabet's would see the need to use the "School Regulations," an official, formal document to enact such elementary canons of behavior as, Children should love their parents (ART. 1, no. 1), respect their teachers (ART. 1, no. 4), and be polite to all members (ART. 1, no. 7). Some rules invite reasonable questions. Everyone might understand why children need to be quiet in class (ART. 1, no. 13). But what justification demanded, as this rule did, that they also maintain silence at meals and in the dormitory? and never make any noise (ART. 1, no. 15)? And if such rules merely stifled the natural ebullience of children, Cabet codified others that raise more frightening questions. What kind of values made it a child's duty to submit to punishment "*sans murmure,*" without complaint (ART. 1, no. 20)? Why would Cabet, who had made much of compassion in his imaginary Icaria, prohibit crying in Nauvoo (ART. 1, no. 14)? And what did he have in mind by forcing children to march from one activity to another "in ranks" of two or three (ART. 18), where "one must not break ranks until the Director gives the signal," and where an "overseer" reports infractions (ART. 20)? Such regulations seem more appropriate for hammering out Spartans than for lovingly nurturing the new humans, Icaria's hope for the future.

Maria Marchand remembered the Iowa colony's teachers. They included Antoine von Gauvin, a university graduate from Berlin who had served as an officer in the Prussian army. Though a staunch Icarian tested in the stormy Cabet years in Nauvoo two decades earlier and though well-liked by all, he nevertheless remained a far cry from the educator that Cabet's fiction demanded. His teaching reflected his desultory interests: he gave the students lessons in history, literature, and shorthand but paid no attention to grammar or spelling. For a time he taught vegetarianism but dropped it when it no longer attracted him. William Moore, the teacher who preceded Gauvin, though not a college graduate, taught the children geography, chemistry, physical science, physiology, and hygiene. Moore had been a Shaker, hardly the best background for an educator of future Icarians.[8] But if the Icarians had remained true to their principles, Moore would have been disqualified for a more important reason.

In fictional Icaria, reading and writing come first. There, educators give the highest priority to those basic skills. For example, recognizing the difficulties in learning French, Cabet's imaginary, ideal republic, as one of its first acts, abolished all irregular verbs and silent letters (may that at least come to pass someday in our own less-than ideal world). Because the books for young readers affect their development so significantly, the Republic of Icaria chooses only the best authors to write them. The basic text is *Amis des Enfants* (The Children's Friend), adopted from a competition among many authors. An attractive little book, each graded volume has excellent typography, fine paper, and charming illustrations in full color. The republic checks every word and every idea carefully to be sure they make learning enjoyable for the designated level of study.

In the real Icaria in Iowa, William Moore used the commonplace McGuffey's Readers – they were in English, of course – and taught spelling by making the children, almost all of whom knew only French, tediously memorize ten words each day from a *Webster's* English Dictionary. Obviously, he had not read the rather advanced educational ideas Cabet presented in *Voyage en Icarie.* In fact, he could not do so because he, the teacher in a French colony, could not read or speak French. Therefore, Moore could not teach the principles of Icarian morality, the sine qua non for Cabet's perfection of humanity. And that deficiency clearly epitomizes the betrayal of Icarian educational ideals.

After a couple of decades in Iowa, the members gave up any pretense of providing an Icarian education and combined their classes with those of the district school.

One might argue, of course, that fairness ought to moderate any harsh criticism of Icaria in its formative years. After all, the achievement of the perfect society might be expected to take a long time. But in fact, Cabet did cover that question. In the Icaria of his imagination he establishes a fifty-year transitional period beginning "immediately," and outlines a comprehensive program for it. Points 21 to 23 of that plan contain his agenda for education, "the main object of public solicitude." Significantly, Cabet assures everyone that the "transitional system . . . differs as little as possible from the definitive system." In fictional Icaria, the people's representatives make ready the provisional schools using the most beautiful public buildings for this purpose, they arrange for the writing of the educational books, and they provide for all the necessary instructors, "the most important of the public functionaries." And they carry this out "as soon as possible," so obviously Cabet considered these the most urgent first steps in the transition.[9]

But if Cabet and the "people's representatives" in the real Icarian colonies took those guidelines seriously, they showed no sense of urgency – witness their foot dragging on building a school. Moreover, in Cabet's fictional Icaria he assigns such a crucial role to education in the transitional program that he unhesitatingly commits "up to 100 million" [francs] each year for it. But in Nauvoo, that poorly planned, pinchpenny attempt to perfect humanity, he turned to begging for educational materials – any kind he could get – from supporters back in France. Then he unabashedly published lists of these haphazard, often educationally useless donations in the colony newspaper.

The colony library in Iowa did have several dictionaries, including a *Webster's* and a few other books appropriate for education. Among its remnants I found one for children, Lafontaine's *Fables*. Its dilapidated condition shows that it heroically filled a need. However, the records contain nothing to suggest that Cabet or his followers approached education in a way even remotely resembling the mandate of *Voyage en Icarie:* no outstanding teachers, no special books, no extraordinary expenditures.

Education in Nauvoo deviated from the promises of *Voyage en Icarie* in other, more inhumane respects. Cabet emphasized family values and their vital role in society. In the fictional Icaria the schoolchildren live at home, cultivated in the warmth of the family circle. However, in the real world Cabet mistrusted the influence that the older generation and even teenagers might have on children. So despite the attractive domesticity and family life espoused in Cabet's novel, in Nauvoo he separated the children from their parents. (The Shakers also followed this practice.) All young children except infants had to live in the boarding school.

This obsession with protecting future Icarians from traditionalist influence also led to hardship and injustice for older children arriving in Nauvoo. For example, the colony closed the school door to Doris Eberdt, who came there at fourteen, because having been raised in the Old World (Germany), she might "set a bad example" for other youngsters.[10]

The tactic of separating little children from their families angered members and fanned the embers of discord. Cabet admitted that. Determined parents might still manage to catch a glimpse of their children by going to the school while the children came outside for recreation periods. But the adults would have to slip off from work for this, a laxity Cabet would never tolerate.

Cabet permitted children to go to the room of their parents for a Sunday afternoon visit, but he granted the visit as a privilege, not a right. He withheld permission from those who became entangled in his complex web of regulations – a tiny misstep could do it – and from other unfortunates who might have stumbled across his headstrong temperament. Thus he could interdict even this little weekly reunion of the family. And when he did, he would be trampling on another axiom of his fictional Icaria: children learn through love not punishment.

Finally, there is Cabet's real-world attitude toward women, which, as I pointed out in the previous chapter, brought second-class education to the girls of the Nauvoo colony. It accounts for one of the gravest contradictions in his thinking. Thus, the neglect and undoing of Icarian education, the key to an Icarian future, stand out as crucial inconsistencies in Cabet's and his followers' attempts to build an ideal society by perfecting humanity.

Here again, fairness might argue against harsh criticism because a lack of funds prohibited a greater effort. Indeed, other experiments throughout the movement that defaulted on education raised that defense. Albert Shaw, who visited the Iowa Icarians during the 1870s, saw that they had come through a very difficult period, and concluded that "care and toil" had made them lose sight of their goals.[11] Still, better times did come along and then they could have made a more principled effort for education. But they did not do so.

The facts of the Icarian experiments show that this fault did not arise from adversity. Rather, it stemmed from distorted priorities. If the new way of life did depend on education, the leaders should have delayed the experiment until they had the means to do justice to what they proclaimed as their hope for the future. Such things tell us that from the beginning Cabet's education represented good intentions perhaps, but not an irrevocable duty.

The records also suggest a membership so imbued with trust in their leader's wisdom and vision that these people, ordinary human beings after all, could set out for America without questioning him closely on the details. How many times throughout history have we seen the tragic consequences of such blind faith?

THE PROFIT MOTIVE

Adversity in this movement, although not a valid defense, accounted for many other defaults on the educational promise. On the other hand, prosperity did not necessarily assure a principled effort for education. The history of one of the most prosperous experiments, Wisconsin Phalanx, illustrates this statement convincingly. Its neglect of education can be traced directly to the propaganda that generated interest in Fourierism, from which the founders learned how to succeed in business without really trying the utopian rationale.

The colony became a reality after a few months of Fourierist meetings in Southport (now Kenosha), Wisconsin Territory. The town's newspaper, the *Telegraph*, played a key role by publishing excerpts from a recent book by Parke Godwin that attempted to explain some of Fourier's ideas. Although Fourier's sweeping speculations fill volumes, Godwin took only a little more than one hundred pages for his commentaries. Not a digest, his slender book ignores most topics and glosses over a basic Fourier premise: All aspects of society are interdependent, and none can be considered apart from the others.

Thus, in Godwin's brevity the emphasis falls too heavily on economic aspects. That heightened its appeal to entrepreneurial instincts and left some people with the impression that Fourier simply promoted a new profit system rather than a new social system. The excerpts in the *Telegraph* added to that distortion. For example, one article illustrating the advantages of Association (April 16, 1844) cites Godwin's example of steamboat owners who formed a syndicate to restrain competition. Fourier's broad social vision, of course, looked much higher than petty commercial schemes. But on such a flimsy basis, Warren Chase and some of his followers, quick converts from the *Telegraph* articles and a few meetings, founded Wisconsin Phalanx.

A year later, rumors about its imminent collapse began spreading. The *Harbinger* published a letter (August 30, 1845) countering the gossip. The letter asserts that the colony has "never been in a more prosperous condition" and mentions with pride the "excellent free school" where everyone can receive a good education. The following week's *Harbinger* contains a letter from Chase, the colony's president, confirming his colony's prosperity.

Significantly, Chase makes this promise, "We are Associationists of the Fourier school, and intend to reduce his system to practice as fast as possible, consistent with our situation." However, inconsistencies diminish that affirmation. Although he says that they have school constantly," Chase reveals that "we have as yet been unable to do much towards that department." Moreover, he confesses that his group would have to depend on the *Harbinger* and Brook Farm for guidance in this "branch," an odd position for a leader in a movement that had made education its hope for the future.

A few months later Chase gave the movement's press the colony's first annual statement, which the *Harbinger* promptly published (December 27, 1845), as it did for subsequent statements. It contains a detailed summary of their progress. In a tone of barely suppressed boasting Chase tells of their 400 acres in wheat, 60 in corn, 20 in potatoes, 20 in buckwheat, 30 in beans, and so forth. They cut 400 tons of hay, and now own over 250 head of livestock. They put up 5 miles of fence, dug a mill race, and then built a grist mill and a saw mill valued at $1000 and $2000 respectively. And most important, they have no debt, and are self-sustaining.

These accomplishments would surely be quite impressive if the colony had merely set out to establish a successful farm, as a few cooperative families in the West were doing. But as Fourierists they had grander goals, and for these the vaunting vanished. First the good news: they had a one-room schoolhouse. And now the bad news: they did not use it. Chase had an excuse, one that would soon become a familiar refrain. "We have approximated as far towards the plan of Fourier as the difficulties incident to a new organization in an uncultivated country would permit."

They valued the schoolhouse at four hundred dollars. A quick comparison of that amount with the values they placed on farm buildings tells us where education stood in their scale of social values. And their building specifications matched that scale, being a stingy twenty by thirty feet, much too meager to serve seventy-two children and eighty adults.

After two years the council finally voted to put the little house to use as a "juvenile school." But the school held only one class each week. William Stillwell sat in for a session of the one-room one-day school, and unimpressed, described it in a letter to his wife, Sarah. It had fifty children, and they learned "all branches" of education. The method consisted of a recitation by each child, after which the "superintendent" asked a few questions. Then they had singing, and with that the schoolday ended. Stillwell noticed the books: a skimpy supply and worn out.[12]

The next annual statement (January 27, 1848) reported another successful year in farming. But in education Wisconsin Phalanx had made little progress. Chase's typically inept and wordy attempt to explain the delay contains embarrassing admissions and discrepancies. "[We are] too busily engaged in making such improvements as were required to supply the necessaries of life to devote the means and labor necessary to prepare such buildings as are required. Having but one schoolhouse, the male and female children have been taught alternately. . . . We have not yet been able to teach [music] to much extent, more for want of room and system in our arrangements than for want of competent teachers."

Reading between the lines, we can see that education took a back seat in their farm wagon. Notice also that, although they espoused womens' equality, they perpetuated a custom of the past in their segregation by sex. Moreover, the point about teaching music contradicts the previous statement, which unambiguously says: "Many . . . study . . . vocal and instrumental music; in this there is constant progress visible."

The statement for the following year (January 29, 1848) speaks out clearly on economic issues. Business: "never been so prosperous." Industrial organization: "never better." Hope: "never more fully aroused." However, when it comes to education the colony's president turns his head aside, mumbling and stumbling uneasily through another foggy apology, quoted here word for word. "We have not yet been able to make this improvement which we desire owing to the want of sufficient buildings and conveniences for reducing the management of this branch to that regular system, which by an adaptation of external circumstances to the internal nature, harmoniously unfolds that 'variety in unity' without which there is no complete educational development."

As for music, Chase says they are teaching it "to some extent." Actually, a council vote that year did approve a weekly singing class. Isabella Hunter recalled its sessions as enjoyable. However, Fourier's doctrines explain the necessity for a large music program built around opera. He designates it as one of two absolute essentials for raising children in the Phalanx. But of that requirement, these "Fourierists" knew nothing. And that is what they spent for it. The colony records list no entries for a music teacher, none for music, and none for instruments.

With déjà vu, we quickly spot the ritual apology in their next annual statement (February 10, 1849). It claims that "for the want of means" the colony could not set up any special program for the children. "We do no more than sustain a common school . . . waiting, when our condition will justify a more extended operation."

At first glance, these annual statements seem like an enigma. On the one hand, the figures tell of a business whose bountiful surpluses would warm the heart of any investor. Indeed, over this four-year period we can add up nearly $15,000 plowed back into farm buildings and more than $3,000 into livestock. (To judge those values, consider, for example, that in those days room and board could be had in New York City for $2.50 per week.) On the other hand, when it came to education, they unashamedly pleaded poverty.

Why would they want to keep publishing a seeming contradiction – strong in business, weak in education – in the movement's press? The explanation can be traced to a tactic called the "Model Phalanx," which leaders of Association in the East had adopted. Having watched countless experiments go under, they decided to concentrate all financial and moral support in one well-run demonstration of the benefits of Fourierism. Chase made a determined effort to convince them that Wisconsin Phalanx should be designated the Model Phalanx. So he used the annual statements to tell the movement back East that his experiment had the efficient business operation that social reorganization sought. And in an attempt to turn the colony's neglect into an advantage, he let the statements imply that, with the infusion of additional funds, the experiment could simply add on the education Fourier had called for. The movement remained unconvinced, and for a good reason.

Obviously, the leaders of Wisconsin Phalanx had only a superficial understanding of education's role in Fourier's plan. Therefore, they continued to think of education simply as an add-on, the superposed veneer they knew in traditional society. They never grasped Fourier's concept of education as both forming the basis of the Phalanx and growing out of the Phalanx, an intrinsic thread woven throughout its web.

When the men who were to found Wisconsin Phalanx looked into Godwin's slender interpretation of Fourier at those first Associationist meetings in Southport they probably saw nothing but dollar signs. The evidence for that shows up in the mercantile spirit that directed many of their later decisions. For example, the council, which would pay forty dollars for a horse, allowed Almira Hoit the sum of fifteen dollars for one year's teaching. Harriet Haven taught French to the Sewing Group, but she did that while busily stitching away with the rest of them in production work. She recorded her daily results for the council: two dozen regular sacks for the colony's flour mill.[13] Of results in regular verbs the council asked for no records.

In 1848 the council actually voted to charge for schoolbooks. Then, a year later, the council even considered a motion to discontinue the school. However, the motion failed when a financial report showed that the school, which had been taking in outside pupils, turned a profit. Still, the school may not have brought in enough income, or perhaps it detracted from the more profitable farm operation because six months later the council again took up the motion to close the school. This time it carried with an amendment to continue only "until the District School is organized."[14] No document indicates a raised eyebrow at this heresy: placing their hope for the future back into the traditional hands of the past.

Actually, the colony school was closed at the time of the vote, and apparently the boys had been behaving like boys. Fourier believed that youngsters in a Phalanx, following the natural tendencies of their individual personalities, would of themselves gravitate into work they found attractive. The leadership, ignoring or ignorant of Fourier's position on children's effervescence, decided to do something about the boys. For this they hired M. E. Morse, formerly a teacher. But the colony had no interest in his pedagogical skills. They wanted him to keep the boys in line by organizing them into a labor gang. Significantly, the council voted to pay Morse as a laborer, not as a teacher. At the same time, the council decided to get a woman teacher for the little children until the district school opened. And once again the three Rs took on the shape of dollar signs. From a letter that Charlotte Haven wrote to her brother William in Champlain, New York, we learn that the colony school had been closed for a month when the council offered her the teaching position. She had been giving it thought, and confided to her brother that she might accept "if I can get enough to pay my expenses." Finally, as the fall of 1849 began, the council voted to rent the colony's little schoolhouse to the school district and any pretense of carrying on a program for social change dropped with the autumn leaves.[15]

A year later the members dissolved the Phalanx. Riding the crest of inflating land prices in the Midwest and the rapidly expanding markets for produce, their vision of profits ameliorated any faults they might have seen in traditional society. Unlike most other experiments in social reorganization, which left members and sympathizers with worthless shares of stock that drained their life savings, Wisconsin Phalanx not only paid off all shares in full but also added on a tidy gain.

The reluctance of the leaders to divert efforts and funds from the farm reflects their superficial knowledge of the movement's goal. That fault shows up in Chase's response to criticism of Wisconsin Phalanx's educational effort. The issue arose when a New Englander visited the colony and sent negative comments about its school to the *Harbinger* (November 6, 1847). Chase had his pat response ready, and soon *Harbinger* readers were assessing his side of the story (January 8, 1848). In this defense of the colony, Chase's misconceptions of Fourier's ideas stand out clearly. First of all, he claims that the colony school is as good as any in the Wisconsin Territory and that it is open more months than the others. Chase then counterattacks by implying a regional bias on the part of eastern critics. He contends that the West cannot be compared to the older cities and states, "We must be compared to the country in which we live."

His parochial defense exposed his insensitivity to the movement's cosmopolitan spirit. In the scope of what social reorganization hoped to achieve, the standards of farm-village schools had no relevance. In fact, comparing the colony's school to the lowest common denominator of traditional society, or to any of its schools for that matter, simply elevated symbol over substance.

With leadership in the hands of profit-minded men who equated a short-term gain with success, substantive education never had a chance. For them, real estate, plowing, and husbandry paid immediate and tangible dividends. That attracted them more than the abstract dividends that might someday accrue from education. So they defaulted from the outset, just as the Icarians did, on their obligation to establish programs appropriate to the principles that underlay the experiment. But in this case the records show that they did not lack the educational money, only the educational mentality.

MISDIRECTION

New-Harmony's educational program began with advantages that most later experiments lacked. These included money, support from educators, and a definite objective. More specifically, it had Owen's wealth, his international connections, and his goal: using education to form character. He claimed that his plan, based on methods vindicated in the schools he set up for the workers' families at his Scotland mill, would turn New-Harmony children into moral, rational, useful members of the New Social System. Among his first steps he established a New-Harmony school for infants, one for children, and another for youths. The schools seemed to open the door to one of the great utopian promises: free, universal education.

However, those first steps began on the wrong foot. Owen's management skills that brought wealth in Scotland, fell victim to muddled priorities not unlike the "go-first-and-build-later" method for starting a colony that was discussed in chapter 3. More important than buildings, item 1 on his shopping list should have been teachers trained in or at least sympathetic to his all-important educational ideas, key to the future. He should have overseen their selection. But he left that to chance and then left for Europe. Members began to complain. Six months went by until young William Owen, saddled with all the responsibilities of the colony in his father's absence, reminded him in an urgent letter that with one possible exception "we have no teachers . . . who understand how to teach at all according to the New Principles."[16]

Robert Owen returned early the following year with what he thought would be a solution. Through his connections he brought to the experiment some famous scientists from the Academy of Natural Science in Philadelphia and several European disciples of Pestalozzi, the educational reformer. They arrived by riverboat, and the Owenites dubbed them the "Boatland of Knowledge." They surely added impressive credentials to Owen's educational program. But nearly eight critical months, perhaps the most crucial in the colony's brief history, had passed without Owenite teachers. During that time neglect of the schools had contributed its own abrasions to an experiment already eroding from improper management. That early wear and tear became yet another factor in the experiment's ultimate disintegration.

Owen, textile mill owner and defender of the poor, developed clear educational values. Those values, which appraised all things in terms of their usefulness to society, defined the schools. They determined what to teach and how to teach. What would the New Social System need, well-read thinkers or workers with manual skills? Owen's experience answered: people who can submerge self and dependably play a role on the production team.

A careful search of the colony ledgers offers convincing clues to how the educational program tried to fulfill those needs. The schools bought large quantities of needles, thread, thimbles, scissors, irons, and coarse fabrics. They invested in many saws, planes, and files. But except for a large map, the only hint of academics comes in money spent for slates, quills, and paper. Marie Fretageot, an educator from France, did bring some supplies and items for teaching geometry. But nowhere on those hundreds of pages of neatly inscribed New-Harmony accounts can we find an entry for the purchase of schoolbooks, not even a dictionary or a book of fables for the children. William Maclure brought his large library, but as we shall see in the next chapter, it would have been of little use to these schools.

The lack of schoolbook purchases may reflect the educational notions of leading members, which appear frequently in *Gazette* articles. Basically, they reject the elements of a liberal education. In one article, two influential teachers say they believe in "cautiously avoiding the delusions of imagination, the constant source of ignorance and error" (February 15, 1826). Fables and even novels would fall under that kind of axe. A series of six *Gazette* articles (April 12 to May 24, 1826) raises strong objections to the "early" study of languages. They argue against Latin in particular as a tool of "the priesthood" by which the people are "duped" and "hoodwinked" and which brings "the young under the immediate modification of the priesthood." Moreover, Latin "does nothing toward modifying [children's] temper, or subduing the violence of their passions." Thinking of children in such terms certainly seems incongruous in a movement with humanistic concerns. These *Gazette* articles further maintain that languages take time away from more useful studies. In a related argument, one article creates a strange polarity between "words" and "things." The writer looks for "utility" in the knowledge of words, and decides that "the science of words (if it be worthy the name of a science) is of far less importance than the science of things."

With that kind of thinking, who would need a dictionary? No surprise, documents from the colony show a decided weakness in spelling and grammar. And the most disturbing examples come from the pens of some of the educators.

The teachers aimed to keep things simple, "preferring the useful to the ornamental." Children learned basic facts that could be grasped in direct experience of the world around them. For example, Miner Kellogg, the artist, then about twelve years old, said his school often held classes in the woods and in these sessions he learned about plants and animals from living examples. The teachers shunned abstractions.

Obviously, vocational training stood at the heart of the education program. The older boys learned trades such as cabinetmaking and printing. As for the girls, the many entries in the colony ledgers for needles and thread speak eloquently of the role that the New Social System had in store for them.

The pupils took classes in gymnastics, a relatively progressive idea, but even there the utilitarian rationale ruled. Owen saw military drills, marching, and carefully regulated dancing as a "powerful means to form good . . . character" because they inculcated, in Owen's words, "discipline" and "obedience," traits the New Social System needed. So gymnastics emphasized marching and climbing, the kind of activities "that lead to utility." The pupils usually marched from one place to another – squad formation – with drums to keep them in step.[17]

The remarkable group of educators and scholars Owen attracted to this provincial outpost should have strengthened the experiment the moment they stepped off the boat. But not all saw eye to eye on education or understood the need to follow Owen's plan. Some could not even be counted as Owenites, although Robert Owen's ego and naïveté surely blocked out that fatal defect in the "Boatland of Knowledge." Owen's plan called for a departmental school system. As Owen conceived it, all teachers in every department would gear their classes to his social and educational ideas. But in a *Gazette* article (May 9, 1827), he complains that some teachers, like traditional masters, have been selecting a few children, setting up their own "schools" for that small group, and teaching according to their own belief. Thus, rather than instilling the values of one large happy family, which the New Social System needed, their blatant disregard for the plan simply fostered chaos. As it turned out, some of the learned group that Owen brought in actually disagreed with his ideas. William Maclure, a president of the Academy of Natural Sciences and dedicated to education, at first eagerly added his own wealth and influence to Owen's effort. But within a year he began to distance himself from Owen, charging that Owen had no idea what a good education meant. Maclure derided Owen's methods as suitable for parrots. His criticism went even further, to the very fundamentals of Owenism, saying that rejecting competition in the schools would reduce all pupils to the same low level. He called one of Owen's favored teachers a madman, ignorant of science and opposed to it. Such destructive differences ran deep within this group of educators and scholars. For example, Maclure had a favorable opinion of another teacher, Joseph Neef. But Marie Fretageot, one of the educators from France, disparaged Neef's ability and would not allow her own son to be placed under his tutelage. She pointed to Neef's children as proof: one dull and thoughtless, another spending her time reading novels. Fretageot also attacked the idea of having the two famous scientists Thomas Say and Gerard Troost and the French artist Charles Lesueur there, enjoying themselves with research and drawing but doing nothing for the experiment to justify their expense. She went in the opposite direction from Maclure and even further, condemning science itself as useless.[18] So these people who had the potential to add so much to what the experiment needed, added to the one thing it did not need: discord.

Antagonisms sprang from other aspects of the educational system too. Owen, like Cabet, believed that children had to be separated from parents to remove them from the influence of tradition. Marie Fretageot, affirming that Owen's principles agreed with hers, described the essence of their philosophy in a letter written shortly before he began the New-Harmony experiment. Children must be taken from their parents when born, she explained, in order to write on those "blank pages" what she thought was correct. And now she saw an opportunity in New-Harmony to apply her theories to "little babies who will be absolutely mine." But some parents seemed reluctant to hand over their children to that way of thinking. Besides, the schools imposed painful restrictions. For example, a letter from Thomas Pears, a colony bookkeeper, tells how his son, Ben, leaves the school on Sundays to visit him and the child's mother. The rules, however, prohibited that perfectly natural impulse.[19]

Moreover, the schools made pupils involuntary participants in a labor program. As we saw from Marie Fretageot's work schedule in the previous chapter, the boys started their day with a two-hour class at 4:30 A.M. That rigorous if not inhumane program had a purpose: it allowed time for them to take part in the colony's industries during the day. Therefore, following that early class they went to their jobs until 8:00 A.M., after which they finally got breakfast. That stint represented part of their obligation to the school. Maclure, who put much of his philanthropy into "industrial education," believed that while learning a trade children could be efficient producers, and their labor could yield enough to sustain a school. Like Fourier, who imagined that "little hordes" could do the dirty work of society that no one relished, Maclure greatly overestimated the capacities of schoolchildren. The New-Harmony experience proved Maclure wrong.

Nonmembers too might have had reason to grumble at the idea of expecting children to produce income for the schools. Looking for nothing more, perhaps, than a good education for their children, they had to pay the then considerable sum of one hundred dollars for each one. Yet New-Harmony's many school advertisements, which listed all the attractive benefits, never mentioned the word *work*.

Among all these negatives of New-Harmony's education program, positive aspects can easily get lost. Its most important principle held that children should be educated without resorting to punishments or rewards, a principle that many today think of as a modern idea. New-Harmony people pioneered in nursery schools, kindergartens, and trade schools long before such concepts became accepted anywhere else in the country. And, of course, they championed free education. Unfortunately, the experiment did not last long enough for the members to enjoy the fruits of their radical innovations.

The Right Stuff

Brook Farm did not have to go out and locate teachers as New-Harmony did. The organizers themselves formed the core of the school as well as the educational spirit there and taught without pretense or propaganda. They made education "the business" of the colony. Ripley explained, "We are a company of teachers. The branch of industry which we pursue as our primary objective and chief means of support is teaching."[20] The school had a regular program of liberal studies and courses for college preparation. Later it advertised for pupils, stressing its faculty of experienced teachers and offering lessons in music, dancing, drawing, and painting "without any extra charge." The school remained the principal source of income – at times the only one – throughout the colony's history.

But Brook Farm educators did not look on this enterprise as a business in the usual sense. Georgiana Bruce found them to be "cultivated persons filled with a missionary spirit" ready to give their "intellectual wealth" to those who had been "deprived." Unlike most other colonies in the movement, Brook Farm did not hesitate to invest in buildings for education. These buildings may have lacked in functional design, but they reflected Brook Farm values. For example, the Cottage, shaped like a plus sign, had a central stairway and a classroom in each arm. The rooms, exposed on three sides to the weather, did not take kindly to the New England climate. But the Cottage had a picturesque quality that suited the more important aesthetic climate of the colony. Amelia Russell, who taught in the Cottage, said the teachers thought that the charm of its design would make school more attractive to the pupils. Such thinking on the part of the teachers illustrates how they used every means to make education pleasant.[21] In this way they created an atmosphere that exalted learning and encouraged children and adults alike to put their efforts into study.

Brook Farm offered "industrial education." Pupils in this program took part in colony labor on the farm and in the household and kitchen, the workshops, and, during the *Harbinger* years, the print shop. Those old enough to work put in one or two hours each day at some manual occupation, which brought them labor-time credit. But unlike Owen's experiment, Brook Farm offered alternative arrangements. For example, "boarders," who paid four dollars a week, could study there without work obligations.

The colony differed from New-Harmony in other, more fundamental ways. For example, Brook Farmers never saw the dangers in individualism that froze the Owenites. John Dwight, in a *Harbinger* editorial (October 4, 1845), warns against silencing the passions and tendencies of the individual. "Study them," he urged; they are "the distracted cries" of each person seeking a place in the scheme of things. Moreover, in contrast to the limited scope of Owen's educational program, Dwight, recognizes children's need for variety and the benefits in letting "natural instincts" guide them in selecting their studies and their teachers, as he explains in another *Harbinger* article (October 10, 1846).

Although these ideas come from Dwight's writings during the Fourier phase of Brook Farm, the colony had applied similar educational principles from the beginning, long before anyone there spoke of Phalanxes. Pupils could select their courses; and unlike New-Harmony, Brook Farm offered variety and choices in the humanities that included modern and classical languages. They could study French, taught by Amelia Russell; German, and Greek taught by Charles Dana; Italian, by Sophia Ripley; Latin, by John Dwight; and Spanish by Manuel Diaz. In addition, George Ripley taught philosophy and mathematics; Sophia Ripley, history and English. The school offered dancing and even stenography. Marianne Dwight taught drawing, for which the colony's records show recurring purchases of paints, Bristol board, paper, and other art materials. Teachers, like other productive members, received labor-time credit for their work.

In music, the school had John Dwight who opened new vistas for the students. Octavius Frothingham saw Brook Farm boys and girls becoming familiar with the works of Haydn, Mozart, Beethoven, and Schubert, an enrichment that would not be found in general education anywhere else in the country for decades. He attributed such advances to "a genuine passion for improvement" and "a thirst for knowledge" there. For those impulses, Brook Farm's school provided a natural environment, as Charles Lane discovered on his visit. He described it as "a really free school" where both young pupils and older ones "are held . . . by the power of love." Calling it superior to traditional New England schools, he saw in it a plan "better calculated to excite originality of thought, and the native energies of the mind." Lane described the teachers as "spontaneous."

Others experienced those same qualities. Nora Schelter remembered her English teacher Sophia Ripley. In the relaxed informality the youngsters addressed her as Sophia, but not out of disrespect. They held her in the highest esteem, "the Supreme Spirit of the school," because of her patience and dedication, which helped even the slowest learners keep pace. And they learned, according to Georgiana Bruce, without the pressures that existed in the elite schools.[22]

Most Brook Farmers brought their books and placed them in the colony library, a special room in the Aerie, the building for lectures and musical events. The Ripleys' excellent collection stood at the heart of this educational facility, unique in the movement. The library also grew because of the many review copies the *Harbinger* received. These included introductory texts in languages, grammar, the sciences, history, and drawing. The music students also benefited from the large number of easy piano pieces, vocal selections, and music theory books that came in for review. This topic will be covered more fully in the following chapters.

Orestes Brownson, though he had ideological differences with Brook Farm, called its school "the best school I ever saw" and described some of its details. For the youngest children, a teacher took two or three, and worked with them for an hour or so and then let them play. They never had to sit still and do nothing and so suffered none of the "bad physical and moral effects of confinement." As a result, they learned more than in "ordinary schools" and did not become "troublesome" to others. Ora Gannett, a teenager at Brook Farm, made a similar observation. She noticed that the boys there did not get into fights as at other schools.[23]

Still, even Brook Farm youngsters had their pranks and escapades, but the colony viewed such things with tolerance. Amelia Russell gave the example of a boy who had found a way to evade the 10:00 P.M. curfew, one of the few rules, by climbing through the pantry window. As punishment, they merely embarrassed him. By their reluctance to impose strict rules, Brook Farmers acknowledged that children differed. Arthur Sumner, for example, admitted that he had learned "very little" while a pupil there. The fields and the river simply attracted him, a teenager, more than studying. But there would be "plenty of time for that afterwards," he pointed out.[24]

Contrast Brook Farm attitudes toward children with those in the other principal experiments. Owen distrusted youthful effervescence and seemed obsessed with curbing it. In Icaria Cabet told mothers to stop meddling in the rearing of their children. Maternal tenderness, he warned, would only stimulate a taste for finery and encourage "intractability." In Brook Farm they applied their ethical principles to children as well as adults.

The Brook Farmers had two well-defined educational goals: to make the highest culture available to each individual, and to teach children the ethics of human relationships. In this one aspect of the experiment, education, they started out prepared for the task. Then, throughout most of the colony's existence they kept those goals clearly in focus without wrangling and discord. Because of that, they came closer than any other experiment in the movement to carrying out their educational objectives.

Educating the Older Generation

Throughout the movement the rank and file and even some leaders showed by their actions that they knew little if anything about the underlying principles of their experiments. That defect made them easy prey for demagogues, cranks, misleaders, and inevitable frustrations. Those dangers made it imperative for each colony to begin immediately the second of the four educational programs listed earlier in the chapter. It required that the founders teach all members the rationale, the plan, and the goals of the experiment. A few people in the movement understood that need intuitively, and a few learned it from tragic experience.

Elijah Grant, president of Ohio Phalanx, saw the need within weeks after the experiment's start, when early problems jarred his idealism. He wrote to Brisbane, the sage of American Fourierism, about proceeding more slowly, holding off investment in buildings and equipment "until the members become somewhat more enlightened" about Fourier's doctrines. He feared that the experiment's elevated goals would be degraded because the members lacked the aesthetic awareness and "good taste" Fourier required in a Phalanx. We have seen how that kind of ignorance led to the perversion of values in the case of Wisconsin Phalanx.[25]

In Grant's uneasiness he displayed considerably more sensitivity to the ideas of Fourier than did leaders such as those in Alphadelphia who measured programs in terms of immediate utility. Alphadelphia's leaders had access to sound advice on the importance of understanding their doctrines from William Gailbraith of Integral Phalanx. In an important letter he issues this basic caveat: people who call themselves Associationists "must study the Science of Association" if they want to succeed. Gailbraith makes some key recommendations, among them that every Association must have at least one if not more "who are qualified to teach the Science, and will exert themselves to do so." He urges a program of nightly meetings for that purpose.[26] But nothing in Alphadelphia's records indicates that its leaders heeded such advice. Dozens of other groups that took the name Association or Phalanx but that had no one "qualified to teach the Science" disappeared in the movement's mass extinctions of the mid-1840s.

A few colonies hoped to accomplish something with occasional lectures. For example, Northampton brought in William Adam, a graduate of Edinburgh University and professor of oriental languages at Harvard, for a series on social economy to illustrate "the principles and practices of the Association."[27] But sporadic lectures could not compare in effectiveness with a steady, day-in-day-out program with a clear goal.

New-Harmony made an unmethodical stab at instructing members in Owenite principles. In one of his first acts, Owen set aside Wednesday evenings for lectures. The colony used that time for discussing a wide range of topics, from those of general interest to the research of the resident Philadelphia scientists. Owen, when in town, did lecture frequently on the New Social System, but such hit-or-miss events could not substitute for a systematic course. Anything else in the records that suggests the study of society or social change stands out by its rarity. For example, William Pelham's letters mention a Sunday meeting at which they had a reading and discussion of William Thompson's *Inquiry into the Distribution of Wealth.* The members did have one other way to learn about Owenism: articles in the *Gazette* (a topic I cover in a later chapter under propaganda). But even those intermittent items did little for most of the members, who knew virtually nothing about how the great plan would work.

They desperately needed an orderly, step-by-step program that would educate them about it. Yet Owen, who placed the future entirely in the hands of education, never took that need seriously enough, and the effect of the colony remains as a historical discredit to him and his followers.

In Icaria, Cabet conducted *Cours icariens* (Icarian lectures) on Sundays. As part of each session he instructed the members in basic principles, especially the foundation of Icarianism in the teachings of Christ and that Christianity required community of property. For example, he would read from Scripture, Acts 2 and 3, to show that Jesus and the Apostles held everything in common and shared according to need. Acts 5, the punishment of Ananias, became the text for a lesson to warn against greed and making private gain from the common fund. Cabet also read from *Le Vrai Christianisme* and his other works and gave instruction from his "Conditions of Admission." Emile Vallet, a member for six years, described Cabet as a forceful and eloquent speaker who could always attract an audience. Apparently, Cabet did not depend on his eloquence alone, because he included singing, instrumental music, or other entertainment as part of each lecture.

Icarians should have known more about their doctrine than any other group. The colony's strict rules required every member to have a "little library" of Cabet's writings to study and to be conversant with. The collection consisted of *Voyage en Icarie* (Voyage to Icaria), *Comment je suis Communiste* (Why I Am a Communist), *Mon credo communiste* (My Communist Credo), *Le Vrai Christianisme* (True Christianity), and *Colonie icarienne* . . . (the colony's history and its laws).

In Iowa, the Icarians, after struggling at the margin of survival for a couple of decades, began to recover and in the process brought back their Sunday afternoon lectures. Maria Marchand remembered that Arsene Sauva conducted them. An Icarian stalwart who had stayed with Cabet when the colony expelled the founder back in 1856, Sauva tried to retain the form of the lectures as they had been conducted in the original colony in Nauvoo. But now, along with the usual Cabet works, the Iowa Icarians wanted readings from any author they found interesting, as well as group singing and recitations. In the tired, waning years of the colony, after doctrinal differences had shredded the membership, education in the principles, long neglected, lost its meaning.

Not surprisingly, among the Fourier groups Brook Farmers made the most organized and consistent effort to tackle the job of teaching doctrine. At least six months before coming into the Fourier fold, the colony established a regular program on his writings. No translations existed, but French, even Fourier's recondite style, posed no obstacle to the Brook Farm scholars. Ripley taught the classes, which met on Monday and Thursday evenings. On Sundays, many of the Brook Farmers met for Fourier readings. Still, the lack of an authentic translation impeded progress. Soon after Brook Farm became a Phalanx in 1845, Brisbane went to the colony in order to work with Ripley on a translation. They promised a publication within a few months. It might have been a boon to the American Fourierists in that year of growing public interest, but nothing came of their effort. When a translation of Fourier's first book did appear in the 1850s, interest in the Fourierist phase of the movement had long since passed its peak.

In the meantime, Dwight and others used the columns of the *Harbinger* for interpretations and occasional translations of brief Fourier excerpts. These benefited the membership, of course, but they had a bigger target on the outside: sympathizers, and the vast body of unconvinced. Dwight and Ripley also tried to reach these people by conducting Fourier classes in Boston.

The leaders of the North American Phalanx unwisely neglected to teach their own members the principles of Fourierism and instead planned to invest their energy on the outside, hoping to convince their New Jersey neighbors. The strategy, as spelled out in the minutes of the meeting where they adopted the plan, directed that "unusual and technical phrases be avoided . . . with a view to impress most strongly . . . the practical features of our movement."[28] The emphasis on practicality reveals either a disingenuous leadership or, more likely, one lacking a full understanding of Fourier. To speak of "the practical features" implies the existence of the "impractical." But in the indivisible unity of Fourier's world each aspect stands in harmony with every other; to diminish or weed out one would affect all. A small point perhaps, but a basic one, suggesting again the importance of more homework for a movement that wanted to make its experiments into a school for the world. The North American Phalanx members did not do their homework in guiding principles and soon found themselves in a devastating doctrinal feud that splintered their colony and contributed to its end.

7

The Life of the Mind

THE PROPONENTS OF SOCIAL REORGANIZATION promised an enhanced intellectual life. That promise offered great humanistic possibilities, especially in an age when free education hardly existed, when free libraries were rare, and when the cost of books made them a luxury for most people in the world. Members from rural and less-affluent backgrounds would have undreamed-of opportunities for self-improvement. Everyone would have access to stimulating discussions and lectures. But most important, a cooperative colony would be able to do what individuals alone could not do; it would provide the membership with a wide selection of books and periodicals that individuals in traditional society could never afford. Books would be essential not only for the obvious use in self-improvement but, more significantly, for the pleasure and enjoyment they could bring to the bountiful leisure hours that the new way of life promised.

But here again, tenuous assumptions could not bridge the vast gulf that existed and would probably continue to exist for a long time between expectations and realization. Moreover, the leadership, particularly middle-class intellectuals, did not anticipate the differences in priorities that would surface between educated and less-educated, between sophisticated and naïve members. Together with the vague strategy for starting a far-reaching social experiment, these differences added yet more frictions for goups struggling in a state of perpetual crisis. But as in all other aspects of the movement, positives appear side by side with negatives. Readers rubbed shoulders with censors, and while some pointed to new horizons for the mind, know-nothings turned their backs.

Utopian speculations saw the monumental colony building as a way to bring not only the basics – food, shelter, work – under one roof but also facilities for intellectual enrichment: lecture halls, library, museum, theater, and concert hall. They specifically identified such resources with the principal goal of social reorganization: happiness. Indeed, the very first New-Harmony constitution equated an increase in "intelligence" with an increase in happiness and concluded, "We seek intelligence . . . as we seek happiness itself."

The Sodus Bay Phalanx Articles of Association set a goal of developing not only agriculture and industry but also the arts. The Sylvania Association constitution includes a promise not usually found in fundamental documents; it guaranteed that the colony would have a library.

Cabet called his system best for improving humanity and developing the fine arts. He had all the points of his credo typographically set in a diamond shape and used it in his propaganda. As you can see in illustration 7, the arts held an important place in his plan. In one of his appeals for support he listed the most essential items he would buy for Icaria if he had $500,000. Books and instruments appear high on his list, along with the necessities.

Brook Farmers considered intellectual development the crucial test of Association's credibility. After one experiment dissolved, the *Harbinger's* editors (July 26, 1845) sharply criticized those in the movement who did nothing to advance the elevated cultural goals. "In ________, the trial has failed, as anyone might have foretold. . . . There was not a single philosophic mind, nay not a philosophic idea even, among the experimenters. They looked upon Fourier as the Messiah of bread buttered on both sides. . . . No system of reform can succeed when its idea rises no higher than to an amelioration of the condition of the human larder."

That tells us that some colonies did not heed or, more likely, did not understand the necessity for devoting resources to intellectual elevation and the arts. Of course, no experiment in all the movement approached this purpose as the Brook Farmers did. One short sentence from a *Harbinger* review proclaimed their credo. "The soul cannot live without beauty."

Intellectual Environment and Membership

The setting for carrying out the promise of opportunities for self-improvement and of greater intellectual fulfillment varied from one experiment to another. The type of members that each attracted had

FRATERNITÉ.

Tous pour chacun.

Chacun pour tous

SOLIDARITÉ
ÉGALITÉ—LIBERTÉ
ÉLIGIBILITÉ
UNITÉ
PAIX.

AMOUR
JUSTICE
SECOURS MUTUEL
ASSURANCE UNIVERSELLE
ORGANISATION DU TRAVAIL
MACHINES AU PROFIT DE TOUS
AUGMENTATION DE LA PRODUCTION
RÉPARTITION ÉQUITABLE DES PRODUITS
SUPPRESSION DE LA MISÈRE
AMELIORATIONS CROISSANTES
MARIAGE ET FAMILLE
PROGRES CONTINUEL
ABONDANCE
ARTS.

ÉDUCATION
INTELLIGENCE—RAISON
MORALITÉ
ORDRE
UNION.

Premier droit,
Vivre.

Premier devoir,
Travailler.

A chacun
suivant ses besoins.

De chacun
suivant ses forces.

BONHEUR COMMUN.

7. Two examples of Cabet's credo typographically set in a diamond shape. The French version is taken from the 1848 edition of Cabet's *Voyage en Icarie*. The English version (*opposite*) appeared in *Colony of Republic of Icaria . . .*, Nauvoo, Ill., 1852.

a decisive effect on the programs that grew or did not grow out of that setting. Four experiments show the broad range of circumstances: Brook Farm, Icaria, La Réunion, and Alphadelphia.

Octavius Frothingham recalled the unique character of Brook Farm. There George Ripley "made a Utopia, quiet, calm, dignified, pervaded by the radiance of mind, the gentle enthusiasm of intellect." As a lifelong friend, he understood Ripley's deep concern for society, an interest "more philosophical than philanthropic."[1]

Almost every aspect of Brook Farm life confirmed those qualities. The members had a way of investing even ordinary things with an intellectual flavor. Their council became the Areopagus, named after the council in ancient Athens, and they called Ripley the Archon, the name for the highest administrator in ancient Greek city-states. They

Fraternity.

Each for all. All for each.

Solidarity.
Equality.--Liberty.
Eligibility.
Unity.
Peace.

Education.
Intelligence.—Reason.
Morality.
Order.
Union.

LOVE
JUSTICE
MUTUAL ASSISTANCE
ORGANIZATION OF LABOR
MACHINERY FOR THE PROFIT OF ALL
INCREASE IN PRODUCTION
EQUITABLE DISTRIBUTION OF PRODUCE
SUPPRESSION OF POVERTY
INCREASING AMELIORATION
MARRIAGE AND FAMILY
CONSTANT PROGRESS
ABUNDANCE
THE ARTS.

From each according to his capacity. To each according to his wants.

First the NECESSARY, then the USEFUL, and at last the AGREEABLE.

Common Happiness.

weeded the garden to Tennyson or Browning. Georgiana Bruce pictured for us a Brook Farm woman ironing collars while memorizing German poetry from a book propped open with two forks. And Amelia Russell remembered that even washtubs became a center for discussing serious subjects.

The character of Brook Farm derived from the kind of members it attracted. The magnet consisted of scholars, teachers, and a diversity of talent in the arts. Frothingham knew them as people with "a thirst for knowledge, a hunger for mental stimulus."[2] Someone always seemed to be available to enrich an evening. For example, they never lacked for music. George Curtis had a fine voice and played guitar; Charles Dana sang bass; Christopher Cranch, who wrote poetry and painted, sang and played the flute; John Dwight played piano at a professional level; and for a time in the early years they had Eliza Ostinelli, later Biscaccianti, America's first opera star. But talent existed among the less-famous too. Jean Palisse, a Swiss engineer, played violin, and they had two fine pianists in Fanny Dwight and Harriet Graupner, daughter of world-renowned Johann Christian Graupner. Mary Bullard, who later married John Dwight, had an excellent soprano voice.

Literature floated in the air. John Drew went through the working day quoting Shakespeare and Byron. In the colony's early period Frank Farley, an experienced farmer skilled in field and barn, gave dramatic readings. The youngster who herded the cattle read Coleridge. And even in the colony's last year, when Nora Schelter joined, she discovered "a choice gathering" of "intellect, wit, and wisdom."[3]

When the experiment ended on a beautiful spring day in 1847, less than a handful of the Brook Farmers went on to North American Phalanx or other Associations. Why so few? I believe the answer lies in their basic devotion, less to Fourierism than to Brook Farm itself, where despite barren fields they found fertile ground for minds to grow.

Icaria had some potential to match Brook Farm. According to Florence Snyder, granddaughter of secretary-general Emile Baxter, Nauvoo attracted a nucleus of cultivated people. Baxter came from a cosmopolitan background: his father, a Scot and a graduate of Edinburgh University, had fought at Waterloo and had settled in France. Emile, educated and trained in France as an artist, emigrated to New York, where he married Annette Powell from Connecticut, a teacher of French and a highly skilled pianist. At the invitation of Cabet they came to Nauvoo with her piano and his art materials. She taught French and played Sunday concerts.[4]

Antoine von Gauvin, one of the teachers mentioned earlier, was a university graduate from Berlin. In New York City, he had edited a French newspaper and taught classical languages. In Nauvoo he lectured on philosophy. Ignacio Montaldo, a professor of mathematics, was said to be a friend of Garibaldi and Chateaubriand. Colony president Alexis Marchand had studied law in Paris and apparently chemistry too because he also served as pharmacist. The census of 1850 gives the name, age, and birthplace of each Icarian and the occupation of each man but, as we might expect, none for women. I analyzed the list in terms of occupations and found two-thirds from the working class. Clothing trades make the largest group (26 percent), and construction came next (21 percent). Farm and kitchen forms the only other sizable category (16 percent). Unlike Brook Farm, few came to Icaria from the professions (6 percent) and the arts (2 percent). However, they did have a trained musician, Claudo Grubert, who directed the band, and the architect Alfred Piquenard (ca. 1826–76), later to be known for several major western landmarks. The census also includes another architect, a sculptor, a physician, engravers, and teachers.[5]

At their fifth anniversary celebration which included instrumental and choral music and an evening performance of a play, *La Mort de Cesar* (Caesar's Death), Cit. Kattman proposed an after-dinner toast. A German, musical activities had made a bridge for him in this French-speaking colony. "I regret I cannot speak your language," he said. "But I have come to understand a language all of us can comprehend without an interpreter. I wish to speak of music. I shall tell you, therefore, in what sense it has spoken to me." He raised his glass to the unity of all nations.[6]

The scene and sentiments have a Brook Farm flavor. They confirm the presence of a few thinkers wanting to rise above the gray austerity that back-breaking toil and shallow mentalities usually impose.

Despite the slogans and fine talk, not all saw intellect as a crucial asset. Soon after the anniversary celebration, their newspaper, *Colonie Icarienne,* listed the members according to where they worked (September 20, 1854). And using a rather curious phrase it also gives the trade or profession that each one "used to practice previously, or could be able to practice." That odd wording undoubtedly shows the operation of rule 15, mandating "useful" work, which may explain why members "previously" in the arts or professions now appear listed among manual workers. It may also reflect rules 16 and 17, which required Icarians to work on the farm or in industry wherever and whenever needed. And these situations lend credence to François Lacour's charges of arbitrary work assignments mentioned in chapter 3. Cit. Montaldo, formerly professor of mathematics, now worked on a flatboat that carried the colony's coal on the Mississippi; Cit. Vallet, a teacher, now made barrels; and Cit. Schroeder, a German artist, painted houses.

Take another look at Cabet's credo in illustration 7. On the lower left of the English version (on the right in the French) the well-known slogan "From each according to his capacity" stands out. Apparently, the Icarians did not know how to evaluate the labor of people who worked with mind not muscle and who used ideas as tools. Had they considered how efficient a professor would be at loading coal? Had they evaluated the cost of wasting a precious resource, a mind? Nothing in the records or the results indicates that they did.

Victor Considérant's La Réunion presents a similar case. His plans made provision for something he called "refinements" for the colony's workers, who might not have had previous opportunities for intellectual elevation. Refinements included the study of French and English, a library, and reading rooms. He believed these opportunities would awaken a "noble ambition" in the workers.[7] And in fact he brought the potential for creating a center for intellectual growth to the tiny frontier settlement that became the city of Dallas.

La Réunion had a nucleus of well-educated people. Considérant, for example, held a degree from the Sorbonne. The colony boasted two good musicians: Charles Capy, a student of Chevé and a proponent of the Galin system of musical ear training that enabled him to develop a colony chorus under difficult conditions, and Allyre Bureau, a former music director of the Odéon in Paris, who brought the first piano to a remote outpost of European civilization in Texas. From the arts the membership included Francis Cantagrel, a graduate in engineering and architecture who had published articles on art criticism in the 1830s. Another member, François Santerre, made the arduous and dangerous overland journey from Houston to Dallas with a small collection of fine books including a 1660 edition of Ovid.

A descendant of one of the Réunionists compiled a list of the members that gives brief biographical sketches for forty-eight of the men.[8] Unfortunately, it tells nothing of the women. I analyzed these sketches in terms of education and occupations. Admittedly, this sample, only 40 percent of the men, may not be large enough for an accurate profile of the colony. But it does suggest a core who might want something more of life than bread and toil. About 27 percent came from the professions and the arts, 40 percent from the skilled trades and farming, and 10 percent had a business background. The others included a military man, a former Jesuit, a jeweler, and seven with no occupation given. At least two of the latter had superior educations.

When Considérant arrived at La Réunion in the summer of 1855, his party included two legislators exiled by the Second Empire and newspaper editors from Brussels and Paris as well as Madame Considérant and her mother, whom colony pioneer Kalikst Wolski called ladies "of the highest Parisian society." Madame Considérant, young, beautiful, educated, and wealthy – her dowry was said to have been 1 million francs – established an al fresco "salon" in a cedar grove where erudite conversation went on until one or two o'clock in the morning. Wolski, discouraged by the way life had been developing in the experiment, hoped that "the high culture of those who have now joined us will make the hardships more endurable." And the cosmopolitan Wolski did indeed find them an "enlightened and congenial company."[9]

But what of the other, less sophisticated members, who might have been uncomfortable in this elite clique? Did the educated organize any program to share their intellectual wealth as Considérant had promised? Dr. Savardan, in his angry recollections of the experiment, brought up Considérant's visions of stimulating the workers' intellects, of raising their dignity through French and English studies, libraries, and reading rooms. He repeated Considérant's grand pronouncements on the need for music as a source of pleasure and education, in the fields and gardens, the cafe, the meetings, games, and so forth. And then he demanded, "Well then! What came of all those beautiful ideas?" His answer, "Nothing! Absolutely nothing!" sums up the intellectual miscarriage in La Réunion.[10]

The Alphadelphia records contain inquiries from prospective members with more than just a rudimentary education, people who could contribute to the experiment's intellectual growth. S. Ripley, a physician-surgeon applied, as did his sister-in-law, M. C. Richmond, an "instructress." At an annual meeting, John White, a "scribe," was proposed. An Alphadelphia agent wrote a letter recommending John Porter of Ann Arbor and underlined his profession: "He is an Artist." None of these names, however, turn up on the membership rolls. John Sherwin's letter of application tells of a background more typical of the membership. Experienced as a joiner, he had tools, would work at anything, and could bring two cows and a calf. His sixteen-year-old son already worked in the same trade, and his wife had experience in what he called "woman's work."[11]

The colony had a shortsighted but not unusual selection process. For example, Sodus Bay Phalanx received an application from a Syracuse music teacher, a Mrs. Hoyt, who offered to bring her piano and invest two hundred dollars. The colony, which had no piano, should have welcomed her. But the name Hoyt cannot be found in the membership lists of the Sodus Bay colony.

The Alphadelphia records contain a list of members' occupations,

Occupations of our members, without counting our friends from Bellevue.

96 are Farmers
5 Farmers & Carpenters
38 House Carpenters
3 Machinists
4 Millwrights
2 Millers
5 Waggon-makers
5 Wheelwrights
2 Chair-makers
2 Painters
1 Chemist
2 Brick-makers
4 Coopers
1 Plough-maker
4 Blacksmiths
4 Masons
4 Furnace-men
~~5 Laborers~~

5 Laborers
2 Gun-smiths
3 Hatters
2 Printers
1 News-paper Agent
4 Physicians
4 Male Teachers
[illegible] Female Teachers
1 Merchant
1 Merchant's Clerk
1 Pump-maker
1 Watch-maker
1 Cabinet-maker
1 Pail-maker
3 Tailors
15 Shoemakers
6 Harness-makers
2 Tanners
1 Tinner

8. Occupations of Alphadelphia's members. By permission of the Bentley Historical Library, University of Michigan.

reproduced in illustration 8. It embraces 242 people, although not all resided in the colony when the founders compiled that list. Still, it suggests a reasonable cross section of the membership. Notice that farmers and low-skilled workers make up nearly half. The building and mechanical trades account for another third. When these Alphadelphians grew up earlier in the century, free public schools did not yet exist in most areas, and more than likely, their educational opportunities would not have extended much beyond the three Rs. Of the members listed, probably fewer than 10 percent would have had the good fortune to get schooling more advanced than that level. But the list does not tell the whole story. For example, because leaders and members saw no urgency about establishing a school, the colony had no need for educators. So teacher Paul Tabor worked as a joiner, teacher Edward James as a clerk. Their situations tell something of the environment for intellectual improvement.[12]

Henry Schetterly, founder of the Alphadelphia experiment, had the advantage of a good education. Born and educated in Germany, he was frequently addressed as "doctor" although what degree he had earned, if any, is not clear. When he arrived his "Appraisal of Property" included medical and laboratory equipment, chemicals, supplies, a globe, and an orrery and tellurian (astronomical instruments). My analysis of all other "Appraisals" shows his as exceptional. For along with their pots and pans, cows, and tools, not one Alphadelphian entered the colony with a book or a print, not even a guitar. Moreover, the colony's own "List of Property" for 1846, after more than two years of operation, contains no hint that it encouraged any activity other than work.

The records do show members' orders for five books over the course of the colony's existence: a hymnal, an Owenite songbook, a history, and two books on Association. Some members did order personal copies of magazines. Over a two-year period, when membership averaged 188, when Alphadelphia had no library, members took a total of thirty-nine subscriptions, many for one year only. The records list twenty-three titles. Farm magazines make up the largest category. Next comes general-interest and fashion publications and then titles of fads—*Phrenology Almanac* was a favorite. A few of the magazines tended to rise above the generally pedestrian level for literature, *Graham's*, for example, had contributions by Bryant, Thoreau, and Longfellow.[13]

Thus, the Alphadelphia records do not suggest a colony striving for a more enriched life or for intellectual improvement. The experiment offered nothing more than farmers and mechanics in traditional society could expect then. If any Alphadelphians expressed disappointment over this lack, their thoughts have probably not survived.

A similar situation turns up in many colonies, large and small, that promised to change the world. Dr. Thomas Steel belonged to Equality, a little-known experiment in southeastern Wisconsin. From his letters to his sister Lilly and to his father, we learn that the colony never met as a group for discussions. Steel complained that working from dawn till night left little time for "mental recreation – which I miss."[14] However, in colonies where such things mattered, members did manage to find the time. So if those in Equality would not exert themselves for what Steel saw as a more rounded way of life, it means they did not see that as important.

His experience has a parallel in what William Owen learned while on business at Father Rapp's Harmonie colony. This group, of course, had no interest in changing society or in the promise of intellectual fulfillment. The congregation of a charismatic leader, these people only wanted a sin-free enclave where they could work and pray for the salvation of their souls. William, Robert Owen's oldest son, spent several months there during the negotiations for the Harmonie colony's property. During that time he complained to his diary, "We find it uncommonly dull and stupid having so little to interest the mind." When James Buckingham visited Harmonie in its new location many years later, he had the same reaction. Rapp's congregation lacked a "relish for education, literature, the fine arts, . . . the cultivation of the mind, and the enjoyment of intellectual pleasures." He attributed that fault to the fact that neither Rapp nor his followers had much education, and found their "chief pleasure" in working and accumulating wealth.[15] That Alphadelphia and similar shallow trials in Association would set their sights just as low in a movement that promised goals so high remains one of the tragic ironies of the utopian episodes.

Intellect and Activities

When Kalikst Wolski visited North American Phalanx, he found people "refreshing themselves mentally" with evening discussions. Brook Farmer Amelia Russell recalled that "a few bright words" in the evening "lifted them above their occupations" the next day. Informal discussions on serious subjects seem to have been the prevalent type of activity, probably a stimulating one given the heterogeneous mix of people with strong convictions that some groups attracted and tolerated.[16]

But such exchanges could also produce detrimental side effects. George Stetson recalled that at Northampton, members took part in discussions "with spirit," that sometimes led to "personal antagonisms." But he believed that ultimately such things created "better understanding and confidence." In Raritan Bay Union, a group born of schism, we can feel similar heat in a letter Lydia Arnold wrote to her sister. "We have some very spirited discussions on religion and morals. There is just difference enough in opinion to make it interesting, but I trust there is too much charity here to separate for opinion's sake."

Charles Codman characterized his fellow Modern Timers as "philosophers" who tried footfall and gave it up in favor of discussions. "They were better at talking than at kicking," he quipped. Moncure Conway described them in his novel about Modern Times as "thoughtful" people who enjoyed "long evenings" discussing economic and social principles.[17]

Brook Farmer John Codman, remembered many evenings in the parlor where he sat among "inspired men and women" discussing the lives of the great painters, musicians, and reformers, or dissecting science and religion. But, gentle soul, he avoided "the arguers and disputants who talked anti-this and anti-that . . . the water cure and homeopathy . . . community of property, western lands, politics, approaching war with Mexico, etc., etc." But Georgiana Bruce, an early member of the colony, said she "never heard the words 'fashion' or 'beau'; no shallow, purposeless words such as you were often bored with elsewhere."[18]

Most colonies had a more formal type of discussion on a regular basis. North American Phalanx had a series to which they gave the name Debates on Current Public Questions. Raritan Bay Union, the splinter group from North American chose the name Saturday Debates for their series. In Modern Times the Philosophers Club met on Sunday evenings and opened with music. Recitations, debates, and readings "on topics of current interest" followed. Northampton offered a similar program series, which they entitled Sunday Lyceums, and frequently, one of the brilliant orators of abolition, George Thompson, Henry Wright, Wendell Phillips, or most often William Lloyd Garrison visited and brought unmatched thunder to the discussions.

Several other colonies instituted a regular lecture program usually held once a week. The quality, of course, varied from place to place. Wisconsin Phalanx's Philolothian Society met on Tuesdays, but its program suffered from a lack of organization, and it tended to emphasize agricultural topics. That changed with the advent of lectures by H. H. Van Amringe, one of those inveterate colony gadabouts who seemed to drift from one experiment to the next. His strange recipe for reform, a pound of millennialism and a pinch of Fourier, did not always find a welcome at his way stations. However, in Wisconsin Phalanx, where members looked up to Fourier but did not look up what he actually said, Van Amringe found his true audience. He came to give two lectures, one on the prophecies in the Old Testament and in the Book of Revelations and the other on the evils of Europe. Believing him accredited by his knack for Fourierist jargon, the leaders let him linger for a year, the colony's last as it turned out, lecturing or preaching once a week.[19]

Two groups, Brook Farm and Raritan Bay Union, made a practice of bringing in well-known visiting lecturers. Charles Dana found that such events gave Brook Farm "a character and reputation . . . it never would have got from the more prosaic mowing and haying that went on in the daytime."[20] The colony generally held all activities in the evening, but John Sears remembered Sunday afternoon lectures too, outdoors in a grove of trees. Lecturers usually received standard fees. The names Alcott, Emerson, and Margaret Fuller are some of the well-known ones that appeared in Brook Farm programs.

Fuller's Journals bring some of these events to life for us and incidentally reveal her character and her attitude toward Brook Farm and its rationale. Her notes cover a week she spent there in 1842 that included several of her "conversations" on a variety of topics, "The Nature of Beauty," for example. On Saturday evening she spoke on education, making these points: the aim is perfection, patience the road; let us not be too ambitious in our hopes as to immediate results; and parents and teachers expect to do too much. In the typical format, she began with prepared remarks, and after that the audience could ask questions or could comment. Some members took the second option a little too eagerly to suit her. Skepticism, a Brook Farm characteristic, aroused her extreme displeasure, which she expressed privately and perhaps haughtily to her journal, "I am accustomed to deference." But independent-minded Brook Farmers apparently saw no reason to oblige her. Fuller's annoyance at one dissenter comes through sharply in her journal in which she calls his comments "philosophical bull."[21] It must have been an invigorating evening.

For Wednesday she chose impulse as a topic because of "the great tendency here to advocate spontaneousness at the expense of reflection." About thirty-five people attended, a large enough circle, she told her journal, but some sat or lay casually on the floor, an informality that belittled her self-esteem. "I defended nature, as I always do; the spirit ascending through, not superseding nature. But in the scale of Sense, Intellect, Spirit, I advocated tonight the claims of Intellect, because those present were rather disposed to postpone them." Though we have no other information on her talk that night, we can well imagine an enthusiastic question period. But questions may have been outnumbered by comments – probably the candid variety – because "those present," from everything we know about them, had clearly and without pretense incorporated the "claims of intellect" into their daily lives.

Raritan Bay Union engaged well-known lecturers, mainly through the efforts of both Marcus Spring, the influential, wealthy sympathizer, and Theodore Weld, director of the colony's innovative school. Lecturers included Alcott, Emerson, Thoreau, and Bryant. A few of the former devotees of Brook Farm – now the spirit of the decade past – added their luster. Then, in the waning days of Raritan Bay, Caroline Kirkland, writer and former editor of *Union Magazine,* built a house on the grounds and contributed to its intellectual life.

At one of the Wednesday lyceums, James Birney, twice the Liberty party's candidate for president of the United States, read a paper. Sundays brought a different emphasis: the colony opened its doors to the neighboring farmers and, like many of the experiments in social reorganization, held a lecture on some agricultural topic.

New-Harmony, unique in this respect, had science lectures. For example, Dr. Philip Price lectured on blood circulation. He traced the history of the subject, spoke of William Harvey's work, and illustrated with the dissection of a calf's heart. Not all lecturers had professional backgrounds. Samuel Bolton, who had little formal education but who had become a good chemist and geologist through self-study, lectured frequently there and elsewhere.

New-Harmony also had lectures by the scientists Owen brought from the Academy of Natural Sciences in Philadelphia. In the spring of 1826 Dr. Gerard Troost (1776–1850), the Dutch naturalist and founder and former president of the academy, lectured in the colony's Town Hall on mineralogy, and the *Gazette* gave his presentation full coverage (May 17, 1826).

That event may be notable in American intellectual history. But in the history of utopianism it has greater significance because his remarks bear directly on the place of intellectual pursuits in the colonies of social reorganization. Two points stand out: the values Troost saw in his work and the role of intellectual work in the colony. Projecting each of these against the movement as a whole lights up the contradictions that lay across the path to the utopian promise.

Values and intellect. Obviously, mineralogy had utility, an Owenite requirement, because it provided society with a source of material wealth. In addition, an expert such as Troost satisfied the usefulness principle because he could teach materials and methods. However, Troost did not speak of any of these things. He discussed three aspects. First, he expanded on "the pleasures" that could be derived from the study of mineralogy. Second, in a key statement on values, he said he thought of his work "independently of . . . utility." Finally, he dwelt on the great beauty of gems. In the somber gray of Owen's utilitarianism, each of these points sparkles like those of a diamond. First, Troost's emphasis on satisfying personal interests ignored the spirit of Owen's battle against any hint of individualism. Second, and even more striking, his values clashed head-on with Owen's, which held a thing or activity worthwhile only in terms of its use to society. Finally, Owen set out to erase the oppressive trappings of traditional society, such as symbols of wealth and royalty, and certainly any infatuation with gems that have no practical or productive application would have fallen under his guillotine.

Values similar to Owen's, which appraised activities in terms of their usefulness, turn up in almost all later experiments except Brook Farm and Modern Times. Cabet, for example, evaluated everything against his well-known scale of priorities, which you can see at the bottom of the English version of his diamond-shaped credo in illustration 7. "First the Necessary, then the Useful, and at last the Agreeable." Some Icarians, at least in Nauvoo, had enough aesthetic sensibility to insist on the "Agreeable" even as they struggled under the restraints of the first two steps. Still, the establishment of these priorities inevitably led to acceptance of austerity as a way of life.

Unlike Owen and Cabet, Fourier unequivocally elevated individual satisfaction and pleasure as the first principle of all activities. His value system for Association gave the highest place to aesthetics. Even so, many of the experiments that called Fourier mentor incongruously adopted the three levels of priority – Necessary, Useful, Agreeable – and as a result they too found austerity their lot. Admittedly, in most of these Associations members and leaders simply did not know enough about Fourier's plan to see the contradiction in such priorities. But North American Phalanx had leaders who knew better. Yet they persisted in extracting only "the practical part" of Fourier and ignored the rest.

So with utility the measure of all things, and in the absence of an initial and determined commitment to the enrichment of life, the "Agreeable" usually ended up on some back burner. Wisconsin Phalanx, finishing its fourth year, boasted in its annual statement of one hundred cattle, three hundred sheep, four hundred hogs, three hundred acres in wheat, and freedom from debt. But the leadership admitted that "We have not yet had time or opportunity to attend to the elegancies of life." They never did get around to that.

Role of intellectual work. This is the second aspect of Troost's New-Harmony lecture that bears on the movement's attitude toward thought as a medium for work. If Troost's research in the colony had a rationale within Owen's utilitarian value system, no such justification could apply to a field trip he made that took him away from New-Harmony. He and another member, Charles Lesueur (1778–1846), a French artist, went to Missouri to collect specimens. When they returned, they had the time to write up their work and publish a report in four successive issues of the *Gazette.* The report advanced scientific knowledge, to be sure, but some in the colony wondered what it did to advance the cause many had been sacrificing for.

Similarly, William Maclure (1763–1840), president of the Academy of Natural Sciences in Philadelphia, and Thomas Say (1787–1834), the entomologist, left the colony to gather specimens in the West. Some of that fieldwork materialized in a lengthy article that Say published in the academy's journal. This shows that even though he worked in the colony's garden, he too could continue his profession as a scientist on a fully committed basis.

These lengthy periods away from colony obligations have special significance because most groups had regulations that severely restricted time off. When Icarians in Iowa wanted to visit people "outside," even nearby, they had to be granted special permission by the general assembly. In Wisconsin Phalanx, leaving the grounds could result in expulsion.

Thus, the values implied in the Troost remarks suggest an exceptional situation in New-Harmony, borne out by the kind of work he and a few others were allowed to do there. Such opportunities existed partly because of an inherent contradiction in the Owenite value system. On the one hand, it named happiness the highest good. On the other, it suppressed individual expression even though such pursuits might bring happiness to some. That contradiction, together with the arbitrary rules in Owen's code of conduct that we considered in chapter 4, and the special privileges for the intellectual elite, helped to incite grumbling among the colony's less educated. Owen did nothing to reconcile the disparities.

Clearly, the research work of the scientists was inconsistent with an Owenite test of utility. However, that opportunity existed for the scientists in New-Harmony partly because Owen, needing their luster to brighten his experiment, offered them privileges in order to attract them, and partly because the colony had a core of people interested in intellectual growth. Significantly, the colony imposed no restrictions on them and made no claims on the results of their efforts.

Compare their situation with the one in Sylvania Association, for example, where the leaders carefully spelled out the rules in their constitution. "Any member may, by permission of the executive council, pursue any branch of business connected with the arts and sciences, in what are termed "working hours," provided he or she shall have labored for the common good to such an extent as to liquidate the debts contracted by himself and family towards the Association." They also provided that 25 percent of any money earned from that work would go to the Association.

In only three utopian experiments could professionals and intellectuals pursue their chosen fields freely. New-Harmony permitted them to do so in spite of Owen's values; Brook Farm offered a congenial environment, but no remuneration; and Modern Times allowed members to pursue any interest as long as it harmed no one else, but there, of course, each had to be self-supporting.

Alphadelphia expected its physician to put in an eight-hour day. But surprisingly, in one of the many inconsistencies in this movement, it allowed him to devote two hours of that credited time to study. Possibly Henry Schetterly, who used the title "doctor," had urged that unusual perquisite.

Among the ranks of Association some did aspire to the kind of goals Fourier had in mind. The Leraysville group in northeastern Pennsylvania wanted to go beyond the agricultural products and clothing that most colonies typically hoped to sell. The colony's leaders told the *Phalanx* (April 1, 1844) that they intended to market books, pianos, oil paintings, and "other productions of skill and art." However, this short-lived experiment never got past the basics. They had the usual nucleus: farmers, a handful in the skilled trades, a few ministers, a doctor, and a lawyer, but no one who could create the intellectual products they wanted to market – no typographers, writers, musicians, or artists.

During this period Brisbane issued a call for creative people to join the Associationist cause. "Artists! Artists! You men of brilliant imagination, of hearts of poetry, here is a new and noble sphere open to you. What are you doing in this prosaic world? Do you feel yourselves at ease in the industrial and commercial society which surrounds you?"[22] Very few answered the call. Although many colonies had at least one or two creative people, only Brook Farm attracted a solid core of members in the arts. There they could pursue creative work or work of an intellectual nature. But, as we saw in the chapter on work, the Brook Farm account books show no labor-time credit to anyone for creative work.

On the other hand, and unlike Sylvania's work mandate, Brook Farm did not require productive work; in fact, they actually had boarders. But they did apply any productive work time as a credit against room and board charges. That made a cash-free existence a theoretical possibility. So Brook Farmers who wished to do so could pursue nonremunerative intellectual work, partially or completely. Of course, if they lacked personal resources, they might run short of cash.

John Dwight, who quit the pulpit to work for reform and pursue his interest in music, had that problem. Like other Brook Farmers he did not care to accumulate money, but he had to supplement a meager income. The word got around, and he found work. In 1842 and 1843 the *Boston Miscellany* invited him to send translations of German poetry; he did a review for the *Christian Examiner*, wrote articles on composers for the *United States Magazine and Democratic Review*, and gave a series of lectures in Boston. But apparently such work paid very little, so Dwight asked a friend in New York City to line up some lectures for him. How much could Dwight earn from such pursuits? Correspondence between him and James Russell Lowell provides a clue. The poet asked Dwight to write music criticism for his *Pioneer*, and offered to pay ten dollars for three pages and two dollars a page for shorter pieces. Dwight's reply shows the situation at Brook Farm in the early years. He said he was happy to have a column and "in these hard times I shall be glad of any additional resources, however small, to eke out what is exceedingly small."[23]

Activities and the Individual

Brook Farm provided a variety of activities, and because of this members could select those that interested them, and ignore or avoid others. They rarely showed timidity in demonstrating their intellectual independence. For example, we have George Curtis's reaction to one of Bronson Alcott's lectures there: "the solemn sphinx, Alcott, dispensing his great discourse on one of his visitations." Alcott was dull and the glorious June evening inviting, so Curtis simply slipped out through one of the Aerie's tall French windows and went for a walk. The "grave philosopher," as Curtis called him, was oblivious to the youthful, positive spirit of Brook Farm. And similarly, Margaret Fuller's pompous "conversations" frequently suffered that fate. Although Frothingham said they all enjoyed her "oracular talks," by Fuller's own account Brook Farmers unabashedly yawned as she spoke, and some simply got up and left.[24]

One of the best examples of this diversity and independence of interests can be gleaned from the letters of Elizabeth Curson to her sister Mary. Elizabeth Curson, in her early twenties, headed up the Dormitory Group. Her letters show us a person who enjoyed books more than music, who would rather spend time in some purely solitary pursuit, drawing or reading, while others went off to crowded group activities.[25]

In one letter she tells Mary that on Wednesday evening they had a musical program "again." But instead of joining the others she remained in her room drawing and mending stockings and then went ice skating. Brook Farm had frequent musical performances in this period, but ten days later Curson admitted, "I have been very little to hear them play because I have been too busy," although earlier in the same letter she had complained that she did not have much to write about. Actually, she had used her free time in skating. Several weeks later, after the regular Sunday Fourier readings they had singing. But she passed that up too because "it was pleasanter" to sit and chat quietly with a friend.

She did go to musical performances. At one Sunday meeting they had psalm singing, Mary Bullard sang and Fanny [Dwight] played "all sorts of pretty things." However, the next day she had the afternoon off and passed the entire time in her room "all by myself" with her sketch pad and a book. And she planned to spend the evening in the same way.

A few weeks later, at the Sunday musicale, "Miss Bullard sings finely, but I am too busy or to _____ [illegible] to trudge to the Aerie to hear her." The next Sunday, they had "great singing" at the Aerie but she had other things to do. She kept to her room, drawing, reading, and writing. And again on Wednesday evening, "Mary Bullard and Fanny were singing, practicing Freischütz, and many fine things." But that was not enough to attract her. "If it had not been so cold and the Aerie was nearer I should have wanted to go there." Actually, the Aerie stood only a short walk away, and the fresh light snow did not deter others. Curson spent the following Sunday in her room curled up with *The Cricket on the Hearth* (Dickens, 1845). She told Mary that she had been reading more lately.

Obviously, Elizabeth Curson could occupy her free time alone reading or drawing because Brook Farmers accepted such pursuits not only as a norm but also as worthy. And as a result they respected the need for the quiet environment these activities required. Other colonies held different attitudes toward the value and importance of reading and striking disparities appear in their efforts to provide reading material. Reading, of course, is an individual activity, and some circumstances may not be conducive to it. Recall the situation in Wisconsin Phalanx's crowded longhouse described in chapter 3. In that sociable environment Charlotte Haven had trouble finding enough privacy just to finish writing a letter. But the value placed on books by a colony and, equally important, the environment it encouraged for reading tells much about that colony's interest in carrying out the great cultural promises of social reorganization.

Reading

Wisconsin Phalanx, which developed the most successful farm in the movement, made little effort to develop a library, create a reading room, or encourage the reading of books. The members put most of their effort into cultivating the soil and hardly any into cultivating minds. In each annual statement, Warren Chase and the other leaders boasted in detail about advances in crops and livestock. As for the lack of progress in tending to intellectual needs, they usually had some excuse: no room or no materials. But they always promised to do something soon. As we saw in tracking their educational efforts through the annual statements, which the *Harbinger* published, this became a litany with diminishing credibility. A few excerpts from annual statements make that clear.

1846. We have not yet opened our library or reading room but intend to do so in the present month.

1847. We have not yet established our reading room and library more for the want of rooms than for a lack of materials.

1848. For want of materials, and from the determination to free ourselves from debt, and contract none for any improvements, we have not yet built so as to establish a Library and Reading Room.

1849. In the absence of a Reading Room and Library, one of our greatest facilities for knowledge and general information is a great number of newspapers and periodicals.

Chase frequently claimed that his Wisconsin Phalanx people avidly read newspapers and magazines. For example, in the statement for 1845 he said that twenty-four subscriptions came to the colony. The population averaged over 160 then, and because some people got more than one item each, obviously many got none. These subscriptions went to individuals, and the records contain no assurance that those who bought them shared their copies. In fact, evidence points the other way. In March, the council voted to appoint a "librarian" with the specific responsibility of collecting all the newspapers and periodicals in the colony, putting them in order, and making them available to everyone. The council asked Jacob Woodruff, the blacksmith, to do the job. Did they now share? Consider the case of William Stillwell, who arrived in the colony ten weeks after the council vote. One month later, fourteen weeks after the council vote, he wrote his wife, Sarah, who had remained home in Pleasant Valley, New York, about his mail. "I also __________ [received?] a paper which was of the utmost importance as it was the first one I had read since I left Milwaukee and furthermore I wish you or someone would mail one each week." The records at this time show at least eleven subscriptions to the *Harbinger.* Individuals there also got the *New York Tribune, Southport Telegraph, Prairie Farmer, Fond Du Lac Journal, Ploughshare and Pruninghook,* and *Practical Christian.* Yet in this experiment dedicated to cooperation, we see that William Stillwell had no access to any of them.[26]

Nevertheless, Chase continued to maintain that people in his colony had greater cultural advantages than farmers in the surrounding part of the country. That contention can be tested against subscriptions taken by others in the area, almost all farmers. Not long after the experiment ended, the population in the town surrounding it stood at about 2,170, and these people got 616 weekly papers plus some dailies.[27] That works out to an average of one weekly per 3.5 people in the town, about the same as in the Phalanx at its peak.

But even if that proved false, and Chase's boast turned out to be true, his position would still contradict two claims the Associationists made for their system: economy and provisions for self-improvement.

Economy. Association is a superior system because it uses resources more efficiently. One large kitchen, for example, serves many families at a lower unit cost than several individual family kitchens. Following the logic of that argument for Association's advantages, buying a few copies of a newspaper and making them available to everyone would have been more efficient than many individual subscriptions. But Wisconsin Phalanx encouraged the old way. In 1847 the council winked at a Phalanx rule that prohibited advances against credited labor and decided to allow advances if the money went for personal subscriptions.[28]

Self-improvement. Association promised to provide for enlarging each member's intellectual horizons. But the Phalanx leaders placed the burden for selecting and securing the necessary items for this purpose on the individual, just where it had always been in the traditional society that Associationists condemned.

Shortly before the leadership of Wisconsin Phalanx published the 1847 statement, its progress came under attack in the Associationist press. It began where M. Hine visited the Phalanx and sent an enthusiastic, laudatory description to the *Tribune.* The letter prompted an editorial caveat by Horace Greeley (August 14, 1847) about the perception of partisan observers. It surely applies to all movements for social change – then and now. "Writers of letters from the Associative experiments are apt to blend what they desire and hope to see with what they actually *do* see [original emphasis]."

Following that a writer for the *Harbinger,* Joseph Cook from Rhode Island, visited the Phalanx, and sent back an objective report on what he had found (November 6, 1847). While there, he boldly asked members if published reports had given "a correct impression of your real, existing condition." Invariably, they answered no. His report included the fact that the colony still had no library or reading room. When the Associationist spotlight fell on that embarrassment, it must have touched a raw nerve in Chase because he fired back an intemperate blast, which the *Harbinger* published (January 8, 1848). He charged that Cook, from "the rich and elegant city of Providence," knew nothing of the West. As always, Chase contended that in comparison with the area's farmers his members had cultural advantages. And once again he assured the movement that the colony would soon have its library and reading room. It never happened.

Charlotte Haven, a Wisconsin Phalanx member during its final two years, observed that people in the colony generally had a "common education" and lacked in "cultivation" but seemed interested in "improvement." Nothing, however, indicates any effort to bring in people who would work toward building up the supply of reading material. In 1848 a person presumably of that kind came from the East Coast to join, having hauled his own library halfway across the continent. But the Phalanx turned down his application, and in order to raise cash to pay for the trip back, he had to sell his books and pictures. Colony members bought none of them. If the Wisconsin Phalanx people did read books or attach any value to them, they left little record of it. In all of the colony's documents, I could find the mention of only three titles, and two of them belonged to Charlotte Haven, a Brook Farmer at heart whose application to join the colony of her choice had been thwarted by its room shortage. Her sister in St. Louis had sent her Macaulay's *History [of England]*, and from home she had received a copy of *Shirley* (Brontë).[29]

The third title, a most revealing one in terms of the colony's history, appears in the journal of Cutting Marsh, who visited Wisconsin Phalanx during its final days. He said he found twelve copies of "Jack Davis's Pretended Revelations." This popular handbook of spiritualism by Andrew Jackson Davis, *The Principles of Nature, Her Divine Revelations* . . . (1847), rode the crest of one of those mass absurdities that spread through traditional society around midcentury. Chase himself had earlier embraced the idea of communicating with the dead and had published his own bizarre notions of spiritualism.[30] The existence of so many copies of this Davis work in a small and virtually bookless colony conjures up an image of a shallow, credulous membership with aspirations far short of the intellectual enrichment the movement promised. In an another example of a utopian episode with an ironic twist, they effectively showed that they had given up the ghost on changing this world when they turned to communion with the ghosts of the spirit world.

A clear example of the disregard for books occurred in La Réunion. Supporters in France had donated a good collection, but Considérant, certainly not an anti-intellectual but an inept and arrogant manager, had the shipment unloaded into a barn loft. Savardan described it as being "heaped pell-mell" on the floor. Considérant decided not to spend money then for a library room to straighten out the mess he had created and even rejected using time and material for some plain shelves in the barn. So for all practical purposes the books remained inaccessible. Finally, in the desperate, waning months of the experiment, the leaders sold them, and the books never contributed toward the colony's original, noble mission.[31]

A somewhat similar fate almost overtook Icaria's library. The inventory of 1853 placed a value on the books at seven hundred dollars. Assuming a nominal value of one dollar per book implies about seven hundred volumes. That means the Icarians must have had an unmatched cultural advantage in that place and in that time. Moreover, sympathizers in France constantly sent gifts. For example, *Colonie Icarienne* (July 26 and August 2, 1854) reported receiving music from friends in Lyon and Paris and two crates of books from Grenoble. The books included: *Mécanique* by Armengaud, *L'Histoire de la Révolution de 1848* by Mme. d'Agoult (Stern), and a book of plays. Cabet claimed that by 1855 Icaria had four thousand volumes, and although he clearly exaggerated, he did encourage reading. He installed a table at one end of the big Nauvoo dining hall, and filled it with current French newspapers from Paris, New York, Mexico, Montreal, New Orleans, and nearby St. Louis. Icaria also received German newspapers.[32]

Cabet understood the strength books could add to a colony in this movement. That explains why he permitted his cohorts to carry out a cruel act of terrorism against the colony library. It came in the aftermath of bitter factional strife when the majority voted to expel Cabet and his partisans. As they left they took brutal revenge against the colony's soul, its defenseless library. They wantonly tore out engravings, and systematically confiscated a volume or two from certain sets in order to diminish their usefulness.[33]

When the Icarians quit Nauvoo for Iowa late in the 1850s, they took the remnants of the library with them, and in a situation reminiscent of La Réunion, dumped it on the floor in a shambles. The books remained in a log hut until the 1870s when someone moved it to a room above the new dining hall. There it stayed in disorderly heaps on the floor because the colony allowed no labor time to do anything more. Only the farm and the workshops counted.

But unlike the tragedy of La Réunion's library, Icaria's had a happier ending. Little Maria Marchand had an early interest in reading, and rummaged the piles for children's books. She learned to read with the La Fontaine fables. The collection of Icarian papers in Iowa has a tattered old copy that includes a brief biography of Aesop, and a stylized engraving for each fable. The missing cover and other signs of hard use show that it served the Icarian children well. It may have been the very copy that started little Maria on her reading. Before the age of nine she had gone through *Voyage en Icarie*, George Sand's *La petite Fedette, and Misères des enfants trouvés* by Eugene Sue. At ten she became a willing librarian when Cite. Mourot asked her to help put the books on shelves the room had. It took a whole summer to make some order because she was allowed to do this only in her spare time. In Icaria even youngsters had duties, and these took precedence. Yet every Saturday little Maria found time to clean the old books and keep them neat. That gave her a chance to work her way through the collection as she grew up. She recalled that early in the 1880s the members put up special shelves in the dining hall for some books and pigeonholes for magazines.

Some of the old volumes remained in the family of Eugene Bettanier, last president of the colony, and the family gave them to the State of Iowa.[34] Of these, eighteen come from the Nauvoo period that ended in the late 1850s, twelve date from the 1870s, and none from the years between, which tends to confirm the long period of cultural decline after the colony moved. Most of the books show the marks of considerable handling, and judging by that indicator, the members favored a French dictionary, Hugo's works, and Cabet's *Histoire de la Révolution française*.

Cabet preferred didactic works. The Des Moines collection of Icarian manuscripts includes some old books, and one of them, *Moralistes anciens* (Moralists of Antiquity), exemplifies the type that Cabet would have chosen. Thoroughly dog-eared and lacking pages throughout, it surely felt the grip of many hands in its time. It has commentaries on Socrates; excerpts from Marcus Aurelius, Epictatus, and Pythagorus; and the didactic aphorisms of Phocylides and others. Its organization resembles a series of articles that appeared in *Colonie Icarienne* called "Communistes célèbres" (Celebrated Communists). These promoted a favorite Cabet theme: the great philosophers of the past were Icaria's antecedents and like Jesus were simply teachers of morality. Cabet considered himself simply a teacher of morality.

When Albert Shaw visited the Icarians in 1883 he found humble cabins with few furnishings. However, he saw books and even a print here and there. Moreover, Shaw said the two Icarian villages that existed at that time each had a library of about one thousand volumes, consisting of standard French works in literature, philosophy, history, and science.[35]

Fortunately, the colony's manuscript records include a large notebook that has a neatly written catalog of the library during this period. It lists well over eight hundred titles, not as many as estimated by Shaw, who stayed in the colony only a few days, but it does provide convincing documentary evidence of an impressive library that needs no overstatement to enhance its stature. A glance through its pages reveals two things: first, the titles, of course; second, how the character of the collection countered a general tendency in the movement to limit the type of books that members ought to read.

On the first point: they had a surprisingly large number of books in English, nearly 40 percent. These included Milton, Byron, the complete Shakespeare, Dante's *Inferno* and *Purgatory,* and biographies of artists and composers. There were several dictionaries, including Samuel Johnson's and an unabridged *Webster's.* The members could have read works on astronomy, chemistry, natural history, and travel in Asia, Africa, and the Arctic. The French volumes included Balzac, the complete Racine, Louis Blanc's *Histoire de la Révolution,* and books on painting technique and on music theory. There were some old editions, one inscribed in 1775, and a Schiller in German.

But the most remarkable aspect of this library in a colony of social reorganization was the large collection of fiction. The collection included English and French novelists, many represented by both languages, and quite a few by sets of complete works. Some examples: Cooper, Collins, Dickens, the Dumas, Hugo, Irving, Melville, Scott, Sand, Sue, Thackeray, the Trollopes, Verne, Zola, and others unheard-of today.

That brings up the second revelation in this list of books: more than 85 percent of the titles fall into the category of fiction. Why is that significant? Because it went against a tendency in the movement to oppose reading novels. Limiting the type of books people read has an ancient and ugly history in traditional society, of course, and even today it casts oppressive shadows across our library shelves. However, in a movement dedicated to freeing the mind from the restraints of the past, such efforts do seem alien.

Two factors militated against reading novels: the yardstick of utility, which measured all things against the bottom line, and a puritanical obsession with idle time, time that had to be used for something worthwhile, such as self-improvement. The following passage by Richard Thornton in the *Primitive Expounder,* published in Alphadelphia (November 28, 1844), typifies these attitudes. "Novel Reading. It is strange that a Christian should seek to fill his mind with fiction when there are so many useful sciences, or suffer his mind to be arrested by false narratives when there are so many works of history, biography, travels, and especially the great ______ [illegible] volume of Divine Truth. . . . That tendency is without doubt deleterious, weakening the understanding and relish for useful sciences and truth."

Novel readers were often associated with certain traits. Maria Marchand, for example, described her friend Caroline as "romantic" because she read novels, an odd comment because Maria read them too. An unhappier example comes from the Oneida Community, not a group dedicated to social reorganization. There, Meron Kneeland came under this sort of criticism for numerous faults: she is inefficient in business, overeats, and "spends a great deal of time in reading novels." As a result, the Oneida leaders told her to leave. In a grotesque sequel, she wrote them a letter five months later asking for some money she had left there, and assured them that she had not read a novel "or looked into one" since she left.[36]

In New-Harmony, Marie Fretageot, one of the teachers, criticized the instruction that Joseph Neef, another teacher, gave his own daughter, Louise. Fretageot criticized Louise for spending her time reading novels, calling her unfit. As a teacher, her educational position dovetailed with Owen's belief that any activity should be evaluated according to its utility. In that system, reading would be useful to the extent that it taught practical things or morality. A *Gazette* article on Byron (December 20, 1826) evaluates his work in this way. "The wayward and gigantic powers of Byron's mind are proof to us how much of what is useful and admirable may be lost to the world by misdirection. . . . [Byron] knew how . . . to astonish, to enchant, but rarely to improve or to instruct."

Another issue of the *Gazette* (August 2, 1826), has an article that applies those criteria, improvement and instruction, as a test in order to determine what books would be considered acceptable for New-Harmony people to read. And there in a utopian skin the wolf of censorship howls softly. The item, submitted by an Owenite who claims he can distinguish between "literary works of real utility, and those which are merely amusing," reprints some literary criticism by Henry Fielding. Obviously, Fielding would not be against reading novels, only certain kinds. First, he attacks the idea that the function of reading is amusement. He allows that wit and humor could be acceptable when used to attack vice, "when the agreeable is blended with the useful," and when they are "only the vehicle of instruction." Given that, a novel might be considered worthy. "But when no moral, no lesson, no instruction is conveyed to the reader . . . the writer comes very near the character of a buffoon."

Why, he asks, do "scribblers" find so many readers? Because "the bulk of mankind" has no taste. So he planned to "lay down some rules" for readers, but in the meantime he urged everyone to "cautiously avoid the perusal of any modern book till it has had the sanction of some wise and learned man." Finally, he warned in eye-catching italics, "*Evil books corrupt . . . our manners and taste.*"

Nothing indicates that anyone in New-Harmony took any action relative to "evil books." Perhaps the experiment did not last long enough, or perhaps the serious problems of the colony took the attention of anyone inclined to "lay down some rules" about which books people could read. But the principle had been enunciated, and since the person who sent the item to the *Gazette* told the editors to publish it "if you approve," its appearance in print had to lend it an aura of "sanction," not unlike the kind Henry Fielding favored.

However, among the significant contributions of a New-Harmony to our culture we must count the forum it could and did provide for competing ideas. That, of course, strengthened our evolving democracy, but unfortunately, as we shall see in a later chapter, it diverted the experiment from its main purpose, and actually contributed to its destruction. Still, the members had an immediate benefit: they could read arguments against allowing an authority to sit in judgment over ideas. These arguments appear in Frances Wright's book *A Few Days in Athens,* which the *Gazette* published in weekly installments (October 4 to December 27, 1826).

The book concerns the philosophy of Epicurus, but instead of dry exposition, Wright broadens its appeal by making it into a fictional narrative. In the story, Theon, a lad of eighteen, comes to ancient Athens to study philosophy, and despite his early prejudice against Epicurus, becomes his disciple. When Theon looks to Epicurus to supply him with a moral judgment, the sage scorns philosophers who say, "The master said so." And with emphasis he advises Theon, "I wish you to think nothing good, or bad either, upon *my* decision. The first and last thing I would say to a man is *think for yourself.*" Then, in a later installment, when Theon mentions rumors of Epicurean interest in vice and depravity, Epicurus cautions him to form judgments based on knowledge, not rumor. "Credulity is always a ridiculous, often a dangerous failing: it has made of many a clever man a fool; and of many a good man, a knave."

Wright's point should have been chiseled in stone, and everyone in the movement made to study it, because their efforts fell victim so easily to the credulous. The book, of course, stands the Owenite test of utility: it instructs, even though some of its thoughts sit uneasily among Owen's precepts. But significantly, it left room in New-Harmony for the growth of intellectual values more in keeping with the humanistic promise of a better life.

The colony did not have a library as such, but collections of books did exist there. Robert Jennings kept a small library in his busy editorial office at the *Gazette,* and other members may have brought theirs too, although with one exception, no documentary information about the character of their books remains. A hint of this comes up in the the case of Louise Neef, the girl who allegedly spent all her time reading novels. If true, her consuming literary interest suggests that a good stock of novels must have existed somewhere in the colony.

The major collection of books in New-Harmony belonged to William Maclure, the geologist. He had joined Owen in this social experiment because it presented opportunities for educational innovations, his interest. He brought his personal library, and documents show that he shared it with his colleagues. Generous, wealthy, and firmly committed to education, he may have made it available to others too. What kinds of books did Maclure have? Unfortunately, no list of them exists for the period of the experiment. But about eight years after it ended he offered to give the Academy of Natural Sciences in Philadelphia a selection of books from his library. Dr. Charles Pickering made the trip to Indiana on behalf of the academy, and wrote up the list. His manuscript provides a clue to the type of books that might have been available to members during the time of the experiment. Pickering's list has more than nine hundred titles consisting of nearly two thousand volumes. When shipped they weighed five tons. Nearly one-fourth of the books that Pickering chose are listed as folio size, which means that a rather large room must have existed somewhere in the colony to hold the whole library at its maximum.[37]

A majority of the books are in French, and at first glance it might appear to be a library dedicated to science. However, about one-third come from the humanities: history, philosophy, literature, and the arts. These books cover an impressive range from the classical Rome of Vitruvius to the Renaissance of Vasari, to Palladio and Piranesi. They include a collection of Raphael prints and books on painters, on sculpture, and on music. Many schools of philosophy are represented, from Plato's *Republic* to Rousseau and Locke and in poetry from Ovid to Pope. Pickering chose Rabelais, Chaucer, and Don Quixote, but the list contains no modern novels except for some works of de Staël. The list has dozens of maps and dictionaries. But more important than individual items, the breadth of these selections suggests that Pickering took a representative sampling.

Another manuscript lists books Maclure donated to a school in Germantown, Pennsylvania, and here the humanities predominate.[38] But the essential character of his library remains the same. Both of these documents tell of an excellent resource for well-educated people. However, it would not have met the needs of New-Harmony's schools, particularly given Owen's belief in practical education based on direct experience with tangible objects. And the general membership probably would have had difficulties with such an esoteric library even if Maclure had made it available to them.

Brook Farmers, on the other hand, could use George and Sophia Ripley's collection of books. The Aerie, the building for cultural activities, became the home for this library of philosophy, religion, and modern European literature. It included the fourteen-volume *Specimens of Foreign Standard Literature,* which George Ripley had edited, and which included his translations of contemporary French philosophy and political theory. Such an esoteric library, with books in foreign languages, was appropriate for this colony, in contrast to New-Harmony, because Brook Farmers, especially in the early years, had educations that enabled them to make use of it. Many read foreign languages, and most pupils in the Brook Farm School studied at least one.

Books held a more important place in the daily life of Brook Farm than in any other utopian colony. Proof for that does not come merely from comparing volume counts; Brook Farmers had their personal libraries, but so did people elsewhere. Just as Marianne Dwight brought her books to Brook Farm and shelved them in her room, so did Robert Jennings bring his to New-Harmony, to his office at the *Gazette.* Rather, the importance of books shines through in the numerous references to them in Brook Farm's records, documents, and letters, and by the value the members placed on reading. When Nathaniel Hawthorne sued Brook Farm to get back money he had put up for the founding of the colony, Ripley had to sell his library to satisfy the lien. The comment he is said to have made then typifies those values: "I can now understand how a man would feel if he could attend his own funeral."[39]

Brook Farmers had a comfortable familiarity with literature. A comparison of attitudes in New-Harmony and in Brook Farm illustrates this clearly. The *Gazette* (November 15, 1826) made fun of the German writer Jean Paul with a tired old "joke" tinged with smug anti-intellectualism. In it, "John Paul" is asked to explain a certain passage in one of his books, and confesses that he too does not understand it. On the other hand, a *Harbinger* review (August 23, 1845) called him a great human being, who writes with "pathos and exquisite humor . . . [and] veneration for . . . man." Brook Farmers celebrated him by decorating their Christmas tree "as described by Jean Paul," with sugar plums, fairy figures, candles, blown eggs, gilt, and so forth. Brook Farmers stayed close to their reading. When Marianne Dwight wrote to her friend Anna Parsons about the character she portrayed in a tableau vivant (living picture), a favorite game they played there, she could refer to it quite casually as "my Jeanie Deanes" (referring to a character in Scott's *Heart of Midlothian*) with no further explanation. That anecdote tells us that they also discussed the books they read.[40]

Moreover, because Brook Farmers read widely, unexpected titles show up there. For example, Georgiana Bruce said she had problems with Law's *Spirit of Love* and the works of Madame Guyon. But these books "were like common bread and butter" to the other Brook Farmers, who she said also read Fenelon. Those names are associated with a mystical idea that originated a century earlier called quietism. It sought perfection through the complete renunciation of self. Such ideas seem out of place among the free spirits of Brook Farm, but it shows how far afield they went in their reading. They also read skeptically. Marianne Dwight read an occult work, *The Seeress,* and though she found it pleasing at first, she quickly turned analytical. "There are so many stories told in it which I can't believe, that it takes much from the satisfaction I should have in the rest of the book." After Georgiana Bruce read a life of St. Augustine, she decided that she "had no sympathy with a man who found religion and natural affection at variance."[41]

When a quarterly meeting of Associationists met at Brook Farm in 1844, it took precedence over other activities no matter how desirable. In a letter to her brother, Frank, Marianne Dwight barely suppressed her clear preference. She characterized the meeting as "interesting" but said they had to pay a price, giving up their beloved Shakespeare reading group for it.[42] They clearly favored Shakespeare, but other names turn up often in their comments: Homer, Plato, Plutarch, Kant, Carlyle, Bryant, and the German romantic poets Novalis and Heine.

Members circulated books freely among themselves. In addition, the daybook, where the colony recorded daily transactions, has entries for library charges. For example, in July 1845 the account of José Corrales, a pupil from Manila, twice had charges of twenty-five cents for "Library Books." Other similar entries range as high as forty-five cents, but none of them tells the library's name. The accounts also list book purchases, most of them propaganda items intended for resale. But occasionally an item like a volume of Spanish plays enlivens those dispassionate ledger columns.

In addition to the members' usual sources of books, during the years the *Harbinger* called Brook Farm home they tapped a rich lode of reading material unique in all the movement. The newspaper featured literary reviews, and because the main reviewers, Charles Dana, John Dwight, and Ripley, lived there, a constant stream of books, periodicals, and music flowed into the old farmhouse called the Hive. A fourth reviewer, Francis Shaw, lived just up the road, and he and his family took part in all of the colony's activities. (His daughters Anna and Ellen both married Brook Farmers.) Shaw translated George Sand's *Consuelo,* which the *Harbinger* serialized.

After a reviewer finished an item it wound up in the hands of the membership. Hints about this obvious situation often appear in reviews: "We laid this book aside"; and in a review of sheet music, "These pretty things have been lying on the piano for some weeks"; and of a favorably reviewed set of books, "They lay about our rooms, and circulated among our little band of fellow workers."

Thus the *Harbinger* reviews make it possible to compile an easily documented Brook Farm reading list. We can even correlate a review with a member reading the book. For example, one day after the *Harbinger* included a notice of Dickens's *Cricket on the Hearth* (February 8, 1846), Elizabeth Curson told her sister in the letter quoted earlier that she had remained in her room to read the story.

During the two-year period that the *Harbinger* was published on the colony grounds, the resident writers reviewed and members had access to some three hundred items. Fiction, the largest category, accounts for nearly one-fourth, with a wide variety from Andersen to Zschokke, including Cooper, Melville, Poe, and Dickens. Poetry and other literature embrace a slightly smaller number. The reviewers covered eighteen books of poems, among them works of Shelley and Thomas Hood, the latter beloved for the social message members saw in his lines. Books by Goethe, Schiller, Fichte, and Jean Paul reflect the leadership's interest in German literature. Carlyle, another of their favorites, has two reviews. Next come equal helpings of religion, travel, politics, and society. Surprisingly, only two of the books reviewed concern Association. But plenty of provocative sociological books get noticed: Dorothea Dix's pioneering work on prisons, one on psychology and crime, another defending capital punishment. Three reviews deal with items on women's equality.

These literary riches found eager eyes at Brook Farm. But not everyone hungered for them. During the *Harbinger* years – the Phalanx period – Association leaders made a drive to attract the working class. Although these new members wanted self-improvement, their priorities emphasized the immediate necessities more than the books and the long-range views of the middle-class Brook Farmers who made up the colony's foundation. That created an unexpected gulf in the life of the colony and generated difficult questions for intellectuals who wanted to change the world but who had not quite thought it all through. "Should they take among them men and women endowed only with practical, everyday talents, able to . . . make shoes and sew garments; to strike with a sledge and a blacksmith's arm . . . but who had never read Goethe or Schiller, and possibly neither Shakespeare, Scott nor Robert Burns, and might not care to read or study Latin, French, German, or philosophy." John Codman said that Ripley and the Brook Farmers had pondered these questions.[43]

They did not come up with answers. As the working-class representation increased, the dilemma grew. An uneasy relationship between the middle-class intellectuals and those who lacked educational advantages set up tensions in Brook Farm and indeed wherever this polarity existed throughout the movement. The architects of social reorganization had made no provisions for this in the perfect worlds their imaginations spawned, and leaders who understood it could not resolve the stresses it created. During the despondent days of 1846 when the cracks in Brook Farm's foundation became obvious to all and membership dwindled sharply, Marianne Dwight wrote to her confidante, Anna Parsons, that she was glad that those who "lack that refinement which is indispensable to give a good tone to the place" had gone. "Those of us who will be left are capable of improving . . . but it always seemed to me a great mistake to admit coarse people upon the place. Now we need not fear subjecting our pupils to evil influences from such quarters."[44]

So even in the best of circumstances, which Brook Farm offered, the promises of intellectual pleasures and of opportunities for self-improvement became mired in confusion over what at first glance had seemed to be clear needs and clear goals. The needs, interests, and goals of different people turned out to be eminently more complex than the ivory-tower revolutionists could have imagined.

Life in Music

DURING THE BITTER WINTER OF 1846, a time of crisis for Brook Farm, John Allen went on the road to raise desperately needed funds. In Vermont a blizzard held him up, so he dozed by the hearth of an inn and dreamed of the glorious days to come. Suddenly the sky was a deep azure, the earth green and decorated with flowers, and myriads of joyful people worked happily. Then, "Art led the universal throng in worship at the shrine of Beauty. . . . Music inspired all with unity as one soul, and uttered those deep emotions which could never struggle up into speech." His fantasy, which the *Harbinger* published (February 20, 1846), came out of an Associationist axiom: music brings us together because it touches feelings we all share but cannot express in words. In the Phalanx, music became the highest art.

Fourier named the qualities to look for in selecting members, and "a precise musical ear" topped the list. He designated opera the principal cultural activity of the Phalanx, and made training for it the core of children's education.[1]

John Dwight said every colony should have at least one member responsible for the arts. That person would ensure an environment of grace and music. "There should be music floating about in the air. . . . Snatches of melody should visit the workman in the field or shop, should impart a rhythm . . . to idle thoughts, . . . should soften and refine all hearts and manners. The presence of good music is the presence of a good spirit."

Like Fourier, who considered opera just as important in a Phalanx as economics, Victor Considérant started La Réunion with this as a guiding principle: "The culture of music is as urgent as that of the fields and gardens."[2]

Cabet differed with Fourier on fundamentals, but in *Colonie Icarienne* (July 19, 1854) he called music "an absolute necessity," especially for Icaria given its goal of fraternity. He said the colony gladly gave up luxuries in order to develop music there. And Brook Farm anecdotes tell of similar sacrifices for the advantages of music.

Brook Farmers, just city folk after all, found that farm life strains the body. Naïve experimenters, they soon learned that changing the world stresses the soul as well. For these ills they had a cure. Worn out or worried when evening came, they sought rejuvenation in music. During one period when doctrinal disputes threatened friendships, Marianne Dwight said they needed more music because it could unite them socially. John Codman recalled that singing made the winter go fast. One colony performance raised his spirits so high that it inspired in him "new ideas of duty and destiny." And John Dwight cherished the excitement they had in hearing a Beethoven symphony; it gave the group "a new good genius, beautiful and strong, to help them through the next day's labors."[3]

However, most people who claimed to be Fourierists distorted or ignored his instruction on the necessity of music. A confederation of upstate New York Associations held a conference in 1844 and passed recommendations governing work and activities in their colonies. The *Phalanx* report on it (June 15, 1844) says they established three categories: Necessity, Usefulness, and Attractiveness. Necessity included industrial operations. They relegated the teaching of music – performance is not even mentioned – to the category of Usefulness. The report gives no hint of music at the conference, not even a traditional hymn.

Most groups who took the name of Association and called Fourier mentor adopted the priorities of Necessary, Useful, Attractive. But such divisions, whatever their rationale, contradict the essence of his concept of Association, in which the Attractive functions as the organizing principle, the only priority.

Cabet, as we saw in the last chapter, also took as an organizing principle: "First the Necessary, then the Useful, and at last the Agreeable." And in that scheme arts and pleasures did have a place in line. But unlike Fourier, he did not predicate his ideal world on individual differences and on the need for what Fourier called "attractive industry" to satisfy those differences. Cabet made no intrinsic connection between life and aesthetics. In Fourier's ideal world, on the other hand, arts and pleasures stand at the head of the line. A Phalanx without an aesthetic life, without music woven into every facet of life, would be meaningless.

The Boston supporters of Association always had music at their gatherings. Of course, having John Dwight handy at Brook Farm, about eight miles away, made it possible. His interest and knowledge generated and sustained the movement's musical activities in the colony and in town. Sometimes the Boston supporters held ambitious and even elaborate programs. For example, when the Union of Associationists held a Fourier birthday gala, Dwight brought his chorus for two larger works: an excerpt from a Rossini opera, and part of a mass. According to the *Harbinger* (April 17, 1847) the vocal music also included Beethoven's "Adelaide" and other "songs of the highest sentiment." They had piano works by Schubert, Mendelssohn, and Liszt, performed on a "magnificent Chickering grand." The editor of the *Boston Chronotype* called it an evening of "never-to-be-forgotten music." And when several clergymen organized the Religious Union of Associationists at the home of James Fisher, Dwight provided a musical program, and a few Brook Farmers and Mary Bullard, his future wife, served as a choir.[4]

Compare the situation in Philadelphia. Supporters there included a pianist, Elizabeth Blackwell, who used to play for the meetings. But she left to study medicine – she became the country's first woman doctor – and they had no one to take her place. James Kay, a leader of the Philadelphia Associationists, wrote to his counterpart in Boston about their plight. He conceded that they could not hope to emulate the movement in Boston. But they did want to get their own hall. However, that would force them into buying a piano, and they simply could not afford it.[5]

Clearly, the musical programs of the Boston supporters stood out for its leadership. The music they chose, however, represented the religious impulses and the tastes of the elite at the helm of Brook Farm. Along with other cultural achievements, that music immeasurably enhanced the quality of life in the colony. But, as we shall see, it did not necessarily harmonize with the new script they created for Association, which turned Fourier's universality into a movement directed toward the working class.

Spontaneous Music

Almost all colonies in the movement had some spontaneous music, the equivalent of the informal discussions described in the previous chapter. I distinguish between spontaneous and planned music because most groups made no effort to encourage anything more than a little impromptu singing. Even in groups that had some regular, organized musical activities, they took place less often than the analogous organized intellectual activities. Two reasons account for that: music requires time – preparation, rehearsals, practice – that few colonies wanted to give up, and it also called for skills that few members had. As you might expect, those groups that cultivated lectures and books generally did the same for music.

What did it take to start a little spontaneous music? The singing spirit sufficed, but an instrument or two – a piano, a guitar, or maybe a fiddle – though not absolutely necessary, helped. Shared work and every utopian's sense of taking part in a great mission for humanity tended to create an atmosphere natural for singing. In North American Phalanx, for example, people would gather in the kitchen after the pea harvest, and as they joined in the shelling they also joined in singing old songs. This anecdote shows how music could help invigorate their efforts, as some in the movement believed. Georgiana Bruce described a similar scene in Brook Farm's kitchen, where she and a partner, Sylvia, faced a mountain of potatoes and carrots. As they peeled and scraped, Sylvia sang stirring Methodist hymns in her full and clear but undisciplined voice: "Oh I'm bound for the Kingdom / will you go to glory with me?" Her singing carried through the windows, where members stopped to listen and went away inspired.[6]

More information survives about the spontaneous music created after working hours, both by groups and by individuals. An example of the latter comes from Moncure Conway's observations made during his visit to nonconformist Modern Times. There he heard a male voice serenading a female in the moonlight. His comment: some old traditions would survive no matter how radically we changed society. Similarly, in New-Harmony, young Miner Kellogg carved a little fife to amuse himself and the other boys. Pleased, his father bought him a flute, and he and his father, who played the jew's-harp, then entertained friends with popular favorites: "Robin Adair," "Charlie Over the Water," and "Auld Lang Syne." Harriet Haven of Wisconsin Phalanx tells in her journal about a new member who played the guitar but could not speak English. As a result he tended to keep to his room evenings, making music for his own enjoyment. But members passing through the narrow central hall of the long building soon began to stop, listen, and open his door. Through music they soon became friends despite the language barrier.[7]

Every group had a member who could sing. But surprisingly, many also had the instrument most suitable for group music making, a piano. North American Phalanx had at least six according to one report. Kalikst Wolski saw two in the large recreation room that the colony used for a theater. Raritan Bay Union kept a piano in the school parlor, a typical arrangement, and it became the focus of impromptu singing early on Sunday mornings.[8]

Each building at Brook Farm had at least one piano. Marianne Dwight brought hers when she arrived and moved into the Pilgrim House. The Hive, the building that housed the dining room, had one in the parlor, and dancing often sprang up there as soon as members cleared the supper dishes. The Cottage had a piano in one of its classrooms, and in the evening students would claim it on the spur of the moment for dancing or singing. During the day, these buildings echoed with scales and finger exercises. The Aerie, the house on the hill, had a large grand piano in the salon, a spacious room framed with picturesque French windows. The colony's best pianists practiced there, often attracting a small, unbidden audience who would sit quietly, appreciating the unexpected recital.

John Dwight worked there almost every day one summer and gives us a picture of such a scene in one of his *Harbinger* reviews (September 12, 1846).

> With spirits clear and calm, thoughts undistracted, . . . one sits down to the piano with a sonata of Beethoven or Mozart, or a set of Chopin's Mazurkas . . . and reads thoughtfully, . . . lingers . . . until [it] unfolds all its beauty. . . . This is worth a thousand concerts. . . . And instead of suffocating halls and glaring lights and whispering, giggling, unappreciating audiences . . . you may have the green shades and the blessed skies of morning, noon, or sunset for surroundings, and perchance a friend or two at your elbow whose souls are in it, and who can keep still without ceremonious effort.

Sometimes Brook Farmers would stop at the salon in the Aerie and find Dwight improvising, "lost in the musical world wherever his thoughts led him," as one member described it.[9] More often, he would be hard at work, going through music he had to review in the *Harbinger.* He spent one summer studying a new edition of Mendelssohn's *Songs Without Words* in preparation for a review (September 12 and 19, 1846). In that case, members had an unforeseen opportunity to become familiar with a recent work from the European repertoire, something few Americans could hope for. In reviewing some waltzes (April 17, 1847), Dwight confided that he had left them lying around for weeks. Such music quickly became part of the colony's shared repertoire; everybody had a chance to try it and criticize it. The result: even more spontaneous music.

New-Harmony had several pianos, including a fine instrument said to be a Clementi that Virginia Dupalais brought from France. In the anecdote told by visitor Duke Bernhard, which was related in chapter 3, she was the young woman who cried when the cow milking interrupted her piano playing. In the finale to the story, after she returned from her chores in the barn some young people invited her to their moonlight boating party, where she entertained them with her singing.

When Marie Fretageot came to New-Harmony to teach, she brought music, a small grand piano, and a "piano transpositor." The piano had an unusual device that could change the sound and possibly the pitch, allowing it to fill a variety of musical situations, just what a colony like New-Harmony needed.[10] The transpositor made it possible for a pianist, even one lacking in technical knowledge, to play in any key, a skill that usually requires considerable practice. With the transpositer a relatively unskilled pianist would be able to find the right key for a few casual singers who liked to get together for some informal musical fun. Singing at moonlight boating parties and gathering around the piano to revisit some favorite tunes are genuine, down-to-earth pleasures. Unfortunately, the good times that members must have had from such harmonious, everyday activities rarely survive in the histories, which dwell on bad times and discord.

Other colonies had keyboard instruments suited to spontaneous music and singing. The Icarians in Nauvoo had the Baxter piano, mentioned earlier. In Iowa they had an orguinette that produced popular airs and hymns from a punched paper roll. They also had a parlor organ (a small reed organ or harmonium), and after supper some of the young people would gather around it and join in singing.

The guitar, found in just about every movement for social change, turns up in this one too, even in colonies with no hint of a musical life. For example, Communia's inventory, which shows absolutely nothing else related to the arts, lists one guitar. Wisconsin Phalanx, another utopian experiment without much music, also had one. Francis Bolton of New-Harmony recalled that his mother played guitar and sang with a sweet voice, making her a great favorite at social events. Many Brook Farmers recalled the enjoyable times when George Curtis, a good guitarist with a "marvelous voice," would sing for them. Christopher Cranch, a frequent visitor with guitar, always entered the gate ready to sing and usually did so with little prompting. In a newspaper item about Modern Times, the reporter discussed its production, and in his description of the village square, with its shoemakers, masons, and tinsmiths, he included a girl sitting on a windowsill strumming away. One of the few examples of utopian speculation realized if only in an impromptu way, it shows that music could be brought to the workplace.[11]

The fiddle, in those colonies lucky enough to have someone who could play it, made it possible to enjoy a little country dancing on the spur of the moment. Icaria, New-Harmony, La Réunion, and even Alphadelphia, where documents tell of a life of all work and no play, had their fiddler. Brook Farm had Jean Palisse, a Swiss engineer and a skilled viollinist, but he only played waltzes.

Of course, just because a colony had instruments does not mean the members used them or had the spirit to do so. A visitor at North American Phalanx who enjoyed his time there found one think lacking: music. He reported in the *Harbinger* (August 28, 1847) that the colony had instruments, but the members claimed they simply did not have enough time to make music. However, groups that cultivated music managed to find the time. Brook Farmers, for example, saw music as a necessary means of expression, and as such it simply became part of daily life. John Codman remembered an evocative little scene that illustrates the point. "It was the time of the full moon, when its transcendent beauty led the young folks to wander over the farm from house to house, to sit a while on the doorsteps or the knoll at the Hive: to sing "Das Klinket" or such part songs as "Row gently here, my gondolier," or "The lone starry hours give me love, when calm is the beautiful night," or anything else to let out the joyousness of their hearts."[12]

Songs of Social Reorganization

Unlike many other radicals, people in the movement for social reorganization never developed a symbolic expression of their ideas. They left us no memorable anthem like *La Marseillaise,* no powerful graphic like the hammer and sickle. The Associationists, more than all the others, had musical talent capable of creating a rallying song. However, little evidence of their interest exists. In 1844 Dewitt Throop, an activist in central New York, wrote his wife, Almira, asking her to "prepare a Fourier Hymn for us."[13] If she wrote anything, it, or information about it, has not survived. In fact, I found only a few examples of songs unambiguously expressing the ideas and ideals of social reorganization, and almost all of these came from the Icarians.

Folk-singers today still sing, "Oleana," a song often associated with this movement. It supposedly describes life in a colony known as Oleana. However, that place had nothing to do with social organization. Oleana refers to a philanthropic effort by a world-famous Norwegian violinist, Ole Bull, who decided to use his wealth to provide land in America for his less fortunate countrymen. His goal, helping them become independent farmers, had long been a traditional solution to society's ills, the opposite of social reorganization. Bull bought a large tract in Pennsylvania and called it New Norway, but when unscrupulous land agents and mismanagement made it look bad, his name, Ole, became the root for its derisive name. The song says that in Oleana the land is free, the crops grow without effort, the cows milk themselves and make the cheese. In short, one can live well there without working.

What should we look for in a true song of social reorganization? In other movements for radical change, the most effective songs have many if not all of these five traits: (1) a singable melody; (2) a stirring anthem-like quality; (3) a clear statement of goals; (4) a direct call for action; (5) emotional words and images. Only a few songs with these characteristics can be found in this movement.

Radicals rarely attract skilled composers. So writing new words to a well-known tune, a traditional practice in religion, has always been a standard means for creating songs in most social movements. "Association Song," set to the tune of a popular minstrel song of the time, belongs to that class. It appeared in the Fall River *Mechanic* (November 16, 1844) and was linked to the Sylvania experiment in Pennsylvania.[14] The tune, singable though not inspirational, satisfies the first trait, and the new words cover the third and fourth: they tell the benefits of the new social order and make a direct appeal for members. But they do that in an inept, mechanical singsong, and without rousing images and emotional appeal.

O come where love makes labor light,
Where toil with pleasure we unite,
Where industry with wisdom blends,
And bliss on social life attends
O come with us we all are brothers,
Each one tries to bless the others.

And so it goes for six verses. The tune "Ole Dan Tucker" gained national popularity in 1843 after Daniel Emmett with face painted black used it in his minstrel show based on white-invented caricatures of slaves. Cleaned up in some songbooks, the original text had stereotypes such as the black stealing a chicken from the coop and "de massa," a kind and gentle soul. A tune associated in the public mind with those images would do little to enhance the credibility of these noble sentiments in the new text.

Behold in each that treads the sod,
Your brother and a child of God.
O make yourselves a band of brothers;
Every one will help the others.

Even if it could overcome its connection with ideas that stand in contradiction to Associationist principles, the clumsy text still would remain a poor example of a song intended to attract the masses.

The Alphadelphia records show the purchase of *Social Hymns for the Use of the Friends of the Rational System of Society.* Owenites in England published this songbook and used it in all their activities. Alphadelphia had English members, and several months before the colony ordered *Social Hymns,* George Davis, an English Owenite, showed an interest in joining. Strange to say, members in Alphadelphia, an experiment based on Fourier not Owen, his opposite, would have found few difficulties with the broad generalities in these songs. For us, the songbook provides some key insights into how Owenites used music in the movement.

Social Hymns has over 150 texts, and as with "Association Song," they are intended to be sung to well-known tunes. These include popular English and Scotch airs such as "Auld Lang Syne" and "Gloomy Winter's Now Awa'." Some appear to be adaptations of traditional Christian hymns, as in this example.

Joy to the world! the light is come!
The only lawful king:

Let every heart prepare it room,
And moral nature sing.

Joy to the earth! now Reason reigns:
[etc.]

In fact, *Social Hymns* has the style of a typical hymnal without music. Each hymn has a number; the meter for each is given using the special abbreviations of hymnody; and the book has an index of subjects. The subjects include death, life, virtue, dismission, and others. But the editor did not simply treat them as traditional subjects; rather, he adapted them to fit the needs of Owenite philosophy and the visions of social reorganization. One noteworthy item, no. 66, includes the word *socialist,* probably the earliest use of that term in a song. Community, the subject with the most hymns overflows with utopian fantasies. No. 40 is typical.

[1] Community! our sole desire,
Our only end and aim!
What blissful scenes our hearts inspire,
At thy delightful name.

[3] Here, at their ease, the social band
Their lightsome labours ply;
Where roses bloom on every hand,
And songbirds carol by.

[4] Blithe health, in this elysian sphere,
With pleasure is combined;
And man's severest duty here
Is love to all mankind.

Many songs use a tired, old metaphor: the past is the night or darkness; the new system is the sun, or the dawn, or the day. But overuse makes the image trite, and it loses its persuasive power. Some texts serve as rhymed vehicles for a boring reiteration of Owen's beliefs. Both of these aspects appear in no. 130, which celebrates his New Social System.

[1] The Social System, wisdom's gift,
We hail it as the rising ray
Of welcome morn, at whose approach
The darkness changes into day.

[3] Sacred to truth! from mystery free!
On its bright banner is display'd;
Man forms not his own character,
It is for him by others made.

[4] These principles, when understood,
To man will ev'ry good ensure:
And cause him to prevent the ills
Which now he tries in vain to cure.

[5] Hail, then the social system hail!
[etc.]

Perhaps these feeble attempts at persuasion convinced someone to join the Owenites or strengthened some member's resolve, but no documentary information confirms that. In the Preface to *Social Hymns* the editor deals with the problem of hanging a text onto an established tune. He points out that very little poetry can be set to music, and even less can be adapted to the New Views.

In fact, most of the texts fail as lyrics for songs, especially songs of social reorganization. Yes, they dutifully fulfilled their obligations to the New Views, but without emotion, powerful images, or calls to action. In a movement that needed rousing words, easy to sing and remember, the book offers only bland expression and unmusical phrases. Had these ideologues only listened to the songs of the masses they hoped to lead they would have discovered the simple wisdom in an old saying, "You can't sing while you're mumbling."

The *Hopedale Collection of Hymns* comes closer to a traditional hymnal than *Social Hymns.* Adin Ballou, the Hopedale colony's leader, took many hymns from various Christian denominations, and using the customary index, he grouped them under standard subjects: devotional, repentance, Jesus Christ, prayer, contrition, and others. However, Ballou also strode forth into subjects rarely heard in churches then: the New Social State, antislavery, nonresistance. The hymns of social activism that Ballou and other members wrote represent a quarter of the more than three hundred texts. Ballou called them "well-adapted to further the great ends we were seeking to secure." Ballou had a scriptural sanction and a rationale in 1 Cor. 14:15 for mingling social and sacred tenets in a hymnal, and he put it on the title page. "I will sing with the spirit, / and I will sing with the understanding also."

The hymns from the New Social State do not dwell on utopian fantasies as much as those in the Owenite book do. Rather, they tend to express noble, ethical social values with a simple eloquence, as in no. 252.

> Ye speak of independence;
> There is no such thing on earth.
> We depend upon each other
> still for all that life is worth.
> To every mind that ponders,
> is every heart that feels.

Affective it is, but not effective enough to be a true movement song.

Brook Farm's musical mentor, John Dwight, kept his head so far in the clouds that he lost sight of the direction he and his colleagues had chosen for Association. Carried away by a new edition of Handel's *Messiah,* he urged it on readers of the *Harbinger* (January 24, 1846) as a symbol for the movement. For him "The Hallelujah Chorus" became "the voice of all humanity." It linked Associationist ideas on universal unity to an "act of worship" and Fourierism to the "prophecies of old." The world remained unmoved by his raptures.

Dwight's advocacy reflected the tastes of intellectuals oblivious to the diversity of a world they wanted to attract. As a result, they followed their own narrow inclinations when, in fact, the movement's imperatives and their own strategy cried out for breadth.

A broader appeal and a rich font of music suited for the kind of movement they wanted came their way in the Hutchinson Family Singers. This homespun musical group had enjoyed successful tours around the country with songs of social reform as well as songs of mawkish sentimentality. In their tours they performed at various colonies of the movement including Northampton and North American Phalanx, and in 1843 they visited Brook Farm. There they sang such songs of social protest as "Right Over Wrong" and "The Good Time Coming." Their repertoire and later their popular songbook included others of that kind, and they could have provided Dwight with a valuable source of songs to recommend for the movement. Unfortunately, their repertoire also included a worthless collection of banalities that surely repelled Brook Farmers. You can identify them just by glancing at titles: "Lament of the Blind Orphan Girl" and "Lament of the Widowed Inebriate." A brief excerpt from "My Mother's Bible" illustrates the point.

This book is all that's left me now,
Tears will unbidden start.
With faltering lip and throbbing brow
I press it to my heart.

The Hutchinson's songbook also has a piece by Henry Russell, a craftsman of trite, teary tunes. Dwight rejected Russell and everything related to his style in a contemptuous sneering *Harbinger* review (January 17, 1846). But the Hutchinsons did not reject Brook Farm. They found it "in full accord with our loftiest aspiration," and they left determined "to do everything in our power to prove . . . the practicability of those high ideals."[15]

Obviously, the Hutchinsons could have helped the movement. They reached a much wider audience, and they knew how to communicate with the masses. Moreover, they already had the songs to put momentum in the movement. "There's a Good Time Coming," easy to learn, has an infectious spirit that quickly gets audiences stamping, clapping, and then believing as music can do far better than speeches. This excerpt from the second stanza illustrates that quality.

[2] There's a good time coming boys,
A good time coming.
The pen shall supersede the sword,
And right not might shall be the lord
in the good time coming.
Worth not birth shall rule mankind.

The song's simplicity made it musically versatile. Moncure Conway heard the members at Modern Times treat it like an anthem. They took their seats quietly for the Sunday meeting held in the large room. An air of seriousness hung over them, and for a while no one spoke. Then spontaneously, a man and a woman began to sing "There's a Good Time Coming," and then everyone solemnly added their voices.[16]

The Hutchinson's had songs that could serve as rallying cries: "The Liberty Ball is rolling on / and with it we'll gather the free." They also had songs to unite and restore hope: "Have Faith in One Another / and the truth will triumph still." Their repertoire included settings of Thomas Hood's "Song of the Shirt" and "Bridge of Sighs." As poems, both of these Hood works stirred the Brook Farmers deeply, and Hood received extensive and serious coverage in the *Harbinger* and other movement newspapers.

So possibilities existed. These needed improvements, to be sure, but leaders made no attempt to turn to this source for songs. Dwight, surely because of his fixed values and his bias against the genre, never reviewed the Hutchinsons, not in the *Harbinger* nor in three decades of *Dwight's Journal of Music.* From here the absence of reviews looks like a shunning. In the *Harbinger*'s first issue (June 14, 1845) Dwight set the tone: "It shall be our business constantly to note and uphold for study . . . music which is deep and earnest, which does not merely seek to amuse." That walled him off from people who enjoyed other kinds of music, perhaps the very people he wanted to attract for his great new world a-coming.

On the other hand, Georgiana Bruce and other members heard ideas in the Hutchinsons that escaped the aesthetes. The popular singing group impressed her, and she wondered about their applying their talent "to a better class of music. However, they touched the hearts of the masses, and inspired moral enthusiasm in the cause of reform. . . . Who shall say this was of less importance than classical music?"[17] Reaching the essential balance between personal taste and what it takes to achieve a goal often eludes people who bury their heads in the clouds.

ICARIAN SONGS

Most of the music that can qualify as serving the movement comes from the Icarians. They more than the others imbued their culture with a strong ideological content. And sad to tell, they, unlike any of the others, had a committee to censor songs and other creative works.

The collection of Icarian papers in Iowa contains some loose music manuscript sheets, which yield many clues to the character of the colony's music. One item, a song, "Ma Commune" (My Commune), clearly differs from other music in the collection. Its neatly inscribed cover and three pages of skillfully penned music have the appearance of a ceremonial copy. The cover has a faint inscription, "New York, le 15 Mars 188–[7?]." That places it worlds away from life in the West and quite late in Icaria's life.

As you can see from page 1 in illustration 9, the poet Eugene Chatelain and the composer Charles Schütz dedicated the song to the *Communistes Icariens.* Significantly, neither Chatelain nor Schütz appears on any Icarian colony membership list. That absence confirms the impression that "Ma Commune" came from the hands of big-city sym-

9. "Ma Commune," an Icarian song, page 1. By permission of the State Historical Society of Iowa.

pathizers who probably never tasted the hunger and smelled the sweat of colony life. People of that sort, in town and out-of-touch, always try to impose their fantasies on the real world. In fact, this song does just that. Here is the first stanza (freely translated, as are all subsequent texts).

> I am the child of a commune where people are united.
> The forests, the songs: everything belongs to everyone in our domain.
> We made into firewood the fences that have separated us.
> Now men and women are equal and live in brotherhood.
>
> [Refrain]
>
> It is not like times past when only water was held in common.
> If there ever was a paradise, it is my commune.

The first stanza enunciates two Icarian ideals: community of property and fraternity, eloquently expressed through the metaphor of the fences. Subsequent verses boast that Icaria takes care of its old people and its children; it needs no soldiers, no medals nor ministers; it has no police, no thieves, and no poor. These words do enunciate the Icarian ideals, but in truth the Icarians had not escaped theft, and in Iowa they had lived not much better than the poor. The fourth verse calls the colony an "Eden," and the fifth tells us, "My domain is no fantasy, it is here on earth." But it was indeed a fantasy, because only in the imagination of the poet could Icaria be a "paradise," an "Eden." As we have seen, education, the Icarians' hope for humanity, remained an empty promise; they denied equality to women; and with all the back-breaking toil they still fell short in basic material satisfactions. Their decades of sacrifice had yielded little more than a few crude farmhouses.

The composer, with perhaps an exaggerated sense of drama for a children's song, arranged it for an elaborate chorus of six parts and a solo voice. Surely impractical for the dwindling membership in the Iowa colony, it would have been impressive at a big rally in the city. The melody has a catchy lilt, but its technical difficulties make it unlikely that the masses would walk out of the hall humming the tune. Still, it is a significant work because it is one of the few surviving examples of an original song that expresses the ideas of social reorganization.

The collection of Icarian papers also includes some loose sheets of music manuscript that appear to be the remnants of choral partbooks. Many pages are missing, but from those that remain I have been able to put together five incomplete partbooks containing eight songs arranged for a typical chorus. The titles give you an idea of the kind of songs the Icarians favored.

"La Moisson" (The Harvest).
"Chant et travail" (Sing and Work!).
"Marche des deux journées" (The Two-day March).
"Chœur des soldats *d'Oedipe*" (Soldier's Chorus from *Oedipus*).
"Les enfans de Paris" (The Children of Paris).
"Vive l'harmonie" (Long Live Harmony!).
"Le Chant du départ" (Departure Song).
"Hymne à la concorde" (Hymn to Concord).

A brief look at these sheets of music tells some surprising things about people who set out to change the world. The sheets have the well-used air of rehearsals and performances (compare illustrations 10

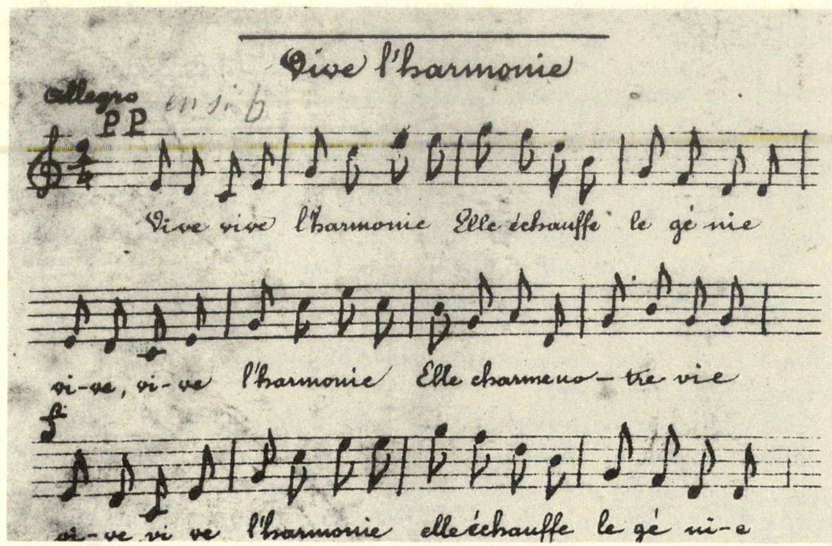

10. "Vive l'harmonie," an Icarian song. Notice the penciled instruction at the beginning: *en si. b.* By permission of the State Historical Society of Iowa.

and 11 with illustration 9). They sing of labor, fraternity, and unity. The last has special significance because of the toll that discord took in Icaria.

"The Harvest," an example of the labor song, glorifies the rewards of working in the fields. It says that through work and song we, the people, make the earth fertile. It is joyous labor. We embellish the work with our songs, and now we have blessed abundance. The melody part is missing but a transparent construction characterizes this song: one note per syllable, simple harmonies, and no complications. The melody would undoubtedly reflect this style, creating a choral setting for this song – unlike the others – that could be learned quickly by untrained singers.

"Sing and Work!" stirs with a martial cadence that comes from short syllables hammered out like a drum beat and from the repetition in its lines.

> United, we face the future,
> and brave the blows of fate.
> United, we learn to brave the blows of fate.

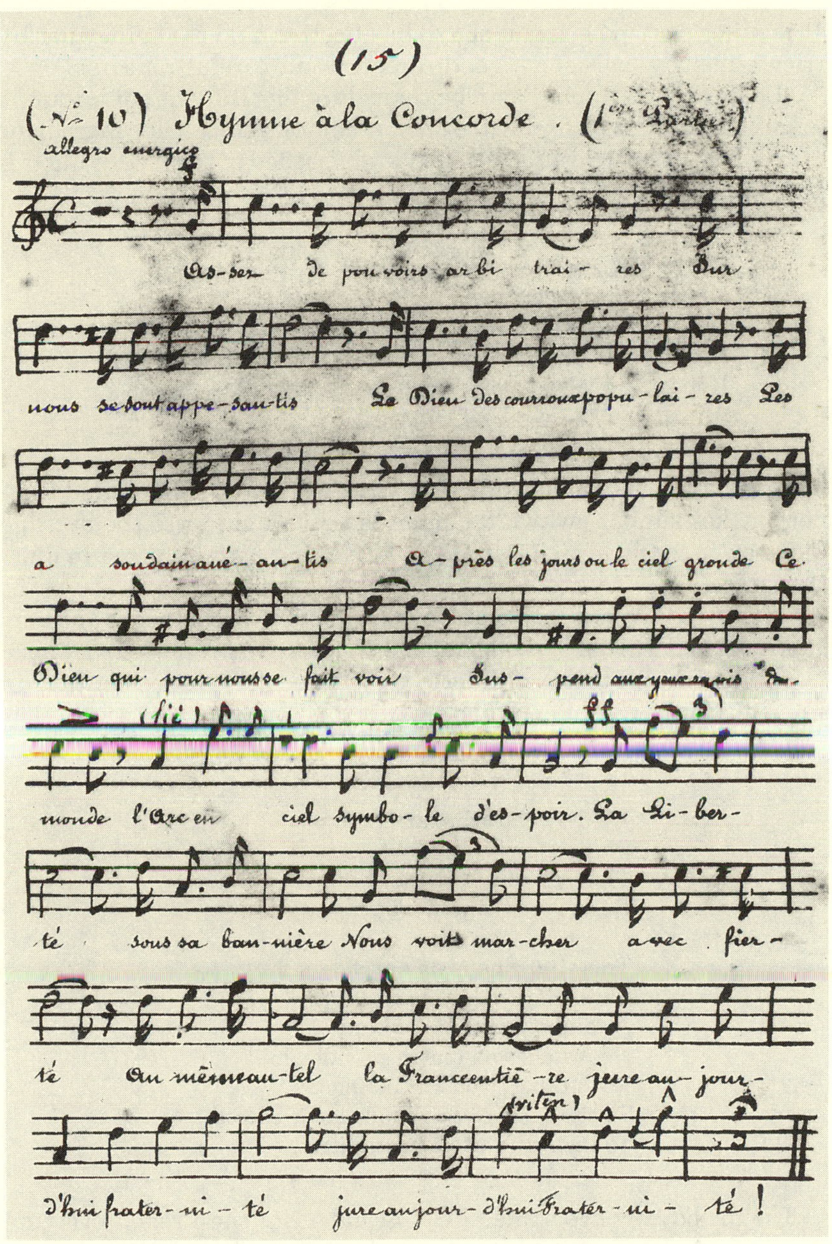

11. "Hymne à la concorde," an Icarian song. By permission of the State Historical Society of Iowa.

It requires a crisp performance to be effective, and the somewhat intricate melody calls for a good director and careful rehearsal.

"Long Live Harmony!" can be taken literally. But the song sounds more convincing as a figurative call for comradeship, a key ingredient of colony life that Icarians so desperately needed in the face of Cabet's provocative manner.

> Long live, long live harmony!
> It gives spirit to genius.
> Long live, long live harmony!
> It exalts our life.
> It inspires the poet with verses most sweet and touching.
> And its lyre enriches our songs.

The melody, spirited and wide-ranging like "The Star-Spangled Banner," makes similar awkward demands that would force the average partisan to grope for its steps. The beginning is reproduced in illustration 10.

"Hymn to Concord" has many of the qualities of a genuine anthem. It speaks in universal symbolism, and it invokes a people's God, angry at oppression, protector of liberty and fraternity. Notice that, as in so many causes throughout history, just and unjust, it presumes that God is "on our side."

> We defy the arbitrary powers
> . . . .
> The God of the people's wrath
> Destroyed them in a flash.
> . . . .
> This God who is on our side
> Showed us . . .
> A rainbow, symbol of hope.
> He watches us march proudly,
> With Liberty on our banner,
> To the same altar France holds sacred.
> To the same altar: Fraternity!

The melody evokes some of the grandeur of the French overture through its alternation of long and short notes (see illustration 11). Yet it has a simple melody, and a clear, predictable harmony that makes it easy to learn and remember. It comes close to meeting the requirements of a true movement song.

"Departure Song" could fill that need. Although not identified as such in the manuscript, I found it to be an old song dating back to the ugly wars arising out of the French Revolution. Originally published as "Hymne de guerre" (War Hymn), it later became known as "Chant du départ" (Departure Song). Several versions exist, and one of them holds a special place in the movement's history. However, the original version, the one found among these Iowa manuscripts, has aspects that fray the edges of utopian values.

Victory holds us in its spell.
We open the barrier.
Liberty guides our steps,
And from North to South
the war trumpet sounds the hour of battle.
Tremble, enemies of France!

[Refrain]

The Republic calls us!
Learn how to conquer or learn to perish!
A Frenchman must live for it!
For it, Frenchmen are ready to die!

Strange, that the Icarians could accept its implicit nationalism while preaching the oneness of all peoples. Strange too that they let its martial spirit and its bellicose allusions invade their pacifist sanctuary. There it had to make an uneasy truce with the noble slogan Cabet hung across the vast Nauvoo dining hall: No More War! Perhaps some of the choristers thought of themselves as Frenchmen first and Icarians second.

A later version has none of those contradictions. Felix Lamb, who wrote new words, changed the title significantly to "Chant de Départ Icarien" ("Icarian Departure Song"), but kept the original "Departure Song" tune. The words appeared in *Le Populaire,* the Parisian organ of the Icarians, a few days before the first contingent of Icarians sailed for the New World. As the ship got ready to depart, these pioneers of social change stood on the deck and sang the new words while the Icarians remaining in France stood on the wharf and joined in. They had other songs, but this one has a special significance.

[The Pioneers]
Arise, workers, mired in poverty!
Reveille has sounded.
Let us see the banner of sacred Community
Floating on the American shore.
No more vice! no more suffering!
No more crime! no more sorrow!
Noble Equality goes forward.
Proletarian, dry your tears.
We go to build our Icaria.
Soldiers of Fraternity,
We go to establish in Icaria
The happiness of humanity.

[Refrains]

[The Pioneers]	[Those Remaining]
Soldiers of Fraternity We go to establish in Icaria The happiness of humanity	Soldiers of Fraternity Go establish in Icaria The happiness of humanity.

As you can see, the refrain comes out of the last four lines of the verse. Both "The Pioneers" and "Those Remaining," sing refrains, but their texts differ slightly in verbs: "we go" and "go."

The printed version does not tell how the two refrains should be performed, they could be sung simultaneously or one could follow the other. Now, that is not one of those hair-splitting, academic questions because the answer takes us to the very human heart of the utopian impulse. And there we come upon an insight about people that aloof political histories never see.

The form the poet imposes on the text strongly implies sequential refrains. If the two groups sang their refrains at the same time, they would obscure the distinction between "we go" and "go." If they sang their refrains one after the other, that difference would stand out.

More than just new words, Lamb's version reaches for a grander, more striking performance. After the verse for the Pioneers, each of the next four verses introduces another role in the drama of the Pioneers, thereby heightening it. The second is "Men," third "Women," fourth "Girls," and fifth "All." Together they create a form akin to the classical French five-act drama Cabet knew and loved.

The theatrical elements suggest that this departure from France had enormous symbolism for the Icarians; after all, people embarking on an ordinary voyage would not put on a show. Decades later, when Icaria was in Iowa, old-timers often retold the story of that sailing like an ancient epic. Alexis Marchand taught his daughter Maria a version of the song when she was four years old, and she acknowledged that even decades later it still stirred her deepest emotions whenever she heard the refrain. Cabet, who considered theater the highest of the arts, understood the power of spectacle. He could see the drama in antiphonal choirs (i.e., two choruses answering each other in the tradition of great cathedral music). That magnificence would satisfy his ceremonious inclinations as the Icarians set forth on what he considered his historic mission to change the world. A dramatic send-off would not only elevate the spectacle but would also constitute a rite, something he worshiped as much as a good play.

Scene: the busy port of Le Havre on a clear spring morning. *Stage left:* the good ship *Rome,* preparing for an Atlantic crossing. *On deck:* the Icarian pioneers in handsome new uniforms, ready to take a giant step for humanity in the wilderness across the sea. *Stage right:* the wharf jammed with the Icarians remaining in France. *Background:* a multitude of sympathizers and curious townsfolk. The ship weighs anchor, excitement builds. All eyes look to the Pioneers on deck who intone the exalting verse of "Icarian Departure Song," followed by their refrain. Now Those Remaining dramatically send back their refrain from the wharf. And as the Pioneers fill the air with five verses each answered by a refrain from the wharf, the thrilling scene sends a tingle through their souls. At that moment their eyes see other scenes: a triumphant return to France; banners flying over grand Parisian plazas; brilliant skies; throngs of grateful people massed along the boulevards offering flowers and homage, cheering their noble sacrifice for humanity. What glorious victory parades must have passed through the triumphal arches of their minds that day.

Unfortunately, history makes a cold audience. It only remembers the humble log cabins in Iowa where the miseries of the real world brought the Icarians to their knees and plowed their social fantasies under in desolate prairie sod.

But the special form this music takes lets us see and feel their dreams of glory as they did. For that reason this setting of "Departure Song" holds a significant place in the history of utopianism. Yet, even as an unadorned solo song it remains an important document. Divorced from the martial allusions of the original text, it becomes the best example I have found of a true song of social reorganization. It makes a forthright call to social change, and it does so with words and images appropriate to a mass movement.

Planned Musical Activities

The Icarians organized various activities for "pleasure and diversion" soon after they moved into Nauvoo in 1849. Many members and visitors mention them. Frédéric Olinet said he belonged to a singing club. Emile Vallet, who was an Icarian during most of the Nauvoo years, called the singing group a choir. Cabet claimed the colony had concerts that featured vocal and instrumental music.[18] Did vocal music mean a little informal group singing, or did they have a real chorus that could put on programs with quality performances? The partbook fragments in the collection of Icarian papers in Iowa contain clues that help answer that question.

Technical aspects in the music suggest that they used it for a program with high standards and not for the casual amusement of a few members gathered around a parlor piano. One indication comes from the manuscript itself. Whoever copied out the parts had a professional familiarity with the conventions of notation and choral practice, as well as the repertoire. Such experienced people would understand the precision that choral performance requires and would know how to work toward it.

Moreover, the music abounds in subtleties that require plenty of rehearsal time. They include sudden changes from slow to fast; gradual increases from soft to loud; a crisp enunciation of syllables suggesting drumbeats in "The Two-Day March"; extended silences for basses; and other dramatic effects. Music such as this requires a conductor to give the cues, and one skilled enough to achieve the discipline that distinguishes choral performance from group singing.

Did the Icarians have a conductor? A short passage in one song has the French word for chorus leader, masculine form, written in the tenor part. So with those two clues we know they did have a conductor, a male one: no surprise given the status of women in Icaria.

No indication for an accompanist appears, But if you look carefully at the song in illustration 10, "Vive l'harmonie," you will notice the penciled direction "*en si b*" at the beginning. Through that means someone wanted to indicate that the song should be performed in a lower range of tones than as written (in B rather than C). Information of that kind would not mean much to a typical singer in a chorus. But it would be highly significant to a pianist working as an accompanist at a rehearsal. That tells us that this manuscript must have been used by a pianist. Obviously, the singers had to strain for the highest notes, so the director, probably an experienced musician who knew how to get the most out of an amateur chorus, told the pianist to play in the lower key. This bit of improvisation would have led to a better performance.

A similar situation appears in "Chœur des soldats *d'Oedipe*" (Soldier's Chorus from *Oedipus*). Though not otherwise identified, this turns out to be a selection from an opera, *Oedipe à Colonne* (*Oedipus at Colonus,* 1786, by a composer virtually forgotten today, Antonio Sacchini, 1730–86). The music makes stern demands and, of course, requires the powerful voices of opera professionals. However, the person who copied these Icarian manuscripts transposed the music to a range lower than that of the original. That adjustment probably made it possible for the Icarians, amateurs after all, to perform the work. And it shows again that they had a director who knew how to adapt ambition to ability.

They did have women in their chorus; convincing evidence in "The Harvest" and "Children of Paris" supports that fact. Even though the soprano parts are missing from the manuscripts, the musical construction makes it clear that these two songs require sopranos and are most effective when the characteristic quality of women's voices sing that part.

On special occasions the Icarians put on plays and musical performances. Some descriptions of these survive. For example, the fifth anniversary celebration included a "labor song" sung by a chorus of "about 15 young men." On another festive occasion, according to Cabet, a chorus of about fifty gave a program that included a "national air" and other works.[19]

What might a choral performance be like in Icaria? The eight songs in these partbooks could be the vestige of one. They have numbers, and in that order, as listed in the previous section, they appear to make up a nicely balanced program. It would take about forty minutes, and build to a moving climax. The curtain raiser puts the audience in a good mood with "The Harvest," a joyful tune for mixed chorus. The program then turns to three relatively dramatic pieces for male chorus: "Sing and Work!" (the "labor song"?), "The Two-day March," and the soldier's chorus. Contrast in mood and sound then comes with the charming, perhaps even sentimental "The Children of Paris" for mixed chorus, possibly including children. Next comes the brilliant and vigorous "Long Live Harmony!" for mixed chorus. After "Departure Song," (the "national air"?) the program ends on a peak of exhilaration, perhaps even exaltation, with the "Hymn to Concord." That would leave the audience humming the tune, clapping, and cheering with revived faith and unity.

The manuscripts give no hints of dates. But they surely belong to the Nauvoo period, the early 1850s, when as the membership lists show, the colony had enough people to form a chorus capable of responding to the musical demands in these partbooks. That would be less likely in the Iowa colony, where most of the original Nauvoo settlers quickly gave up, leaving a population that averaged only a few dozen, including children. Although the Icarians undoubtedly brought these manuscripts in the migration from Nauvoo, the long years of hardship in Iowa hushed the musical impulses evident in them.

As for the instrumental music, the evidence points towards a lesser quality of performance than that implied in the choral manuscripts. The Icarians had a band, but little information about its programs remain. François Lacour described in his journal a picnic at which the band played "military marches." Later in the afternoon the musicians "organized a dance orchestra," and everyone danced until the musicians became too tired to play. The bank often performed on holidays and at special festival banquets. On the Fourth of July they invited in their American neighbors, who left full of admiration for the Icarian musical achievements. Lacour pointed out that although the band occasionally entertained the membershp with "some pretty tunes," for the most part it played music for the theater. Cabet considered drama the greatest of the arts.[20]

How well did the band play? It is said that a U.S. Army general who visited Icaria called the band "unexcelled in the union." Of course, a brass hat may not be the most convincing credential for a critic of brass music. But, in this case we need not depend on apocryphal accounts to form a judgment.[21] Fortunately, *Colonie Icarienne* published a list of the musicians and the instruments they played (September 27, 1854). That makes it possible to develop a better idea of the band's character and an objective evaluation of its potential.

With thirty-six members, it surely impressed by size and volume; army bands at that time had only sixteen. Similar to the marching bands we now see at college games, it consisted almost entirely of wind instruments, with trumpets, trombones, tubas, and drums.

Cabet also mentioned in a letter that two violins were available "when needed." Obviously these instruments had no place in a band, but they probably played for the picnic dancing that Lacour attended.

The director, Claude Grubert, thought this combination satisfactory. Nevertheless, the list shows that it suffered from a lack of balance: too many brasses, not enough softer sounds. Moreover, the general quality of performances can be gauged from the assignment of the instruments. Assignment is the appropriate word in this case for the following reason. More than half the band members were children, average age about eleven, and they played the smaller instruments while the adults played the larger ones and the big drums. Clearly, such a distribution could not happen by chance or choice. As we saw in chapter 3, Icarians did not select occupations; the colony assigned them, and apparently the same system applied to band instruments. Director Grubert probably decided who played what. Horns make technical demands that often usher in unpredictable squawks. But their size undoubtedly made them practical for small bodies, because five horns turn up in the hands of children, average age ten. All these factors would have definitely limited the band to a rather simple kind of music, or else it would have produced the kind of sounds that make parents with ears squirm at elementary school concerts.

For a time the Icarians counted among their comrades a musician from the highest level of the profession. H. F. Albrecht, a violist and clarinetist, had been a member of the Germania Orchestra, a world-famous chamber group that toured Europe until it disbanded in 1854. Albrecht had read *Voyage en Icarie* and sympathized with Cabet's aims. As reported in *Colonie Icarienne* (October 25, 1854) he decided to join the colony in Nauvoo. Albrecht brought his sophistication, skill, and an excellent music library of 478 works. Unfortunately, he arrived just as the terrible factional fights began to dominate Icarian life. Disenchanted, Albrecht left after a year. Icaria lost his library and his musical professionalism.

Cabet sought and received gifts and donations from supporters in the United States and in France, and these may have mitigated the sacrifices the Icarians had to make for music. For example, *Colonie Icarienne* (July 10, 1854) reported that the colony had recently received four brass instruments and a couple of accordions. Partisans in Lyon sent them music notebooks. In addition, they got donations of music. But beggars could not be choosers: a shameless sympathizer in Grenoble sent a horn "in poor condition"; another contributed a flute, an instrument that was not used by French bands of the Icarian type; and another sent the music for the old concert commonplace *William Tell Overture,* a work far beyond their skills.

Still, the donations had a spiritual value that cannot be quantified. But the monetary value can be. The colony inventory for 1852, when a loaf of bread cost three cents, listed musical items at an impressive $170; the folloiwng year the total went to $278.

Some people tried to hire the Icarian musicians for functions outside the colony. In one case they were offered one hundred dollars, an enormous sum then, to play for the opening of a railroad. But the colony's English language newspaper, *Popular Tribune,* reported (February 11, 1851) that Cabet had turned all of the offers down. He declared that Icarian musicians did not perform to make money; they did so only "to promote and keep up sentiments of harmony, union, fraternity, and pleasurable satisfaction" in the colony. In a key statement reflecting his values, he pointed out that Icarian musicians "are not like ordinary musicians"; they are workers who "cannot be taken from their work for study, rehearsals, and musical performances without disorganizing our workshops and labor."

Similarly, the children musicians could give only Sundays and summers to the band. Therefore, a critical and realistic appraisal of the band needs to incorporate its relationship to colony life. In such terms, the Icarian musicians clearly made a positive contribution toward an important goal. Cabet enunciated it in the history of his experiment: they "added to the charm of colony life" and contributed to the pleasure of their meetings and fetes.[22]

The struggling Icarians in Iowa had almost none of those blessings. Maria Marchand remembered a poignant moment when that outpost experienced the exaltation that only real music can evoke. One of their teachers somehow managed through a friend to bring to the colony an Italian orchestra then on tour. For the young Icarians it turned into a revelation; never before had they heard a harp, violins, clarinets, flutes. It affected them deeply. That musical event has a tragic flip side, an incident whose irony seems so characteristic of these utopian episodes. When the Icarians moved to Iowa they found room in their covered wagons for Nauvoo's instruments. But early on, the battle to survive in Iowa left little inclination to strain for the joy music can bring. So they locked the old instruments away in a log cabin, where for over a decade they lay moldering along with the remnants of the Nauvoo library. Then in the mid-1870s a stranger arrived at the Iowa colony and began to drum up enthusiasm for organizing a band. It must have taken salesmanship to convince the members to clean up the old horns and clarinets in their spare moments and devote precious time to skirmishes with the rudiments of music. But before this program got very far their new Iowa "Music Man," certainly not a Harold Hill from River City, was exposed as a thief who had stolen the treasury of a "socialist local" in New York. With that the music program went back to subsisting mainly on hymns and old songs "contributed by each willing member." Adversity sapped the Icarians' will to continue the musical efforts that had enriched the old colony in Nauvoo.[23]

New-Harmony established regular musical activities unmatched by other experiments in social reorganization. Owenites set aside one night each week for a dance and one for a concert. In no time the *Gazette* had to publish notices in each issue (fall of 1825) saying that on those nights the doors to the Town Hall would not be opened until seven o'clock. Evidently, people were so eager for such events that they began to form crowds outside the Town Hall doors right after dinner.

What kind of performances did they have in that remote place in that era? What music did they play and what did they use for instruments? Unfortunately, nothing specific about the programs remains, and the *Gazette* never reviewed concerts. It did mention that "the regular band" performed weekly. That phrase of course implies more than one instrumental group. Other New-Harmony people also mention the "band." However, the visitor Duke Bernhard, the only eyewitness to provide details, refers to an "orchestra." He described a concert he attended. "The orchestra was not substantial. . . . In the beginning it only had a violin, bass viol, clarinet, and two flutes. Still, to my surprise, the concert was good, especially since the musicians had been together less than a year." He did not name the pieces he heard, but "concert" must have meant something other than a seated audience listening to music. As he described it, the evening probably did open with an instrumental group because the duke mentioned things that came "later." These included the clarinetist entertaining on the "Beagle Horn," a poetry reading, a singing group. During the concert everyone danced, and the evening ended with a lively cotillion.[24] That description does not sound like a concert in the usual sense, and given the modest size of the Town Hall and the space required for promenading dances, not everyone could have been seated in the traditional concert fashion. Many would have had to remain standing, but that necessity seems appropriate for the kind of event. Rather than a concert, it seems to have been more like an evening at a resort club featuring a variety show interspersed with dancing by the patrons.

To find out what kind of pieces could have been played, let's do a little musical detective work. We begin by looking for clues and find these three items to enter as evidence: exhibit A, a collection of manuscript and printed music that belonged to member Virginia Dupalais; exhibit B, Robert Dale Owen's collection of music; and exhibit C, the most important, William Pelham's oblong, music manuscript book.[25]

Like good sleuths, we keep in mind information about the people involved. Dupalais and Owen, as we have seen, both had liberal educations and cosmopolitan backgrounds. Pelham served as editor of the *Gazette* and taught in one of the colony schools. He typifies the urbane core the experiment attracted; his roots reach back to early American cultural circles. His grandfather was Peter Pelham, the colonial artist and teacher of John Singleton Copley. The manuscript book shows Pelham's knowledge of the masterpieces of music, and his access to authentic sources for copying them. Among other works it includes accurately copied excerpts from Handel's *Messiah.*

Although the music in Pelham's book is copied in ink, some pieces have a number penciled in at the top. These numbers follow no order, and have no relation to page sequence. Conductors routinely use numbers in that fashion as a performance shorthand to remind musicians about which selection comes next. But people who get together to play for their own amusement have no need for such reminders. That is our first clue.

Some items in Pelham's manuscript book also turn up in Dupalais's sheet music and in another book found in the New-Harmony collection. Our supposition that New-Harmony musicians used them for performance is reinforced by handwritten cross cues on the printed sheet music such as "No. I, Blue Book" and "White book, II." Unfortunately, the Blue and the White books may no longer exist. One of the Robert Dale Owen partbooks contains this note: "These two last tunes has got no parts in the other books you will therefore not number them." The phrase "in the other books" proves that others existed although we now only have two. Further proof that these collections do have performance links comes from associating some technical oddities that appear in each of the parts.

All of these clues come out of a surprising collection. At a time when most Old World culture had not yet found its way to the frontier, these collections provided the colony with a taste of the European opera and concert repertoire. Famous names abound: Handel, Haydn, Mozart, and others. Like good detectives, we would suspect forgeries with boasting like that, and we would be right. But many turn out to be genuine and readily identifiable. These include "Haydn's Surprise" (variations from his G Major Symphony), and "Handel's Water Piece" (from the third suite of his *Water Music*). One collection has popular airs from the *Magic Flute* arranged for flutes. The true heritage of a few works claiming no famous name can also be certified. For example, one piece for instruments turns out to be an arrangement of a Mozart vocal duet. Arias with the text, particularly from Rossini's operas, suggest that New-Harmony had vocal performances too.

Nevertheless, all of these pieces, appropriate for concerts in the traditional sense, add up to a small minority of the total. The rest, the vast majority, consists of dance music and marches. For example, Robert Dale Owen's partbooks contain mostly jigs and other dances, many appropriate for what we now call square dancing. He admitted that like most other young people in the colony, he was "passionately fond of dancing."

That takes our musical detective work onto a new trail. Knowing what kind of instruments they had can help answer a crucial question: what function did music serve in New-Harmony? After arriving in the colony, Pelham copied some marches into his book that require instruments whose names he omitted. In "Bassoon Quick March" the lowest part looks just right for a bassoon, but some passages in it require two performers. Therefore, New-Harmony must have had another bassoon or some other instrument covering the same range. In fact one page has a penciled-in cross cue: "Basso p. 32," which must refer to another book, probably lost. What instrument could that signal refer to?

The museum in present-day New Harmony has a collection of old musical instruments. When I saw them stored away in its dark attic, several appeared to date from Owen's time. One of them, an old metal horn, ancestor of our modern tuba, answers the question about the other bass perfectly. And sitting near it, an old glockenspiel with its rows of metal bars gathering dust, might provide another clue to the character of New-Harmony music. When we think of its high, sparkling, metallic, jingle, we think of parades and marching bands.

Other clues turn up in the remaining music books. For example, one flute part alerts the player to a horn solo, and another tells the flutist to play together with the piccolo. Yet neither horn nor piccolo parts can be found in any of the New-Harmony archives. In another book someone used a blank back page to write a scale with a number for each note. The numbers obviously represent the trombone slide positions and that clue suggests that New-Harmony may have had one of those instruments. Finally, an entry in a New-Harmony ledger under the "Public Amusements" account shows one dollar for a trumpet mouthpiece, so the colony must have had at least one of the high brasses, too. When you have trombones and trumpets you can create loud music.

As the list grows, a larger combination than the one the duke described at the evening entertainment begins to take shape. It differs markedly in character and in volume. All of these instruments deduced from the evidence would have been suitable for outdoor music, more specifically for a military-type band.

A military band in a utopian colony? That sounds like a strident contradiction. But, in fact, New-Harmony had its own militia from the start. It included a company of infantry, one of artillery, and a corps of riflemen: 250 men in all. They paraded and appeared with the band on ceremonial occasions. The *Gazette* (November 23, 1825) describes a "Military Ball" given by the Light Infantry Company "in full uniform" in the Town Hall. For a Masonic installation the light infantry led the procession through the colony, and the riflemen brought up the rear. According to the *Gazette* (November 19, 1825), the band supplied "appropriate airs."

Why the martial emphasis when Owen preached nonviolence? Owen, who believed the New Social System had to reshape human character and suppress individualism, saw in highly ordered rhythmic activities such as marching and structured group dances a way to inculcate discipline. In New Lanark, his great industrial achievement in Scotland, he had tried it in the schools he had established for his workers. Owen applied this educational concept in New-Harmony; pupils learned the orderly patterns of group dances, and teachers put them through "military evolutions." Miner Kellogg recalled that experienced military men drilled the boys in "squads" and that in going from one activity to another, they had to march to the beat of drums "in a prescribed and military manner."[26]

No other experiment in social reorganization, not even Icaria, undertook such militaristic activities. Most would have recoiled in horror at the very thought of them. From Hopedale's Practical Christians, who followed Jesus' precept of turning the other cheek, to the freethinkers of Modern Times, war and everything associated with it, that is, militarism, killing, and particularly regimentation, all belonged to the past, to the cruel, evil ways of the society they wanted to replace.

Our detective work done, we can now present our case. The regimental aspects of Owen's social philosophy give greater weight to a band than to an orchestra, to a wind group that could serve for military parades and dancing. Most of the surviving music meets that need. Based on the evidence in that music and in the museum's instruments, the band would have had a piccolo, flutes, clarinet, and trumpet for the higher registers; horns for the middle; and bassoons for the low notes, together with a tubalike instrument and possibly a trombone. The drums Kellogg mentioned would provide the beat. Such an ensemble would sound like a military-style marching band. We might add to that combination the old glockenspiel stored in the museum's attic, but it is not certain that it came from the time of Owen's experiment. If that were determined to be the case it would simply make an even more convincing argument for a military band.

That group of about fifteen, though unbalanced and not dazzling, could produce a sound boisterous enough for outdoor spectacles. That undoubtedly would be the "regular band" the *Gazette* mentioned. Based on the evidence in the same body of music, the "orchestra" the duke described would perform music from the recent European repertoire, but only occasionally.

Unlike all other experiments in social reorganization, the New-Harmony ledgers show actual expenditures for things musical: "7 Music books, $5.25," the trumpet mouthpiece, and others. One entry shows a payment to Josiah Warren of $14.69 for "Sundry articles relating to Music." Warren, the renaissance man who later became the mentor of Modern Times, had the responsibility of the musical performances. Robert Dale Owen characterized him as an excellent leader and his performances as "much beyond what I expected in the backwoods."[27] A lucky find, Warren represents a key ingredient of colony life, and one that tragically few leaders of the movement planned for or even thought about.

Although other details of New-Harmony's musical life have not survived, enough remains to reveal two discordant trends. Owen saw in music a means to suppress individualism through regimented exercises, which he used to foster uniformity and conformity. The band provided music for military parades and for a type of restrained group dancing. But the large number of jigs, waltzes, and other free-spirited dances in the music collections defy the restricted confines of Owen's plan. They suggest that no matter what Owen had in mind for them, the members meant to have a good time. These musical cross-purposes surely introduced yet another sour note into the taps that would ultimately sound for this experiment.

Brook Farmers had more music than any other experiment in the movement. Yet they never organized an orchestra, a band, or other instrumental group. The criticism John Dwight wrote for the *Harbinger* provides a good source of clues to their musical life. Dwight, an excellent pianist, reviewed the publication of well over one hundred musical works while at Brook Farm, and the review copies wound up in the music rooms of the colony and ultimately in their performances. In that way they became part of a repertoire that we can easily characterize. With one exception, this body of music contains only vocal or piano pieces and therefore, as we might expect, Brook Farm music consisted almost exclusively of selections from these two categories. Letters and reminiscences of Brook Farmers name compositions performed in the colony, and those documents confirm our conclusion.

Obviously, the realities of life in the colonies of social reorganization should have always favored vocal or piano music over orchestras and bands. But the Brook Farmers' musical repertoire, which avoided the problems and cost of developing a large ensemble, derives from their particular circumstances. Their choice relates directly to the larger question of where an experiment ought to be located, a subject few utopians thought about.

Brook Farm's location on the outskirts of a great city, unique in the movement, placed the experiment within walking distance of incomparable cultural advantages. Members in the New Jersey experiments, North American Phalanx and Raritan Bay Union, could almost manage a one-day visit to a great cultural center, New York City, but the trip by stage coach, railroad, and ferry would have left only a few midday hours in town. Those in western experiments, of course, had no such opportunities. Brook Farmers, however, had the nation's best orchestra virtually at their doorstep. This enabled them to adopt an efficient, twofold strategy for satisfying their musical appetites. For vocal or piano music they created fine performances at home, and they could do that without straining the always meager resources all utopians suffered. For orchestral concerts and other fine performances, something no colony could hope to emulate at home, they went to Boston.

They usually walked the eight or so miles to downtown Boston as a group, undeterred even by snow. Returning late at night tired but inspired, they vigorously dissected the concert all the way home. Brook Farmers approached music with the same intensity as literature. For example, in 1844 world-famous virtuoso Ole Bull, the Norwegian violinist, toured the United States, and a large contingent of Brook Farmers walked to his concert. He overwhelmed them with Paganini's difficult, flamboyant *Carnival of Venice,* and its fireworks lit up their discussion on the long walk home and for months after. Marianne Dwight sided with the glowing review in the *Boston Courier.*[28] But her brother John threw cold water on the showy music, and it spilled over into two of his reviews (June 28, and November 1, 1845). Both tell something special about him as the movement's musical mentor: in the first review he was not above prejudice; in the second: he knew how to apply utopian beliefs to music.

Lured by romantic notions, Dwight in his criticism sometimes wandered off into positions that countered the movement. In the first review such notions led him into a fallacy that belittled the *Courier*'s reviewer, Lydia Child, friend of the movement and a friend of his, a strong and courageous champion of social progress in her own right. His assertion: she responds to Ole Bull not as an objective critic but as a kindred soul. So "she writes what she feels, and feels it because she cannot help it." Dwight's criticism usually keeps to a higher level, often marked by keen aesthetic insights. He grounds these in a social context that allows him to link art, Fourier, and the utopian future.

The second Ole Bull concert, according to Dwight, attracted a smaller audience because the novelty had dissipated and enthusiasm is "more for novelties . . . than for Art." Virtuosos such as Ole Bull, he contends, bring in crowds who want only a display of individual prowess. This intense individualism is a trend of the times and the mark of a society in decay. Virtuosos are part of that society. They cannot play together; each must stand alone. But in the New Social Order where unity reigns and each great musician contributes to a joint effort, there we shall have orchestras of genius. And there, he concludes in a visionary synthesis, "society itself shall be music." A Fourier purist might have argued that storming the barricades of individualism should be left to Owen, because the Phalanx existed (as an idea) to protect a personality type, an Ole Bull, for example, who found the display of individual skill an attractive form of work.

If virtuosos gnawed at Brook Farm values, musical and social, Beethoven steeled their fundamental beliefs about art and society. His symphonies, of which they had ample hearings, became significant experiences for them. Dwight saw a clear relationship between the advent of Beethoven's Fifth Symphony in Boston and the birth of the Brook Farm idea. "It was to a great extent the young souls drawn to 'Transcendentalism' . . . who were most drawn also to the great, deep music which we began to hear at that time. For be it remembered, the first great awakening of the musical interest here was when the [Fifth] Symphony of Beethoven was played."[29] Brook Farmers, passionate about social meaning in the arts, heard a prime example in the Fifth Symphony. Undoubtedly, they interpreted the triumphal ending that rises out of the somber third movement as their own story, their own hope of overcoming fate.

No better example of their conviction occurs than in Dwight's review of the Ninth Symphony (June 13, 1846). At a desperate time for the experiment, his words echoed members' innermost feelings. "We went away physically exhausted by the excitement of listening to so great a work, but unspeakably confirmed in our highest faith. The Symphony had actually lifted the leaden cloud which weighed upon us for days. . . . The sins and follies of Humanity are apparently coming to a crisis. The battle will be closely fought . . . between the powers of darkness and Light. But we trust our own hearts and God's word and the Symphony that Light will prevail."

Clearly, the availability of such experiences outside the colony belongs to Brook Farm's history just as Icaria's and New-Harmony's ensemble music does to theirs. Brook Farmers did without the homegrown variety, but their unique location enabled them to hear the best and to avoid the sacrifice and frustration the others endured.

Brook Farmers enjoyed a musical world within the colony. The Aerie, the house on the hill where they held many events, became a home for piano music, for Mendelssohn and the sonatas of Mozart and Beethoven. There the Brook Farmers also heard technically demanding piano transcriptions from modern operas including those of Bellini and Weber. They could do that because they had excellent pianists among the membership and the stream of regular visitors. John Dwight's talent is well-known, of course; but, for example, they also had his sister Fanny, a fine pianist in her own right, and Harriet Graupner (1829–95), daughter of renowned Johann Christian Graupner, oboist in Haydn's London orchestra and a key figure in the development of the symphony orchestra in America. She visited the colony frequently, performed there often, and went on to become one of America's foremost pianists. Moreover, visiting musicians brought in significant, new repertoire. For example, a Norwegian pianist, Sophy Jertz, performed there in 1844 and gave the Brook Farmers an opportunity to hear a recent work by Schumann, *Carnaval*.[30] Such performances confirm that Brook Farmers knew the latest in German Romanticism, a significant fact because its spirit pervaded not only the poetry and the other literature they loved but even the way they lived their lives.

Vocal music was the mainstay of their programs. They heard a wide range, from opera scenes to oratorios, from "Wood Robin" to Beethoven's "Adelaide." As with pianists, Brook Farm had excellent singers available among the membership and among the frequent visitors from Boston. John Dwight conducted the singing groups and headed the unit that planned and provided entertainment during the early Phalanx period. John Sears remembered that Dwight always had a musical program in reserve that could be brought forward on short notice. For these he often depended on the soprano Mary Bullard, his future wife. John Codman recalled her program of Schubert, their favorite among the German Romantics. It included "Ave Maria," "Serenade," "Elegy," and "The Wanderer." Codman remembered another evening when George Curtis sang such popular songs as "Kathleen Mavourneen," "Good Night to Julia," and "Erl King." That performance also made a lasting impression on Georgiana Bruce. Decades later she still recalled how "Erl King" had affected her with its "mysterious and awe inspiring piano accompaniment."

Bruce's reminiscences include a revealing description of a colony performance. When she arrived the concert had already begun. "We went up the steps [of the Aerie] with caution lest a note of the melody that floated through the open French windows should be lost to us. It was surprising that, entering the high room, we found not only the chairs and sofas occupied, but the floor well-covered with seated listeners whose stillness left the singer ignorant of their presence." During the performance she turned around and noticed young people – most of the audience – holding hands, "lost in a dream of bliss."[31]

Dwight organized singing groups in the colony, somewhat similar to the glee clubs found in our high schools. In fact, the groups did sing glees, a kind of short, simple piece for two or three parts. Many Brook Farmers mention the glees of John Callcott (1766–1821) as being very popular among the members, and several of the anthologies favored by them contain his music. For example, Annie Salisbury, an early member, said she used *The Boston School Song Book,* "a sweet collection." Its well-known Callcott glee, "The Might with the Right," seems remarkably attuned to the Brook Farm credo. The Modern Timers also favored this glee and sang it like a hymn.

> Let good men ne'er of truth despair,
> Though humble efforts fail;
> Oh! give not o'er until once more
> The righteous cause prevail.
> In vain, and long, enduring wrong,
> The weak may strive against the strong.
>
> But the day shall yet appear,
> When the might with the right
> and the truth shall be.
> And come what there may
> To stand in the way
> That day the world shall see.

Another anthology, the *Boston Glee Book,* gave Brook Farmers many more Callcott glees, a selection of rounds, a happy form for these utopians who liked to burst into song at any moment, and most notably, several well-known songs from the late Renaissance, including Morley's "Now Is the Month of Maying."[32] But that lively, ever-popular tune falls on hard times in this edition because of a stuffy, nineteenth-century adaptation. Otherwise unimportant, the existence of this expurgated Morley becomes significant in the story of Brook Farm for what it tells of a facet of colony life not strictly musical. The original Morley, which throbs with spring's fertility and the joy of youth, would have unleashed a salvo of gossip from the colony's puritan neighbors, who often accused the happy young Brook Farmers of loose morals. However, prying eyes could have seen little ammunition in the *Boston Glee Book* adaptation, one that betrays the heavy hand of an editor turned censor. The songbook's preface assured proper Bostonians that "Bacchanalian subjects have been, of course, excluded as inconsistent both with correct moral principles and public opinion." So the editor put a drape over Morley's earthiness and laced the form into a tight Victorian girdle that squeezed in its Renaissance verve.

Fortunately for the Brook Farmers, they also had authentic music to enrich their lives. They found it in a favorite three-volume anthology they referred to informally as "Kingsley's Choir."[33] Actually titled *The Social Choir,* the collection contains well over two hundred compositions of all types except sacred. The Brook Farmers might have been partial to this anthology because it included Dwight's translation of a Goethe song. But inexplicably, none of Dwight's many music reviews mention Kingsley's work. Still, it remains an important artifact of Brook Farm life.

Unlike many anthologies of the period that filled pages with spurious works, everything in *The Social Choir* appears to be genuine. The selections make greater demands on singers, and several are quite long, particularly the excerpts from recent European operas. Moreover, almost all have piano parts, which – unlike the usual oom-pah-pah variety that debased anthologies of that era – make a valid contribution to drama or mood. Brook Farm certainly had the pianists who could handle those technical difficulties. A scene from the perennial favorite *William Tell* exemplifies these aspects. It calls for a level of professionalism that, among the experiments dedicated to social reorganization, only Brook Farm could muster. Its political message and its romantic strain surely harmonized with their beliefs.

Reminiscences name other opera scenes produced there that appear in *The Social Choir.* John Codman remembered a performance of excerpts from Rossini's *Moses in Egypt.* John Sears tells of scenes from several Parisian hits of the 1830s performed with all the parts and full chorus. For these performances the dining room in the Hive, the main house, became the Brook Farm opera house. They needed the dining room because these scenes required more space than they had in their usual concert room in the Aerie. Sears also said they presented an entire oratorio, Mendelssohn's *St. Paul,* "the most ambitious performance in my time" at Brook Farm. They gave it twice and invited the public. However, for this they needed the spaciousness of a natural amphitheater located in a pine grove, a hallowed spot for all Brook Farmers.[34] You can still make out the place as you walk toward the Charles River from the remains of the Hive in the cemetery that took the place where the Brook Farm spirit once lived.

Dissonance in Music

Musical life at Brook Farm included the Catholic mass. The significance of that fact has less to do with music, and more with a tendency for the utopians to confuse their goals. In an experiment that shied away from what members called religious forms, the link with prescribed observances had a negative effect on daily life and ultimately on the experiment itself.

Among the composers of masses heard there, Mozart was the favorite. Georgiana Bruce remembered two specific works, which she referred to as "Mozart's Seventh and Twelfth Masses." John Codman also recalled singing these same works and said they used a recent anthology published in London. Undoubtedly, that was the edition Dwight had ecstatically reviewed in the *Harbinger* (August 23, 1845). The review advised the movement, "Get a little company of four, eight, or twelve voices to join . . . in the magnificent [Mozart] Twelfth Mass. . . . In no way can you get better study or deeper communion." And with that, Dwight began to champion the work. His Brook Farm chorus sang it in Boston at the inception of the Religious Union of Associationists, and he directed them in it again at the Fourier birthday celebration. In preparation, Dwight had worked with the Brook Farmers on the Kyrie, Gloria, and Agnus Dei until, as John Codman said, "they became as familiar to us as household words."[35]

Some did not share in the enthusiasm. For example, Arthur Sumner (nephew of Senator Charles Sumner) recalled that they "sang Kyrie Eleison night and day. It seemed to me they sang it rather too often." And even Dwight felt it necessary, then and in later years, to justify singing masses as a part of movement functions, something he had not done for any other genre of music. An example shows in his *Harbinger* response (June 19, 1847) to criticism in the *American Review* (May 1847) that chided him for bringing the mass into a meeting of the Religious Union of Associationists. Dwight argued that the critic had seized on the mass with Latin text as a formally adopted rite and so had linked Dwight with "the establishment." Dwight denied it. All that his singers wanted was good music, no matter where it came from. "The taste and experience of the choir led them . . . [to] these Masses, because the music seemed to them so warm, so reverent, so beautifully expressive of the heart's best aspirations, and of the true religion." They had no objection to the Latin words, he continued, because the words are "beautiful and true," and simplicity makes them musical, whereas the ordinary practice of singing long didactic poems to psalm tunes is incongruous. Then, half a century later, when Brook Farm had long been laid to rest, Codman revived a defense of Dwight's position in his memoirs. He asked his readers, Do you think it strange that these "radical thinkers" and protesters against the religious establishment would take up the music of "a profoundly conservative church"? Codman answered no, because "having freed their minds from sectarian prejudices, they recognized beauty and genius wherever found, and did not care what church or creed they had served."[36]

But the experiment's founders, clergymen themselves, saw the threat of doctrinal disputes lurking in forms that served established churches and creeds. So they intended to keep the colony free of rituals associated with any denomination.

Dwight tried to minimize the religious component of the mass; still it crept into his advocacy of it. His enthusiastic *Harbinger* review spoke ambiguously of the "deeper communion" the mass can bring. And his reply to the *American Review* critique compared the mass with "the ordinary practice of singing a long didactic poem to a psalm tune." But he glossed over the clear relationship between such singing and worship. Moreover, he suppressed an important detail: the mass at the meeting of the Religious Union of Associationists had, in fact, been part of a religious rite albeit not Catholic. Rev. William Henry Channing directed a communion service at that meeting. He substituted water for the wine – the alcohol taboo – but the ritual and its symbols, which Brook Farmers had always shunned, stood out.[37] Finally, Dwight's claim that the choir selected the music seems disingenuous; his ideas on music carried the force of authority throughout the movement. Everyone looked to him for guidance. He studied the music; he reviewed it; he made the choices.

The historical significance of these events stems from the fact that a few zealots led by Rev. William Henry Channing had intensified their efforts during this period to impose a formal religious life on the tolerant Brook Farmers. Channing, a movement gadabout but never a member of Brook Farm, a talker in a cause that needed doers, tried to thrust his own evangelical visions on this experiment in social reorganization. He warned them that "without the religious element no attempt at association could possibly succeed," and he pressed them to build a "temple of worship" in Brook Farm. Finally, on Sunday, October 19, 1845, he violated the Brook Farm Articles of Association and other fundamental documents that expressly prohibited any "religious test." He urged those who favored his religious plan for Brook Farm to follow him into the next room and join hands in a circle. Not everyone went along with his divisive move. So now the experiment added a schism as one more burden to carry to its grave.

Years later Channing admitted, "My heart was set on quite another movement." He wanted to "organize and embody a living Church" in the system of Association. Perhaps the Brook Farmers did not see where his zeal would lead. Marianne Dwight, present at the crucial events, said Channing would not be considered a priest; "we do not want a priest." However, she said that they would now have "services," and that these would include music. But "most carefully" she affirmed, "will we guard against sectarianism and against dead forms."[38] In the midst of that period of turmoil her brother John studied the new edition from London and began teaching his singers the masses it contained.

Given this volatile situation, links to the rites of the religious establishment raised fears that the experiment would be led down a road into the past. Marx Lazarus, an early and dedicated Jewish Brook Farmer who left the colony but continued to aid the movement, wrote to a key supporter of Association, James Fisher, about Channing. Characterizing Channing as simplistic, Lazarus warned that his revivalist impulses countered "the spirit of our movement," and "did not inspire to spade work."[39]

Clearly, in this context Dwight's long-range focus must have blurred his view of short-range practical consequences. He introduced music that, in a quiet way, could have enriched the musical life of the colony. But his emphasis turned up the volume and amplified the voices of schism. And because other leaders did not question that emphasis for its potentially adverse effects, they too allowed it to contribute its own tiny but insidious dissonance to other noises disturbing the experiment. With a decibel here and a decibel there, the discord soon became painful.

This utopian episode, like many of the movement's efforts, has its ironic twist. It involves the two masses for which Dwight proselytized, works he called the product of one of the greatest musical minds. Those two works, the so-called Mozart Seventh and Twelfth Masses, turn out to be forgeries, probably the product of a couple of second-rate musicians known only to avid readers of musicological footnotes.

Another example of this secular movement's thoughtless sanction of sacred interests through music surfaces during the decline of North American Phalanx. Little is known about the colony's musical life; I found only one primary document related to the subject. Yet that document, a manuscript, shows how music can open a window on utopian history. It discloses misguided leadership that allowed irrelevant, sectarian agendas to weaken a united effort. And it reveals Channing as misreading the goals of social reorganization at North American Phalanx as he had done at Brook Farm before it succumbed. Moreover, the manuscript supports the contention of Charles Sears, a president of North American, that the sectarian efforts of a few zealots split a membership whose religious views he characterized as liberal.[40]

The document has a portentous historical context: it comes from the inaugural dinner for North American Phalanx's new hall in 1851. Not long after that, persevering zealots finally succeeded in taking their splinter group out of the Phalanx to create Raritan Bay Union, a new colony that had an establishment of religion in its organizing principles. The split left a gaping wound in the original colony that festered until the end.

The document is a handwritten menu from the inaugural dinner. It also lists the evening's program as follows: 1. Opening hymn; 2. Channing prayer; 3. Channing speech; 4. Closing hymn. It includes the texts for both hymns, which not only express traditional ideas of Sin and Salvation, but capitalize both words. In the movement for social reorganization, the words *sin* and *salvation* are rare indeed and almost never capitalized. The hymns contrast sharply with Fourier's ideas on the social source of evil and on the need to end evil through social change. The opening hymn, "Thy Kingdom Come," concludes, "Righteousness . . . makes an end of Sin." However, Fourier saw iniquity not in people but in a social order that went against human nature. Therefore, he had no concern with sin and righteousness. In the closing hymn the gates of Salvation obviously do not open into a Phalanx.

> Hear what God the Lord have spoken,
> O my people faint and few.
> Comfortless, afflicted, broken;
> Fair abodes I build for you.
> Scenes of heartfelt tribulation,
> Shall no more perplex your ways;
> You shall name your walls Salvation,
> And your gates shall all be praise.

The question here is not about religion. Rather, the question is, How should a movement with nontraditional ideas and a universal goal represent itself honestly and effectively before its members and before the world it wants to win? That inaugural dinner program, in which music contradicted an essential tenet of the movement, does not seem like the right answer. It could only sow confusion in a membership already weak in its doctrines and encourage zealots pushing their own agenda to the detriment of the movement's goal, social reorganization.

If they had other music at the inaugural dinner no one took the trouble to note that fact. The *New York Tribune* printed a detailed, two-column story (May 12, 1851), which mentioned music only once. "After appropriate music [the opening hymn], reading of the Scripture, and prayer, the dedicatory address was delivered by William H. Channing." It might have been fitting at the dedication of a new hall to perform music more closely associated with the movement's goals or to explain Fourier's ideas on the role of opera in a Phalanx or on the importance of instruments and lessons there. But these hymns in this colony of that time bear witness to leadership and membership so ignorant of the doctrines they supposedly believed in that they let people with a different goal take over their movement.

All of this shows how music could affect life in and the life of these experiments. It brought joy to some of them, as it should, and as utopian speculations promised. But this most natural, most human form of expression sometimes embroiled gentle utopians in unnatural, inhuman conflicts. In some places music took a heavy sacrifice for its pleasures, and in others it became distorted under conflicting doctrines. Here again, the complex tendencies and counter-trends that the hunger for music generated in the movement argue against simple interpretations of its history.

Life in Words

THE BURDENS OF PUTTING TOGETHER a colony that satisfied the utopian ideals would seem to be daunting enough for most people. But these social experimenters gave themselves yet another handicap: they published newspapers. The movement had at least two dozen, and most hold surprising clues to the early end of the utopian dream. They also give us unexpected insights into colony life.

Why did these fledgling societies need their own newspapers? The first issue of the *New-Harmony Gazette* (October 1, 1825) said it wanted nothing more than to tell the world Owen's principles because people suffer from ignorance, not inherent vice. But after a year's experience in trying to change society the editors decided that they would need a more provocative tactic. Otherwise, "the human mind would continue to be occupied with superstition, trade, and politics . . . with pompous nothings. It is surely high time that the lethargy in which . . . the rational faculties . . . have been held, should terminate" (October 4, 1826).

The Brook Farmers said they needed a newspaper "to aid us in our progress towards the truth and beauty, the possession of which is the ultimate destiny of mankind." The first issue of the *Harbinger* (June 14, 1845) set the goal: to examine all questions in politics, literature, the fine arts, and most of all "Social Reform" in order to find "the whole truth." Four issues later the editors justified this effort as essential "to us whose especial office it is to watch everything that bears upon the movement of society."

Integral Phalanx planned its newspaper, *Ploughshare and Pruning-hook,* as soon as the members bought their land, before they even put a plough to the earth or pruned a tree. Their object: "to study truth as a science."

News and Propaganda

Obviously then, most of the movement's newspapers were not *news* papers. In fact, they offered little on world events and even less on their own colonies. They functioned primarily as organs of propaganda.

The propaganda hammered away on two points: the colony's condition is sound, and the plan has proven itself in practice. Items develop around four topics: (1) the old society – poverty, ignorance, waste, etc.; (2) the promise – visions of life in the new society; (3) the doctrine – explanations of the underlying principles; and (4) the practice – generalizations on how to build utopian colonies. The articles in an issue of *Ploughshare and Pruninghook* (February 15, 1846), provide a clear example of how these four topics generated the content of a newspaper devoted to propaganda.

Article	*Topic*
"Economy of Association"	the doctrine
"Mode of Living in Association"	the promise
"The Integral Phalanx"	the practice
"Fifth Period, or Civilization"	the old society
"Infidelity in Association"	the doctrine
"How a Phalanx May Be Developed"	the practice
"What Is Association?"	the promise
"Property Rights in Association"	the doctrine
"Women in Association"	the promise
"Our Third Number"	the practice
"Government of the United States"	the doctrine

The propaganda often hides behind a literary disguise, lurking between the lines of fiction, arts criticism, and in poems. Mostly, it strides forth directly from editorial and essays.

Even when an item about life in the colony does appear in one of these newspapers, it contains no hint of problems and no rumblings of discord. So to an unknowing world outside everything seems fine; the members have seen the future, and it works. This applies to all the newspapers of the movement's Owenite and Associationist phases, most notably New-Harmony's *Gazette* and Brook Farm's *Harbinger* and to a lesser extent those published by the Icarians.

The *Gazette* provides the egregious example. William Pelham, one of the editors, writing his son shortly after it began publishing, admitted that "news is a secondary objective, the first being to disseminate a correct knowledge of the principles, practice, and local affairs of the Society."[1] But, in fact, you need patience and strong eyes to spot a word or two on "local affairs" in the *Gazette*'s densely packed pages. When Owen returned to New-Harmony from abroad in January 1826, he abruptly decided to make a revolutionary change in the basic principle of the experiment. Yet no inkling of his intentions and no reports of crucial meetings and discussions that preceded this fundamental shift appeared in the *Gazette.* The information might have been known to the few who had access to the handwritten minutes of the committee that drafted the new constitution. But all that the rest of the world knew came from two brief sentences in the *Gazette* (February 8). They mention the adoption of a new constitution and promise an abstract of the convention proceedings in the next issue. The text of the constitution did appear there as promised, but not one word of the proceedings, none of the debate or the thought that created this momentous and controversial upheaval ever found its way into the *Gazette.*

Moreover, for almost the entire life of the experiment none of the serious ferment and factional strife within the colony got through to the *Gazette*'s readers. So when a four-column article about discord finally did break onto the editorial page a year later, its ominous implications must have shocked outside supporters. How could they have suspected such a situation from a reading of earlier issues? Occasionally, Owen himself would comment on "local affairs" in the *Gazette,* but always in such benign and optimistic terms that a distant subscriber could never doubt both the wisdom of his social ideas and their vindication in New-Harmony. What else could outsiders think after reading these words from a lengthy first-anniversary article (May 23, 1826)? "In one short year the mass of confusion, and in many cases, of bad and irregular habits, have been formed into a community of mutual cooperation and equality." And if that did not convince them, he concluded with a startling announcement that ought to have reverberated more than the shot heard round the world. "The friends of the system everywhere may rejoice and be exceeding glad, for they may be assured that the deliverance from poverty and ignorance, and the oppression of riches is at hand."

Similar fantasies by others appeared in the *Gazette* during the life of the experiment. For example, in the midst of an extreme crisis, in a time of rampant discord and disorder, the editors painted this typical, rosy picture (October 11, 1826). But, as a skeptic can see with eyes born of hindsight, the Pollyanna spirit does not quite hide the serious problems that peer out between the lines.

> For several weeks past the steady progress in good habits and substantial improvement among the younger part of the population has been obvious to everyone. . . . They are punctual in their attendance upon the lectures, and take an extraordinary interest in them. . . . They have abandoned . . . their wild irrational mode of conduct; they are now seldom heard to swear or seen engaged in quarrels. . . . The parents have also made a considerable advance in temperance and industry. There are but two or three among the whole population who are seen occasionally to trespass against the former virtue.

Even if this assumed confidence had any propaganda value outside the colony, the *Gazette* must have paid a heavy price in credibility among the colony residents. Sarah Pears, a member, wrote to her aunt in Pittsburgh, a *Gazette* subscriber, not to believe "the lies" they printed about happiness and contentment. The Associationist press, two decades down the utopian road, blundered into the same dead end. Elijah Grant, president of the Ohio Phalanx, wrote to Horace Greeley that he was "pained" because "no reliance can be placed upon the published accounts of the various associations" in the movement's newspapers. He charged that they started with a bit of truth and expanded it into what he called "fancy sketches," barely above the level of "fables."[2]

The *Harbinger* contained that kind of distorting optimism, and ironically its first number carried such an article about Ohio Phalanx. "The affairs of that Association wear a very promising aspect," it reported, "and there can be no reasonable doubt of its success." But its editors and Associationist leaders knew full well from Grant's letters to them that the Ohio Phalanx lay on its deathbed. When the end came a few weeks later, it could not have been a surprise to them. The *Harbinger* editors had promised "the whole truth," but they printed reports about Associations in which facts and hopes mingle without distinction. That defect proved to be destructive in two ways. First, it eroded the credibility the paper needed to fulfill its assumed role as the voice of Association. Second, it placed false hopes in the hearts of the faithful and left their spirits vulnerable to being crushed by the ambush of later events. Moreover, it illustrates how people of integrity, good folks, impelled by visions of a higher law, can tamper with facts in the service of a cause.

Admittedly, that fault stemmed in part from the inability of the misty-eyed Brook Farm leaders to gauge the magnitude of the task they set for the *Harbinger*. In the first issue, the editors, middle-class intellectuals to the core, realistically defined their natural readership. "We look for an audience among the refined and educated circles, to which the character of our paper will win its way." Unrealistically, they also expected to create a kinship with another social class, but a touch of romanticism exposes them as aliens in that sphere. "We shall also be read by the swart and sweaty artisan; the laborer will find in us another champion."

Actually, little in the *Harbinger* deals with the concerns of artisans and laborers. One of the few exceptions, the article "What Do Workers Want?" (July 5, 1845), had the potential to win converts among them. But a more typical example comes in "Labor in New York," a series of thirteen articles (September 6, 1845 to June 17, 1846). Today we would call it investigative journalism. The appalling factory conditions these articles describe would hold no surprise for workers, but the series clearly functioned as an eye-opener for the essentially middle-class readership, who knew nothing of that exotic world. The same can be said for "Letter from a Factory Worker" (July 4, 1846). The editors characterized it as "testimony of actual experience." And with *actual* they let slip a subtle clue to something they themselves lacked.

Such articles and editorials reflect the *Harbinger*'s split personality, a birth defect that can be traced to the odd marriage of incongruous parents. It was mothered tenderly back at the farm by bookish expatriates from Harvard, while the absentee father Parke Godwin, off in New York City with his Fourierist friends and their visions of a laborers' mass movement, sent support.

Plans for the *Harbinger* began in the fall of 1844 when Godwin proposed that the movement replace the defunct propaganda sheet *Phalanx* with a new publication edited by the Brook Farmers. Charles Dana wrote Godwin that he and Ripley liked the idea; John Dwight could supply music criticism, Ripley could write on social reform movements, and he, Dana, could contribute literary and philosophical criticism. However, there seemed to be some disagreement about the paper's style and content. Dana instructed Godwin, "Experience shows the best journals are the likeliest to obtain the public favor." And he pointed out the difference in their outlook. Godwin's mind was set, his "public teachings purely affirmative." But the Brook Farm leaders "pursue unimaginable phantoms and exult in the discovery of half truths," and such people are the ones who can "take the general mind captive and head the movement of the masses."[3]

So even though the Godwins of Association sought a movement paper with a broad appeal and wide circulation, the Brook Farm writers thought in terms of the "best journals." How did these writers go about taking the general mind captive and leading a movement of the masses? They wrote material directed toward people who had a good education and the leisure time and the money to pursue the kind of interests extolled in the *Harbinger*'s columns. Such people could buy and appreciate the books it reviewed, could attend the concerts in Boston or New York it discussed, and had the skills needed to play or sing the new musical editions it recommended. In closing the newspaper's third volume (December 12, 1846), the editors admitted what had been obvious from the first: they wrote for "a friendly circle," not for the general public. Years later, the sculptor William Wetmore Story, who had been one of the *Harbinger*'s writers and a contributor of many of its poems, expressed this idea more frankly in a letter to the poet James Russell Lowell. "No my friend, you and I want an audience which is intelligent and sympathetic, which can understand and stamp what is good and what is bad. We do not write for idiots or boors. We gather strength from sympathy. We must have our sounding board to give effect to the tune we play."[4]

As the voice of Associationism, the *Harbinger* did carry some news about the experiments, mostly unreliable. But it included relatively few of these items to begin with, and the number dwindled sharply, from twenty-four in the first volume to just five in the last. In actual lines, news of Associationist colonies occupied about 2 percent at first and an even more insignificant amount thereafter.

As for news of Brook Farm itself, the editors said that although they printed the paper there, it would not be the "exclusive organ" of their colony but would represent "the interests of the general movement." They did promise to publish accounts of Brook Farm "from time to time" but only those "we may think suited to promote the advancement of the common cause" (June 28, 1845). But that selectivity damaged their credibility. First, it corrupted their pledge to provide "the whole truth." Second, since they never did publish accounts of Brook Farm life, with one minor exception, they told the world in effect that they had no news that could "promote the advancement of the common cause."

The Icarian papers, especially *Colonie Icarienne*, did provide some real information about colony life. Through the open window of its columns we can look into such things as the names and trades of the people who worked in each shop; the names of members who died, along with the cause of death; the progress in farm production; the items ordered from Paris; the gifts the colony received from supporters in France; and rules concerning daily life.

Still, the Icarians found room in their publications for an abundance of propaganda. *Colonie Icarienne,* for example, ran a series "Communistes célèbres" (beginning September 13, 1854), which presented Cabet as the legitimate heir to the thought of Socrates, Plato, Moses, the Essenes, Jesus, and St. Augustine. Cabet inserted many doctrinal harangues into colony publications that promoted and justified his tactics. Such items materialized as about six dozen pamphlets and circulars. He aimed some at internal opposition; the historic broadside reproduced in illustration 12 shows how he used this tool in the last of his factional battles before being expelled. Notice the old rabble-rouser's skill at work with the power of emotional appeals. Most often, however, he targeted his propaganda outside the movement, hoping to win converts and support. Significantly, only Cabet, the most ideological of the utopians, used mass distribution items of that type. In one of these pamphlets he adopted the crude promotional device of inserting a page of unsolicited endorsements for his vision of a better world. One of the fourteen letters there made this appeal: "Brethren, can we believe our eyes? Can it be true that, by this simple and divine plan, the hour of departure for the promised land will sound for us?" Another has a stronger religious ring to it. "We were like those who live not, but your [Cabet's] courage has re-animated us." And a third goes beyond to a full-fledged epiphany: "How many years have I remained in darkness? but my eyes at length have seen the light. Count on me."[5]

Propaganda and Its Costs

These social experimenters paid a heavy price for their publishing ventures. Obviously, it included precious cash and, less obviously, resourceful and skilled labor, an asset in short supply. But the greatest cost, one that cannot be quantified, came from the controversies they generated and the fallacies they tolerated, all barriers to their goal.

Soon after the Icarians arrived in Nauvoo Cabet bought out a local press and went into publishing. Some costs are easy to see. The American printer had no French diacritics and ligatures, so they had to specially order them from France. Moreover, according to Etienne Ravat,

FAREWELL OF Mr. CABET AND THE TRUE ICARIANS
TO THE INHABITANTS OF NAUVOO.

Since the 15th of March 1849 we are your fellow-citizens, and, since several years, many of us have the honor to be naturalized American citizens.

We hoped that our principles of evangelical Fraternity, of morality in respect to marriage and family, of education and instruction for all our children, of temperance, order, labor and industry, would make us live happily in a fraternal union.

Unfortunately, after a more or less considerable time, discord has glided among us.

A systematical Opposition, developping itself by means it would be too long to ennumerate, became a Majority of 91 against a Minority of 74 and exerted itself to destroy the Icarian Community and its fundamental basis, substituing for devotedness, sensuality and for Democracy, Demagogism.

After having elected me 7 consecutive times, unanimously, their President; after having called me, for nearly 20 years, their father; after having boasted themselves, my children and disciples; after having acknowledged me as worthy, not only of their gratitude, respect and love, but of their admiration and even of the admiration of the World; the ambitious leaders of this Majority suddenly attempted to remove me, all at once, violently from Office, in February and May 1856, exerting themselves to crush me with insults, injuries and outrages, though acknowledging all the while, that I was the Idol of the Minority, being nearly as numerous as their adversaries.

The life in common with them, being, in this situation, insupportable to us, I, agreeing with the Minority, proposed an amicable Separation, and we even offered the choice between the Colonies at Nauvoo and in Iowa.

I even proposed to buy all the assets and to pay the debts or give the Majority the same chance; but they constantly refused all and everything, answering : **All or Nothing**!...

This Majority then constituted itself as a secret Society, with an occult Government, preparing all their manœuvres in partial and clandestine meetings, and did not attend the general Assemblies but for oppressing and tyrannizing the Minority.

To escape this oppression and tyranny, the Minority declared to separate ; not to attend any longer the pretended general Assembly, to constitute themselves in a particular Assembly for the Minority, and to apply to the Circuit Court of Hancock County or to the Legislature of the State of Illinois for obtaining a dissolution and liquidation of the Society.

At the ordinary time of the elections, towards the 4th of August, the Majority, violating the Bill of Incorporation and our Icarian Constitution in relation to elections, arranged these elections in a manner as to control them entirely, attending them alone and without a general Assembly ; and though the new Gerance was only the Gerance of the Majority, they pretended to be the Gerance of the Community ; and disregarding our protestations, took hold of the administration and of the whole fortune of the Community by force and violence, removed from Office all the ancient functionaries, belonging to the Minority and put in their places new functionaries, belonging to the Majority, unwilling to wait for a decision of the Court, concerning the validity or nullity of these operations.

The Minority then leaving work by necessity and for *defending* themselves, while the Majority did so for the purpose of *attacking*, the Majority had recourse to the most illegal, atrocious and barbarous measures, going so far as to deprive the whole Minority (81 men, the provisionally admitted included, 45 women and 43 children), of food, clothing, lodging, washing, fuel, even of tools and admission fees.

All these abuses and excesses, on the part of the Majority against the Minority, roused in France the most lively indignation, as manifested in a multitude of addresses, covered with thousands of signatures.

If the Minority had listened to nothing but their sentiments of human dignity and love for Liberty, they would have preferred war to tyranny : but our principles of Fraternity, especially the desire not to create embarassment to the magistrates of the City of Nauvoo, and not to trouble the peace of the City, induced us to a resignation and a courage more difficult than violence.

After having commenced a lawsuit for a dissolution of the Society and having given powers of attorney to pursue this aim and to have, if necessary, our Bill of Incorporation repealed, we leave, all of us, to recommence or to continue at St. Louis our Community and our Icaria.

We leave at our own expenses, which are enormous, by means of loans and fraternal aid by the Icarians of France, without asking any thing, for the present, from this barbarous Majority, who, trampling under foot the principles of Humanity of the American laws which protect indigence and the tools of laboring men, have exposed us to die from hunger or cold, who even refused us the tools necessary to make our life by laboring, and whom we denounce to the whole world as pitiless spoilers, among whom we obviously see the hand of several polices.

However, we do not leave, without addressing our gratitude to those of the inhabitants of Nauvoo, whose esteem, kindness and good wishes will follow us !..

Nauvoo, October 22d, 1856.

CABET.

NAUVOO, *New Icarian Printing Office.*

12. A broadside from Cabet's arsenal of propaganda. By permission of the State Historical Society of Iowa.

who ran the press, they had to make all their own typesetting items, surely an imprudent allocation of labor for an experiment struggling to get on its feet.[6]

The intangible costs lie deeper. Cabet's strategy of reaching for converts far and wide with printed propaganda remained as a legacy among the Icarians. A poignant example of it surfaces in the Iowa period during the bitter split between the "young faction" and the "old." Reason should have urged them to use scarce resources to strengthen their respective colonies as a way to win supporters. But they chose printed words as a tactic and succeeded only in using print to harden their views beyond reconciliation. The young group had the press of Jules Leroux, and in 1877 they came out with *L'Etoile du Kansas et de l'Iowa* (Kansas and Iowa Star). The old faction managed to convert an old lithographic press to print from type and answered with a revival of *Revue Icarienne.* Then, in 1880, just as strife between young and old began to abate, Jean-Baptiste Gerard rekindled it with *L'Observateur.*

The press run of *Revue Icarienne* in Iowa never exceeded eight hundred, but typically it came out far below that. Three volunteers did the work: Arsene Sauva and Charles Levy the writing, and John Dye, an American who knew no French, the typesetting and printing. Their regular duties came first, so they had to squeeze publication work into spare moments. Under those conditions they could publish only intermittently. They exchanged copies with like-minded journals in Europe and America, but without a consistent publication schedule they felt they could not even charge for the newspaper.[7] So unlike other colonies, they never made a drive to get subscriptions. And they never reached the people who needed convincing.

The Alphadelphia records show that the leaders did make a drive for subscriptions to the colony newspaper from the beginning. And they also show that the drive generated discord there almost at once. When the board of directors hired outside agents to sign up readers, Edward Camp protested. He argued that, in violation of their constitution, board members were using their office to run a business.[8] And, in fact, the colony books and correspondence reveal that the secretary, Henry Schetterly, put more official time into subscriptions than into the vital needs of the newborn experiment.

The *Harbinger* staff avidly pursued subscriptions. According to the daybooks, where they kept these accounts, even resident members had to pay for theirs, and that included the printers. Circulation probably peaked early at about one thousand and then declined. With virtually no advertising except in the last year, the newspaper had to depend on the two-dollar subscriptions for revenue. Even at maximum that brought in only about thirty-eight dollars a week, barely enough to cover labor, but not materials. Fortunately, Brook Farm received two large donations that covered the price tag of five hundred dollars on the press. The production cost took its toll. For example, in mid-1846, when the colony suffered shortages that could have been alleviated by income-producing labor, the print-shop took eight people. And those eight garnered from 225 to over 300 hours of labor time credits each week.[9]

Less obviously, the writing and managing jobs had their costs too. George Ripley, Charles Dana, and John Dwight, who did most of that work, also taught in the Brook Farm School. Moreover, the quality of their teaching accounted for its fine reputation, which had made it a key source of income for the experiment. But churning out articles, reviews, and translations to beat the mail deadline every Saturday took its toll in the classroom. After ten months of the *Harbinger,* Marianne Dwight, who also taught in the school, complained that "our school has lost reputation abroad not from want of talent here to conduct it, but because that talent has been diverted from it."[10]

Three factors detracted from the *Harbinger*'s contribution to the movement: inept management, confusion over a newspaper's function, and a general unfamiliarity with Fourier's notions and their implications.

Inept management. In the correspondence of James Fisher, a leading Boston sympathizer, two letters testify to long-standing inner conflicts over the operation and the role of the *Harbinger.* In one, Edward Tweedy discusses the agenda for the next meeing of the Phalansterian Realization Fund Society, and he warns that "the affairs of The Harbinger will be discussed too by those who are competent to decide on its *real* [condition ?]." That statement clearly implies the fatal weakness of the movement I mentioned earlier: unrealistic people whose faith in an ideal outweighed their ability to handle practical matters. Newspapers, even noncommercial ones, need management skills to keep them going, and for those skills sincere commitment to a good cause cannot substitute. Recognition of their lack surfaces in occasional, muted criticism of leaders otherwise venerated. For example, Marianne Dwight made this "confidential" admission to her closest friend, "We have not had businessmen to conduct our affairs, we have had no strictly business transactions from the beginning." Similarly, Amelia Russell acknowledged that the leaders were "unused to commercial pursuits" and needed most of all someone "practical."[11]

The newspaper's function. In the other Fisher letter the writer expresses fierce opposition to the *Harbinger*'s giving space to "partial reformers," particularly to Channing's antislavery propaganda. He insists that the paper be devoted only to Association. "If it is to become the instrument of any party or fraction, I shall withdraw from it instantly."[12]

Such confusion over basic policy trapped the *Harbinger* into exposing in public the movement's lack of direction. A few strategists had discussed throwing all support behind one experiment and designating it the "Model Phalanx." Warren Chase proposed his Wisconsin colony as the best choice in a lengthy *Harbinger* article (April 3, 1847). A year passed in talking. Chase then complained in a Boston newspaper that the *Harbinger* had failed to carry items about his colony. A testy *Harbinger* editorial (July 8, 1848) shot back: "Mr. Chase is laboring under an unaccountable delusion." The editors maintained that they welcomed articles from Wisconsin Phalanx but claimed that a letter intended for publication had never arrived. They also admitted having "declined" another article. Finally, hammering yet another nail in unity's coffin, they gave voice to gossip of the movement's enemies about "irreligion" at Wisconsin Phalanx. "It is the first time we ever heard of its irreligion," they wrote disingenuously.

Unfamiliarity with Fourier notions. One of the best examples of controversy spawned by muddled thinking on the *Harbinger* comes from its publication of "Cosmogony" (December 12, 1845, to January 3, 1846). This series consisted of several translated excerpts from Fourier's speculations on the physical world. The editors blundered badly with them and attracted ridicule when the movement needed converts. They knew they had put their foot into a sticky web, judging by their unusual steps: defending, explaining, and finally backing away as supporters and others who read no French began to come face-to-face with the real Fourier for the first time. This episode, in fact, marks the beginning of attempts by the editors to put a little distance between the *Harbinger* and Fourier. And it attests to the rampant ignorance of Fourier's ideas in a movement that called him mentor.

Fourier characterized the material in "Cosmogony" as "the medical science of the planet." He claimed that this "science" would make it possible to grow oranges in the polar regions within five years. He cataloged the "aromas" of the planets and stars. These imperceptible aromas are familiar to humans. Jupiter, for example, has the aroma of the jonquil; Earth, the violet; Mercury, the rose. Aromas control creation; the aroma of Jupiter created the ox; the aroma of Saturn, the horse and also the flea.

All of this might have been delightfully amusing to most *Harbinger* readers if not for three things: (1) the mind from which those thoughts sprang had been absolutely serious; (2) that mind was supposed to guide them in what leaders of Association called "the science of society"; and (3) Fourier's invasion of a sacred precinct, creation according to Scripture, alienated allies both committed and potential, and it placed another powerful weapon in the hands of those opposed to social reorganization.

Negative reaction to "Cosmogony" appeared quickly from both inside and outside the Associationist camp. From the outside, John Humphrey Noyes, founder of Oneida, said in his Bible paper the *Perfectionist,* "If the Fourierists received this as a direct revelation, we have no fault to find, except with their credulity. But if it is to pass for the result of human investigation, it is evidently very silly, impudent stuff."

John Dwight's response, including quotations from Noyes, took most of a *Harbinger* page (January 17, 1846) for a general and sometimes eloquent defense of Fourier, "our Guide." But he glibly talked around the "obscurities" and "technicalities" in Fourier's Cosmogony. And he surely did not win the hearts and minds in Noyes's group and perhaps elsewhere with these words: "Perfectionist [Noyes] himself has his Cosmogony, we doubt not, which may need *perfecting* as much as many other things."

From inside the Associationist camp, Alphadelphia's *Tocsin,* under the direction of Schetterly, attacked Fourier, their mentor. Schetterly charged him with infidelity because he had ascribed creative powers to planets and stars, something reserved only to God. Of course, one might argue that Schetterly as a leader should have studied Fourier's works long before he committed himself and dozens of families to schemes unknown.

Charles Dana answered for the *Harbinger* (February 21, 1846), and like Dwight he tried to skate gingerly over Fourier's thin ice. On the defensive although he denied it, he replied to the *Tocsin* in his characteristically snide and abrasive style, which did little to make friends either outside or within the movement.

Finally, the *Harbinger* editors published "Statement of the American Union of Associationists with Reference to Recent Attacks" in place of their regular editorial (August 15, 1846). They did not explain *attacks.* "As to Fourier's theories of Marriage, of Cosmogony, and the immortality of the soul, we do not accept them, and this is the position which the Associative school in this country and in Europe have always taken and never varied from." Despite these words, this stands as the first disavowal of any of Fourier's ideas by the Associationists. By implication, it affirmed the depth of controversy that "Cosmogony" and kindred writings had brought down on the heads of the movement.

Very little documentary information remains on how the *Harbinger*'s leaders made editorial decisions. For example, how in the world did they choose to go ahead with an item like "Cosmogony"? But clues suggest that the decision making did generate lingering and unproductive disputes. A letter from Godwin to Dana, written just as the Brook Farmers struggled past the paper's birth pangs, briefly opens the editor's door for us and reveals a minor but telling example of the dogmatic quibbling on which these radical doctrinaires wasted their energies. Godwin argues: "How could you commit The Harbinger to the decimal [metric] system of Weights and Measures? Fourier [inveighs ?] against its falseness in right good round [terms ?]. And [the] decimal system of dollars and cents is the devil. The old system which proceeds by twelves is better."[13]

A more intriguing hint about the editorial process surfaces in Dana's response to the *Tocsin*'s "Cosmogony" criticism. According to Dana, the editors thought that reading "Cosmogony" would whet people's interest in "the more practical parts" of Fourier. "Against the expediency of this course any person has a right to protest, though we do not think that any one who conceives aright the doctrine of the Cosmogony will be likely to do so." Could it be possible that Dana and perhaps others really believed those wild ravings in "the doctrine"? It sounds like that. And it certainly hints at differences of opinion on "the expediency" of taking the course they did.

Evidence of Dana's credulity turns up in, among other places, his *Harbinger* review of a pamphlet on clairvoyance (September 6, 1846). This morsel describes a visit someone made to Saturn while in a "magnetic sleep." It attracted Dana into its weave of the same bizarre filaments that hold together Fourier's cosmic visions. After a lengthy quotation from the outlandish account, Dana admitted that: "The description of the people of Saturn . . . does not excite entire skepticism in our minds. Saturn we believe to be, from various indications, in a state of harmony, having passed through the dark ages of ignorance and discord which are attendant upon the social infancy . . . of every Race upon every planet."

The historically significant aspect of the Cosmogony scandal turns up in Dwight's reply to the *Perfectionist.* In a damaging admission he conceded that the editors went ahead with this material "fully conscious" that it would "provoke not a few." Provoke it did, and to the movement's detriment. No Brook Farmer claimed that the trauma and effort of that tactic helped the cause by winning new friends or that it contributed to improving their lot in the severe crisis they suffered that winter.

Why is it historically significant? Because this provocative tactic repeated a blunder that New-Harmony had made two decades earlier with damaging consequences. The Associationists could have learned from the New-Harmony experience, but they never labored to seek out the lessons of utopian history.

The editors of the *Gazette* deliberately published items designed to provoke. They acknowledged their tactic when they began the second year (October 4, 1826). "It is true, the prejudices of the world have been aroused, and as was purposely intended, put into considerable excitement." That admission contradicts the principle they espoused in the first issue (October 1, 1825). "Averse from differing with others whenever we can consistently agree with them, we desire not to combat the errors or prejudices of mankind."

The provocative path begins in that very first issue, when the editors offered to print items by readers. They made no restrictions and emphasized their sincerity with italics. "Our columns . . . will ever be opened to the free expression of sentiment believing that the expression of opinions, however erroneous, may become useful where reason and truth are left free to combat them." They provided a convenient letter box near Robert Jennings's window for "Communications" and even invited outsiders to participate. With that they opened the door to virtually any eccentric with a quill.

Almost immediately a writer who referred to himself as a "hair-brained fellow" demanded and got space for an assault on religion (October 22, 1825). The following week "J." answered his tirade and took an entire column to define religion and charity. That marked the onset of an absurd war of words on religion fought up and down the columns of the *Gazette* for months. The editors themselves initiated most of it with page-length polemics. Then they would give over an equal amount of space for rebuttal. They often rebutted the rebuttal, sometimes in a caustic tone sure to elicit angry reactions. They favored battles involving inflammatory topics, those that anyone seeking unity with the multitude would have left at rest. These issues included attacks on religion, the existence of God, and arcane interpretations of Scripture. An early editorial on free will brought on volleys of philosophical disputes that answered back and forth week after week for half a year. That kind of war makes no friends and has no winners.

At one point the *Gazette*'s editors seemed inclined to call a truce. They reminded everyone of their goal: to devote the paper to basic principles, politics, and literature, not "religious controversies." But with skewed priorities they allowed this foolhardy tactic to continue.

The point here concerns those priorities, not the propaganda, whatever its merits. Actually, some of it did have validity, particularly items exposing the hypocrisy of the establishment. Validity, however, does not necessarily make an item essential or appropriate. In "The Third General Epistle of Peter," the *Gazette* editors turned to literature as a weapon in the religious debates (August 2, 1826). They identified this item as a translation of a recently discovered manuscript suppressed by "The Council of Nice." A parody, but with no hints about that for the gullible – the movement had plenty of them – the editors made it look like a set of rules for the church and the clergy. Biblical language and the familiar system of numbers for chapter and verse lend a flavor of authenticity.

> 3:9. [on preaching]. If a brother shall raise up the banner of war against a brother, and Christians against Christians, rebuke them not; . . . tell the one host that God is on their side, and the other, that He is on their side.
>
> 3:12. [on slave traders]. And though he sell them into foreign slavery to toil beneath the lash all their days, tell him not that his doings are of antichrist; for lo, he is rich and giveth unto the church, and is esteemed pious, so shall ye not offend him lest peradventure he withdraw himself from your flock.

Humanity, of course, had to confront such matters. And the New Social System was supposed to, if the experiment could somehow get off the ground. But the *Gazette*'s editors, whenever tempted by such challenges, could not discriminate between *now* and *later,* between *essential* and *important.* In each case they ignored a basic question that cried out for an answer: If we take this action, how will it help New-Harmony fulfill the grand promise? That neglect cost the experiment dearly.

The editors eventually saw the necessity for a truce in these destructive crusades. They maintained that they had no time for polemics because their hopes rested on "convincing the common sense of the world" through "an exhibition of practical results." So they did not intend "to combat the metaphysical errors of the age to which there is no assignable limit" (April 26, 1826).

The cease-fire held for two months. Then Owen himself violated it with his "Declaration of Mental Independence," which the *Gazette* duly published (July 12, 1826). Owen aimed this cluster bomb at what he called the "trinity of evils," which he identified as "Individual Property, Irrational Systems of Religion, and Marriage based on these." Such a blast could not miss anyone in the broad array of New-Harmony observers. Those people, sympathetic, or not, had surely watched patiently through this critical early period for any sign of "practical results." So Owen's attack on religion and marriage must have been especially exasperating to them because he never showed its relevance to the urgent and real problems facing the experiment. Like the *Harbinger*'s "Cosmogony" fiasco, it generated immediate enemies when the movement needed long-term friends. It simply placed one more immovable object on the path to the goal.

What price in the alienation of supporters did the *Gazette* pay for Owen's doctrinal blast? None at all, according to the editorial starting the second year (October 4, 1826). "When we determined to publish the Declaration of Mental Independence, a document directly opposed to the ignorance and prejudices of mankind, we naturally anticipated a reduction of nearly one half our list of subscribers." That admission, if true, surely demonstrates a short-sighted imprudence if not a cavalier recklessness. After all, the editors' actions affected the futures of all the other people in the colony. The explanation continues with a startling boast. "But to our surprise, and to the credit of the advance of intellect in this country, the subscription list has increased every week since its publication, four only have withdrawn their names, and none that we know on account of that publication."

But an analysis of their printing paper use tells another story. The account books for April 29, 1826, show a delivery of fifty-one reams of royal (a large size). That supply covered the *Gazette*'s usual needs for three months, a time that included the period before the "Declaration" and the two weeks after. Then two changes take place. (1) Instead of putting in their normal stock of paper, they begin to take monthly shipments, a tactic that businesses use in times of uncertainty. (2) The monthly quantities for the period show a gradual decline from seventeen reams to a low of only nine in the October shipment. So the *Gazette* used an average of about 1,960 sheets per issue in the period before Owen's "Declaration." Then over the eighteen-week period following his bombshell, usage fell below 1,100, a significant drop of about 44 percent.[14] What thoughts could have gone through the bookkeeper's mind as he entered those nine reams knowing that his editors had that day claimed the *Gazette* lost no subscribers?

The events of this period of crisis, the fall of 1826, also hint at dissension among the editors, something not otherwise disclosed. But to make sense of it, we need to go to the vantage point of New-Harmony's final crisis the following spring, when the *Gazette* suspended publication for one issue. That happened only once, on June 6, 1827, five days after Owen left New-Harmony, the nominal end of Owen's experiment. In the next number, June 13 (incorrectly dated May 13, a clue to print-shop turmoil), the *Gazette* buried one sentence on a back page about the missing issue. The explanation: they could not get paper. The records, unfortunately, provide no way to verify that.

But now we look back to that post-"Declaration" crisis of the previous fall and discover a curious parallel. The paper use for that period told us the truth about the state of circulation. And just then, in the issue of November 3, 1826, the editors warned of a possible suspension of publication because they could not get paper. But here again the account books tell the true story: they show an entry for paper received on that very day. So these publication excuses appear to be manufactured and indicate that the unwarranted threat of suspension in November, like the actual suspension the following June, stemmed from editorial problems, not from production problems.

The experiment paid a huge price for these follies, and although Owen picked up the bills, even he had his limits. Moreover, every dollar allocated to the *Gazette* had to be taken from elsewhere. How many dollars? The account books show that during the crucial April-to-November period of 1826, expendable printing materials totaled nearly seven hundred dollars. That amount translates into perhaps fifteen to twenty thousand dollars today. It paid for paper, ink, type, lead, and other supplies, but it did not include the big price tag: machinery. And the dollar amount does not account for the enormous labor time to write and edit some sixteen thousand words each week, hand-set them in 7 1/2- and 9-point type, and print, fold, address, and get it all into the mail every Wednesday.

This utopian episode, like so many others, has its ironic twist. It falls into the category of hidden costs. The editors reported (February 8, 1826) that people had been stealing *Gazette*s from post offices around the country, apparently because they considered newspapers common property. The editorial concluded wryly, "[Our] subscribers, however much they admire the system of Community of Property as advocated in our columns, will no doubt readily admit the injustice of a partial application of it to practice."

Admittedly, the *Gazette*'s editors made an important contribution to American intellectual history by providing a forum for religious and philosophical dissent that might have otherwise remained stifled. But their digressions did nothing to advance an experiment that held the hopes of so many people.

Principles and Prose

Colony papers, except in Icaria, offered fiction and poetry. When they slipped across the border from editorial land into the imaginative states, they took their carpetbags of propaganda, but tried to conceal the message under a cover of allegory. With a few exceptions, this strategy led to obvious, didactic items in which writing style had no role. Why did such low quality see print? Because ideology became the muse. Most of the material was written by, directed toward, and accepted by uncritical people.

Hopedale's *Mammoth* carried such items almost exclusively. The title makes a comical reference to its initial format: postcard size, four pages. It had a witty Latin motto, *De omnibus rebus cum multis aliis,* or virtually, "All things considered along with many others," which reinforced the humorous implications. But behind that smiling mask a stern-faced moralizer, awkwardly disguised as a narrative, a verse, or a quip, stands ready to preach.

A typical example occurs in "Sketch of Benedict Brassface" (July 26, 1848), part of *Mammoth*'s "Story Teller" series. Brassface, a cruel young man, works for old Peregrene Greedygain, and produces double his wages in profits. They fall out when each claims all the gain.

Brassface abuses the old man, who can only return a small insult. "What do I care," Brassface gloats, "he's used up." Motivated only by greed, Brassface boasts, "I never knock under to any one but the old lady." So in this way, the writer makes Brassface into a crude symbol for the selfish, aggressive, and evil men the Hopedale leaders saw in the competitive system. That provided a loaded and fit subject for glib moralizing.

Surprisingly, while the moralizing continues up front, contradictions slip quietly in the back door, and negate Hopedale's noble ideal of bringing all of the human race together. Stories perpetuate derogatory images of women as incessant talkers, vain, shallow, fit only for housework. I mentioned some instances of *Mammoth* stereotypes in the chapter on women's life. "The Widow's Daughter" stands out as the most blatant. Its message, a woman's place is in the home, and those in other stories like it raised no eyebrows in Hopedale. That tells us that given a bit of propaganda about values among the common people, Hopedale members accepted without criticism a story whose moral countered what the experiment set out to achieve.

The *Mammoth* filled out columns with short "jokes." Many of them belittled blacks, Indians, or the Irish by assigning them a stereotyped role such as the slow-witted one, the shiftless, the sly, or the greedy. Here is one example. "A negro out South bought a hat, and upon going out into the rain was observed to take it off his head and try to keep it from getting wet. And being asked why he did so, answered, 'Hat mine, head massa's.'" We know, of course, that material of that sort appeared in all kinds of media across the country. But the people of Hopedale had proclaimed brotherhood and had demonstrated their adherence to it by, for example, promoting the books of the former slave Frederick Douglass. Still, their dedication would have been more convincing if the *Mammoth* had looked higher for its humor and sentiment than the lowest common denominator of the society it condemned.

Admittedly, the *Mammoth* came from the mind of a boy of just thirteen. Adin Augustus Ballou, the son of Hopedale's president. His age, however, should not change our critical appraisal of the attitudes found in its pages. First of all, it did go out under the name of Hopedale; so to the outside world these words spoke for the colony. Second, the senior Adin Ballou knew the contents and wrote of his son's efforts with pride.[15]

Hopedale also published the *Practical Christian,* a paper devoted primarily to religion in social issues. It too included sentimental short stories with a moral message, and these differed little from those in the *Mammoth* except in length. "My Washerwoman" (March 16, 1844) tells of the awakening of Mrs. Mary Elwood to the meaning of poverty. When her husband, Mr. George Elwood, comes home from work and discovers that she neglected to pay the washerwoman her day's wages of fifty cents, he decides to bring the money to Nancy himself. Unlike white people, all called Mr. or Mrs., the story identifies the washerwoman only by her first name. Mr. Elwood goes to the other side of town where she lives and sees life among the poor. He tells his wife, and from his grim description Mrs. Elwood sees the true light.

In "The Sleigh Ride" (May 15, 1847), a girl becomes bored with the simple home her father keeps. He takes her to a starving family, and they distribute firewood and food. Now she begins to see things differently and devotes her life to Christian charity. These stories promoted Hopedale's belief in charity as a response to the evils of the world. That belief sets it apart from the mainstream of the movement, which derided individual action or partial measures as the failed methods of past reform efforts.

The *New-Harmony Gazette* often used allegorical tales, parodies, and little didactic pieces to present the leadership's position, hoping perhaps to reach people who might shun its usually dull editorials. The earliest such story (October 8, 1825) sent a clear message to the membership. It tells of a harmonious family, mother and four children, each considerate and helpful to the others. The mother has to leave for a month because of certain obligations, and when she returns, she finds a sad change. The children quarrel and no longer cooperate. Rather than scold them, the gentle mother has them play separately, each child in a corner. But they soon tire of that and beg for some other means of amusement. She answers: "'I know but one way to make you happy. . . . You seem to have forgotten it.' . . . They all [responded] 'Dear mother, we heartily wish to recollect it,' and then they stood attentive. . . . 'What you . . . have forgotten, is the mutual love and friendship which you once had for each other, and which was so delightful'." Needless to say, they lived happily ever after. But the editors did not direct this childish piece toward children. Owen left for England three months before it appeared, and in that brief time the members began to quarrel, and cooperation faded. They would have had no trouble with the moral here. Just substitute paternalistic Owen, who often treated his followers like children, for the gentle mother, and the editorial shines through this embarrassingly transparent fable.

Among the little didactic pieces we find "The Art of Happiness" (January 24, 1827), which pretends to be a story about two friends, Arachne and Melissa. The names are obviously allegorical, Greek for *spider* and *bee*. In the story, Melissa gathers honey from every weed, while Arachne sucks poison from the fairest flowers. Arachne always looks at the dark side of things; Melissa does the opposite. Melissa is happy because she looks at the bright side, and "by this practice may every person arrive at that agreeableness of temper, of which the natural and never failing fruit is happiness." This piece ran early in 1827, during the last months of the experiment, when carping and discord had become rampant, when any member who did want to look at the bright side would have difficulty finding it; only the dark side of New-Harmony life remained visible. In that context, the story becomes an Owenite appeal for unity.

The *Gazette* editors included items that reinforce prejudices against Indians, blacks, and women. I cited some examples of the *Gazette*'s bias in the chapter on women's life. The following illustrates a black caricature (October 29, 1845). "'Where is the hoe?' said a master to his negro. 'Wid de harra.' 'Where is the harrow?' 'Wid de hoe.' 'And where are both?' 'Why bofe togeder; good L——d, do you wan make a fuss wid poor nigger dis mornin?'"

Owen frequently used the *Gazette* to instruct members to treat their fellow beings with respect and dignity. But neither he nor the other leaders asked why items so characteristic of the despised old social system should appear in a newspaper dedicated to the New Social System.

The *Harbinger*, with one exception, did not use allegory as a vehicle for doctrine, although its writers did not hesitate to use its columns to promote Associationist ideas. And the Brook Farm editors generally did not fill out columns with hackneyed quips, so they had none of the desecrating of principles that other colonies tolerated with such things.

The *Harbinger*, alone among the colony papers, generally kept to high standards in its fiction. Certainly, the editors' decision to publish, in serial form, the first English translation of George Sand's huge novels *Consuelo* and its sequel, *The Countess of Rudolstadt*, represents a significant achievement. Why did they attempt this massive translation and publication? Certainly not to relieve the editors' burden by filling out pages for nearly two years, as some historians have said. On the contrary, they favored George Sand because her vision reinforced theirs.[16]

The following passage from her nonfiction, translated for the *Harbinger* as "Skepticism of the Age" (August 9, 1845), shows the affinity between her ideas and those promoted by Brook Farm. "In the age in which we live, the elements of a new social and religious unity are floating, scattered throughout a great conflict of efforts and wishes. . . . [Their] object . . . is just beginning to be understood, and [their] links of connection to be forged by some superior spirits." The Brook Farm leaders thought of themselves as the "spirits" who "understood"; they stressed the "new social unity" in their writings on every topic; they had committed themselves to forging its links. And as the George Sand text continues we can sense them, writers all, nodding agreement with an experience they knew. "How many of us have taken the pen to tell the deep wounds our souls have received, and to reproach contemporary humanity with not having built for us an ark in which we could find a refuge from the tempest. . . . The higher our claim to be sincerely and loyally converted to new doctrines, the more we ought to . . . allow others the right of judging our past doubts and errors. It is solely on this condition that they can know and appreciate our actual belief."

Therefore, in the minds of Brook Farm's literati George Sand, like most material in the *Harbinger*, had a doctrinal contribution to make. Her fiction defined their otherwise indefinable reactions to the real world and real dilemmas of the 1840s.

Consuelo and its sequel tell about a good woman, Consuelo (consolation), a singer who touches all with her inspired music and soul. The complex narrative roams freely over Europe from gloomy castles to brilliant opera houses. Real people, Haydn, Frederick II, and others, mingle with a host of fictional characters in a romantic world of mystical coincidences.

John Dwight explained the book's purpose (June 14, 1845) from the Associationist point of view: it teaches morality in relation to art. Brook Farmers found in George Sand's fiction links between beauty, truth, and good, a goal they themselves had set for the *Harbinger*. She said metaphorically in fiction what they wanted to say editorially. So they saw this, their major effort in fiction, as both entertainment and education.

When the final installment came off the *Harbinger*'s press in 1847, the Brook Farm experiment had already run its course; the vote to dissolve had come two weeks earlier. Shortly afterward, pragmatic

New York leaders, more interested in mass movements than in metaphors, took the *Harbinger* from the farmhouse hush to the hubbub of lower Manhattan. There it published no more fiction.

The Brook Farm editors made literary and arts criticism their hallmark from the beginning. But it varied from incisive to hack work. The latter quality came from two factors. First, the pressure of getting sixteen printed pages into the mail every Saturday forced shortcuts on the small staff. In one critique Dana filled nearly nine columns with quotations from the item under review, and stitched these together here and there with a few of his own words.

The second and more damaging factor that led to hack work came from a belief that everything could be seen more clearly through the lens of Fourier doctrines. Thus, with the slightest prod from the work being reviewed, a *Harbinger* critic would drag in social significance, often forcing transitions that butchered style and even effective persuasion. A review-book then became a foil for Associationist propaganda. Dana manages this almost too obviously in his review of *Cosmos,* Humboldt's comprehensive study of the physical world (October 4, 1845). First he looks deep within the work and comes up with the link he needs: "It is an eloquent and profound expression of the great idea which this age is inspired with, the idea of Unity." Having started the engine, he veers off into his own cosmos: "While the science of Nature more and more positively affirms the Unity of things, can thoughtful men long overlook a higher branch of science, the science of Social Unity." Dana promises Humboldt but gives us Fourier.

Of the two hundred *Harbinger* book reviews from the Brook Farm years, Dana wrote more than half. In these reviews his arrogant, sharp-tongued manner, like a lawn mower running wild, hacked both weeds and flowers, and surely cut a swath through the literary world wider than the *Harbinger* intended or needed to reach its lofty goal. The *Harbinger* named its reviewers only in a yearly index. Therefore, Dana's reviews, which appeared in almost every issue, were in effect anonymous, possibly prompting some readers to attribute the caustic style of the reviews to a general editorial attitude. Such misunderstandings surely did not help the *Harbinger*'s cause. These two examples typify the Dana sickle at work (April 18, 1846 and July 26, 1845).

> *The Retrospect.* This book is a three-fold misfortune: first, in its design; second, in its execution; and third, in its publica-

> tion. . . . Some friends ought to have prevented the author from making himself publicly ridiculous.
>
> *The Bustle, A Philosophical Poem.* We are surprised that any reputable publisher should attach his name to such a mass of garbage. . . . Any man who could knowingly put such a book into circulation deserves a severer punishment than any merely critical tribunal can inflict on him.

Dana tiptoes more tactfully into a review of George Foster's new edition of Shelley (January 10, 1846). As he starts on the work of "friend Foster," a New York writer for the *Harbinger,* Dana apologizes: "We know well what it is to put the cold water of criticism upon the fire of ardent feeling." But then he opens the hydrant all the way with an obscure doctrinal attack: "Mr. Foster seems to us to have fallen into a most serious error. We mean his assertion that Shelley's system and that of Fourier are identical." Whatever value, if any, that Dana's hair-splitting ultimately had for Association, such family squabbles certainly belonged in a meeting for members, not in a newspaper trying to unite a fragile movement and reach a broad audience. What seeds fell from Dana's threshing in this field? The paper carried Foster poems in the next two issues – they had undoubtedly been scheduled earlier – and then Foster's name simply disappears from the *Harbinger* forever.

Dwight, the other principal reviewer, also found unlikely arenas to conduct doctrinal bouts. Reviewing an edition of Burns (September 20, 1845), he drifts from the poet's humanity into a Fourier thicket. Here he comes upon a favorite topic, the Passions, and asserts that traditional society has restricted them. But he concludes that "true Social Science" will change the dissonance of our society into "the perfect accord of Harmony." What does this all have to do with Burns? He never makes that clear.

Dwight reviewed the transcendentalist writers, friends all, but he gave them no more favorable treatment than anyone else. However, Dwight can be deceptive; unlike Dana, who criticized with a scythe, he worked with a scalpel. His lengthy reviews of poetry by Emerson and William Wetmore Story (January 16 and 23, 1847) begin cautiously: "To the tasting of this honey we should come too grateful to be overcritical." However, he is not so grateful as to overlook faults in Emerson. He quibbles a bit over form, but content is the devil that launches Dwight into a holy war. "What passion of the soul inspired [these poems]? . . . They yield no warmth. . . . They shine aloft . . . like

Orion on a frosty night, cold and distant; they counsel loneliness, and they call that true life." Then he turns the heavy artillery of Fourierism on basic Emerson. "The great reconciling thought of Universal Unity . . . teaches us that all things are organic, harmonious, mutually implied constituents of the complete whole. And whoso lives in any part, if that part be in harmony, . . . rides upon the wave which our one-sided transcendentalist is doomed to chase. . . . Mr. Emerson and all his poems . . . treat life as a retreating wave."

Dwight zeroes in on Emerson's "gospel of self-reliance" and argues that there is unity in hearts reaching out to other hearts. "But by communing with his own heart alone . . . by isolated self reliance, no man ever came near that unity of which the heart whispers." Finally, Dwight delivers the decisive blow: "We love the transcendental in Poetry. . . . But we also demand that it be human."

William Wetmore Story, a staunch ally who wrote more poetry for the *Harbinger* than anyone else, did not escape Dwight's incisive probing. In his application of Fourierism to art, he found Story's poems delinquent on a major obligation. Their sin: they had "no distinct theory, or constructive vision of man's social destiny perceptible in them."

Dwight did not withhold favorable comments, and I do not want to imply that he did by my choice of illustrations. But he always stated his criticisms in stronger terms, and based these in social and aesthetic jargon that had the ring of authority. So one negative nugget tips the scales against a whole paragraph of positive remarks.

Only one work by anyone associated with transcendentalism received an entirely favorable review, Hawthorne's *Mosses from an Old Manse* (June 27, 1846). As in many other *Harbinger* reviews, issues external to the subject color the criticism, but here doctrines and social questions play no part.

Hawthorne had begun as ugly lawsuit against Ripley and Dana and, in effect, against Brook Farm, to get back money he had put in as an early member. With no funds, Ripley faced the immediate prospect of personal ruin. Given that situation, why review Hawthorne at all? It seems probable that the editors, perhaps as a gesture of conciliation, hoped that a benign review might move Hawthorne to call off his lawyer. They gave the job to William Henry Channing, who had written only one other review for the *Harbinger,* a trivial item. Obviously, they must have thought Channing, neutral and bland, could be their olive branch. Besides, they never could have entrusted this delicate matter to the others, especially Dana, who even in this ticklish situation could not curb his snide manner. He let a phrase slip into his review of some other book that appeared a few columns away from Channing's Hawthorne review. In an oblique reference Dana said of the Hawthorne book, "We [the *Harbinger*] have done such justice as we could." Dana had his say, but as usual it mocked unity, a value that got so much lip service in his columns. The movement's publications always seemed prone to fumbling when they took the ball on a drive for unity and always fell short of the goal. Hawthorne won.

Poses and Poetry

Only one author of note, Thomas Hood (1799–1845), got the *Harbinger*'s unhedged approval. Several articles and reviews had nothing but good things to say about him. The *Harbinger* reprinted fifteen of his poems, far more than those of any other poet, including its regular contributors of original poetry. Two of his qualities account for this partiality: the romantic spirit and his "humanitarianism," about which the reviewers commented at great length. One article (August 2, 1845) called him "a true good man" who fought a "fierce, uncompromising war" against the evils, abuses, and corruption of the world. Hood cried out against "the oppression of Woman," and unlike other popular writers, who shaped their style to satisfy the vested interests of "the present system," Hood "wrote to the mighty and struggling heart of . . . humanity." One review (May 16, 1846) declared that "Bridge of Sighs" and "Song of the Shirt" had endeared Hood to "every friend of humanity, to every suffering wretch whose soul is greater than his lot."

Those two poems touched deep, sensitive chords in Brook Farmers, and they repeated them over and over with great emotion. Clearly, his appeal stemmed from his special talent, one rarely encountered in the movement's newspapers, for reducing a social message to terms everyone could understand. He enhanced it without affectation and with imagery drawn from common experience, as in this excerpt from "The Root of All Evil," popular in the movement's press.

> Gold! Gold! Gold! Gold!
> Bright and yellow, hard and cold,
> Molten, graven, hammer'd and rolled;
> Heavy to get, and light to hold;
> Hoarded, bartered, bought and sold;

Stolen, borrow'd, squander'd, doled;
Spurn'd by the young, but hugged by the old
To the very verge of the church yard mould;
Price of many a crime untold.

The movement newspapers usually included verse, some original, some copied from other publications. Much of it could easily be dismissed as crude, meaningless jingles of no consequence or historical interest. However, most of these items command our attention because they had a special mission, namely, to represent the movement, to carry the message of social change, to teach, or to inspire. And here, where we ought to expect the movement's finest efforts, we find, with a few exceptions, incredibly bad stuff. Possibly, unknowing enthusiasts assumed that imposing a rhyme scheme on an inspirational idea created inspiring poetry or supposed that merely versifying editorial prose elevated it. Some editors apparently considered a poetry column just another voice in the propaganda ensemble.

In the case of Alphadelphia's *Tocsin,* pretentiousness also motivated its interest in poetry. Henry Schetterly, secretary of the Association and editor of the paper, said he was "very anxious to give our paper a high literary character."[17] That goal seems far removed from the needs of the membership, who, for the most part, never had the opportunity for anything but a minimal education. This Schetterly affectation fits in with what the colony records tell us about the leadership. As I showed earlier, they had two serious faults: they favored the pompous manner of would-be intellectuals, and they made little effort in behalf of books and education.

Consistent with that, we find obviously mannered verse in the *Tocsin.* For example, a column called "Ladies Department"–a stereotype, to be sure–gives us "The Maiden's Reason" (December 6, 1844). Its message and rhythms lean heavily and awkwardly on Hood's famous poem of 1843, "Song of the Shirt." Hood creates vivid images beginning with this memorable first stanza. "With fingers weary and worn / With eyelids heavy and red / A woman sat in unwomanly rags / plying her needle and thread." The *Tocsin*'s pale imitation tries to copy the shape of Hood's poem but cannot muster his evocative power.

[1] A maiden sat by her window low,
And wrought the silken thread,
And flowers, and birds, and beautiful things,
On the silken robe were shed.

A stranger sees her labor, and assumes it brought her wealth.

[6] Then the maiden raised her soft blue eye,
to the aged man and said
"Through days and years alone I toil
To gain my daily bread,"
And hurriedly on with her work she sped.

The versifiers of the movement usually included its jargon in their poems. They favored universals: *Truth,* always capital T, no *the,* and used as if everyone knew what it meant. This naïve reliance on stock words and phrases, perhaps in the belief that the mere utterance of them would inspire, often forces awkward construction. Ironically, poems put together that way fail in their reason for being, inspiration.

Yes, yes, Dear Friends, we'll meet again
On Alphadelphia's wide domain!
Then Truth and love shall ever be
Our polar star: From every envy free,
We'll then extend our sphere of love
Till we shall meet in heaven above.

The editors of the *New-Harmony Gazette* sought original verse that could serve as instruction on Owenite themes. They preferred these subjects: the New Social System, evils of the old system, irrationality of religion, overcoming individualism, and "female vanity." A clear example of verse used in that way is "To the Children of the New-Harmony Boarding School" (October 8, 1825). It opens by calling the pupils to "Wake Up!" and do battle against "the Demon" of the schools. The lessons, based on Truth, of course, begin in the second stanza:

Away with studied form and phrase,
Away with cant and bigot zeal,
Let Truth's unclouded beacon blaze,
[etc.]

"The Passions, An Ode in Imitation of Horace" stands out as a typical example of the *Gazette*'s bad didactic verse (October 5, 1827). Its twenty-four long lines with their jumble of feet stumble through some major targets of Owenite moralizing: individualism, ambition, greed, and religion. But a point that comes up in stanza 6 makes this banality worthy of notice. It presents an unusual opportunity to illustrate Owen's concern with human feelings, "the passions." Set free, they inspire individualism, the poison of Owen's collective society. That contrasts sharply with Fourier's view of human nature. He saw the passions as the normal expression of humanity, to be encouraged, not suppressed. He embraced and cultivated them as a force for social good. These lines from stanza 1 and stanza 6 give the Owenite line.

> [1] When the Passions are the Masters, what becomes of the Man?
> He will run to destruction as fast as he can. . . .
>
> [6] Consult then with thy Reason since the passions are such!
> She will curb them. Rather none than too much.
> The Pleasures they yield, they are vastly too dear.
> For a Moment of heart's joy, you'll mourn for a year.

Always ready for controversy, the editors found some "disbolical verses" called "Devil's Tour," in a Philadelphia newspaper, and reprinted them (January 11, 1826). In these verses Satan hears about New-Harmony, and realizes that not since Adam's fall has he had such an opportunity to promote sin. He thinks back on his efforts in behalf of evil and names the best. But never before could he say, "Here's a plan that beats the Devil!" The poem ends as Satan makes hell ready for the people of New-Harmony.

Quickly, the *Gazette* came up with a rhymed rebuttal of twenty-three stanzas (January 25, 1826). These show a laughing Satan overseeing traditional society, a vicious world run by corrupt clergy and greedy politicians. In stanza 20 Satan learns that he cannot take the Owenites into his fold; they are "honest husbandmen and sawyers / [but] hell is crammed with brokers, priests, and lawyers." Stanza 22, invoking the usual capitalized universals, makes a clumsy attempt at inspiration.

> Meanwhile the Owenites with warm devotion
> To Truth's, to Nature's, and to Virtue's cause
> Still pushed their shallop [ship] o'er life's ocean,
> Fearless of blame, and heedless of applause
> Skillful to steer in tempest, surge, or swell,
> Without the fear of heav'n, or the hope of hell.

With this item the editors began a regular practice of copying poetry from other publications and using it to trigger a propaganda blast. This shows that their selection criteria had less to do with poetic merits, and more with a poem's potential for editorial exploitation. The strategy became increasingly prevalent during the second year but waned and disappeared after Owen left the colony in June 1827. Typical of that type, the editors reprinted from the *European Magazine* fourteen extremely maudlin stanzas called "The Orphan Boy" ("Alas! I am an Orphan Boy / With nought on earth to cheer my heart"). Unabashed by its shallow sentiment, the editors (October 4, 1826) promised that in the New Social System "the Orphan will not experience destitution. There will not . . . be such an unfortunate being known as an Orphan" because society will give children care and kindness.

While that promise at least sounds plausible and certainly laudable, such selections usually brought forth the kind of editorial commentary that gives seekers after a better world a bad name. For example, in their observations on the poem "Twilight Reverie," the editors offer reassurance to all lovers: broken hearts will be unknown in the New Social System. And with the poem "Death" they consoled mourners: no need for gloom; grief is brought on by an irrational social system.

Two poems generated editorials that, given Owenite values, point the way to state control of creativity. The first poem, a tribute to Byron, prompted the editors to attack imaginative writing and to criticize Byron because his fantasies fail to teach the moral lessons of this world (December 20, 1826). They warned that "talents . . . falsely directed or altogether perverted to useless or injurious effects" impede the perfecting of human nature. The key Owenite test, usefulness, coupled to the idea that words could be injurious must have brought little encouragement to poets, even if friendly to the cause.

The editors restated these principles in their comments on "The Past" (February 21, 1827). The poem venerated bygone things ("The visions of the buried time come thronging dearer far / Than joys the present hour can give"). They traced this longing for "the good old days" to traditional schooling that fails to give children "useful ideas." Then, when they grow up the real world does not match their expectations. But educators could avoid this if they would "*cultivate the senses and the judgment rather than the imagination*" [original emphasis]. Then children would know the world "*by objects and experience only.*" Moreover, "If poets instead of merely . . . complaining of evils and miseries were to endeavor to discover a remedy, then poetry, if it were less beautiful (which we doubt) would at least be more rational; if it astonished less it would instruct more."

Not all of the poetry selected for the *Gazette* became grist for the editorial mill. The editors included a sentimental trifle or two, an occasional bit of nonsense verse, and even two verses about love, an emotion rarely mentioned on these pages concerned with human needs. But the poetic muse never seemed free to inspire lines in these columns.

◉ ◉ ◉

Hopedale's *Mammoth* did open the door to her for a moment with a little fantasy on dawn clouds (March 8, 1848) that drifts along the border of imaginative writing.

> Beings of light and love we are,
> We dwell in the heavens, we dwell in the air;
> We come to the earth with the morning light,
> And children are our constant care.

In the following stanzas we discover that these ethereal beings have a Hopedale function: they help children to do right, and when death comes, they take the children up into the sky to live among the clouds.

After that one brush with celestial invention, the *Mammoth* returns to its usual down-to-earth view in "Get up Early," (June 14, 1848). Notice that it associates an ordinary, purely human feeling that all of us know with sin.

> [1] Get up early! time is precious,
> Waste it not in bed;
> Get up early! while the dew drops
> O'er the fields are spread
> . . . .
> [2] Get up early! it is sinful
> To be wasting time;

Now, *sin* is a word rarely used by groups who traced the world's problems to a defective social system. So this shows yet again the position Hopedale occupied at the edge of the movement's spectrum. Its body stood in the ranks of social reorganization; its soul drifted toward individual salvation. We see it in "On the Death of a Rabbit" (October 6, 1827). It tells of a pet that some animal has killed despite the protection of a specially built pen. The poem concludes with a moral that could fall more readily from the lips of those dedicated to saving souls rather than society: "And then we discovered that all our pleasure, / When doting on an earthly treasure / Is quite ill-founded."

"A New Generation" (February 23, 1847) typifies the inspirational verse of social reorganization. Notice the two characteristics that mark this type here and everywhere else in the movement's press: an assertive, even militant tone and a generous sprinkling of exclamation points.

> We come! we come! a new generation!
> The fathers are gone, or fast are going;
> And we now advance to take our station.

Its sixty-six lines enumerate the movement's goals: end poverty; restore human dignity; build brotherhood; abolish war. Unfortunately, the writer, prone to a major fault of the movement's poets, pretension, mangles what could have been a rousing appeal. In the end the bungled technique distracts and so stifles inspiration. Compare stanzas 4 and 9:

> [4] Now come to the conflict, O new generation,
> And fear not to grapple these monsters of night!
> Let no one be lacking in self-consecration,
> Let none be behind in his love of the right.
>
> [9] Off with those manacles! take them right off!
> Shall a new generation go down to their graves
> And leave these men chained? No! now let the scoff
> Of the despot cease – to these pining slaves;
> Proclaim we liberty throughout the earth;
> Man as a man has his freedom by birth!

But even these irregularities offend less than the bellicose mood that transgresses the spirit of a Practical Christian commandment, nonviolence.

Undoubtedly, the Hopedale people found the quality of such verses sufficient. They certainly made no claims to high literary standards as, for example, the Brook Farmers did. Indeed, their leader, Ballou, saw this difference as one of several that convinced him to turn down a possible union with Brook Farm. He pointed out that Brook Farm "abounded . . . in literary accomplishments and aesthetic tastes. . . . In this respect we were poor."[18] Having recognized that, he could have directed Hopedale's limited resources, physical as well as aesthetic, into more suitable activities. But he did not.

◉ ◉ ◉

Brook Farm did indeed have a wealth of literary talent, but even there standards could waver. That shows up in four ways: (1) for inspirational verse, the *Harbinger*'s editors tolerated glaring banalities; (2) they took erudite poems unsuited to the goal of reaching the masses; (3) they permitted untenable ideas if the poet had good intentions; and (4) they indulged friendship even if the poet-friend opposed social reorganization. The following four examples illustrate these.

First, in didactic and inspirational verse the editors often accepted clichés and clumsiness. "Look Aloft! Look Abroad!" (May 16, 1846) typifies this class.

[1] Men of hoping souls whose vision
Pierceth through the future's curtain,
Ye who scorn the world's derision,
Ye whose trust hath still been certain,
Look aloft! your hope is sunward!
Look abroad! your course is onward!

[2] In old European nations
Throbs with joy each freeman's bosom;
Ye who waited long with patience,
Now behold your hopes in blossom.
Look aloft! . . .

Second, the editors included verse inappropriate for a mass-movement newspaper. Dana's attempt to inspire with "Ad Arma" (June 21, 1845) exemplifies this type. In it he calls to the people to become active on the battlefield of social change.

Oh loiterer that dalliest with thy dreams,
. . . .
Is there no Spartan nerve in all thy frame
That feels the summons to that solemn field?
And canst thou then its sacred honors yield,
And the high guerdon of Eternal fame,

For purple skies and wreaths of fading flowers,
And the short lustre of these flitting hours.

Perhaps such stilted language had found praise at Harvard, where Dana studied before joining Brook Farm. But in the *Harbinger* it made a mockery of Dana's boast, in the letter to Godwin quoted earlier, that the paper would "take the general mind captive and head the movement of the masses." How many among the masses would know the meaning of *guerdon?*

Third, the editors would even let untenable ideas into the *Harbinger* if the author's heart was in the right place. John Dwight's "Work While It Is Day" (June 28, 1845) illustrates the point.

[1] Work, and thou wilt bless the day
Ere the toil be done;
They that work not cannot pray,
Cannot feel the sun.
. . . .
Work, or lose the power to will,
Lose the power to love.

Dwight says things about "they who work not" that would be hard to defend. In fact, the movement condemned the past precisely because "they that work not" *could* pray, *could* feel the sun. So a poem of this type slipped by Brook Farm critics because the poet meant well and invoked their favorite nostrums, work and love.

Fourth, the editors diluted a principled position by publishing the verse of a friend, even though he stood unalterably opposed to the movement. George Curtis, whose poetry and reviews appeared in the *Harbinger* throughout its Brook Farm years, fits that description. He had little sympathy for its social goals. In 1844, before the birth of the paper, he wrote John Dwight a candid letter with an admission outrageously at odds with the Brook Farm spirit. "With respect to association as a means of reform I have seen no reason to change my view. . . . I live only for myself. . . . I feel that our evils are entirely individual, not social. What is society but the shadow of the single man behind it. That there is a slave on my plantation or a servant in my kitchen is no evil; but that the slave and servant should be unwilling to be so, that is the difficulty."

Curtis had been a student at the Brook Farm School when Dwight had urged poets to become active in behalf of social change. "The truest poetry for us at present is to carry out in practice the ideal principles of human brotherhood and justice. . . . We believe then, that the most ideal and poetic impulse of our people is engaged in the movement for reform."[19] But Curtis's poetic inclinations rejected such a call, just as he rejected the key axioms of the movement. Still, he retained his friendship with the Brook Farmers. And they found a spot in the *Harbinger* for his poems and reviews.

How did this fourth contradiction show up? Both Curtis and Thomas Wentworth Higginson wrote poems for the *Harbinger* with the same title "The Railroad." Both poems deal with a train trip, but they provide an instructive contrast. Higginson brings out the unity of the collective experience, a Brook Farm axiom, and most appropriate for the *Harbinger.* Curtis said of his own poem, "It is so different from Higginson's that I do not feel as if the same road had been run over by us." The difference, however, came not from the railroad, but from their outlook.[20]

Curtis sees the world only in terms of himself, a trait that many people in the movement associated with life in traditional society. His train drifts in slow-moving blank verse through a silent landscape shaped by his meditations, and colored by his moods. He goes by a town "Remembering the heavy debt I owed / To the dim arches of dingy bricks / Which sternly smiled upon my youngest years / And gravely greeted now, as through the crowd / By all unknown and knowing none, I passed" (April 25, 1846).

On the other hand Higginson's poem (April 4, 1846) travels the movement's tracks. It starts out as a lyric composition, the song of a poet carried away by the new mode of transportation. With its robust, repetitive rhythms evoking the mechanical throbbing of a train and with its complex eighteen-line stanzas creating a sense of extended time, it appears to be a vehicle for displaying technical facility.

Onward, ever onward!
How the miles have faded by
As in ceaseless course we've wandered
Underneath a morning sky!
Chanting one eternal song,
As we restless speed along—
As the sunbeams round us glowing,
Firm and constant is our going;
While our strong mechanic forces

Know no limit to their courses,
While the glittering path of steel
Knows no pressure from our heel
Who shall dictate stop or stay
To our still unwearied way.
Till the thread of Fate unravel
Till our mortal days be gone,
Earth may echo in our travel
Onward, onward, ever on!

Higginson's eyes and ears catalog sensations: smoke mingling with clouds, groaning rails, echoes from the cliffs, and so forth. But as we travel down its seven stanzas the scenery shifts from lyrical to inspirational. Not among his best poems, it undoubtedly sprang from a *Harbinger* editorial (February 28, 1846). In it, the editor reminds us that although railroads were ridiculed at first, everyone can see that they pose "no alarming consequences to Church and State." And if we can improve locomotion over old-fashioned ways, then why not social organization? The editorial predicts that the time will come when the good sense of locomotion will be applied to society.

Higginson picks up on this link between social and technological progress, and on his railroad people discover nature's secrets and thus the eternal truths about the unity of life, about brotherhood, and so forth. The ride ends with this imperative: "work on for Use, for Beauty, / Labor on for Truth and Duty." So while Curtis's railroad passes through his thoughts without social allusions, far off the movement's main line, Higginson's turns out to be a metaphor for the road to the utopian goal, just what the movement needed.

Brook Farm's abundance of literary taste did bring a few superior poems to the *Harbinger.* They came from the pens of Higginson and William Wetmore Story, the only regular contributors to offer well-written poems appropriate to the medium. The high point in inspirational verse, Higginson's "Sonnet," appeared in the *Harbinger* during Brook Farm's low point. At a time when only faith and raw sacrifice kept the experiment alive, when every member needed inspiring words, he extolled its men and women as an inspiration to the movement. "Sonnet" (January 30, 1847) speaks in a language moving and eloquent yet comprehensible to the masses. And for well-educated readers, his finesse in handling the five-foot lines with enjambment and with rhyme must have brought a welcome relief from the many *Harbinger* poems that too readily sacrificed art on the altar of doctrine.

There are great souls among us! In the prime
Of Grecian strength or England's loftiest days
I find no names more meet for reverent praise,
Than theirs who 'mid us now work on sublime;
Teachers whose deep words lead this selfish time
To heaven-wide musings; patriot orators
Whose Christ-anointed lips are rich with stores
Of burning, fearless Truth; poets, whose rhyme
Hath never stooped to sound a meaner song
Than love for all God's children; women pure
Who lend their stainless hands to labors strong,
Deeming their birthright to such duty
Though fools deride. Dear native land, how long
Against such prophets shall thy crimes endure?

Perhaps none saw the irony then in the fact that the *Harbinger* editors published a Curtis when they had a Higginson who so closely matched the movement's mood. But they made other incongruous choices. They also included poetry by members, sympathizers, and friends that countered the characteristic spirit of the movement through melancholy, passivity, uncertainty, and even cynicism. Each of these negative moods tended to neutralize the attractions of utopianism: its optimism, its confidence that for all perplexing social questions there existed positive answers, and its assurance that the "law of progress" promised a bright future for humanity.

Poetry has a special talent for opening a view to deep within the soul of this movement where its true pulse beats. So it is significant that poems in a negative mood started appearing in the *Harbinger* early in 1846, a year before Brook Farm's terminal crisis. Retrenchment had reached a physical limit, membership had dwindled, and the world remained unmoved by the Brook Farm message. The Brook Farmers and their friends began to notice omens, and some wrote poems that reveal thoughts and feelings lurking far below the words on the page. William Ellery Channing (nephew of the Unitarian leader, cousin of William Henry Channing) wrote a poem for the *Harbinger* (August 1, 1846), that takes to task people "vainly striving" for "some unanswering good" in the future. "The mocking future" he calls it and compares it to a fish net. In "The Hanging Moss," which Frederick Hedge wrote for the *Harbinger* (September 12, 1846), he expresses a desire to escape from the struggle.

[1] I would I were yon lock of moss
Upon the tressed pine,

Free in the buxom air to toss
And with the breeze to twine.

Then he would be free of passion, strife, and thought. He only wanted "perfect peace" and "a vegetable soul." And in that way he would live in the lonely forest, "erased from human nature's page." It is a far cry from the movement's exclamation points.

Not long after that strange poem, Story's "Pledge" appeared in the *Harbinger* (December 12, 1846), just as winter and the end began at a despondent Brook Farm. One of his inferior efforts, its significance lies in its mood. Ostensibly an inspirational poem, "Pledge" brings a hollow ring of confidence to the funereal stage he sets with phantoms and dark images.

[1] I sit alone, my friends have all departed;
By our deserted board alone I sit,
The silent midnight makes me lonely-hearted,
And visions of the past around me flit.

The visions are friends from his youth, but now a profound unity of souls replaces their laughter and singing. They rebuke his "doubting fear," his "slumbering Faith." And that prompts the Pledge: "Never to yield this heart to time's annealing, / To bear our youthful hope forever up." Story ends with the question that surely haunts all who have hoped to change the world, then and always: What if we fail?

[6] What though Truth's fair reflection seem to quiver
Upon the restless waves of whirling life?
The image only fleets – the star forever
Lives, journeying on unharmed by mortal strife.

So even if the dream falters today, we still have the future. But the future now becomes even more remote, a star deep in space. That thought must have brought small consolation to those who had sacrificed so much for the dream.

The *Harbinger* has more of this type, and similar examples can be found elsewhere in the movement's press. The following excerpt shows negativism and gloom in the *New-Harmony Gazette* (June 20, 1827).

We are hastening on—we are hastening on,
To the sleep of the years that are vanished and gone
To the voiceless chambers that lie beneath,
To the silent halls of darkness and death.

Each stanza ends with the dirge "Ye are hastening to dust. Ye are hastening to dust." Surely no coincidence, this poem appeared in the *Gazette* just after Owen left the colony for good and it became clear that for all practical purposes the grand dream had gone to dust.

The Romantic Spirit

The melancholy, negativism, and escapism in the movement grew in part from the emergence of a depressing thought: changing the world might not be so simple. Most vulnerable to that malaise were the unrealistic visionaries who thought that with the mere pronouncement of Truth humanity would see the light. But to a greater extent, those moods came out of a related deeper current than ran through the movement and particularly through its intellectual leader, Brook Farm.

A clue to it appears in an article Ripley wrote for the *Harbinger* on the difficulties of starting an Association (December 20, 1845). Here he admits that even the sacrifices "are not without a certain romantic charm." And that spirit permeated life at Brook Farm. Dana had his German class translate from the hymns of Novalis. The teachers and writers translated the German Romantics for publication, Ripley doing Schlegel and Fichte, and John Dwight the poetry. With a few exceptions the only translated poems to appear in the *Harbinger* came from the German Romantics: Heine, Ruckert, Seidl, and Uhland. Dwight canonized Schubert and Mendelssohn and saw only the romantic side of Beethoven. John Codman said, as quoted in the previous chapter, that he and his young friends sang a gondolier's song. More than likely he referred to Schumann's "Leis rudern hin" (Row Gently There), and it shows in yet another way the familiarity that Brook Farmers had with the very latest in German romanticism.

The romantic spirit, particularly elevating imagination to the point where it obscures reality, abounds in Brook Farm thought. A clear illustration comes from Marianne Dwight's widely circulated description of the fire that destroyed Brook Farm's new building on March 3,

1846. The members had invested their last hopes in it, not to mention their life savings, so the disaster clearly tolled the death knell for their grand dream. The fire started late in the evening, and members spotted it as they left a meeting in a nearby house. Dwight sent a lengthy account to her friend Anna in Boston.

> It was glorious beyond description. How grand when the immense heavy column of smoke first rose up to heaven! There was no wind, and it ascended almost perpendicularly, sometimes inclining towards the Aerie. Then it was spangled with fiery sparks, and tinged with glowing colors, ever rolling and wreathing, solemnly and gracefully up, up. An immense, clear blue flame mingled for a while with the others and rose high in the air, like liquid turquoise and topaz. . . . The whole front was on fire – that was beautiful indeed – the whole colonnade was wreathed spirally with fire, and every window glowing.

She supplied brilliant images: a temple of molten gold, trees turned to silver, and rockets of glittering gems "like our July 4th fireworks." Nearly two hundred spectators gathered from miles around. At the end everyone went to the Hive, where, she said, they "feasted" on bread, cheese, and hot coffee – a rare treat in Brook Farm's hardship. Someone rushed to town for milk. Morning had come when Dwight sat down to write to Anna. "We look towards the hill and all seems like a strange dream. You can't think of how it struck me last night towards the close of the fireworks when, after watching the constantly rolling, changing flames for two hours, I looked up to the sky and saw Orion looking down so steadily, so calmly, reminding me of the unchanging, the eternal."[21]

Glorious beyond description? Fireworks? Beautiful? Reason would have shielded its eyes from such a cataclysm and certainly would not have waxed poetical. In any case, physical facts suggest that imagination dominated her observations. Dwight said she "looked up" near the end and saw Orion "looking down so steadily, so calmly." That would have been after eleven o'clock. But on the third day of March at latitude 42°22′ north, the approximate location of Brook Farm, Orion, in the course of its yearly cycle, is low in the southwestern sky at that hour, tilting close to the horizon. Moreover, Dwight would have been looking southwest toward the new building, and the hill behind it would have formed her horizon and cut off some of the southwestern sky. Thus from Dwight's point of view the lower part of Orion would have been hidden. Only Betelgeuse and possibly Bellatrix might have been seen above the hill if the hovering smoke, which she alluded to, did not obscure them. Oddly, she never mentioned the moon. On March 3, 1846, it neared first quarter. Due to set just after midnight, its brightness would have dominated the western sky at the time the fire ended and would have seized the limelight from the stars there.[22]

So, for Dwight, as for most Brook Farmers, subjective interpretations had greater force than reality. And in this way, one of the great catastrophes in the history of social reorganization comes down to us as a bit of romantic fantasy. Brook Farmers believed in the power of poetic vision. When John Dwight reviewed Thomas Carlyle's *French Revolution* for the *Harbinger* (December 12, 1846), he decided that this work was actually a poem rather than a history. From this he arrived at a principle: you need "a poet to either record things, or see things truly."

The thought that the Brook Farmers could conceive of making this disaster into a special occasion by bringing out their precious hoard of coffee and scurrying around at midnight for milk evokes a grotesque image of people who perhaps enjoyed the tragic mood and wanted to savor it to the full.

Their souls would be in tune with a *Harbinger* sonnet, "Why Are Poets Sad?" (March 6, 1847). It says that if you have ever seen beauty made ugly or watched a loved one dying, then you know why poets are sad. Poets need these "daily thwartings" to survive. Poets moan in secret for humanity's sorrows and shed warm, hidden tears for the world's woes. So: "No Poet's he who can be glad / With so much round to make him sad."

That kind of delight in dolor also stands out in the poems of Thomas Hood, and the *Harbinger* chose them for that quality as much as for the social content. John Codman said that at Brook Farm they talked about Hood day and night, "by the roadside, in the shops, on the farm, in fact everywhere." His friend Thomas Blake was "wild" over "Bridge of Sighs." "It was so full of sentiment, it was so tender, it displayed so touchingly the sorrows of a young heart, and was so in harmony with the humanitarian sentiment of our lives, that he and the others could but repeat it over and over."[23]

These *Harbinger* selections, typified by "The Death Bed," overflow with teary sentiment: "We watched her breathing through the night / Her breathing soft and low / As on her breast the wave of life / Kept heaving to and fro." Hood's "Ode to Melancholy" laments, "The world!

it is a wilderness / Where tears are hung on every tree." It ends with a romantic trait, mixing opposite emotions: "There's not a string attuned to mirth / But has its chords of Melancholy."

Another aspect of the romantic spirit shows up in the acceptance of bizarre characters in many colonies. Proportionately, the short-lived, tiny Fruitlands had the most. But Brook Farm had the model case: Charles Newcomb, a frail, reclusive mystic. Barely in his twenties when he arrived shortly after the colony began, he found escape there from a domineering mother.

Newcomb made pretensions to being a writer, a profound and inscrutable one, and as a boarder he had no obligation to work. In nearly five years as a Brook Farmer he turned out only one short piece, "The Two Dolons."[24] A bit of arty trivia, it deserves notice only because it shows the potential that nonconformist groups have for attracting outlandish individuals. Until his last day there, the colony cultivated his idiosyncrasies and deferred to him as a genius, delicate and precious. Brook Farmers gave him special privileges at the table when shortages forced the productive people to do without.

Over the years his mother's letters constantly urge him to come home. She tempts him with gifts. These include an edition of Plato he wants, and as we learn from her letter written late in 1845, he finally gives in. Don't delay, she prods; activities are already planned: reading Shakespeare, going to the Catholic church. "My heart is leaping to see you," she gushes, and then reminds him to take his laxative. He is twenty-six years old. "Come dear, your Mother waits, Plato waits, and Jesus waits – last, not least of course." Marianne Dwight continually mentions "the sweet sad youth" in her letters. Writing her friend Anna about his departure, she expresses her concern about his return to the outside world. "Think of him in city life, if you can, Oh! it will kill him body and soul."[25]

Romantic notions may have contributed to the charm of some colonies. But as life got its toe in the front door, charm slipped out the back. The Philadelphia Industrial Association, an experiment near the northern border of Indiana, had a member, A. E. Winter. When he arrived he called it a "romantic place." But that ill-fated attempt succumbed after eighteen months of terrible suffering. And then he wrote to his sister back home in Belchertown, Massachusetts, that "when sickness came the romance vanished but sad reality remained."[26]

Many of those who saw a social experiment as a romantic experience had difficulty coping with its ups and downs. They reacted too readily to advances and declines with mood swings that erased the boundary between elation and despair. Never stopping to count the cost of such subjective responses to the real world, Brook Farmers tolerated and even encouraged this romantic confusion of opposites. And those subtle traumas did their little bit to hasten the end.

The romantic spirit associated with Brook Farm did have some happy consequences, most notably in William Wetmore Story's *Harbinger* poems. A lawyer in his mid-twenties at the time, he stood on the threshold of his career as one of America's foremost sculptors, his priorities not quite sorted out. In many of the *Harbinger* poems we find him groping for aesthetic as well as social goals. Thus his long poem "The Future," ostensibly an inspirational piece for the *Harbinger,* actually speaks on a more personal level, probing his doubts and yearnings (June 28, 1845). It refers to two futures, his own and society's. He begins by looking at the dreary world and becomes discouraged by the "false part men are playing." He turns to "youth's auroral dream," which he describes in a fanciful way. And throughout it, despite life's cares and pains,

> Faith commanded me, and kept me strong.
> The hands of mighty dreams my own were clasping,
> And I was pledged to do away with wrong.

And as he nourishes his soul he sees the link between Truth and Beauty, and that decides his own future.

> Then did I swear in full and sweet affiance
> To wed the beautiful and be its priest,
> And strengthened by heroic self-reliance,
> To struggle on till Art should be released.

He knows the goal, but he still has important work to do now, so Story turns from subjective musing to objective thoughts about the Associationist world to come. Yet even here his speculations cannot escape the inner component that fuels them: "The dim and distant Future haunts my being / With a rich music swelling like the sea."

Story's best *Harbinger* poem is "The Mountain Stream" (December 13, 1845). Its one hundred lines of free verse could be taken as nothing more than a romantic evocation of the picturesque in nature: a stream rushing down the mountain into the valley. As such, it offers passages sparkling with evocative imagery. He talks to the stream:

Thou callest to the mountains
"Wake from thy dream of quiet,"
And they answer with the voices of their pines;
Thou smilest to the morning,
And the morning stoops to kiss thee,
Painting rainbows on the incense of thy spray;
Within thy shaded hollow
The cold fair moon comes seeking
For thy sleepless spirit whitening in the night.

However, he has clearly chosen the stream as a metaphor for a current he found in his own soul and for the fun-loving free spirit he saw bubbling in his young friends at Brook Farm as they struggled under great hardship to reach the utopian horizon. He salutes the stream, actually the vibrant Brook Farmers, with admiration and affection:

Wild mountain youth!
Thou that laughest at despair,
Thou that scornest every danger,
Thou free impetuous heart,
That hateth dull inaction,
That fleeteth from the Present,
That panteth for the Future,
My spirit yearns to thine!

But then a negative idea intrudes: the stream, an impatient youth, may struggle on undaunted, but it seeks something it can never gain. On this wistful, ambivalent note the poem ends. "With joy my heart thou stirrest, / Yet thou makest me to sigh."

That delicious uncertainty delighted the Brook Farmers, but its romantic wavering between extremes describes too truthfully their fatal weakness.

In the wake of the experiments some poems of despair appeared, characterized by bitter and poignant expressions of disappointment, frustration, even cynicism. These poems, of course, did not see print in the movement press. Warren Chase included two of this type in his autobiography. One, "Dirge of the Phalanx" overflows with sentiment. The poet speculates on an appropriate personal burial site and rejects many places but chooses the lonesome prairie. There friends, presumably from the town of Ceresco where the Wisconsin Phalanx had been located, could stop after work and visit the grave. The other poem generates more genuine emotion as N. Brown, the poet, contemplates with gloomy disillusionment the idea of returning to the old society.

> [2] Behold the struggle! the mad, selfish rush
> For shining baubles or a beggar's crust!
> In vain, divines, ye try the tides to hush,
> Though hearts are dead or bleeding in the dust.
> There kneels the nabob, drawling out a prayer;
> Here dies the o'er-worked victim in despair.

The following stanzas then describe the eternal evils of the world: the lust for wealth and fame, the hate, the human mind "chained," and the failure of religion to overcome these evils. The poem ends in hopeless dejection.

> [8] The world is rich in musty lore and creeds,
> In mysticism, and in temple show,
> In spirit chains; but poor in brother deeds
> To the great brotherhood of man below.
> The central truth designed the world to save
> Is crushed by self to a dishonored grave.[27]

The most moving of these poems of despair comes from the hand of George Ripley. He wrote it in the spring of 1847, when the fate of Brook Farm had already been sealed; but although the *Harbinger* still carried on, he published "The Angels of the Past" elsewhere.[28]

> [1] My buried days! in bitter tears
> I sit beside your tomb,
> And ghostly forms of vanished years
> Flit through my spirit's gloom.
>
> [2] In throngs around my soul they press,
> They fill my dreamy sight
> With visions of past loveliness
> And shapes of lost delight.

[4] And as they pass, the conscious air
Is stirred to music round,
And a murmur of harmonious prayer
Is breathed along the ground.

[6] The past and future o'er my head
Their sacred grasp entwine,
And the eyes of all the holy dead
Around, before me, shine.

Unlike many others who suffered tragic personal defeat in the movement, Ripley's human qualities and his great inner strength sustain him, bolstered perhaps by the shield of utopian faith.

[7] And I rise to life and duty,
From nights of fear and death,
With a deeper sense of duty
And fuller strength of faith.

◉ ◉ ◉

Did these colony publications make sense? I looked for indications that, despite the enormous individual and financial sacrifices that left immediate needs unsatisfied, the movement for social reorganization actually benefited from them. When L. M. Richmond saw a copy of Alphadelphia's *Tocsin* in the spring of 1845, it impressed him, and he thought it "well-calculated to accomplish great reforms in society." He had considered joining Alphadelphia, but an uncle who had belonged to an Association in New York State dissuaded him. However, "since seeing your paper," he wrote enthusiastically, "I have renewed ideas of joining you." Still, his name never turned up on the membership roll. When the Brook Farmers began the *Harbinger* in 1845, Marianne Dwight liked it very much. "It ought to be an instrument of much good," she told her friend Anna. "May it bring many to the good work."[29]

But I have not been able to find documentary evidence showing that these newspapers actually brought anyone to "the good work." Rather, the constant struggle for circulation and funds and the sectarian aspects of these papers suggest just the opposite. In every case, the drain on limited resources, financial and human, weakened the colony, encouraged discord, and hastened its end. And then the world could sneer at the utopian boasts. A stronger colony with a softer voice might have made more noise.

As always, however, the intangible benefits elude such evaluations. Among the leaden propaganda pieces, the provocations and venomous reviews, the maudlin stories, the controversial jokes, and the jingles passing as poetry, they did indeed bring a few moments of elevation, exaltation, and even beauty for some members. After all, among the utopian promises such joys attracted like the light of a Bethlehem star, but in reality remained a goal lightly touched, light-years from fulfillment.

10

After Life

Failure and Success

EVERYONE KNOWS, of course, that the movement for social reorganization did not succeed in bringing about the radical change its members and supporters envisioned for the world. But the question asked in the Introduction remains: why did its colonies fall apart so quickly? And what should we make of their story? Should we mark those experiments down as failures plain and simple, or can we find in them some elements of success? *Success* – the concept itself raises difficult questions that need to be addressed, especially in evaluating colonies established to provide ideal conditions.

Shortly after Brook Farm started, a friend of the experiment, Elizabeth Peabody, wrote an article explaining how its ethical values derived from the teachings of Jesus. But apparently many Americans looked to another value system, one in which the bottom line stands at the top of the list. For example, a well-known Unitarian zealot, Harm Jan Huidekoper, active in public efforts to encourage spiritual values, reacted to her article with crass materialism. Rather than "Miss Peabody's description," he said he would prefer to see "Mr. Ripley's ledger . . . at the end of the year."[1] He typifies our deplorable trait of quantifying an abstraction such as success, of making the accumulation of wealth the sine qua non of success. It introduces yet another complication in attempts to understand the ideal colonies of that time.

The conventional wisdom in the field attributes success to the Shakers, to the Inspirationists in Amana, and to similar groups that established their ideal havens for what I call individual salvation. Almost every writer on the subject finds success in the longevity of those colonies and in the wealth and property they accumulated.

However, as soon as we look at the implications of that attribution, we see why the concept of success requires scrutiny. For example, Father Rapp's evangelical group acquired huge tracts of land early in the century, particularly in Indiana, and those acquisitions brought windfall profits from soaring real estate prices in later decades. Their wealth also came from oil wells, railroads, and mining. But what had that to do with Rapp's holy mission? These riches, accumulated over the colony's long existence, stand as far removed from his spiritual goals as is earth from heaven. A nitpicker might even argue that though the members filled the colony's coffers, nothing indicates that they heeded the instruction of Jesus: sell all you have and give the money to the poor, and you will have riches in heaven (Matt. 19:21 and Mark 10:21).

In any case, the fact that Father Rapp's and other colonies dedicated to individual salvation amassed wealth can hardly be a standard for determining whether they succeeded in their stated objective: admission to heaven and eternal life. Some believe those groups did succeed in that objective, and no one can disagree, of course, when it comes to a matter of faith. But obviously that success cannot be established as a matter of fact. For similar reasons the longevity of their colonies cannot be used as a measure of success. We need to remember that such groups created an ideal haven from sin only as an earthly way station, a temporary stop in eternity, and to exalt that temporal means depreciates the spiritual significance of their sacred ends.

Moreover, their economic prosperity needs to be seen against the demands that the members made of their colonies. Rapp and his followers, peasants with little education, had fled the religious oppression of a still-feudal Württemberg when they came to the United States early in the century. They wanted nothing more than an environment that allowed them to follow their heavenbound path. Isolated from secular, materialistic America by their colony's early priorities, their expectations and aspirations remained the simple wants they had known on their native soil. A British traveler, James Buckingham, visited them in their fourth decade, and noticed that working to accumulate stock was their chief pleasure. In their seventh decade a reporter, Charles Nordhoff, visited the colony to observe their way of life and concluded that they "have failed of the proper and just development" in their "inattention to the higher and intellectual wants."[2]

Obviously, the fewer demands members made, the fewer problems a colony had to solve. Groups dedicated to individual salvation, having no concern with changing the world and achieving universal happiness, had a much smaller burden than the colonies dedicated to social reorganization. In contrast, the movement for radical change demanded the satisfaction of wants more complex and more diverse. And even the colonies that butchered its elevated goals had to live with and eventually die with the burden of those promises. Simply put, social reorganization asked more out of life than members in the colonies of individual salvation accepted.

Indeed, people in the movement could not conceive of living the monastic life those colonies offered. John Dwight visited the Shakers in New Lebanon and wrote a lengthy two-part article in the *Harbinger* (August 14 and 21, 1847) on what he saw there. He found among other things a shallow existence, their dancing "ghost-like" and bloodless, their music empty. He called their success superficial, "purchased by the extraction of so many human wants." Fred Cabot, looking back on his Brook Farm experience, compared it with life in the evangelical groups and applied a test of success that illustrates the thinking of social reorganization. He would not concede success to a society "which fails to do justice to all the faculties . . . of the human soul." Robert Dale Owen, reflecting on his New-Harmony experience, left us another perspective on how the movement thought about success. He noticed that the evangelical groups led by charismatic leaders could amass large reserves of capital and property because their congregations asked for nothing more in their earthly existence than necessities. In an ominous foreshadowing of our own time, he concluded that if people want only food, clothing, and shelter, "they can readily obtain all of this . . . provided the dictator to whom they submit is a good business manager."[3]

In fact, many of the charismatic leaders of individual salvation did manage their business enterprises very well, and that aptitude for commerce marks a major distinction between them and the leaders of social reorganization. It provides one explanation for the prosperity of those groups, and for the general lack of it in the colonies dedicated to radical social change.

Many activists in social reorganization pondered the question of success and failure in those terms. Nathaniel Meeker, who had been a member of Trumbull Phalanx and other experiments, took issue with the conventional wisdom about the movement's short life. This veteran of utopian battles looked into the causes for the fall of New-

Harmony and found that the role of religion did not matter. He identified the key fault as poor management. Based on his own utopian experiences, he concluded that social reorganization could achieve success only by providing what the present social system offered, "material advantages."[4]

However, a businesslike approach, the factor Meeker identified, is just one among many that directly affected the longevity of social reorganization's experiments. As we have seen in the previous chapters, the characters of those colonies and thus their problems were eminently more complex, at least as complex as the people that gathered in them. The disasters that overcame the utopian episodes do not admit of simple explanations, and those who attribute their collapse to a single cause, or even to two or three, fall far short of the mark.

More than a dozen decisive faults and errors in thinking and strategy necessarily prevented the people in social reorganization from ever achieving their goal. The following summary includes one or two typical examples for each kind of fault or error. Needless to say, each did not appear in every colony, and did not act with the same force everywhere. Some defects were completely destructive, and some merely created frustration and discord, but even these traumas eventually took their insidious toll in fragile experiments, and ultimately, in the movement itself.

One characteristic failing ran through the movement like a genetic defect. Members immersed themselves so deeply in the brilliant glow of the future that they came away blinded to the prosaic obstacles that blocked their path to its glory. Believing so completely in the rightness and righteousness of their cause made them see success as the only possible outcome of their efforts. So they observed situations through rose-colored glasses, and sometimes, buoyed by the confidence of true believers, they did not even bother with observing the situation at all. Thus, they quite naturally saw no barriers. And if a mountain did happen to fall within their ken, they tended to minimize or underestimate it. In this way, they consistently oversimplified every task that lay before them.

I call this flaw *visionary vision.* Nearly half the weaknesses enumerated below can be traced to its effects, and it actually made every experiment in the movement susceptible to early mortality.

Victor Considérant provides the egregious example of a leader so afflicted with visionary vision that he missed things obvious to any careful observer. In 1853 he visited Texas and returned with the starry-eyed conviction that he had found the best location in America for a new and grand experiment in Association. In two of his books he describes the area he chose as perfect in every respect. He never noticed the lack of water, the unbearable heat, and inaccessible markets, omens of the fate that would overcome the men and women in his La Réunion colony. These obstacles defeated their labor and brought terrible suffering, disease, and early death. The results bear tragic witness to the power that an ideal has to warp the perception of people in this movement.

Even after more than two bitter years of La Réunion, Considérant persisted in his Panglossian appraisal of the site. Dr. Augustin Savardan, who suffered through those years in the colony, scorned Considérant as "one who wanted to see all in beauty" and berated him as "more than blind."[5] Thus people with visionary vision see what they want to see and miss what stands out clearly to others.

Factors That Precluded Success

The dozen fatal errors described below stem from three basic causes: (1) people in the movement for social reorganization thrived on illusions; (2) they had no working strategy; and (3) they had foggy ideas about principles. Their illusions included the folly that conjectures were facts, that life was simple, and that zeal alone could change the world. In the absence of a working strategy, they adopted red tape instead of planning, made no preparation for emergencies, and never took advantage of the potential in a movement. In their fogginess about principles they went off on sidetracks, became obsessed with trivia, and floundered in endless meetings. Not surprisingly, with a slight adjustment for ideologies, you can find parallels for most of these blunders in the radical movements of our own time. In fact, those who have aspired to change the world of our century, and those who still do, might ponder the following summary for signs of their own errors and weaknesses.

ILLUSIONS

Imaginative speculations about the ideal world of the future kept the people of social reorganization out-of-touch with the present. When New-Harmony had yet to pass its first birthday, a writer for the *Gazette* put considerable effort into compiling a long list of fanciful names that he believed they would need for all the colonies New-Harmony would father, a premature concern given the age of the would-be parent. The *Harbinger* devoted eight pages to outlining the pleasures several individuals enjoy on a typical day in the society to come: pleasant work, relaxed socializing, healthful meals in a germ-free environment, and theater finer than any we now know. Ironically, this colorful fantasia appeared just as Brook Farm staggered through its final, gray weeks of existence.

Faith seduced members into oversimplifying the task. This error often appears as facile, almost smug predictions about their imminent success. New-Harmony had been in operation barely eight months when the *Gazette*'s editors put on airs of self-satisfaction with their revolutionary skills. Although eight months of experience hardly seems like a qualification for the job of changing the world, they boasted (April 12, 1826) that the creation of additional New-Harmonys "is now pretty well understood among us, and is entered upon like a matter of ordinary business."

Faith instilled a confidence that blotted out the plain facts. Early in 1827 blunders and discord rocked the New-Harmony experiment to its foundations, a clear sign of impending doom. Stedman Whitwell, designer of Owenite utopian palaces, an architect, should have been able to recognize a house of cards when he saw one. But with visionary vision he saw something else: "With all the difficulties of New-Harmony I am far more convinced of the happy tendency and easy practicability of the new system." Similarly, when a potential member for Ohio Phalanx inquired about the colony's prospects, Elijah Grant, the president, wrote back, "It has encountered many difficulties, and doubtless has many more to encounter before complete success, but . . . it is secure against failure."[6] Grant's faith in illusions surely blocked out reality, because shortly thereafter the colony finally succumbed.

Visionary vision gave rise to a powerful illusion: we are living in revolutionary times with humanity about to stride forth into a new age. Some even saw the millennium. Its spirit comes through in words like these from the *Gazette* (January 31, 1827). "How extremely gratifying to live even in the anticipation of the great and important change that must soon take place." In 1826 the editors added to the issue date: "Fifty-first Year of Political Independence, First Year of Mental Independence," a reference to Owen's declaration that was supposed to usher in the new age.

For people with visionary vision, complete success seemed only natural, and many expected to see it soon. And then, as Benoni Pixley declared in a letter to Alphadelphia, "the sun of millennial glory would encircle the globe." William Owen, Robert's son, made a prediction in the *Gazette* (October 29, 1825) about when the glorious event would happen. "I think I am not too sanguine when I say . . . even before this generation shall pass away." A generation passed. Then the editors of *Ploughshare and Pruninghook,* perhaps more sanguine than Owen, said (February 15, 1846) it would only take between ten and twenty-five years. After that time "Integral Phalanx will be operating fully under the system of . . . Fourier," a society "never equalled in earthly beauty . . . since . . . Eden." Two more generations passed. The movement had long since slipped below the choppy waves of history when John Codman looked back to the time Brook Farm broke up. He claimed that the members had never considered that to be the end. And he, like them, still believed that soon "the country would be dotted with little Phalanxes." Four generations passed since the movement began. In 1904, when only a feeble few even knew of its existence, Charles Codman, John's brother and one of the last surviving Modern Timers, still saw the utopian light at the end of the tunnel. Now seventy-eight, he maintained that "we are only on the edge of things, but the progress will be rapid."[7] For some, old illusions never die.

Conjecture equals fact. This means that their ideal world stood on a wobbly foundation of a priori assumptions. Cabet, for example, believed that humans are born naturally affectionate and good and are therefore perfectible. Owen thought humans are born neither good nor bad; society arranges that. Others asserted that because humans are social beings, all interests would be harmonized in a utopian society. No empirical evidence supported any of these speculations, and no one in the movement ever searched for it. For example, in the third decade of the movement, when the ruins of countless experiments lay strewn across the American landscape for all to see, Considérant presumed to lead the Associationists. With no experience in building a utopian colony, and without a shred of proof, he told the world that if an experiment gets off to a good start it "naturally advances rapidly."[8]

Founders of these experiments assumed that all members would be equally industrious, capable, and sincere. Yet reality showed otherwise. North American Phalanx, for example, went through a decade of agonizing over the fair division of profits. In their tenth year they tried to adjust their labor standard of ninety cents per day by applying a complex "Scale of Differences in Performance" and "Scale of Differences Between Functions" to the members. The industrious got more; the not so industrious – obviously, they had them – got less, based on dozens of arcane "degrees."[9] That table evaluating work, just the dry facts, reveals a human situation never imagined by library revolutionaries: some members would be more highly motivated than others. It speaks more eloquently than reams of speculations about how an ideal society would work. Moreover, as Moncure Conway discovered at Modern Times, not everyone joined to build a new society; some merely came looking for a refuge from the old one.

For many members, the image of a better world came to them as a revelation. But they received it from propaganda; it did not grow from objectively studying the actual words of utopian mentors and scrutinizing their schemes for inconsistencies. The force of this apocalypse they themselves experienced led them into an abiding faith in the efficacy of "Truth" as a weapon against evil. Show the world Truth, they said, and all would soon be right. Of course, that belief implied that the world responds to reason and that people always act in behalf of their own best interests, both obvious conjectures with little or no support in history. Yet no one tested the validity of such notions.

Believing their goal moral, their cause noble, and their ultimate success just, people in the movement fell prey to another shaky notion: a "law of progress" governs human existence. From there they needed but one false step to the trap door of a final, even more precarious, supposition: "progress is inevitable." Giles Stebbins, a member of Northampton, put it this way, "Right outlives wrong, and so the world moves upward."[10] People in the movement regarded such conjectures as fact and never demanded proof. They tended to accept rather than to question.

Life seen in simple terms. The detailed description of ideal societies in the movement's propaganda stemmed from a belief that one could actually foresee exactly how life at some time in the future would go. With that in mind, utopian thinkers tried to provide in advance for every facet of life, every situation, every problem.

That prompted many leaders to reduce all human activity to the clauses of exceptionally detailed constitutions and involved rules. Frédéric Olinet, in Icaria for a year, described the rules, which members had to obey, as "excessive minutiae."[11] Some thought the movement could do nothing without such instruments. In 1844 the western Associationists held a three-day meeting at which useful and practical programs could have been developed to strengthen the ties within the movement. Instead, they squandered this rare opportunity by spending virtually the whole time arguing over words in a constitution. The movement generally maintained a naïve faith in these documents as propaganda tools. Many colonies, thinking that potential members would actually read such tedious writ and be convinced to join, wasted valuable resources in printing and distributing them wherever and however they could.

The simple-minded belief that constitutions or similar documents could account for all human activity derived from social reorganization's most provocative assumption: society can find a solution for every social dilemma. That dubious proposition lured the movement's people into glib answers for the most vexing social questions. More dangerous yet, it snared them in the trap of *doctrine-correct positions,* the belief that for each question about society, the arts, or life itself there existed only one answer. It spawned the devastating controversies in the *Gazette* and the brutally destructive polemics in Icaria.

"We were children in the ways of the world," admitted Amelia Russell as she looked back on her Brook Farm years. For a movement that set out to change the world, an undertaking that would seem to call for worldly people, the folks in social reorganization turned out to be quite unsophisticated. A good example of their innocence and its cost comes from the experience of John Allen as he barnstormed New England trying to raise funds and sign up new members for Association. The progress letter he sent back exposes the parochialism rampant in the movement. In a Vermont town hall that could hold a thousand, he and John Orvis held forth to a couple of dozen. Eloquent and convincing, so they thought, they made but two "converts" and did not get one *Harbinger* subscription. "We are encountering the rough realities," Allen complained. But his sudden awareness that the business of remaking society might not be as simple as the movement claimed elicited a surprising attitude toward the hearts and minds they hoped to win over. Shocked by the audience's hesitance when offered the principle of friendship and love, Allen called them "boors" and "brutes."[12] Oversimplifying a complex world made events incomprehensible to the people of social reorganization and caused many to stub their toes on basic principles.

Zeal alone can change the world. People in social reorganization deceived themselves with a belief that dedicated members could move mountains and that fervor could substitute for skill. John Dwight, Brook Farm's leading authority on doctrine, captured the idea in one short line when he wrote, "A true purpose is power, though it have no hands." In a characteristic error, he confused the possession of what the movement called "Truth" with the possession of strength, and he overlooked the obvious: it does take hands to make a true purpose into something tangible. Charles Codman of Modern Times thought that "enthusiasm" would carry them through "the howling wilderness" to the utopian goal.[13] But as a few people came to realize, a colony with a preponderance of intellectuals and members whose only tool had been a pen lacked an indispensable ingredient to overcome the wilderness into which they had wandered.

Amelia Russell, in retrospect, recognized that ingredient. What Brook Farm wanted most "in the time of our great need" was a "good, practical, experienced" person who could oversee the various operations.[14] In fact, except for Brook Farm's school, the history of most of these experiments demonstrates their poverty in capable people at every level and for every task. They could never create an effective, productive society from the ground up – one that could satisfy their humanistic goals – without experts in agriculture, construction, manufacturing, and trade and without the managers who could coordinate everything. Their illusions made them think small even as they blithely undertook the largest venture in history: changing the world. They approached it like a do-it-yourself project instead of a monumental task that required a full spectrum of skills.

Incompetent people in authority could damage the united effort in many ways. In Icaria, those who had the responsibility for finding a new location in Iowa gave the experiment a grave handicap because they chose a site seventy-five miles from a supply town. Still, that town stood closer than the one where the parent colony had done its buying. Records from the original Icaria show purchases of cleaning supplies, dishes, glasses, glue, medicines, paper, sandpaper. All of these items could be had from American sources, but unqualified buyers simply ordered everything from France, paying a high premium they could not afford. And when a group of men in Icaria blistered their soft hands chopping firewood, their inability to be productive also became a loss to the entire experiment. But the director who sent such men on this job typifies the crux of the problem: allowing people to be managers who did not know how to manage. A cause surely needs people with hearts in the right place, but on the world scale this cause had in mind, good intentions were not enough.

What kind of leadership does a successful revolutionary change require? Obviously, such a fundamental reconstruction of society has two phases: the old and the new. During phase I, in the old society, leaders need to agitate, desecrate what people have always accepted, and make them ready to leave it all behind. Leaders in phase 2, the new society, need to consolidate, get the new system running in an orderly fashion, and promptly satisfy the promises made in the first phase. Once launched, the new society cannot tolerate for long any similarities with what came before.

It seems to me that, given two phases so distinctly opposite in character, each phase ought to require a leadership temperamentally attuned to its special demands. The first calls for leaders impatient with the past, and temperamentally disposed to an irreverent break with tradition. They must be agitators who can fan the flames of discontent and gather forces with the strength to tear down the old. They act in noisy, broad spheres and need to know about such things as mass meetings, speeches, and leaflets. Many of the leaders of social reorganization, though not fiery rabble-rousers, suited the first phase.

However, phase 2, the new society, calls for the opposite type: patient leaders, people temperamentally disposed of careful evaluating and building up. Owen, the successful industrialist in Scotland, had those qualities. But in New-Harmony, as Thomas Pears, one of his clerks put it, "Owen's heart ran away with his head."[15] Leaders in the new society function in quiet planning sessions. They need to know about such things as bushels of wheat per acre and how to sell it, the labor in a pair of shoes, how much coffee to buy, how big a school should be, and how many people a job requires and where to get them. This stage calls for bookkeepers – but not bureaucrats – dedicated to radical change who can precisely measure and record the true day-to-day situation objectively and without losing patience.

Restive temperaments with grand illusions have always found their way into radical movements, and social reorganization had its share. Its shortage came with the second type, the businesslike ones who know how to build up. But such people have skills and personalities that more readily assure them a satisfying place in traditional society, so they have no reason to tear down; their interest naturally gravitates toward the status quo and conservative social views. You generally do not find them in radical causes.

Alphadelphia's leaders, as one of their first acts, ordered a beautiful set of account books, leather-bound and gold-stamped. These large volumes, with a few random entries but mostly barren white pages, unfilled and unfulfilled in a quiet archive in Michigan, bear mute witness to the movement's illusions and its lack of people of the second type.

NO WORKING STRATEGY

Groups launched colonies without carefully thinking through the implications of what they set out to do and what options they had. Moreover, for people committed to the premise of social planning, who wrote elaborate constitutions that seemed to embody its essence, they did little planning themselves. In their most basic error, they imprudently began by moving to rural land and then attempting to build a fully functioning human environment with the random skills of a small group. Few gave any thought to the alternative. Thus, their noble goal of improving the human condition got lost in the crucial start-up period, actually the most vulnerable stage, as they struggled desperately to scrape together enough for just their daily bread. Soon the world saw them backtracking on the utopian promise, making excuses, rationalizing, and then spending energy quelling discontent. In each case, a circle of staunch people, often the founders, hung on while less resolute members, sympathizers, and curious outsiders quickly became disenchanted. More than anything else, this lack of planning materialized as the grim reaper of the utopian episodes.

Almost every group started out with little cash and took on the added burden of a heavy mortgage that imposed erratic zigzags on their graphs of progress. Charles Sears said that when he and the other founders of North American Phalanx had proposed the experiment, they had tried to raise enough cash to avoid debt. However, when their fund raising did not meet the goal, they decided to go ahead anyway, an unstrategic move, as the colony's history shows. Sears described his dilemmas, so typical of the movement, as he tried to keep the colony afloat. The lack of funds inevitably drove him to counterproductive choices. For example, if he put money into the vegetable farm, he fell short in the dairy.[16] As a result the colony had to appeal continually for funds, which surely turned the skeptics away.

The movement fell into an unwise strategy of depending on the soil for its main source of income. The error stems in part from romantic, back-to-nature yearnings. But its roots grow out of a classical fallacy held by city folks, the notion that farming can produce enough to support a group aspiring to a life of elevated culture. The surpluses they would have needed from it in order to get the refinements, the leisure, and the manufactured goods their ideal society called for would have been impossible even for experienced and efficient farmers able to cope with the physical burdens.

But the urban, middle-class class leaders of social reorganization never understood that, and they did not attract enough people who did so. Fourierists especially tended to confuse dabbling in a flower garden or orchard with agriculture. When they came up against the hard work that farming demands, it usurped their energies, and ironically, instead of a means, it soon became an end in itself. The soil extracts a price for its riches, but those with visionary vision never saw the relationship between what they wanted to do and what they had to pay to do it.

In addition, most groups typically and foolishly picked remote locations, as the Icarians in Iowa did, and for them even a surplus would have little value because of the great distance to markets. The founders of Modern Times chose their site because of favorable terms: low cash down, five years to pay. As city dwellers ignorant of farming, they readily bought the land unaware of its unproductive soil, the arid conditions, and the area plagued by fires from the sparks of passing locomotives. Thomas Steel's letters from Equality on the Wisconsin frontier tell how, in their need for housing, they tried to build log cabins. Neighbors came to help, and went away laughing at the ignorance of these genteel Londoners.

In Brook Farm, Ripley and his colleagues from Harvard tried their delicate hands at husbandry. Elizabeth Peabody warned them of their folly: even if they succeeded they would only be able to prove that intellectuals who gave over their bodies to backbreaking toil from dawn to dusk might become laborers.

Her point leads us to a basic error in the movement's thinking. Supposing that, through the most ardent efforts of a dedicated few, a utopian model could be shown to work. It still would not necessarily confirm that ordinary individuals subject to normal human weakness could themselves produce and maintain a society with ideal conditions.

The situation in New-Harmony made it somewhat atypical, particularly because of Owen's background. His great success in Scotland came from expertise in textile manufacturing. In fact, the potential he saw in the workshops of Father Rapp's group helped persuade him to buy the colony. But in America, Owen the Scottish industrial expert turned out to be an amateur. His heedless opening of the colony doors before taking the three basic steps of industry – make the crucial market decisions; plan production and distribution; get the manufacturing facilities ready – proved to be a fatal error. Moreover, his course of action – opening the colony doors and then immediately trotting off to Europe in search of support—convinces me that he had no strategy for running an industrial experiment.

Many colonies expended scarce dollars and valuable labor time on producing propaganda media. Uncertainty existed in some minds about whether that took first or second place. For example, the *Harbinger* editors (January 31, 1846) supported the idea that propaganda should take precedence over establishing Phalanxes. The following year (January 16, 1847) they called a "practical trial" one of the "primary objects" of the movement. But they still insisted on "a thorough system of propagation . . . a Press." Apparently no one in the movement, from its earliest days to its last, questioned the wisdom of spending labor time and dollars for propaganda.

The penchant for propaganda created debilitating problems through controversies and misplaced efforts. And in more fundamental terms, it shows how little they planned strategy. If they had thought it through, they would have seen the two essential steps. First, in each case, they should have made sure that the experiment worked and that it had excellent living conditions to at least clearly show the potential if not the immediate fulfillment of the utopian promise. Then, and only then, could they dare boast of the new system and hold up the colony to the scrutiny of a skeptical, pragmatic America.

Red tape instead of planning. In the absence of a carefully worked-out strategy for dealing with the day-to-day organizational procedures, most colonies fell back on traditional administrative formalities. To the untrained eye, such steps looked like well-planned control. In fact, the colonies simply adopted vexatious commercial systems for the operation of experiments in brotherhood. These procedures generated paperwork and disenchantment. Some mandated daily production reports, official requisitions for even minor needs, and despite avowals of mutual trust, exacting methods to account for charges, credits, and exchanges.

Some people consider the dreary, distracting business of filling out forms and writing up reports a necessary evil. But such demanding expressions of emerging bureaucracy, always a danger in any society, had a tendency to become petty at times and ultimately destructive to many colonies. Yet no one in the movement made a serious attempt to control the growth of red tape or mitigate its effects. Paul Brown, whose time in New-Harmony brought him little cheer, castigated the paperwork the Owenites had instituted. "This depending on accounts, notes, bills, receipts, certificates, and reports on paper" conjured up for him ghosts of the old society. He had expected that in this new society the cooperative spirit should have reigned, but these things appeared to him as a revival of traditional "mercantile feelings."[17]

The elaborate systems for recording and rewarding labor time shows the utopian dream perverted into a bureaucratic nightmare. Surprisingly, remuneration generated more controversy and more red tape than any other aspect of operations. That happened because no one had given much thought to operational details before launching a colony. For example, Elijah Grant, founder of Ohio Phalanx, wrote Brisbane for advice on dividing income between labor and shareholders. But seven months of irritating paydays had already gone by before he looked for an authoritative answer. Members everywhere negotiated and renegotiated and often ended up with solutions more complex than equitable, a clear example of how the absence of a carefully planned strategy for compensation damaged the movement. North American Phalanx's scales for adjusting the labor standard, mentioned earlier, typifies these. Brook Farmers arrived at a supposedly fair system, but it could actually produce the opposite effect: absurd inequities. For example, their account book shows that Fred Cabot missed eleven and one-half days of work during February 1845. Still, in that shortest of months he somehow managed to accumulate credited time of twenty two days, one hour and forty minutes.

No anticipation of ordinary calamities. People who could see the extraordinary wonders of humanity's future should have been able to foresee the ordinary troubles that beset us every day. But the movement never had a strategy for drought, floods, frost, and especially sickness.

The labor records of Brook Farm and of Alphadelphia disclose considerable time lost when members became ill. Not surprisingly, illnesses often increased with the hard work and stress of key production periods. That situation posed a grave problem for these farm-dependent colonies because the loss of a few days at harvest could mangle their hopes for a year. But they did not plan for an orderly, routine transfer of people from low-priority jobs to crucial, time-dependent work whenever illness or some other cause required it.

Moreover, they made no reasonable preparations for the always inconstant weather, and they suffered for it. The usual spring rains made the roads impassable and forced Ohio Phalanx members to stop their building program for the season although they had based the colony's success on its completion. Colonies never set aside funds to cover disasters. Thus, a summer drought retarded the peach crop in North American Phalanx and brought on unplanned-for financial headaches.

Owen, Fourier, Cabet, and people of visionary vision in this movement, though they pondered the nature of society, gave little thought to nature itself. They never considered the expected and common ways in which it could affect their grandiose schemes. In the beautiful worlds of their speculations, no one ever gets sick, no bad weather darkens blue skies. But in the real world, unpreparedness creates unsurmountable obstacles.

Neglected the potential in a movement. The leaders of social reorganization overlooked one of their most important assets: the strength that large groups of people working together for a common goal can muster. This error showed most of all in the proliferation of puny experiments when they only needed one robust colony to demonstrate that their ideas could work in practice. Early in social reorganization, the Owenites squandered the potential inherent in a single, concerted effort. Foolishly, they allowed the fragmenting of New-Harmony into separate colonies, a dead end for this movement. In the years after that debacle, they continued to sprinkle small attempts here and there in the East and the Midwest, all of them isolated droplets in place of the Owenite boast of a torrent.

The 1840s phase had the same tendency toward scattering the forces of social reorganization across the country. The Associationists, more than any other division of social reorganization, could have released the hidden power of a movement. They had a much larger following than the others, and many wealthy and influential sympathizers such as Horace Greeley. A few voices did call on all Associationists to raise money for and to unite behind a "Model Phalanx." But petty jealousies and concern for protecting minor fiefdoms—even here—overrode the logic of one well-planned experiment.

They never developed any central organization to direct and coordinate the popular interest in Association. They could have used it to integrate the dozens of Fourier Clubs and committees that had sprung up almost everywhere. They could have gathered all of the piggy-bank treasuries into one large fund, and used it to adequately finance one experiment built to match the promises of their propaganda. Instead, they watched the utopian impulse peter out in scores of disjunct, haphazard ventures built on a foundation of pennies.

The parallel lack of strategy on a press for Association grew directly from the thoughtless approach to colony formation. If they did need a propaganda medium, a doubtful proposition, they surely wasted resources on separate newspapers published in Alphadelphia, Integral Phalanx, Brook Farm, and elsewhere. Moreover, that same neglect of a carefully planned strategy for the Associationist press led to a practice of ignoring the real problems in every experiment. Tampering with the news, inimical to a free society, came back to haunt, as it always must. Since each colony knew little of the fatal errors waylaying others left and right, each in a macabre scenario repeated those same deadly blunders.

The absence of a strategy on centralized guidance also encouraged individual schemes destructive to the movement. The secretary of Integral Phalanx wrote to his counterpart in Alphadelphia that one of the groups in Ohio, in an unfriendly act, had tried to "draw off our members." Some evidence does exist to support his complaint. Ohio Phalanx, for example, hired independent agents, not necessarily sympathizers of Association, to sign up members on a commission basis, a tactic brimming with possible mischief. The correspondence of these colonies show that people interested in joining shopped around. For example, Philandor Tabor wrote to Ohio Phalanx to inquire about the advantages it offered. At about the same time, he also sent a similar inquiry to Alphadelphia. His name later shows up on Alphadelphia's membership list, but his reasons have not found their way into the records.[18]

The leaders of Association liked to spout a Fourier catchword, "Universal Unity." Yet they did not plan a strategy to do whatever it took to unite with the other divisions of social reorganization. People representing its variety came together during this phase of the movement in several congresses and conventions lasting a day or two. Yet the talk always centered on differences rather than similarities, and nothing came of these meetings.

Admittedly, the special tenets of certain groups created difficulties. Ballou pointed to these differences when he rejected a union of his Practical Christians with Brook Farm. And the Brook Farmers accepted that without soul searching for compromise.

Thomas Higginson recalled a more violent barrier to unity between divisions. Social reformers of all persuasions held frequent public discussions in Boston on current issues, and various factions of social reorganization attended. Clearly, they thought they could exploit the meetings as forums for getting their own message out to the general public. Instead, partisans of Association used to clash there in fierce, even ugly ideological battles with supporters of John Collins, a founder of a colony in Skaneateles, New York, based on Owenite ideas.[19] In the absence of a sound strategy to encourage unity, people in social reorganization took part in such follies and dissipated the latent energy of a young movement.

Ironically, their messages never did get out to the general public. Typically, the movement's leadership, like performers in a round dance with arms linked, saw only the center of their circle. And as they wheeled in their own special orbit, they separated themselves ideologically, intellectually, and socially from the masses they hoped to win over. Visionary vision took them to the distant realm of sectarianism, home for many – then and now – who talked of changing the world.

FOGGY IDEAS ABOUT PRINCIPLES

The movement required more than just good management. It also needed people at every level who fully understood its basic rationale. But most colonies had only a few, and perhaps none who looked seriously into its principles. So even if a colony did have leaders with good management skills and expertise in business, that would not have mattered unless they used these in accordance with the utopian promise. Wisconsin Phalanx had good businessmen at the helm. But the skill they knew directed them toward profits as an end, not a means. Consequently, in their drive to make money they ignored and ultimately perverted the movement's elevated objectives. And the membership went along. Mentalities of that sort made no effort for education; no music, no books; not even a Bible shows up in the inventories of their colonies.

Elijah Grant, president of Ohio Phalanx, said people with that outlook had ambitions only for huge crops of wheat and corn, but "they do not see even dimly the importance of . . . refinements." Having suffered those types in his own colony, Grant learned from its collapse. He vowed never to try an Association again "unless it should be under the permanent management of persons who understood both business and the principles of Association." He complained of one Illinois group in which neither the president nor the members had any idea of what the movement stood for.[20]

How could such colonies come into being? Grant provides a good clue in a letter he sent to Brisbane describing the Fourier convention in Pittsburgh. He points out that the delegates knew nothing of Fourier's objectives. They came only to promote their own peculiar schemes for establishing colonies, and they inaccurately called these

Associations. Grant also provides cogent insight on one group: "excellent people, conscientious, self-sacrificing, but stung to madness by the wrongs of civilization, they have leaped abruptly to their present position without pausing to seek for Truth."[21] By seeking for Truth he meant, of course, studying Fourier. Grant saw little hope in their efforts.

Many groups came together in that way with only a vague cooperative arrangement in mind, and they could not wait to attack the soil. In fact, most of the short-lived disasters that took the name "Association" in upstate New York and Ohio during 1844 and 1845 came out of that fatal mold.

Even at the core of Association, one of the few places where people actually read Fourier, confusion existed about the character of the Phalanx. While Fourier envisioned an amalgam and balance of all classes, including laborers and capitalists, the *Harbinger,* under pressure from the New York faction, a small group of middle-class altruists, pushed for a movement directed toward the working class. The ideological confusion this misinterpretation of Fourier generated showed up quickly in the turmoil of Brook Farm and other groups.

Owen's New-Harmony came out of a desire to help the downtrodden, and it too attracted a coterie of wealthy sophisticates with benevolent inclinations. However, when confronted with the laboring classes there, with equality as a fact instead of an abstraction, they retreated behind an uneasy aloofness. Their reaction confirms how little they really understood about the catchwords they spouted. That fault opened a ravine between altruism and need, one the experiment could never bridge.

Too many sidetracks. Most colonies encouraged democracy and pluralism, a virtue that had hidden costs. People far off the mainline to social reorganization found easy access to the membership in these experiments and took advantage of the opportunity to harangue an interested audience ready for some intellectual stimulation. The editors of the *Gazette* established a policy with untold potential for mischief when they agreed to publish all letters. The torrent of diatribes that followed on free will, religion, and a host of other topics having nothing to do with New-Harmony's goal started the movement off on the wrong foot.

Visitors could walk in the open door of most colonies and create distractions, usually innocuous but unnecessary, from the difficult work of building a society. At a Brook Farm meeting, a prim guest raised the issue of swearing in Association, and thereby set off a lengthy but improvident discussion. In Wisconsin Phalanx the same arguments actually led to a rule against swearing, and the colony enforced it. Rules like that encourage busybodies more than busy people. Besides, such rules negate a basic Fourier tenet that calls the suppression of human emotion a social evil. A silly issue, perhaps, but it does show how easily these experiments could be sidetracked.

Free discussion took more serious turns, of course. But in making their lecterns available to visiting proselytizers from a spectrum of religious sects as well as atheism, members quickly found themselves fighting over issues totally irrelevant to the movement's program. Given the hazy understanding of the movement's objectives by most members, this atmosphere could only make the path to the distant goal more foggy. When the partisans of abolition and the hucksters of free love, spiritualism, and other extraneous causes brought their inflammatory proposals to the floor, they easily shunted these fragile experiments off the mainline to social reorganization. The heated debates and often angry controversies these visitors could produce worked against the unity every group desperated needed. Although the mental stimulation that such discussions generated might seem like a tonic, it actually turned out to be a lethal potion, even in small doses, to these prematurely born democracies.

The movement's hunger for members made it possible for people with goals quite different and even antagonistic to social reorganization to infiltrate its ranks. Some joined up simply because they thought of its members as potential recruits for their own causes. In addition, the character of the movement as a social protest attracted into its ranks come-outers (opponents of social conservatism in the church) and other dissidents. Many of them had only a nebulous impression of what the movement hoped to achieve. Faddists and eccentrics saw it as a place where their oddities or fringe concepts might be more readily accepted.

Current fads, such as the water cure, ran through several colonies but probably did no harm. However, the attention and energy devoted to spiritualism and bizarre notions about communicating with the dead, clearly disrupted Wisconsin Phalanx and several others, and became a decisive factor in their dissolution. The followers of Emanuel Swedenborg, a mystic who interpreted the Bible from dreams and visions – he claimed he had beheld the Last Judgment – joined several colonies in order to convert the members. Grant complained to Greeley about how the Swedenborgians had exploited Ohio Associations for their own purposes. He called them arrogant and intolerant, and he pointed out that when they could no longer make converts, they simply deserted a colony, leaving a destructive effect on its stability.[22] The antireligionists in New-Harmony, though they proclaimed devotion to the New Social System, effectively derailed the experiment by pointing it down a sidetrack.

In every colony that opened the gate into these byways the wrong turnoff affected its ability to go forward. The shakiest needed only a few steps down the wrong turn to reach the end of the road.

Too much trivia. The proper approach to activities and organizational details loomed large in the minds of people weak on principles. That happened because they did not know how to evaluate the basic aspects of colony life in terms of the movement's goal. As a result, their colonies ran into trouble in discriminating between major and minor, and these two disparate concerns easily ended up getting the same attention. In that way, leaders and often the entire membership allowed themselves to become mired in some petty problem or in getting some unimportant task done while more pressing work waited in line.

In some of the groups operating as joint stock companies, new members could exchange personal property for shares of the colony. When a new family arrived, the colony had to make a detailed inventory of items tendered for exchange. Their property often consisted of nothing more than kitchen utensils of low value. Still, no matter how inconsequential, a price for each piece had to be negotiated, and the appraisal sessions could be disputatious. After that, members could still appeal for adjustments. One member of an Association in central New York called it a "dollar and cents business" that should have reached "a higher note." It led directly to the aborting of his colony.[23]

Cabet, unlike most others, did not offer his Icarians democratic niceties. In accord with his strict rules mandating community of property, members had no choice but to surrender to the general fund everything they owned. Nothing could be held back, not even trinkets or sentimental items of no value. In the great context of changing the world, some might call such matters unimportant. But Emile Valet said he saw these little irritants gradually contribute to the decline of Icaria during his six years there.

Too many meetings. Like the fault of spending time on trivia this one comes directly out of the uncertainties that leaders had about the movement's goal and principles. Typically, they would make no decisions, not even insignificant ones, without calling a meeting of all the members and without full discussion and a majority mandate. These sessions generally opened the floor to anyone with a point to make, valid or not, and even to people with their own agenda. As we have seen, the utopian colonies had plenty of them.

Democratic in intent out of a noble impulse to show absolute fairness to all voices on all questions, the penchant for talk still came with a price tag. Special daytime meetings interrupted work, but frequent evening meetings had more insidious effects. They leached away relaxation hours that these tender, novice laborers needed, and took time from educational and cultural activities, the promise that distinguished utopian life from ordinary farm life. At the least, frequent meetings simply became one more distraction along the road to steady progress. In Icaria, however, where Cabet made attendance at all meetings mandatory, they became self-defeating. Cabet's headstrong ways produced stormy sessions, and each successive meeting alienated more members and raised the discord index.

A democratic society needs councils, committees and subcommittees and consensus. But this movement allowed these to become ends instead of the means to a smoothly functioning democracy. If everyone in these experiments based on cooperation understood the principles, volunteers should have been able to handle minor decisions and details without the need for motions, points of order, and calling the question. But in the absence of that essential understanding, meetings just became a way of life. For example, North American Phalanx's Industrial Council could not cope with Fourier's complex schedule of operations without meeting every night to work out the details of the following day's labor schedule. The council had to finish this chore no matter how long it took, because the new lists for each day had to be posted on the wall before breakfast. In Fourier's speculative world people always choose tasks according to what attracts them personally. Here they found out what to do from a schedule made by a committee whose decisions came after a day of farm labor.

At least one more factor needs to be added to these dozen that precluded success. The utopian experiments generated irreconcilable animosity in the establishment. Of course, that cannot be counted as a fault of the movement. Admittedly, social reorganization, by definition, stood as a threat to the very foundations of traditional society. But, in fact, the antagonism came as much from what the members said and the way they said it as it did from the movement's goal. Although none of the groups covered in this book advocated violence and although only a small number opposed private property, they did seize every opportunity to expose without restraint what they perceived as the wrongs and hypocrisy of the present social system. They held these aloft not as isolated problems of the times but as the inherent flaws of a social system so defective it had to be replaced.

In comparison, the groups dedicated to individual salvation such as the Shakers and Amana did in fact commit a cardinal sin against traditional society by holding all property in common. Yet, the establishment saw no threat from that quarter because these groups did not make an ideological issue of private property, but went quietly about their mission. More important, their monastic austerity held little attraction for the poor and discontented of traditional society. Indeed, the asceticism and stern way of life itself served as a vindication for defenders of the competitive system.

Social reorganization did not go about its business quietly but continued to pound away at social evils whenever and wherever the opportunity came up. Defenders of the status quo reacted in various ways, none pleasant. Edgar Allen Poe dubbed the experiment outside Boston "Snook Farm" and publicly branded its members "crazyites." John Dwight found his social life in his hometown ruined because people viewed him as "a member of a despised sect."[24]

Moreover, some groups relaxed traditional social conventions and seemed, in the eyes of conservative New Englanders, to be thumbing their noses at the establishment. A backlash may have taken forms more destructive than mere name calling. The fire of unexplained cause that wiped out Brook Farm's new building and all hope for the experiment left the members with uneasy thoughts. John Sears, a youngster there, delighted in the colony's pleasant informalities. He surmised as others did that the stern specter of puritanism still haunting Boston's countryside could not abide the colony's free spirits and that it impelled bigoted neighbors to arson. The potential for terrorism undoubtedly existed elsewhere too. Warren Chase of Wisconsin Phalanx, for example, mentioned hostility in the area, and he said the colony had to guard their mill around the clock to protect it from a similar fate.[25]

Aftermath

These factors and other less important ones remorselessly dragged every experiment of social reorganization down to a tragic end. Perhaps the most depressing aspect came from the ominous feeling that began to haunt members long before the actual collapse. It materialized in an unthinkable thought: all the sacrifices, hard work, and loss of life savings would simply go to waste.

John Collins, leader of the Skaneateles experiment, visited Sodus Bay Phalanx early in what turned out to be its final year. His gloomy report touched deep nerves throughout the movement, and to Sodus Bay members it must have sounded like a eulogy although the colony still breathed then. He found it painful to think that these people "who for nearly two years had struggled against great odds, . . . must be dispersed and thrown back again to . . . strife and competition." But worst of all, he characterized their efforts as "useless." Similarly, Elijah Grant began looking critically at what the movement had begotten once he recognized the inevitable in his Ohio Phalanx. In addition to his emotional investment, which had been heavy, he had also lost a thousand dollars, a considerable sum then. He applied his experience to what he saw in Brook Farm, and his thoughts surely brought no cheer to its members. He called their situation a shame because "so many interesting and devoted people were laboring and sacrificing themselves to so little purpose."[26]

How did these gentle revolutionaries, ordinary humans after all, deal with dreams shattered and the enormity of a world lost? For utopians who never allowed the dreaded word failure to enter their minds, the cold steel of reality cut deeply. Augustin Savardan described the mood at La Réunion when a day of bitter discord and recrimination finally told everyone the end had come. "It was a deplorable scene. [Allyre] Bureau was somber, so disheartened, so preoccupied with thoughts of suicide that it was hardly possible to get a few monosyllables of response out him."[27] After Alphadelphia went under, members refused to talk about the experiment – even decades later – saying they had banished its memory.

Disenchantment and slamming the door on a credo seem to be understandable human reactions when a beautiful future turns out to be an ugly past. Most people in the movement groped for reasons, and many came up with a scapegoat: the masses, the very people they had hoped to win over. Maria Marchand of Icaria gave the typical if not the most prevalent explanation when she called the masses ignorant. A correspondent for the *Harbinger* blamed prosperity and gloated that the next depression would teach the masses its bitter lesson. Josiah Warren left the disaster of New-Harmony convinced of the inherent selfishness of the human race.

Some utopians merely modified their thinking and looked for other ways to continue what they thought of as good works. After Raritan Bay Union had gone the way of other experiments he had helped underwrite, Marcus Spring, the wealthy New York sympathizer of Association, turned to education as the only hope for the future. In fact, teaching became a favorite agency for thwarted revolutionaries. On the other hand, Adin Ballou found a different path more in accord with his religious beliefs when Hopedale broke up after fourteen years. He turned to charitable work, convinced that people should attempt no more than they are able to do and "let the rest find its proper doer."[28]

Some former revolutionaries turned their backs completely on what they had professed and went off in the opposite direction in their political, religious, and social views. Charles A. Dana, one of the most famous reversals, closeted reams of his radical *Harbinger* articles and later became famous for the arch-conservatism of the *New York Sun*, which he owned and edited.

A surprising number of Brook Farm members and friends went from the colony's spirit of personal, unbounded religious expression, free of prescribed observances, to the cloistered mysticism and formalized rites of the Roman Catholic church. They include Sophia Ripley, Sarah Stearns, and Orestes Brownson. Members in other groups also took that route, sometimes creating surprising changes. For example, Thomas Nichols of Modern Times, whose strident espousal of sexual promiscuity stigmatized the colony, later became a devout Catholic.

Some transformations strain credibility. Charles Lane, who had imposed the most stringent regimen on the members of Fruitlands—only vegetables, fruits, and clear, cold water—went to the Shakers. Like most groups dedicated to individual salvation, they had no food taboos and gave no thought to such items as pork and wine. Fruitlanders had also abhorred anything of cotton because it came from the evil of slavery. When the colony broke up, Sam Larned, in an even more astonishing turnabout than Lane's, moved to the South and married a slave owner.

As for Ripley, who later became an important literary critic and editor, the spirit of Brook Farm still animated him although he tended toward political but not religious conservatism. However, two late manuscript fragments I found among his papers do disclose more poignantly than anything else how the soul of this humanitarian, who wanted so much to elevate men and women everywhere, must have churned. On one of these pieces of paper he listed, for some unknown purpose, "Leaders of Thought," which contains twenty-two names, from Plato to Spencer. One person's name remains conspicuous by its absence, the one Ripley venerated in Brook Farm days as a foremost leader of thought and for whom he had once given over his entire life without reserve: Fourier. On the other manuscript Ripley used what he considered his most important contributions to periodical literature. His voluminous work for the *Harbinger* does not appear there.[29]

This preponderance of negatives seems to load the historical balance completely on the side of failure. On the other hand, an impressive number of individuals did come away from these colonies with highly positive reactions to their experience, and they lift the beam slightly toward the other side. For them, the words *success* and *failure* do not stand like the rigid absolutes of a computer's binary world, the mechanical yes or no, but bend in more pliant, more human interpretations. So despite the harsh conditions they endured, they found mitigating aspects of life in their colonies that qualified the concepts of success and failure for them. To those who look only skin-deep, success and failure might seem like incompatible opposites. But to these members, whose responses represented innermost thoughts and feelings, success and failure could actually emerge from the utopian episodes side by side.

For example, when Giles Stebbins recalled the people and life in Northampton, he found a simple but essential balance: "It may be said that we did not succeed, but surely we did not wholly fail, for the memory of those days has been pleasant and helpful to all." Another member of Northampton, George Stetson, saw it from a different perspective. He explained in his reminiscences that the colony's leaders believed that through a liberal and moral education for their children they could influence society. He reviewed the subsequent lives and characters of people there and decided that "the results desired have been generally obtained." Moreover, he pointed out that although the enterprise "failed materially," it did achieve something: these people remained an influence for good in the surrounding area long after the colony had been forgotten.[30] Indeed, as we shall see, that legacy stands as one of the valuable contributions of the movement.

Social reorganization made happiness its objective, and in fact the word *happiness* appears not only in reminiscences but also in descriptions from the midst of the colony experience. Ripley confirmed that, "We are conscious of a happiness which we never knew until we embarked in this career." He cautioned that "a hasty and superficial observer" would notice only the "great imperfections and embarrassments," but he characterized life there as "far superior" to anything in "Civilization." Earlier, James Curtis had written his father that he was "decidedly contented here" and if given a choice of any style of life "from royalty to serfdom," he would take Brook Farm.[31] Chester Adkins summed up his six years of Wisconsin Phalanx in one short phrase, "the happiest years of my life." Isabella Hunter, who also spent six years there, used a similar phrase, "the happiest days of my life," and characterized it as "a little taste of the millennium." Moreover, half a century later, she declared that the friendships made there had lasted throughout the ensuing years.[32] This phenomenon came out of certain other colonies too. Undoubtedly, the fellowship and camaraderie and even the few good times those places knew, accounted for part of it. But certainly, like soldiers who go through battle together, the members experienced a uniting force that grew out of the sense of shared sacrifice. Moreover, many saw what they did in larger terms, as a noble act for humanity's sake, and that conviction intensified bonds of comradeship.

Analogously, at least eight marriages came out of Brook Farm. Undoubtedly, the fervent spirit of purpose and all of its emotional overtones that characterized Brook Farm, served as matchmaker. Though the number seems proportionately high for so small a group, incomplete information about marriages in other colonies makes comparisons difficult. Of course, Brook Farmers, seemed more inclined than any other group to record for posterity the details of their feelings and lives, and that propensity may distort the ratio.

However, their tendency does provide us with insights into the quality of life there. They said they felt happier at Brook Farm than anywhere else; they found life more rewarding, more exhilarating, and better than any they had ever known. Frank Sanborn, not a member but an intimate friend of Brook Farmers who knew their deepest feelings, referred to the colony as "that lost paradise" and "that arcadia," and his allusions come through in the words of the members. Thus, John Codman remembered most its poetic atmosphere, and Willard Saxton saw his life there as a beautiful picture.

Amelia Russell believed that their Brook Farm experience later helped members cope with the world. She claimed that the new vigor and freshness she felt in her first days there remained with her even after four decades. Strange as it may seem, others attested to that same feeling. In 1880, half a lifetime after her student days at Brook Farm, Nora Schelter Blair wrote to Ripley to ask for a photograph to show her grandchildren. "I feel an emotion of rejuvenation whenever I look back on the time spent at Brook Farm," she confided. And he replied – his usually fine handwriting now blurred by his final illness – that he too rejoiced in the "beautiful remembrances."[33]

Legacies

The leaders of Association, Greeley, Brisbane, and others, refused to admit failure, saying there had never been a valid trial. By this, they meant an adequately funded, properly run experiment based on the ideas of Fourier or at least as these American revisionists of Fourier had adapted and diluted them. So in their view, the downfall of paltry and totally inadequate colonies offering substandard living conditions meant nothing.

However, Ripley found success even in disaster. "The great cause which we advocate has rather gained than lost by these failures. They have been schools for training, heavy as the cost has been." And with a sure instinct for continuity, he passed the torch to the future. "We are only preparing materials which . . . will help those who come after us."[34]

Ripley's insight suggests a link between social reorganization and the growth of a radical tradition in America. Only a few people saw, as Ripley did, the subtle threads that tied all of social reorganization's diversity into a single force for social change, a movement. No matter, the threads did exist; they ran through the movement and eventually continued on into other causes. We can trace one weaving through the decades, connecting Owenites to Fourierists to the followers of Cabet.

At the beginning, the Owenite phase, we see New-Harmony leaders studying and discussing Fourier, unknown in America then, and calling his ideas excellent. The connection gels as the movement's Fourier phase gets under way while the other fades. Owen's experiment, long since gone, becomes a generic term, as when Samuel Osgood, Dwight's friend, learns of plans for Brook Farm, and asks, "Did you hear of the New Harmony which is about to be established?"[35]

Then, after Brook Farm passes from the scene, North American Phalanx dedicates its new hall with a ritual that shows another link. As members and guests hold hands around a circle, Channing intones a prayer, and James Fisher, the wealthy sympathizer of Association, unfurls a banner. Blue cloth with "Universal Unity" in silver letters, it had belonged to Brook Farm, a symbol they created long ago for

Fourier celebrations. And now it becomes a bond across the years.

Later, Fisher visits Icaria, a colony diametrically opposite to Association on the basic question of private property. He carries a letter from Greeley introducing him to Cabet as "a true socialist" and "a friendly observer." Some years after that, Fisher, still dedicated to Association, receives a letter from Alcander Longley of Cincinnati, publisher of the *Communist Monthly,* thanking him for his support. Later still, Longley, a member in nine Associations and other experiments over the years, advertises the *Communist Monthly* as available at all "liberal and progressive book stores." A curious phrase, it suggests the jargon of other movements and a widening diffusion of radicals. Finally, in the 1880s, Moncure Conway, who has been at Modern Times but who is too young to have been at Brook Farm, still senses the spirit of Brook Farm after four decades. The property has passed though several hands and different uses over the decades, and a few vestiges of the old colony remain. Yet he feels compelled to "make a pilgrimage" to those hallowed grounds.[36] Through all of this a vital essence of the movement passes, touching hands across differences.

Tracing that thread discloses one of the legacies of the movement: the rise of the professional radical, a new phenomenon in America. A person of that calling, unlike most earlier activists, labors for a cause – often unpopular – not as an evening or weekend volunteer but as a full-time occupation. Some, like New-Harmony's leaders, have money, but most, like John Dwight, must find time between agitation and propaganda to eke out their daily bread as best they can. Like Alcander Longley's, their names appear and reappear in documents of the movement as its various efforts come and go. People of that mold show up in latter-day social movements of every persuasion.

The most important legacies of the movement come out of the issues they raised and the programs they tried to establish. Many seemed radical then, but as an original Brook Farmer, George Bradford, recognized late in the century, some gained general acceptance over the years. Today, many seem ordinary.

For example, social reorganization advocated education as the single most important remedy for all the ills of society. Admittedly, others had seen the social importance of education. But the movement elevated it from a quiet philosophical proposition into a rallying cry. Horace Greeley proclaimed the wondrous future to the world: education shall "banish evil and wretchedness from the face of the earth."[37] Moreover, the movement's propaganda raised the stakes in education by calling for a program both free and universal, a possibility beyond the imagination of those times. That most colonies ultimately defaulted on the promise does not detract from it. And even where that happened, colonies still brought the first school into many remote parts of our country. It then became, as in the case of Wisconsin Phalanx's demise, the district school, the movement's unexpected legacy to the surrounding countryside.

The same holds true for the elevation of the arts that the movement brought into the hinterlands. In the 1820s ordinary people in New-Harmony heard Mozart and Haydn, music otherwise rare on the frontier, and elsewhere available only to the elite. Moreover, the Owenites introduced stage plays into the colony, and those first performances led to a drama tradition and a fine theater that lived on in the little town of New Harmony, Indiana, for decades after their experiment died. Such things along with the schools the town inherited from the Owenites made it into a cultural center. Its advantages held members there and attracted newcomers.

A similar legacy endured in the wake of other colonies. Raritan Bay Union, which taught art in its school, had a collection of European prints, musical performances, and excellent lectures by people of letters and noted poets. These refinements outlived the experiment and brought painters George Inness and William Page as well as prominent writers and actors to the area and to the school that arose from the ashes of Raritan Bay Union. People from the former colony's band and from its philosophers' club continued to provide the area with an intellectual climate that rural towns then could not hope to enjoy.

Experiments like New-Harmony, for all their faults, did offer a public arena where serious questions normally kept in the establishment's closet could be openly raised. These questions often dealt with issues that would sooner or later find their way onto the national agenda and prod America into thinking about its values. For an illustration of just how far ahead of their time the Owenites might have been, let us take notice that in the year 1825 the *Gazette* chose to publish a letter from a Native American (October 22). His name was Red Jacket, a member of the Onondaga Nation, and the editors made space available to him so that he could describe the suffering of his people. Ideas like that, barely heard then, have only recently begun to catch the national ear. Giving such voices a forum remains a legacy of the movement.

The ministers who came out of their pulpits to found Brook Farm,

Hopedale, and other experiments did so because they saw the established churches standing aloof from the suffering of humanity. The wrongs they cried out against would not go away, and in time others took up the call to the public soul. Their efforts remain as a legacy in the idea of a church with a social conscience, and today most people seem comfortable with its mission of protecting the exploited and taking a political stand in behalf of the downtrodden and the defenseless.

Icaria destroyed itself with incessant polemics over dogma. But its bickering did not extend to ethnic relations. A French colony, it included Germans, Italians, Poles, and Spaniards who, as the Icarian song "My Commune" says, made into firewood the fences that separated them. It showed the possibilities of a pluralistic society, something America, then on the road to the melting pot, needed to learn – and still does.

Programs to combat the hazards of alcohol and to raise questions about the use of tobacco certainly did not originate with the advent of social reorganization. However the movement's colonies almost without exception institutionalized these concerns with a novel argument, extreme then but a standard now, that society has a duty to protect its citizens against harmful substances. And when colonies dissolved, members returned to traditional society as vigorous defenders of that principle.

Finally, in its most significant legacy, the movement challenged the time-worn inferiority that society had imposed on women. And it raised the consciousness of women – and men – within and outside the movement long before traditional society even began to give any thought to the question. Moreover, the movement did not simply look for a few quiet reforms. And it went far beyond its historically important championship of freedom in dress styles for women, which made it easier for them to expand their work and recreation horizons. It said that women should have the right to determine their roles in life, guaranteed of a full and equal education and equal rights not only in society but also in marriage. Brook Farm and the *Harbinger* made comparatively good strides in this. But even in colonies that dragged their feet, where words outdistanced deeds, the words themselves remain a contribution to our time because the words shook the silence and reinforced voices long stifled by society. It should be to the everlasting credit of those utopians that their early stand contributed to the winning of rights that have only recently begun to filter into the lives of half our population.

Through all of these things, the movement helped confront old assumptions about the values and goals of humanity. In that way, the people of social reorganization contributed a voice to the conscience of society, an essential of democracy sadly quiet through much of our history. And when the New-Harmonies of America came to an end, a legacy of tolerance and concern with human needs lingered on in their respective localities. That legacy animated and invigorated the democratic spirit and reinforced the axiom that a good society cares about the welfare and happiness of its people.

Postscript

People of later times who have looked back critically on our utopians have typically found it easy to sneer at their naïveté. In truth, the utopians really believed that by now their ideal society would be here, bringing universal happiness. But before we recommit them to the obscure footnotes where they have managed to survive, we might wonder what they would say if they could see our world and realize how far off the mark their faith had been.

Undoubtedly, our technology would impress them, particularly with respect to health. But then they would get down to other basics in the quality of life and might even return our sneers. They would see that from "Star Trek" to Star Wars, real and fictional, we still accept violence as a way of settling disagreements. Indeed, as a nation we seem bewitched by violence. They would marvel at resources not even a utopian could imagine and would then ask why hunger and malnutrition still remain a plague for millions. They would be astonished that with an educational system outstripping the fantasies of a Cabet, illiteracy and ignorance still haunt us. They might be appalled that we, knowing history, still let inequality and bigotry stalk the land. And they would dismiss our values, which recognize ethics and morality as annoying guests in the houses of power – and even in ordinary homes. Utopians denounced those evils more than a century ago.

That does not mean they had the solution to our problems. Social change comes out of two related questions, What is wrong? and How can we fix it? But even though some people present answers to the first that appear convincing, it does not necessarily follow that their answers to the second will be equally sound. That seems obvious, but people in social reorganization missed the logic and fell into a basic error. They assumed that compelling evidence on the first naturally made them right on the second.

Actually, given the glaring faults in society there will undoubtedly always be a good supply of answers to What is wrong, the easy part. Owen, Fourier, Cabet, Marx, and a long list of others have developed them, often with persuasive arguments. However, the difficulty always comes with How can we fix it, the hard part. Those who want to remake society tend to propose ideal solutions. But in our complex society, where change that benefits one person often harms another, we need workable solutions. The people of social reorganization proceeded on the assumption that one ideal fits all, and never gave any thought to the possibility that their ideal solution might not be ideal for everyone.

Change has its cost, not necessarily in money but in its effect on the soul of society. And herein lies another basic error of social reorganization. It never looked for informed consent on a question a good society must always ask of its people: How much are you willing to bear for change? In this balanced summary of social reorganization, that dereliction weighs heavily on the negative side.

Still, that movement and its people should command a higher place than the obscurity history has assigned to them if for nothing else than their role as voices of social conscience. Their spirits must surely be deriding present-day values. They would certainly denounce late twentieth-century leaders who encourage personal greed without concern for where it takes society. As spirits of social conscience, they would then turn to those who accept that as moral and throw down this challenge, "Yes, we failed, but at least we tried; what have *you* done about society's faults and the cynicism and despair it imposes on millions? What have *you* done to prevent the social cataclysms that inevitably flare up from hopelessness?" Recent events answer all too clearly.

Finally, we cannot pack the utopian episodes away without exalting their positive attraction, one that gave them life: their optimism. Perhaps nothing characterizes it as well as a toast that John Dwight made at one of the movement's celebrations not long after the young, sanguine hearts of Brook Farm beheld its tragic end: "To Joy! to Liberty! to Childhood's Mirth! to Youth's Enthusiasm!" By keeping alive aspirations for a better world, they elevated human spirits; by lifting eyes above the ground, they sustained hope that society would somehow find a way to ameliorate the human condition. In our social wisdom we ought to remember the voices of society's conscience and its messengers of hope.

Appendix A

Brief Notes about People Frequently Mentioned

A. Bronson Alcott. Teacher, itinerant peddler. Founded Fruitlands at age forty-five. Father of Louisa May Alcott.

Albert Brisbane. Early champion of Fourier in America. Wrote several books explaining "the practical part" of Fourier. In his thirties when movement peaked, he became ideological godfather of Association.

Georgiana Bruce. At twenty-two, became early member of Brook Farm. Taught in its school. After leaving, she married, and under her married name, Kirby, wrote of colony experience. She is identified in this book by the name associated with her colony life, Bruce.

William Henry Channing. Clergyman. Nephew of renowned Unitarian William Ellery Channing. In his mid-thirties preached Fourierism with evangelical fervor, but never joined any colony. Agitated for establishment of religion on frequent visits to Brook Farm, North American Phalanx, and Raritan Bay Union.

Warren Chase. At thirty-two, one of the founders and a president of Wisconsin Phalanx, key experiment in West. Socialist candidate for governor.

Charles Codman. Came to Brook Farm as a boy with brother John. Later went on to Modern Times and left manuscript history of that colony.

John Codman. Came to Brook Farm as a boy with brother Charles. Wrote book about life in Brook Farm.

Victor Considérant. Disciple of Fourier. Came to America at forty-six to found La Réunion. Wrote books promoting Texas as ideal for an experiment.

Charles A. Dana. Quit Harvard and went to Brook Farm. Wrote literary criticism for its newspaper. Later in Lincoln's cabinet; then owned and edited *New York Sun.*

John Sullivan Dwight. Harvard divinity graduate. Disillusioned with pulpit; joined Brook Farm soon after it began. Was music and literary critic for its paper. Later published influential *Dwight's Journal of Music.* Helped found Boston Philharmonic.

Marianne Dwight. Came to Brook Farm in her late twenties. Skilled in drawing. Taught in its school. Before experiment ended, she married Brook Farmer John Otis but is identified in this book by the name associated with her colony life, Dwight.

Elijah Grant. Yale graduate. In his mid-thirties, founded Ohio Phalanx.

Horace Greeley. Publisher of *New York Tribune.* Active supporter of Association though never well-versed in its goals and spirit. Gave movement use of a column in his paper for propaganda. Later Republican candidate for president of the United States.

Maria Marchand. Grew up in the Icaria of Iowa and wrote of her experience there. During its late period, she married William Ross, but because most events she described come from the years before, she is identified in this book as Marchand.

Robert Dale Owen. Son of Robert Owen. At twenty-four came to New-Harmony and joined his older brother William. Took active role in its cultural life. Later a congressman.

George Ripley. Harvard divinity graduate. Disillusioned with pulpit; founded Brook Farm at age thirty-nine with wife, Sophia. Both taught in its school. He edited its newspaper. Later literary critic and editor for *Harper's.*

Amelia Russell. Daughter of a diplomat. Joined Brook Farm in its second year and stayed till the end. Teacher in its school. Wrote of her experiences there.

Emile Vallet. Came to Icaria in Nauvoo at sixteen. Served as teacher. Opposed Cabet's dictatorial ways. Left after six years, just before Cabet's ouster. Wrote of his experiences there.

Appendix B

Colony Names, Locations, and Principal Newspapers

Name and Location	*Year*	*Formal Name*	*Principal Newspaper*
Alphadelphia			
Comstock, Mich.	1844–48	Alphadelphia Industrial Association	
Brook Farm			
West Roxbury, Mass.	1841–44	Brook Farm Institute of Agriculture and Education	
	1844–45	Brook Farm Association for Industry and Education	
	1845–47	Brook Farm Phalanx	
	1845–48		*Harbinger*
Fruitland			
near Harvard, Mass.	1843		
Hopedale			
near Mendon, Mass.	1841	Fraternal Community No. 1	
near Milford, Mass.	1842–56	Hopedale Community	
Icaria			
Nauvoo, Ill.	1849–60	Icarian Community	
Corning, Iowa	1856–95		
	1879–86	Jeune Icaria	
	1851, 1852		*Popular Tribune*

Appendix B (*continued*)

Name and Location	*Year*	*Formal Name*	*Principal Newspaper*
	1854		*Colonie Icarienne*
	1855, 1856, 1857, 1878		*Revue Icarienne*
La Réunion now Dallas, Tex.	1855–58		
Modern Times now Brentwood, N.Y.	1851–late 1850s		
New-Harmony New Harmony, Ind.	1825–26	Preliminary Society of New-Harmony	
	1826–27	New-Harmony Community of Equality	
	1825–28		*Gazette*
North American Phalanx near Red Bank, N.J.	1843–55		
Northampton Florence, Mass.	1842–46	Northampton Association of Education and Industry	
Ohio Phalanx near Bellaire, Ohio	1844–45	(also called American Phalanx)	
Raritan Bay Union Perth Amboy, N.J.	1853–56		
Sodus Bay Sodus and Huron Twps., N.Y.	1844–45	Sodus Bay Phalanx	
Wisconsin Phalanx now Ripon, Wis.	1844–50	(also called Ceresco Community)	

Notes

Abbreviations

ARCHIVES, manuscript collections, and certain frequently cites sources with lengthy names are identified by the following special abbreviations. Otherwise, items in the Notes are generally cited in a shortened form, details of which can be located in the Bibliography. A few peripheral items are not included in the Bibliography, and for them the full references are given in the Notes.

Alpha	Alphadelphia Association Papers. Michigan Historical Collections, Bentley Historical Library, Univ. of Michigan.
Bryant	Bryant-Godwin Collection. Rare Books and Manuscripts Division, New York Public Library, Astor, Lenox and Tilden Foundations.
Cabet	Etienne Cabet, *Colonia icarienne aux Etats-Unis d'Amérique, sa constitution, ses lois, sa situation matérielle et morale après le premier semestre de 1855* (Paris, 1856).
Ceresco	Ceresco Community Papers. State Historical Society of Wisconsin, Division of Archives and Manuscripts, Madison.
Dwight J	John Sullivan Dwight Papers. Boston Public Library.
Dwight M	Marianne Dwight, *Letters from Brook Farm, 1844–1847,* ed. Amy L. Reed (Poughkeepsie, N.Y., 1928).
Fisher	James T. Fisher Papers. Massachusetts Historical Society, Boston.
Fourier Q	Charles Fourier, *Théorie des quatre mouvements et des destinées générales,* 2d ed. (Paris: Aux Bureau de la Phalange, 1841).
Fourier U	Charles Fourier, *Théorie de l'unité universelle,* 2d ed., 4 vols. (Paris: La Société pour la propagation et pour la réalization de la théorie de Fourier, 1840–43).
Grant	Elijah P. Grant Papers. Special Collections, Joseph Regenstein Library, Univ. of Chicago.
Harvard	Houghton Library, Harvard Univ.
Icaria MS	Icarian Community Manuscripts. State Historical Society of Iowa, Des Moines.
Illinois	Illinois Historical Survey, Univ. of Illinois, Urbana.
Ill-StLib	Illinois State Historical Library, Springfield.

Macdonald	A. J. Macdonald Collection. Yale Collection of American Literature, Beinecke Rare Book and Manuscript Library, Yale Univ.
MHS	Massachusetts Historical Society, Boston.
NH	New Harmony Community Records. Library of New Harmony Workingmen's Institute, New Harmony, Indiana.
NJHS	New Jersey Historical Society, Newark.
Steel	Thomas Steel Papers. State Historical Society of Wisconsin, Division of Archives and Manuscripts, Madison.
Throop	George Addison Throop Papers. Collection no. 218, Department of Manuscripts and University Archives, Cornell Univ.

1. The Who, What, When, and Where of the Utopian Episodes

1. Articles of Agreement and Association between the members of the Institute for Agriculture and Education.

2. Josiah Warren, "Natural Liberty Consistent with Social Order," MS, NH.

3. Hymn 242, *Hopedale Hymns;* Ballou's characterization: *Harbinger,* Feb. 28, 1846; the religious test: Ballou, *Practical Christian Socialism,* 520– 21, and *Hopedale Community,* 2–4.

4. Letter from William Owen to Henry, *New-Harmony Gazette,* Oct. 29, 1825; George Ripley, "Sign of the Times," *Harbinger,* Nov. 21, 1846; Victor Hennequin, *Love in the Phalanstery* (New York, 1849), 3.

5. [Cabet], *Community of Icaria,* 14.

6. Frothingham, *Ripley,* 118.

7. Statement by John Dwight, *Boston Chronotype,* Aug. 23, 1849, quoted in Cooke, *Dwight,* 138; Ballou's list: Ballou, *Practical Christian Socialism,* 26; Cabet, "Communistes Célèbres," *Colonie Icarienne,* Oct. 4, 1854.

8. "Clermont Phalanx," *Phalanx,* May 18, 1844; Elijah Grant to Albert Brisbane, Mar. 31, 1845, Grant; Marianne Dwight to Anna, Mar. 22, 1846, Dwight M; Nichols, "Institute of Desarollo," *Hopedale Community,* 8; *New-Harmony Gazette,* May 24, 1826.

9. "Social Utopias," in vol. 3, William and Robert Chambers, *Chambers's Papers for the People,* 12 vols. (London and Edinburgh, 1856).

2. The Spur to a Utopian Life

1. Russell, *Home Life,* 4; Louisa Sheldon to Abigail Sheldon, Oct. 1, 1847, Ceresco.

2. Savardan, *Un naufrage,* 130–35; Wolski, *Impressions,* 178–83.

3. Wolski, *Impressions,* 187.

4. Frances Judd, "Reminiscences," in Sheffield, *History,* 116.

5. Horace Greeley to Charles A. Dana, Aug. 29, 1842, Wilson, *Dana,* 42.

6. George Throop to Dewitt Throop, Mar. 17, 1844, Throop.

7. Frederick Douglass, "What I Found at the Northampton Association," in Sheffield, *History,* 130.

8. Considérant, *European Colonization,* 10–11; [Cabet], *Community of Icaria,* 1; Bradford, "Reminiscences," 142.

9. Sears, *Fruitlands,* 47.

10. Bremer, *Homes* 2:621–22.

11. John Bliss to H. R. Schetterly, Jan. 30, 1845, Alpha.
12. Fourier Q, 192.
13. "Mr. Ballou's Address," *Harbinger*, Feb. 28, 1846.
14. Bradford, "Philosophic Thought," 313.
15. Cabet, 116.
16. Considérant, *Great West*, 54.
17. Lane, "Brook Farm," 351; Russell, *Home Life*, 46; Georgiana Bruce Kirby, "My First Visit," 15.
18. [Olinet], *Socialisme*, 18–19; George Throop to Dewitt Throop, Oct. 4, 1843, Throop.
19. Conway, *Pine and Palm*, 226–27, 244; Sophia Ripley to John Dwight, Aug. 1840, Dwight J; A. Bloomer Hart, "Brook Farm," *Phalanx*, July 27, 1844.
20. Newspaper clipping, n.d., Macdonald.
21. Marcus Spring to Elizabeth Chace, Sept. 1843, in Lillie Buffum Chace Wyman and Arthur C. Wyman, *Elizabeth Buffum Chace, 1806–1899: Her Life and its Environment*, 2 vols. (Boston, 1914), 92–93.
22. Art. I, sec. 1, *Constitution, By-Laws, Rules and Regulations of the Hopedale Community*.
23. "Our New Jersey Correspondence," *New York Herald*, June 4, 1853.
24. "Hopedale Community," *Sunday Dispatch* [1853?], a clipping in Macdonald.
25. Frothingham, *Recollections*, 288–89, 236; William Throop to George Throop, Jan. 16, 1844, Throop.

3. Daily Life: The Necessities

1. Sears, *Fruitlands*, 50, 107.
2. Huldah Bayley to Calvin Bayley, Dec. 20 [1846?], Calvin C. Bayley Papers.
3. Labor record book of Hannibal Taylor, Alpha.
4. Elizabeth Curson (Hoxie) to Mary Curson (Russell), Jan. 17, 184[6], Harvard; Hawthorne, *Note-Books*, Apr. 22 and June 1, 1841.
5. Wolski, *Impressions*, 181; Marianne Dwight to Frank, Apr. 14, 1844, Dwight M.
6. Elizabeth Curson (Hoxie) to Mary Curson (Russell), Dec. 23, 1845, and Jan. 7, 26, and Feb. 8, 15, 1846, Harvard; Emerson, "Historic Notes," 345.
7. Sears, *My Friends* 144; Journal, Brook Farm Records, MHS.
8. (The German words are *verwünschte . . . der . . . Gleichheit*), Bernhard, *Reise durch Nord-Amerika* 2:148.
9. Rude, *Deux ouvriers*, 152.
10. Finch, *An English Woman*, 245; Proceedings Book, June 18, 1844, Sodus Bay Records.
11. Bernhard, *Reise durch Nord-Amerika* 2:142.
12. Sumner, "A Boy's Recollection," 311; John Dwight to My Dear Friend, Jan. 14, 1847, Bryant.
13. Catherine H. Birney, *The Sisters Grimké* (Boston, 1885), 275.
14. Cabet, 146.
15. Rude, *Deux ouvriers*, 150–51; [Olinet], *Socialisme*, 120–21, 132; Vallet, 20.
16. Bill of Fare, North American Phalanx, Harvard.
17. Minutes, Brook Farm Records, MHS; Marianne Dwight to Anna, Dec. 14, 1844, and Mar. 22, 1846, Dwight M.
18. Russell, *Home Life*, 130–31; J. Codman, *Memoirs*, 98.

19. "Memorandum of Sugar Weighed from Box . . . ," Day Book, Alpha; Minutes, May 5, 1844; [Samuel W. Durant], *History of Kalamazoo County, Michigan* (Philadelphia, 1880), 337.

20. Charlotte Haven to Hannah, Oct. 26, 1848; Harriet Haven journal, Oct. 8, 1848; both in Ceresco.

21. Otis Capron to George [Swinington], Oct. 19, 1845, Ceresco.

22. A. E. Winter to Sarah Winter, Oct. 10, 1847, Illinois; Thomas Steel to James Steel, Oct. 5, 1843, Steel.

23. Wolski, *Impressions,* 182, 189, 191.

24. Sears, *Fruitlands,* 31, 68.

25. Chase, "To the Friends of Organization," Dec. 23, 1848.

26. New-Harmony account book 6, 315, 317, 319, NH; Agreement, Robert Owen to Jonathan Rogers, Apr. 1, 1827, Lucius C. Embree Collection, Indiana State Library, Indianapolis.

27. Cabet, 189–90; "Dépenses. Voyage à St. Louis," Icarian Society Papers, Burton Historical Collection, Detroit Public Library.

28. *Inventaire de la colonie,* 10–11.

29. Conway, *Autobiography* 1:268; Conway, *Pine and Palm,* 228; C. Codman, "Modern Times," MS, 15.

30. "Model Phalanx," *Harbinger,* Oct. 2, 1847; "To the Friends of Social Reform," *Spirit of the Age,* Oct. 1, 1849, p. 260; [Chase], *Autobiography,* 119.

31. The French words are *brequer le canon contre ceux qui approcheraient.* Fourier U 3:430.

32. A. Bronson Alcott to Junius S. Alcott, June 18, 1843, *Letters of Bronson Alcott;* Sears, *Fruitlands,* 14.

33. Russell, *Home Life,* 58.

34. William Owen to Robert Owen, Dec. 16, 1825.

35. George and Lydia Arnold to Marcus and Rebecca Spring, June 8, 1853, NJHS.

36. Fourier U 3:423–70.

37. Wolski, *Impressions,* 177, 179; Savardan, *Un naufrage,* 57; William G. Pearse to John S. Williams, Dec. 15, 1846, Ill-StLib; *Ploughshare and Pruninghook,* Feb. 15, 1846.

38. Elijah Grant to Robert Wheatly, Dec. 30, 1844, Grant.

39. Extrapolated from Report of the Committee on Rents, Proceedings for Aug. 6, 30, and 31, 1844, Sodus Bay Records.

40. Charlotte Haven to Hannah, Oct. 26, 1848, Ceresco; [Chase], *Autobiography,* 122.

41. Interview with Eugenia Mason (Mrs. Robert Mason) in 1903, S. T. Kidder MS book, 261; Charlotte Haven to Hannah, Oct. 26, 1848, and to William (her brother), July 8, 1849; all in Ceresco. Henry Thoreau to his sister Sophia, Nov. 1, 1856, in *Correspondence of Henry David Thoreau,* ed. Walter Harding and Carl Bode (New York, 1958).

42. Vallet, 24; Rude, *Deux ouvriers,* 149.

43. "City of Modern Times," *Brooklyn Daily Eagle,* June 5, 1904; Conway, "Modern Times," 425.

44. Bremer, *Homes* 1:80; Bernhard, *Reise durch Nord-Amerika* 2:140; Pears, *New Harmony,* 42, 82.

45. Finch, *An English Woman,* 248; Julia Bucklin Giles, "North American Phalanx," *Red Bank Register,* Jan. 24, 1935; Conway, "Modern Times," 426.

46. J. Codman, *Memoirs,* 134; Nora Schelter Blair, "School Memories," 2; Marianne Dwight to Anna, Apr. 17, 1844, Dwight M.

47. Cabet, 147–48.

48. *Inventaire de la colonie,* 11; also "Trousseau d'homme, de femme de petite garçon au-dessons de 10 ans et de petite fille au-dessons de 10 ans," Etienne Cabet, *Prospectus: émigration icarienne* (Paris, 1852), 27–32.

49. Maria Marchand Ross, *Child of Icaria,* 57, 101.

50. Curtis, "Hawthorne and Brook Farm," 159; J. Codman, *Memoirs,* 64; Nora Schelter Blair, "School Memories," 2.

51. Brownson, "Brook Farm," 494; J. Codman, "Brook Farm Association," 35, 37.

4. Civil Life: Freedom, Tolerance, Equality, and Fraternity

1. Wilson, *Dana,* 528, 31; Georgiana Bruce Kirby, *Experience,* 99; Wolski, "North American Phalanx," 160.

2. Savardan, *Un naufrage,* 119–20.

3. Chase, "Wisconsin Phalanx"; "Interview with Mrs. Isabella Hunter," by Ada Clark Merrill, clippings from *Milwaukee Sentinel,* Jan. 31, 1904, and *Ripon Commonwealth,* Oct. 21, 1904, Pedrick; Louisa Sheldon to Abigail Sheldon, Jan. 28 [1848?], Ceresco.

4. William Pelham to William (his son), Sept. 8, 1825, in Pelham, William; Miner K. Kellogg, "Remembrances and Sketches of incidents in the life of the author, being merely for his own and his family's gratification – being mostly personal and consequently *Private,*" New Harmony manuscripts, Indiana Historical Society; Pears, *New Harmony,* Nov. 18, 1825.

5. [Olinet], *Socialisme,* 138; Cabet, 37, 36.

6. Elijah Grant to Osborne Macdaniel, Jan. 19, 1845, and to Jacob Shriver, Jan. 1, 1845, Grant; J. Codman, *Memoirs,* 167, 187; Thomas Pears to Benjamin Bakewell, Sept. 2, 1825, Pears, *New Harmony.*

7. "Appraisals of Property," "Agreements to Leave," "Council of Arbitration Reports," typical examples: Aug. 21, 1845 and June 17, 1846.

8. Huldah Bayley Leavens to Calvin C. Bayley, Feb. 22 [1845?], Calvin C. Bayley Papers; Thomas Steel to James Steel, Dec. 2, 1843, Steel.

9. "A Week in the Phalanstery," *Life Illustrated,* Aug. 11, 18, 1855.

10. Elijah Grant to Horace Greeley, Aug. 11, 1844, Grant.

11. C. Codman, "Modern Times," MS, 10; Everett Chamberlain as quoted in *History of the City of Ripon . . .* (Milwaukee, 1873), 92.

12. Almira Throop to George Throop, Dec. 3, 1843, Throop; John Bliss to H. R. Schetterly, Jan. 30, 1845, Alpha; information about Marcus Spring in Rebecca Spring to William Cullen Bryant, Apr. 24, 1865, NJHS, and in Elizabeth Curson (Hoxie) to Mary Curson (Russell), Dec. 23, 1845, Harvard; William Henry Channing to James Fisher, Dec. 4, 1846, Fisher.

13. Jason Lathrop, *Southport Telegraph,* May 6, 1845; Franklin G. Sherrill to Executive Committee of the American Home Missionary Society, Jan. 16, 1851, Pedrick Collection; Otis Capron to George [Swinington], Oct. 19, 1845; William Stillwell to Sarah Stillwell, June 30, 1846, both Ceresco; Franklin G. Sherrill to American Home Missionary Society, Jan. 16, 1851, Pedrick.

14. *Phalanx,* July 27, 1844.

15. J. Codman, *Memoirs,* 72.

16. Kellogg, "Recollections," 56.

17. Frothingham, *Ripley,* 119.

18. Kellogg, "Recollections," 59; William Pelham to William (his son), Sept. 7, 1825, in Pelham, William.

19. W. G. Miller, *Thirty Years in the Itinerancy* (Milwaukee, 1875), 50, 52; *Phalanx,* Sept. 12, 1844.

20. Cabet, 35.

21. Brown, *Twelve Months,* 33.

22. Ballou, *Practical Christian Socialism,* 495.

23. Kirby, *Experience,* 79.

24. [Olinet], *Socialisme,* 129–37.

25. Rude, *Deux ouvriers,* 152; Vallet, 21, 29.

26. Thomas Pears to Benjamin Bakewell, Sept. 29, 1825, Pears, *New Harmony;* Robert Dale Owen, *Threading My Way,* 277.

27. Savardan, *Un naufrage,* 124; Considérant, *European Colonization,* 27, 36.

28. Nichols, *Forty Years of American Life,* 251–65, 270; Chase, "Trinity."

29. Fourier, *Publication des manuscrits* 2: part 1, 74; J. Codman, *Memoirs,* 165; Leonora Cranch Scott, *The Life and Letters of Christopher Pearce Cranch* (Boston, 1917), 26.

5. Life for Women

1. *New-Harmony Gazette,* Aug. 9, 1826; Thomas Steel to James Steel, Oct. 23, 1843, Steel.

2. Fourier, Q, 195–96.

3. de Gamond, Gatti [Zoe Charlotte], *The Phalanstery or Attractive Industry and Moral Harmony* (London, 1841), 118, 120.

4. Elijah Grant to Mrs. Gore, June 15, 1845, Grant.

5. Charles Sears to James Fisher, Dec. 14, 1852, Fisher.

6. Frances Judd, "Reminiscences," in Sheffield, *History,* 117.

7. Alcott, *Journals,* Jan. 7, 1844.

8. Sarah Pears to her aunt, Jan. 6, 1826, Pears, *New Harmony.*

9. Wolski, "North American Phalanx," 154, 155.

10. "Roll of Female members" and "Report of the Committee to Organize and Equalize Labor," Alpha.

11. Marie Fretageot to William Maclure, Mar. 2, 1827, NH.

12. E. to Henry Schetterly, n.d. [1845], Alpha.

13. Cabet, 138.

14. [Cabet], *Community of Icaria,* 5.

15. Shaw, *Icaria,* 117.

16. [Cabet], *Community of Icaria,* 5.

17. Sept. 15, 1850, "Le Temoignage d'un satisfait," Rude, *Deux ouvriers,* 254.

18. "Inscriptions: Principes Divers," Cabet, 121; Ross, *Child of Icaria,* 126.

19. Emerson, "Historic Notes," 345.

20. J. Codman, *Memoirs,* 188.

21. *New York Tribune,* Mar. 1, 5, 6, 12, 17, 19, 24, 28, and Apr. 7, 21, 30, 1860. All are reprinted in Greeley, *Recollections,* 571–617.

6. Life for the Future: Education

1. *Popular Tribune,* Feb. 15, 1851. The paper attributed the words to Horace Greeley.

2. "Inscriptions: Principes Divers," Cabet, 121; Cabet, 13.

3. Charles Sears to Horace Greeley, Nov. 24, 1852, Bryant; Charles Sears to James Fisher, Dec. 14, 1852, Fisher; Sarah Pears to her aunt, Mar. 10, 1826, in Pears, *New Harmony;* Donald Macdonald, *Diaries of Donald Macdonald,* Jan. 9, 1826.

4. Cabet, 7.

5. Cabet, *Voyage,* 74, 89.

6. Cabet, *Voyage,* 83.

7. Holynski, "Cabet et les Icariens," 296; Vallet, 30.

8. Ross, *Child of Icaria,* 74–75.

9. Cabet, *Voyage,* 359, 368.

10. Vallet, 30–31.

11. Shaw, *Icaria,* 83–84.

12. Minutes, vol. 1, Apr. 16, 1846; William Stillwell to his wife, Sarah, June 30, 1846; both Ceresco.

13. Minutes, vol. 1, Mar. 11, 1847; Harriet Haven journal, Oct. 8, 1848; both Ceresco.

14. Minutes, vol. 2, Jan. 24, 1848, and Jan. 15, July 2, 1849; Ceresco.

15. Minutes, vol. 2, June 18, 1849; Charlotte Haven to William, July 8, 1849; Minutes, vol. 2, Sept. 24, 1849; all Ceresco.

16. William Owen to Robert Owen, Dec. 16, 1825.

17. Robert Owen, *Life of Robert Owen,* 319–20; Kellogg, "Recollections," 50.

18. William Maclure to Marie Fretageot, Feb. 8, 24, and Jan. 3, 1827, and Marie Fretageot to William Maclure, Mar. 2, 1827, Bestor, *Correspondence of William Maclure and Marie Fretageot.*

19. Marie Fretageot to Robert Owen, Nov. 1824, NH.

20. Brownson, "Brook Farm," 489.

21. Kirby, *Experience,* 90; Russell, *Home Life.* 63–64.

22. Frothingham, *Ripley,* 128; Charles Lane, "Brook Farm," 351; Nora Schelter Blair, "School Memories," 3, 4.

23. Brownson, "Brook Farm," 491; Ora Gannett Sedgwick, "Girl of Sixteen," 399.

24. Sumner, "A Boy's Recollection," 309.

25. Elijah Grant to Albert Brisbane, Feb. 12, 1844, Grant.

26. William Gailbraith to William Gould, Feb. 12, 1847, Ill-StLib.

27. Sheffield, *History,* 81.

28. North American Phalanx, Minutes.

7. The Life of the Mind

1. Frothingham, *Recollections,* 236–37.

2. Frothingham, *Ripley,* 129.

3. Blair, "School Memories," 3.

4. I am indebted to Mrs. Florence Snyder for biographical material on her grandfather, Emile Baxter, which she kindly supplied when I spoke to her in Nauvoo, Ill., on Jan. 30, 1977.

5. Personal Sketches, IcariaMS; "Members of the Icarian Community listed in the 1850 . . . censes," Ill-StLib.

6. *Célébration par les icariens,* 17.

7. Considérant, *Great West,* 45 and 37.

8. George Santerre, *White Cliffs of Dallas: The Story of La Reunion, The Old French Colony* (Dallas, 1955), 95–146; see also Savardan, *Un naufrage,* 93–97.

9. Wolski, *Impressions,* 183–85.

10. Savardan, *Un naufrage,* 94–97.

11. "Proposals for Membership;" "Proposals for Membership at the annual meeting of 1844;" John Sherwin to Mr. Schetterly, Apr. 27, 1845; all Alpha.

12. "Occupations of our members" and "Roll of Original Members," Alpha.

13. "Tocsin Accounts," Alpha.

14. Thomas Steel to Lilly, Dec. 13, 1843, and to his father, Oct. 5, 1843, Steel.

15. William Owen, *Diary,* Jan. 16, 1825; Buckingham, *Eastern and Western States* 2:220.

16. Wolski, "North American Phalanx," 153; Russell, *Home Life,* 12.

17. George Stetson, "When I was a Boy," in Sheffield, *History,* 120; Lydia Arnold to Marcus and Rebecca Spring, June 8, 1853, NJHS; C. Codman, "Modern Times," MS, 22; Conway, *Pine and Palm,* 236.

18. Kirby, "My First Visit," 10; J. Codman, *Memoirs,* 219 and 55.

19. Charlotte Haven to William (her brother), July 16, 1849, Ceresco.

20. Wilson, *Dana,* 527.

21. The Fuller quotations and those that follow: Emerson, Channing, and Clarke, eds., *Memoirs of Margaret Fuller* 2:73–77. Channing edited that section.

22. Brisbane, *Association, or Concise Exposition,* 25.

23. Henry Tuckerman to John Dwight, Nov. 2, 1842; Henry Bellows to John Dwight, Nov. 25, Dec. 18, 1842; all Dwight J. James Russell Lowell to John Dwight, quoted in Cooke, *Dwight,* 69–72.

24. Edward Cary, *George William Curtis* (Boston, 1896), 23; Frothingham, *Ripley,* 129, Emerson, Channing, and Clarke, eds., *Memoirs of Margaret Fuller* 2:74.

25. Elizabeth Curson (Hoxie) to Mary Curson (Russell), Jan. 7, 17, 26, and Feb. 8, 15, 1846, Harvard.

26. Minutes, Mar. 17, 1846; William Stillwell to Sarah, June 30, 1846; Minutes, Mar. 2, 24 and June 1, 29, 1846, June 8, 1847, and July 28, 1848; all Ceresco.

27. "Ceresco," Martin Mitchel, *History of Fond du Lac County* (Fond du Lac, 1854).

28. Minutes, Sept. 13, 1847, Ceresco.

29. Charlotte Haven to Hannah, Oct. 26, 1848; Harriet Haven journal, Oct. 13, 1848; Charlotte Haven to Isabella, Feb. 20, 1850; all Ceresco.

30. Journals of Rev. Cutting Marsh, June 24, 1850, Ceresco; Chase, "Psychology."

31. Savardan, *Un naufrage,* 96.

32. *Inventaire de la colonie,* 9; Rude, *Deux ouvriers,* 155–56.

33. Vallet, 36.

34. "Part of the Library," IcariaMS.

35. Shaw, *Icaria,* 115, 118.

36. *Daily Journal of the Oneida Community,* July 18 and Dec. 18, 1866.

37. Maxmillian [Alexander Philip], Fürst von Wied-Neuwied, *Reise in das innere Nord-Amerika in den Jahren 1832 bis 1834,* 2 vols. (Coblenz, 1839–1841), 163–64; Minutes of the Academy of Natural Science, Philadelphia, Sept. 23, 1835; "Books Selected by Doctor Pickering," MS, NH.

38. "Books presented to the Germantown School," MS, NH.

39. J. Codman, *Memoirs,* 235.

40. James Curtis to his father, Christmas 1842, Illinois; Marianne Dwight to Anna, June 4, 1844, Dwight M.

41. Kirby, *Experience,* 135; Marianne Dwight to Anna, Aug. 1, 1845, Dwight M; Kirby, "My First Visit," 16.

42. Marianne Dwight to Frank, Nov. 1, 1844, Dwight M.

43. J. Codman, *Memoirs,* 30.

44. Marianne Dwight to Anna, Apr. 19, 1846, Dwight M.

8. Life in Music

1. Fourier U 1:230–31 and 4:6; see also Fourier, *Le Nouveau monde industriel,* 148.

2. John Dwight, *Lecture on Association in its Connection with Education,* 16; Considérant, *Great West,* 37.

3. Marianne Dwight to Anna, Feb. 15, 1846, Dwight M; J. Codman, *Memoirs,* 99, 168; John Dwight, "Music as a Means of Culture," 304.

4. Handwritten notes, "A meeting of persons interested in the formation of a religious Union . . . ," Fisher.

5. James Kay to James Fisher, Nov. 26, 1847, Fisher.

6. Julia Bucklin Giles. "North American Phalanx," *Red Bank Register,* Jan. 24, 1935; Kirby, *Experience,* 100.

7. Conway, "Modern Times," 425, 426; Kellogg, "Recollections," 53–54; Harriet Haven journal, "Thursday" [Oct. 12, 1848], Ceresco.

8. Bremer, *Homes* 1:82; Wolski, "North American Phalanx," 150; Lydia Arnold to Marcus and Rebecca Spring, June 8, 1853, NJHS; Mary Peabody Mann to Horace Mann, July 12, 1856, Horace Mann Papers, MHS.

9. Willard Saxton, "A Few Reminiscences of Brook Farm," 381.

10. Marie Fretageot Correspondence, June 16, 1821, transcript, NH. Marie Fretageot's piano was in the home of Miss Helen Elliot in New Harmony, Ind., when I saw it some years ago. I want to express my appreciation to her for her exceptional kindness in allowing me to examine and photograph it. The "transpositer" was stored in the attic of the Museum of the Workingmen's Institute in New Harmony when I saw it some years ago, but a close examination of it and the other instruments there was not permitted and could not be arranged.

11. Francis D. Bolton, "Autobiography," NH; "Modern Times," *Sunday Dispatch,* n.d., a clipping in Macdonald.

12. J. Codman, *Memoirs,* 82–83.

13. Dewitt Throop to George Throop, Jan. 7, 1844, Throop.

14. Fall River *Mechanic,* Fall River (Massachusetts) Public Library. The text can also be found in Philip Foner, *American Labor Songs of the Nineteenth Century* (Urbana, Ill., 1975), 47.

15. Hutchinson, *Story of the Hutchinsons,* 84; *Granite Songster: Songs of the Hutchinson Family.*

16. Conway, "Modern Times," 426.

17. Kirby, *Experience,* 104.

18. [Olinet], *Socialisme,* 112; Vallet, 20; Cabet, 16.

19. Cabet, 123, and *Célébration par les icariens,* 16; Cabet, 111–12.

20. Rude, *Deux ouvriers,* 154, 155; *Popular Tribune,* Feb. 11, 1851; *Colonie Icarienne,* July 19, 1854.

21. I. G. Miller, "The Icarian Community of Nauvoo, Illinois." *Illinois State Historical Society Transactions* 11:105, quotes from the general's report to the President, who sent him to investigate the situation in Nauvoo. In an attempt to locate his report, I searched indexes of government documents including the following: *A Compilation of the Messages and Papers of the Presidents* (New York, 1897), vol. 6; Benjamin Perley Poore, *A Descriptive Catalogue of the Government Publications of the United States, 1774–1881,* repr. ed. (Ann Arbor, 1953); *Master Keyword Index to the Publication-issuing Offices of the United States Government, 1789–1970,* vol. 5; and *Mereness Calendar: Federal Documents on the Upper Mississippi Valley, 1780–1890,* 13 vols. (Boston, 1971). They turned up no clues. I asked Agnes Ferruso, head of the Government Publications Section, Serial and Government Publications Division, Library of Congress, for additional help. I would like to express my appreciation to her for her efforts. Unfortunately, the report could not be found.

22. Cabet, 160.

23. Ross, *Child of Icaria,* 43, 62–69, 108.

24. Bernhard, *Reise durch Nord-Amerika* 2:139.

25. Virginia Dupalais collection of MS and printed music, NH; Robert Dale Owen collection of MS and printed music, Indiana Historical Society, Indianapolis; William Pelham, oblong music MS book, NH.

26. Robert Owen, *Life of Robert Owen,* 319–20; Robert Dale Owen, "Outline of the System of Education at New-Lanark," 4th installment, *New-Harmony Gazette,* Nov. 30, 1825; Kellogg, "Recollections," 50, 56.

27. Robert Dale Owen, *Threading My Way,* 275.

28. Marianne Dwight to Frank, May 29, 1844, Dwight M.

29. Dwight, "Music as a Means of Culture," 304.

30. Marianne Dwight to Frank, Aug. 27, 1844, and to Anna, Aug. 30, 1844, Dwight M.

31. J. Codman, *Memoirs,* 168–69, 219; Kirby, *Experience,* 101, and "My First Visit," 15.

32. Annie M. Salisbury, *Brook Farm* (Marlboro, Mass., n.d.), 15; *The Boston School Song Book,* published under the sanction of the Boston Academy of Music, original and selected by Lowell Mason (Boston, 1841); Conway, "Modern Times," 426– 27; *The Boston Glee Book,* arranged by Lowell Mason and George Webb (Boston, 1846). There was an 1838 edition, but my copy, which I used for this research, is dated 1846.

33. *The Social Choir: Designed for a Class Book, or the Domestic Circle,* ed. George Kingsley, 3 vols. (Boston, 1835–1844).

34. J. Codman, *Memoirs,* 168; Sears, *My Friends,* 81, 82.

35. Kirby, *Experience,* 103; J. Codman, *Memoirs,* 167.

36. Sumner, "Boy's Recollections," 311; J. Codman, *Memoirs,* 167–68.

37. Frothingham, *Channing,* 225–26.

38. Frothingham, *Channing,* 209–10, 217–18; Marianne Dwight to Anna, Aug. 31 and Oct. 5, 19, 1845.

39. Marx Lazarus to James Fisher, June [?], 1847, Fisher.

40. MS program for the Dedication of the Hall, Fisher; Charles Sears, *North American Phalanx,* 12–14.

9. Life in Words

1. William Pelham to William (his son), Nov. 11, 1825, in Pelham, William.

2. Sarah Pears to Sally Bakewell, Mar. 10, 1826, in Pears, *New Harmony;* Elijah Grant to [Horace] Greeley, Aug. 11, 1844, Grant.

3. Charles Dana to Parke Godwin, Nov. 20, 1844, Bryant.

4. William Wetmore Story to James Russell Lowell, Dec. 30, 1855, *Browning to his American Friends: Letters Between the Brownings, the Storys, and James Russell Lowell, 1841–1890,* ed. Gertrude Reese Hudson (New York, 1965).

5. [Cabet], *Community of Icaria,* 4.

6. Cabet, 159; Rude, *Deux ouvriers,* 250–51.

7. Ross, *Child of Icaria,* 91, 93–95, 96, 109.

8. Edward Camp to Board of Directors, May 6, 1844, Alpha.

9. Marianne Dwight to Frank, Feb. 15, 1845, Dwight M; "Printing Group," Journal, Brook Farm Records, MHS.

10. Marianne Dwight to Anna, Apr. 24, 1846, Dwight M.

11. Edward Tweedy to James Fisher, Jan. 4, 1849, Fisher; Marianne Dwight to Anna, Dec. 7, 1845, Dwight M; Russell, *Home Life,* 46–48.

12. [?] to James Fisher, Feb. 14, [184-], Fisher.

13. Parke Godwin to Charles A. Dana, Oct. 1, 1845, Bryant.

14. New-Harmony account book 6:109, 113, NH. In August 1826 only, all supplies, ink, type, and paper, were entered under one total. Therefore, I extrapolated the quantity for August from the relationship between price and quantity for the period. That showed twelve reams for the month, plus or minus one ream.

15. Adin Ballou, *Memoir of A. A. Ballou,* chap. 3.

16. Clarence Gohdes, *The Periodicals of American Transcendentalism* (Durham, N.C., 1931), 112.

17. Henry Schetterly to Benoni [?] Pixley, Jan. 13, 1845, Alpha.

18. Adin Ballou, *History of the Hopedale Community,* 26.

19. George Curtis to John Dwight, Mar. 3, 1844, Curtis, *Early Letters;* Dwight, Review of Poets and Poetry, *Christian Examiner,* Sept. 1842, p. 33.

20. George Curtis to John Dwight, Apr. 12, 1846, in Curtis, *Early Letters.*

21. Marianne Dwight to Anna, Mar. 4, 1846, Dwight M.

22. Moon set for Boston, Mar. 3, 1846: *The American Almanac and Repository of Useful Knowledge for the Year 1846* (Boston, 1845), 15.

23. J. Codman, *Memoirs,* 107–8.

24. Charles Newcomb, "The Two Dolons" *Dial* 4:112–23.

25. Rhoda Newcomb to her son Charles, Dec. 4, 1845, Rhoda Newcomb letters; Marianne Dwight to Anna, Dec. 12, 1845, Dwight M.

26. A. E. Winter to Sarah Winter, Sept. 20, 1847, Illinois.

27. [Chase], *Autobiography,* 127–29.

28. *Christian Examiner and Religious Miscellany* 42 (May 1847).

29. L. M. Richmond to Henry Schetterly, May 8, 1845, Alpha; Marianne Dwight to Anna [summer 1845], Dwight M.

10. After Life: Failure and Success

1. Harm Jan Huidekoper to his daughter Anna, Sept. 16, 1851, in Nina Moore Tiffany and Francis Tiffany, *Harm Jan Huidekoper* (Cambridge, Mass., 1902), 288.

2. Buckingham, *Eastern and Western States* 2:220; Nordhoff, *The Communistic Societies,* 39.

3. F[rederick] S. C[abot], "Brook Farm and Fourier," *American Socialist,* Feb. 13, 1879; Robert Dale Owen, *Threading My Way,* 244.

4. Nathaniel C. Meeker, "Why Owen Failed," *American Socialist,* Nov. 22, 1877.

5. Savardan, *Un naufrage,* 220.

6. Whitwell, "New Harmony," 48; Elijah Grant to T. E. Fortune, Mar. 21, 1845, Grant.

7. Benoni [?] Pixley to [Henry Schetterly ?], Mar. 4, 1845, Alpha; J. Codman, "Brook Farm Association," 97; Charles Codman, quoted in "City of Modern Times . . . ," *Brooklyn Eagle,* June 5, 1904.

8. Considérant, *European Colonization,* 23.

9. "Key to Scale of . . . Awards for Labor and . . . Capital," 1853. Fisher.

10. "A Young Man in the Community," Sheffield, *History,* 129.

11. [Olinet], *Socialisme,* 170.

12. Russell, *Home Life,* 47; John Allen to Mary Anne [Marianne Dwight], Jan. 16, 1846, Bryant.

13. John Dwight to his sister, May 1839, in Cooke, *Dwight,* 33; C. Codman, "Modern Times," MS, 3.

14. Russell, *Home Life,* 48.

15. Thomas Pears to Benjamin Bakewell, Sept. 2, 1825 and Mar. 4, 1826, in Pears, *New Harmony.*

16. Sears, *North American Phalanx,* 3–4; Charles Sears to Horace Greeley, Nov. 17, 1852, Bryant.

17. Brown, *Twelve Months,* 27.

18. Secretary of Integral Phalanx to Henry Schetterly, Oct. 21, [1845?]; Philandor Tabor to President, May 24, 1844; both in Alpha. Tabor's letter to Ohio Phalanx acknowledged by Grant, May 17, 1844, in Grant.

19. Ballou, *History of the Hopedale Community,* 26; Higginson, *Cheerful Yesterdays,* 85.

20. Elijah Grant to H. Barnard, Nov. 13, 1844, to Jerry Doty, Dec. 12, 1845, and to Albert Brisbane, July 16, 1845, Grant.

21. Elijah Grant to Albert Brisbane, Sept. 26 and June 12, 1843, Grant.

22. Elijah Grant to Horace Greeley, Feb. 12, 1844, Grant.

23. [Dewitt Throop?] to George Throop, Mar. 7, 1844, Throop.

24. Edgar Allen Poe, "Brook Farm," *Broadway Journal,* Dec. 13, 1845; John Dwight to Lydia Maria Child, Oct. 23, 1844, Dwight J.

25. Sears, *My Friends,* 143, 170; [Chase], *Autobiography,* 122.

26. *Harbinger,* Jan. 31, 1846; Elijah Grant to James D. Thornburgh, Jan. 28, 1846, Grant.

27. Savardan, *Un naufrage,* 205.

28. Adin Ballou to Sarah Grimké, Dec. 22 and 23, 1856, Weld-Grimké Papers, William L. Clements Library, Univ. of Michigan.

29. "Leaders of Thought" (misc. notes), and "List of my most important contributions to Periodical Literature," n.d., two manuscript fragments, George Ripley Papers, MHS.

30. Giles Stebbins, "A Young Man in the Community," and George Stetson, "When I was a Boy," in Sheffield, *History,* 126, 118–23.

31. George Ripley, "Our Present Attempt," *Harbinger,* Dec. 20, 1845; James Curtis to his father, George Curtis, June 19, 1842, James Burrill Curtis Collection, Illinois.

32. Two interviews by Ada Clark Merrill, "Chester Adkins and the Ceresco Community," a clipping dated Jan. 27, 1904, and "Reminiscences of Early Days," a clipping dated Jan. 31, 1904, Pedrick.

33. Nora Schelter Blair to George Ripley, Mar. 5, 1880, and Ripley's reply, Mar. 9, 1880, George Riley Papers, MHS.

34. George Ripley, "Unsuccessful Attempts," *Harbinger,* Dec. 19, 1846, and his editorial of Dec. 20, 1845.

35. Samuel Osgood to John Dwight, Nov. 21, 1840, Dwight J.

36. Horace Greeley to Etienne Cabet, May 24, 1853; Alcander Longley to James Fisher, Jan. 22, 1858; both in Fisher. Advertisement in *Realization of Communism: Brief History of Icaria.* Moncure Conway to Elizabeth Buffum Chace, Nov. 29, 1886, in Lillie Buffum Chace Wyman and Arthur Crawford Wyman, *Elizabeth Buffum Chace, 1806–1899: Her Life and Its Environment,* 2 vols. (Boston, 1914) 222–23.

37. *Popular Tribune,* Jan. 23, 1851.

Bibliography

THE FIRST TWO SECTIONS of this Bibliography are limited to the documents of social reorganization and to accounts by first-hand observers. These are the items used in researching and writing this book. Therefore, they exclude writings by those who had no direct knowledge of the events and people covered.

MANUSCRIPTS AND ARCHIVAL ITEMS

Alphadelphia Association, Papers. Bentley Historical Library, Michigan Historical Collections, Univ. of Michigan.

- "Agreements to Leave."
- "Appraisals of Property."
- Census, members and their occupations, Mar. 1845.
- Committee Reports, 1843–1844.
- Constitution, Jan. 5, 1844.
- Correspondence:
  - George Davis to Sir, July 31, 1845.
  - Philandor Tabor to President, May 24, 1844.
  - [Schetterly] to Brethren, Jan. 23, 1845.
  - E. Camp to Directors, May 6, 1844.
  - to Henry Schetterly from:
    - James Billings, Sept. 15, 1844.
    - John Bliss, Jan. 30, 1845.
    - Benoni [?] Pixley, Jan. 13, 1845.
    - [L. Richmond ?], May 8, 1845.
    - Secretary of Integral Phalanx, Oct. 21, 184–.
    - John Sherwin, Apr. 27, 1845.
    - Philandor Tabor, Nov. 22, 1844.
  - and: Samuel Denton to [Schetterly], July 15, 1844.

Benoni [?] Pixley to [Schetterly], Mar. 4, 1845.
——————[E?], to [Schetterly ?], –, 1845.
Council of Arbitration Reports, 1845–1846.
Daybook.
Labor book of Hannibal Taylor.
Ledger.
Membership list.
Minutes of the Board of Directors. Record Book (blue).
"Occupations of our members."
Original members and their occupations.
"Proposals for Membership."
Report of H. Keith.
Report of the Committee to Organize and Equalize Labor.
Report of Site Selection Committee.
Roll of Female members.
Roll of original members.
"Supplemental Agreements."
Time Book.
Tocsin accounts.

Bayley, Calvin C., Papers. State Historical Society of Wisconsin, Oshkosh.

Blair, Mrs. Nora Schelter. "Some School Memories of Brook Farm by a former pupil." St. Elmo, Tennessee, Dec. 22, 1892. Library of the Boston Athanaeum.

Brook Farm Records. Massachusetts Historical Society, Boston.
"Articles of Agreement and Association between the members of the Institute of Agriculture and Education," renamed "Constitution of the Brook Farm Association."
Daybook.
Journal.
Minutes.
Painting of Brook Farm, ca. 1845, attributed to Josiah Wolcott.
Record Book.

Bryant-Godwin Collection. Rare Books and Manuscripts Division, New York Public Library, Astor, Lenox and Tilden Foundations.
Charles Sears to Horace Greeley, Nov. 17 and Nov. 24, 1852.
Charles A. Dana to Parke Godwin, Nov. 20, 1844.
John Dwight to My Dear Friend, Jan. 14, 1847.
Parke Godwin to Charles A. Dana, Oct. 1, 1845.
John Allen to Mary Anne [Marianne Dwight], Jan. 15, 1846.

Ceresco Community Papers. State Historical Society of Wisconsin, Division of Archives and Manuscripts, Madison.
Otis Capron to George [Swinington], Oct. 19, 1845 (photostat).
A. Holmes to ——————, Jan. 15, 1846 (photostat).
Diary of Michael Frank, 1844–1847.

Haven, Charlotte (Mason), Papers.
Charlotte Haven letters.
Harriet Haven journal.
Journals of Cutting Marsh.
Minutes of the Organizational and Council Meetings.
"Ripon Historical Society, Recollections of Early Settlers," interviews by S. T. Kidder.
Benjamin and Louisa Sheldon to Abigail Sheldon, Oct. 1, 1847, and Jan. 28 [1848?], TS.
William Stillwell to his wife, Sarah, June 30 and July 29, 1846.
Betsy and Nathan Strong, Jr., to Nathan Strong, Sr., Jan. 5 [1845] (photostat).

Codman, Charles. "History of the City of Modern Times." Suffolk County Historical Society, Riverhead, N.Y.

Dana Family Papers. Massachusetts Historical Society, Boston.
George Ripley to Richard H. Dana, Jr., Dec. 8, 1845.

Dwight, John Sullivan, Papers. By courtesy of the Trustees of the Boston Public Library.
Henry Bellows to Dwight, Nov. 25 and Dec. 18, 1842.
Dwight to Lydia Maria Child, Oct. 23, 1844.
Samuel Osgood to Dwight, Nov. 21, 1840.
Henry Tuckerman to Dwight, Nov. 2, 1842.

Fisher, James T., Papers. Massachusetts Historical Society, Boston.
Boston Union of Associationists, meeting announcement, Dec. 1, 1848.
Bulletin of the Texas Emigration Union no. 1, Aug. 1855.
"A meeting of persons interested in the formation of a religious union" [Jan. 3, 1847].
Phalansterian Record. Cincinnati, Ohio (advertisement).
Record of the proceedings of the Religions Union of Associationists, Jan. 3, 1847.
Religious Union of Associationists, circular, Nov. 20, 1848.
"To the Associationists of the United States," circular, Sept. 1, 1850.
North American Phalanx Documents:
Annual Statements, 1851–1855.
Conditions of Membership and Rules of Admission.
Copy, Balance Sheet, n.d.
"Dedication of the Hall," May 6, 1851 (hymns, program, dinner menu).
Key to Scale of . . . Awards for Labor and . . . Capital, 1853.
Obituary for Emile Guillandeau, n.d.
Resolutions Respecting Losses in 1854, Executive Council, Jan. 7, 1855.
Rules and Conditions of Admission to Resident Membership.
Statement of Expenditure for Improvements, Jan. 10, 1854.
"The Tailors' Group . . . solicit your orders," circular, Nov. 12, 1852.

Letters to Fisher from:
William Henry Channing, Dec. 4, 1846.
S. P. Chapin, Apr. 20, 1849.
Victor Considérant, Mar. 31 and Aug. 11, 1853.
Parke Godwin, Jan. 29, 1852.
Emile Guillandeau, Apr. 21, 1851.
James Kay, Nov. 26, 1847.
Marx E. Lazarus, June 1847.
Alcander Longley, Jan. 22, 1858.
[Monill?], Feb. 11, 1852.
George Ripley, Apr. 16, 1846, Dec. [29?], 1852.
Charles Sears, Nov. 25, 1848, Dec. 14, 1852, July 23, 1853.
Rebecca Spring, Jan. 5, 1853.
Edmund Tweedy, Jan. 1849.
Letters to [Fisher] from:
Cesar Daly, Mar. 29, 1855.
Anna Q. T. Parsons, Dec. 29, 1849, Jan. 15, 1851, Apr. 28, 1852.
————, Monday, Feb. 14, [184-].

Grant, Elijah P., Papers. Joseph Regenstein Library, Special Collections, Univ. of Chicago.
Letterbooks 1 to 5.

Houghton Library, Harvard Univ.
Brook Farm Account Book.
Letters of Elizabeth Curson (Hoxie) to Mary Curson (Russell).
James Burrill Curtis to George Curtis, May 1840.
"Excursions en Harmonie," lithograph by Arnoult.
North American Phalanx documents:
Catalogue of Articles Exhibited (at the county fair).
Bill of Fare, Sept. 11, 1853, May 7, Sept. 6, Oct. 1, and Nov. 19, 1854, and Sept. 16, 1855.
Domain of the North American Phalanx (report form for groups).
Monthly Account of ________ (report form for labor credits).
"Dear Sir," printed appeals for support in Phalanx reorganization, Oct. 17, and 19, 1855.
Map of the Phalanx with terms of sale.
North American Phalanx, color lithograph by T. W. Whitely.
Playbills for Nov. 4 and Dec. 18, 1854.
George Ripley commonplace book.
"La théorie sociétaire de Charles Fourier," lithograph by Charles Daubigny [1817–1878].

Icarian Community Manuscripts. Historical, Memorial, and Art Department of Iowa, Des Moines.
Articles of Incorporation, 1860.
Articles of Incorporation, 1879.

"Le Chant des transportés," Dupont (2d tenor).
"Chœur Icarien – Chant du départ."
"Coup d'Etat de Cabet," broadside.
"Farewell to M. Cabet and the true Icariennes," broadside.
Julien ——— to Alexis Marchand, [?], 1889.
Law upon withdrawal and expulsion from the Icarian Community.
Loose music manuscript sheets.
"Ma Commune," by Eugene Chatelain and Charles Schütz.
Moralistes anciens. [title page missing].
"Ouvrages Français," record book with library catalog and accounts.
"Part of the Library of the Icarian Colony: Gift of Eugene Bettanier, 1975."
"Personnel of Icaria," 1880.
Photographs of Icaria, n.d.
La Sainte Bible, l'ancien et le nouveau testament. Strasbourg, 1863.
Maps and description of property with member's homes.
Regulations of the General Assembly.
"Personal Sketches."

Icarian Society Papers. Burton Historical Collection, Detroit Public Library.
"Dépenses. Voyage à St. Louis," expense account.

Indiana State Library, Indianapolis.
Agreement between Robert Owen and Jonathan Rogers, Apr. 1, 1827.
Minutes of the Convention, Feb. 6, 1826 (photostats).
Proceedings, Preliminary Society, Nov. 2, 1825, to Feb. 28, 1826.

Illinois Historical Survey. Univ. Library, Univ. of Illinois.
A. E. [and Cornelia] Winter to Sarah Winter, Sept. 26, 1847.
James Burrill Curtis Collection.
Letters to his father June 19, 1842, and Christmas 1842.

Illinois State Historical Library, Springfield.
"Members of the Icarian Colony listed in the 1850 . . . census." David Babelay, comp. TS.
"Causes of Deaths" (in Icaria) for year ending June 1, 1850.
Inventory of the Beluze Collection of Books.
Integral Phalanx Records.
W. N. Gailbraith to William Gould, Feb. 12, 1847.
William G. Pearse to John S. Williams, Dec. 15, 1846.

Macdonald, A. J., Collection. Yale Collection of American Literature, Beinecke Rare Book and Manuscript Library, Yale Univ.
"Alphadelphia Association."
"Brook Farm Association."
"Clermont Phalanx."
"Convention at Boston of the Friends of Association, Oct., 1843."
"A Dialogue Concerning the Sylvania Association."
"Fourier Domain – Clermont Co. Ohio," pen and ink sketch.

"Hunt's Experiment–Equality."
Interview with M. Cabet, July 10, 1852.
Leraysville Phalanx certificate 16, for one share of stock.
"New Harmony" engraving.
Newspaper clipping, n.d., Macdonald.
"The North American Phalanx" woodcut.
"Northampton Association."
"Ohio Phalanx."
"Raritan Bay Union."
Sears, Charles. "North American Phalanx," rules and conditions.
Sunday Dispatch, [1853?], a clipping, in Macdonald.
Sunday Dispatch, n.d., a clipping in Macdonald.
"Sylvania Association."
Sylvania Association certificate 81 for 4 shares of stock.
"Sylvanian's Prayer."
"Trumbull Phalanx."
"The Wisconsin Phalanx."

Newcomb, Rhoda, Letters to Charles Newcomb. Brown Univ. Library.

New Harmony Community Records. Library of New Harmony Workingmen's Institute, New Harmony, Ind.
Bolton, Francis. "Autobiography," MS.
Collection of 7 musical instruments.
Duclos, Victor. Recollections of New-Harmony, MS.
"V. P. Dupalais–Musique," 2 bound collections, printed and MS.
"Fauntleroy," dance book with music; also contains "Deceiving and Deceived," a play, MS.
"Fauntleroy," music books, 3 vols., MS.
Marie Fretageot. Extracts from letters, TS.
"List of Books presented to the Germantown Public School by William Maclure delivered by M. D. Fretageot," MS.
"List of Books Selected by Doctor Pickering for the Academy of Natural Sciences," MS.
"List of engravings sold by Marie Fretageot," MS.
New-Harmony account book 6, MS.
William Pelham notebook with song texts, MS.
William Pelham oblong ensemble music book, MS.
"The Racers" and other dances, dance manual, MS.
"Mrs. V. P. Twigg," bound collection of printed music.
Warren, Josiah, "Natural Liberty Coexistant with Social Order," MS.

New Harmony manuscripts and other items. Indiana Historical Society, Indianapolis.
"Deutsche Lieder."
Drawings of New-Harmony by Charles A. Lesueur.
"Ebor Nova, written by Stedman Whitwell, composed [arranged] by Signor Garcia."

Kellogg, Miner K. "Remembrances and Sketches of incidents in the life of the author, merely for his own and his family's gratification—being mostly personal and consequently *Private.*"

"Robert Dale Owen." Bound collections of music:

Clementi, [Muzio]. *Studio per il pianoforte.* London, n.d.

Dance music, 2 vols. [violin 1 and violin 2], MS.

Favorite Scots Songs, vol. 2. London, n.d.

Flute duets, printed [flute 2].

New Jersey Historical Society, Newark.

George Arnold to Marcus Spring, June 8, 1853.

Marcus Spring to Ralph Waldo Emerson, Mar. 10, 1850.

Rebecca Spring to William Cullen Bryant, Apr. 2, 1865.

North American Phalanx Minutes. Monmouth County Historical Association, Freehold, N.J.

Pedrick Collection. Ripon College, Ripon, Wis.

"Chester Adkins and the Ceresco community."

"Reminiscences of the Early days."

Franklin Sherrill to Executive Committee, American Home Missionary Society, Jan. 16, 1851.

Perth Amboy Public Library. Perth Amboy, N.J.

Barbara Bodichon to her father, B. Smith, Nov. 20, 1857.

Eagleswood School, a prospectus, n.d.

Ripley, George, Papers. Massachusetts Historical Society, Boston.

"Leaders of Thought" (misc. notes), MS fragment.

George Ripley, notes, Oct. 1, 1840.

"List of my most important contributions to periodical literature," n.d.

Letters to Ripley from:

George Bancroft, June 8, 1876.

Nora Schetter Blair, May 5, 1880.

Ellis Loring, Apr. 30, 1849.

Letters from Ripley to:

Nora Schetter Blair, Mar. 9, 1880.

[Theodore Parker], July 31, 1852.

John Orvis to his sister Mary, Mar. 15, 1846.

Sodus Bay Records. Rochester Public Library, Rochester, N.Y.

Articles of Association.

Constitution, Oct. 15, 1844.

Group and Series labor credit form.

Petition opposing resignation of Benjamin Fish, president.

Proceedings Book.

Prospective members.

Sodus Bay Phalanx Journal.

Sodus Bay Phalanx Ledger.

Steel, Thomas, Papers. State Historical Society of Wisconsin, Division of Archives and Manuscripts, Madison.

Throop, George Addison, Papers. Collection no. 218, Department of Manuscripts and Univ. Archives, Cornell Univ.

Articles, Books, and Newspapers

Alcott, A. Bronson. *The Journals of A. Bronson Alcott.* Edited by Odell Shepherd. Boston, 1938.

———. *Letters of A. Bronson Alcott.* Edited by Richard L. Herrnstadt. Ames, Iowa, 1969.

The *American Socialist,* Oneida, N.Y., 1876–79.

"Articles of Association of the American Phalanx," *Canton Ohio Repository,* Nov. 25, 1843.

Ballou, Adin. *Autobiography of Adin Ballou.* Completed and edited by William S. Heywood. Lowell, Mass., 1896.

———. *Christian Non-Resistance in All Its Important Bearings. . . .* Philadelphia, 1846.

———. *A Concise Exposition of the Hopedale Community: Descriptive, Statistical, Historical, Constitutional.* N.d., n.p.

———. *History of the Hopedale Community. . . .* Edited by William S. Heywood. Lowell, Mass., 1897.

———. *Memoir of A. A. Ballou,* Hopedale, Mass., 1853.

———. *Practical Christian Socialism.* Hopedale, Mass., 1854.

Bernhard, Karl, Duke Saxe-Weimar Eisenach. *Reise durch Nord-Amerika in den Jahren 1825 und 1826.* Weimar, 1828.

Bestor, Arthur, ed. *Education and Reform at New Harmony: Correspondence of William Maclure and Marie Duclos Fretageot, 1820–1833.* Indianapolis, 1948.

Bradford, George P. "Philosophic Thought in Boston." In vol. 4 of *The Memorial History of Boston,* edited by Justin Winsor. Boston, 1881.

———. "Reminiscences of Brook Farm." *Century Magazine* 45 (1892): 141–48.

Bremer, Fredrika. *Homes in the New World.* 2 vols. New York, 1853.

Brisbane, Albert. *Association, or Concise Exposition of the Practical Part of Fourier's Social Science.* New York, 1843.

———. *General Introduction to Social Science,* Sociological Series no. 1. New York, 1876.

———. *Social Destiny of Man, or Association and Reorganization of Industry. . . .* Philadelphia, 1840.

Brown, Paul. *Twelve Months in New-Harmony, Presenting a Faithful Account. . . .* Cincinnati, 1827.

Brownson, Orestes A. "Brook Farm." *United States Magazine and Democratic Review,* n.s., 9 (1842): 481–96.

Buckingham, James S. The *Eastern and Western States of America.* 3 vols. London, 1842.

Cabet, Etienne. *Colonie icarienne, aux Etats-Unis d'Amérique, sa constitution, ses lois, sa situation materiélle et morale après le premier semestre de 1855*. Paris, 1856.

———. *Colony or Republic of Icaria in the United States: Its History*. Nauvoo, Ill., 1852.

———. *Départ de Nauvoo du Fondateur d'Icarie avec les vrais Icariens*. Paris, 1856.

———. *De que manera communiste, mi credo communiste*. Barcelona, 1848.

———. *La Femme: son malheureux sort dans la société actuelle, son bonheur dans la communauté*. Paris, 1848.

———. *Lettre sur la Réforme icarienne du 21 novembre 1853. Réponse du citoyen Cabet à quelques objections sur cette réforme*. Paris, 1853.

———. *Manifestes de l'opposition et Réponse du citoyen Cabet*. Paris. 1856.

———. *Opinion icarienne sur le marriage. Organization icarienne. Naturalization des Icariens*. Paris, 1855.

———. *Prospectus: émigration icarienne, conditions d'admission*. Paris, 1852.

———. *Voyage en Icarie*. Paris, 1845.

[Cabet, Etienne]. *Adresses des Icariens de Nauvoo au citoyen*. Paris, 1853.

———. *Community of Icarie*. London, 1847 [?].

Cantagrel, F. *The Children at the Phalanstery*. Translated by Francis G. Shaw. Boston, 1848.

Célèbration par les Icariens du cinquième anniversaire. Paris, 1853.

Chase, Warren. "Industrial Association: Plan for Organization, Specific and Incidental Features." *Univercœlum and Spiritual Philosopher*, Oct. 28, 1848, 311.

———. "To the Friends of Organization." *Univercœlum and Spiritual Philosopher*, Oct. 14, 1848, pp. 313–14; Dec. 16, 1848, p. 43; Dec. 23, 1848, p. 59; Feb. 3, 1849, p. 156.

———. "Psychology." *Univercœlum and Spiritual Philosopher*, June 9, 1849, p. 21.

———. "Trinity." *Univercœlum and Spiritual Philosopher*, June 16, 1849, pp. 83–84.

———. "Wisconsin Phalanx." *Univercœlum and Spiritual Philosopher*, June 30, 1849, p. 70.

[Chase, Warren]. *The Life-Line of the Lone One, or Autobiography of the World's Child*. Boston, 1857.

Codman, John Thomas. "The Brook Farm Association." *Coming Age* 2 (1899): 33–38.

———. Brook Farm: *Historic and Personal Memoirs*. Boston, 1894.

Colonie Icarienne. Nauvoo, Ill., Jul. 19, 1854–Dec. 19, 1854.

Colonie icarienne. *Réforme icarienne du 21 novembre 1853*. Paris, 1853.

Colt, Mrs. Miriam Davis. *Went to Kansas: being a thrilling account of an ill-fated expedition. . . .* Watertown, 1862.

Considérant, Victor, *Au Texas,* Brussels, 1854.

———. *European Colonization of Texas.* New York, 1855.

———. *The Great West.* New York, 1854.

Constitution de la communauté icarienne. Nauvoo, Ill., 1851.

Constitution of the Communia Working Men's League. Clayton County, Iowa, July 23, 1852.

Constitution of the Brook Farm Phalanx, Adopted May 1, 1845.

Constitution, By-Laws, Rules and Regulations of Hopedale Community. Revised and approved Aug. 31, 1853.

Constitution of the Icarian Community. Revised and adopted May 4, 1851. Nauvoo, Ill., 1854.

Constitution of the Trumbull Phalanx. Trumbull County, Ohio, n.d.

Contrat de la nouvelle communauté icarienne d'Adams County. Corning, Iowa, 1880.

Conway, Moncure Daniel. *Autobiography, Memories and Experience of Moncure Daniel Conway.* 2 vols. Boston, 1905.

———. "Modern Times, New York." *Fortnightly Review,* July 1, 1865, pp. 421–34.

———. *Pine and Palm, A Novel.* New York, 1887.

Cooke, George W. *John Sullivan Dwight, Brook Farmer, Editor, and Critic of Music.* Boston, 1898.

Curtis, George. *Early Letters to John Sullivan Dwight: Brook Farm and Concord.* New York, 1898.

———. "Hawthorne and Brook Farm." In vol. 3 of *From the Easy Chair.* New York, 1894.

Dall, Caroline Wells [Healey]. *The College, the Market, and the Court, or Woman's Relation to Education....* Boston, 1867.

———. *Women's Right to Labor, or Low Wages and Hard Work: Three Lectures.* Boston, 1860.

Dana, Charles A. *Lecture on Association in Its Connection with Religion.* Boston, 1844.

Dwight, John S. *Lecture on Association in Its Connection with Education.* Boston, 1844.

———. "Music as a Means of Culture." *Dwight's Journal of Music* 30 (1879): 305–6, 313, 314–15.

———. Review of *The Poets and Poetry of America,* by Rufus Griswold. *The Christian Examiner and General Review,* 3d ser., 15 (1842): 25–33.

Dwight, Marianne. *Letters from Brook Farm, 1844–1847.* Edited by Amy L. Reed. Poughkeepsie, N.Y., 1928.

Earle, Pliny. *Memoirs of Pliny Earle.* Edited by F. B. Sanborn. Boston, 1898.

Edgar, Henry. *Modern Times: The Labor Question and the Family.* New York, 1855.

———. *The Positivist Calendar ... with a Brief Exposition of Religious Positivism.* New York, 1856.

Emerson, Ralph Waldo. "Historic Notes of Life and Letters in New England." In *Lectures and Biographical Sketches.* Boston, 1896.

———. *The Journals and Miscellaneous Notebooks of Ralph Waldo Emerson.* 8 vols. Edited by William H. Gilman and J. E. Parsons. Cambridge, Mass., 1970.

———. *The Letters of Ralph Waldo Emerson.* 6 vols. Edited by Ralph L. Rusk. New York, 1939.

Emerson, Ralph Waldo, William H. Channing, and James F. Clarke, eds. *Memoirs of Margaret Fuller Ossoli.* Boston, 1884.

Finch, Marianne. *An English Woman's Experience in America.* London, 1853.

Fisher, William L. *An Examination of the New System of Society by Robert Owen Showing Its Insufficiency.* Philadelphia, 1826.

Fourier, Charles. *Le Nouveau monde industriel et sociétaire. . . .* Paris, 1973.

———. *Publication des manuscrits de Charles Fourier.* Vols. 11 and 12 of *Oeuvres Complète de Charles Fourier.* Paris, 1967.

———. *The Social Destiny of Man, or Theory of the Four Movements.* Translated by Henry Clapp, Jr., with "Treatise on the Function of the Human Passions and an Outline of Fourier's System of Social Science," by Albert Brisbane. New York, 1857.

———. *Théorie des quatre mouvements et des destinées générales.* 2d ed. Paris, 1841.

———. *Théorie de l'unité universelle.* 2d ed. 4 vols. Paris, 1840–43.

Frothingham, Octavius B. *George Ripley.* Boston, 1882.

———. *Memoir of William Henry Channing.* Boston, 1886.

———. *Recollections and Impressions.* New York, 1891.

de Gammond, Gatti [Zoe Charlotte]. The *Phalanstery, or Attractive Industry and Moral Harmony.* [Translated anonymously by Henry James, Sr.] London, 1841.

Godwin, Parke. *A Popular View of the Doctrines of Charles Fourier.* New York, 1844.

The Granite Songster: Comprising the Songs of the Hutchinson Family. Boston, 1847.

Greeley, Horace. *Associationism Discussed. . . .* New York, 1847.

———. *Recollections of a Busy Life Including Reminiscences of American Politics and Politicians.* New York, 1869.

The *Harbinger,* Brook Farm Phalanx, June 14, 1845–Oct. 30, 1847; New York, Nov. 6, 1847–Feb. 10, 1849.

Hawthorne, Nathaniel. *Passages from the American Note-books.* Boston, 1883.

Hennequin, Victor. *Love in the Phalanstery.* New York, 1849.

Higginson, Thomas Wentworth. *Cheerful Yesterdays.* Boston, 1895.

———. *Contemporaries.* Boston, 1899.

Hinds, William Alfred. *American Communities.* 1878, facsimile reproduction Secaucus, N.J., 1973. 2d. ed., rev. Chicago, 1908.

History of the City of Ripon. . . . Milwaukee, 1873.

Holynski, Alexander. "Cabet et les Icariens." *La Revue socialiste*. 32 (1891): 539–50; 33 (1892): 40–49, 201–8, 296–307, 315–21, 449–56.

The Hopedale Collection of Hymns and Songs for the Use of Practical Christians. Compiled by Adin Ballou. Hopedale, Mass., 1859.

The Hopedale Community. N.p., Dec. 1, 1851.

Hopedale Community Constitution, By-Laws, Rules and Regulations. Hopedale, Mass., 1853.

Hudson, H. N. "Religious Union of Associationists." *American Review: A Whig Journal* 5 (1847): 492–502.

Hutchinson, John Wallace. *The Story of the Hutchinsons (Tribe of Jesse).* Compiled and edited by Charles E. Mann. 2 vols. Boston, 1896.

Icarian Community: Conditions of Admission. Jan. 22, 1850. Nauvoo, Ill., 1854.

Inventaire de la Colonie icarienne. 1853. Paris, 1853.

James, Henry. *William Wetmore Story and His Friends, from Letters, Diaries, and Recollections.* 2 vols. Boston, 1903.

Kellogg, Miner K. "Miner K. Kellogg: Recollections of New Harmony." Edited by Lorner Lutes Sylvester. *Indiana Magazine of History* 64 (1968): 39–64.

Kirby, Georgiana Bruce. "My First Visit to Brook Farm." *Overland Monthly* 5 (1870): 9–19.

———. "Reminiscences of Brook Farm." *Old and New* 3 (1870): 425–38; 4 (1871): 347–58; 5 (1872): 517–30.

———. *Years of Experience, An Autobiographical Narrative.* New York, 1887.

Lane, Charles. "Brook Farm." *Dial* 4, (1844): 351–57.

Lazarus, Marx E. *The Human Trinity, or Three Aspects of Life.* New York, 1851.

———. *Love, Marriage, and Divorce, and the Sovereignty of the Individual: A Discussion of Henry James, Horace Greeley. . . .* New York, 1853.

———. *Passional Hygiene and Natural Medicine.* New York, 1852.

Macdonald, Donald. *The Diaries of Donald Macdonald, 1824–1826.* Indianapolis, 1942.

The *Mammoth,* Hopedale, Mass., Nov. 1845–1848.

McLaren, Donald C. *Boa Constrictor, or Fourier Association Self-Exposed. . . .* Rochester, N.Y., 1844.

Miller, Rev. W. G. *Thirty Years in the Itinerancy.* Milwaukee, 1875.

M'Night, James. *Discourse Exposing Robert Owen's System as Practiced by the Franklin Community at Haverstraw. . . .* New York, 1826.

Mott, Lucretia. *Discourses on Woman. . . .* Philadelphia, 1849.

The *New-Harmony Gazette,* New-Harmony, Ind., Oct. 1, 1825–Oct. 22, 1828.

Nichols, Thomas Low. *Forty Years of American Life.* 2 vols. London, 1864.

———. "Institute of Desarrollo." *Nichols' Journal of Health, Water-Cure, and Human Progress* 1 (1853): 49–50.

———. *Woman in All Ages and Nations. . . .* New York, 1854.

Nordhoff, Charles. *The Communistic Societies of the United States from Personal Visit and Observation.* New York, 1875.

Northampton Association of Education and Industry: Principles. Apr. 8, 1842, Northampton, Mass.

Northampton Association of Education and Industry: Preamble and Articles of Association. Feb. 1, 1843, Northampton, Mass.

L'Observateur. Corning, Iowa, 1880.

[Olinet, Frédéric.] *Socialisme: voyage d'un autunois en icarie à la suite de Cabet.* Autun, 1898.

Owen, Robert. *Address . . . at a Public Meeting at the Franklin Institute. . . . June 25, 1827, [with] an Exposition of [His] Pecuniary Transactions [with] William M'clure.* Philadelphia, 1827.

———. *The Book of the New Moral World.* London, 1836.

———. *A Discourse on a New System of Society as Delivered [before] the President of the United States [and] Congress, March 7, 1825.* Washington, D.C., 1825.

———. *The Life of Robert Owen by Himself.* 2 vols. London, 1857–58.

Owen, Robert Dale. *Threading My Way: Twenty-Seven Years of Autobiography.* New York, 1874.

———. *To Holland and to New Harmony: Robert Dale Owen's Travel Journal, 1825–1826.* Edited by Josephine M. Elliot. Indianapolis, 1969.

Owen, William. *The Diary of William Owen from November 10, 1824 to April 20, 1825.* Edited by Joel W. Hiatt. Indianapolis, 1906.

The Peaceful Revolutionist. 1 (1833); and *The Peaceful Revolutionist, Devoted to the Practical Details of Equitable Commerce* 2, no. 1. Utopia, May 1848.

Pears, Thomas and Sarah. *New Harmony: An Adventure in Happiness.* Edited by Thomas Clinton Pears, Jr. Indianapolis, 1933.

Pelham, William. "Letters of William Pelham Written in 1825 and 1826." In *Indiana as Seen by Early Travelers: A Collection of Reprints from Books of Travel, Letters, and Diaries Prior to 1830.* Selected and edited by Harlow Lindley. Indianapolis, 1916.

The *Phalanx.* New York, Oct. 5, 1843–Mar. 25, 1845.

Ploughshare and Pruninghook. Integral Phalanx, Ill., 1846.

Poe, Edgar Allan. "Brook Farm." *Broadway Journal,* Dec. 13, 1845. Reprinted in vol. 13 of *The Complete Works of Edgar Allan Poe.* Edited by James J. Harrison. New York, 1965.

Popular Tribune. Nauvoo, Ill. 1851. Special Collections, Knox College, Galesburg, Ill.

The *Practical Christian,* Mendon and Hopedale, Mass., Apr. 1, 1840–Apr. 14, 1860.

The *Present,* New York, 1843–1844.

The *Primitive Expounder,* Jackson and Ann Arbor, Mich., 1844.

Raritan Bay Union: Preamble and By-Laws. Mar. 22, 1853, Perth Amboy, N.J.

Realization of Communism: Brief History of Icaria, Constitution, Laws, Regulations of the Icarian Community. Corning, Iowa. 1880.
"Red Owl Cottage Hermit." *Brooklyn Times,* July 29, 1893.
Die Republik der Arbeiter. New York. 1850–55.
Revue Icarienne. Nauvoo, Ill., 1855; Corning, Iowa, 1878–1888[?].
Ross, Maria Marchand. *Child of Icaria.* New York, 1938.
———. "Icaria." *Social Gospel* no. 38, n.s. 9 (1901): 3–7.
Rude, Fernand, ed. *Voyage en icarie: deux ouvriers viennois aux Etats-Unis en 1855.* Paris, 1952.
Russell, Amelia E. *Home Life of the Brook Farm Association.* Boston, 1900.
Salisbury, Annie M. *Brook Farm.* Marlboro, Mass., n.d.
Savardan, le Dr. [Augustin]. *Un naufrage au Texas: observations et impressions recueillies pendant deux ans et demi. . . .* Paris, 1858.
Saxton, S. Willard. "A Few Reminiscences of Brook Farm." *History and Proceedings, Pocumtuck Valley Memorial Association* (annual), 1917, pp. 371–86.
Sears, Charles. *The North American Phalanx: An Historical and Descriptive Sketch.* Prescott, Wis., 1886.
———. *Socialism and Christianity, Being a Response to an Inquirer Concerning Religion and the Observance of Religious Forms at the North American Phalanx.* North American Phalanx, 1854.
Sears, Charles et al. *Exposé of the Condition and Progress of the North American Phalanx in Reply to the Inquiries of Horace Greeley. . . .* New York, 1853.
Sears, Clara Endicott, comp. *Bronson Alcott's Fruitlands.* Boston, 1915.
Sears, John Van Der Zee. *My Friends at Brook Farm.* New York, 1912.
Sedgewick, Ora Gannett. "Girl of Sixteen at Brook Farm." *Atlantic Monthly* 85 (1900): 394–404.
Shaw, Albert. *Icaria: A Chapter in the History of Communism.* New York, 1884.
Sheffield, Charles A., ed. *The History of Florence, Massachusetts, Including a Complete Account of the Northampton Association of Education and Industry.* Florence, Mass., 1895.
The *Social Pioneer and Herald of Progress,* Boston, 1844.
Sodus Bay: Constitution and By-laws. 1844.
The *Southport Telegraph,* Southport [later Kenosha], Wis., 1843–50.
The *Spirit of the Age,* New York, 1849–50.
Stanton, Elizabeth Cady. *Address to the Legislature of New York.* Albany, 1854.
Sumner, Arthur. "A Boy's Recollection of Brook Farm." *New England Magazine,* n.s., 10 (1894): 309–13.
Sylvania Association: Constitution and By-Laws. May 29, 1843, New York.
Thompson, William. *Appeal of One Half the Human Race: Women Against the Pretensions of . . . Men. . . .* London, 1825.
The *Tocsin,* Kalamazoo County, Mich., 1844.

Two Essays on the Social System of Charles Fourier. New York, 1838.

Vallet, Emile. *An Icarian Communist in Nauvoo: Commentary by Emile Vallet.* Introduction and notes by H. Roger Grant. Springfield, 1971.

Van Amringe, H. H. *Association and Christianity. . . .* Pittsburgh, 1845.

"A Week in the Phalanstery." *Life Illustrated.* New York, Aug. 11 and 18, 1855.

Weitling, Wilhelm. *Garantieen der Harmonie und Freiheit.* Hamburg, 1849.

———. *Die Menschheit wie sie ist und wie sie sein sollte.* Munich, 1895.

Whitwell, Stedman. *Description of an architectural model . . . for a community upon a principle of united interests as advocated by Robert Owen.* London, 1830.

———. "New Harmony." *Cooperative Magazine* 2 (1827): 48.

Wilson, James H. *The Life of Charles A. Dana.* New York, 1907.

Wisconsin Phalanx: Act of Incorporation. Feb. 6, 1845, Territory of Wisconsin.

Wolski, Kalikst. *American Impressions.* Translated by Marion M. Coleman. Cheshire, Conn., 1968.

———. "A Visit to the North American Phalanx." Translated and edited by Marion Moore Coleman, *Proceedings of the New Jersey Historical Society* 83 (1965): 149–60.

Some Recent Books

Altfest, Karen Caplan. *Robert Owen as Educator.* Boston, 1977.

Beecher, Jonathan. *Charles Fourier: The Visionary and His World.* Berkeley, California, 1987.

Bestor, Arthur. *Backwoods Utopias: The Sectarian Origins and the Owenite Phase of Communitarian Socialism in America, 1663–1829.* Philadelphia, 1970.

Claeys, Gregory. *Machinery, Money, and the Millennium: From Moral Economy to Socialism, 1815–1860.* Princeton, 1987.

Delano, Sterling F. *The Harbinger and New-England Transcendentalism: A Portrait of Associationism in America.* Rutherford, N.J., 1989.

Fogarty, Robert S. *All Things New: American Communes and Utopian Movements, 1860–1914.* Chicago, 1990.

Francis, Claude. *Parton pour Icarie: des Français en Utopie. Une société idéale aux Etats-Unis en 1849.* Paris, 1983.

Guarneri, Carl. *The Utopian Alternative: Fourierism in Nineteenth-Century America.* Ithaca, N.Y., 1991.

Harrison, J. F. C. *Quest for the New Moral World: Robert Owen and the Owenites in Britain and America.* New York, [1969].

Johnson, Christopher H. *Utopian Communism in France: Cabet and the Icarians, 1839–1851.* Ithaca, N.Y., 1974.

Kolmerten, Carol. *Women in Utopia: The Ideology of Gender in the American Owenite Communities.* Bloomington, Ind., 1990.

Levitas, Ruth. *The Concept of Utopia.* Syracuse, 1990.
Morton, A. L. *The Life and Ideas of Robert Owen.* London, 1969.
Riasanovsky, Nicholas. *The Teaching of Charles Fourier.* Berkeley, California, 1969.
Spencer, M. C. *Charles Fourier.* Boston, 1981.
Zeldin, David. *The Educational Ideas of Charles Fourier.* New York, 1969.

Index

Most of the names listed here are placed in context by the information in parentheses. It identifies the colony the person belonged to or visited, or otherwise explains his or her connection to the episodes discussed in the text. Women are listed under the name they were known by during the time they were active in these episodes. Married names, where appropriate, are given in brackets.

D0205464

SKEPTICISM about the EXTERNAL WORLD

SKEPTICISM

about the

EXTERNAL

WORLD

Panayot Butchvarov

New York • Oxford

Oxford University Press

1998

Oxford University Press

Oxford New York
Athens Auckland Bangkok Bogota Bombay
Buenos Aires Calcutta Cape Town Dar es Salaam
Delhi Florence Hong Kong Istanbul Karachi
Kuala Lumpur Madras Madrid Melbourne
Mexico City Nairobi Paris Singapore
Taipei Tokyo Toronto Warsaw

and associated companies in
Berlin Ibadan

Published by Oxford University Press, Inc.
198 Madison Avenue, New York, New York 10016

Library of Congress Cataloging-in-Publication Data
Butchvarov, Panayot, 1933–
Skepticism about the external world / Panayot Butchvarov.
p. cm.
Includes bibliographical references and index.
ISBN 0-19-511719-0
1. Skepticism—Controversial literature. 2. Realism. I. Title.
BD220.B87 1998
121'.2—dc21 97-14104

9 8 7 6 5 4 3 2 1

Printed in the United States of America
on acid-free paper

ACKNOWLEDGMENTS

This book contains material, though heavily revised, from previously published articles, namely: "Adverbial Theories of Consciousness," *Midwest Studies in Philosophy* 5 (1980); "Our Robust Sense of Reality," *Grazer Philosophische Studien* 25/26 (1985–1986), reprinted in Rudolf Haller, ed., *Non-Existence and Predication* (Amsterdam: Rodopi, 1986); "The Untruth and the Truth of Skepticism," *Proceedings and Addresses of the American Philosophical Association* 67, 4 (January 1994); and "Direct Realism without Materialism," *Midwest Studies in Philosophy* 19 (1994). But except for the first, all were extracted, in response to invitations, from earlier versions of this book; it is not a collection of them, they were excerpts from it. Some of those versions of the whole or of its parts have been read by Professors Robert Audi, Albert Casullo, David Stern and Günter Zöller, and by the students in my seminars in epistemology. I am greatly indebted to their comments and suggestions, even though they often sharply disagreed with me.

CONTENTS

SKEPTICISM about the EXTERNAL WORLD

INTRODUCTION

By skepticism about the external world I shall mean what Hume called skepticism with regard to the senses, that is, with regard to our knowledge through sense perception of the existence and qualities of bodies, of material objects. The problem such skepticism poses has dominated modern philosophy ever since the discovery, in the sixteenth century, of Sextus Empiricus's manuscripts,[1] and arguably it also dominated ancient Greek philosophy at least after Aristotle.

The reason is not hard to find. To be skeptical about the existence of an external world is to be skeptical also about the existence of other (embodied) persons, therefore about the existence of society, almost certainly about the existence of anything deserving to be called morality, of anything deserving to be called history, and, on almost all theological views, of (true) premises for any plausible argument for the existence of God.

It may seem that a priori knowledge, which by definition is independent of experience, would not be affected, but even this is not clear. Mathematics may be an a priori discipline, but what would it be like without the use of pencils or sticks, paper or sand, and now computers, and without the tradition of mathematical inquiry, represented by certain human beings and their lectures or writings, all of which would be parts of the external world the reality of which the skeptic questions? There might still be a priori knowledge of a few self-evident propositions, but however necessary this knowledge may be to an a priori discipline, such as mathematics, it would hardly constitute a discipline all by itself.

The problem of skepticism about the external world can thus be seen to be at the very center, even if not at the conceptual foundations, of philosophy. Indeed, it seems to be the most important issue human beings *can* face. Many philosophers may disagree with this assessment, but they would have a right to disagree only if they have a reasoned answer to the skeptic. To my knowledge, they do not.

Even though skepticism about the external world does have this central place in philosophy, it is not the only skepticism on the philosophical scene. The term "skeptic" used to be applied to those questioning the existence of God. There is skepticism about the reality of human minds other

than one's own, and also about the reality of the past. There is skepticism about the legitimacy of inductive reasoning. There is also skepticism about morality and about the claims of mathematics. Many are skeptics about the more esoteric parts of physics. I will not be concerned with these kinds of skepticism, even if, as I have suggested, many bear logical relationships to skepticism about the external world. It is the latter that constitutes the topic of this book.

Of course, by skepticism about the external world I mean *philosophical* skepticism, that is, a denial *reached through philosophical reasoning* that we have knowledge of, or even beliefs based on genuine evidence about, any propositions about material objects, whether about their reality or about their qualities. One can be a philosophical skeptic even if firmly believing such propositions. Hume tells us that he could not believe his skeptical conclusions, but this is philosophically irrelevant, it is of biographical interest; what is philosophically relevant is how he arrived at those conclusions, and he was a philosophical skeptic only if he arrived at them by reasoning (as in fact he did). This is why the skeptic may even *have*, unbeknownst to her, the knowledge and evidence she questions. But knowledge and true beliefs are philosophically irrelevant if we neither do nor can, on reflection, know or have evidence that we have them.

In his noteworthy recent book *Unnatural Doubts* Michael Williams distinguishes between "the discovery that knowledge is impossible under the conditions of philosophical reflection" and "the discovery, under the conditions of philosophical reflection, that knowledge is generally impossible."[2] He seems to mean by the former that philosophical, in particular epistemological, reflection is a special (unnatural) context of thought that by its very nature leads one who is engaged in it to conclude that knowledge is impossible, and by the latter that philosophical reflection, whatever the context, leads to that conclusion. Skepticism is unavoidable in the former context but not in the other contexts. Views about the special nature of philosophy and in particular the special nature of philosophical skepticism have been expressed also by Thompson Clarke, Barry Stroud, P. F. Strawson, Bernard Williams, Thomas Nagel, and many others.[3] Their historical roots perhaps can be traced to Wittgenstein's peculiar attitudes (both Tractarian and later) toward philosophy.

But I believe philosophy is a distinctive discipline only in that it considers the propositions presupposed but not examined by common sense and the sciences, not in that it requires a special frame of mind, or a special context in a sense other than the innocuous one that its topics are different from those of the other disciplines. So Michael Williams's distinction is not the one I made. Mine is simple and unproblematic. Yet the neglect of it has led, for example, to the notorious dispute whether Hume was a skeptic or a naturalist (i.e., for our purposes here, a believer in the existence of bodies and in our ability to know them). I hold that he was a skeptic as a philosopher, and a naturalist as a nonphilosopher.

There is nothing deep, mysterious, puzzling, or even romantic about

this, though Hume's theatrical prose encourages the thought that there is. As Thomas Nagel remarks, "The possibility of complete erosion by skeptical possibilities is built into our ordinary beliefs from the start: it is not created by the philosophical imposition of new standards of justification or certainty. On the contrary, new justifications seem to be required only in response to the threat of erosion from ordinary criticisms, sufficiently generalized."[4] To understand the *natural* possibility of skepticism we should reflect on the natural gap between knowledge and belief. One can be confident about what one knows that one does not know (I am confident today that I will be alive tomorrow but will pay the life insurance premium due today), and one can fail to be confident about what one knows that one knows (consider the person repeatedly returning home to make sure that the door has been locked).[5] Contrary to what Hume supposed, skepticism about the external world *can* be internalized, that is, actually accepted in one's life, although the person presumably would need to be institutionalized. But this is not to say that his position is mistaken. An insane person can be right about what he believes, just as a sane person can be wrong about what *he* believes. Calling someone insane is name-calling, not philosophical reasoning.

Discussions of skepticism about the external world have often been marred by what I consider to be major defects, which here I shall do little more than mention. Later I will return to all of them, often but not always at some length, and will show how they have affected previous discussions of our topic. My enumeration and blunt description of them here as defects are intended to be merely prefatory.

The first defect is the failure to observe the distinction I explained earlier, the failure to see that one cannot answer the skeptic by just holding that the beliefs the skeptic questions are firmly held, perhaps even natural, inescapable, and that the skeptic's questions are therefore unnatural, perhaps not even genuine. The usual additional claim that those beliefs are trustworthy or warranted is just comforting rhetoric, if it is not argued at length, as it usually is not. P. F. Strawson writes: "Skeptical doubts are not to be met by argument. They are simply to be neglected . . . because they are *idle*; powerless against the force of nature, of our naturally implanted dispositions to belief."[6] I have given reasons for thinking that skepticism is not unbelievable. But what matters more is the obvious question, Even if it were, so what? As G. E. Moore said, "[T]he direct object of Ethics is knowledge, and not practice."[7] If this is true of ethics, surely it is true of epistemology.

A second defect is the quick dismissal of direct realism as "naive," and the related obscurantist use of otherwise familiar ordinary expressions such as "sensation" and "experience." A third is the failure to examine the concept of existence, or reality, even though the skeptic questions precisely the *existence* of perceivable material objects. Whole chapters of this book will be devoted to these two topics, and I shall leave them here merely mentioned.

A fourth defect is the hasty and insufficiently critical use of the notion of nondemonstrative evidence, often hidden under the umbrella of the defective notion of justified belief, defective because it is obviously deontic in natural discourse and thus implies a straightforward, simplistic doxastic voluntarism. Surely, such voluntarism is false. As Paul Ziff remarks, "Justification may be required if one claims to know that *p*, but it has nothing whatever to do with judging that one knows that *p*. Knowing or believing are not things one can choose."[8] And William P. Alston writes: "For the most part my beliefs are formed willy-nilly. When I see a truck coming down the street, I am hardly at liberty either to believe that a truck is coming down the street or to refrain from that belief . . . it is clear that for the most part we lack such powers."[9]

A fifth defect is the uncritical use of the related notion of rationality, the vagueness of which is freely admitted even by those who make the most use of it, for example, Hilary Putnam and Richard Foley.[10] This fifth defect (perhaps also the first) is itself probably a manifestation of a sixth defect, the sway of what may be called "the new way of beliefs," the obsessive use in contemporary philosophy of the notion of belief, usually with complete neglect of phenomenology, reminiscent of the obsessive use of the notion of idea in earlier philosophy ("the new way of ideas") and its also striking neglect of serious phenomenological considerations. Since beliefs (I don't mean feelings of confidence or religious faith) constitute a most obscure, perhaps not even genuine, category, it seems easy to do almost anything one wants with them, in particular to describe them as justified or rational or reliable or whatever. The mantra of "rationality" comes to seem to have universal utility when combined with an unbridled but usually unconscious commitment to doxastic voluntarism.

A seventh defect, of which the fourth and fifth may be thought of as species, is the chaotic use of a large number of terms (hence, also of concepts), such as justification, rationality, warrant, internalism, externalism, reliabilism, foundationalism, coherentism, that were either recently invented or recently given invented uses.[11]

An eighth defect is the common appeal to "intuitions" in substantive philosophical discussion, which is admitted by its practitioners to have nothing to do with the traditional and venerable appeal to a particularly trustworthy special source of knowledge, but is not recognized as what in fact it is: a pretentious avowal of confidence in one's opinions. In imitation of the earlier philosophy of ordinary language, the appeal is usually to what we would or would not say, but differs from it by a penchant for raising this question with regard to situations often so contrived as to exceed even science fiction; the question is then answered better by just remaining silent than by agonizing introspection of one's linguistic inclinations.

A ninth defect (I shall qualify this description shortly), which largely explains the presence of the eighth, is the "linguistic turn" philosophy took decades ago under the pressure of logical positivism; the waywardness of that turn continues to disorient, though nowadays less obtrusively, Anglo-

American philosophy and has also waylaid recent continental philosophy, even though neither subscribes to logical positivism. Indeed, in 1978 we find Michael Dummett writing: "[T]o possess a concept is to be a master of a certain fragment of language,"[12] and even as late as 1993 also writing: "What distinguishes analytical philosophy . . . from other schools is the belief . . . that a philosophical account of thought can be attained through a philosophical account of language" and in no other way.[13] But also there has been a move away from such extremism. In discussing Saul Kripke's "puzzle about belief," Keith Donnellan writes forthrightly: "the puzzle we feel really has nothing to do with *language* or with languages at all."[14] And even Michael Dummett admits that "linguistic practice is no more sacrosanct, no more certain to achieve the ends at which it is aimed, no more immune to criticism or proposals for revision, than our social, economic or political practice."[15]

A tenth defect is that the detailed recent discussions of skepticism, which have occurred mainly in Anglo-American philosophy, generally ignore the lessons to be learned from twentieth-century continental philosophy, especially from phenomenology. In the course of this inquiry I shall often have occasion to draw attention to this fact and to deplore its consequences. Indeed, I shall be heavily indebted to themes characteristic of both analytic and continental philosophy. Therefore, purely "analytic" and purely "continental" philosophers will find much of it distasteful, but I hope that such purity of philosophical orientation has become rare as the century draws to a close. Of course, by my frequent appeals to "phenomenology" I shall not mean any particular view that Edmund Husserl, or Martin Heidegger, or Jean-Paul Sartre held, but what I take Husserl's slogan "Back to the things themselves!" to have originally meant, namely a determination to take seriously the facts as we find them, rather than begin with theoretical presuppositions about them, whether metaphysical or scientific. In this respect, phenomenology is not very different from the relaxed empiricism of Hume, who was cheerfully willing to admit counterexamples even to his cherished doctrine that all simple ideas are derived from impressions. And the connection of phenomenology, so understood, with the study of ordinary language, which was the most impressive part of analytic philosophy, should be evident. Surely the phenomenological facts must be reflected in our language. Again, I eschew any commitment to specific doctrines, such as the view that ordinary language, indeed language in general, is the proper subject matter of philosophy, and merely take for granted what Aristotle also took for granted: that a starting point, though a secondary one, for philosophy is what we ordinarily say, even though this is in no way the subject matter of philosophy. I am sure he would also have agreed that another starting point, indeed the primary one, is how things reveal themselves to us. In neither case need we claim that these are more than starting points. They both are in the service of the defining goal of philosophy: the examination of the propositions presupposed but not examined by science or common sense. Neither yields the last word on these

propositions, but philosophy must have a starting point, and what better starting points can there be? Certainly not science, since it is rife with precisely the sort of presuppositions that philosophy must examine. But I shall not engage in a detailed account of phenomenology or of analytic philosophy. I believe the reader is sufficiently familiar with both. I shall only observe that when one makes a phenomenological appeal, or an appeal to ordinary usage, one must not be expected to offer an *argument*. The whole point of such appeals, as both Husserl and Wittgenstein held though in very different ways, is that they involve only *description*.

An eleventh, perhaps the most serious, defect, is the simplistic assumption that skepticism must be either just completely ignored, or straightforwardly refuted, or heroically accepted.

As I said earlier, I shall return to all these defects, though only some will be discussed in detail. But with regard to the eleventh, a warning is needed at the very beginning.

We must guard against intemperate and dogmatic attitudes such as those expressed in the following: "I consider skepticism something worse than unsatisfactory; I consider it nonsense to hold or to imply that just any empirical judgment is as good as any other—because none is warranted. A theory which implies or allows that consequence is not an explanation of anything but merely an intellectual disaster" (C. I. Lewis).[16] Or: "We reject the sceptical view according to which there is no reason to believe that the premises of an inductive argument ever confer evidence upon the conclusion. If this sceptical view were true, then we would know next to nothing about the world around us" (Roderick M. Chisholm).[17] Or: "[A]lligators are material objects and maybe there are no material objects. But this seems a silly thing to worry about, though it may not be a silly project to analyze what it *is* to be a material object" (Henry E. Kyburg, Jr.).[18]

None of the defects I have mentioned is a simple mistake. This is why they are found even in the works of first-rate philosophers. They all are rooted in familiar facts or at least natural assumptions: for example, that perception involves a causal process that produces something "in us"; that people have experiences and sensations; that of course unreal, nonexistent, things do not exist; that there is a clear difference between truth and falsehood, between reality and unreality, and thus between knowledge and ignorance; that generally if someone asserts a proposition we can say that she believes it; that of course some assertions are much better supported by evidence than are their contraries, even though it does not entail them, and therefore one who makes the former rather than the latter is justified in doing so; that language is an indispensable tool of sophisticated thought. But though these assumptions are natural, they are also untutored.

This book attempts to avoid the defects I have mentioned and to deal afresh with the problem of skepticism. It will conclude that its solution cannot be simple, straightforward, or of a familiar kind, and indeed that there is both untruth and truth in skepticism. It will attempt to answer, not refute, the skeptic, but in ways philosophers don't usually expect.

It may seem quixotic to attempt once again to answer (even if not refute) skepticism, rather than just accept it or ignore it. Surely, we must have learned by now that none of the answers so far given is philosophically satisfactory, whether it be that from causal considerations, or from inference to the best explanation, or from the demands of coherence, or from "transcendental" considerations, and so on. Of course, they all still have their proponents, but most philosophers are aware of their weaknesses. Well, then, can the skeptic's challenge be met? I am unaware of a good reason for thinking that it cannot. That despite twenty-five centuries of philosophical work it has not been met, a fact that two hundred years ago Kant described as a scandal to philosophy, is hardly a good reason. There are fundamental problems in the sciences as well that have not been resolved. But why suppose that five centuries of scientific development is a very long time? So, why suppose that twenty-five centuries of *philosophical* development is a very long time? To what measure of "long" can we appeal?

Some so-called postmodernist philosophers propose that we abandon philosophy, without apology or regret, on the grounds that its history has been a series of failures and unredeemed promissory notes. In holding this they exemplify the historical myopia I have just deplored. But their view also shows a misunderstanding of what constitutes progress in philosophy (or for that matter in science). It is not so much the accumulation of more and more "data," but the development of insights, distinctions, conceptual innovations, and, yes, also the discovery of new problems. (Think of the revolution Kant's philosophy caused in the history of philosophy.) To deny that progress, in this sense, has been made since Thales would be absurd. The question whether the skeptic's challenge can be met depends for its answer on how we should understand the word "met" in it.

Just as the birth of modern science constituted a revolution, not a mere further development of already present ideas and principles, so the skeptic's challenge would be met only by radically innovative work, not by relying on our present, rather simplistic, notions of philosophical argument, proof, and refutation.[19] If skepticism is to be answered, this would hardly be done with a valid deductive argument all of the premises of which are beyond question. Indeed, what worthwhile philosophical argument has ever been of this sort? Twenty-five centuries may not be long enough for despair in epistemology, but they should be long enough to have taught us not to expect simple solutions.

Is such innovative work impossible? We may have no reason for pessimism, but also we have no reason for optimism, not even with respect to our task in this book. We may still live in the prehistory of philosophy (perhaps also of science). To say this is not to express optimism, but only to forestall groundless pessimism. We ought to do our work, avoid the familiar ruts, be imaginative, and hope. Just to ignore skepticism is out of the question, since the existence of skepticism is the raison d'être of the philosophy of perception, the latter is the core of epistemology, and without epistemology there can be no coherent philosophy. Nor can we just cheer-

fully agree with Richard Foley that the skeptic cannot be answered.[20] We have no reason for thinking that we have tried hard enough. In this book I shall try again, and try hard.

My programmatic remarks here may become clearer if we note that, in addition to Kant's "Copernican" revolution, we have other actual examples of the sort of innovative work I have advocated. There is much in the history of epistemology that is obviously relevant to our topic, quite familiar, yet not taken seriously at present, for no good reason at all.

One example, relevant to the thesis of chapter 4, is Descartes's argument for the existence of an external world from the existence of God. This argument does not involve the sort of *conceptual* revolution I have mentioned. Yet it is radically innovative. Why is it not taken seriously by philosophers today? One reason is that it is vaguely thought to be a religious argument, and philosophers insist on not mixing religious with philosophical considerations. But, of course, it is religious only in the sense that it involves a discussion of the existence and characteristics of God, not in the proper sense of making an appeal to faith. As such, it belongs legitimately in metaphysics and epistemology. A second reason is that the argument has been thought to be unsound, or at least that Descartes had no right to use some of its premises (e.g., that everything has a cause) after having engaged in his austere methodological doubt. This second reason is legitimate. But is it sufficient? We would know whether it is only after a *rethinking* of the argument has been attempted in detail, and especially after the idea of what is to count as a good argument in philosophy has been reexamined. It is a mere prejudice to judge now that such an attempt at reconstruction would fail. Of course, it would also be a mere prejudice to judge that it would succeed. Why not avoid both judgments and simply make the attempt? But it is possible that we would then discover that to be successful we would need a conceptual revolution.

A second example, relevant to the thesis of chapter 5, can be given. No less familiar than Descartes's argument for the existence of a material world is Plato's argument for its *nonexistence*, at least for its being a world of mere appearance, not of genuine being. In effect, Plato answers the skeptic with regard to the senses by denying that there is anything, or at least anything important, to be skeptical about. Genuine knowledge is concerned with Being, and that is the "world" of the Forms; it is a priori, and thus, for example, not vulnerable to Descartes's dream-argument. Following in Plato's footsteps, Augustine wrote about the skeptics: "Whatever argument they raise against the senses has no weight against all philosophers. For there are those who admit that whatever the mind receives through a sense of the body, can beget opinion, but they deny (that it can beget) knowledge which, however, they wish to be confined to the intellect and to live in the mind, far removed from the senses."[21] Obviously, much more needs to be said about Plato's view, including a defense of my exegesis of it. Though completely different from anything currently held, its direct relevance to our topic is hardly questionable. So is its intrinsic philosophical impor-

tance. But contemporary epistemology just ignores it—again, in my opinion, for no good reason at all. Perhaps it does so just because Plato's view is "unscientific" and thus not in accord with current fashion. Or perhaps the reason is that the view did involve a radical conceptual innovation, and we still cannot understand it.

These are just two examples. I do not endorse (but neither do I reject) either of them. I believe that so far no satisfactory answer to, let alone refutation of, skepticism has been found. In this book I shall offer answers to the skeptic, though by no means unqualified or even unambiguous answers. In chapters 1 and 2 I shall explain and defend in detail an uncompromising version of direct realism. In chapter 3 I shall state and defend in detail what I consider to be the skeptic's most persuasive argument. Then, in chapter 4, I shall offer my first answer to the skeptic; I shall set the necessary context for it by defending the view that though direct realism, contrary to Kant's opinion, does not refute skepticism, it alone makes it plausible that an answer to skepticism can be found; and then I shall explain my answer by developing in detail a consequence of skepticism regarding the reality of material objects *in general* that would be especially unpalatable to philosophers. Chapter 5 will be devoted to an account of the concept of reality, since it is the application of this concept to *particular* objects of perception that the skeptic primarily questions, and if we are not clear about it we shall not be clear about what skepticism says and how it may be answered. Finally, in chapter 6, on the basis of that account of the concept of reality, I shall offer a second answer to the skeptic by arguing that philosophical skepticism regarding the reality of any particular object of perception is in one sense untrue, but in another sense, true.

The impatient reader may wonder why he or she should have to wait until chapters 4 and 6 for my answers. The reason is that if these answers are to be worthwhile, they require careful preparation. Too much has been lost in epistemology in the common rush to answer the skeptic as quickly as possible!

In general, my strategy in answering the skeptic, in solving the major problem of epistemology, the scandal to philosophy, will be to *bypass* standard epistemology. Surely, the bankruptcy of the familiar approaches to our topic is evident by now. It is hardly surprising. It is a direct consequence of the nature of philosophical questions, which I mentioned earlier. No standard answers, whether deductive or inductive or abductive or coherentist or foundational, can be expected for such questions. But I shall by no means ignore the familiar epistemological setting of the skeptic's question or the no less familiar attempts to answer it with abstruse accounts of knowledge, evidence, and justification. Whether my approach is more promising is up to the reader to judge.

1

DIRECT REALISM

1. What Is Direct Realism?

Discussions of our knowledge of "the external world" usually begin with the observation that, although such knowledge rests on the testimony of our senses, this should not be taken to imply that (even in veridical sense perception) we directly perceive material objects. According to Sextus Empiricus, "the faculty of sense does not deliver the external objects to the intellect, but reports its own peculiar affections."[1] Most writers on perception, both before and after him, have agreed. The view that we do directly perceive material objects (but not necessarily *only* material objects) is naturally describable as direct realism, direct in the sense that it denies that perception of objects is mediated by any intermediaries, though it is often called naive realism on the grounds that it is incompatible with some of the most familiar facts about perception. I believe that this appraisal of direct realism is quite unwarranted and will devote this chapter and the next to showing that this is so.[2] Direct realism would deserve to be called naive if it denied that any perceptions are illusory, but as we shall see, it does not and need not deny this.

The direct realism I shall propose represents, though in a somewhat regimented way, our commonsense and phenomenologically firmly grounded view of sense perception, namely, that at least seeing and tactual feeling are simply cases of being mentally confronted with (aware, conscious, of) material objects. Being phenomenologically grounded, it cannot be expected to be proved with an argument. But the direct realist need not hold, as the "naive realist" was defined by H. H. Price as holding,[3] that we cannot also perceive, for example in hallucinations and dreams, material objects that are not real (this is the regimentation) and thus can follow philosophical tradition by speaking of skepticism about the *reality* of the external world.

Indeed, despite his sense-datum theory, Price allowed, probably under the influence of continental phenomenology, that we can have what he called *perceptual consciousness* of unreal objects. He admitted that common sense is happy, "though not without vacillation," with the use of the

word "perception" as a synonym of his "perceptual consciousness" but decided against using it so himself because it would have been against the practice of "several philosophers, including Professor G. E. Moore."[4] And in *The Foundations of Empirical Knowledge* A. J. Ayer wrote: "I am using ['perceive'] here in such a way that to say of an object that it is perceived does not entail saying that it exists in any sense at all. And this is a perfectly correct and familiar usage of the word."[5] I shall try to show that it is essential to direct *realism* even with respect to veridical perception that it allow for the possibility of direct perception of unreal objects, and thus that it include what may be called "direct *irrealism*." But what is the ontological status of unreal, nonexistent objects? If by "ontological status" we mean a mode of existence, then they have none. If we mean their proper ontological classification, then the answer is simple: they are nonexistent.

The reason this is so has to do with a second, no less familiar, formulation of direct realism, namely, that perception, whether veridical or not, involves no intermediaries such as sense data, sensations, ways of being appeared to, sense experiences, mental representations, ideas, images, looks, seemings, appearances, occurrent beliefs or "assents," or anything else.[6] The point is not merely that perceptual judgments are not inferred from, or justified by, judgments about such intermediaries. The point is that the intermediaries are philosophical inventions, whether they are supposed to be particular objects, such as sense data, or properties, such as ways of being appeared to. If so, then a nonveridical perception can only be a perception of an unreal object. I shall return to this claim, of course.

In view of the present temper of the times, it is worth noting that the second formulation of direct realism should make it appealing to a materialist who says what she means, that is, the uncompromising eliminative materialist. (We shall see later why she may still disagree with direct realism, but on a much deeper level.) We may also call such a materialist a physicalist, and I shall do so in order to avoid the needed qualifications. If materialism is the view that all that exists is material, then since it is ultimately up to physics to tell us what it is for something to be material, it would be also up to physics to tell us what exists. This is what would matter metaphysically. Whether the other natural sciences, for example, biology, are "reducible" to physics I shall not discuss. Nor shall I discuss what has been called "supervenience physicalism," beyond avowing that I find it perversely obscurantist. However misguided philosophically we may think him to be, we must admire the forthrightness and lack of false sophistication in J. J. C. Smart's classic statements of materialism, such as the following: "I mean the theory that there is nothing in the world over and above those entities which are postulated by physics. . . . I wish to lay down that it is incompatible with materialism that there should be any irreducibly 'emergent' laws or properties."[7] I shall return to the topic of physicalism in the next section.

That direct realism as I have stated it (it should not be confused with any other so-called direct realism) is at least prima facie true should be evi-

dent from the fact that what I have called intermediaries are invariably described with technical terms or grossly abused ordinary terms.[8] I shall consider here just some of these.

We do not speak of having visual sensations when seeing something unless we mean pains or tickles or itches in the eyes; nor do we say that we experience, or have a sense experience of, a person just because we see the person.[9] Indeed, it need not be true that in such a case we have any experiences at all, in the proper sense of the word, for example, emotions, pains, tickles, itches. This point is, of course, familiar to readers of Gilbert Ryle's works.[10] What may be less familiar is that G. E. Moore, in "A Defense of Common Sense," expressed doubt that "there is a certain intrinsic property . . . which might be called that of 'being an experience'," and that whenever one is conscious there is an event that has that property.[11] If Ryle's grounds were linguistic, Moore's, I believe, were strictly phenomenological. The difference need not be as great as it seems. It would be surprising if ordinary language failed to reflect the phenomenological facts. Indeed, in the case of tactual perception we often use the verb "to feel" ("I feel a rough surface"), but to infer from this that such tactual feelings are sensations or experiences would be to ignore the obvious ambiguity of the English word "feel." (Feeling pain, which can be quite properly described as a sensation as well as an experience, is categorially different from feeling a rough surface.)

As to beliefs, surely they are not occurrences, for if they were it should make sense to say such things as "I am believing that p," which it does not. They may be behavioral dispositions (they cannot be dispositions to entertain certain occurrent beliefs if there are no occurrent beliefs), but then they would hardly be logically involved in perceiving, which is a kind of occurrence. The acquisition of a disposition may be an occurrence, as David Armstrong and George Pitcher, who defended accounts of perception in terms of belief, have pointed out,[12] but they admit that there are perceivings that involve no such acquisitions and so feel compelled to appeal to acquisitions of such things as inclinations to believe, potential beliefs, even suppressed inclinations to believe. But while we have a very clear idea of what it is to perceive something, we have only the vaguest idea of what, if any, dispositional beliefs, to say nothing of inclinations to such beliefs, suppressed such inclinations, or potential beliefs, we acquire then. The robustness of perception can hardly be captured with gaseous notions such as these. ("Belief" is sometimes used to refer to a feeling of confidence or conviction attached to a judgment, but I doubt that anyone would hold the occurrence of such feelings to be necessary for the occurrence of perception.) Paul Ziff quotes W. V. Quine and J. S. Ullian: "One's repertoire of beliefs changes at least slightly in nearly every waking moment, since the slightest chirp of a bird or chug of a passing motor, when recognized as such, adds a belief—however trivial and temporary—to our fluctuating store." Ziff remarks that one "cannot take seriously talk about a 'store' of beliefs, unless one is prepared to countenance intrinsically indefinite col-

lections."[13] The new way of beliefs leads us astray in our thinking about perception, just as the "new way of ideas" did and still does (though now using a different terminology).

Very often, the notion of occurrent belief seems indispensable in epistemology, for example, when we speak of the unthinkability or inconceivability of mistake in believing that p. I suggest, however, that in such cases the proper word to use is "judgment" or one of its cognates. The philosophical tradition supports this suggestion, although only recently it has been seen that beliefs are not occurrences. The standard term has been "judgment," and if belief was mentioned at all it was understood in terms either of judgment, sometimes even identified with it, or of certain special feelings. For example, Hume wrote: "[T]he *belief* or *assent*, which always attends the memory and the senses, is nothing but the vivacity of those perceptions they present; and . . . this alone distinguishes them from the imagination. . . . 'Tis merely the force and liveliness of the perception, which constitutes the first act of judgment."[14] And in the appendix of the *Treatise* he remarked that "belief consists merely in a certain feeling or sentiment; in something that does not depend on the will. . . . [W]hen we are convinc'd of any matter of fact, we do nothing but conceive it, along with a certain feeling, different from what attends the mere *reveries* of imagination" (624). Kant wrote: "The holding of a thing to be true, or the subjective validity of the judgment . . . has the following three degrees. . . . Opining is such holding of a judgment as is consciously insufficient, not only objectively, but also subjectively. If our holding to the judgment be only subjectively sufficient . . . we have what is termed *believing*. Lastly, when the holding of a thing to be true is sufficient both subjectively and objectively, it is *knowledge*. The subjective sufficiency is termed *conviction* (for myself), the objective sufficiency is termed *certainty* (for everyone)."[15] And recently William G. Lycan has written: "It is an interesting question whether we ever introspect beliefs. On both phenomenological and theoretical grounds, I doubt that . . . ; [W]hat we introspect, in the way of cognitive items, are judgments, and we infer our knowledge of our beliefs from those."[16]

A judgment is an occurrent mental act, or a disposition to engage in such acts. But when occurrent it is merely an act of consciousness, not a private object or inhabitant of consciousness; it is a way of being directly related to a state of affairs (real or not). There is, of course, no more plausibility to analyzing perception in terms of the occurrence of such acts or the acquisitions of such dispositions than there was to analyzing it in terms of beliefs or dispositions to believe. But we do need to refer to them in other epistemological contexts. And, unlike the case of beliefs, there is nothing questionable about occurrent judgments. Surely they are as familiar as the occurrences we call statements with which they are expressed sometimes (by no means always—fortunately we do not always speak, even "in our minds," when we think). I shall not offer here a theory of judgment, beyond my earlier suggestion that a judgment is a distinctive and not further ana-

lyzable way of being conscious of a (real or unreal) state of affairs. When Hume described a belief as an especially lively idea ("perception"), he was not far from giving a description of what a judgment is. For stylistic reasons, however, I shall feel free to use the words "belief" and "believe" where this would be philosophically harmless, especially in chapter 4.

The account of perception in terms of belief almost inevitably turns out to be a version of the causal theory of perception, and the wide acceptance of the latter has wrought devastation in epistemology. Of course, for veridical perception to occur certain causal conditions must be satisfied. For example, in vision, light must be reflected or emitted by the object seen, it must stimulate the retina, and the optic nerve and the brain must be functioning properly. But this, I suggest, is a topic for science, not for philosophy. According to the *philosophical* causal theory of perception, however, perception logically involves the causal efficacy of the object perceived (thus the theory does not allow us to speak, even though we regularly do so, of perceiving, e.g., seeing, objects that are not real, as in hallucinations and dreams). And the theory ordinarily holds that the relevant causal effect of the object is precisely one of the intermediaries I have mentioned. This is so even if the effect is described just as the *experience* of the object (a good example of why we should avoid this technical use of "experience"). Indeed this is the view of P. F. Strawson, who attempts to combine direct realism with the causal theory. But he does this by denying that causation need be a relation between "distinct existences."[17] As Hilary Putnam puts it in his Dewey Lectures, "[Strawson] frequently mixes a genuine strain of natural [direct] realism with a wholly incompatible 'causal theory of perception'" by holding that the common sense view that "we normally have experiences because of the presence of their objects . . . is . . . tantamount to the causal theory of perception."[18]

Putnam also adds:

> [I]t may be helpful to distinguish between what is commonly called "direct realism" and what I shall call from now on *natural realism*. . . . A natural realist, in my sense, does hold that the objects of normal,"veridical," perception are usually "external" things. But the philosopher whose "direct realism" is just the old causal theory of perception with a bit of linguistic cover-up can easily go along. "We perceive external things—that is, we are caused to have certain subjective experiences in the appropriate way by those external things," such a philosopher can say. The natural realist, in [William] James's sense, in contrast, holds that successful perception is just seeing, or hearing, or feeling, etc., of things "out there," and not mere affectation of a person's subjectivity by those things. . . . James's idea is that the traditional claim that we must conceive of our sensory experiences as *intermediaries* between us and the world has no sound arguments to support it, and, worse, makes it impossible to see how persons can be in genuine cognitive contact with a world at all.

In a footnote to this passage Putnam remarks: "Note that even the materialist version conceives them so; it is just that for this version altera-

tions of our brain's states is what the affectations of our subjectivity *are*" (453–54).

The so-called intuition behind the causal theory is that the object perceived is somehow necessary for the occurrence of the perceiving. But our direct realism acknowledges this: the object, even if not real, is a *logically* necessary element of the perceiving.

In fact, as H. P. Grice admitted in his classic defense of the causal theory of perception, the intuition in question seems rather to preclude a causal theory.[19] He wrote: "There is no natural use for such a sentence as 'The presence of a cat caused it to look to X as if there were a cat before him.'" To meet the objection, Grice suggests that we should not restrict the causal theory to using the verb "to cause" and that we should allow it to use such expressions as "accounts for," "explains," "is part of the explanation of," "is partly responsible for." But all these expressions also have a natural logical sense, and therefore so stated the "causal theory" is no longer a causal theory but a family of theories, of which the original theory is at best only one member, direct realism being another. Of course, Grice is right that in cases where appropriate causal connections are missing (as in his example of the clock on the shelf, which is not seen even though one's "visual impression" is just as if it were, because the impression is caused by posthypnotic suggestion or direct manipulation of one's brain) we withhold the judgment that the object the perceiver claims to perceive is really perceived. But a sufficient explanation of this is that ordinarily we take for granted that perception is veridical and that in veridical perception a suitable causal connection is present, as a matter of fact, not of logic, and on discovering in a particular situation the extraordinary circumstance that it is not, we hesitate to say that perception of the object occurs, or perhaps are just left speechless. Indeed, it may be said that the presence of an appropriate causal connection is pragmatically implied, but not entailed, by a perceptual statement, somewhat as one's making a statement implies, but does not entail, that one believes it. This is a good example of how wary we should be of relying on linguistic "intuitions." But I shall not appeal to this explanation, since the direct realist has a much simpler explanation of such hallucinations as that of Grice's clock. The perceiver sees not the real clock on the shelf but an unreal ("hallucinatory") clock that is otherwise just like it.

It is an illusion to suppose, as some defenders of the adverbial theory of sensing do, that if the relevant causal effect is a way of being appeared to, then the causally efficacious object is directly perceived.[20] What one is really aware of, according to this theory, is the way one is appeared to, which according to the leading defender of the theory, Roderick M. Chisholm, is a self-presenting property of one, one's having that property being self-evident to one. (Chisholm offers a purely epistemic definition of "self-presenting," but I believe he would also use the phrase in its usual sense. Indeed, he describes purely psychological properties such as being appeared to in a certain way as "those properties to which we have privileged

access," though he then proceeds to add his epistemic description of them).[21] In the latest (1989) edition of his *Theory of Knowledge*, he writes: "In the case of being appeared to, there is something, one's being appeared to in a certain way, that one interprets as being a *sign* of some external fact"[22] (Chisholm's italics). And: "[I]f, for example, you look outside and see a dog, then you see it by means of visual sensations that are called up as a result of the way the dog is related to your eyes and nervous system. In seeing the dog, you are also aware of the visual sensations (but it would be a mistake to say that you *see* them). Whether sensations ever *do* present us with such things as dogs is a difficult question" (18, Chisholm's italics). Another adverbialist, Alvin Plantinga, writes: "My perceptual beliefs are not ordinarily formed on the basis of *propositions about* my experience; nonetheless they are formed on the basis of my experience. . . . [You] form the belief . . . on *the basis of* this phenomenal imagery, this way of being appeared to"[23] (Plantinga's italics). And: "[T]o be aware of [the tiger-lily] I must be aware of something else, namely the tiger-lily appearances; the latter, not the former, is what I am directly aware of" (189)—although Plantinga also proceeds to say, in parentheses, "Of course, in another and perfectly good sense of 'directly aware of', I *am* directly aware of the tiger-lily."

Such theories can (and usually do) stipulate that the object causing the way one is appeared to is perceived, but this violates the ordinary sense of "perception," according to which perception is a mode of awareness. On the other hand, if they allow that one is aware of the object, the state of being appeared to being logically independent from that awareness and also vice versa,[24] then we have at best a rather uneconomical version of direct realism, moreover one encumbered with all the difficulties of the adverbial theory I shall discuss in chapter 2. It might be said that the adverbial theory acknowledges that in perception we *seem* to be directly aware of a material object, but that this is just an illusion and we need the theory to free us from it. This, however, would be just a dogmatic assertion. But more needs to be said about the adverbial theory, which today is the chief alternative to our direct realism, and I shall do so in chapter 2.

Of course, we can say that a perceived object appears to the perceiver, but so far we have just a strained way of saying that the perceiver perceives the object, not a theory of perception. And the standard locutions of the forms "appears F," or "seems F" or "looks F," which mention a *quality* of the object, are in most cases used as cautious substitutes for "is perceived to be F" or "is perceived as F." But it is best to avoid these locutions in the philosophy of perception because they encourage us to speak also of "appearances" and "ways of being appeared to." How can we do this? We do it simply by speaking of perceiving qualities *in* the material objects we perceive even if the objects do not really have those qualities, that is, even if the qualities perceived are not qualities of the objects. If an object is blue and "appears" blue to us, we may say that we perceive blue in the object

and that the object is blue. If the object is white but "appears" blue to us, then we may say that we still perceive blue in the object but the object is not blue. All this would be especially clear if we followed G. F. Stout, D. C. Williams, and Keith Campbell in regarding the qualities of particular things as being themselves *particulars*, "tropes."[25] I shall return to this point.

A similar remark can be made regarding theories that appeal to the occurrence of "perceptual experiences." If by "perceptual experience" they simply mean perceiving, then they introduce needless terminological confusion. If they mean something *caused* by the object perceived, then a perceptual experience is likely to be what I have called an intermediary, and the absence of such a peculiar event from the phenomenological field should be evident.

The direct realist view is that all that is *logically* involved in perceiving is the perceiver, the awareness or consciousness properly called perceiving in ordinary discourse, and the object perceived. But the object perceived need not exist. It is chiefly in this respect that our direct realism differs from the so-called disjunctive view defended by J. M. Hinton, Paul Snowdon, and John McDowell.[26] Roughly, this view (at least as presented by Hinton) accepts direct realism with respect to veridical perception and avoids commitment to objects or events such as sense data and experiences by denying that veridical and nonveridical perception have a common element, a "common factor." The proposal is that a disjunction such as "It is either a perception or an illusion" is the best description of a putative perception.

Why not accept this view? One reason is that it tells us nothing philosophically informative about the second disjunct by merely labeling it "illusion" (or "appearance"). But the main reason is that it does not do justice to the undeniable phenomenological fact the sense-datum theorists relied upon, namely, that there is no intrinsic difference between (veridical) perception and illusion. Our direct realism, however, does do justice to it in the most obvious and natural way: by regarding both as perception and identifying the difference between them as one between their objects, namely, respectively, real and unreal objects, a difference that we shall see in chapter 5 is not itself an object of perception. (Hinton quotes Gilbert Ryle's well-known admission that "There is something in common between having an afterimage and seeing a misprint. Both are visual affairs."[27] Ryle recognizes that this constitutes a problem for his denial that there are visual sensations in the philosophical sense. It is equally a problem for Hinton's disjunctive theory, but he does not seem to recognize it.)

In his important book *Mind and World* John McDowell repeatedly describes experience as "openness to the world" (a welcome sign of the influence of continental philosophy) but considers the objection that "experience can be misleading." His response is that this objection "would be appropriate if I were aiming to answer traditional sceptical questions,

to address the predicament of traditional philosophy. . . . But my talk of openness is a rejection of the traditional predicament, not an attempt to respond to it. . . . The aim here is not to answer sceptical questions, but to begin to show how it might be intellectually respectable to ignore them, to treat them as unreal, the way common sense has always wanted to."[28] But we shall find that the skeptical questions arise and must be answered even if we adopt direct realism, even if we agree that experience is "openness to the world," and that they do so quite independently of the "Myth of the Given," to the demolition of which McDowell's book is largely devoted.

We can now see why direct realism must include what I called "direct irrealism." Only thus can commitment to intermediaries be avoided without ignoring the fact of there being no intrinsic difference between veridical and nonveridical perception. I suggested at the very beginning of this chapter that direct realism is supported by common sense and phenomenological reflection. I can add that (as Price and Ayer recognized) it has this support even in the cases involving unreal objects: consider our natural descriptions of dreams and hallucinations as cases of seeing, tactually feeling, et cetera, and our descriptions of their objects with predicates applicable to real material objects.[29] Of course, these are not our only natural descriptions of such cases: we sometimes describe them as cases of only seeming to see, or to feel, et cetera, and this fact prompted me to describe what I call direct realism as involving a regimentation of common sense. But the phenomenological evidence is overwhelmingly in favor of such regimentation, as the "no intrinsic difference" argument shows. If direct realism, so understood, did not face philosophical objections, for example, to its acknowledgment of unreal objects, it would never occur to us to question it. This chapter is devoted to meeting those objections, including the one just mentioned.

I shall limit my discussion to vision and tactual feeling, partly because hearing, smelling, and tasting, even though they can be given a direct realist account, require that the account be quite complex, but mainly because for philosophical purposes direct realism would be sufficiently vindicated if it is true of seeing and tactual feeling.[30] Our conception of the material world is almost entirely that of the world of sight and touch.

I shall also take perceiving to be expressed by statements of the form "x perceives y," not by statements of the form "x perceives that y is F" or of the form "x perceives y as F." The second kind of statement is usually understood as entailing knowledge that y is F and thus is unsuitable as a starting point in a discussion of skepticism. And statements of the third kind are ambiguous. They may mean "x perceives an F'y y," and then they would really belong to our first kind. Or they may mean "x perceives y and applies the concept F to y" or "x perceives y and is under the impression that y is F or resembles something that is F." Understood in either way, only the first conjunct, "x perceives y," would be a statement of perception. I shall have more to say about the various senses of "perceive" in chapter 2.

2. Direct Realism and Physicalism

At least five reasons have been given for the view that direct realism is false, that we are never directly aware of material objects: (1) the commonsense fact of perceptual relativity (I shall call it the objection from perceptual relativity); (2) the scientific facts about the circumstances (causal or not) in which states of perceptual awareness occur (I shall call it the scientific objection); (3) the phenomenological assumption that, if there are mental states or events such as direct perceptual awarenesses, they can only be "ghostly," occult, spooky (I shall call it the phenomenological objection); (4) the assumption that direct realism commits us to the being of nonexistent objects in the cases of existentially illusory perceptual awareness, such as hallucinations and dreams (I shall call it the ontological objection); and (5) the fact that direct realism cannot tell us how to distinguish between veridical and nonveridical perceptual awareness (I shall call it the epistemological objection).

The power of skepticism can now be understood without appeals to philosophical fantasies about deceiving demons or brains in vats; it seems to follow if direct realism is true, precisely for the reason mentioned in the epistemological objection, and it seems to follow if direct realism is false, for the familiar traditional reason that if our awareness is limited to the intermediaries discussed earlier, to "our ideas and sensations," then we can never get outside their circle, behind their veil, because no deductive, inductive, abductive, coherentist, or any other known kind of inference can penetrate it. It is seldom recognized, perhaps because of the influence of Kant's "refutation of empirical idealism," that the mere acceptance of direct realism does not entail the rejection of skepticism.

The first three objections are related. The first, that from perceptual relativity, is often supposed to provide support for the relevance of 2, that from science, and 2 is often supposed to support 3, that from phenomenology. In this and the next section of this chapter, I shall consider 1 only very briefly and 2 somewhat more fully, and I will concentrate on 3 and 4, which together with 2 constitute what I shall call the general *physicalist* objection to direct realism. As to 5, this whole book is devoted to it.

Neither of the first two objections against the view that we can be directly aware of material objects is impressive. As to 1, from the fact that different qualities are perceived in objects in different situations even though there need not be, and indeed there is not, any perceived intrinsic difference between the perceived qualities the objects do have and the perceived qualities they do not have, that is, even though there need not be an intrinsic difference between qualitatively veridical perception and qualitatively illusory perception, or indeed between existentially veridical perception and existentially illusory perception, it does not follow that in the case of completely veridical perception we are not directly aware of real material objects and of the qualities they really have. Direct realism is the view that in perception we can be, and perhaps often are, directly aware of

real material objects and of their real qualities, not that we always are, or that it is only of real material objects and of their real qualities that we are directly aware in perception. It may be that we cannot *know* about any particular case whether or not it is one of veridical perception, but this is a different question, it is a part of the epistemological objection.

And as to 2, from the scientific fact that veridical perceptual awareness occurs only simultaneously with or after the last link in the physical causal chain that, say, begins with the object's reflecting light and ends in a specific event in the brain, whether further localized or not, it does not follow that the perceptual awareness that occurs simultaneously with or after that last event in the brain is itself somehow "in the head," rather than a direct relation to the object, that is, a state that includes the object as a logical component, even if the object is earlier in time than the awareness.[31] Analogously, the fact that I come to be 240 miles from Chicago as a result of a fairly long and complex causal process of driving does not entail that this end-result, my being 240 miles from Chicago, is not my being in a direct spatial relation to Chicago, which is neither in me nor in Chicago, but rather is a state that includes me and Chicago as *logical* components. My being 240 miles from Chicago is not at all the same as, nor does it include, the largely causal process of driving that led to it. Moreover, the fact that I *was* in Chicago some hours ago is quite compatible with my being *now* 240 miles from Chicago.

Of course, direct perceptual awareness, this peculiar relation of oneself to an external object, is not and perhaps cannot be acknowledged by the physical sciences. If direct realism is rejected just for this reason, then the real issue is the truth of physicalism, not the truth of direct realism. We thus arrive at what I called the general physicalist objection. I cannot discuss in detail the global issue of physicalism here, except insofar as it relates to direct realism, but the following observations are needed. If physicalism is not supported by argument, it deserves no discussion since it is hardly offered as a self-evident truth. (Avowals of commitment to "the scientific image" of the world are not arguments, they are expressions of faith. In this respect there is an analogy between recent Anglo-American philosophy and some parts of medieval philosophy.) If it is supported by argument, this is likely to be the familiar phenomenological argument against there being "ghostly" events or things, in other words, what I have called the phenomenological objection. But our version of direct realism also rejects the existence of the ghostly events or things relevant to it, namely those I have called intermediaries. Therefore, if physicalism is incompatible with direct realism, this must be at a deeper level, or perhaps the incompatibility is a mere appearance due to misunderstanding.

The widespread acceptance of physicalism is probably the most distinctive feature of contemporary Anglo-American philosophy. Why is physicalism so attractive today? Doubtless, part of the explanation is to be found in the pervasive influence of modern science, in the desire of philosophers to be "scientific," to conform to "the scientific image" of the

world, to be included, however vicariously, in the scientific community. But another part of the explanation is that the alternative to physicalism has seemed to be to accept a realm of being populated with irreducibly and unequivocally mental things such as images, ideas, thoughts, sensations, representations, an ego, perhaps even a soul, to say nothing of the ubiquitous "experiences" and "beliefs," all in some, perhaps causal, relation to physical things, in particular the brain, but a relation which, unless confused with mere correlation between brain states and behavior, verbal or nonverbal, the physical sciences cannot study since *ex hypothesi* one of the relata falls under none of their distinctive concepts and principles (e.g., mass, motion, the conservation of energy). Impressed by this fact, the philosophizing scientist or the scientizing philosopher assumes that the only alternatives are either simply to deny that there is anything corresponding to ordinary psychological talk, or to identify what corresponds to it with certain physiological events and states, though perhaps only functionally described.[32] Although direct realism suggests that the former alternative is closer to the mark, it seems, on the face of it, just crazy, and so our philosopher-scientist is more likely to opt for the latter. He begins to talk about *neural* representations that are identical with the alleged ghostly events, thus combining the structure of the theory of the ghost in the machine with a perverse application of the concept of identity, perverse because it accords with none of the paradigms of its application.

But how else can the integrity of scientific causal explanation of human actions be preserved, or the existence of epiphenomena, mere nomological danglers that play no causal role, be denied? Perhaps the clearest brief account of what a dualist regarding mental and physical properties (not substances) would say is still J. L. Mackie's. He points out that no mental properties seem to be analyzable or reducible to uncompromisingly physical features. The often-appealed-to analogy with identities in science (e.g, of lightning with electrical discharge), which are understood by distinguishing what the event really is and what it appears to be, "will not do for experiences themselves and their contents. Its looking thus and so to us is one of the features that is embarrassing to the physicalist, and the explanation that it only looks to us as if it looks thus and so is not only absurd but useless: it would leave us with an unexplained item of the same sort on our hands."[33] But physical (neurophysiological) and mental properties can be equally legitimately assigned (nonconflicting) causal roles if the "connection between the neurophysiological basis [of the mental features] and the mental features" could not have been missing. Then it would not "make sense to say that the mental features are idle: the actions could not have occurred without them. Two items neither of which could have occurred without the other do not compete for a causal role: even if one is a sufficient as well as a necessary cause of some outcome, the other will be a necessary and sufficient cause of it too."[34]

But my present purpose is not to evaluate the merits of specific proposals (such as Mackie's) of how to reconcile the rejection of physicalism with

scientific integrity, or how to avoid epiphenomenalism. It is to respond to what I called the phenomenological objection to direct realism, which is a part of the general physicalist objection, by drawing attention to the fact that as *usually* understood it ignores the general conception of consciousness in which direct realism is grounded, a conception familiar to phenomenologists and existentialists, versions of which I suggest were held by four of the most important twentieth-century philosophers: G. E. Moore, Ludwig Wittgenstein, Martin Heidegger, and Jean-Paul Sartre. (I could also have added Gilbert Ryle, especially since, unlike Moore and Wittgenstein, he exhibited knowledge and appreciation of Heidegger and Sartre. See discussion in note 10.) None of them accepted the existence of the ghostly realm physicalists so abhor, but also none of them was a physicalist. I shall call it the direct realist conception of consciousness and contrast it with what I shall call the mental-contents conception, which is essentially that of the mind as populated with the sort of things I called intermediaries in the case of perception, a prime example being "sensations." My reference to these philosophers is intended merely as a convenient way to remind the reader of the ultimate ground for accepting the direct realist conception, which is phenomenological and therefore not the conclusion of a "proof."

3. The Direct Realist Conception of Consciousness

It should be evident that Wittgenstein did not subscribe to the mental-contents conception.[35] One of his chief concerns was with getting "rid of the idea of the private object" generally, with getting rid of what Sartre called "inhabitants of consciousness."[36] His assertion that being in pain "is not a *something* but not a *nothing* either" fits well with the views of the mental defended (at various times) by Sartre, Moore, and Heidegger.[37]

In his revolutionary 1903 article "The Refutation of Idealism," Moore argued against the mental-contents theory (he did not use the phrase), according to which "the object of experience is in reality merely a content or inseparable aspect of that experience," whether the experience be a sensation, a mental image, or a thought, and defended what has been called the act-object, or intentionality, theory, according to which the "peculiar relation . . . of 'awareness of anything' . . . is involved equally in the analysis of *every* experience . . . [and is] the only thing which gives us reason to call any fact mental."[38] And he described consciousness as something that seems to be "transparent" (20), is "diaphanous," and thus seems to be "a mere emptiness" (25). He suggested that "many people fail to distinguish it at all," which "is sufficiently shown by the fact that there are materialists" (20). Applying this conception of consciousness to perception, he asserted: "There is, therefore, no question of how we are to 'get outside the circle of our own ideas and sensations'. Merely to have a sensation is already to be outside that circle" (27). He went on to say, "I am as directly

aware of the existence of material things in space as of my own sensations" (30). Indeed, later, Moore accepted the sense-datum theory, but he interpreted it so as to allow for the possibility that the sense datum one senses is identical with the front surface of the material object one perceives, in which case of course one would be directly aware of the object.[39]

Heidegger wrote: "Let us take a natural perception without any theory . . . and let us interrogate this concrete perception in which we live, say, the perception of the window. . . . To what am I directed in this perception? To sensations? Or, when I avoid what is perceived, am I turning aside from representational images and taking care not to fall out of these representational images and sensations into the courtyard of the university building?" He insisted that perceiving, as well as representing, judging, thinking, and willing, are "intentionally structured," that they are by their very nature directed toward an object, whether real or not, but warned against the "*erroneous objectivizing*" of intentionality, against regarding it as "an extant relation between an extant subject and object," as well as against the "*erroneous subjectivizing*" of it, against regarding it as "something which is immanent to the so-called subject and which would first of all be in need of transcendence" (Heidegger's italics). He went on to say that "intentionality is neither objective, extant like an object, nor subjective in the sense of something that occurs within a so-called subject."[40] "Extant" (*vorhanden*) may be understood to mean "existing as a thing."

But the account both most detailed and clearest of the idea that seems common to Wittgenstein's, Moore's, and Heidegger's views was provided by Sartre. He held (1) that a consciousness (or, we may say, an act or a state of consciousness) necessarily has an object, it is always of, directed toward, something, and (2) that the consciousness has no contents, no intrinsic constitution, that everything it is it owes to its object. This view is strikingly similar to Moore's (in the articles mentioned in note 38). It is that if you try to consider the (act of) consciousness you do find something, but something that is entirely transparent, translucent, without any nature or character or content of its own. So a (an act of) consciousness may be said to be nothing, in the sense that it is not a thing that has a nature or intrinsic characteristics, yet it must also be said to be something, in the sense that it does exist. (Sartre explicitly described consciousness as *being*-for-itself.) So, in Wittgenstein's words, if perhaps not meaning, consciousness is not something but neither is it nothing, and in Heidegger's words, it is neither objective nor subjective.

A state of consciousness considered in abstraction from its object is unequivocally *nothing*, since "all physical, psycho-physical, and psychic objects, all truths, all values are outside it. . . . There is no longer an 'inner life.'"[41] "Consciousness does not have by itself any sufficiency of being as an absolute subjectivity . . . it has only a borrowed being."[42] Even if its object does not exist, it has a nature, qualities (e.g., it is a mermaid), and these suffice to guarantee the being of the consciousness directed upon it. Sartre's works abound with applications of this view. "*Representation*, as

a psychic event, is a pure invention of philosophers" (217; see also 125). "As soon as we abandon the hypothesis of the contents of consciousness, we must recognize that there is never a motive in consciousness; motives are only *for* consciousness" (34). As we might expect, Sartre also vigorously rejected the philosophical notion of sensation (314), and so did Merleau-Ponty.[43] The phrase "material object" is the obvious sortal term for the usual objects of perceptual consciousness, for such things as trees, people, snakes, and rivers, whether they are real or not, just as "number" is the obvious sortal term even for numbers the nonexistence of which can be proved. What is true of perceptual consciousness is not the presence of sensations *in* it but the presence (usually) of material objects *before* it.

I pointed out earlier that contemporary physicalists ignore the direct realist conception of consciousness and instead usually take themselves to be arguing against the existence of the mind as a ghostly realm, as a system of psychic, "spooky," entities, perhaps representations, a mental machine. But, as we have just seen, the direct realist conception also rejects such a realm. To what extent would awareness by them of this conception influence their opposition to direct realism in the philosophy of perception? It ought to have a major influence insofar as they are chiefly motivated by the thought that the existence in perceptual consciousness of a realm of ghostly things is sheer fantasy; for perceptual consciousness, as understood, for example, by Heidegger and Sartre, is no such realm, it is indeed not a thing at all. But insofar as their chief motive is the one I mentioned earlier, namely, their commitment to scientism, to the "scientific image" of the world, obviously the direct realist conception of consciousness might still be unacceptable to them. Consciousness, so understood, is not a physical thing or property or relation, it has no place in the scientific image. Presumably, this is why in his earlier works Hilary Putnam writes that "postulating" that "the mind has a faculty of *referring to external objects* (or perhaps properties) [a faculty called "by the good old name 'intentionality'"] would be found by naturalistically minded philosophers (and, of course, psychologists) . . . unhelpful epistemology and almost certainly bad science as well."[44] So, clearly, even the theory I have attributed to our four philosophers would not be acceptable to some physicalists. If this is the case, so much the worse for them, we may say, and dismiss what I called the physicalist objection to direct realism with just a sigh. For the direct realist conception of consciousness is hardly a postulate, whether scientific or nonscientific; it does not pretend to be science, good or bad. It is a straightforward acknowledgment of the most intimately known fact about ourselves. Nor is it intended as an explanation, which might be "helpful" to epistemology or to psychology, nor does there seem to be any prospect of finding a genuine explanation, whether scientific or nonscientific, of the fact of consciousness. In this sense Putnam is right in describing consciousness as mysterious[45] but wrong if he supposes that it is not completely familiar to us or that its existence is questionable. After all, the difference between being conscious and being unconscious or nonconscious

is something we need to learn neither from science nor from philosophy. The direct realist conception of consciousness is too fundamental to follow from any argument, yet phenomenologically it is obviously true.

Putnam is not a physicalist. In fact, even in an earlier work he expresses the opinion that "scientism . . . is one of the most dangerous contemporary intellectual tendencies" and that its most influential contemporary form is materialism.[40] He is chiefly interested in arguing against what he calls metaphysical realism, "the myth of comparing our representations directly with unconceptualized reality" (143). This theme is repeated in almost all of his works. I shall confine myself here to just two remarks about it.

The first is that he usually regards representations as linguistic entities, even if they occur in "mentalese." And the core of his argument is that we cannot even think of a unique relation of "correspondence" between any mental state and any external object or event because such a relation would itself be something external to the mind. Of course, the argument is fallacious: at most it follows that we cannot *know* any such relation. But for our purposes the argument is significant in that it displays particularly vividly the mental-contents theory's naive picture of the relationship between the mind and its objects. If there are no mental representations to begin with, if we are in direct touch with the objects of our perception and thought, then the view, which is central to Putnam's model-theoretic argument, that any representations can be given an indefinite number of different interpretations rests on a false presupposition, on what Ryle called "Descartes's myth," the myth of there being mental representations, a species of what I have called mental contents, a myth to which Putnam seems to manifest allegiance by saying that "we have no direct access to . . . mind-independent things" (207). He admits that "if the mind has direct access to the things in themselves, then there is no problem about how it can put them in correspondence with its 'signs'" (225). Putnam seems to have intellectual intuition in mind as the sort of direct access he claims we do not have, but this merely shows that he takes for granted that perception cannot constitute such a direct access.

My second remark is that our acceptance of the direct realist account does not commit us to regarding the objects of perception as "unconceptualized," though neither does it give us reason for holding the opposite position. Direct realism is compatible with either view about this issue. Nevertheless, it is not hard to see that something is wrong with Putnam's claim that we have no direct access to unconceptualized reality. As H. H. Price pointed out long ago, in *Perception* (the context was an argument against the earlier idealist position that Putnam's resembles), *of course* we must have direct access to *something* that is unconceptualized if we are to conceptualize it! On the other hand, the description of it as "reality" presupposes, trivially, that it has been conceptualized by the application to it of the concept of reality. And if we say, as we should, that knowledge involves at least in part the application of concepts and that its general object is re-

ality, we can agree also that we cannot have *knowledge* of something without conceptualizing it. But surely this would be a tautology. I shall return to this topic often, in chapters 3, 5, and 6.

Now, in his 1994 Dewey Lectures, Putnam adopts (perhaps under the acknowledged influence of John McDowell) a very different view. He writes:

> Just think: How could the question "How does language hook on to the world?" even appear to pose a difficulty, unless the retort "How can there be a problem about talking about, say, houses and trees when we *see* them all the time?" had not already been rejected in advance as question begging or "hopelessly naive"? The "how does language hook on to the world" issue is, at bottom, a replay of the old "how does perception hook on to the world" issue. . . . Is it any wonder that one cannot see how thought and language hook on to the world if one never mentions perception?[47]

And Putnam explains his earlier model-theoretic argument from "the huge multiplicity of unintended interpretations, including quite bizarre ones" by his having accepted the view that

> the perceptual outputs are the outer limit of our cognitive processing; everything that lies beyond those inputs is connected to our mental processes only causally, not cognitively. . . . Thus I concluded that, if the sort of realism we have been familiar with since the early modern period, including the causal theory of perception, is right, then everything that happens within the sphere of cognition leaves the objective reference of our terms, for the most part, almost wholly undetermined (60).

All this is a very welcome development in his thought and largely in harmony with what I have been saying. The reason I considered briefly his earlier views is their independent merit and the prominence they have had and continue to have.

Earlier I suggested that a judicious, nonideological version of physicalism is compatible with the direct realist theory of *perception*. That would be a version that takes seriously the claim that perceptual consciousness involves no intermediaries. But I remarked that the physicalist might balk at the direct realist conception of consciousness as something nonphysical. Would the judicious physicalist be mollified by the direct realist's further claim that consciousness itself is not a thing, or a property, or a relation, that it has no contents, whether objective ("physical") or subjective ("mental"), that in a sense it is *nothing*, that is, it is not a *thing*? Doesn't this give physicalists what they really wanted? Whether such a version of physicalism would still deserve to be called physicalism is another, perhaps unimportant question. Of course, it would still be not compatible with any view that allows for the existence of irreducibly mental ("psychic") objects such as pains and itches, that is, sensations in the ordinary sense of the term. These are not inhabitants, contents, of consciousness, and they are not intentional.[48] They are *objects* of consciousness. Perhaps they are not something, but certainly they are not nothing. The question of their nature

is irrelevant to our topic, which lies squarely in the philosophy of *perception.* But it is quite relevant to the truth of physicalism, and thus to our overall response to the physicalist objection. Therefore, I shall return to it after we respond to the ontological objection to direct realism. We shall find that our response will provide us with the resources for a treatment of the reality of sensations that, though motivated very differently and quite independently of worries about physicalism, might be acceptable to judicious physicalists.

4. Existential and Qualitative Illusion

We now come to the ontological objection to direct realism. Although this is not our chief concern here, it connects with our earlier discussion of physicalism. For, despite its far more general motivation, it might be eagerly, though misguidedly as we shall see, embraced by the physicalist. According to the direct realist conception of consciousness, some acts of consciousness have objects that are not real, that do not exist. And a physicalist may regard this as a reductio ad absurdum of direct realism. But whether this is so must be decided now on phenomenological grounds, not on the grounds appealed to by the simplistic physicalism motivated by mere scientism, which we have already rejected, and not even on any grounds that what I have been calling judicious, nonideological physicalism might have. For the ontological objection has a far more general and deeper motivation. When Alexius Meinong and Bertrand Russell disagreed about objects that have no being, physicalism was hardly on their minds.

In chapter 5 I shall have far more to say about it, but here let me bluntly assert that the ontological objection is based more on prejudice than on reason. (Unlike Meinong, I shall use "existence" and "reality" as synonyms. The latter is actually preferable because it expresses the concept more vividly. On the other hand, much of the literature employs "existence," and so shall I occasionally. Saying that the dagger Macbeth saw did not exist may sound strange, but surely saying that the dagger Macbeth saw was not real does not; it is something we all readily understand and, unless we are philosophers, also readily accept.)

That some objects of consciousness are not real is a direct consequence of the thesis of the intentionality of consciousness: that all acts of consciousness are directed toward an object. One of the principles of phenomenology, indeed of all rational thought, is to accept the facts as we find them, at least as our starting point, and not to be swayed by preconceived ideas. It is obviously a fact that sometimes we think of things that do not exist, as Meinong pointed out. The things in question are ordinarily mountains, people, life situations; our thought is not directed toward some peculiar spiritual photographs of these "in our minds," or toward extraordinarily complex general ("quantified") states of affairs, as implied by Russell's theory of definite descriptions. Almost a century ago, Husserl put the phenomenological point bluntly as follows: "If I represent God to my-

self, or an angel, or an intelligible thing-in-itself, or a physical thing or a round square etc., I mean the transcendent object named in each case, in other words my intentional object: it makes no difference whether this object exists or is imaginary or absurd."[49] So, there are things that do not exist. But, as we shall see in chapter 5, perhaps some of the examples Meinong and Husserl used were too extravagant to be phenomenologically plausible. This, of course, does not detract from the general thesis that some of the objects of consciousness do not exist. And we shall not appeal to any extravagant examples in our phenomenology of perception, with which alone we are here concerned.

I described the ontological objection as based largely on prejudice, for it rests on two assumptions that are not sufficiently thought out and indeed are obviously false. The first is that to allow for nonexistent objects of consciousness is to allow for a special realm of being. The second is that to say that there are such objects is to say that there *exist* such objects, and thus to contradict oneself. The first assumption is explicitly rejected by anyone who has held the view against which the objection is directed and uses "being," "existence, "and "reality" as synonyms; nonexistent objects have no being *at all*. The second assumption fails to recognize that "there are" has a common use in which it is not a synonym of "there exist" (e.g., in "There are many fantastic things I dream about. Let me tell you about them"), and that in any case we can express the view simply by saying "Some things we are conscious of do not exist." It is worth noting that the synonymous expressions in German and French are, respectively, *es gibt* and *il y a*, which do not contain forms of the German and French synonyms of the English verb "to be." Meinong's opponent, in denying that there are things that do not exist, is asserting the logically equivalent proposition that all things exist, that all things are real. It is incumbent upon her to tell us what she means by "exist" or "real" in making this startling claim. Anti-Meinongians have not offered an explanation. For example, Russell's account of existence as satisfaction of a propositional function[50] obviously presupposes a more fundamental notion of existence, which we would employ in deciding what to allow as arguments satisfying a function, for example, whether to allow Secretariat but not Pegasus as an argument of "x is a horse"; but he never explained this notion, indeed seemed not even to notice that he presupposed it. I shall return to this point in chapter 5.

What then lies behind the two assumptions I have mentioned? Why are they made, if there is so little to be said in their favor? I think the answer is that it is natural to fail to distinguish between being conscious of nothing and being conscious of something that does not exist. This is natural since on the level of language the distinction is not clear, probably because it seldom needs to be made explicitly. It is, however, quite clear on the level of the facts to which we give linguistic expression. There is an obvious difference between not imagining anything and imagining something that does not exist. Anti-Meinongianism fails to take this difference seriously, and views such as the early Russell's (in *The Principles of Mathematics,*

published in 1903) that ascribe being to all objects, existent and nonexistent, take it too seriously. Both are influenced by a picture of nonexistence as nothingness, as an undifferentiated darkness out of which emerge lit-up distinct objects, "beings." But the realm of nonexistence is not such an undifferentiated darkness, it is not sheer emptiness, nothingness, though it is easily confused with one. Once the confusion is made, we do indeed find it senseless to suppose that there are nonexistent things, for to suppose this would seem to be to suppose that the emptiness has occupants. But sheer nothingness is occupied by nothing. The realm of nonexistents is not sheer nothingness; it contains differentiable objects of thought, of imagination, of perception, and so forth, and seems to be impossible only if confused with sheer nothingness, which of course is not a realm of anything at all, whether dark or lit-up.[51]

But how would the direct realist describe *qualitative* perceptual illusion, in which what is perceived is a material object that does exist but does not have some property that is perceived in it? I have already noted that the simplest proposal, one which I do not accept, but neither wholly reject, for ontological reasons I cannot go into here,[52] is to treat the qualities of particular things as themselves particulars, "tropes," rather than universals. Then the account of qualitative illusion would be quite the same as that of existential illusion. The illusory quality, though perceived in the object, does not exist, is not real. Instead, some other, unperceived, quality exists in the object. The white book that looks blue exists, but the particular blue color that is perceived in it does not; rather, a particular but unperceived white color does.

But while this would be the simplest treatment of qualitative illusion, it is not the only one available to us. Let us suppose that the qualities of particular individual things are not particulars, that they are universals. But let us allow for disembodied "surfaces," or, better, for nonexistent "surfaces," for unreal perceptual expanses.[53] The notion of a perceptual expanse is employed by H. H. Price and by Frank Jackson in discussing their (not to be identified!) notions of a sense datum.[54] Price argues that a perceptual expanse cannot be identical with a surface of a body on the grounds that a surface is not a particular existent but an attribute.[55] But, as he seems to recognize, we predicate of surfaces first-order attributes, for example, colors and shapes, and therefore surfaces cannot be attributes, they must be particulars. Moreover, he introduces his term "sense datum" by giving a red *patch* as an example (3). The idea of a perceptual expanse is in need of elucidation but is not incoherent. Shadows, flashes of lightning, and rainbows provide a ready starting point for understanding it. Now in a case of qualitative illusion there is a real material object but one perceives a perceptual expanse that could be and is perceived as being, but in fact is not, the front surface of the object or indeed of any real object. It is indistinguishable from a part of the surface of an object, and could have been identical with such a part, but in fact is not.

The view I have suggested differs from Price's and any other sense-

datum theory in allowing for nonexistent expanses. In effect, according to it, qualitative illusion is simply a kind of existential illusion. That in our account of *qualitative* perceptual illusion we make an appeal to nonexistent, unreal objects, namely mere perceptual expanses, is a natural extension of our appeal to such objects in our account of *existential* perceptual illusion. The much larger number of nonexistent, unreal, objects we would thus need to accept should not disturb us. If Ockham's razor has a legitimate function, surely it is to protect us from multiplication of existents, not of nonexistents. We do not overpopulate the universe by acknowledging a large number of nonexistent objects. Mere (i.e., illusory) perceptual expanses are not existent, real objects, and the general defense of allowing for them would be like that of allowing for nonexistent material objects. If so, we can point out the important consequence that since a mere perceptual expanse does not exist, the question whether it is or is not mind-dependent does not arise. A mere perceptual expanse, so understood, does not exist at all, and therefore is neither "dependent" nor "independent," though in every other respect is just like perceptual expanses that do exist, namely, the existent surfaces of existent material objects, and perhaps things such as shadows, flashes of lightning, and rainbows. It makes no sense to say that it is logically or causally dependent on us, if it does not exist at all!

Our general view can be seen now to incorporate the virtues of the sense-datum theory, indeed to coincide with a drastically revised version of it, a version compatible with direct realism as well as with any plausible phenomenology of perception. Sense data, according to this version, are indeed what we perceive directly. They are what could be but need not be the real facing surfaces of real material objects. If they are not, then they are nonexistent, unreal, but nonetheless perceived perceptual expanses. If they are, then to perceive them would be, of course, to perceive (as "directly" as it makes sense to say that we could) the real material objects of which they are the facing surfaces. We must not make the mistake of supposing that since we cannot perceive a material object without perceiving a surface of it, it is only the latter that is directly perceived. (As Thompson Clarke has pointed out, this would be like supposing that we cannot be eating a sandwich because we can do so only by chewing a part of it at any one time.)[56] And, of course, to perceive what could be but is not a real surface of a material object would be indistinguishable from perceiving an unreal material object.

The reader may have noted that if understood as I have suggested, my answer to the ontological objection need not be rejected by the physicalist. After all, why should she not admit that some things do not exist and still hold that all those that do are physical? In what way could this be incompatible with physicalism? The truth is that physicalism is incompatible with direct realism with respect to perception only if it rejects the *general* direct realist conception of consciousness, described in the previous section. But would it reject it if it understood it properly, for example, in Sartre's way?[57] Why should it deny that there is something that is in itself

not a thing, namely, consciousness? Would physics need to deny it?[58] Or would it instead acknowledge its own limitations, not falsehood? I believe that a thoughtful physicist would do the latter (as he may also regarding the existence of God), and that so should a thoughtful physicalist. But would this still be physicalism? Perhaps after what has been said it no longer matters what we call it.

Our response to the ontological objection may suggest now how the physicalist could deal even with what seems to be the intractable problem of the existence of sensations in the ordinary sense of the word, for example, headaches. On a Sartrean view, they are not inhabitants but objects of consciousness. Now what cannot be rejected is the consciousness of the headache, but I have already said that consciousness, if understood in Sartre's way as a no-thing, might be acceptable to the physicalist. What about the headache itself, however? Could it be that, though an object of consciousness, it is an unreal one? The answer would depend on what is meant by "reality," a question we shall consider in detail in chapter 5. But suppose we anticipate and say that for something to be real is for it to be indefinitely identifiable, by oneself as well as by others. Is a headache real, then? Wittgenstein argued that in his private-language argument he was not asserting that a sensation is nothing but only that neither is it something. I shall ignore his further explanation that in the language game a nothing would serve as well as a something, because I think one can offer an explanation deeper than one that has to do with language. What is this explanation? The reader would guess of course that it is to be found in Wittgenstein's claim that a sensation, understood as a private object, is not reidentifiable. Though he did not draw this conclusion, we can immediately say that it follows that a sensation, so understood, is not something real. It is not literally nothing, of course, since after all it was the subject of the question whether *it* was reidentifiable; we knew which item the question was concerned with. But, like Meinong, perhaps Wittgenstein was aware that there is no simple dichotomy between something and nothing. Even to raise the question of the reality or nonreality of something, we must at least think of that something.

Now a reasoning like this may offer support to an intelligent eliminative materialism with respect to sensations. But the extent to which it may do so would depend very much on how we see our sensations. I shall limit myself here to illustrating my point. A person experiences a headache when going to bed, awakes in the middle of the night with a qualitatively similar headache, and arises in the morning again with a similar headache. She can see the objects of the three experiences as distinct but ephemeral events and for this reason may refuse to ascribe to them genuine reality. (The experiences, of course, she would continue to regard as "real," since they are merely acts of consciousness and are in themselves no-thing; my point concerns only their objects.) But she could also see them as one and the same headache, unfelt for long periods of time but nevertheless the same. In other words, she may apply the concept of identity to them or

deny it. If she does apply it, I suggest, she would be much more inclined to view the headache as a real event of some duration. Which would be the right thing for her to do? Common sense inclines in both directions, but when confronted bluntly with the question whether headaches can exist even if unfelt it might recoil. If this reaction would be right, then we could declare headaches, and surely any other sensations, to be unreal objects of consciousness and thus perhaps free the physicalist from the major objection to her view, though hardly in the way she might have expected. To be sure, there are these objects of consciousness. But they are not parts of reality.

This completes our discussion of the ontological objection to direct realism. But it is the epistemological objection that, I believe, is the really serious objection, not the objections from perceptual relativity, from science, from phenomenology, from ontology, or from the sort of physicalism motivated solely by scientism. Unfortunately, Sartre does not cast much light on the epistemological question that the objection poses, nor do Moore, Wittgenstein, and Heidegger, even though Moore and Wittgenstein devoted much attention to it. Yet it is a question we can hardly ignore, for it is probably the first question that would occur to the reader when confronted with the direct realist's acknowledgment that some objects of consciousness are not real, do not exist. I believe that no other theory offered so far has a satisfactory answer to this question, and therefore that it would not be a distinctive fact about, or argument against, direct realism if it did not; but I believe also that, unlike the competing theories, the direct realist theory offers a brighter prospect that an answer is possible, for it brings us, so to speak, at least halfway toward an answer, simply by allowing us to be directly aware of material objects even if they do not exist. I shall explain this further in chapter 4.

But first we must consider in greater detail the adverbial theory, which is the chief rival of direct realism, if this defense of direct realism is to be complete. As I have suggested, the standard third alternative, the sense-datum theory, if interpreted in a defensible way, would be quite compatible, indeed could be said to coincide, with direct realism. I should warn the reader that my rejection of the adverbial theory will be mainly phenomenological, and so not based on argument. But philosophers have for too long been preoccupied with the search for arguments, perhaps because of the Cartesian illusion that philosophy should be like mathematics or natural science. But surely philosophy is sui generis. Husserl and the later Wittgenstein should have taught us this.

2

THE ADVERBIAL THEORY

1. The Several Senses of Perceptual Verbs

In recent American philosophy, discussions of perception often contain expressions such as 'being aware here-ly', 'is appeared to redly', 'senses redly', 'senses rhomboidally', 'sensation of the of-a-red-triangle kind', 'senses a-pink-cube-ly'. We owe this innovation in philosophical terminology to the so-called adverbial theory.[1] But, the adverbial theory of what? The answers usually given are: of appearing, of sensing, of sense-impressions, of sensation. But, as we saw in chapter 1, all these terms are suitable in this context only if understood as technical terms, of unclear sense and uncertain reference, not as they would be understood in common discourse. And the adverbial theory is precisely a theory of that which is supposed to require their introduction as technical terms and an explanation of how they should be understood. Therefore, it is not with a statement of the adverbial theory that we can begin a discussion of the adverbial theory. We must begin with the conceptual roots the theory must have in common discourse if it is to be even intelligible.

If we speak as we do before our immersion in philosophy, we may say that it is a characteristic feature of perceiving (seeing, tactile feeling, hearing, smelling, tasting), of imagining, of thinking, perhaps of everything that is, or in some manner involves, what may conveniently be called consciousness, that one can perceive, imagine, think of, perhaps in general be conscious of, things that do not exist. That this is so in the case of imagination and thought is unequivocally supported by common discourse. As we have seen, in the case of perception common discourse is not unequivocal. I shall use seeing as my example of perceiving, but whatever I say about it can be said also about the other modes of sense perception.

Now we may correctly say of the delirious drunk, about whom philosophers often write, that he sees a pink rat, and of an ophthalmologist's patient that she sees stripes where there are none. But we may also say that the drunk only thinks he sees a pink rat and that the patient only thinks she sees stripes. Should we conclude from this that "see" has at least two senses? Pace J. L. Austin,[2] I think that we should, though mainly for the

sake of terminological convenience. What is important for our purposes here is that we recognize the distinction, not that we regard it as a distinction between senses. For it is only in that distinction in common discourse that some of the central terminological proposals of the philosophy of perception can be anchored. Indeed, for our purposes in this chapter we may even allow (despite our arguments against it in chapter 1) for a third sense of "see," in which what one sees must not only exist but also be causally related in an appropriate way to oneself. (Not: to one's seeing, for in this third sense of "see" the seeing would include the causal relation.) And let us allow that, possibly, there is a fourth sense: that, in addition to what one of the first three requires, the perceiver have some belief, that is, make a judgment, about the thing he sees, in particular that it exists and has the qualities it is seen to have. The evidence for there being such a sense would be *at best* that, as we noted in chapter 1, sincere first-person uses of "see" usually pragmatically imply (not entail!) that the seeing is veridical and so they might be taken to presuppose that the speaker, who is the perceiver, has the relevant beliefs, makes the relevant judgments; sincere other-person uses might then be held to presuppose this regarding the other person but not, of course, regarding the speaker. Corresponding distinctions of senses can be made with respect to all perceptual verbs, and so they may be thought of as four senses of "perceive."

One reason I have been so generous here in allowing for such an unlikely multiplicity of senses of "see" (and generally of "perceive") is that even if they all were present in ordinary discourse there would be no genuine philosophical question about which of them is the most common or the correct one. To appeal to a distinction Gilbert Ryle made, but for a purpose of which he would have disapproved, that would be a question about usages, not uses, of perceptual verbs.[3] But my main reason is that surely the first sense, that in which what is perceived need not exist, has *epistemological* primacy and therefore is the one that should mainly concern us. For only in that sense can we plausibly say that perception is the source of our knowledge of the existence of material things. In the second and third senses, the use of the perceptual verb *presupposes* that what is said to be perceived exists. And, in the fourth sense, it is not the mere occurence of one's judgment that one can intelligibly regard as evidence for the existence or qualitative character of what one perceives or thinks one perceives; such a judgment is precisely what requires, not what constitutes, evidential support (except in the irrelevant case in which it may serve as indirect, inductive evidence, e.g., if we know of a person that usually she does not make perceptual mistakes, her making a certain judgment on the basis of perception may count as evidence for its truth). The philosophy of perception begins, insofar as it is concerned with language at all, with a question regarding the first sense of perceptual verbs: How can one perceive something that does not exist? (We may also begin by asking, How can one perceive qualities in a thing that the thing does not have? But if we do, we quickly see, as I suggested in chapter 1, that our answer must

wait upon the answer we would give to the general question about perceiving things that do not exist.)

One answer to this question is that no special explanation is required, that sometimes we just do perceive things that do not exist, that we know that this is possible because it is actual. Of course, this answer faces immediate difficulties concerning the status of nonexistent things and the notion of existence, but they are difficulties we would need to face because of the facts about imagination and thought, which surely often have objects that do not exist, even if we steadfastly refused to speak of *perceiving* nonexistent things. In chapter one I suggested how these difficulties can be met, and chapter 5 is reserved for a detailed discussion of this topic.[4] I shall not go into it in the present chapter beyond observing that an important advantage of this answer to our question is that it is the natural one, the prima facie correct one, the one that seems phenomenologically obvious. But it is not the only answer that philosophers have offered.

Another answer is that what is ordinarily described as a case of someone's perceiving something that does not exist is really a case of the person's perceiving (seeing, hearing, etc.) something else that does exist but is such that it is naturally confused with the former. This other thing is usually called a sense datum and, in the central cases of visual and tactual perception, is described as a mere perceptual expanse that has precisely some of the sort of qualities we ordinarily say we perceive material things as having, for example, colors and shapes. This is why, we would be told, it is natural to confuse a sense datum with the front surface of a material thing, to confuse perceiving a sense datum with perceiving a material thing.[5] And to reflect the fact that ordinarily we speak of perceiving material things, it may be proposed, solely for the sake of terminological clarity, that we use a technical term for our perception of sense data, namely, the term 'sensing'. But if it is added that in the case of veridical perception the sense datum, the perceptual object, which one senses is identical with the front surface of a material thing, an addition essential I think to any plausible sense-datum theory, then in that case one's sensing a sense datum would be identical with one's perceiving a material thing (as directly and immediately as it would make sense to suppose), and, as we saw in chapter 1,[6] the sense-datum theory would coincide with direct realism, insofar as the latter is merely the claim that we *can* directly perceive real material objects.

A third answer that has been proposed by some is that one's perceiving something that does not exist is essentially one's judging falsely that the thing does exist. But this answer is a nonstarter, since perception (in the sense expressed by sentences of the form "x perceives y" rather than "x perceives that y is F" or "x perceives y as an F"), whether veridical or nonveridical, need not and ordinarily does not involve judgments at all, certainly not occurrent ones, and in most cases not even judgments that are merely dispositions. At any rate, to what extent, if at all, it involves judgments is an issue best left to psychologists, and it has no bearing, as far as

I can see, on any philosophical issue, at least not on that to which this book is devoted. We did allow for a sense of "see" that requires that the perceiver make some judgment about the object perceived, but that was not the only sense, indeed we ought to doubt that it is genuine at all.

A fourth answer is that what is ordinarily described as a case of someone's perceiving something that does not exist is really not a case of perception, or of any other kind of consciousness, of an object at all, whether of the object we ordinarily take it to have (a material thing) or of any other object (e.g., a sense datum), even though it *seems* to be such. It is really a case of someone's being in a state of consciousness that has a certain nonrelational (whether sortal or qualitative) characteristic. Since a state of consciousness is expressed most naturally with a psychological verb, its characteristics would be expressed most naturally with adverbs modifying that verb. Hence the designation of this fourth answer as the adverbial theory. Because its proponents allow (seldom on the basis of argument) for the use of perceptual verbs only in the case of existentially veridical perception, they too introduce a technical term, indeed, usually, again 'sensing,' for the kind or mode of consciousness characteristic of sense perception, and describe the theory as the adverbial theory of sensing. Adverbial theories of thinking, imagining, and believing have also been proposed,[7] for reasons similar to those behind the adverbial theory of sensing. We may therefore speak generally of the adverbial theory (or theories) of consciousness. This would make explicit the fact that what is at stake in a discussion of the adverbial theory of sensing is far more general than any issues specific to the philosophy of perception. But I shall be concerned directly only with the adverbial theory of sensing, though in a manner relevant to adverbial theories of other modes of consciousness. In addition to the obvious reason that this book is about perception, there is the fact that only the adverbial theory of sensing has been developed in any detail.

The adverbial theory of sensing may be understood in three distinguishable, though not always distinguished, ways. First, it is a method of reformulating, or paraphrasing, statements in ordinary language that seem to commit us to philosophical views the adverbial theorist wishes to reject: specifically, the view that sometimes we perceive things that do not exist and the view that sometimes, perhaps always, we perceive ("sense") things that do exist but are not material objects, such as sense data and after-images.

Second, the adverbial theory may be understood as a philosophical description of the nature of at least some kinds of consciousness. Clearly, such a description must be phenomenological; it must be defended with phenomenological considerations. For what else can a philosophical description of a certain state of consciousness be? Even if a certain state of consciousness were identical with a certain state of a brain, we could know this only if we had an independent conception of the former as well as an independent conception of the latter. (To know that the evening star is identical with the morning star we must first know what we are asserting

to be identical with what.) And whereas the conception of the latter would be based on anatomical and physiological facts, the conception of the former surely must be based on the phenomenological facts. It should be noted that the examination of the ordinary uses of psychological terms need not be an alternative to the phenomenological approach. When practiced at its best, it can be regarded as a methodological variety of that approach.[8]

Third, the adverbial theory may be understood as a postulation of certain entities (perhaps "sense impressions") possessing certain characteristics, a postulation intended to provide an explanation of various phenomena, especially of the perceptual reports (both correct and incorrect) we make and of our so-called conceptual representations.[9] Chisholm's ways of being appeared to may be thought of as merely postulated entities, though this is not how he thinks of them.

I shall first consider the adverbial theory as a method of reformulation. Then I shall consider it as a phenomenological description. I shall not consider its third version, partly because of my skepticism about philosophers' *explaining* phenomena, partly because of my skepticism about philosophers' *postulating* entities, but especially because it seems obvious to me that both its rivals, the sense-datum theory and the quasi-Meinongian theory mentioned earlier, would serve any needed explanatory role much better than would the adverbial theory.

2. The Adverbial Theory as a Method of Reformulation

Roderick M. Chisholm recommends that we say of a man who has "spots before his eyes" that "the man senses (is appeared to) 'spottily', or 'in a spotty manner'," rather than that he senses "a spotty appearance" or simply, as ordinarily we would, that he sees spots.[10] Elsewhere Chisholm recommends that in order "to eliminate the reference to the thing that appears," we say, "I am appeared whitely to" or "I sense whitely," instead of "Something appears white to me."[11] More recently, he has described the "*sensible* properties" of philosophy in the empirical tradition as "the ways in which we *sense*, or are *appeared* to."[12] And Wilfrid Sellars has suggested that to have a sensation of a red rectangle is not to stand in a peculiar relation to a red rectangle, but rather to a-red-rectangle-ly sense.[13] But it should be noted that Sellars's version of the adverbial theory is part of a rich metaphysics and philosophy of mind. It is by no means a proposal of a mere reformulation, for the purpose of avoiding puzzlement. And although Chisholm often writes as if that is all his version is, clearly it too is motivated by deep ontological and epistemological considerations.

I will not comment here on the value of reformulation as a general method for the solution of philosophical problems or on the conception of philosophy that encourages its practice. And I shall postpone until the next section the really important question regarding any proposed reformula-

tion, and therefore regarding those offered by the adverbial theory, namely, whether the reformulation captures the structure of the situation described by the original statement, whether it casts light on it, whether it reflects the crucial similarities and differences between it and other kinds of situation, in terms of which we may make it intelligible to ourselves. (Whether the reformulation succeeds in dissolving superficial puzzlement occasioned by the original statement seems to me of little philosophical importance.) Here I shall raise only a question so elementary as to be out of place in most cases of the practice of philosophical reformulation, but certainly not in this case, namely, whether the reformulations proposed by the adverbial theory even make sense. If we think of the Russellian reformulation of a statement containing a definite description as the paradigm of a philosophical reformulation ("analysis"), then the corresponding question about it would be not, for example, one of those Strawson asks in "On Referring,"[14] but one that to my knowledge has never been asked, namely, whether it even makes sense. This question has not been asked about the Russellian reformulations because the answer to it is obvious: they do. Even if "There is one and only one thing that is now King of France, and that thing is bald" is not an adequate reformulation of "The present King of France is bald," there can be no question that it is a perfectly meaningful and clear, though rather long-winded, statement.

Let us take the example "Something appears white to me" and its paraphrase as "I am appeared whitely to." We must keep in mind that we are asked to understand the latter in such a way that it does not entail either that something is appearing to me or that something is white. How should we understand it then? The first obvious observation is that 'whitely' is rarely used in English and then not at all in the sense the adverbial theory needs. But of course we should recognize that in general it is in accord with English grammar to form an adverb from an adjective by adding the suffix 'ly' and that we might try to understand 'whitely' as we understand the familiar results of that procedure. Thus we may appeal to an analogy with statements like "She runs slowly."[15] But such an appeal would be useless. We mean by "She runs slowly" exactly what we mean by "Her run(ning) is (tends to be) slow," and if we were told that the former should be so understood that it is not equivalent to the latter, we would avow that then we have no idea of what it means. But we cannot understand "I am appeared whitely to" as meaning the same as "My (present) being appeared to is white," since the latter sentence is either necessarily false or senseless. And if it made sense and also were true, then the curious result would follow, that after all "I am appeared whitely to" does entail that something is white, though not that a material thing or a sense datum is white, but that a state of consciousness is white. The paradox is even more striking when by a similar reasoning the conclusion is reached that a state of consciousness is rhomboidal!

Indeed, C. J. Ducasse did hold that "'blue', 'bitter', 'sweet', etc., are names not of objects of experience, nor of species of objects of experience, but of

species of experience itself. What this means is perhaps made clearest by saying that to sense blue is to sense *bluely*, just as to dance the waltz is to dance 'waltzily'."[16] He claimed that "blue stands to sensing blue . . . as kind stands to occurrence of a case thereof," and explained that what he meant is that the sensing, the awareness, is "of the determinate sort *called 'blue'*, and not that it has, like lapis lazuli, the property of being blue." He also explained that "when I assert of lapis lazuli that it is blue, what I mean is that it is such that whenever I turn my eyes upon it in daylight it causes me to experience something called 'blue'."[17] And in *Perceiving* Chisholm did distinguish three uses of the word "blue" and claimed that "frequently the word 'blue' is used to designate a kind or species of appearing."[18] And Herbert Heidelberger did suggest, in defense of Ducasse's view, that "being-a-blue-patch, being-a-blue-speck, being-a-blue-line, and being-a-blue-spot are qualities, just as being blue is a quality, and . . . all are exemplified by acts of sensing."[19]

It may seem that Ducasse and Chisholm would be willing to say that an awareness, or a sensing, or an appearing (a state of sensory consciousness) is blue as long as we understand saying this as analogous to saying that Jessie is a cow rather than to saying that Jessie is white. (Compare Aristotle's distinction in the *Categories* between being-said-of and being-present-in.) And I assume that Heidelberger's statement entails, together with the reasonable assumption that there are blue patches, that some acts of sensing are blue patches. But I suggest that it makes no more sense to speak of a state of consciousness as being of the species blue or as being a blue patch than it does to speak of it as having the property of being blue. It should be noted that Sellars's version of the adverbial theory is not open to this objection, since he holds that the attributes of sense impressions are only analogous to those of the (facing sides) of the material things that are their standard causes.[20] But I tend to think that in this manner—through transcategorial analogies between characteristics of states of things and characteristics of things—absurdity is avoided only at the cost of excessive vagueness and perhaps vacuity.

There is a second difficulty. It is not true that "I am appeared whitely to" does not entail that something appears white to me. (That it does not is essential to the adverbial theory for dealing with the crucial case of existentially illusory perception.) Since 'to appear' is not intended to be understood as a technical term, but is the term with which the admittedly technical 'to sense' is explained, this statement, on the surface singular and nonrelational, makes sense only if understood as elliptical for the general and relational statement "I am appeared whitely to by something." An analogy may make this clearer. The fact that the statement "John was shot" contains no reference to the person who shot John merely shows that it is elliptical for a certain general relational statement, namely "John was shot by someone" or "Someone shot John" (in very special circumstances, we may need to replace "someone" with "something"); it certainly does not show that the statement is genuinely singular and moreover nonrelational,

that John could have been shot even if no one (not even he himself or *something*) shot him. It should be noted that to introduce the verb "to sense" as a technical synonym of "to be appeared to" would not help. The ordinary verb "to sense" is transitive and therefore requires an object if it is to be used grammatically. On the other hand, it cannot be intransitive if introduced as a technical synonym of "to be appeared to," since, as we have just seen, one's being appeared to in some way entails that something appears to one in that way.

A third general difficulty arises when we consider adverbial reformulations of more complex statements such as "I see a triangular red after-image to the left of a circular blue after-image." (Some specific difficulties that such statements pose for the adverbial theory are discussed in detail by Frank Jackson, and I shall not repeat them here.[21] But I think that, contrary to what Jackson supposes, they do not directly affect Sellars's version of the theory.)[22] What would be the adverb that a reformulation of this statement would contain? "Triangularly-redly-to-the-leftly-of-circularly-bluely" or "Triangular-red-to-the-left-of-circular-blue-ly" can only be described as a syntactical monstrosity. To suggest that the use of such a phrase would save us from philosophical puzzlement and befuddlement would be disingenuous. Chisholm attempts to deal with this objection in *Person and Object*:

> And what of the sort of thing the sense datum philosopher is trying to describe when he says "I sense a triangular red sense datum located to the left of a circular blue one"? We needn't coin an adverb to describe the situation. We could say merely: "There is a way of appearing which is such that (i) it is the way one is appeared to under optimum conditions for perceiving that a red triangle is to the left of a blue circle and (ii) I am appeared to in that way."[23]

But it is not true that we could say merely this. Chisholm's reformulation is a *general* statement about ways of appearing, that is, exactly about what would be expressed by the adverbs we need not coin. Such a general statement is no more intelligible than its singular substitution instances would be. But a substitution instance of this statement would be a conjunction, the first conjunct of which (that corresponding to i) would contain a phrase that replaces "it" and contains the adverb we have been told we needn't coin, and the second conjunct of which (that corresponding to ii) would have the form "I am appeared to . . . ," the empty place being filled again with that adverb. Unless we can construct such an adverb, we cannot construct the conjunction. And unless we can construct the conjunction, we cannot attach sense to Chisholm's general statement about ways of appearing that the conjunction would instantiate. A general statement cannot make sense if its singular substitution instances do not make sense. And a true general statement must have at least one true singular substitution instance. If "There are horses" makes sense and is true, then some singular statement of the form "x is a horse" must also make sense and be true. This is an elementary point about our understanding of quantification.

Surprisingly, this rather simple point is ignored also by Michael Tye, who is otherwise quite aware of the extraordinary difficulties the adverbial theory faces. His elaborate version of the theory rests on the initial assertion: "[A]n event *e* is a sensing *F*-ly if, and only if, *e* is a sensing having the qualitative character of sensings which are typically brought about in normal perceivers by their viewing *F* objects in standard circumstances." He goes on to offer a similar account in defending his translations of "Jones hallucinates a red circular object and a blue rectangular object" as "Jones senses (redly-coincidental with-circularly)-ly and (bluely-coincidental with-triangularly)-ly," and of "Jones has exactly one red after-image" as "Jones senses redly but it is not the case that Jones senses (redly-spatially separated from-redly)-ly."[24]

Another defender of the adverbial theory, Romane Clark, also seems to ignore that simple point. In an otherwise most judicious article on the subject, he simply assumes that "the technical usage, to 'sense redly', as Chisholm's discussion makes clear, is intended to denote the sort of experience which normally sighted persons have when facing middle-sized red objects from a reasonable distance."[25] If "sense redly" is to be understood in this way as purely technical, it might as well be replaced with, say, the undisguisedly technical verb "Fs," the denotation of which is fixed by the definite description "the sort of experience which. . . . " Then, depending on how the blank is filled, "x Fs" could mean what Chisholm and Clark want it to mean, but it could also mean what the sense-datum theorist would want it to mean, namely, "x senses a red sense datum." For sensing a sense datum is supposed to be, of course, a sort of experience, just as sensing redly is supposed to be. To be offering a distinctive view, the adverbial theorist must be willing to employ adverbs understood as *adverbs*. And even if "redly" were to appear innocent, the elaborate adverbial constructions that Chisholm (but not Tye) says are not needed must at least be constructible and *intelligible*. An appeal to general statements such as Chisholm's, Tye's, and Clark's could not suffice since a general statement must have intelligible singular substitution instances.

3. The Adverbial Theory as a Phenomenological Description

But the adverbial theory can also be taken as a description, sufficiently general to count as philosophical, of a certain kind of consciousness, the kind it would call sensory consciousness, and its puzzling alleged reformulations of the ordinary statements describing states of such consciousness may be thought of not as reformulations at all but as purely technical though phenomenologically more adequate descriptions of those states. The required adverbs would be coined, and both the verb "to appear," as well as the verb "to sense," would be assigned explicitly technical senses. Whether and how this might be accomplished is not clear to me. But let us ignore this question. Let us ask, instead, is the adverbial theory phenome-

nologically adequate in general? If it is not, then even if it succeeds in providing intelligible technical descriptions of particular states of consciousness, these descriptions would be false or misleading or inadequate in some other, much deeper, way. If it is, then we would have reason to think that the required technical descriptions can be provided and explained adequately, some day, by someone. It may be objected that it is a mistake to take the adverbial theory as phenomenological, that at least since Ducasse's work no expositions of the theory have contained serious phenomenological descriptions. But to say this is not to defend the theory; it is to point out a glaring methodological defect of it. As I have repeatedly said, a description of a state of consciousness must be ultimately phenomenological.

I shall begin by recalling several (by no means all!) phenomenological objections to the theory that may be found in the literature. Then I shall attempt to identify the common and deeper ground on which they rest. But they must not be regarded as formal arguments against, or counter examples to, the adverbial theory. A phenomenological objection to a theory can only consist in drawing attention to a phenomenon, or to a feature of a phenomenon, that the theory does not fit adequately or plausibly. I do not doubt that the adverbial theorist can respond to each of the objections by providing some sort of adverbialist description of the phenomenon or feature in question. What I do doubt is that this description would be phenomenologically plausible (even if it were grammatical and intelligible).

Perhaps the simplest phenomenological ground for rejecting the adverbial theory was well stated by J. L. Mackie, even though he rejected its relevance. He wrote:

> [T]he only entity involved is, for example, Tom's having an experience of a certain sort. Talk about its intentional object can be no more than a way of characterizing it, of saying what sort of an experience it is by indicating its content. But what gives rise to the difficulties and to the mistakes we are constantly tempted to make in this area is that this content, though it is really only a feature of the experience . . . presents itself as if it were a more or less distinct object to which the subject is related, this whole relational situation then being the experience.[26]

I am not concerned here with Mackie's reasons for thinking that the phenomenological fact he so honestly describes is in some sense an illusion. It is significant that he acknowledges that *phenomenological* fact, and this is what is relevant to us in this section.

But there have been more detailed discussions of such phenomenological facts. Perhaps the most serious phenomenological discussion of the adverbial theory is still to be found in the exchange between G. E. Moore and C. J. Ducasse, though neither used the words "phenomenological" or "adverbial." Regarding Ducasse's view that "when I see the sensible quality 'blue', this quality is related to my seeing of it, in the same way in which,

when a cricketer makes a particular stroke at cricket, say a 'cut', the kind of stroke he makes is related to the striking of it," Moore observed: "It seems to me evident that I cannot see the *sensible* quality 'blue', without *directly seeing* something which has that quality—a blue patch, or a blue speck, or a blue line, or a blue spot, etc., in the sense in which an after-image, seen with closed eyes, may be any of these things."[27] Ducasse responded by suggesting that "if the sensible quality blue qualifies anything, what it qualifies is only some region of sensible space."[28] But Moore observed, "An after-image may gradually grow fainter, while it remains in the same sensible region: but that sensible region does not grow fainter. And an after-image may sensibly move from one region in sensible space to another: but no region in sensible space can move from one place to another in sensible space." Moore also urged that

> in order that you may be seeing a resting blue spot, it is necessary that you should not only (1) be seeing the colour, blue, but also (2) seeing a region (or 'place') in sensible space, and also (3) seeing the colour blue *as* occupying that seen place. And even if the colour blue could be related to your seeing as is a stroke at cricket to the hitting of it, I do not at all understand how a place could be related to an act of seeing in the same way, and still less what account can be given of seeing a colour *as* occupying a place.[29]

Ducasse's reply to this was that "when I observe the 'after-image' moving, all I observe is that different but continuous regions of sensible space sensibly become occupied by sensible blue at continuously successive sensible times," that "to say that the after-image gradually grows fainter while it remains in the same sensible region [means] that the sensible blues seen there at continuously successive times are blues of continuously smaller intensities," and that "the seeing of a place is an 'emergent' of two specific acts, each of which is related to a species of sensing as a 'cut' is related to hitting. . . . [T]he seeing a specific sensible place . . . is the psychological *emergent* of [sensing kinaesthetically in a specific way] and of possession of superior 'clearness' by some one of the color qualities seen at the time."[30] Later he suggested that we "may or must speak of being aware not only *bluely*, but also *briefly* (or perhaps lengthily), *extensionally* (or perhaps punctually), *here-ly* (or perhaps there-ly), *abundantly* (or perhaps scantily), etc."[31] Readers may judge for themselves the phenomenological adequacy of Ducasse's reply to Moore.

As Sellars has pointed out, Chisholm 's "sensing redly" would not do as an adequate description of any sensory state; a phrase such as "a-red-rectangle-ly sensing" is required.[32] But even the latter phrase would sometimes be inadequate, as becomes evident when we note the fact we would ordinarily describe by saying that a person may see two red rectangles, for example, two red and rectangular after-images, at the same time. (This point is related to Jackson's but is concerned with the phenomenological adequacy of the adverbial theory, not with the adequacy of its reformula-

tions of certain ordinary statements.) The adverbial theory must allow for phrases such as "*this*-red-rectangle-ly sensing" and "*that*-red-rectangle-ly sensing" if it is to do justice, first, to the phenomenological fact we would ordinarily describe by saying that we see, not *mere* kinds of after-images, which presumably would be abstract entities, but *particular*, individual after-images; and, second, to the logical fact that if we can say, for example, that a cow is grazing in the field, then we must be able, in principle, to say that this cow, or that cow, is grazing in the field, since we do not mean that a certain abstract zoological species is grazing in the field. But, of course, the phrases I have suggested, if they make sense at all, contain reference, in virtue of the inclusion of "this" and "that," to what in such contexts may only be individual things, not any properties or sets of properties of sensings. As the case of the two red and rectangular *after-images* shows, it is not true that, as Sellars says, "the question Impression of *which* red rectangle? makes sense only as a request to know which red and rectangular object is *causing* the impression, rather than how the impression is to be *described*."[33] Red and rectangular after-images are not caused by red and rectangular objects, at least not in the relevant way.

Reinhardt Grossmann has pointed out that when a painter sees a rectangular object as trapezoidal he may draw what he sees by producing a trapezoidal shape on his canvas. And he may do this by carefully reproducing the shape he sees on the canvas. Surely he attends to a certain shape he sees, even though it is not the real shape of the object; he does not attend to his inner states of consciousness and their monadic properties. And even if he does the latter, why does he draw a trapezoidal shape, since no state of consciousness is trapezoidal?[34] Sellars, of course, would reply that the painter's visual impression of a trapezoidal shape, though not trapezoidal itself, is analogous in certain respects to physical objects that are trapezoidal on the facing side, that the latter are the model of the former. But, as Romane Clark has remarked, "the model does not illuminate what is special and interesting about sense impressions as mental phenomenon: the fact that, and the way in which, the havings of sense impressions are awarenesses of the sensible qualities of material things, or, more accurately, of the way in which they are impressions of sensibly qualified things."[35]

We can strengthen Grossmann's example by revising it as follows. A novice at drawing wishes to represent the rectangular side of a building as it appears to her, that is, as trapezoidal. She looks at it through a piece of clear glass and with crayon traces on the glass the shape the side appears to her (through the glass) to have. She produces on the glass a trapezoidal shape. She simply draws the shape segment by segment so that each segment obliterates a segment of the shape the side appears to her to have. She does not look at the side of the building and then attempt to produce on the glass a shape that would appear to her in the same way that the shape of the side of the building appears to her. No doubt some sort of adverbial analysis of what she does can be offered. But what phenomenological plausibility would it have?[36]

Chisholm himself has drawn attention to a difficulty the adverbial theory faces in the case of the perception of a complex thing *as complex*. Ordinarily, when we see a thing we also see some of its parts. For example, we may see a hen and also see one of its feathers as well as the tip of that feather. What would be the sensory state corresponding to such a case of seeing? Chisholm suggests that we may say: "The way in which a man senses with respect to a thing includes ways in which he senses with respect to some, but not all, of the parts of the thing, and the way in which he senses with respect to any part of the thing is included in the way in which he senses with respect to the thing."[37] James Cornman complained that "the notion of one way of sensing being included in another is at best unclear and perhaps meaningless."[38] The truth, I suggest, is that it is unclear and perhaps meaningless not because the notion of inclusion just happens to be inapplicable, or not clearly applicable, to ways of sensing, but because the application of any notion, except those in terms of which the notion of a way of sensing has been introduced, to ways of sensing is unclear and indeterminate. And this is so because the notion of a way of sensing has no independent phenomenological grounding. What properties do we find ways of sensing to have? What relations? Are ways of sensing countable? To say, with Sellars, that these questions are to be answered with appeals to analogies hardly suffices.

This becomes especially evident when we enlarge the scope of Chisholm's example and ask for an adverbial phenomenological description of one's total visual experience at a given time, of a whole "visual field." Not only would the number of parts and the complexity of their organization be likely to be greater; entirely novel phenomena must be taken into account. There is the familiar figure-ground phenomenon. Merleau-Ponty observed:

> Already a "figure" on a "background" contains . . . much more than the qualities presented at a given time. It has an "outline," which does not "belong" to the background and which "stands out" from it; it is "stable" and offers a "compact" area of colour, the background on the other hand having no bounds, being of indefinite colouring and "running on" under the figure. The different parts of the whole—for example, the portions of the figure nearest to the background—possess, then, beside a colour and qualities, a particular *significance*.[39]

There are also the differences between the part of the visual field one attends to, the immediate context of that part, and the rest of the visual field. As Aron Gurwitsch argued,

> "[E]very total field of consciousness consists of three domains, each domain exhibiting a specific type of organization of its own. The first domain is the *theme*, that which engrosses the mind of the experiencing subject, or as it is often expressed, which stands in the "focus of his attention." Second is the *thematic field*, defined as the totality of those data, co-present with the theme, which are experienced as materially

> relevant or pertinent to the theme and form the background or horizon out of which the theme emerges as the center. The third includes data which, though co-present with, have no relevancy to, the theme and comprise in their totality what we propose to call the *margin*.[40]

Indeed, the very distinction between attending to what one perceives (senses) and not attending to it but still perceiving (sensing) it is phenomenologically crucial. I can see an after-image but not attend to it (I may be preoccupied with other things), or I can see it and also attend to it, but not to its shape or color or to any other quality it may have, or attend to its color or shape but not to both and even not to the after-image itself. Even if what we would ordinarily call the seeing of the after-image were objectless, surely the *attending* to the after-image is not. But to attend to it is precisely to attend to *what* one sees. It is certainly to be distinguished from attending to one's *seeing* the after-image; one may attend to the after-image but not to one's seeing it (e.g., if one is interested in the kind of after-image it is, in its peculiar color or shape), or to one's seeing it but not to the after-image (e.g., if one is interested in the fact, perhaps in a psychological experiment, that one is seeing an after-image, but not at all in its specific characteristics). Indeed, O. R. Jones observed that "one can be said to look at an after-image"; that one "can focus one's eyes on an after-image that is directly in front of one's eyes and thereby see it very clearly, or focus one's eyes on something in the far distance that happens to be in one's direct line of vision, thereby taking scant notice of the after-image or perhaps not noticing it at all"; that "there is such a thing as having a second look at the same after-image, which also means that we could take a second count of the features of the after-image [e.g., the number of the points of a star-shaped after-image], thereby checking on the first count"; and that one can make sure that an after-image "is in the direct line of vision as against being to the one side."[41]

Moreover, an adequate phenomenology must take into account not only the internal organization of a visual field but also the fact that a visual field ordinarily includes reference to the preceding visual fields, as well as to those that will succeed it, that it is given as continuous with a certain past as well as with a certain future visual field, that in a sense the awareness of it includes awareness of what precedes it and of what will follow it. Husserl wrote: "A bird just now flies through the sunlit garden. In the phase which I have just seized, I find the retentional consciousness of the past shadings of the duration likewise in every fresh now. . . . The bird changes its place; it flies. In every situation, the echo of earlier appearances clings to it (i.e., to its appearance)."[42] And elsewhere he remarked that also "there belongs to every external perception its reference from the 'genuinely perceived' sides of the object of perception to the sides 'also meant'—not yet perceived, but only anticipated and, at first, with a non-intuitional emptiness (as the sides that are 'coming' now perceptually): a continuous *protention*, which, with each phase of the perception, has a new sense."[43]

The adverbial theory ignores such subtler yet quite unquestionable, indeed essential, features of sensory states. Can it give an account of them in adverbial terms? And, far more important, would such an account be phenomenologically plausible?

4. The Chief Phenomenological Objection to the Adverbial Theory

I have mentioned a number of phenomenological difficulties the adverbial theory faces. Do they have a common ground? Is there a single, chief phenomenological objection to the theory? I think that there is. The adverbial theory is incapable of doing justice to what in chapter 1 I argued is the most obvious and indeed essential phenomenological fact about perceptual consciousness, namely, its intentionality, its object-directedness.

Indeed, insofar as it is applied to existentially illusory, for example, hallucinatory, perceptual consciousness, the adverbial theory *begins* precisely with the denial of the intentionality of such consciousness (though it may admit its *seeming* intentionality) and *consists* in an attempt to make sense of that denial. If a hallucination were intentional, if it were necessarily directed toward an object, then there would be hallucinatory objects, whether these be existent "wild" sense data, or nonexistent perceptual expanses, or nonexistent quasi-Meinongian material objects. Many of the objections in the preceding section consisted in drawing attention to respects in which the denial of the intentionality of existentially illusory perceptual consciousness is phenomenologically implausible.

But does the adverbial theory do justice to the intentionality even of existentially *veridical* perceptual consciousness? It should be noted that it is not a theory of (veridical) perception but of certain states of consciousness it calls being appeared to or sensing, which it sharply distinguishes from perception. Nevertheless, it is usually offered as a component of a theory of perception, namely, of a causal theory. Thus in *Perceiving* Chisholm goes scientific and defines what he calls "the simplest of the nonpropositional senses of 'see'" as follows: "'S *sees* x' means that, as a consequence of x being a proper *visual* stimulus of S, S senses in a way that is functionally dependent upon the stimulus energy produced in S by x."[44] Now a state of *sensing* is, according to the adverbial theory, not directed toward an object. So if *seeing*, in the sense defined, is to be understood as directed toward an object, this fact could consist only in the causal relation between the object and the perceiver's sensing in a certain way. This relation is dyadic and therefore there is perhaps a sense in which the perceiver's sensing is directed toward an object. But, clearly, neither is the causal relation *itself* a case of consciousness. Perception, so understood, is a case of consciousness in virtue of the state of sensing it involves, not in virtue of any causal relation in which that state enters. But that element of perceiving, which alone can be described as a case of consciousness, is also the one the adverbial theory requires us to regard as not being object-

directed. To be sure, the adverbial theorist can admit all this and still insist that perceiving is (by definition) a case of consciousness and also object-directed in virtue of its involving the causal relation, and just ignore the fact that what makes it object-directed is not what makes it a case of consciousness. But such a reply would conflict with the spirit, if not the letter, of the thesis of the intentionality of consciousness.

The fact that x is causally related to S's sensing in a certain way can no more reasonably be described as S's being conscious of x than the fact that the presence of carbon monoxide in the air is causally related to S's having a headache can be described as S's being conscious of carbon monoxide. The classical causal theories (e.g., Locke's) are also sense-datum theories and thus can legitimately ascribe to one and the same element of perception (namely, to the sensing of the sense datum) both the characteristic of being a state of consciousness and the characteristic of being object-directed. But they deny that the perceiver is conscious of the material object perceived and for this reason usually hold that it is the sense datum, not the material object, that is "directly," "immediately," perceived. Hence the familiar epistemological difficulties of causal theories. There is a clear sense in which according to them we can never get at material objects but only at our sensations. Chisholm concluded his book *Perceiving* by saying: "[O]ne *can* get at them—in the only relevant sense of this expression—by *perceiving* them."[45] But the only relevant sense is that of our being conscious or aware of them, and this is precisely what we cannot do in Chisholm's simplest nonpropositional sense of 'perceiving'.

In *Perceiving* Chisholm proceeded to introduce a more complex sense of "see," in which S sees x only if S takes x to have some characteristic. It can be argued that this sense does capture the intentionality of perception, though, so to speak, through the back door, through the intentionality of the judgment (the "taking") that is a component of perceiving in this sense. Indeed, this is exactly what Chisholm does argue, for example, in "Thought and Its Reference."[46] The chief thesis of that article, applied to perception as well as to thought, belief, and imagination, is that "we need not appeal to any 'dimension of intentionality' other than what is involved in a propositional attitude," that "given the concept of a propositional attitude—for example, *acceptance*, *entertainment*, or *endeavor*—we have all that is needed to add a theory of objective reference, or intentionality, to logic and ontology." The application of this view to perception is contained in the following series of definitions. (1) "*S* perceives *x* = Df. There is a property such that *S* perceives *x* to have that property." (2) "*S* perceives *x* to have the property *F* = Df. There is a proposition *p* which is such that: *S* perceives *p*; and *p* implies *x* to have the property *F*." (3) "*p* implies *x* to have the property *F* = Df. There is a property *G* such that (i) only one thing can have *G* at a time, (ii) *p* entails the conjunction of *G* and the property *F*, and (iii) *x* has *G*." (4) "*p* entails the property of being *F* = Df. *p* entails a proposition which is necessarily such that it is true if and only if something has the property *F*." Chisholm adds: "Now we may say that a proposition *p per-*

tains to—or *is about*—a particular thing *x*, provided only that *p* implies *x* to have some property."

I think that the sense of 'about' Chisholm's definitions capture is that which corresponds to the sense in which the *statement* "There is one and only one baby who will be born first in Mercy Hospital next year, and that baby will receive a gift from the Chamber of Commerce" may be said to be, if true, about a certain baby, *whoever* that baby may happen to be. And the sense of "intentionality," or of "objective reference," they capture is that corresponding to the sense in which someone who knows that the above statement is true would have been said by Bertrand Russell to have *knowledge by description* of that baby. This would be so regardless of how unusual the property *G* in definition 3 is supposed to be. But the phrase "intentionality of consciousness," or "objective reference" ("reference to an object"), has ordinarily been understood by philosophers as having a very different sense and is relevant to the issue before us only if so understood. This is the sense that corresponds, even if only roughly, to what Russell meant by "*knowledge by acquaintance*,"[47] and in the philosophy of language to what is meant by "referential use of a definite description" as contrasted with "attributive use of a definite description."[48] Not only does Chisholm's theory of intentionality fail to capture this standard concept of intentionality, or of objective reference, it seems to leave no room for it. He defines even acquaintance as follows: "*S* is acquainted with *x* at *t* = Df. There is a *p* such that (i) *p* is self-presenting for *S* at *t* and (ii) there is a property that *p* implies *x* to have,"[49] a self-presenting proposition for *S* at *t* being one that is true and necessarily such that whenever it is true then it is certain for *S*. And oneself is the only object of one's acquaintance, even in this peculiar sense of "acquaintance," since, according to Chisholm, a self-presenting proposition can imply only oneself to have some property.[50] It is fair to conclude, I think, that Chisholm's theory, when applied to perception, does not do justice to the intentionality of perception, in the standard sense of "intentionality"; it does not really allow us to say that we can get at material objects by perceiving them in the usual sense in which saying this would be understood; it allows us to be "aware" of material objects only by description.

Of course, one can still hold, independently of Chisholm's theory of intentionality, that the intentionality of perception consists in the intentionality of the judgments involved in perception, rather than in any intentionality of the "sense experience" that is also involved in perception. But this view, though common, seems to me incredibly muddled. What does the intentionality of my present true judgment that this page is white consist in? The answer becomes evident when we consider the *statement* expressing that judgment and ask, In what sense is the statement "This page is white" *about* this page? The usual answer is that the subject term is used to refer to this page. But what does this successful referential use consist in? In part, though necessarily so, in the fact that I pick out (single out, identify) this page. And how do I accomplish this? Obviously, by *per-*

ceiving the page, since the statement is one expressing a perceptual judgment. We should now say that the intentionality of the perceptual judgment also consists, at least in part, in the fact that it is a judgment about something I have picked out by perceiving it. And this perceiving is nonpropositional and *its* intentionality is direct, not mediated by any judgment that may happen to accompany it.[51]

It is the intentionality of perception so understood that alone explains the crucial phenomenological fact about perception Sartre expressed by saying that, unlike the imagination, perception leads to knowledge, that prima facie it provides us with evidence for the existence of material objects, that it appears to us as a sort of contact with the external world. Whether it *really* provides us with such evidence is of course one of the chief problems of epistemology, which is the subject matter of this book. Its solution would rest not only on phenomenological considerations but also on a detailed philosophical elucidation and defense of the notions of reality and evidence that could yield such a solution, if these notions are taken as primitive; and if they are to be defined, then in a detailed philosophical elucidation and defense, dialectical as well as phenomenological, of the *primitive* notions in terms of which they would be defined. This is how the task of this book should be understood.

Now both alternatives to the adverbial theory mentioned in section 1 do justice to the phenomenological fact I have described. According to one of them, in a case of perception the perceiver is ordinarily conscious of a material object, even though the object might not exist. According to the other, in a case of perception the perceiver is conscious of an existent object, that is, a sense datum, that has properties the front surface of a material object could have and that could even be identical with the front surface of a material object. For both, the phenomenological fact that we regard perception as providing us with evidence for the existence of material objects, that it *appears* to us as providing us with such evidence, is completely understandable. Indeed, this is why we began our inquiry with a defense of direct realism, understood as incorporating a defensible version of the sense datum theory. But according to the adverbial theory, a state of sensory consciousness is an objectless state. Its occurrence may in fact constitute evidence for the existence of a material object, but it can hardly *appear* to one to do so. It is not directed toward such an object, or toward an object that is just like the front surface of a material object; it is not directed toward an object at all. Nor, of course, does it itself have any of the distinctive properties of a material object, even if the properties it does have were analogous to some of those of material objects. Indeed, it may be caused by a material object, but this would be precisely the sort of fact for which we require perceptual evidence, not the sort of fact that constitutes perceptual evidence. The occurrence of such a sensory state would not *appear* to one as evidence for the existence of the material object that stands in the appropriate causal relation to it, just as the occurrence of a headache caused by the presence of carbon monoxide in the

air does not appear to one as evidence for the presence of carbon monoxide in the air.[52]

5. Concluding Remarks

Of course, as I warned at the outset, the foregoing phenomenological appeals are not conclusive. Each can be rejected by the adverbial theorist as either question-begging or phenomenologically unsound. To some extent their inconclusiveness is due to the very nature of such appeals: they are intended as phenomenological descriptions, not as logically conclusive arguments (so dear to the hearts of most philosophers and also so rare). But, I suggest, it is also due to the fact that the adverbial theory is proposed as an account of the nature of what *philosophers* and *psychologists* have called sensations, sense impressions, sense experience. It has been argued repeatedly and by many that there are no such things at all, unless the terms "sensation," "sense impression," and "sense experience" are understood in ways that make them useless to the adverbial theory. If so, then we should not be surprised that our phenomenological objections to its description of them seem inconclusive. It is not so much that the adverbial theory is mistaken as that it has no subject matter. This was pointed out in chapter 1 but perhaps deserves repeating here.

That the terms "sense impression" and "sense experience" are philosophical (or psychological) creatures, introduced for a variety of reasons and in many, very different ways, should require no argument. The latter term might be relatively innocuous, since it might be understood as a synonym of "sense perception," which is the general term corresponding to specific terms such as "seeing," "hearing," "smelling," "tasting," "(tactual) feeling," perhaps also "feeling" as used in speaking of feeling pains in various parts of our bodies as well as feeling the motions of such parts. But the former term is not innocuous. It clearly suggests the pseudoscientific picture of sense perception as consisting in an elaborate causal chain that begins with the object perceived and terminates in a "mental event." Since the chain itself is the perception, this mental event must be something else, and the term "sense impression" is coined as the name of that postulated last link of the chain. In this picture the zoological ("naturalistic") conception of human being and the conception of the human mind as a ghost in a machine form a curious but unholy union. Of course, if the last link is supposed to be just a brain state, then we would have a philosophically unobjectionable account because the account would no longer be philosophical. We would have a bit of biology, that unfortunately but harmlessly uses the word "perception."

The term "sensation" is, of course, not a philosophical creature. But, as Gilbert Ryle repeatedly pointed out, its ordinary uses are not at all those required by philosophers.[53] Sometimes it is a name of our consciousness of such things as pains and tickles, sometimes it is applied to the objects of such consciousness. Thus it is a rough synonym of "feeling," in one of

the latter's uses, and shares its ambiguity. (I should remark that we do not speak of sensing or feeling painfully, but of sensing or feeling, or having, pain in some part, or even the whole, of our body; or we speak of some part, or the whole, of our body *hurting*.) That there are sensations (and sensings) in this sense is phenomenologically obvious, even if, for metaphysical reasons, which I argued in chapter 1 would be misguided, we were to identify them with states of the brain. But this is not the sense the adverbial theory needs. The sense it needs is that in which we may also speak, for example, of visual sensations. But common discourse is entirely silent on the existence of such things. If someone were to speak of having a sensation when seeing something, she would be understood most probably as meaning that her eyes hurt or tickle, or that she is feeling nauseous or excited, and so on. And we say that the drunk *sees* pink rats, or at least that he "thinks" he sees them, not (unless we are philosophers or psychologists) that he senses, or has a sensation of, pink rats.

How seriously should we take these facts about common discourse? Perhaps not very seriously if introspection revealed the sorts of occurrences the adverbialist appeals to. But does it? Regarding the *philosophers'* notion of a sensation, Sartre remarked: "[I]t is pure fiction. It does not correspond to anything which I experience in myself or with regard to the Other,"[54] and Merleau-Ponty optimistically concurred: "It is unnecessary to show, since authors are agreed on it, that this notion corresponds to nothing in our experience."[55] The similar views held by Moore, Wittgenstein, Ryle, and Heidegger were noted in chapter 1.

Of course, the term "sensation" could be introduced as a technical substitute for "perception" in the latter's first sense, distinguished in section 1, in which we may be said to perceive both existent and nonexistent things; or, if we accept the sense-datum theory, as a technical term for our perception ("apprehension") of sense data; or, for the purposes of psychology, as a technical term for our perception of "a simple quality like 'hot,' 'cold,' 'red,' 'noise,' 'pain,' apprehended irrelatively to other things."[56] These technical uses of "sensation" would be entirely explicable, as they ought to be, in terms of our ordinary perceptual verbs and would be of no use to the adverbial theory, which requires that sensations be objectless states of consciousness.

I shall end this chapter by drawing attention to the larger implications of the view that there are objectless states of consciousness. In the previous section I argued that it is incompatible with the thesis of the intentionality of perception. But it is also incompatible with the more general and more fundamental thesis of the intentionality of all consciousness. Is intentionality, object-directedness, an essential characteristic of consciousness (not of the psychological or mental, as Brentano held, for we saw in chapter 1 that, for example, pains are nonintentional but are naturally classifiable as mental or psychological)? Can anything be both a state of consciousness and nonintentional? This, I suggest, is the most important question to be raised in regard to the adverbial theory. If the correct answer

to it is negative, then the adverbial theory is false, for reasons far deeper than those I have discussed so far. Is the answer negative? We are told that at least being in pain and being depressed (in general, not by anything in particular) are states of consciousness that have no objects. But surely to be in pain is to feel, to be conscious of, pain in some part of one's body (even if only a phantom part), or in the whole of one's body, to be conscious of that part's or one's body's hurting (not of one's mind hurting!); and it is plausible to say that to be depressed in general is to be conscious of the world as a whole, or of one's life, or of oneself, as depressing.[57] The pain is an object, not a state, of consciousness, and so is something's being depressing. But the defense of the intentionality of consciousness must rest on firmer foundations than ping-pong games with examples and counter examples. It must issue from an account of the nature of intentionality and of the nature of consciousness. As we saw in chapter 1, Sartre argued (as Moore in effect had also done, in "The Refutation of Idealism") that to take the intentionality of consciousness seriously is to recognize that consciousness is perfectly transparent, that it has no contents, that it exhausts itself in its object, that its being (though genuine) consists in the revelation of its object.[58] If this is so, then of course the adverbial theory must be false, since it consists precisely in the claim that certain states of consciousness have an elaborate structure of monadic characteristics ("ways of sensing"), that they are, as Sartre would say, centers of opacity within consciousness.

But if Sartre's rather Moorean view of consciousness is accepted, together with its inseparable companion, his Humean and perhaps also Moorean view that not only is the self, if understood as the subjective pole of a relation of consciousness, unobservable but the very idea of such a self is unintelligible,[59] then we are led to the Sartrean conclusion that consciousness is nothing distinct from its object. This conclusion is, so to speak, the mirror image of the adverbial theory. Consciousness indeed cannot be straightforwardly a relation, since it lacks one of the needed relata, but the relatum it lacks is the subject, the self, not the object. So, the further conclusion seems to follow that consciousness can be only a monadic characteristic, though not a characteristic of the subject but a characteristic of the object.[60] But these considerations go far beyond the aims of this chapter.[61] They will be directly relevant to chapter 6, section 6, where a discussion of them will be provided.

I have now completed my defense of direct realism and am ready to state, and eventually respond to, the skeptic's argument. I have clarified, to the best of my ability, its phenomenological setting, in terms of which this argument and my response to it must be understood. It should be evident by now that, contrary to accepted opinion, whether Thomas Reid's and Kant's in the eighteenth century or Hilary Putnam's and John McDowell's in 1994, direct realism does not constitute an answer to the skeptic. Nevertheless, I shall argue, it alone makes an answer possible.

3

THE SKEPTIC'S ARGUMENT

1. Several Skeptical Questions

We are now ready to embark on an explicit discussion of our topic, skepticism about the external world. I shall devote this chapter to an exposition and defense of what I regard to be the skeptic's strongest argument. But it cannot be fully appreciated without a discussion of the numerous objections to it and of several ways they can be answered, which will require strengthening the argument in what may be unfamiliar ways. Hence the length of the chapter. But I think it is unavoidable if the skeptic's argument is to be done justice. In the remaining three chapters I shall try to answer it, though not to refute it.

There are four pairs of questions our skeptic may ask. The first is, *Do* we know, or at least have evidence, in at least one particular perceptual situation, that the material object of the perceptual consciousness, say, a snake, is real? I shall refer to it as the *particular nonmodal epistemic question.* But the skeptic may also ask, Do we know, or at least have evidence, that in general there are real perceivable material objects, a real external world? I shall refer to this as the *general nonmodal epistemic question.* Corresponding to the particular *modal* epistemic question, *Can* we know, or at least have evidence, in at least one particular perceptual situation, that the material object of the perceptual consciousness, say, a snake, is real? there is the general *modal* epistemic question, Can we know, or at least have evidence, that in general there are real perceivable material objects, a real external world? Corresponding to the particular nonmodal *nonepistemic* question, *Is* the material object of the perceptual consciousness in at least one particular perceptual situation real? there is the general nonmodal *nonepistemic* question, Are there real perceivable material objects, a real external world? And there are also the particular *modal nonepistemic* question, Can the material object of the perceptual consciousness in at least one particular perceptual situation be real? and the general *modal nonepistemic* question, Can there be real perceivable material objects, a real external world? The distinction between particular and general questions (no less than eight of them!) is no pettifoggery; it is epistemologically

crucial. An affirmative answer to one of the particular questions entails an affirmative answer to the corresponding general question, but the converse is not the case. This opens the possibility that we may be able to answer one of the general questions affirmatively even if we cannot answer affirmatively the corresponding particular question. Indeed, this seems to have been the strategy of Descartes and Kant, and it will be my strategy in chapter 4, though not in chapter 6.

All eight questions concern the *existence* of material objects. I shall not discuss here the corresponding questions concerning the *qualities* of existent material objects, though I shall consider them briefly in chapter 6. There are three reasons for this choice. First, as I argued in chapter 1, a qualitative illusion can be taken to be the unreality of a perceived perceptual expanse, and thus the problem of its distinguishability from qualitatively veridical perception can be understood as a special case of the problem of the distinguishability of unreal objects of perception from real ones (if there are any). Second, the reality of material objects is of far greater importance than the reality of the qualities we ascribe to them. Third, questions about what qualities a perceived material object really has can arise only if we have answered affirmatively the question whether the object is real. An unreal (say, hallucinatory) object has qualities that are perceived, but it makes no sense to ask whether it has those qualities really or only apparently.

As explained in chapter 1, I am using the phrase "material object" as a sortal, not as one presupposing reality, and by "the external world" I mean the totality of material objects so understood and thus allow that a world may be external, that is, external to consciousness, but not real. So, the phrase "skepticism about the external world" means, as it usually does in the philosophical tradition, skepticism mainly about the reality, the existence, of the external world. And I use "to perceive" roughly as a synonym of H. H. Price's "to be perceptually conscious of,"[1] thus allowing that one can perceive what does not exist, what is unreal, as in hallucinations and dreams. But, for the sake of simplicity of exposition, in this chapter I shall often omit these qualifications.

Now, by definition, the *epistemic* questions are the ones the skeptic asks. But in this book I shall take the *nonepistemic* questions as primary; surely, they are also the ones in which we, including the skeptic, are really interested. The traditional approach to skepticism has been to focus on the epistemic questions. I suggest that this is why what Kant called a scandal to philosophy is still with us. For with that approach we become preoccupied with so-called "analyses," often Ptolemaic in complexity, of the concepts of knowledge, evidence, justification, and so forth, and with the search for convincing deductive, inductive, abductive, coherentist, transcendental, or whatever, arguments for the reality of an external world. Surely, the futility of this approach has become evident by now, even though it has been pursued with brilliance and with valuable results on topics other than skepticism. As I suggested in the introduction, to solve the chief problem

of epistemology we must bypass epistemology. In particular, we must concentrate on the nonepistemic questions, which means that we must approach our topic from the standpoint of metaphysics, as we should have learned from classical and medieval philosophy. To understand being qua known or at least knowable, we must first understand being qua being. But what this amounts to cannot be fully explained until chapters 5 and 6.

I shall usually ignore the epistemic modal questions, not only because they are epistemic but also for the following reason. It may well be that in some sense of "can" they are to be answered affirmatively, that in some "possible world" one's epistemic situation with respect to the reality of some perceived material object is the same as one's epistemic situation with respect to, say, the reality of one's having a headache. For a similar reason, I shall also ignore the nonepistemic modal questions. Whether there are such possible worlds need not detain us. It suffices to point out that even if there are, the skeptic would not really have been answered, since his (and our!) concern is whether we *do*, not just *can*, know or at least have evidence, in at least one particular perceptual situation, that the perceived object is real and that in general there are real material objects; or whether the object *is* real and there *are* real material objects. This becomes clearer when we note that it need not be true of other kinds of skepticism. In ethics we may be primarily interested in the question whether moral knowledge is possible, perhaps because we are interested in the question whether moral realism is true, whether there are moral facts, and only secondarily interested in the question whether we actually do have moral knowledge. (A utilitarian ought to give a positive answer to the former but, unless in possession of supernatural cognition of the future, almost certainly a negative answer to the latter.)[2] In metaphysics we are likely to ask whether we *can* know why there is something rather than nothing, not whether we *do* know this.

I said that by definition the skeptic asks the *epistemic* questions, partly because skepticism is an epistemological position, partly because the skeptic himself expresses his concerns by asking the epistemic questions, rather than by asking the *nonepistemic* questions. Indeed, as I have announced, in my answers to the skeptic my strategy will be to focus on the nonepistemic questions. However, the present chapter is devoted to presenting the skeptic's case as persuasively as we can, not to providing those answers. We must take skepticism seriously, we must do it full justice, and speak its own language if eventually we are to answer it adequately; we don't want to fight a skeptic made of straw, as so often happens in discussions of skepticism.

I should remark nonetheless that since by an answer to the skeptic we mean, of course, a *reasoned* answer, that is, an answer based on something like an argument, ordinarily we should expect such an answer to one of the *nonepistemic* questions to provide an answer also to the corresponding *epistemic* question. This is why our taking the nonepistemic questions as primary does not mean ignoring the epistemic questions. Logically, the an-

swers do belong to different levels, but we should be able to manage not to let this confuse us.[3] Reaching a conclusion by means of an argument can constitute (if the argument meets appropriate standards) an answer to the corresponding epistemic question about the truth of the conclusion even if the latter employs no epistemic terms. The fact, emphasized by William P. Alston, that in order to know or have evidence ("justification") for a proposition one need not know or have evidence ("justification") that one knows or has evidence for the proposition, though legitimate and important, cannot be used to silence the skeptic, who, as Paul K. Moser points out, asks whether we have "an effective, non-questionbegging reason for thinking we have ontological knowledge or ontologically reliable justification."[4] Moser goes on to say, "Epistemologists thus must explain justification and standards of justification in the most cogent manner available, even if the first-order unreflective having of justification does not require the same."[5] Just as it is no part of skepticism to deny that a certain proposition (e.g., that one has two hands) is true but only to deny that we know (have evidence, etc.) that it is true, so it is really no part of skepticism to deny that we know (have evidence for, etc.) that proposition but only to deny that we know (have evidence, etc.) *that we know* (have evidence for, etc.) the proposition. The reason skepticism is usually silent on this matter is most skeptics' belief that if one knows (has evidence, etc.) that p then one can know (have evidence, etc.), *just by reflection*, that one knows (has evidence) that p. Since they deny the consequent of this conditional (when p is one of the propositions they question), naturally they also deny its antecedent. And if told that knowledge, evidence, and so forth, can exist unbeknownst to us, they would ask us how acknowledging this would answer their concerns; they would properly accuse us of ignoratio elenchi.

But while we may expect that the answers to the epistemic and the nonepistemic questions are connected in the way I have described, they need not be. For our answer to a nonepistemic question may be reasoned, it may be based on something like an argument, yet not provide an answer to the corresponding epistemic question, perhaps because the reasoning and the argumentation are not good enough, but more likely because they may not, in any clear sense, provide us with the *knowledge* or the *evidence* asked for in the epistemic question. The latter can happen if the reasoning or the argumentation is of a rather unusual nature, which I believe is what is needed if the skeptic is to be answered. I should recall the warning issued in the introduction, that the sort of reasoning and argumentation I shall offer in answering the skeptic, in chapters 4 and 6, will be sufficiently unusual to preclude us from claiming that it refutes the skeptic, and I have made the foregoing distinctions for that reason. In this respect my approach differs radically from that common in epistemology, where the starting point is the provision of accounts of knowledge, evidence, and justification, on the basis of which, it is hoped, an affirmative answer to the epistemic questions may be given, and only then also an affirmative answer to the nonepistemic questions. As I have already remarked, this approach has

not been successful, and this is one reason why I shall attempt to reverse it, even though not as smoothly as we might wish. Indeed, I shall have a great deal to say about knowledge, evidence, and justification, but I shall attempt to answer the nonepistemic questions independently of specific views about these topics.

Typically, the skeptic with regard to the senses gives negative answers to both the general and the particular (modal or nonmodal) epistemic questions I have distinguished, whether or not the negative answer to one of them is given on the basis of an inference from the negative answer to the other. As I have pointed out, an affirmative answer to one of the particular epistemic questions entails an affirmative answer to the corresponding general epistemic question, but the converse is not true. This is a major difference between the two. Moreover, obviously, the general question is by far the more important one for philosophy. The two have not usually been distinguished. And this is one reason why many philosophers, for example Heidegger, thinking, in my opinion rightly, that the general question is the really important one, and also thinking, in my opinion wrongly, that the answer to it is obvious, dismiss skepticism, indeed epistemology altogether, even though they have nothing to say about the particular question. But there is also another reason. If what I have called the direct realist conception of perceptual consciousness is accepted, then it may also seem that the answer to the particular question is obvious. This too is evident in Heidegger, as well as in Moore's "Refutation of Idealism." But it is a mistake. The direct realist conception of consciousness may show that an affirmative answer to the particular question is *possible*, while its competitors may fail to do even this much, but it does not itself provide or imply such an answer. I shall try to explain the complex dialectic these remarks suggest in chapter 4.

2. The Advantages of Beginning with Descartes's Dream-Argument

> How often, asleep at night, am I convinced of just such familiar events—that I am here in my dressing gown, sitting by the fire—when in fact I am lying undressed in bed! Yet at the moment my eyes are certainly wide awake when I look at this piece of paper; I shake my head and it is not asleep; as I stretch out and feel my hand I do so deliberately, and I know what I am doing. All this would not happen with such distinctness to someone asleep. Indeed! As if I do not remember other occasions when I have been tricked by exactly similar thoughts while asleep! As I think about this more carefully, I see plainly that there are never any sure signs by means of which being awake can be distinguished from being asleep. The result is that I begin to feel dazed, and this feeling only reinforces the notion that I may be asleep. (Descartes, First Meditation)[6]

In the next section I shall state Descartes's dream-argument in my own words and more fully. But here I want to explain why in a discussion of

skepticism with regard to the senses we still cannot do better than to start with it. The argument is so clear and well-known that it requires no immediate explanation. But my selection of it as the centerpiece of skepticism about the external world does.

To begin with, I should point out that the usual objection (e.g., Thomas Reid's, Kant's, Hegel's) to skepticism, namely, that it presupposes "the new way of ideas," the view of perception as a veil, in short, representationalism, or what in chapter 1 I called the mental-contents theory, is quite misplaced if directed against the dream-argument. To be sure, Descartes was a representationalist. But his dream-argument does not depend on his representationalism at all, as even the most cursory reading of it would show.[7]

A more serious charge is that Descartes's argument presupposes an "unnatural, spectator's standpoint" (he is sitting by the fire, with a piece of paper in his hand, contemplating the possibility that he might be dreaming). But the natural standpoint of a human being is that of being immersed in the world through action, together with others. It would be much more representative of our situation in the world, someone like Heidegger might say, if Descartes gave as his example his stoking the fire, in the company of others, who perhaps also bring him wood and converse about the falling snow. Now all this may be granted, but it is irrelevant, since the latter situation might itself be just a dream. At most one might say that in such a more representative situation one would not even consider whether one might be dreaming, and thus that epistemology is not rooted in considerations about a state representative of the human condition. One might draw from this the conclusion that epistemology does not have the overwhelming importance accorded to it in modern philosophy and should be concerned with (if with anything at all) matters characteristic of a representative situation. Indeed, this seems to have been the attitude of Heidegger, Wittgenstein, and Sartre. But adopting it merely shows a philosophical preference, not a contribution to epistemology, although almost certainly it is a contribution to philosophy in general to have pointed out that the spectator's standpoint is woefully inadequate to what it is for us to *be* in the world (*if* there is a world!).

There are, on the other hand, important positive advantages of approaching our topic through Descartes's dream-argument. One is that, unlike his demon-argument and contemporary science fiction arguments about brains in vats, it has immediate intuitive power and comprehensibility. As Hilary Putnam says, "Descartes's choice of dreams was, in a way, a happy one for his purpose. . . . We all dream . . . and when our dreams are vivid and realistic enough, they give us a paradigm of an experience in which it is *as if* we were seeing or hearing or feeling something or other when nothing of that kind is physically present for us to see or hear or feel."[8] The other arguments are inevitably subject to doubts about their intelligibility. (The dream-argument has been questioned in this respect mainly by Norman Malcolm, but only by carrying verificationism to absurdity.[9] I shall come back to this.)

Consider the brain-in-a-vat argument. Your brain has been removed from your body and placed in a vat of nutrients. Evil scientists have connected its nerve-endings to a supercomputer with which they cause you to have the illusion that everything is normal. It would seem that you could not know that you are in this predicament. But Hilary Putnam argued in an earlier work that this hypothesis could not possibly be true "because it is, in a certain way, self-refuting." You can say or think the words expressing the hypothesis but you cannot refer to what they ordinarily refer. The reason is that "one cannot refer to certain kinds of things . . . if one has no causal interaction at all with them." The brain has no causal interaction with the vat or indeed with anything in the real world (except, in a quite deviant sense, with the scientists and their computer). We can put this better by saying that it does not have the sort of causal interaction that would be relevant to reference.[10] Robert Nozick, however, pointed out that "for any reasoning purporting to show this skeptical hypothesis cannot occur, we can imagine the psychologists of our science fiction story feeding *it* to their tank-subject, along with the (inaccurate) feeling that the reasoning is cogent. So how much trust can be placed in the apparent cogency of an argument to show that the skeptical possibility isn't coherent?"[11] I shall not attempt to adjudicate the dispute, partly because (at least on Putnam's side) it rests on a theory of reference I cannot accept. For my purposes it is sufficient that the dispute exists and has no obvious resolution.

The brain-in-a-vat hypothesis has also been questioned on purely scientific grounds by Daniel Dennett.[12] He points out that, for example, the evil scientists' causing the brain to have the experience of wiggling "its" index finger in the sand must take into account the fact that how the sand will feel depends on just how the brain "decides" to move its finger. He argues that "[t]he problem of calculating the proper feedback, generating or composing it, and then presenting it to you in real time is going to be computationally intractable on even the fastest computer, and if the evil scientists decide to solve the real-time problem by precalculating and 'canning' all the possible responses for playback, they will just trade one insoluble problem for another: there are too many possibilities to store."[13] Dennett thinks that this is an argument against skepticism, but of course if adequate (something I shall not discuss) it is only an argument against resting skepticism on the brain-in-a-vat hypothesis.

We don't need to consider scientific matters in order to see why we should not rest skepticism on the evil-demon hypothesis. Descartes's notion of an evil demon with almost divine powers to deceive us about virtually everything (except that we exist) is obviously derived from the notion of God and is no easier to understand than that notion. A standard argument for atheism has been precisely that we do not have a genuine concept of God. Whether the argument is sound or not is irrelevant to my purposes here. It suffices that it has some plausibility. And if it applies to the notion of an evil demon (not because the demon is evil and deceiving but because of what a demon is supposed to be—a fallen angel, moreover one

of almost divine powers, according to the hypothesis), then this is a sufficient reason for avoiding this skeptical argument. We may recall that Descartes originally entertained the hypothesis that he was deceived by God and replaced it with the evil-demon hypothesis only for the obvious theological reasons.

Another, for us much greater, advantage of beginning with the dream-argument is that the skeptical challenge it poses does not depend on any specific, and therefore highly controversial, understanding of the key epistemological concepts of knowledge and evidence,[14] and that it frees us also of the hold of the concept of "justified belief." It is hardly controversial that dreaming provides the dreamer, while dreaming, with neither knowledge nor any evidence, even on the loosest conceptions of knowledge and evidence. And we might say that a dreamer is "justified" in judging to be true whatever she happens to be dreaming about, but by this we would mean nothing epistemic: we would simply mean that she is not to blame for her judgment. We would not say that she has *evidence* for what she judges, for *we* would not regard as evidence what absolves her from blame, namely something she is dreaming. A person can be justified in judging a proposition to be true even if no one else (including those who know all the relevant facts) is justified in making this judgment, but a person cannot have evidence for a proposition unless there is such evidence and therefore unless anyone else who knew of it and possessed the needed concepts would regard it as evidence for that proposition. (We may label this difference by saying that evidence has the property of public transmissibility, while justification does not, and this is so presumably because, unlike evidence, justification is perspectival.)[15] This is why we would not say that the person has *knowledge* of what she is dreaming, even if what she is dreaming (e.g., that she is in bed) is true. As Alvin Plantinga remarks, "Where you lack warrant . . . it is clear, of course, that you may nonetheless have *justification*. You may be perfectly within all of your rights; you may have been flouting no duties whatsoever; you may have been doing your level best to achieve the truth."[16] I believe he would be willing to use "evidence" instead of "warrant" here. His distinction between the two terms is not at all clear, but the distinction between either one and "justification" is throughout respected by him, as of course it should be.

We have here a good example of why we should avoid the slippery notion of justification when we do epistemology and distinguish it sharply from the notions of knowledge and evidence. The notion of epistemic justification, if genuine at all, is a notion of something subjective, in the sense just explained. Moreover, it is clearly normative. The notion of evidence, on the other hand, is a notion of a relation between propositions, or between a fact and a proposition, even if the fact happens to be psychological. And, contrary to recent opinions, there is nothing normative about it. One may be justified, that is, not blameworthy, in judging a proposition to be true even if one has no evidence for it. (The judgment might be quite trivial and made by flipping a coin.) And one can have ev-

idence for a proposition but not be justified in judging the proposition to be true, not because there is contravening evidence but because one's evidence is too weak. (How weak? The uselessness of the notion of epistemic justification becomes especially evident when we recognize that we have no principled answer to this question.) Moreover, the notion of justification is not only normative but essentially deontic, and even if we allowed for doxastic voluntarism (which we should not, at least not without major qualifications[17] that would render the notion of epistemic justification almost worthless for epistemology) it must be kept out of the traditional purely epistemic, nonnormative domain of the concepts of knowledge and evidence.[18]

That the issue is not purely verbal can be seen easily from two examples. First, one may have evidence neither for a certain proposition nor for its contradictory. But it is intelligible to hold that in such a case believing either proposition is justified ("permitted"), and some philosophers have in fact adopted this view, thus explicitly severing the connection between the notion of justified belief and the notions of truth and knowledge. The second example is the frequent claim that if a Cartesian demon produced in us only false beliefs, the beliefs we regard as justified would remain justified. Again, this is intelligible if by "justified" we meant "permitted," "not to be blamed for," but the severance of the connection between the notion of justified belief and the notions of truth and knowledge becomes even more dramatic. Of what use, then, is the notion of justified belief to epistemology?

Similar remarks may be made about relying on the even vaguer (and also normative) concept of rationality. Our dreamer may well be described as rational, both in the judgments she makes and in the actions she undertakes in her dream. But the propriety of such a description would have no greater epistemological significance than the propriety of the description of her beliefs or judgments as justified. Even the notion of epistemic rationality developed in detail by Richard Foley, which is not vague, may apply to her, as Foley admits by implication. (According to Foley, it consists in judging, on careful reflection, that what we judge is likely to be true.) He does not consider the dream-hypothesis, but regarding the evil-demon hypothesis he writes: "Are not some of the propositions we believe epistemically rational for us to believe? And would not whatever it is that makes these propositions epistemically rational for us also be present in a world where these propositions are regularly false but where a demon hid this from us. . . . The intuitive answer is yes."[19] Perhaps this is why he begins his book by pointing out how removed "the theory of epistemic rationality" is from the concerns of traditional epistemology and by writing, in the crucial chapter on epistemic rationality and truth, that "an account of epistemic rationality . . . may be only marginally useful in developing an account of knowledge."[20]

A comparison with ethics may be helpful here. Being rational is analogous to doing one's subjective duty, that is, doing what one *judges* (even if

only on careful reflection) to be one's duty. Knowing is analogous to doing what *is* one's objective duty, that is, doing what one ought to do. Since the notion of subjective duty is obviously parasitic on that of objective duty, ethics has been chiefly concerned with the latter.[21] And since the notion of epistemic rationality presupposes the epistemic, not the statistical, notion of likelihood of truth, it is parasitic on the epistemic notion of a judgment that *is* likely to be true, and the latter should be the one of chief concern to epistemology.

Epistemology is by definition the theory of knowledge, and, by extension, since the concept of knowledge includes that of evidence and supposedly we often have no knowledge but do have evidence, also the theory of evidence. This is why the problem of skepticism has been central in epistemology: for the skeptic, by definition, denies that we have knowledge or even evidence, whether in general or in some particular domain. And the concepts of knowledge and evidence are not in any obvious way normative. Only confusion results from ignoring this fact and introducing into epistemology normative notions such as justification and rationality. Our understanding of the normative is far more deficient than our understanding of the epistemic, and it would be poor strategy to look to the former for help in improving the latter. Epistemology is not the most developed branch of philosophy, but ethics is even less so. In epistemology, at most we can allow for normative statements of the form "If you want to judge what is true and not to judge what is false, then you ought to judge that p." It may be allowed that the usual task of epistemology has been to discover true statements of that form. But the crucial connection between what the antecedent and the consequent of such a statement are about is hardly normative. It is merely the means-end relation. Kant's categorical, not his hypothetical, imperatives were his concern in uncovering the foundations of morality. Indeed, one who violates an imperative may thereby display ignorance, mental incompetence, or weakness of the will, all of which (let us suppose) are intrinsically bad, and this provides the normative element made explicit by the occurrence of "ought" in the imperative. But *badness* is the normative characteristic, not ignorance, mental incompetence, or weakness of the will. We must avoid the error of thinking that what has a normative characteristic must itself be normative. Being truthful is good, but while being good is a normative characteristic, being truthful is not. Similarly, having knowledge may be an intrinsic intellectual good, but its goodness is the normative characteristic, not the having of knowledge. If we did not observe this distinction, the number of normative characteristics would turn out to be enormous, and that of nonnormative characteristics perhaps rather small!

All this becomes especially clear when we consider the applications of the notions of knowledge, evidence, justification, rationality, and normativity to the case of dreaming, and the dream-argument is especially likely to be free, and to free us, from the confusions engendered by their misapplications.

3. Descartes's Dream-Argument

I shall now state Descartes's dream-argument in my own words and in a somewhat expanded version.

Any knowledge we may have of material objects *ultimately*, though not necessarily wholly, rests on the testimony of our senses. But it is a commonplace that our senses often deceive us. Objects look different from different points of view and in different conditions. Through experience we may have learned to correct or withhold judgments in which we have been, or may be, misled by the variable ways objects look to us, for example, to refrain from jumping to the conclusion that the moon is small just because it looks small. But there are also the facts of hallucination and dreaming. Perhaps in the case of hallucination we can still make appropriate corrections of our judgments, for example, by trying to touch but failing to feel a visually hallucinated object. Not so in the case of dreams. Any corrections of perceptual judgments made when we dream would themselves be part of the dream and therefore without value. The point is not that if I am dreaming that p, p being a proposition ordinarily accepted on the basis of perception, then p is false. I may be dreaming that I am in bed while I am in bed. The point is that if I am dreaming that p then I do not *know*, or even have any *evidence*, that p. I may be justified or even rational in judging ("believing") that p, in the general normative and epistemologically irrelevant sense that I am not to blame for making the judgment, nor am I to be regarded as stupid or insane. But I don't have knowledge or even evidence that p, for if I did, then anyone else who knew about it (e.g., heard my dream-report in the morning) would also have (secondhand) evidence that p. Dream-reports, however, are not admissible as evidence in a court of law, except in support of psychiatric statements about the dreamer.

If I dream that I see an object and wonder whether it really exists, it would be pointless to try to touch the object, for I might also merely dream that I am touching it. It would be pointless to appeal to any alleged inductive evidence, which I could do in the case of a hallucination; the past to which I appeal would be the dreamt past or at most the past stages of the dream. It would be also pointless to appeal to common sense or to science, which I could do in the case of a hallucination, for the common sense or the science to which I appeal in my dream would be merely what I dream to be common sense or science. And even if my dreams had a distinctive feature, say a certain incoherence, I could not rely on this fact in judging that I am dreaming, for while dreaming I would just be dreaming that the real world does not also have that feature. I could not rely on my memory of what the real world is like, since the memory available to me is itself part of the dream.[22] Commonsense and scientific judgments about the real world must be in principle checkable by perceptions, but these have no epistemic worth if taking place in a dream. In any case, a dream can be as coherent as a wakeful experience, which is why appeals to coherence in justifying claims to perceptual knowledge are *ultimately* misplaced (of

course, they have an important place in the secondary stages of the cognitive enterprise, e.g., in the sciences), and why we would be justified in ignoring attempts to answer the skeptic by relying on a coherentist theory of justification.

The so-called "externalist" theories of justification, such as reliabilism, are even more obviously irrelevant to the issue before us, namely, How can *I* tell whether *I* am dreaming or awake? (Moreover, if the externalist were to appeal to any scientific facts, she would beg the question against the skeptic, who would certainly be also a skeptic with regard to science.)[23] As Paul K. Moser repeatedly argues in a recent book, "The pressing question is: what non-questionbegging epistemic reason have we to think that (a) our cognitive processes such as memory or perception, (b) predictive theoretical success relative to experience, or (c) inference to the best explanation relative to experience ever provides accurate indications of a conceiving-independent world?"[24] And Simon Blackburn points out: "The power of scepticism is quite underrated if it is seen as merely an attempt to shake confidence by invoking possibilities that can normally be ignored. Its real power comes with the absence of any sense of our own reliability. . . . We might try to say, blankly, that we know that these possibilities are not realized. But can we regard ourselves as reliable on just this *kind* of point?"[25]

Does all this mean that the answer to skepticism must be foundationalist? We shall find that both answers to skepticism I shall offer in this book fail to satisfy any familiar conception of foundationalism. And the history of the subject has shown that Descartes's dream-argument cannot be answered by adopting any familiar foundationalist approach, for example, by deduction or induction or abduction from the "given." On the other hand, the traditional skeptic would usually subscribe to the doctrine of the given and to the doctrine that *if* empirical knowledge were possible it would need foundations. Contrary to the recent rhetoric against these doctrines, they can be readily understood and respected.

To begin with, it is evident that any discussion of the dream-argument and of skepticism generally must be from the "first-person perspective." The philosophical question is whether *I* can tell that *I* am not dreaming, not whether others can tell that I am not dreaming (asking the latter obviously begs the question against any skepticism about the external world, since it presupposes that there are other, presumably embodied, knowers). So externalism is immediately seen to be irrelevant. And the first-person perspective cannot be just abandoned, because to abandon it would be epistemically to abandon ourselves, and what could that mean? It is an illusion that it is abandoned in the sciences; there it is just left unmentioned, tacit. However social and cooperative a scientific investigation may be, the individual scientist participating in it may only rely ultimately on his or her own judgment, even if this is just to defer to the judgments of one or more of the other participants.

And we must acknowledge that in any questioning or inquiry there must be a starting point that is not itself in question in that inquiry. But is there

a starting point that is not in question at all? It seems obvious that perception, as understood in chapter 1 (i.e., as having no implications regarding the reality of its objects), is one, and that so is our consciousness of sensations such as pains and itches, and of truths such as that 2 and 2 is 4. I made this point already in the introduction, where I described phenomenology as providing such a starting point. Only false sophistication could lead one to deny this. The sentences about them may be questionable on semantical and grammatical grounds. And the corresponding judgments may be questionable on conceptual grounds. But the starting point is what the sentences and the judgments are *about*, and *that* is what is unquestionable. (I shall consider later in this chapter what such unquestionability consists in.) To be sure, stripped of the concepts applied to it, it cannot enter in any logical relations, and thus cannot be properly called an *epistemic foundation*, though it can still quite properly be called a *given*,[26] indeed the phenomenological given. But to go further and deny that there could be an unconceptualized starting point would lead to the paradox that conceptualization is not the application of concepts to *something* but a sort of creation *ex nihilo*, and to the implausible view that infants and nonhuman animals have no experiences.[27] Nor should we just assume that all conceptualization is questionable. If the concepts are sufficiently general (e.g., dark, not-square), the conceptualization of something that is unquestionable might itself be unquestionable. Now, if all this amounts to a commitment to the given and to foundationalism, and if recognizing the unavoidability of our first-person perspective amounts to acceptance of "internalism," then so be it.

Let me explain further. There can be no question that there is a given that is not or at least need not be conceptualized. But this does not entail that it is the foundation of empirical knowledge, the view properly called foundationalism. If something is to ground a judgment it has to have logical form, because the judgment does. Does the given have a logical form qua given? To be sure, it is usually complex, but (contrary to Wittgenstein's early view) not all complexity is propositional (i.e., logical). At any rate, the logical form the given must have if it is to serve as a foundation for a judgment would not be on a par with the colors, shapes, and so forth, that would ordinarily be attributed to it. Thinking along these lines, it becomes plausible to say that the logical form of something in the world (or in the given) is due to us (our language or our conceptual faculties). Using Wittgenstein's terms again, the world may be the totality of facts, not of things, but if what I have suggested is right, we should rather say (if we agreed) that the world is propositional. If the given is also propositional, as it must be if it is to be the foundation of a belief or judgment, then it must be such because of our "contribution" to it, not because of what it is in itself. This is why I've used the word "proposition," not just because logical relations are best understood as holding between propositions. "Fact" covers too much, since in ordinary language things can be said to be facts. And a judgment has logical form and enters in logical relations

only in the sense that the proposition it expresses does so. Notice that the notion of logical form has paradigmatic application to sentences and judgments, not to "facts." And sentences and judgments are paradigms of the conceptual. So the given itself need not be conceptualized since in itself it is not propositional. It is phenomenologically absurd to suppose that an experience must be expressed in language with a sentence, rather than just named, that it consists of "facts" rather than of "things." But to serve an epistemic role as a foundation of knowledge it must be contaminated by what F. H. Bradley called "the relational way of thinking," it must be *thought* of as propositional, that is, as consisting of states of affairs or facts, not just of things. I shall return to this point in chapters 5 and 6.

But after having admitted this, we must note its irrelevance to the skeptic, or at least to his dream-argument. Even if the skeptic accepts the presence of a conceptualized given, in the sense I have suggested, he would not describe it as an epistemic foundation, since he questions that there is anything that can rest on it. Therefore, he would just lack any interest in the question whether foundationalism is true and therefore probably also in the (distinguishable) question whether there is a given. He would find them just boring! Nothing in the dream-argument mentions, or requires mentioning, either of them.[28] As to his internalism, he would say that this is merely another way of describing his question as asking, "How do *I* know that *I* am not dreaming now?" And can we, with clear conscience, reject that question as unintelligible, or incoherent, or irrelevant, or unimportant?

Yet another advantage of approaching our topic through a consideration of Descartes's dream-argument is that it makes all this quite obvious and frees us from the need of discussing general epistemological theories such as foundationalism, coherentism, and externalism on their own merits.[29]

Saying this is no expression of dogmatism on my part. For example, if one wishes to confer the honorific titles of "evident" or "knowledge" on judgments that have some property such as cohering with other judgments or issuing from reliable processes, I shall not argue against this but merely point out that so understood these titles are irrelevant to the epistemological problem with which I am concerned in this book. Of course, they are not irrelevant to other traditional epistemological concerns, for example, Which are the sources of knowledge that are reliable?, and How is coherence to be understood? And there is much to be said for holding that philosophical reasoning itself is essentially coherentist, though not as envisaged by contemporary coherentists, but rather as envisaged by Socrates and Plato, in their conception of dialectic, and by Hegel, in his account of the essential presuppositionlessness and hence circularity, of philosophy.[30] For any appeal to self-evidence in support of a *philosophical* position is of course subject to scrutiny that does not consist in merely appealing to other alleged cases of self-evidence. Even phenomenological appeals are faced at least with the task of dealing with eliminative materialism, and therefore a

complete philosophical system cannot just rest on them; I have made such appeals only because of the limited nature of my project.

It's a frequent objection to the dream-argument that we know that there are dreams only on the basis of past experience, and thus that we could not consistently appeal to the occurrence of dreams in raising a general doubt about knowledge based on experience. But this is a misunderstanding. What matters to the philosophical skeptic is the *possibility* of dreaming, not its actuality, and we can describe such a possibility even if we have never had a dream. And what is at issue need not be the possibility that all of one's experiences have been a dream, but the possibility of one's finding oneself at any one time having the experience we would call "awakening" and as a result either concluding (even if falsely) that what one had earlier taken to be real had been just a dream, or at least facing the decision whether this experience, and the experiences that follow it, are veridical, or whether the ones that preceded it were veridical. (I shall return to this point in chapter 6.) But could we have a conception of that experience except on the basis of past experience? Perhaps not, but the past experience itself could have been just a dream. We can dream that we are "awakening."[31] But we need not follow Russell in supposing that our whole life may have been a dream.[32] The reason is that the concept of a whole life has no clear application with respect to a dream.

Nonetheless, these remain vexing questions, and if the skeptic had only the dream-argument to rely on, they would need to be answered by him in detail. But if adequate answers cannot be given, then the skeptic, like Descartes himself, can fall back on the demon-argument, or perhaps even on the brain-in-a-vat argument. Then skepticism would lose its intuitive power and appear to be merely an intellectual puzzle. Just about anyone can find the dream-argument compelling; we sometimes do wonder whether or not we are dreaming, without having even heard of philosophy. Not so with the demon-argument or the brain-in-a-vat argument. And the intuitive power of the dream-argument suggests that the vexing questions mentioned earlier can be answered satisfactorily by the skeptic. I shall not attempt to do so myself, since my arguments *against* the skeptic will not depend on whether or how those questions are answered. We must also keep in mind that the root of any argument for skepticism about the external world is the fact that the occurrence of sense perception (or, if you like, "sense experience") does not entail or bear an intelligible evidential relation to the reality of its objects.[33] The dream-argument merely makes this especially obvious. It is not the specific facts about dreaming that ultimately matter. Saying this should not be confused with the familiar argument from "the veil of perception." I understand sense perception in the direct realist manner explained in chapter 1. It involves no intermediaries, no veil, but since its objects might be unreal its occurrence by itself provides no argument against the skeptic. We shall come back shortly to this point.

An example of the intuitive power of the dream-argument (as contrasted

with the demon-argument and the brain-in-a-vat argument) is that it seems impervious to the thesis that knowledge is not closed under known logical implication. We need not evaluate this general thesis here beyond noting that (at least in Robert Nozick's formulation of it)[34] it depends on an externalist conception of knowledge, heavily encumbered with an account of subjunctive conditionals in terms of "closeness" of possible worlds, which would be quite foreign to Descartes's (and our) concerns. Descartes would simply insist that if one knows that p is true then *of course* one knows that nothing incompatible with the truth of p is the case, even if one has not canvassed all possibilities and even if one does not independently know with respect to some that they are not the case (perhaps because one has just not thought of them). Even if all this were not obvious in the abstract, it is surely obvious in the case of the dream-argument. (This is an additional advantage of approaching the topic of skepticism by considering that argument.) There is overwhelming power to the intuitive conviction that one's dreaming that p (where p is a proposition ordinarily accepted on the basis of present perception) would be incompatible with one's knowing or even having evidence that p, in any standard sense of "know" or "evidence," that the possibility that one is dreaming that p can easily be considered, and indeed sometimes actually is, and that obviously if one does not know or have evidence that one is not dreaming that p then one does not know or have evidence that p.[35] As Michael Williams points out, "[T]he sceptic can put forward knowing that one is not dreaming as an independent and intuitively plausible condition on acquiring perceptual knowledge of the world, so his argument need not involve any general principle of closure [of knowledge under known logical implication]. . . . [This] condition seems likely to prove as plausible as any theoretical account of knowledge conjured up to rebut it."[36]

Barry Stroud distinguishes between the conditionals "If I know that p, then I am not dreaming that p" and "If I know that p, then I know that I am not dreaming that p."[37] For the reasons I have already given, we can accept the first conditional as obviously true in the case of perceptual judgments, but the skeptic requires the second conditional. Her denial that she knows she is not dreaming that p can lead, by modus tollens, to the skeptical conclusion that she does not know that p only if the second conditional is true. But, in general, it is false, if for no other reason than that one seldom considers whether one is dreaming or perhaps even lacks the concept of dreaming. The fact remains, however, that one *can* consider this and one *can* acquire the concept. Moreover, the dream possibility is easy to entertain and sometimes actually entertained in nonphilosophical contexts (unlike the brain-in-a-vat or the evil-demon hypotheses), and when we entertain it we easily reach the conclusion that the consequent, and therefore the antecedent as well, of the second conditional is false, that is, we arrive at skepticism.

This last point is relevant to the question whether Descartes's argument applies to both the particular and the general questions I distinguished ear-

lier. That it does apply to the former seems evident. And this may be enough for the skeptic. For though a *negative* answer to the particular question does not entail a negative answer to the general question, it does seem to provide the latter with overwhelming support. With respect to *any* particular perceptual situation it is false that we know (or have evidence) that the object of our perception exists, for we do not know (or have evidence) that we are not dreaming. If so, then for the negative answer to the general question to follow we need only the assumption that our knowledge that in general material objects exist can rest only on an affirmative answer to the particular question. But in chapter 4 I shall question this assumption, at least as it is ordinarily understood.

4. Abduction and Causality

The most common attempts to meet Descartes's dream-argument have been appeals to "the best explanation," and I shall devote this section to showing the general weakness, indeed the irrelevance, of any such appeal. In *The Problems of Philosophy* Bertrand Russell wrote: "[I]t is possible that life is one long dream, and that the outer world has only that degree of reality that the objects of dreams have; but although such a view does not seem inconsistent with known facts, there is no reason to prefer it to the common-sense view, according to which other people and things do really exist" (122). Earlier he had claimed that the former view is "a less simple hypothesis, viewed as a means of accounting for the facts of our life" (22–23). (But the reasons he had given for this claim concerned the general possibility that there are no material objects, there being instead only "sense data.") However, the fact is that appeals to the best explanation in discussing our present topic are irrelevant, because even if we had a clear notion of what to count as an explanation and especially as a *good* explanation, we could not use it to distinguish between dreaming and being awake. The reason is simple. Anything one might appeal to in evaluating the explanation (e.g., greater simplicity, elegance, predictive success, coherence with other theories) would be worthless if it were merely part of a dream.

This is why it is pointless to appeal to the best explanation of the "subjective contents of one's experiences," as Paul Moser does in *Knowledge and Evidence*, which is perhaps the best nonskeptical foundationalist work in recent epistemology.[38] But there is also the fact that the notion of explanation is too vague, too indeterminate, to play the crucial role any such appeal would impose upon it. (How vague it is, is described well and in detail by William G. Lycan in his *Judgment and Justification*, even though he defends "explanationism"!)[39] Moser dismisses Descartes's dream argument by saying that the subjective contents of one's experiences are better explained by the proposition that there are physical objects before one than they are by the proposition that one is dreaming, and therefore that the former proposition is justified for one (162–63, 259). The

vagueness, indeterminacy, of the notion of explanation is apparent from Moser's supposition that Descartes was trying to *explain* anything with his hypothesis. For the purposes of epistemology, what is distinctive about a dream is that it is a perception of unreal objects. What would the dream-hypothesis purport to explain? Certainly not the unreality of the objects (it would be part of the explanandum), nor the occurrence of the perception (the best explanation of the latter might be Freudian!). At any rate, suffice it here to ask Moser what relevance would the allegedly greater explanatory power of the real-physical-objects hypothesis have for a person who is dreaming but wonders whether she is dreaming or is awake. Would her knowledge of it help resolve her wonderment?

(Laurence BonJour, who has provided us with what is perhaps the best version of the coherentist theory of justification,[40] considers only Descartes's demon-hypothesis, which indeed can be thought of as an explanation, and argues that it is substantially less likely to be true than our ordinary hypothesis that our experiences are caused by material objects, even though the latter is still "highly unlikely."[41] I shall not consider whether this is so, but merely ask BonJour, too, the question I just asked Moser. What relevance would knowing all this have for a person who is wondering whether he is dreaming or is awake, and tries to resolve his wonderment?)

Moser is, of course, aware of the problems with the notion of explanation. They are familiar to all epistemologists and philosophers of science. Presumably this is why he contents himself with describing it as follows: "[O]ne thing explains another when and only when the former makes it, to some extent, *understandable*, why the latter thing is as it is" (*Knowledge and Evidence*, p. 93). He carefully avoids describing the understandability in question as knowability of a causal relation, even though in the case of perception this would be the natural description of it. Why does he do so? Unless, like Berkeley, he was bothered by the idea that "body can act upon spirit," I can only speculate that, being a consummately careful philosopher, he was aware that the ordinary notion of causality is notoriously controversial, perhaps, as Hume in effect argued, unintelligible, and that one cannot plausibly appeal to it in describing the foundations of empirical knowledge. Let me explain this in greater detail (without at all suggesting that Moser would agree with what I shall say), since the concept of causality has played such an important role in attempts to answer the skeptic.

Hume's most familiar contribution to the topic of causality was his claim that in observing what we ordinarily would describe as one moving billiard ball causing another billiard ball to move, we do not observe any necessary connection between the two billiard balls or between their motions. (Unlike some modern "Humeans," he regarded necessary connection as essential to our idea of causality.) If we assume that what physics tells us about billiard balls and motion is true, then we should not be surprised by Hume's claim. Obviously, he was right. If there is any necessary connec-

tion between the motion of the one billiard ball and the motion of the other, it could only obtain between the particles constituting the one ball and the particles constituting the other, or between the properties and relations of those particles. None of these are observable. No wonder that any necessary connection present in such an alleged paradigm of causality would also not be observable.

But is there genuine causality in the physical world (I shall ignore the "mental world"), real necessary connections between what Hume called "distinct existences"? It should be evident that only a physicist can give a responsible answer to this question. (Of course, a philosopher might also happen to be a physicist.) A philosopher's claim that she can provide the physicist with an "analysis" of the concept of necessary connection or of causality would be like a claim that she can provide the physicist with an analysis of the concept of particle, or of wave, or of force, or of electron. That she can provide something some might call an analysis is indisputable. But it is also indisputable that her analyses of these concepts would be neither needed by the physicist nor likely to be useful or even relevant to his work. I suggest that the same is true of philosophical analyses of the concept of causality. My conclusion applies even more obviously to philosophical theories of the *nature* of causality, for example, that it is a relation between universals, theories that are *not* offered as analyses of concepts. A philosophical theory of a scientific subject matter, say, the nature of the electron, can be true or useful only *per accidens*. Evan Fales has argued that we have a direct experience of causality in tactual perception of pressure, in the kinesthetic perception of muscular force, and in our experience, through our sense of balance, of gravitational and centrifugal forces.[42] Perhaps he is right. But even if he is, the kind of causality a physicist or an epistemologist like Moser needs is a long way from the kind Fales claims we experience, and Fales is quite aware of this fact. He agrees with Hume that no perception of causation between physical events (e.g., the motions of billiard balls) is possible, since he accepts a causal theory of perception of nonphenomenal states and denies that the causal relation itself has causal powers. His examples of perceived causation are all phenomenal. But Moser needs causation that is not purely phenomenal. The causal relation may be a genus one species of which (the purely phenomenal one) we can experience and form a conception of, while some very different, totally unknown and perhaps for us inconceivable, *other* species is what is needed for causal inference from "subjective contents" to material objects.

What answers might the physicist give to our question whether there is causality, real necessary connection, between "distinct existences" in the physical world? One might be that she does not need the concept of causality or of necessary connection. A second answer might be that she needs it but does not yet know how or to what to apply it. A third might be that she needs it, knows how to apply it, and moreover applies it to something not describable in terms of any other concepts. If this third answer is true,

then the physicist has discovered or at least has good reason to judge that there is causality or necessary connection in nature. The philosopher could deny this conclusion only on the basis of very general philosophical considerations about the nature of science, which have no specific relevance to our present point, or by insisting that he does not mean by causality or necessary connection what the physicist means. To say the latter would be like the philosopher's saying that he does not mean by electron what the physicist means. But suppose the physicist gives the first answer. If she is right, we should conclude that, at least so far, there is no evidence for the existence of causality or necessary connections in nature. The conclusion to be drawn from the second answer presumably would be that we should suspend judgment. Causality (in nature) is a scientific, not a philosophical topic. But even if there were relevant scientific findings about it, even if the physicist did give us the third answer, an appeal to them would merely beg the question against the skeptic with regard to the senses. Any such findings would depend at least in part on alleged findings of our senses.

There is also a short answer to appeals to the best explanation in attempting to refute the skeptic. It is a species of the general answer to any appeals to nondemonstrative evidence. Even if p provides the best explanation for the truth of q, why suppose that p is true, indeed why suppose that the explanatory relation between propositions, however it is understood, is even evidentially relevant, that it is an evidential relation, why suppose that the fact that p provides the best explanation of the truth of q is evidence for the truth of p? As David Armstrong points out, indeed "'There is *a* sense in which 'the best explanation' must be true, for if it is not true, it is not 'the best'. But what would be the best explanation if it were true, need not be true."[43] My point (Armstrong can speak for himself on this) is exactly parallel to the standard skeptical questions about induction, memory, other minds, and coherence of beliefs or judgments. Why suppose that inductive inference is in any sense valid, that past experience is genuine evidence for what is true of future experience or the unexperienced past and present? Why suppose that our seeming to remember something is evidence that it really occurred? Why suppose that others' behavior is ever evidence for their having mental states? Why suppose that the coherence (however understood) of our system of beliefs or judgments is evidence for their truth? The fact that this sort of question is not so familiar with respect to abduction, that is, with respect to inferences to the best explanation, is a sign not of the latter's having any privileged status among the alleged kinds of nondemonstrative evidence, but of the fact that its obscurity has kept philosophers from subjecting it to the sort of epistemological scrutiny that, say, induction has received ever since Hume. At least we understand what induction is supposed to be, be it valid or invalid. We don't understand even that much about abduction. I should add that to some, though not nearly the same, extent, appeals to the coherence of our beliefs or judgments, another and often, as in BonJour, closely related way of answering the skeptic, are also subject to this objection. One can easily

describe what is alleged to be inductive evidence for a proposition. But one must engage in tortuous controversies in order to describe what the coherentist evidence is and what is meant by "coherence" in such appeals. I have dwelt mainly on abduction and largely have ignored coherentism only because it has seemed to foundationalist philosophers (such as Moser in *Knowledge and Evidence*) to be a far more plausible basis for an answer to the skeptic. And, as I have pointed out, the traditional skeptic would classify himself as a foundationalist, if forced to wear some currently faddish tag.

5. Some Other Responses to the Dream-Argument

The conclusion to be reached from our consideration of Descartes's dream-argument so far is thoroughly skeptical, and obviously of enormous significance, though Descartes himself thought he could avoid it by proving the existence of a nondeceiving God, a proof the soundness of which I shall not consider here. (I made some remarks about it in the introduction.) What I do want to emphasize, however, is that Descartes's dream-argument indeed is, as he seems to have thought, central to the theory of empirical knowledge and evidence, and that no theory of empirical knowledge and evidence can be adequate if it does not answer it. A common fatal defect of nonskeptical theories is that they do not. I have already discussed Russell's proposal that the existence of matter is to be accepted because it constitutes the best explanation of the existence and nature of the sense data we sense, even though he admitted, rather disingenuously, that there was "a slight doubt derived from dreams" about the value of this reasoning.[44] (He did not explain why the doubt was "slight"!) But there have been other "answers." For example, J. L. Austin wrote:

> I may have the experience (dubbed "delusive" presumably) of dreaming that I am being presented to the Pope. Could it be seriously suggested that having this dream is "qualitatively indistinguishable" from *actually being* presented to the Pope? Quite obviously not. After all, we have the phrase "a dream-like quality"; some waking experiences are said to have this dream-like quality. . . . If dreams were not "qualitatively" different from waking experiences, then *every* waking experience would be like a dream.[45]

Austin's dreams must have been such that he always knew when dreaming that he was dreaming!

Moore, of course, took skepticism with regard to the senses very seriously, but his answers were singularly unilluminating, consisting of little more than bare assertions to the effect that he knows, for example, that he has a body (see "A Defense of Common Sense"), or that there are two human hands before him (see "Proof of the External World"), or that he is standing up (see his posthumously published article "Certainty").[46] In "Certainty" he did consider the dream-argument in some detail. But he ad-

mitted to being quite dissatisfied with his discussion of it. And the discussion is marred by his adopting there a rather primitive phenomenology of dreaming: he speaks of dream-*images*. Insofar as there is an argument in the paper, it seems to consist in his remark that if he knows that he is standing up then he knows that he is not dreaming, and therefore that the skeptic must give better reasons for his proposition "I do not know that I am not dreaming that I am standing up" than Moore can give for his proposition "I know that I am standing up."[47] (We are given no defense of this assertion. Why must the skeptic give better reasons? Why isn't a "draw" good enough for him, as it was for some of the ancient Greek skeptics?) Moore points out that the reasons the skeptic would give are that it is logically possible that veridical sensory experiences are exactly like dream-experiences, presumably meaning that the two are exactly alike in their intrinsic properties. And the skeptic would hold (Moore does not make this explicit) that any attempt to distinguish them by appealing to nonintrinsic differences such as differences of causal origin would be obviously question-begging. Moore also suggests that in addition to having sensory experiences he might have "memories of the immediate past," and that this might be sufficient to enable him to know that he is not dreaming (250). But, of course, if he were dreaming, these memories would themselves be merely part of the dream.

We find Wittgenstein writing: "The argument 'I may be dreaming' is senseless for this reason: if I am dreaming, this remark is being dreamed as well—and indeed it is also being dreamed that these words have any meaning."[48] But the sentence "I may be dreaming" is not senseless at all; it is sometimes employed with very clear and important sense both when we are awake and when we are dreaming. If I am informed that I have unexpectedly inherited one million dollars, I may well say to myself, "I may be dreaming," and mean this quite literally. And if I dream that I have inherited one million dollars, in my dream I may well again say (silently) to myself, "I may be dreaming," also meaning this quite literally. Wittgenstein's failure to take the dream-argument seriously mars other familiar responses he makes to the skeptic. For example, his remarks about the propriety of epistemic statements about material objects in certain situations, his avowal, "I would like to reserve the expression 'I know' for the cases in which it is used in normal linguistic exchange,"[49] blatantly beg the question against the skeptic, since whether an expression is being in fact used in a normal (wakeful?) linguistic exchange is just the sort of thing the skeptic would say we cannot know.

Wittgenstein also writes: "Suppose now I say 'I'm incapable of being wrong about this: that is a book' while I point to an object. What would a mistake here be like? And have I any *clear* idea of it?" (*On Certainty,* §17). But, of course, one can have a very clear idea of what such a mistake would be like. All one would need to do is to imagine that one will presently have the familiar experience of finding oneself waking up. Exactly the same response can be made to another familiar passage: "It's not a matter of

Moore's knowing that there's a hand there, but rather we should not understand him if he were to say 'Of course I may be wrong about this'. We should ask 'What is it like to make such a mistake as that?—e.g. what's it like to discover that it was a mistake?" (§32). Or to: "There are . . . certain types of case in which I rightly say I cannot be making a mistake, and Moore has given a few examples of such cases" (§674). And to: "I want to say: If one doesn't marvel at the fact that the propositions of arithmetic (e.g. the multiplication tables) are 'absolutely certain', then why should one be astonished that the proposition 'This is my hand' is so equally?" (§448). An essential part of Descartes's dream-argument was that, unlike knowledge of propositions such as "This is a hand," mathematical knowledge was not affected by one's dreaming. Perhaps he was wrong, but this part of his argument cannot be just ignored.

Behind Wittgenstein's claims just quoted lies the conviction that nothing could be more certain than a statement such as Moore's "Here is a hand" when made in normal circumstances, and this is why he questioned the propriety of Moore's use of "I know" with respect to such statements. "One says 'I know' when one is ready to give compelling grounds. . . . But if what he believes is of such a kind that the grounds that he can give are no surer than his assertion, then he cannot say that he knows what he believes" (§243).[50] And in section 115 he writes: "If you tried to doubt everything you would not get as far as doubting anything. The game of doubting itself presupposes certainty." But the conviction that nothing could be more certain than the Moorean statements, even when made in normal circumstances, is false. There is something quite familiar which is both more certain than Moore's statement "Here is a hand" and moreover constitutes the obvious evidence on which the statement rests (*if* anything is such evidence). That is Moore's *seeing* a hand before him, whether or not the hand is real, and whether or not this seeing takes place in a dream. It is noteworthy that this evidence is quite naturally described simply with the ordinary notion of seeing. There is no need to invent technical notions such as those of a sense datum, or sensation, or sense experience, or way of being appeared to. The dreamer sees a human hand, just as he may see a human hand when awake. The difference lies on the side of the object of the seeing, which in both cases is a human hand, but in the first case it is unreal, does not exist, and in the second (let us suppose) it is real, it does exist. This is a perfectly natural use of the notions of seeing and of reality, and to reject them would require philosophical reasons that Wittgenstein does not even attempt to give. (The physiological differences between the two cases must be held to be irrelevant to a discussion of skepticism with regard to the senses, and I think Wittgenstein would have wholeheartedly agreed. He was no worshiper of science.) Of course, if the seeing takes place in a dream, then, as I have argued, it is not evidence that there is a (real) hand. Nevertheless, it is still more certain than the latter could ever be, even when one is awake. A similar response can be made to Anthony Kenny, who writes with regard to Descartes's dream-argument: "There is

no fact better known to me than the fact that I am awake, that I can offer as a reason for saying that I am awake. When I say 'I am awake,' I do so without grounds, but not without justification."[51]

6. A Deeper Way To Understand Wittgenstein's Responses

But Wittgenstein had deeper grounds for rejecting the skepticism Descartes's dream-argument supports, and the remarks I have dismissed so quickly can also be taken to express those grounds. To understand them properly, let us recall our distinction between two questions. The first was, Do we know or at least have evidence, in at least one particular perceptual situation, that the material object of the perception, say, a snake, is real? I called it "the particular question." The second was, Do we know or at least have evidence that in general there are real material objects, a real external world? I called it "the general question." As I have remarked before, an affirmative answer to the particular question entails an affirmative answer to the general question, but the converse is not the case. This is an important difference between the two questions. Moreover, obviously, the general question is of greater interest for philosophy.

Now as answers to the particular question, Wittgenstein's arguments, just quoted, may have little or no value. But they may have considerable value if understood as answers to the general question. Then they can be connected with other grounds he gives for rejecting skepticism. In *On Certainty* he writes: "I want to say: propositions of the form of empirical propositions, and not only propositions of logic, form the foundation of all operating with thoughts (with language)" (§401). He also writes: "So is the *hypothesis* possible, that all of the things around us do not exist? Would that not be like the hypothesis of our having miscalculated in all our calculations?"(§55). In the same work there are also the following striking remarks: "My life shews that I know or am certain that there is a chair over there, or a door, and so on.—I tell a friend e.g. 'Take that chair over there', 'Shut the door', etc. etc." (§7), and "If you are not certain of any fact, you cannot be certain of the meaning of your words either" (§114). He speaks of "the inherited background against which I distinguish between true and false" (§94). He writes: "What would it be like to doubt now whether I have two hands? . . . I have arrived at the rock bottom of my convictions" (§§247–48).

Such arguments have often been described as transcendental because they resemble some of Kant's arguments from the conditions necessary for the very possibility of experience and unified thought. They are obviously directed at what I have called the general question, and for this reason they will be of special interest to us in the next chapter. Essentially, Wittgenstein is claiming that skepticism is an incoherent position because it questions the conditions for the possibility of language and thought. Except for making some brief remarks directly relevant to our topic, I shall not attempt

to evaluate such global arguments, partly because I am skeptical that the needed premises about the nature of language and of conceptual cognition have been adequately worked out, whether by Wittgenstein or any one else. Some of these premises, however plausible when taken outside the context of a discussion of skepticism, appear ludicrous if taken as parts of arguments against it. For example, the assertions "If language is to be a means of communication there must be agreement not only in definitions but also (queer as this may sound) in judgments"[52] and "'So you are saying that human agreement decides what is true and what false?'—It is what human beings *say* that is true and false; and they agree in the *language* they use. This is not agreement in opinions but in form of life" (§241), could both be cheerfully accepted by the skeptic but regarded as irrelevant to his position since he questions even the existence of other persons with whom he may agree or disagree, whether in definitions or in judgements. (Skepticism with regard to the senses entails skepticism with regard to the existence of embodied persons.) The skeptic can also accept the assertion "If you are not certain of any fact, you cannot be certain of the meaning of your words either" (*On Certainty*, §114), since he does not claim to be not certain of *any* fact. He is a skeptic only with regard to the senses! When Wittgenstein writes, "[W]hat could make me doubt whether this person here is N.N., whom I have known for years? Here a doubt would seem to drag everything with it and plunge it into chaos" (§613), the skeptic would simply disagree, he would not even need to appeal to the dream-argument. Mild cases of aphasia are not uncommon and do not plunge everything into chaos for the sufferer.

It may seem that many of the responses the skeptic would make to Wittgenstein's global claims about language and thought presuppose the possibility of a private language insofar as they must be understood as presupposing the possibility that one is dreaming when one is making them. It is significant that Wittgenstein does not make this point. The reason, perhaps, is that he would have agreed with Malcolm's claim that Descartes's view that a dream consists of thoughts, feelings, and impressions, sometimes even mathematical reasoning, is absurd, meaningless, on the extreme verificationist grounds (surely such extreme verificationism is most questionable, and in fact has been questioned by many) that our only method of verification of a dream report is to verify that the report has been made sincerely, and that we have no criterion for distinguishing between veridical and nonveridical sincere dream reports. These would be also grounds for holding that neither do we use a language in a dream, so the question whether we might be using a private language does not even arise. But suppose that, unconvinced by Malcolm's extreme position, *we* raise the question. What would the skeptic's reply be? She could, of course, deny the soundness of the private language argument, as most nonskeptics also have done, or at least point out that it is quite controversial and say that if Wittgenstein's rejection of skepticism with regard to the senses has to depend on that argument then it would rest on very shaky grounds. But the

more likely response would be that there is no reason for supposing that language used in a dream is private, for there is no reason to suppose that it would be *logically* impossible for another person to learn it, which is Wittgenstein's conception of a private language. (After all, the dreamer may awaken and teach it to us!) At any rate, it is the ordinary public language that a dreamer commonly uses in a dream, if she uses a language at all. But if there were no material objects, and therefore no embodied persons, wouldn't the skeptic's language have to be private? No, because it would still be logically possible that someone else could understand it—unless the skeptic adds to her hypothesis that the existence of other persons is logically impossible, something she surely need not do. Of course, one would understand it by understanding the dream-report made when the person is awake. But, *ex hypothesi*, what is understood is still the language used in the dream.

But all these issues are highly complex, and I cannot discuss them further here. Suffice it to say that the skeptic would regard Wittgenstein's global premises about language and thought as much more questionable than her simple and intuitively compelling claim that we have no way of distinguishing between dreaming and being awake. However, Wittgenstein's transcendental arguments do have value by in effect raising what I called the general question and also *suggesting* an answer to it. I shall attempt to give such an answer, though not Wittgenstein's, in the next chapter.

7. The Skeptic's General Argument

The dream-argument has far-reaching general epistemological implications that provide the skeptic with a much more powerful, though less intuitive, *general* argument, of a purely conceptual nature and therefore much wider application. It constitutes strong, though not conclusive, grounds for denying that we have an intelligible or at least usable concept of *nondemonstrative* evidence (i.e., of evidence compatible with the falsehood of what it is evidence for) at all. The usual reason for denying this has been that the concept seems to have no phenomenological grounding; to appeal to this reason is merely to accept a relaxed and up-to-date version of Hume's principle that every genuine primitive idea corresponds to an impression. But a second and for our present purposes the relevant reason is that if we did possess a genuine, substantive, intelligible concept of nondemonstrative evidence, it would help us distinguish between dreaming and being awake. If it could not do this, of what use would it be? Every other use to which we might put it presupposes our being able to make that distinction. If we cannot make it, then we have no use for the concept of nondemonstrative evidence. (For, surely, it is not by demonstration that the distinction can be made.) And if we have no use for it, how can it be a genuine concept?

This reasoning seems to have two immediate and closely related consequences. The first is that the much maligned traditional "strong" concep-

tion of knowledge as infallibility (the Cartesian conception!) is vindicated. For the contrasting "weak" conception of knowledge (true belief or judgment based on nondemonstrative, perhaps strong but neither logically nor metaphysically conclusive, evidence—we shall ignore Edmund Gettier here!) turns out now to have no application at all. The second consequence is that the conception of epistemic probability (which presupposes the concept of nondemonstrative evidence that is part of the weak conception of knowledge) that is supposedly involved in warranting beliefs or judgments that are "justified" but are not knowledge, also turns out to have no application, to be a conceptual phantom. This was seen by Hume, presumably because he attended in detail to the topic of induction where the need for these conceptions is especially vividly felt. Clearly having the traditional, strong conception of knowledge in mind, he wrote: "But knowledge and probability are of such contrary and disagreeing natures, that they cannot well run insensibly into each other, and that because they will not divide, but must be either entirely present, or entirely absent."[53] And almost two centuries later John Cook Wilson wrote: "There is no general character or quality of which the essential natures of both knowledge and opinion are differentiations. . . . It is vain to seek such a common quality in belief. . . . Belief is not knowledge and the man who knows does not believe at all what he knows; he knows it."[54] (Obviously, Cook Wilson would include under belief any so-called justified or epistemically probable belief or any belief based on nondemonstrative evidence.) Of course, the original defender of the view was Plato, who in *Republic* 477e wrote: "Socrates: A short time ago you agreed that knowledge and opinion are not the same.—Glaucon: How can any intelligent man say that a fallible thing is the same as an infallible one?—Socrates: Right." The dream-argument makes all this clear with respect to the judgments that are neither a priori nor introspective, that is, precisely the ones a "weak" conception of knowledge and the concept of nondemonstrative evidence are intended to legitimize. If they fail to do so, then they have no use, no epistemological value, at all.

The concept of *demonstrative* evidence, on the other hand, that required by the concept of knowledge in the traditional Platonic, Cartesian, and Humean sense (in which, for example, I do not know that I will be alive tomorrow regardless of how strong my "evidence" for this proposition may be) remains unaffected by the dream-argument, as Descartes indeed saw. It has two forms. (For the sake of terminological simplicity, I shall diverge somewhat from the dictionary meaning of "demonstrative" by counting as demonstrative evidence also what has traditionally been called self-evidence. The self-evidence of a proposition supposedly guarantees its truth, just as being demonstrated by inference from true premises supposedly guarantees the truth of the demonstrated proposition.) The first is what I have just described as self-evidence (this is the divergence from the dictionary). It is best understood as the unthinkability of mistake or error (not of falsehood, for the proposition in question may be contingent) or, more precisely, as the brute psychological fact of one's finding it unthink-

able, being unable to make anything of the supposition, that one is mistaken in judging the proposition in question to be true.[55] It should not be confused, as it often is, with the concept of infallibility, or of incorrigibility, or of indubitability, or of certainty.

Infallibility trivially entails truth, and so the correct application of the concept of the former presupposes the correct *independent* application of the concept of the latter. Incorrigibility is irrelevant here if it merely implies (as it should) invulnerability to genuine correction by oneself or by others in the *future*.[56] Indubitability is essentially the also irrelevant psychological state of being unable to doubt (a state we often find ourselves in when it is obvious, even to ourselves, that we have no knowledge or even evidence of any kind); as the structure of the word shows, pace Alston,[57] it is not the epistemologically relevant state of there being no *grounds* for doubt. The word "certain" does not wear its meaning on its sleeve, as the others do. A perusal of a good dictionary would show that although its chief current meaning is that of (1) being completely convinced (the highest degree of confidence), it also can mean (2) being necessary (in the sense of being required by the laws of logic, or of physics, mathematics, morals, etc.), or (3) having been proved, that is, known in the strict sense. The first meaning, often called subjective certainty, is irrelevant to our topic; 2 is too narrow, for we wish to speak of knowledge of the laws of logic, and so forth, themselves, as well as of matters that might not follow from any laws (e.g., feeling pain); and 3 of course is just what we had hoped to elucidate with the word "certainty."[58]

Unlike infallibility, unthinkability of mistake does not entail truth. Being unable to make anything out of the supposition that one is mistaken does not entail that one is not mistaken. It is a brute psychological fact. But it is also the closest we can come epistemically to truth, since what is unthinkable, what we are unable to make anything out of, is precisely our *not* possessing truth. That "I find it unthinkable that I am mistaken in judging that I have a headache" (F) does not entail "I have a headache" (H), is obvious. But note that "I am not mistaken in judging that H" (call this "M") does entail H. Now, neither does F entail M, since if it did then it would entail H. But what is striking is that we cannot determine that F does not entail M in the only *ultimate* way we can determine that a given proposition does not entail a certain other proposition, namely, by being able to think of a situation in which the former is true and the latter is false. For F denies precisely that the falsehood of M is thinkable. This is not the same as entailment, of course. But it is as close as we can come epistemically to a case of entailment, and thus as close as we can come epistemically to the truth of M and thus of H. What is the moral to be drawn from this fact? Not that we should tamper with the notion of truth, or with the notion of knowledge. (For example, we must not allow ourselves the luxury of an epistemic definition of truth or succumb to what Sartre derisively called the alimentary conception of knowledge as the ingesting, the absorption, of the known object by the knower.) Rather, I suggest, we should recognize

that the only relevant sense in which we can "get" at the truth of a proposition is epistemic, that is, by employing our epistemic capacities. But, surely, this is a tautology, though one we often forget. And the employment of our epistemic capacities in this sort of case is our trying, but failing, to think of a certain judgment as mistaken. This is a brute psychological fact, as I have said, but it is quite familiar to all of us. It's not unlike trying but failing to lift a heavy object. Indeed, even our recognition of formal entailments depends on our finding their negation to be unthinkable. We accept "If p then p" because its negation is a contradiction. But why do we accept the principle of noncontradiction? No subtle logical or semantical theory could do better than the simple, straightforward answer: because we find any putative exception to it to be unthinkable.

Does all this support global antirealism, according to which we have no access to "objective" truth, our understanding of assertoric discourse being limited to knowing its assertibility-conditions, not any "evidence-transcendent" truth-conditions? If what I have called "getting at the truth" is inherently epistemic, as of course it must be (it does not aim at some sort of physical possession!), then we have no substantive issue between the realist and the antirealist, but just a muddled picture. It is hardly clear what could be meant by saying that truth is epistemic by its very nature, as the antirealist claims, unless it is the tautology that our ultimate epistemic *access* to it is epistemic. If we try to say something about it in itself, it would be best to think of it as a regulative idea, in Kant's sense, which necessarily informs the epistemic enterprise but cannot literally *coincide* with any of its achievements. To use an analogy, competent *ordinary* calculation in arithmetic presupposes the infinity of the series of natural numbers (there is no largest number, we would never run out of numbers), but cannot make it a part of its subject matter (if it did, it would cease to be ordinary). Of course, epistemic definitions of truth have been proposed by C. S. Peirce, Putnam, and others, in terms of warranted assertibility, or what would be agreed to ultimately by all inquirers, or what would be justified in epistemically ideal conditions. I shall not discuss them here. They are too removed from our ordinary concept of truth, and probably are also circular or for us question-begging, the notion of *warranted* assertibility being exactly what the skeptic questions and the notion of truth being probably at least partially involved in the notion of agreement and especially in the notion of *epistemically ideal* conditions. For an excellent criticism of these definitions, the reader may consult William P. Alston's *A Realist Theory of Truth*.[59]

It should be noted that the unthinkability of mistake is self-validating since if mistake is unthinkable in a particular case then so is, in that particular case, mistake in thinking that mistake is unthinkable in that particular case, and this is why it is (if I may use Alston's language) no chauvinism to regard the doxastic practice of appealing to it as privileged, as the Archimedean point from which we can make an impartial evaluation of all other doxastic practices.[60] There can be no question of justifying my

judgment that I find mistake regarding a certain proposition to be unthinkable, though we can certainly say that it is self-justified, that is, self-evident, and thus no infinite regress or epistemic circularity can arise. The notion of self-evidence is guaranteed to be genuine because of its applicability to the brute psychological, but epistemically crucial, fact of one's finding oneself, in a particular situation, unable to think that one is mistaken in judging some proposition to be true (e.g., that one has a stabbing headache). There is no circularity since by the very meaning of "self-evidence" no appeal to another judgment is (or at least needs to be) made. For the same reason no infinite regress arises. Indeed if, perversely, we wanted to appeal to a higher order judgment, for example,"I find mistake in judging that p is unthinkable to be itself unthinkable," going to even higher orders would lead, not to making genuine further judgments, but merely to stammering. Indeed this is true of many alleged infinite regresses. For example, perhaps "I believe (judge) that I believe (judge) that p" is all right, but beyond it (e.g., "I believe that I believe that I believe that p") we express no genuine thought, we merely produce verbiage. (The coherentist may use this point in self-defense against some familiar objections.)

I should emphasize that in the relevant cases mistake is unthinkable not abstractly but with respect to a particular proposition (or state of affairs, if you wish), and by a particular person at a particular time and in a particular context. And, once again, its unthinkability is a brute psychological fact, not a purely conceptual or logical matter. But this is how it should be. It is ultimately *my* knowledge I must appraise, at *this* particular time and in *this* particular context. How could it be otherwise, even if what I allegedly know is that someone else knows something? And if the unthinkability of mistake is in this way bound to a particular factual context, how could it be a purely conceptual or logical matter?

The previous paragraph is directly relevant to the question whether knowing entails knowing that one knows, which we touched upon in section 3. Surely, the answer is no, since an infant has some knowledge but no knowledge that it has that knowledge, simply because (presumably) the infant lacks the concept of knowledge. On the other hand, the temptation to hold that knowing entails knowing that one knows is laudable because it is a symptom of the fact (insisted on by major epistemologists such as H. A. Prichard) that knowing does entail that one can, *on reflection*, know that one knows. Some (e.g., infants) are incapable of such reflection, because they lack developed intelligence or the concept of knowledge. But most of us are not. There is no mystery about any of this. The conception of knowledge as the unthinkability of mistake makes it quite clear. If I find mistake in a certain judgment unthinkable, I need not also find unthinkable mistake in my finding mistake in the original judgment to be unthinkable. But I must be able to do so, as long as I would be entertaining genuine thoughts.

So far I have discussed the first form of demonstrative evidence, namely, self-evidence. The second form (the one properly so-called) is that involv-

ing entailment (whether formal or "synthetic a priori") by something that is self-evident, the entailment itself being self-evident, that is, our finding it unthinkable that the entailing proposition should be true and the entailed proposition false. It is familiar and requires little discussion here. If Descartes is right, an appeal to both kinds of demonstrative evidence in dreaming is quite possible, for example when engaging in mathematical reasoning. But not so with nondemonstrative evidence. For, as we have seen, any appeal to nondemonstrative evidence (inductive, abductive, coherentist, etc.) is legitimate only if the dream-problem has been solved.

Elsewhere, I have argued on general grounds that we do not have (but perhaps some day will develop) an intelligible concept of nondemonstrative evidence.[61] The argument is that nothing seems to resemble demonstrative evidence sufficiently in order to belong with it in the same genus. I shall not go into its details here. Roughly, the point is that no known species of alleged nondemonstrative evidence (inductive, abductive, coherentist, etc.) appears to be sufficiently similar to demonstrative evidence to render their subsumption in the same genus intelligible. (Of course, the word "evidence" could be equivocal, but then the same conclusion would be reached directly.) And demonstrative evidence is the unquestioned paradigm of evidence, for its connection with truth at least *seems* quite clear—the evidence entails that which it is evidence for, the entailing proposition(s) cannot be true unless the entailed proposition is also true. (I say that the connection at least seems clear because of my earlier remarks about what could be meant by "getting" at the truth. But we can say that it is as clear as any such connection could meaningfully be supposed to be.) Nothing even remotely *like* this seems to be the case with the alleged species of nondemonstrative evidence. None entails or can even be thought to entail truth. Indeed, how could anything be *like* entailment in any significant way without *being* entailment? But then what connection can the alleged cases of nondemonstrative evidence have with truth, which they must have in order to deserve to be called evidence? How can they be truth-conducive? It would be useless to suppose that in such cases we have "partial entailment," at least until someone explicates this mysterious notion.

An analogy with ethics may make this clearer. Suppose that the hedonist is right: pleasure is the only intrinsic good. He then faces three options, as Mill did. The first is simply to deny that the other alleged intrinsic goods, for example, virtue, honor, money, are really intrinsic goods. This would be analogous to the skeptic's view about nondemonstrative evidence. The second option, the one actually adopted by Mill, is to count such alleged intrinsic goods as pleasures. This dogmatic and highly implausible view is analogous to the one I have argued against regarding nondemonstrative evidence. The third option is to suspend judgment, to admit that pleasure is a paradigm of an intrinsic good but allow that we may discover a rationale for regarding also virtue, honor, money, and so on, as intrinsic goods (not pleasures), that is, to allow that we may discover that all of these do after all belong with pleasure in a common genus.[62] With re-

spect to nondemonstrative evidence, the analogous option is to suspend judgment on the question whether the appearance of insufficient similarity between it and demonstrative evidence is not deceiving, whether in fact they do belong to the same genus, and simply hope that further inquiry will provide the answer, negative or positive. This is the option I think should be adopted, not that of the skeptic or that of the dogmatist. But the suspension of judgment must be genuine, it must not surreptitiously legitimize our accepting whatever we generally happen to accept, even if it were given the honorific title of common sense.

Earlier I suggested that we must dispense with the alleged notion of epistemic justification and remain true to the traditional view that epistemology is concerned with knowledge and evidence. *If* now we find that the notion of nondemonstrative evidence must be dispensed with as well, or at least not appealed to until made intelligible, we are left with the conclusion that so far knowledge alone is the proper subject matter of epistemology (a tautological result!), since the concept of demonstrative evidence is hardly distinguishable from that of knowledge in the strict, traditional, indeed Cartesian sense, though this sense has often been expressed misleadingly with expressions such as "certainty," "indubitability," "apprehension," "intuition." (It is a myth that the traditional conception of knowledge was justified true belief.) We need not add to it the conditions of judgment ("belief") and truth, for finding mistake in judging a proposition to be true unthinkable entails the making of a judgment and comes so close to truth as to be in any particular case factually (though not conceptually) indistinguishable from it.

In defending direct realism in chapters 1 and 2 I argued that we are in direct contact with material objects. How does this square with what I have said in this section? The answer is that the contact in question is not epistemic, it does not consist in a state of knowledge or a judgment based on evidence; it is a nonconceptual, nonlinguistic, and in general nonsymbolic, nonrepresentational event. Of course, neither is it physical. It is direct perception of an object. There is no circularity or question-begging here, for our direct contact in perception may be with something unreal, something "untrue."

The conception of knowledge I have outlined, though traditional, is austere and does not fit most of the ordinary usages of the word "know." Whether this is a defect would depend on how we view the extent to which divergence from ordinary usage is permissible in philosophy. The fact is that common sense itself readily diverges from ordinary usage when the issue is important. "I know that I'll be in my office tomorrow" (which entails that I'll live that long), I would casually say when nothing important is at stake. But I would not put off renewing my life insurance until tomorrow just because of this fact about ordinary usage, and when reminded of this I would of course withdraw my original statement. Similarly, common sense seldom considers the possibility that one is dreaming and therefore lacking any knowledge or even mere evidence regarding anything ex-

cept what reason and introspection disclose. But it requires no profound reasoning on the part of common sense to recognize this possibility when the question really matters (Did he really say he loved me? Did I really inherit one million dollars? Did my son really have a fatal automobile accident?). And that recognition may swiftly dispel any pretensions to having knowledge or evidence.

It is only philosophers eager to avoid the discomfort of skepticism who seem unaware of this. It is to them that it needs to be said that their favorite less austere conception of knowledge, presumably true belief or judgment based usually on nondemonstrative evidence, would pass the first necessary condition we should insist on, namely, intelligibility, only if the concept of nondemonstrative evidence has been made clear. So far, it has not.

I have engaged in these general epistemological reflections for a particular reason. They show that Descartes's dream-argument leads directly to a *general* skeptical argument. If we can neither know nor have evidence that we are not dreaming by employing nondemonstrative senses of "know" and "evidence," then these are without a use in nonintrospective empirical knowledge, all of which presupposes that the dream-argument can be met. We are left then with the demonstrative senses of these words, those appropriate to a priori and introspective knowledge, which are the only kinds of knowledge the skeptic about the external world recognizes as genuine. This conclusion, though reached on the basis of Descartes's dream-argument, strengthens it by allowing us to see it now in the context of a general account of the concepts of knowledge and evidence, which leads to the same conclusion as Descartes's argument but without appealing to the possibility of dreaming or any other particular skeptical possibilities. For, obviously, in any particular case of perception, neither is it unthinkable that we are mistaken in judging that its object is real nor is such a judgment entailed by other judgments we find it unthinkable to be mistaken about. The concepts of knowledge and evidence on which this general skepticism is based are very much the traditional ones, and thus such skepticism has roots that the bare dream-argument does not have, even though its power is most clearly and vividly seen through the latter.

4

A FIRST ANSWER TO THE SKEPTIC

1. Toward a Direct Realist Answer to the Skeptic

The truth is that neither Descartes's dream-argument nor the skeptic's general argument it leads to has been answered, yet they concern what presumably is the most important question we can ask: Does an external world exist? Philosophy after Descartes was therefore quite justified in concentrating on this question, and thus in according a central status to epistemology. (With Kant being the major exception, the question was usually understood as what I have called the particular question, presumably because of the natural belief, which nevertheless I shall argue is mistaken, that what I have called the general question could be answered only as an inference from an answer to the particular question.) Some philosophers disagree with this assessment, but they would have the right to do so only if they had a solution to the problem of skepticism. In fact, they do not even attempt such a solution, sometimes just saying that it is not a genuine problem at all. But they do not explain why it is not a genuine problem, unless we count as explanations aphorisms such as Austin's and Wittgenstein's, which are reminiscent of Dr. Johnson's "refuting" Berkeley by kicking a stone. It seems to remain true that it is a genuine problem and that we have no solution of it.

Now this conclusion certainly applies, at least with respect to the particular question, to the philosophers who, I suggested in chapter 1, hold a direct realist view. I have already tried to show this in the case of Wittgenstein and Moore, who alone devoted any attention to it. Heidegger did not even discuss the question, he merely dismissed it by denying that knowing is our primary access to the Real.[1] Sartre did consider it briefly, distinguishing (in *The Psychology of the Imagination*) between perception and imagination by saying that by its very nature the former, though fallible, leads to knowledge,[2] and suggesting (in *Being and Nothingness*[3] and elsewhere) that it does so by constituting material objects out of the profiles they present to us. This Husserlian notion of consciousness constituting its objects may seem to be no longer an answer to our original question but a

rejection of it, because of its idealist implications that were made explicit by Husserl himself. But to suppose this would be a mistake. Husserl's was not Kant's transcendental idealism, which was committed to the doctrine of there being unknowable things-in-themselves, and what I have called direct realism need not be incompatible with it; just as Kant's "empirical realism" was not, even though it presupposes the contribution consciousness makes to its objects and thus has idealist implications, which however must not be confused with his official transcendental idealism. But we need not pursue this issue here further. I shall return to it in chapter 6. What is relevant to our present purposes is that if we interpret Sartre to be saying that perception leads to knowledge in the sense that our initial judgments about what material objects are before us can be confirmed, indefinitely, by further perceivings, we must admit that he is begging the question against the skeptic, since the latter would of course question the assumption that genuine confirmations can be expected. But I believe this would be a misinterpretation of Sartre. His view that, unlike imagination, perception leads to knowledge is phenomenological, not epistemological; it is in effect my own view that if understood in accordance with direct realism perception provides us with direct access to, though not knowledge of the reality of, material objects, that we "see" perception as leading to knowledge, whether or not it really does so. (Indeed, later in his life, Sartre avowed that he had never had an interest in epistemology.)[4]

It is also true that none of our four philosophers took seriously Descartes's particular concern that we may not be able to tell whether we are dreaming or are awake. We have seen that Wittgenstein returned to it repeatedly but only to brush it aside, and that Moore's discussion of it in "Certainty" was singularly sketchy and regarded as unsatisfactory even by him. Sartre did devote a chapter to it in *The Psychology of Imagination*,[5] but rejected it on the unbelievable grounds that one can tell whether one is dreaming or awake because dreaming is *phenomenologically* a kind of imagination, and he had argued convincingly much earlier in the book that there are fundamental and phenomenologically evident differences between imagination and perception.

Yet the intuitive power of Descartes's concern is obvious. It cannot be just ignored. Wittgenstein's view of language, Heidegger's view of the relationship of Dasein to the world, Moore's conviction on a certain occasion that there is a human hand before him, and Sartre's view of perception as leading to knowledge, provide no answer to Descartes's question. Dasein presumably is capable of dreaming, and Sartre's "confirming" his experiences (if that's how we understand him), Moore's seeing his hands, and Wittgenstein's uses of language could all be just events in a dream. So, not even the major twentieth-century philosophers who held the direct realist conception of consciousness met the Cartesian challenge regarding the particular epistemological question, though, as I shall argue now, they were in a better position with respect to it, and especially with respect to the general question, than the defenders of what I have called the mental-contents

theory of consciousness have been, or indeed the defenders of any other theory known to me. This argument will be my first, obviously insufficient, but in my view indispensable, step toward answering the skeptic. Let me explain.

While the direct realist conception of consciousness, like any of the competing conceptions, does not provide a solution to the problem of how we may know in a particular perceptual situation that there is a real material object before us, at least it allows us to regard such a solution as *possible.* On the main opposing conception of consciousness, the mental-contents theory, we are encircled by our ideas and sensations; what we are aware of is only the contents of our minds. (I shall ignore the materialist conception because of its obvious irrelevance to the epistemological issue before us. What good would accepting materialism do one who wonders whether he or she is dreaming or awake?) If so, our task is to explain how we may know that there is an external object in the first place, whether real or unreal, when no such object is given to perceptual consciousness at all, and this task is that of inferring that there is such an object from the contents of our minds. If it is suggested (e.g., by some adverbial theorists who, unlike Chisholm, have not thought out the *ontology* their theory presupposes) that no such inference is needed, then our knowledge of the external world becomes even more mysterious.

It may seem peculiar to speak of knowing that there is an unreal object. But let us recall that quantification over unreal objects is not only intelligible but common. And the knowledge in question need not result from a process of investigation. It could be, indeed ordinarily would be, direct, immediate, as for example knowing what one is thinking or imagining usually is. Of course, in speaking of knowledge here I am not begging the question against the skeptic. On any theory of perceptual knowledge that is at all plausible, there is something in perceiving that is known directly and immediately, and on none so far offered that is defensible is what is so known the reality of a material object. The distinguishing feature of the direct realist theory is that what is known is that there is such an object, but not that this object is real. Knowing the latter would be an additional item of knowledge. (This is why direct realism does not commit us to foundationalism, as the latter is usually understood.) And it is a virtue of direct realism that it makes perspicuous the connection between these two steps. It's an a priori, logical connection. The second step logically presupposes the first step. They correspond to Stanley Cavell's distinction between "knowledge as the identification or recognition of things" and "knowledge of a thing's existence."[6] It's one thing to perceptually identify or recognize a thing as such and such, or to be able to call it by the right name, it's quite another to know that it exists. Yet if one could not do the former, one could not do the latter.

But if the reader still finds all this unpalatable, she might be satisfied with the assertion that the first step, that is, knowing that there is an external, material object, even if that object is unreal, could be described just

as the having of a clear conception of that the reality of which is in question. This makes the a priori status of the connection between the two steps explicit. As Richard Fumerton remarks,"One ought to accept the responsibility of analyzing propositions about the physical world in such a way that one accounts for the fact that we believe them and believe we are justified in so doing."[7] And our present objection to the mental-contents theorist would be that she is unable to explain how such a conception and such beliefs (judgments) would be arrived at. To just suppose that this can be done in some manner or other, and that then we can come to have knowledge of the existence of the object, would be to engage in empty speculation. It is worth remembering that Berkeley's chief argument against the existence of material objects was that we have no conception of such objects. This argument has no force against direct realism; if direct realism is true, then the (ordinary, not the scientific) conception of a material object is derived from the perceptual awareness of what it is a conception of, and so there is not the slightest reason for thinking that we don't have this conception. And it is quite obvious why we judge (even if mistakenly) that material objects exist and why we judge (even if mistakenly) that we are justified in judging this: we *perceive* material objects. A realism that is based on a mental-contents theory, on the other hand, *is* faced with Berkeley's objection, and I don't think it has an answer to it; a fortiori, it has no answer to the question why we judge that material objects exist and that we are justified in judging this. Let me explain further.

First, there is the difficulty of making clear what the "contents" of our minds are supposed to be, and indeed that there are any such things at all. Appeals to vague ordinary notions, such as those of idea and sensation, or to technical notions of doubtful intelligibility, such as those of a sense datum (as ordinarily understood by philosophers, as a private, mental entity, not as, following G. E. Moore, I suggested in chapter 1 it could be understood), or a way of being appeared to, or a "representation" (whether mental or physical), are hardly helpful. Second, there is the difficulty of explaining why our mental contents should prompt us to believe, without any inference usually, that there are real *material* objects before us. Third, if as philosophers we attempt such an inference, presumably by an appeal to "the best explanation," and if by a good explanation we mean in part a deep one, then it is not at all clear that the object, the existence of which we ought to infer from our mental contents, would be at all like what we ordinarily mean by a material object. The esoteric "objects" of quantum physics would seem far more suitable, but, as I shall point out presently, inferences to them appeal, in however chaotic a fashion, to facts about nonesoteric, ordinary material objects. And, fourth, the validity of the inference would be quite questionable. The validity of ordinary scientific inferences to "the best explanation" is notoriously difficult to understand and defend, partly because of the vagueness of the notion of "the best explanation," indeed of the general notion of explanation, to which I drew attention in the previous chapter. And, as we have seen, in the case under

consideration we bear the additional burden of being most unclear about the explanandum, since the explanandum is supposed to be such things as ideas and sensations, not familiar characteristics of material objects and events, such as readings of instruments, which are what in fact we appeal to in science. Scientific inferences to the best explanation proceed ultimately from what are taken to be facts about directly observable material objects and we have no conception of what these inferences would be like if they did not, if they proceeded from alleged facts about "mental contents." All four difficulties are familiar from the history of modern philosophy and do not need further exploration here.[8]

Now the case with the direct realist conception is very different. According to it (again, I shall use G. E. Moore's vivid words), "Merely to have a sensation is already to *be* outside . . . the circle of our own ideas and sensations."[9] Moore continued this sentence by saying, "It is to know something which is as truly *not* a part of *my* experience, as anything which I can ever know." I assume that he did not mean to deny that there could be hallucinations and dreams. I take his point to be that to have a sensation, in the sense he used this term, for example, a sensation of (something) blue, can only be to be in direct epistemic contact with something, an object, which is not a part of one's perceptual consciousness. But that object need not be a real object, and in the article from which I have quoted, Moore says nothing about how we can know that it is real. Nevertheless, on the direct realist view, we can be assured that at least *there is* an object we perceive, and the problem is how to find out the *further* fact about it (*if* it is a fact) that the object exists, is real. We may have no adequate philosophical solution of this problem, but in ordinary life we think we have a very clear idea of how to go about resolving it (in particular cases, with respect to which alone it is here relevant), and the general nature of the challenge is also clear—it is not such that it renders the possibility of our meeting it obviously implausible, as in the case of any mental-contents theory.

Our task is, in general, that of explaining how we may discover that a certain object before us has, in addition to the properties it is given as having, also another property or, better, characteristic or feature, namely, reality, which it is not (and probably, as Kant argued, cannot be) *given* as having. Presumably, the reason this feature is not given is not that it is somehow hidden. It might not be given simply because it is, very broadly speaking, a highly complex relational property which, at least to human minds, cannot be given as a whole. The relational property may be coherence with other objects, or, as I shall argue later, indefinite identifiability by oneself and by others. There is no need to take a stand here on its exact nature; I shall do so in chapter 5. But its not being given as some of the other characteristics of the object are given need not mean that there is something mysterious about it. This is why a view such as Sartre's or Moore's, though it does not answer the question whether we know, or even have evidence, in some particular perceptual situation, that there is a real material object before us, at least makes it not obviously implausible that

an answer can be found. The mental-contents view, on the contrary, makes this quite implausible. To that extent the direct realist view is not only superior as a phenomenological account of the nature of perceptual consciousness, but indispensable for any adequate answer to skepticism.

2. The Kind of Answer We Need

At the end of chapter 3 I seemed to have exhausted all possibilities of answering Descartes's dream-argument. Direct realism may offer us the prospect that an answer can be found but does not constitute such an answer. If at no time do we know or even have evidence that we are not dreaming, then surely at no time do we know or have evidence that we perceive real material objects. And since all empirical knowledge and evidentially based judgment about material objects, both in everyday life and in science, presuppose perceptual knowledge and evidence, we have no empirical knowledge or even evidentially based judgments about material objects, about an external world. So, the skeptic seems to have won.

But let us remember that there is also what I called the *general* question, namely, Do we know or at least have evidence that there exist perceivable material objects in general, that an external world exists? If we had been able to answer what I called the *particular* question, Do we know or at least have evidence, in at least one particular perceptual situation, that there exists a material object before us? we would have had also an answer to the general question. But perhaps we can answer the general question even if we cannot answer the particular question. As we recall, this was the deeper lesson to be learned from Wittgenstein's objections to the dream-argument. We may know that some material objects are real, without knowing with respect to any one in particular that it is real. How may we know this? Clearly, not in any of the familiar ways we have already considered of trying to answer the particular question in the context of Descartes's dream-argument. Perhaps our best hope lies in finding a reductio ad absurdum argument, but only if we use the term "absurdity" in its ordinary sense, not in the sense of formal contradiction.

This approach is a familiar theme in discussions of skepticism. For example, Hume eloquently pointed out the impossibility of genuine, sustained withdrawal of assent from the propositions the skeptic challenges. And there are the arguments, usually called transcendental, that skepticism is conceptually incoherent or even self-refuting, because it implies the incoherence of our conceptual scheme, which it itself employs. In what follows I shall offer a different reductio ad absurdum argument against the skeptic. I shall be concerned with a less familiar implication of skepticism regarding the reality of the external world. It resembles Hume's point (I do not believe he intended it as an *argument* against skepticism—any arguments from the unlivability or the irrelevance of skepticism to our everyday decisions are blatantly question-begging), and like it might be said to be essentially psychological, thus needing to be distinguished from the ar-

guments alleging conceptual incoherence or self-refutation, which may be called logical. It is different from Hume's point, since, unlike the latter, it will not focus on the unbelievability or even unlivability of the skeptic's conclusion, which the skeptic may be the first to admit. The skeptic we (unlike psychiatrists) are interested in is a philosopher, and a philosopher has the professional obligation "to follow the argument wherever it may lead," regardless of her personal beliefs and circumstances. Hence the impropriety, at least in a philosophical context, of Robert J. Fogelin's distinction between what he calls "theoretical skepticism" and "prescriptive skepticism."[10]

And my argument will differ from what I have called the logical arguments in that it will not depend on the acceptance of highly abstruse, technical philosophical theories about conceptual cognition, meaning, and understanding, which are at least as controversial as the skeptic's argument and in most of their versions beg the question against it. It is strategically incoherent to address such abstruse arguments to one who questions whether, to use G. E. Moore's example, there are such things as human hands. For example, my argument will not rely on Crispin Wright's suggestion that "cogent intellection" (such as the skeptic's reasoning) is just as incompatible with dreaming as is (veridical) perception, a claim explicitly denied by Descartes and defended by Wright on the basis of the assumption (which I reject) that the difference between cogent and illusory intellection as well as the difference between (veridical) perception and dreaming are at least in part aetiological.[11] My argument will be much more modest and for that reason, I hope, more likely to be adequate.

In accordance with the strategy of this book, announced in the introduction and chapter 3, namely, to attempt to solve the chief epistemological problem by bypassing epistemology, my argument will focus on the implications of the general *nonepistemic* proposition that there are no material objects, *not* on the implications of the general *epistemic* proposition that we do not know, or even have evidence, that there are material objects. Of course, by definition, the skeptic asserts the epistemic proposition; he does not deny that there are material objects. This is why I began with and took seriously the epistemic proposition. Yet, if the implications of the nonepistemic proposition are absurd, then this may be a sufficient reason for regarding the epistemic proposition as false. It may be a reason strong enough to justify our holding even that we know that there are material objects. My hesitancy on this, and my use of the vague word "justify," are due to the fact that the argument I shall offer is sufficiently peculiar as to leave unclear whether it renders the concepts of knowledge and of judgment based on evidence applicable to its conclusion. But then this is exactly what should be expected from our strategy. We do not *want* to stay in the rut of standard epistemology. In addition, since there is more to knowledge and evidentially based judgment than truth (indeed, according to the standard view, an evidentially based judgment need not be true at all), any attempted reductio ad absurdum argument, even if successful, against the

epistemic proposition may tell us nothing about what we are really interested in, namely, the nonepistemic proposition, for the absurdity may be due solely to features of the concepts of knowledge and evidentially based judgment other than truth. For example, a Gettier-type argument against the epistemic proposition would depend entirely on the vagaries of the concept of knowledge in terms of which it is understood, and have no bearing whatever on the truth of the corresponding nonepistemic proposition. I may be wrong in thinking that I know that a certain person owns a Ford but not at all wrong in thinking that the person does own a Ford. An example closer to our topic would be that of being wrong in thinking that I know there is a real barn before me, if unbeknownst to me there are many fake barns in the area, even though there *is* a real barn before me. To be sure, these cases arise because of the acceptance of a conception of knowledge (that of justified true belief) that, as I indirectly argued in chapter 3, should never have been taken seriously. But something similar may also happen to a reductio argument of ours against the skeptic's epistemic proposition.

3. The Skeptic's General Question Answered

It is of the very essence of all reductio arguments in support of our belief in the reality of an external world that they recognize how extraordinarily fundamental that belief is. In the previous chapter I argued that the dream argument is the most intuitive and readily comprehensible of the several skeptical arguments, and offered the best defense of it I could manage. But I did not argue that its conclusion is to be accepted or even that it is believable. (Clearly, it's not. Anyone who really did not believe that he could ever tell dreams from reality would be counted as insane, not as a profound philosopher.) But here I want to draw attention to a way of recognizing this that is less familiar than the usual, for example, Hume's, way. It is far less general, quite nontechnical, yet closer to our philosophical home. Unlike Hume's, it is of a purely philosophical nature. But it rests on no philosophical (and therefore controversial) assumptions. It begins with the observation that the skeptic's *general* epistemic proposition, that we do not know or even have evidence that material objects, an external world, exist, is one that, by definition, only a philosopher would assert or even entertain; at least, by definition, it is one that only a philosopher can defend with reasoning that is at all adequate. (The dream-argument may be simple but, as we have seen, the defense of it must be highly sophisticated.) A corollary of this observation is that the only rational basis for asserting this proposition is the skeptic's *philosophical* reasoning. And my argument is concerned with that reasoning itself. There are two parts of the argument. Both rely on the fact that the really challenging sort of skepticism is a complex, highly sophisticated, technical, professional view. It is by no means just Descartes's brief argument that he could not tell whether he was dreaming or awake. Descartes's project, after all, was not to defend the

skeptical position, but to refute it. Hume's philosophy would be a better example of the sort of sophisticated and detailed skepticism I have in mind. But perhaps the best example I can give of sophisticated skeptical reasoning is the Cartesian dream-argument developed, even if not exactly embraced, in Barry Stroud's *The Significance of Philosophical Scepticism*.[12] In chapter 3 I stated the skeptic's argument using Descartes's dream-argument as my example because of its intuitive power, freedom from questionable assumptions (with which Hume's philosophy is rife), and the relative ease with which the standard objections to skepticism (coherentist, abductive, etc.) could be answered in the case of that argument. And for these reasons it will be the explicit target of the counterargument I shall offer here, although it will be evident that if my counterargument is successful it will apply to any version of skepticism about the external world. Of course, just as in chapter 3 I went far beyond what Descartes said or even could have said in his time, so will I in this chapter.

The first part of my argument begins with the observation that skepticism regarding the reality of material objects concerns also the reality of other people, since there are people (who are not mere souls) only if there are human bodies, and human bodies are material objects. And our view of ourselves largely depends on our regarding ourselves as members of a community of people which has had a certain history. We regard most of our knowledge as having been obtained from other people, and most of the language we speak, including that employed in technical reasoning, as having been learned from other people. Now, to even *suppose* that there exist no material objects (this is the general *nonepistemic* proposition), that the external world is one great illusion, is therefore to suppose also that the reasoning that leads us to this extraordinary supposition, which only a philosopher would make and the only basis for which is that philosophical reasoning, is itself, in a peculiar but deeply disturbing way, illusory. (I do not say that it is senseless or conceptually incoherent or self-refuting.) For, as G. E. Moore pointed out in "A Defense of Common Sense," it is to suppose that *philosophers* do not exist, have never existed, will never exist.[13] In effect it is to suppose that philosophy itself does not exist, even though the skeptical conclusion, insofar as it deserves philosophical consideration at all, is believed to arise out of philosophy, indeed to be a part of philosophy, since it is the result of *professional* philosophical reasoning (in the broad sense of "professional" that implies nothing about social position or source of income). Even the skeptic is not a philosopher, that is, a human being with a certain fairly extensive training, whether formal or informal.

The skeptical reasoning takes place in what we *believe* to be the context of our knowledge of philosophy, which is inseparable from what we believe to be our knowledge of the history of philosophy, for example, of Descartes's and Hume's works, from what we believe we have read in current philosophical books and journals, the lectures we believe we have heard in classrooms, and the discussions in which we believe we have en-

gaged in seminar rooms. We believe that the philosophical reasoning that leads to the skeptical conclusion takes place in, and depends on, at least the *philosophical* social and historical circumstances in which we find ourselves. Notoriously, we believe that a philosopher is to a very large extent a creature of her teachers, and more generally of the environment in which she happens to be. Even when she strikes out on her own, the marks of how she began stay with her. We believe that we inherit from our teachers philosophical attitudes, interests, and orientations that play a major role in what we do as philosophers. One takes skepticism seriously, or instead dismisses it as a purely technical puzzle, often because of one's teachers' attitudes toward and arguments about skepticism. And this is true even when one forms one's own attitudes and arguments in opposition to those of one's teachers, even when one rebels. Moreover, the skeptic almost certainly believes that he is *writing*, or has *written*, his exposition and defense of skepticism, probably going through many versions of the paper or book, if he is professionally responsible. Probably he believes he has lectured on skepticism many times before students and colleagues, and has tested his arguments in private discussions with other philosophers. He probably expects or at least hopes that his arguments as written down in papers or books will be read and appreciated by other philosophers. Indeed, ordinarily his aim is to convince *other* philosophers that he is right!

If material objects did not exist, none of these beliefs would be true, this dependence of the skeptic's reasoning on material objects, whether philosophers or his own scribblings on paper, would be purely illusory. Of course, the skeptic would not include any of these beliefs (judgments) as premises of his argument, for if he did he would be inconsistent in the special but important sense that his conclusion would entail that he does not know or even have evidence that all of his premises are true, and my argument against him would then be that *in that sense* skepticism is inconsistent and therefore *in a corresponding sense* self-refuting. My much more modest argument, however, is only that the judgments in question, though not part of the skeptic's argument, must nevertheless be presupposed by the skeptic if he is to *take his own argument seriously*. Without them, the skeptic would have to understand his own skepticism as originating, so to speak, *ex nihilo*. It is not that he could not state it coherently or consistently, but rather, I suggest, that he could not take it *seriously* as a *philosopher*, not merely (as Hume held) as a human being, that he could not take *his own* skepticism seriously as the conclusion of a professional philosophical argument, just as we do not take seriously what goes on in a dream if we judge that it is a dream. If you dream that you have inherited one million dollars but judge (as you might well do) that you are just dreaming, or at least are uncertain that you are not, you would not count yourself a millionaire. But when I speak of his not taking his own argument seriously I don't mean merely that the skeptic does not actually cease to believe in the external world as a result of the argument, that the skeptic does not actually believe his own conclusion. As I pointed out in the introduction,

whether he does or does not is philosophically irrelevant. I mean that the skeptic can not take his argument seriously as *an argument*. Yet that argument is the only basis for his skeptical conclusion as a philosopher.

The second part of my argument also concerns the skeptic's philosophical reasoning but does not appeal to his beliefs about its social and historical setting. It begins by noting that he would ordinarily claim that his reasoning is a priori, at least in the sense that it is not based on perceptual evidence. Of course a premise such as that perception does not entail the reality of its objects, or that there need not be any intrinsic difference between perception in a dream and a perception when awake, might not be a priori in the usual sense of the term, though this is not obvious. But I shall ignore this terminological complication, allow the skeptic to hold that his ultimate premises are all a priori, and recall that, as Descartes indeed held, a priori judgments would not be invalidated by being made in a dream. But any sustained argument or reasoning, such as the skeptic's dream-argument, even if intended to be a priori, takes time; it involves relying on memory, on a continuing, steady, and sober grasp of a manifold of connections. And surely one's memory of these would be far more doubtful if it occurred in a dream than it would be if it occurred in wakeful life. Since knowledge based on memory is not purely a priori, even if it is knowledge of truths knowable a priori, the a priori knowledge the dreamer could have would be limited to immediately, noninferentially apprehended truths. But the conclusion of the skeptic's reasoning is hardly such a truth, and therefore it must presuppose at least that his memory of the earlier steps of her reasoning is veridical. Such dependence on memory may not matter in ordinary cases of reasoning from a priori premises, though Hume argued that it did. But, obviously, it does matter in the case of a complex reasoning that takes place in a dream.

Indeed, since dreaming is only a kind of nonveridical *perception*, we cannot argue that our very conception of a dream is such that one who seems to remember something in a dream only dreams that one remembers it, any more than we can argue that one who experiences joy or fear in a dream only dreams that one experiences joy or fear (the joy or fear often stays with one even after awakening). Nevertheless, while the dream-memory may be veridical, if what is remembered is a perception that occurred in the dream or anything inferred from such a perception, directly or indirectly, the memory would have no evidential worth regarding the object of the perception, for the perception had no evidential worth that the memory could inherit from it, since (as explained in chapter 3) no dream-perception has evidential worth. Of course, the skeptic's reasoning might not rely on perceptual memories. But at each stage it must rely on memory of the earlier stages of the reasoning itself. And ordinarily one's confidence with respect to any memory that it is veridical is to some extent a function of one's confidence that one's present and past perceptions are veridical. For example, my confidence in the veridicality of my memory of what I read on page 76 of a certain book is reinforced by my confidence that it is

continuous with, that it fits in with, what I judge I now *see* on page 77, and also by what I remember to have seen on page 75. And if I am engaged in serious philosophical reasoning, I try to keep track of it by recording it on *paper* (perhaps tape or disk). The skeptic cannot, without abandoning her skepticism, hold that memory of the earlier stages of her reasoning receives that sort of reinforcement (though it can be reinforced by cohering with her other judgments and memories). Even if the judgments made at those stages were purely a priori, the memory of them, it would seem, still needs perceptual reinforcement, if not by perceptual knowledge of discussions with other philosophers and of books and articles, at least by perceptual knowledge of what the skeptic has put on *paper*. A serious, complex philosophical reasoning can be done "in one's head," but a professional philosopher would not place much trust in it until it has been presented to other philosophers or at least has been put down on paper and then checked out by herself—often going through many sheets of paper, containing detailed expositions of various actual or possible objections to the reasoning and of her replies to those objections (there had better be replies if the reasoning is accepted). But, by definition, the skeptic cannot assume that she has talked to other philosophers about her argument or that she has put it on paper. Philosophers are, at least in part, material objects, and paper is a sort of material stuff. My point is not Crispin Wright's, which I mentioned earlier, that "cogent intellection," including the sustained and subtle intellection that any skeptical argument worth considering represents, cannot take place in a dream, but that the skeptic cannot take its outcome seriously unless she assumes that it did not take place in a dream.

In general, with respect to both parts of the argument, we must remember that the interesting sort of skepticism is that involving sophistication, knowledge of numerous relevant distinctions and considerations, awareness of modes of argument, and the employment of all these in a sustained process of some duration. (Of course, these conditions need be satisfied only to a reasonable degree. No exceptional erudition or reasoning ability is required!) For example, the skeptic must have a good grasp of the literature on causality, since many antiskeptical arguments appeal to causal considerations. The skeptic must have a good grasp of the literature on inference to the best explanation, again since many antiskeptical arguments rely on such inferences. Numerous other examples can be given. We all know that the sophomoric skeptic is easily silenced by his fellow sophomores' objections, for example, that he can tell whether he is dreaming by pinching himself, or that, like Dr. Johnson, he can prove that there are material objects by kicking a stone. The mark of a professional philosophical position is that it takes into account, and offers responses to, the objections it has faced or may face. And this, we believe, is only possible if one has considerable knowledge of what other philosophers have said and written, and of one's extensive exposition on paper of one's own arguments. However intuitively powerful Descartes's dream-argument may be, to rest a skeptical position just on it and fail to consider the very many antiskeptical views

(e.g., Kant's, Wittgenstein's) that have been proposed and defended in detail, and to fail to write down, also in detail, one's responses to them, would be a mark of philosophical ignorance or irresponsibility. It would be unprofessional. It would be what a sophomore, who has just read Descartes, might hold after a couple of beers.

Combining the two parts of my argument, I can state it briefly as follows. We would ask the skeptic who denies that he can tell that he is dreaming or that he is awake whether if he were to suppose that he is dreaming he would take his skepticism as a serious *philosophical* view, one arrived at in possession of extensive knowledge, and through careful consideration, of the various alternatives, concepts, distinctions, subsidiary arguments, objections, replies to objections, all of which are what we ordinarily believe one learns, through years of training as a philosopher, mainly from the writings, lectures, and discussions of other philosophers, ancient, medieval, modern, and contemporary, none of whom would have existed if material objects did not exist. My argument is that if the skeptic supposed that he is dreaming, he would have to acknowledge that he would not take his skepticism as a serious philosophical view. This would be so even if the skeptic supposed that he arrived at his skeptical conclusion in a rich and vivid dream that duplicated what ordinarily leads to it: the knowledge of the history of philosophy, and so forth.[14] Of course, the skeptic does not deny the general *nonepistemic* proposition that (some) material objects exist, but only the general *epistemic* proposition that he knows or even has evidence that they do. My argument is intended to show that the skeptic cannot take his own skepticism seriously unless he takes for granted that nonepistemic proposition, and thus takes for granted exactly what he claims to not know or even have evidence for. (I shall not consider the possibility that the skeptic merely denies that he knows that there are material objects but affirms that he has evidence for their existence, though not evidence sufficient for knowledge, and that he can take his skeptical argument seriously because of his possession of that evidence. Such a position would be inconsistent with the skeptic's general argument, explained in section 7 of chapter 3. It would ignore the fact that the challenge of answering the skeptic is largely that of making clear such a notion of evidence. At any rate, as we have seen, in the case now under consideration it would be question-begging, since in a dream nothing counts even as mere evidence for the existence of material objects.)

It seems reasonable therefore to accept the proposition that an external world of material objects exists, at least insofar as it includes the historical institution of philosophy, and also paper and writing instruments. So we can reject the skeptic's claim that we do not know or even have evidence that there are material objects. But this rejection need not imply that we *do* know or at least have evidence that material objects exist. Rejection is not a claim to refutation. We have not refuted the skeptic, we have not proved and thus provided ourselves with knowledge that there is an external world. To have expected such refutation and proof would have been un-

reasonable, as I suggested in the Introduction. I have not shown that skepticism involves contradiction or conceptual incoherence or any other familiar epistemic defect. I have not made the Hegelian claim that a philosophical position or concept logically (or metaphysically, or conceptually) presupposes a historical setting and therefore entails the existence of that setting. Such a claim would be too questionable to serve as an answer to the skeptic. Nor have I appealed to how in fact philosophical positions and concepts are arrived at, in particular that they are arrived at in a historical, intersubjective setting, for such an appeal would have been flagrantly question-begging against the skeptic. But the argument I have offered does provide a reason for *rejecting* skepticism with regard to the general question, since the alternative to its conclusion is that material objects do not exist, and this entails (as I have explained in some detail) that the skeptical reasoning cannot be taken seriously. Put somewhat paradoxically, the reason for rejecting skepticism is that the more seriously the skeptic takes the conclusion of his reasoning, that is, that for all he knows or has evidence about, material objects do not exist, the less seriously can he take that reasoning.

This reason for rejecting skepticism is of course epistemic in character but it is hardly describable as evidence, whether demonstrative or nondemonstrative, since it bears little resemblance to the paradigmatic kinds of evidence: deductive, inductive, abductive, and so forth. It is not just a psychological reason, at least not in the way Hume's was; after all, it concerns the question whether a certain *argument* can be taken seriously *as an argument*. We might call it a dialectical reason, since our argument resembles some arguments that Socrates employed. But, of course, nothing prevents us from calling it psychological, as long as we clearly distinguish it from Hume's and others' claims about the unbelievability or even the unlivability of skepticism. What we call it does not matter. What matters is whether it stands or falls on its own. But surely this is as it should be. Surely the time when we could expect to argue against skepticism in familiar ways is long gone. We can redeem traditional epistemology only by bypassing it.

At most the skeptic can reply that if he cannot take his reasoning seriously, neither can his opponent. But this would not be a happy dialectical ploy. Indeed, if I were to suppose seriously that I was dreaming while developing my antiskeptical argument, I would be unable to take this argument seriously, just as the skeptic would be unable to take his argument seriously. But I am not supposing that I am dreaming. The skeptic is. *He* faces the difficulty my argument poses because he makes that supposition. *I* do not. My argument in effect points out a peculiar inconsistency, dissonance, absurdity in the skeptic's position. The moral to be drawn is not that my argument begs the question against the skeptic but that if the supposition against which it is directed, namely, that one is dreaming now, or that material objects do not exist at all, is taken seriously, as by definition it must be so taken by the skeptic, even though of course not claimed by him to be

known to be true or to be based on evidence, then it is impossible to take seriously *any* complex, sophisticated, genuinely philosophical argument.

But couldn't the skeptic respond by saying that what she can or cannot take seriously does not matter, that the only issue is whether her argument is sound, that is, both valid and having only true premises? Well, on the assumption that she wishes to assure herself of its soundness, how would she do so? It is a complex argument (think of Stroud's exposition and defense of it), and to determine whether it is valid one must survey it and at each step remember the previous steps. I have already drawn attention to the problem of relying on memory if material objects do not exist. What about the truth of the premises? Presumably, one premise is that there is no intrinsic difference between one's perceptual consciousness when dreaming and one's perceptual consciousness when awake. Is this premise true? Does the skeptic rely just on her own experience? That too would involve memory, but the new problem is that she can hardly be sure that she has not just failed to notice some intrinsic difference. The truth is that the skeptic who accepts this premise does so largely on authority, on her judgments about what Descartes, many other philosophers (e.g., Stroud), some psychologists, and her friends and acquaintances have written or said about the subject, on her judgment that she is sufficiently familiar with the literature not to have missed some well-known evidence that the premise is not true. Moreover, has she taken into account the *possible* objections to her premise? She may have thought of some of them on her own, but surely she assumes that there are likely to be many that have never occurred to her. Does she look for them in the existing literature, to find out what, for example, Austin, Wittgenstein, and Malcolm have written on dreaming? Does she ask her colleagues for help? But if there are no material objects there is no such literature and there have never been such persons as Austin, Wittgenstein, Malcolm, and her colleagues.

I have been concerned with skepticism with regard to the senses. But the reader may have become aware that my argument against it is also an argument against skepticism with regard to the existence of a past and of other minds. Indeed, it includes such arguments, though perhaps it does not include or imply an argument against skepticism with regard to induction. The presupposition of the existence of a past and of other minds is essential to the performance of the sophisticated philosophical procedure that leads to skepticism. And my argument is also, implicitly, an argument against skepticism with regard to reason, though now for a familiar reason: the skeptic's argument, to be taken seriously, must itself be supposed to constitute a defensible exercise of reason. So we arrive at the perhaps unexpected conclusion that if skepticism with regard to the senses is rejected for the reasons I have given, skepticism with regard to reason and with regard to the existence of a past and of other minds can also be rejected. But I shall not develop this point here, even though if correct it would be of philosophical importance. I shall only note the reasons for my reservations regarding skepticism about induction.

In the case of perception, the past, and other minds, the skeptic questions the reality of what she herself takes, explicitly or implicitly, to constitute the context of her reasoning, indeed of any serious, informed, sophisticated philosophical reasoning. This is not so with induction. The skeptic regarding induction does not question the reality of material objects, though perhaps she ought to do so if our knowledge of, or evidence for, the latter is necessarily in part inductive (a disputable assumption on which it would be premature to take a stand now, before chapter 6). She only questions that we have knowledge or rational judgments based on past experience; the veridicality of that experience she does not question. The most obvious such knowledge and judgments are those about the future. The skeptic probably does presuppose the truth of some such judgments, for example, that she will live long enough to complete the page she is writing. And if she did not, then her reasoning might well come to a stop. But it need not. Her reasoning could still proceed even if she did not make that presupposition. She may be willing to gamble! Contrast this with skepticism regarding perception. Its conclusion is that our judgments about the existence of material objects have no support worth having. This implies that for all we know or have reason to believe there have never been any philosophers, or philosophical books and papers, or philosophical lectures and discussions, or our own scribblings on paper. I have argued that one who reaches this conclusion cannot take her own reasoning seriously. But one who reaches the conclusion that for all she knows or has reason to believe she may not live long enough to finish the page she is writing *can* take her reasoning seriously, though also perhaps become rather pessimistic about its future.

If we take the implications of the skeptic's argument into account, then we are apt to see the skeptic's position as not unlike that of the logician Mrs. Christine Ladd-Franklin, who is reported by Bertrand Russell to have written to him that she was a solipsist and was surprised that there were no other solipsists.[15] There are important differences between the two positions, of course, but the similarity is that Ladd-Franklin could not have taken her solipsism seriously.

Am I not begging the question against the skeptic by describing the reasoning skeptics engage in or at least ought to engage in if they are professional philosophers? No. It is sufficient for my purposes to take what I have been describing to be, not what *other* philosophers do and can or cannot take seriously, but what *I* do and can or cannot take seriously when engaged in skeptical reasoning. And my argument is that, given what I believe to be the facts about my own skeptical reasoning (not merely hypothetical—I have engaged in it in the past, have written on it, have rehearsed it in front of students, and indeed at one time accepted Hume's skeptical conclusions!), I cannot take it seriously and therefore cannot be a skeptic. The conclusion applies, of course, to anyone else who may have engaged in a sufficiently similar reasoning. It is possible that a philosophical mind superior to mine would work out the skeptical argument entirely on its own,

without relying on judgments about other philosophers, about books, lectures, conversations, indeed perhaps even instantaneously and thus without writing or relying even on memory. But I don't have such a mind, and any worked-out skeptical reasoning I can perform and of which I have a clear, distinct, and detailed conception would be subject to my argument. Of course, I can speak only for myself, as I should, given the requirement that no questions against the skeptic be begged. In speaking of the skeptic I have been speaking of myself in one role I think I can play and indeed have played, which I believe has been played by other philosophers, but I do not assume in my argument that this belief is true.

I defined the skeptic with whom we are concerned as one who gives a negative answer to the two (nonmodal) epistemic questions I have called the particular and the general question. Since we are concerned here only with the general question, and only with a skeptic who gives her answers on the basis of a sophisticated, professionally responsible, genuinely philosophical argument, let us, for our present purposes, restrict the word "skeptic" to one who holds, on the basis of a sophisticated, professionally responsible, genuinely philosophical argument, that we do not know or even have any evidence that material objects exist; and let us restrict the phrase "skeptical argument" to the argument on the basis of which the skeptic holds this. Now my counterargument can be summarized in just three sentences. (1) Unless we hold, explicitly or implicitly, that material objects exist, we can take no skeptical argument seriously. But, (2) a skeptical argument is the only basis for holding that we do not know or even have any evidence that material objects exist. Therefore, (3) we can take seriously the only basis for holding that we do not know or even have any evidence that material objects exist only if we hold, explicitly or implicitly, that material objects exist.

The argument is valid. I think the second premise is unquestionable. And most of what I have said in this section has been a defense of the first premise. If I am the author of the skeptical argument, then of course I cannot take it seriously, for the reasons I have given in detail. If someone else is, I cannot take it seriously if for no other reason than that the person and his spoken or written argument would be material objects, the sort of objects the existence of which is just what the skeptical argument questions. Can the other person take his argument seriously? He would have to be a philosopher who does not take for granted that his argument has any connections to what has been said or written by other philosophers, or that it has been put down on paper or developed in a lecture, or that there may be a mistake in its earlier, now just remembered, stages. I cannot take such a philosopher seriously, and he should not take himself seriously.

Nevertheless, the modesty of my argument should be evident. And, in keeping with the counsel offered in the Introduction, this is as it should be. We would have been wasting our time if we sought a conclusive argument against the skeptic. It might have been less modest if we could assume (1) that a judgment is "innocent until proven guilty," that there is a presump-

tion in favor of the truth of the judgment that material objects exist, unless there is a good reason for thinking that it is false; and (2) that the skeptic's argument, which alone could be such a reason, is not a good reason. I have tried to argue for 2. But I would not accept 1, and at any rate would not wish to appeal to it since it is a controversial *epistemological* assumption. My argument would have been even less modest if we could assume (3) that every skeptical argument contains premises entailing the existence of material objects; my argument then would have been what I called a logical argument, in particular, one charging incoherence though not self-refutation (since the skeptic does not deny the existence of material objects, he only questions it). But 3 is clearly false, since a careful skeptic can always avoid such premises and still state his argument. (For example, instead of the premise "It is generally recognized that there is no intrinsic difference between wakeful and dream experiences," he could simply say, "There is no intrinsic difference between wakeful and dream experiences.") Of course, I have argued that even then the philosophical skeptic takes such revised premises seriously only because he makes related judgments that do entail the existence of material objects. But these related judgments need not be part of his argument. I have merely claimed that the skeptic takes (or ought to take) his own reasoning *seriously* only if he holds these judgments to be true.

Moreover, my argument concerns only the general question. We still face the particular question. To be sure, we could argue that even in a particular case, with regard to a particular perceived object, one can take seriously one's *philosophical* reasoning that leads to the conclusion that one does not know or even have evidence that one is not dreaming only if one takes for granted, explicitly or implicitly, that one has not been dreaming while engaged in that reasoning, and thus that the reasoning cannot be taken seriously. But, and this is the power of Descartes's dream-argument, which led us to focus on it, one need not engage in any philosophical reasoning or indeed even be a philosopher to ask innocently, at any one time, Do I know or even have evidence that I am not dreaming now? perhaps not even giving an answer to the question, whether skeptical or nonskeptical, or giving an answer but one that is not backed by an argument at all. If someone asks me this question about herself, it would be absurd for me to try to help her by giving her this chapter to read. It would be absurd to suppose that my argument in this chapter, even if sound, can be used to answer that sort of question whenever and by whoever it is asked, that this chapter can serve as a manual to be kept in one's pocket for consultation whenever one is tempted to ask such a question. The judgments that material objects do not exist, or at least that we do not know or even have evidence that they do, or that we can *never* tell whether we are dreaming or awake, are strictly philosophical and for that reason deserve philosophical attention only if backed by philosophical reasoning. Therefore, they are vulnerable to my argument. But the judgment "I am dreaming now" is not philosophical; it is sometimes made in everyday *particular* cases. Yet it deserves philo-

sophical attention even if not backed by a philosophical argument. The attention it deserves would consist in trying to determine whether in a particular situation we can know or at least have evidence that it is false, and if we can, what sort of knowledge or evidence that would be. We might conclude that we cannot have the needed knowledge or evidence, that with respect to the particular question the skeptic is right, even if wrong with respect to the general question, as I have argued. Let me repeat that skepticism about the latter entails skepticism about the former, but not vice versa. If I do not know that material objects exist then I do not know that this computer exists, but I may know that material objects exist, perhaps through a kind of divine guarantee, even if I do not know that this computer exists, perhaps because I do not know that I am not dreaming now. Of course, one can ask the particular question without considering the possibility of dreaming, one can ask it even when taking for granted that one is awake, as in fact it has been asked by most philosophers of perception. There is more than one way to skepticism. It's just that Descartes's dream-argument is the most compelling one.

If we accept the argument I have offered against skepticism about the external world, then our conclusion would be not unlike Descartes's, which I mentioned in the introduction.[16] Descartes thought he had in God's existence a guarantee of the *general* judgment that material objects, an external world, do exist. But with respect to *particular* judgments about the existence of material objects he merely advised, in the Sixth Meditation, that we suspend them when they exceeded our knowledge. He said very little about exactly what that knowledge is (though he explicitly appealed to the criterion of coherence) or how it relates logically to the judgments in question, yet, surprisingly, he claimed that, having proved the existence of God, he could tell whether he was dreaming or awake. It is fair to say that while Descartes had an answer (even if perhaps unsatisfactory) to our general question, he did not have anything deserving to be called an answer to the particular question. Whether he was aware of this fact, I cannot judge. Our conclusion also resembles Kant's view that the coherence, the unity, of the representations of inner sense presupposes the reality in general of the objects of outer sense, even though he had very little to say about how we might determine the reality of any particular object of outer sense; it also resembles Kant's view that we have synthetic a priori knowledge that every event has a cause but at best only empirical knowledge of the cause of any particular event, about which again he had very little to say.

4. Concluding Remarks

My reductio argument can be employed by many philosophers, including those who accept the mental-contents theory. But it fits the direct realist conception of consciousness far better, and it has much greater plausibility if combined with it, because an essential feature of this conception is that consciousness consists in a direct relation to what *might* be a real

world, and therefore that we are directly given that the reality of which our reductio attempts to protect from the skeptic's argument. It does not require the intermediate step its rivals require, namely, an explanation of how we even come to have a conception of something other than ourselves, in particular of material objects such as pebbles, lakes, mountains, books, and philosophers, a conception which we do not acquire by abstruse philosophical or scientific reasoning, and the possession of which the reductio arguments employed by the opponents of direct realism presuppose but surely cannot themselves explain. The explicit and implicit judgments about material objects, such as that there are philosophers and pieces of paper, which I have argued constitute the context of any skeptical argument deserving to be taken seriously, are certainly not arrived at by the *skeptic* through any inference; he questions precisely such inferences. If we are to avoid begging the question against him, we must say that ultimately they can be arrived at only directly, even if they are false, through the direct confrontation of some material objects, even if these are unreal. (Fortunately, this is not just a requirement my argument must meet; it happens also to be the plain truth!) My argument in the previous section could not even begin without the direct realist conception of consciousness. If so, then the direct realist view of consciousness is epistemologically, not just phenomenologically, superior to the alternative views in respect to the general question.

The philosophers I have identified as accepting the direct realist view can be easily interpreted as defending something like a reductio argument, though not the specific argument I have delineated. Wittgenstein is doing so, in *On Certainty*, when he writes: "So is the *hypothesis* possible, that all the things around us don't exist? Would that not be like the hypothesis of our having miscalculated in all our calculations?"[17] The argument is implied also by what Heidegger says about the nature of Dasein as Being-in-the-World, "together with others," by Sartre's "ontological proof" of Being-in-itself as a necessary condition for the being of consciousness, of Being-for-itself, and by much of what Moore says in "A Defense of Common Sense." But their arguments, unlike mine, are global in their presuppositions and for that reason perhaps less convincing and open to more objections.

Even though my answer to the general question is far more plausible when combined with the direct realist conception of consciousness, this still does not render it conclusive. Indeed, as we have seen, the fact that to believe that material objects might not exist is to believe that one's own philosophical reasoning might be illusory is of extraordinary importance and does constitute an epistemic reason for giving an affirmative answer to the general (though, as we have seen, not to the particular) question. But it can hardly be said to prove that answer, and the sort of reason it is remains problematic. Of course, it seems to be a powerful *psychological* reason, a motive, for the rejection of skepticism, and as such differs from Hume's

only by appealing to the professional, philosophical nature of skepticism. But I have suggested that there is more to it than that, that it is a sort of *epistemic* reason. (I shall not lean on the weak reed of saying that at least it "justifies" the rejection of skepticism.) Yet, at most it shows that skepticism regarding the general question whether material objects exist cannot be taken seriously as a professional philosophical doctrine. The argument does not show that material objects do exist. Therefore, it also does not show that we *know* that they do. But an additional reason why it does not show the latter is that the epistemic reason the argument provides may not be sufficiently strong for knowledge, even if we hold a rather lax conception of knowledge.

Moreover, as we have seen, neither does the direct realist conception of consciousness provide us with an answer to the particular epistemological question, even though, unlike its competitors, it renders plausible the possibility that such an answer can be found, by regarding us as being directly in touch with that the reality of which is in question. And although the particular and the general questions are distinguishable, and the general question is the one of special philosophical importance, the fact remains that unless we answer also the particular question we cannot be secure in the answer we have obtained to the general question. Indeed, an affirmative answer to the particular question (i.e., that in some perceptual situation we know or at least have evidence that the perceived object exists) entails an affirmative answer to the general question (i.e., that we know or at least have evidence that material objects exist), but in chapter 6 we shall see that at a crucial point the former still requires the argument I have given in this chapter for the latter. So the two answers, or arguments, are both needed. I should remark here that if we take our argument to have shown that *generally* our perceptual judgments about material objects are true and then infer from this, with respect to a particular such judgment, that it is *probably* true, we would need to be employing not the statistical but the epistemic notion of probability, if the inference is to have epistemological import. But the latter notion is essentially the notion of nondemonstrative evidence that the skeptic rejected with her general argument in chapter 3, section 7, and we have found no reasons for questioning that argument.

Hence the modesty of my two conclusions so far reached in this book: that the direct realist conception of consciousness brings us one major step *closer* to an answer to skepticism about the external world, and that the reductio argument I have stated provides us with what seems to be an epistemic reason for accepting a nonskeptical answer to the general though not to the particular question. To have greater confidence in these two conclusions, especially in the second, we must have an answer also to the particular question. Moreover, though the general question is of greater philosophical importance, the particular question still does have great philosophical importance, which is not limited to the fact that an affirmative answer to it entails an affirmative answer to the general question. We

embark now on the search for such an answer. We shall consider the particular question in chapter 6 but we shall begin, in chapter 5, with an account of the concept of reality, which is largely what is at stake (a fact of which epistemologists seem seldom aware) when we ask, Do we know or at least have evidence, in some particular perceptual situation, that the object perceived is *real*?

5

OUR CONCEPT OF REALITY

1. Meinong and Russell on the Concept of Reality

It is striking that, though the skeptic questions the *reality* of material objects, especially of those we perceive, in recent discussions of skepticism there is very little said about what obviously is the crucial concept, that of reality. Instead, we have detailed discussions of the concepts of knowledge, evidence, and justification, as if it mattered little what precisely is that of which we may or may not have knowledge, or make evidentially based or justified judgments about. This was not always the case. For example, as I pointed out in the introduction, Plato in effect undercut the motivation behind skepticism by denying that the objects of sense perception have real being. In modern philosophy we are also familiar with Berkeley's view that in the case of the objects of perception to be is to be perceived, whether by oneself or by another, including God. We are also familiar with John Stuart Mill's view that the reality of a so-called material object is nothing but the permanent possibility of certain sensations. And we know that Heidegger sought an understanding of Being by explicitly denying that it is *a* being, and hoped for a very special grasp of it, one grounded in an interpretation of time.

What accounts for the scarcity of such bold opinions in more recent Anglo-American epistemology? Doubtless, it is the influence of Bertrand Russell's view of reality, or existence, as what is expressed by the so-called existential quantifier. The view had its origin, of course, in Gottlob Frege, but it was Russell who forced it on Anglo-American philosophy, in the course of a series of arguments against Alexius Meinong.

Meinong deplored what he called our prejudice in favor of the actual, indeed, more generally, our prejudice in favor of what has being, whether its being is actuality or existence (concrete being in space and time) or subsistence (the sort of being abstract objects have). He made what he acknowledged to be a paradoxical assertion, that there are objects of which it is true that there are no such objects. And he gave as examples of such objects the golden mountain and the round square, about which he claimed

we can make true statements such as "The golden mountain is golden" and "The round square is round."[1] Russell responded, in part, by writing: "In such theories, it seems to me, there is a failure of that feeling for reality which ought to be preserved even in the most abstract studies. . . . A robust sense of reality is very necessary in framing a correct analysis of propositions about unicorns, golden mountains, round squares, and other such pseudo-objects."[2]

What is this robust sense of reality to which Russell appealed? I shall argue that what Russell says is not just a flight of Russellian rhetoric, and that the question I have asked requires an answer both by anti-Meinongians and by Meinongians. I shall follow Russell (at that stage of his philosophical development) in using the terms "reality," "existence," "being," and "actuality" interchangeably, thus ignoring Meinong's (and Russell's earlier) important distinctions between them, because these distinctions are not relevant to the topic with which I am concerned, though very relevant to other philosophical topics.

What does Russell mean by "reality" when he writes of the need for a robust sense of reality? It may seem that he had answered the question just a few pages earlier. There he writes:

> The notion of "existence" has several forms, one of which will occupy us in the next chapter [where he discusses indefinite and definite descriptions]; but the fundamental form is that which is derived immediately from the notion of "sometimes true." We say that an argument a "satisfies" a function ϕx if ϕa is true; this is the same sense in which the roots of an equation are said to satisfy the equation. Now if ϕx is sometimes true, we may say there are x's for which it is true, or we may say "arguments satisfying ϕx *exist*." This is the fundamental meaning of the word "existence." Other meanings are either derived from this, or embody mere confusion of thought.[3]

But this notion of existence, to which Russell had appealed also as early as 1905, in his article "On Denoting," as well as in *Principia Mathematica* and in "The Philosophy of Logical Atomism," cannot be what he means by "reality" in the phrase "a robust sense of reality." The reason is simple. Are we to allow as arguments satisfying ϕx only objects that exist or also objects that do not exist? If the latter alternative is adopted, then we have at most a highly idiosyncratic proposal as to what "existence" is to mean and nothing that will distinguish Russell's own views from Meinong's; for example, the theory of definite descriptions could then be accepted without the slightest suggestion that it provides us with an alternative to Meinong's view that there are true propositions about objects that do not exist. If we accept the former alternative, that only objects that exist are to be allowed as arguments satisfying the propositional function, which of course is the alternative Russell accepts, then in enforcing, indeed in even *understanding*, this rule we must be employing another, obviously more fundamental notion of existence than the one Russell defined. It is the notion that would allow us to tell what to count as arguments satisfying a propositional func-

tion and what not to so count, for example, that Secretariat is, while Pegasus is not, an argument satisfying the propositional function "x is a horse." I suggest that it is this more fundamental notion that Russell must have had in mind when he wrote of a robust sense of reality. But he said nothing about it. He did not even attempt to answer our question.

I should remark that my point stands even if we add to Russell's view his theory of logically proper names, and allow as substituends for the variable in the propositional function only logically proper names. Indeed, Russell held that a logically proper name can name only something that exists. But then we need the more fundamental notion of existence in order to decide what to count as a logically proper name. He also held that logically proper names name only objects of acquaintance. But according to him nothing counts as acquaintance unless its object exists, and so we would need the more fundamental notion of existence in order to determine that a particular case is indeed a case of acquaintance. And, as G. E. Moore remarked concerning sense data (which were regarded by Russell as the most likely candidates for being objects of acquaintance and bearers of logically proper names), even if we are not clear about what might be meant by saying "This sense-datum exists," we are quite clear about what would be meant by saying "This sense-datum might not have existed."[4] We need what I called the more fundamental notion of existence in order to be clear about this. What I have already said should suffice to show that this notion of existence is also presupposed by definitions of existence such as the following: (1) A exists = df "A" is a genuine name; (2) A exists = df $(\exists x)(x = A)$; (3) A exists = df A = A. It should also suffice to forestall the possible answer that nonexistent objects could only be referred to with definite descriptions and that Russell's theory of descriptions has shown that such reference is bogus, the definite descriptions being eliminable. Russell's theory of descriptions was motivated in part precisely by the conviction that there are no nonexistent objects. And, in any case, why could not Meinong have referred to his golden mountain with a proper name? He could have "baptized" it, and the reference of its name could then be understood even in accordance with an ontologically subtle causal theory of reference, according to which the initial cause is the baptism, not the baptized!

Indeed, Russell also held that logically proper names designate simples, and obviously the golden mountain or any other example Meinong gave of a nonexistent object is not a simple. Perhaps Russell's conviction that there are no nonexistent objects was in part motivated by his conviction that no examples of *simple* nonexistent objects could be given. If so, he was wrong. I can imagine or think of a white patch, which if sensed would be called a sense datum (Russell's favorite example of a simple particular), and give it a proper name, but the patch does not exist. Russell might have tried to avoid such an example by holding that what I have named is only a (existent) mental image, not a white patch. But then he could have said the same about imagining or thinking of the golden mountain. The appeal to sim-

plicity has thus accomplished nothing; it has only brought to our attention a primitive phenomenology of imagination and of thought. And, in any case, the notion of a simple object is too unclear to bear the weight placed upon it. Is a white patch really a simple object? What about its color and shape? Doesn't it have spatial parts, for example, a left and a right half? And don't even its color and shape have parts, for example, in the case of chromatic color, its hue, saturation, and brightness, and in the case of, say, a rectangle its four sides? On the other hand, if we say that a shade of color or a rectangle has no parts, is a simple, what about Hume's missing shade of blue, that is, a shade of which we have an idea but, by hypothesis, not an impression, or any of the shapes which we can easily imagine and perhaps describe but which nothing exemplifies? If we are not Platonists, presumably we should hold that the shade of blue and those shapes do not exist. Yet surely we can name them. As Wittgenstein was to realize in his later philosophy, the notion of simplicity is too vague to be of much value in philosophy, even though it was central in his earlier (Tractarian) philosophy.

Russell's use of the notion "sometimes true" as basic[5] must not mislead us into supposing that it can do duty for what I have called the more fundamental notion of existence. I have in mind the supposition that even if there were nonexistent objects they could not satisfy propositional functions because there could be no true propositions about nonexistent objects, presumably because nonexistent objects could not have properties. To suppose this would be to beg the question against Meinong, but, more importantly, it would be also dialectically misconceived. One believes that the seemingly analytic proposition "The golden mountain is golden" is not true, on the grounds that the golden mountain has no properties, not even that of being golden, because one is convinced that there is no such object as the golden mountain. One does not believe that there is no such object as the golden mountain because one is convinced that it has no properties, that there are no true propositions about it.[6]

If by "reality" Russell meant what I have called the more fundamental notion of existence, what did he mean by "a robust sense of reality"? If he was suggesting that Meinong lacked a sense for the difference between what is real and what is not, what exists and what does not, then he would have been guilty of a travesty of Meinong's position with which he cannot be fairly charged. (Others have been guilty of that travesty, namely, all those who have accused Meinong of having a jungle ontology, or of over-populating the world; i.e., all those who have ignored Meinong's explicit view that the objects in question have no being at all.) Nor could he have meant by a sense of reality knowledge of his own account of existence; he did not accuse all earlier philosophers and all nonphilosophers of lacking a sense of reality. I have suggested that we should think of the notion of reality, to our sense of which Russell appeals, as the notion of reality that allows us to determine what according to Russell would count as an argument satisfying a propositional function and what would not. Could

Russell have meant by "sense of reality" simply this notion? But that is just the ordinary notion of reality, which allows us to say, for example, that the actor playing Santa Claus exists while Santa Claus does not. If so, then Russell has admitted the heart of Meinong's theory: some objects exist and others do not; and in stating his theory Meinong certainly had that ordinary notion of reality in mind. Russell would say, of course, that objects that do not exist cannot be arguments satisfying propositional functions, that there can be no truths about them, that it cannot be true, for example, that Santa Claus is jolly. But surely he would need to say this on the basis of argument; it is hardly evident once we grant that some objects do not exist. But no argument is provided.

2. "Our Robust Sense of Reality"

There must be more, therefore, to Russell's appeal to a robust sense of reality. Indeed, the notion of reality he must have in mind in it is not that which he has defined but that which he would use in deciding how to apply the notion he has defined, that is, what to count as arguments satisfying propositional functions. But something else is also involved in his appeal to a robust sense of reality than that *notion* of reality. I suggest that the additional element, which justifies the use of the words "robust sense," is the powerful conviction that it is false that some objects do not exist, that is, the powerful conviction that all objects exist, that all objects are real, that there are no nonexistent, unreal objects. One has a robust sense of reality when one has this *conviction.*[7] Indeed, one needs all the strength of one's convictions one can muster in order to accept the proposition that all objects exist, that everything is real.

It is important that we regard this proposition as substantive and logically fundamental, as resting neither on a particular view of the meaning of "exist" nor on technical considerations about difficulties faced by the opposing view. For it employs what I called the more fundamental notion of existence, not that defined by Russell, not that expressed by the "existential" quantifier. And the power of the belief in it far exceeds anything that might have been derived from a recognition of particular difficulties in which Meinong's theory, like *all* philosophical theories, may be involved. This is why few philosophical disagreements are as passionate, basic, and seemingly unresolvable as that between the Meinongian and the anti-Meinongian. Each claims to *know* something that is obviously true; yet they disagree.

The power of the conviction that everything exists, that, as Quine puts it, everything has being (see note 7), is especially striking in the thought of three distinguished contemporary American philosophers who are also distinguished Meinong scholars. Roderick M. Chisholm writes: "Surely no one who takes ontology seriously would maintain that there are certain things that are merely possible and not actual. States of affairs—whether or not they obtain and whether or not they are self-consistent—are not 'merely

possible entities'; like everything else, they exist."[8] Gustav Bergmann writes: "To *exist*, to be an *entity*, to have *ontological status* are the same. One who uses these words differently I cannot even hope to understand,"[9] but proceeds to endorse "The belief that whatever we think of has ontological status (exists)," including those complexes ("facts") that have the mode of potentiality (unactuality) rather than the mode of actuality; yet (at least in the work cited) he denies that he is presented with either mode.[10] In a later work he asserts: "As I use the word here, technically, to be an *existent*, to have *ontological status*, and, most crucially, to be *thinkable*, are all one and the same."[11] What is striking about Chisholm's and Bergmann's views is the fusion of basic agreement and basic disagreement with at least one part of Meinong's theory. They agree that "there are" what according to Meinong are objectives that have no being, but insist that such objectives ("states of affairs" in Chisholm's terminology, "complexes" in Bergmann's) *do* have being, do exist; what distinguishes them from the objectives that according to Meinong have no being is that (Chisholm) they do not obtain or (Bergmann) they have the mode of potentiality. We must save the conviction that all things exist, whatever the cost! And Reinhardt Grossmann agrees with Meinong that some objects of thought do not exist but denies that they can have properties; they can only be *imagined* to have properties.[12] If we must grant Meinong's thesis that some objects do not exist, we can still drain it of all significance by insisting that such objects have no nature, no character, no features, and thus after all are nothing at all! Yet, for Grossmann, they do have the property of being imagined!

No reader of Bergmann, Chisholm, or Grossmann would suppose that their views on our topic are merely terminological (even though Bergmann sometimes writes as if to suggest that they are—a suggestion I am sure he would have repudiated). They are no less substantive, indeed no less robustly felt, than Russell's view. But now if the conviction that all objects exist and therefore the disagreement about its truth are substantive, then the anti-Meinongian must be saying something substantive about all objects when he says that they exist, he must be expressing a genuine concept by the verb "exist," whether or not that concept is to be thought of as a concept of a *property*. He must have *something* in mind regarding all objects when he asserts that they all exist. He must *mean* something. Otherwise, what is there to feel so strongly about? He can hardly be taken to be merely asserting that all objects are objects, to be identifying the concept of being an object with that of being an existent. Were he doing that, then there might be no difference between his concept of existence and Meinong's concept of *Quasisein*, which was supposed to apply to all objects, and which Meinong abandoned on the reasonable grounds (I am somewhat diverging here from what he actually wrote) that nothing can count as a genuine concept unless we can make sense of what it would be for it to *fail* to apply to something.

The serious anti-Meinongian must therefore be taken to understand what she says as something *worth saying*. She must be taken to have a con-

cept of existence in terms of which what she is saying is to be *understood*, at least by herself. To my knowledge, no anti-Meinongian has given an account of that concept. If it were held to be a primitive, indefinable concept, we should still expect to be told whether it is a concept of an individual thing, or of a property, or of a relation, and to be given an elucidation of it through comparisons, contrasts, analogies. An indefinable concept is hardly one we can say nothing illuminating about; we merely cannot define it. (Compare Moore's discussion of the nature of goodness in *Principia Ethica*. He did not define it, indeed claimed it was indefinable, yet said enough about it to set the course of twentieth-century Anglo-American ethics.) Yet, clearly, the anti-Meinongian, or at least Russell, would reject all of these alternatives.

But this is not the feature of the anti-Meinongian's position with which I am now concerned. What I am concerned with is the fact that if the anti-Meinongian understands at all what she is saying, if she is making a genuine claim, then she is in effect allowing that there is a certain concept, namely, that of existence, which, for whatever reason, applies to everything, to all objects, and that the fact that it applies to all objects is nothing trivial (like the fact that all objects are self-identical) or purely verbal (as it would be if "existent" and "object" were synonyms), but a fact of philosophical importance, one that is worth arguing for and feeling robustly about, and that indeed has been denied by some, most notably by Meinong. But if all this is so, then the anti-Meinongian owes us an answer to the question, how does she know such an extraordinary fact, namely that the concept in question, whatever it might be, applies to *all* objects, all things? It is noteworthy that anti-Meinongians not only do not answer this question but generally are unaware of it, of the fact that they need to say what they mean when they say "There are no nonexistent objects, all objects exist." Generally, they just sense robustly about these matters.

Is the anti-Meinongian right in holding that all objects exist? For the sake of simplicity of exposition, let us use the word "feature" for that, whatever it is, that renders an object an existent, without suggesting that it is a property, even one that is *ausserkonstitutorisch* ("extranuclear," "noncharacterizing"), that is, not part of the nature of the object. The anti-Meinongian holds that all objects have that feature, that no object fails to have it, that it is false that some objects do not have it. (I ignore here the thoughtless anti-Meinongian who holds that it is false that there are objects that do not exist and then informs us that by "there are" he means the same as "there exist." The obvious alternative is to interpret quantification in terms of the truth of singular statements, whether about existent or nonexistent objects, that are instantiations of the quantified statement.) What grounds does he have for holding this? Once again, it cannot be that the proposition is a straightforward tautology, for it would be such a tautology only if by "existing" he meant being an object, in which case, as we have seen, he might be a Meinongian who has held onto the theory of Quasisein. Nor could the proposition be a disguised tautology, for the notions of being

an object or thing and of existing hardly have the kind of complexity that might generate such a disguise. (Of course, it would be a tautology on Russell's defined notion of existence, but we are discussing now what I have called the more fundamental notion of existence, which I have argued is presupposed by Russell's defined notion.) The anti-Meinongian must therefore allow that it is logically possible that some objects *do not* exist. But once he allows this, his view begins to unravel. For, surely, in holding that though logically possible this is not the case, he would not appeal to there being an a priori but synthetic connection between being an object and existing. And it would be absurd for him to appeal to some empirical generalization such as "We have never seen a nonexistent object," or to the fact that physics does not need nonexistent objects for its explanations. If by perception we mean veridical perception, then the first assertion is true but trivially so; if we allow also for nonveridical perception, for example, hallucination, then it is empirically false. And if science does not knowingly appeal to nonexistent objects in its explanations, this would be no more surprising than that we do not try to build existent houses with nonexistent timber.

Indeed, once the anti-Meinongian thesis has begun to unravel in the way I have described, we see easily that it is *obviously* false. Many of the objects of our thought, imagination, dreams, fantasies, and perception (in the "regimented" sense of "perception" explained in chapters 1 and 2) do not exist. But there is nothing mysterious about them. Indeed, as I remarked in chapter 1 and shortly will further explain, it makes no sense to say that they are logically or causally dependent on us. But ordinarily they are perceived (if they are the sort of objects that are perceivable at all) as having the usual perceivable properties and relations. (The rat I hallucinate is pink or gray, etc., and it is to the left of me or in front of me, etc. In a sexual dream one may be vividly aware of an unreal person's properties and find them exciting.) We all know this, and our knowledge of it and our judicious application of this knowledge in particular cases is essential to our living and thinking. Of course, this is just what Meinong argued at great length and in great detail. It can even be reasonably called our robust sense of reality.

3. The Power of the Conviction That All Things Exist

But what explains the *power* of the conviction that all objects exist? Why do most philosophers share it, if it is so plainly wrong? There are the misunderstandings mentioned in chapter 1, section 4, especially the failure to distinguish between being conscious of nothing and being conscious of something that does not exist. But the main reason, I suggest, is the special character of the concept of existence. Although we do have this concept and it is genuinely classificatory, that is, it applies to some objects and not to others, it is not a concept that itself stands for anything, real or unreal,

an individual or a property or a relation. We must not say circularly, with Rudolf Carnap, that it stands for the relational property of being a part of the real world, "that [a real thing] fits together with the other things recognized as real, according to the rules of the framework."[13] Nor must we say that it stands for the property of being causally efficacious, as if the distinction between reality and unreality had no application to causal efficacy (do we mean real or just imaginary causal efficacy?) and as if the existence of objects outside the causal order, for example, numbers, were to be ruled out without argument. (Nonexistent mountains are causally inefficacious, but so too are existent numbers.) Any of these all too familiar proposals are blatantly circular, whether explicitly or implicitly. The truth is that there is *nothing* before our minds, whether in perception or imagination or thought, that all existent objects possess and all nonexistent objects lack. There is nothing in reality that *is* existence. This is why it is natural to fail to understand how there could be such a concept as the concept of existence. And if we do not understand how there could be such a concept, then we do not understand how the concept of existence can be classificatory. If we do not understand this, then we do not understand how there can be nonexistent objects as well as existent objects. We find ourselves compelled to think that all objects are the same with respect to existence. Either none exist or all exist. Not surprisingly, we choose to say that all exist.

I shall call a concept that has classificatory application, that is, may *apply* to some things and not to others, but does not *stand* for anything in, of, or between the things to which it applies, a transcendental concept. That the concept of existence is transcendental in this sense (I must not be taken to mean by "transcendental" anything else) is of course suggested by Kant's familiar argument. He writes:

> "*Being*" is obviously not a real predicate, that is, it is not a concept of something which could be added to the concept of a thing. . . . The real contains no more than the merely possible. A hundred real thalers do not contain the least coin more than a hundred possible thalers. For as the latter signify the concept, and the former the object and the positing of the object, should the former contain more than the latter, my concept would not, in that case, express the whole object, and would not therefore be an adequate concept of it. . . . If we attempt to think existence through the pure category [of existence] alone, we cannot specify a single mark distinguishing it from mere possibility. Whatever, therefore, and however much, our concept of object may contain, we must go outside it, if we are to ascribe existence to the object.[14]

But the exegesis of this argument is not at all easy. For example, Kant also writes: "In the *mere concept* of a thing no mark of its existence is to be found," existence has to do

> only with the question whether such a thing be so given us that the perception of it can, if need be, precede the concept. For that the concept precedes the perception signifies the concept's mere possibility; the per-

> ception which supplies the content to the concept is the sole mark of actuality. We can also, however, know the existence of the thing prior to the perception . . . if only it be bound with certain perceptions, in accordance with the principles of their empirical connection (the analogies). For the existence of the thing being thus bound up with our perceptions in a possible experience, we are able in the series of possible perceptions and under the guidance of the analogies, to make the transition from our actual perception to the thing in question (A225/B272–A226/B273).

And elsewhere he writes:

> The empirical truth of appearances in space and time is, however, sufficiently secured; it is adequately distinguished from dreams, if both dreams and genuine appearances cohere truly and completely in one experience, in accordance with empirical laws. . . . That there may be inhabitants in the moon, although no one has ever perceived them, must certainly be admitted. This, however, only means that in the possible advance of experience we may encounter them. For everything is real which stands in connection with a perception in accordance with laws of empirical advance. . . . To call an appearance a real thing prior to our perceiving it, either means that in the advance of experience we must meet with such a perception, or it means nothing at all. (B520–21/A492–93).

There is much to be said for holding that Kant in fact held a phenomenalist view of existence, according to which existence is indeed not a monadic property, but is a relational property, namely that of being an object of perception which is appropriately related to other actual and possible objects of perception. If so, his celebrated view of existence resembles John Stuart Mill's view that the existence of a material object is the permanent possibility of certain sensations. He did not claim that existence is not a real predicate in our contemporary sense, and thus his view is not at all Russell's. He merely held that existence is a *relational* predicate (property), not a nonrelational predicate.

Meinong agreed with the negative part of Kant's view. In "The Theory of Objects" he argued that the object as such stands beyond being and nonbeing, that the distinction between being and nonbeing is a matter of the objective, not the object, that neither being nor nonbeing can belong to the object in itself. In replying to Russell's charge that on Meinong's view the existent golden mountain must exist, for the same reason that according to Meinong it must be golden, Meinong distinguished between saying that the existent golden mountain is existent, which is true, and saying that the existent golden mountain exists, which is false, and indeed mentioned Kant's example of the hundred thalers.[15] So, Kant and Meinong agreed that existence is not a *konstitutorisch* property, one that is a part of the intrinsic nature of the object (in the wide sense of "nature" in which what Aristotle would have called accidents of a thing would also be parts of its nature). My claim, however, is that it is not even an ausserkonstitutorisch property (except in the ontologically useless sense of "property" in which just about any open sentence is sometimes said to express a property).

Kant was not the first to hold that existence is not an intrinsic property of objects. In fact, it was the view of Aristotle and most medieval philosophers. Aristotle argued in the *Metaphysics* that Being cannot be a genus, because it would not have differentiae since they would not have being, a genus not being predicable of its differentiae (998b 21–26). But if not a genus, then being is not a category; rather it is one of the *concepts* the medieval followers of Aristotle called transcendental, namely, concepts (among them was also Unity, a fact significant for what I shall be arguing) that range across the Aristotelian ten categories and, since the latter contain everything, correspond to nothing. The difference between Kant, on one hand, and the medieval philosophers and Meinong, on the other, was that Kant not only recognized the existence of such transcendental concepts but also acknowledged their constituting role in what we regard as a *world*, a role for which ultimately *we* are responsible. This, of course, was the distinctively Kantian sense of the term "transcendental."

My purpose here is not to engage in historical exegesis. But since one of Russell's main arguments against Meinong is that already mentioned, that if there is an object such as the existing golden mountain then a golden mountain must exist, it is important to draw attention to the great difference between thinking of the existing golden mountain and thinking just of the golden mountain. That we can do the former merely shows that with respect to any object we can think of it *as* an object of the application, whether correct or incorrect, of the concept of existence. It does not show that the concept of existence stands for anything in or of the object that is being thought, that it stands for anything that can be singled out, whether in perception or in imagination or in thought. For to think of the *existing* golden mountain, I suggest, can only be to think of the golden mountain *as existing* (unless, irrelevantly, it is to think of a golden mountain that, whether we know it or not, happens to exist), and from this of course it does not follow that it exists or that we even think that it exists. (I should make a similar remark about thinking of a state of affairs, an objective, as actual or as "obtaining," if the category of states of affairs is admissible.)[16] Contrast this now with the case of thinking just of the golden mountain. Contrary to Grossmann's view, I suggest, it is not to think of it, or imagine it, as golden and a mountain (*what* would be that which we are only thinking of or imagining as golden and a mountain? a bare particular?); it can only be to think of something that *is* golden and a mountain. But I agree with Chisholm that it would be better to use as our example not a statement such as "The golden mountain is golden," but rather a statement such as "The mountain I am thinking of is golden" or "The object I am thinking of is a golden mountain."[17] For statements such as the latter make clear the phenomenological, and not semantical or logical, basis of a defensible Meinongian theory. As Chisholm says in the passage just cited, the statement "The golden mountain is golden" may leave us speechless! The reason is not that it is about an object that does not exist, but that it does not seem to be about anything at all, since the description functioning as the

subject term, though certainly meaningful, does not seem to be used to refer to anything, existent or nonexistent. A defensible Meinongian theory must take seriously the Strawsonian distinction between meaning and referential use.

In what I have said I do not suggest that there are no nonexistent objects that are not "before the mind." Neither logical nor causal mind-dependence can be coherently ascribed to something that does not exist. (But to say of it that it is *mind-independent* would also be incoherent, or at least misleading. For by "mind-independence" is usually meant *existing* independently of the mind.) As Meinong remarked, "I cannot conceal from myself at present the fact that it is no more necessary to an Object that it be presented in order not to exist than it is in order for it to exist."[18] What I do suggest is only that no genuine *example* of a nonexistent object can be given that is not before the mind, and that the mere construction of a definite description, however significant or meaningful it may be, does not suffice. Contemporary defenders of Meinong tend to ignore this crucial fact, perhaps because they are mainly interested in logic and the philosophy of language. Incidentally, what I have said, if true, casts doubt on Meinong's view that there are impossible objects, such as the round square, to say nothing of his defective objects, if they cannot be before the mind, that is, objects of consciousness. This suggests a simple way of resolving most of the difficulties discussed in the recent literature on Meinong. But it does not conflict with the spirit of Meinong's theory of objects, which (see, e.g., the beginning passages of "The Theory of Objects") is *phenomenological*. And if we remain faithful to that spirit, we would concern ourselves mainly with the philosophically crucial examples of nonexistent objects, namely, those of perception, imagination, and thought, rather than with philosophically peripheral ones such as fictional characters (which are also impure examples because of their logical intermeshing with something that does exist, namely, the work of fiction).

4. Reality as a Transcendental Concept

In the light of what was said in the previous section, it would require little reflection to acknowledge that a proper answer to the question, "What is it for something to exist or be?" would have to be very different from the proper answers to other questions of the form, "What is it for something to ϕ?" We need not follow Heidegger in the rest of his views in order to agree that whatever Being may be, it is not itself a being. It is not an individual, whether material or immaterial. But neither is it a property, monadic or relational, even though it may be expressed with a grammatical predicate that, if the Meinongian is right, applies to some objects and fails to apply to others. To begin with, the concept of existence would be, presumably, applicable to that property itself, and even if there is no logical difficulty in the idea of a property exemplifying itself, surely saying that existence

exemplifies itself would be mere verbiage. At any rate, we do not discover, even in the most basic noninferential cases, that something exists or that it does not by examining its properties and seeing whether they include a property called existence. We do not discern such a property even as one that is not konstitutorisch, that is, is not a part of the nature of the object. (The property of being simple is not a part of the nature of an object that is simple, but surely it is discernible, at least in thought, as a property *of* the object, though not *in* the object, if the object is indeed simple.) We may discern, at least in thought, the complex relational property of some experiences that the phenomenalists (and seemingly also Kant) appeal to, but to make its subject an existent that property, presumably involving spatial, temporal, and perhaps causal relations, must itself exist, be *really* present, and therefore its presence cannot *be* what it is for something to exist. To serve its putative role, the relational property must be taken to be real, not just imagined. Any phenomenalist account of existence is therefore conceptually circular.

In inferential cases we infer that the object exists or that it does not exist (in part) *from its properties*. If we allowed for such an object as the round square, we could infer that it does not exist by relying on truths of logic and geometry. If we found ourselves to be thinking of, or imagining, a golden mountain somewhere in Iowa, we could infer that it does not exist by appealing to truths of geography and geology. But in neither case would we take ourselves to be inferring the absence of a property called existence; it is not at all like inferring the microproperties of an object from its macroproperties. To suppose that it is, that existence is a *hidden* property, one that cannot be discerned directly but must be inferred, would be to indulge in mere fancy. Yet we do distinguish between objects that exist and objects that do not exist. That we have the concept of existence, that it has application, and that it is classificatory cannot be doubted. But it stands for nothing. It is a transcendental concept, *at least* in the medieval but surely also in the Kantian sense, as I shall explain shortly. (Let us not say that it stands for the set of existent objects! Since that set is not arbitrary, what do its members have in common?)

But if the concept of existence is transcendental, we face the obvious question, "How is such a concept possible?" How is it possible for a concept to apply in some cases and not in others, and yet to stand for nothing, whether an individual object or a property or a relation? (Kant and Meinong explained why it cannot stand for an intrinsic property. I have explained why it cannot stand for a relation or a relational property and will say a great deal more about it later. But, like Kant and Meinong, I shall ignore the possibility that it stands for an individual object.) I believe that we can find an answer to our question, and thereby obtain also a much better grasp of the concept of existence, if we recognize that it must be understood in terms of the even more fundamental concept of identity, the transcendental character of which is especially evident.

To see the connection between existence (reality) and identity, let us ask again, what is that more fundamental concept of existence that I accused Russell of ignoring? My example of Pegasus and Secretariat may have suggested that there is nothing particularly mysterious about it, even though the concept does require philosophical discussion. It is our ordinary concept of existence, or reality, freely employed in singular existential statements. But what is the content of that concept? On the surface, there is no particular mystery about this either. It is the element of truth in Mill's view, and freed from his phenomenalism it can be stated simply as follows: For a thing to exist is for it to be indefinitely identifiable. Or, shifting terminology in order to avoid the implied subjunctives, we may say that for a thing to exist is for there to be an indefinite number of perspectives on it, even if no one occupies them. In Frege's terminology, though not view, for a thing to exist is for it to possess an indefinite number of modes of presentation, even if it presents itself to no one. Frege explicitly held that the reference of an expression has an inexhaustible number of modes of presentation. He explained his notion of the sense of an expression as that "wherein the mode of presentation is contained."[19] The notion of a mode of presentation was therefore for him the more fundamental and no longer semantic notion. And he allowed that a mode of presentation need not be a mode of presentation of something that exists; to use his own example, the name "Odysseus" perhaps has no reference, but it does have a sense,[20] and therefore, we *must* say, there is a mode of presentation contained in that sense.

Indeed, this is how we do employ the concept of existence, though we do not use the technical terminology I have used. The kernel of common sense in phenomenalism is that we regard a material object as existent, as real, only if we believe that *it itself* (not some other things, such as sense data) can, in principle, be perceived or in some other manner detected on an indefinite number of occasions and by an indefinite number of observers. And we regard an object as hallucinatory when we believe that it cannot. Perhaps this preliminary account of existence also fits the Stranger's suggestion, in Plato's *Sophist*, that being is power (247e–248e). We ascribe existence (being, reality) to what is not subject to our whim or wishful thinking, to what we must be prepared to confront on any number of occasions and in any number of ways, to what places an ineliminable constraint on our perceptions and thoughts. Even if we tried to eliminate that constraint by destroying the thing, it was such a constraint before we destroyed it, and this fact was perhaps our reason for destroying it. But, after its destruction, ironically, the thing continues to constrain our memories and judgments, it continues to need to be taken into account, to have intellectual power over us, because it *did* exist.

There is the related, venerable Platonic view that true being involves permanence, unchangeability. The reader may recall that in chapter 1 I ap-

pealed to something like this view to provide some rationale for eliminative materialism with respect to ephemeral headaches.

But however attractive these accounts of existence may be, they are not enough. Modal notions, such as Mill's "possibility of sensations," cry out for explanation; the related subjunctive conditionals, essential to any officially phenomenalist account, are probably the most unclear kind of statement, and the use of them can cast little light on any philosophical topic; the Fregean notion of a mode of presentation, as well as my appeal to the notion of a perspective, hardly suffice; Plato's appeal to the notion of power may much too easily suggest some popular but cheap (and almost certainly circular) causal theory; and his appeal to unchangeability requires us to deny reality, true being, not only to ephemeral headaches (which we may be willing to do), but also to stars and planets.

But neither can we rest with the also modal general idea of existence as indefinite identifiability, attractive though it is, even though for terminological brevity I shall continue to employ the *phrase*. At the risk of offending the reader's logical sensibilities, I suggest that we replace that idea with the idea that an object exists if and only if *there is* an indefinite number of objects each *identical* with it, whether or not we have ever encountered any of them. (There is no circularity here. Once we have got beyond Russell's defined notion of existence, we have no special motive for insisting that "there are" and "there exist" are synonyms. If you feel otherwise, simply replace statements of the form "There are things that are F" with statements of the traditional and less wordy form "Some things are F," which surely is not synonymous with "F's exist.") In speaking of an object as identical with other objects, I am merely accepting the fact (to which, of course, I shall return) that an informative identity judgment is always about "two" things, even though if true these two things are one thing. The terminology is awkward, but unavoidable because it is of the essence of our language, and thus expressive of the essence of our thought. My use of it is certainly not intended to imply that two *entities*, beings, may be identical. It may be helpful to say, though with terminological and historical inaccuracy, that what it does imply is that two *intentional objects* may be identical, as long as we allow that an intentional object need not be actually intended by anyone. Elsewhere,[21] I try to remove the awkwardness by explaining in detail a distinction between entities and objects, but I shall not complicate the present discussion by repeating that explanation. What I shall say can be understood without it.

5. Identity as a Transcendental Concept

We must face now what *is* mysterious about the concept of existence, though the concept itself does not seem mysterious. In effect, I have offered an account of it in terms of the concept of identity. But what is the content of the concept of identity? Like Hegel,[22] Wittgenstein ridiculed (I believe

with justification) the usual view that identity is a relation that everything has to itself and to nothing else. He wrote:

> But isn't the *same* at least the same? We seem to have an infallible paradigm of identity in the identity of a thing with itself. I feel like saying: "Here at any rate there can't be a variety of interpretations. If you are seeing a thing you are seeing identity too."
>
> Then are two things the same when they are what *one* thing is? And how am I to apply what the *one* thing shows me to the case of two things?[23]

Well, what about the case in which we apply the concept of identity to "two" things? We must not suppose that any such application would be false, on the grounds that two things cannot be one. Genuine, informative identity statements are always about things that are given, presented, as two, though, if the statement is true, they are in fact one. This is the lasting lesson yet to be learned from Frege's distinction between the entity referred to by an expression and the different modes in which that entity is presented.

Presumably, if there were an entity, a being, that is identity, it could only be a relation. So, let us ask ourselves whether the genuine, informative applications of the concept of identity imply that between the "two" things there is a relation that might be called their identity. Let us consider some cases so simple that if such a relation were present it would surely be readily discernible.

I am now reading this page. Is the page I am holding now in my hands the same as the page I held a few moments ago? Of course. I have no doubt that it is. But is my confidence based on my discerning a relation of identity between the page I hold now and the page I held a few moments ago? Surely not. If any doubt about their identity arose, I might appeal to the fact that the "two" pages have certain common characteristics and occupy the same place, and that at each moment during the period in question there has been in that place, in my hands, a page with those characteristics. By doing so I would seem to be *justifying* my application of the concept of identity. But is this really so, or am I rather just describing the situation in greater detail in order to display more clearly how I employ the concept of identity? The facts to which I appeal are not themselves the identity, for they can be admitted and the identity denied. But neither does the "justification" consist in my inferring from the facts to which I appeal that there is, in addition to those facts, a relation between the page I hold now and the page I held earlier, a relation that might be called identity. If there were such a relation, why could I not discern it directly? Surely it is not hidden or invisible in the way the atoms constituting the page are hidden and invisible. And many philosophers have denied, by implication, that the page I hold now and the page I held earlier are identical, for they have denied that there are continuants, that there are, in David Lewis's terminology,[24]

enduring rather than just perduring, individual things, and have argued that ordinary individual things such as this page are really series of momentary things that are the former's temporal parts, in the general sense of "part" in which they are said to have also spatial parts; and who would identify two spatial parts of a thing just because they are parts of the same thing? Other philosophers have disagreed, and have argued, again by implication, that the page I hold now and the page I held a few moments ago are not two momentary objects but rather are literally identical, one and the same object, which merely happens to exist now as well as to have existed a few moments ago, though presumably undergoing some alteration. I am not interested now in taking a stand in this controversy. (I will do so in the next chapter.) It suffices for my present purposes that there has been such a controversy. How is this to be explained? Surely not by saying that one of the parties in the controversy was fortunate enough to see a relation of identity between, for example, the page I hold now and the page I held earlier, while the other was not, or that one saw that there is no such relation while the other imagined one. And to appeal to the Leibniz-Russell definition of identity would be obviously wrongheaded; whether the page I hold now has the property of having been held by me a few moments earlier, which the page I held then does have, can be decided only if first we decide whether it is identical with the page I held a few moments ago. Identity is the ultimate criterion of complete coincidence of properties, not vice versa. This is especially evident in my next example.

The color of this page, let us suppose, is exactly similar to the color of the next page. Do I detect a relation of identity between the color of the one and the color of the other? Most philosophers have held that it is false that the color of one page can be identical with the color of another page, because they have denied the existence of universals. Suppose that they, the so-called nominalists, are right. Are their opponents, the so-called realists, then just imagining a relation that is not there? Or suppose that the realists are right. Are the nominalists then just partially blind philosophers, who fail to see a relation that is there? In this example surely there can be no question of the relation of identity being hidden and therefore having to be inferred, for example, of inferring the identity of the colors from the coincidence of their properties. Do I know that the color of this page has the property of being instantiated by the next page, which the color of the next page does have? Only if I first know that they are identical.

Of course, one could hold that our puzzlement arises because we fail to see that identity is only the phantom relation that everything has to itself and to nothing else, that the concept of identity has no legitimate informative applications at all, that there is no individual identity through time or qualitative identity or personal identity or any other kind of genuine identity, that all things are in a Heraclitean (we may also say Humean) flux. In the *Theaetetus* Plato showed that such a view entails that no coherent thought or speech is possible.

I have said that a concept is transcendental if it applies to objects even

though it stands for nothing in, of, or between objects. In effect, I have just argued that the concept of identity is transcendental in this sense. If the concept of existence is understood in terms of the concept of identity in the way I explained earlier, then we now understand why it too is transcendental. We can also understand better the profound difference (despite their surface similarity) between our account of existence and the phenomenalist (perhaps also Kantian) relational account. As I mentioned earlier, the latter is at all plausible only if it describes the relationships to which it appeals as real, rather than imaginary, and therefore is a conceptually circular account of what it is to be real, or to exist. Our account of existence appeals to identity, but explicitly denies that identity is anything real or unreal, whether a relation or anything else. Thus it avoids the conceptual circle in which a phenomenalist account inevitably finds itself. But, of course, it also faces an obvious question.

What justifies the application of the concept of identity (and thus of existence) in the primitive, noninferential cases? How do we tell that A is indeed identical with B, and with C, and D, and so on, and then conclude that it exists, is real? Ultimately, I suggest, the answer is that we just find ourselves applying the concept, that we "see" A and B as identical, and, say, M and N as not identical, that we display a certain conceptual habit. And by "habit" I mean simply what we generally *find* ourselves doing in certain situations, not any physical or mental state that supposedly "explains" what we do. A few lines after the passage I quoted earlier, Wittgenstein writes, in connection with the justification of supposing that one is following the *same* rule, "If I have exhausted the justifications [*Begründungen*] I have reached bedrock, and my spade is turned. Then I am inclined to say: 'This is simply what I do.'" Here, I suggest, is the element of truth in conceptual irrealism, an issue much discussed today. (It becomes especially evident when we consider the otherwise hopeless puzzles about personal identity.) Contrary to what philosophers such as Nelson Goodman and Hilary Putnam have held, we can judge the adequacy of our conceptual scheme and of our language by comparing them with reality, with the identities and differences we ascribe to objects and especially to properties. But we cannot so judge the adequacy of the concepts of identity and existence themselves. They are our measures in any such comparison and can be such precisely because they themselves stand for nothing in reality.

The concept of identity (or of reality) has application to things yet it does not itself stand for any thing, whether an individual, a property, or a relation. It is better thought of as imposed by ourselves on the manifold of the objects we confront in perception, imagination, and thought. Of course, the imposition, to be genuine, cannot be random or a mere pretense. Our application of the concept is a matter of genuine, serious judgment, not of mere whimsy. It is a matter of habit, of a way (form) of life. The concepts of identity and reality stand for nothing in the world, and may be equally legitimately applied in very different situations, for there is no objective constraint on their application. (But would not agreement in judgments

with other people act as an objective constraint? No, because we must presuppose the *reality* of any such agreement.) From this it does not follow, however, that they are wanton—they are *concepts* after all.

However, how exactly all this is to be understood is a question of insuperable difficulty. In the *Prolegomena to Any Future Metaphysics*, after arguing that "nature in the material sense" is possible only "by means of the constitution of our sensibility," and that nature "in the formal sense" is possible only "by means of our understanding," Kant wrote: "But how this peculiar property of our sensibility itself is possible, or that of our understanding and of the apperception which is necessarily its basis and that of all thinking, cannot be further analyzed or answered, because it is of them that we are in need for all our answers and for all our thinking about objects."[25] One need not be a Kantian to acknowledge that at least with respect to the concepts of identity and reality no genuine explanation of their origin, function, or possibility can be given, since any such explanation must presuppose them. Anyone who thinks that it can be given by science, or by some facts about our language or about our culture, simply has failed to sense the depth of the issue.

The crucial fact about existence is that it cannot be thought of as a property of objects. It certainly is not observable, and it would be mere fancy to suppose that it is somehow hidden in or behind the object that exists. I have suggested that we should think of it as the indefinite identifiability of the object to which it is ascribed, but (thus avoiding the subjunctive mood) only in the sense that there is an indefinite number of objects with each of which it is identical. This fits our actual conception of what it is for the object of an ordinary case of perception to exist, and resembles the philosophical conception behind the accounts offered by phenomenalists as well as by phenomenologists (for example, by Mill, Husserl, and Sartre). It is to be able to see the object again, to touch it, perhaps smell it, taste it, or hear it, in various circumstances and in agreement with the perceivings by other persons. But the view I have suggested is, I believe, superior to the phenomenalist and the phenomenological views, and much closer to common sense, in at least three respects. First, it appeals to the identity of the object, rather than to the synthesis of it out of discrete existents, whether things or aspects of things, whether sense data or appearances or profiles (*abschattungen*), a synthesis notoriously difficult to elucidate. Second, it avoids any ultimate appeal to modal notions and thus to subjunctive conditionals in its account of what it is for a perceptual object to be indefinitely identifiable. An object exists if and only if *there is* an indefinite number of objects with each of which it is identical. And third, as I have pointed out already, it avoids the conceptual circularity of those other views by holding that identity and existence do not themselves exist, are not elements in reality, not because they are nonexistent things but because they are not things at all, whether individuals, or properties, or relations.

Identity is not an entity, a being. It falls under no category, nor is it itself a category, a *summum genus*. (Is it just a coincidence that this is ex-

actly what in the *Metaphysics* Aristotle held regarding being?) This is why the identity of an object with "another" object is not a matter of fact, something to be discovered. It can only be thought of as *imposed* by us, as the result of a certain conceptual *decision* by us. And that there is an indefinite number of objects with each of which the object is identical, and thus that it exists, is red, is simply our willingness to impose the concept of identity in any relevant context we may be presented with. It is not something we discover, it is something we just do, as it should be if what I have said about identity is true and if reality is reducible to identity.[26]

This view of identity casts light on the otherwise mysterious nature of existence, its seeming elusiveness, which, I have argued, explains the power of the conviction that all objects exist. For we have a much firmer grasp of the concept of identity than we have of the concept of existence. And its transcendental character is much more evident. The view I have proposed allows us to understand why the concept of existence is transcendental. The reason is that the concept of identity is transcendental, and that the concept of existence is to be understood in terms of the concept of identity. And we can see why existence is not a property or a relation: identity is not a property or a relation.

If there is such a thing as a robust sense of reality, we must emphasize in our description of it the word "sense" and not the word "reality." There is no reality (or, for that matter, unreality) that might be the object of that sense. But there is such a sense, although now it would be more properly called a habit of applying the concept of reality, a habit that indeed is ordinarily robust. It manifests itself in strong conviction because of the fundamental role of the concept of reality. Without that concept we could have no understanding of what objects are real and therefore no understanding of what objects are unreal. Therefore we could have no understanding of what it is for something to be a world. But the concept itself does not stand for anything in reality or outside reality. It is imposed by us on the manifold of objects we confront in perception, imagination, and thought. And these objects must not be thought of as a category of things: they are what things are built of.

Are there other concepts that in this respect are like the concepts of identity and reality, indispensable for our understanding and knowledge of reality but not corresponding to anything in reality? Plausible examples would be the concepts of the logical quantifiers and the propositional connectives, the concept of a state of affairs, the concept of relation. None of these seem given to perception or to any other mode of consciousness, nor of course are they inferred in the way theoretical entities in science are inferred. They are not indispensable for the worldliness of the world; that is a function of the application of the concepts of identity and existence, which even a young child not yet capable of sustained thinking and the use of language may possess, exhibiting them in acts of recognition and some distinctions between what is and what is not real. But they are indispens-

able for any (advanced) thought and especially for language *about* the world.

If relations and therefore relational states of affairs seem to be observable, read what their greatest champion, Bertrand Russell, had to say toward the end of his life:

> For my part, I think it is as certain as anything that there are relational facts such as "A is earlier than B." But does it follow that there is an object of which the name is "earlier"? It is very difficult to make out what can be meant by such a question, and still more difficult to see how an answer can be found. There certainly are complex wholes which have a structure, and we cannot describe the structure without relation-words. But if we try to descry some entity denoted by these relation-words and capable of some shadowy kind of subsistence outside the complex in which it is embodied, it is not at all clear that we can succeed.[27]

Some of these additional concepts may be defined in terms of the others (e.g., the particular quantifier in terms of the universal quantifier and negation), and which are taken as primitive may be a matter of convention, but what is not a matter of convention is that we need *some* such primitives. This is evident in the case of the purely logical concepts. And the concept of a state of affairs, of an entity to which an indicative sentence corresponds and which if actual renders this sentence true, does not seem reducible to any other concepts, for what is distinctive of a state of affairs is not its constituents but the peculiar unity of these, a topic much but inconclusively discussed by Bradley and Russell early in this century. It is hardly plausible to claim that we find states of affairs in the world. It is even less plausible to claim that we find entities in the world corresponding to the quantifiers and the propositional connectives.[28] But developed language and thought seem impossible without these, and our understanding the sentential structure of language and our even most informal and most general notion of truth as correspondence seem impossible without the supposition that true sentences are *somehow* related to states of affairs.

Of course, much more detail needs to be provided in the way of an explanation of the need for such additional transcendental concepts. In the case of identity and existence, the explanation is readily forthcoming. By their very nature they serve to reduce the manifold of the objects of consciousness, the brute "matter" with which we are confronted, to a much more manageable number and thus make the emergence of a world out of that manifold comprehensible. (E.g., we regard Jack as one person rather than as an indefinite number of persons corresponding to the various occasions on which we say we perceived or remembered, or imagined, or thought of him.)[29] They are thus prior to any other transcendental concepts, since the latter generally presuppose that what they are applicable to is a *world* and thus may be described as secondary transcendental concepts, the concepts of identity and existence being the primary ones. For

example, an explanation of the need for the concepts of state of affairs and relation seems readily forthcoming. By its very nature, our thought takes the form of judgments and is expressed in indicative sentences. Both are propositional, in the general sense of having a form usually describable as propositional. The definitory characteristic of both is to have a truth-value, to be true or false. And the natural understanding of truth is as some sort of "correspondence" to the world of entities, these having been already formed through the imposition of the concepts of identity and existence. We can accommodate these requirements of the nature of thought by imposing propositional forms on the manifold of the *entities* we confront, that is, by "seeing" them as constituents of states of affairs, rather than just as a bare "given." (See the brief discussion of the given and foundationalism in chapter 3.) We may thus be led to the early Wittgenstein's view that all complexity is propositional and that the world is the totality of facts, not of things, as well as to Bradley's view that our way of thinking is unavoidably relational, even though it corresponds to nothing in "reality," that it belongs to "appearance." Of course, the connection between the concepts of a state of affairs and a relation is not at all coincidental. It is obvious in the case of ordinary relational states of affairs. But we must think of even a singular monadic judgment as representing what is really a relational state of affairs, the relation being the "tie" between the logical subject and the logical predicate, the tie of exemplification. We cannot coherently think of a relation except as relating—and what is constituted by this relating if not what we call a state of affairs?

But these are difficult topics, and a full discussion of the secondary transcendental concepts would far exceed the scope of this book.

6

THE UNTRUTH AND THE TRUTH OF SKEPTICISM

1. The Skeptic's Particular Question Answered

We are now ready to attempt another answer to the skeptic, one based on the preceding considerations regarding the concept of reality. Can what I have called the particular (nonmodal epistemic) question, namely, Do we know or at least have evidence, in some particular perceptual situation, that what we perceive is a real material object? be given a nonskeptical answer, just as in chapter 4 I gave a nonskeptical answer to the general (nonmodal epistemic) question, namely, Do we know or at least have evidence that material objects exist? If it can, then we would also have a second nonskeptical answer to the general question, since a nonskeptical answer to the particular question entails a nonskeptical answer to the general question, though not vice versa. Thus my argument in chapter 4 in favor of the latter would receive welcome supplementation. But, as we shall see, we would still need that argument at a crucial point in our search in this chapter for a *complete* nonskeptical answer to the particular question. The fact is that both answers are needed. There is no circularity here, since the argument in chapter 4 is independent of the argument to be offered in this chapter. It's just that the converse is not quite the case.

Clearly, the question whether a certain perceptual object exists, is real, cannot be answered unless an account of the concept of existence, reality, is offered, even though this fact has been generally ignored by recent Anglo-American philosophers of perception (in striking contrast with continental philosophers). I have already said why Russell's account in terms of the satisfaction of a propositional function is unacceptable; it presupposes a more fundamental concept of existence, which would allow us to decide what to count as admissible arguments of the function and what not to so count. And the familiar proposal that the reality of an object consists in its fitting in the spatiotemporal causal system of the world is conceptually circular; it presupposes the concept of reality, for of course the system in question must be a system of real objects, and the causal relations in it must also be real, rather than imaginary, if the "fitting in" is to be even

relevant. For similar reasons, also conceptually circular is the Kantian-phenomenalist account, as I argued in chapter 5.

The failures of these accounts should not be surprising if the existence, the reality, of an object cannot be thought of as one of its properties, relational or nonrelational. It certainly is not observable, and we would be indulging in mere fantasy if we suppose that it is somehow hidden in or behind the object that exists. I have argued that we should think of existence as the indefinite identifiability of the object to which it is attributed, in the sense that there is an indefinite number of objects with each of which it is identical. But their identity is not something in reality. Rather it is imposed on them by our decisions to apply the concept of identity. The same can be said about the concept of existence, reality, since it is to be understood in terms of the concept of identity. Both are transcendental concepts.

Given these conclusions reached in chapter 5, my answer to the skeptic's *particular* epistemic question can now be given in blunt summary as follows. Reality (existence) is not a matter of knowledge or evidentially based judgment, it is a matter of decision, and thus the skeptic's question whether we know or even have evidence with respect to any particular perceptual object that it is real does not even arise, indeed it cannot be sensibly asked. And the skeptic's answer to that question, namely, that we do not, perhaps cannot, know or even have evidence that the object is real, is not false but still it is untrue, for there is no genuine question to which it is an answer. (Of course, the same applies also to the *standard* antiskeptical answer, but this is hardly something the skeptic would wish to appeal to in support of *his* answer.) The reality of the object which the skeptic questions is not a matter of fact, which we may or may not have knowledge of, or evidence for, in the way we may or may not have knowledge of, or evidence for, its properties and relations. It is something we ourselves impose on the object. The imposition cannot be true or false, right or wrong, though it can be genuine or facetious (i.e., a serious application of the concept, a genuine judgment, or merely a whimsical utterance).

Of course, I am speaking here only of the primary, noninferential judgments of identity and reality. After the initial applications of the two concepts (which surely precede the acquisition of language—after all, words themselves have to be recognized, seen as the same again and as parts of reality, if they are to be learned), a presumably intersubjective conceptual structure is built up, or joined in, that *guides* (not *causes* or *justifies*) our conceptual decisions about reality and identity. It is only then that it would make sense to speak of *criteria* and of *paradigms* of reality and identity. Inferential judgments, for example about the reality of objects in the distant past, though in themselves they too are neither true nor false, can be epistemically defective if the inference is logically defective or a premise, other than one asserting identity or reality, is false. Such an inferential judgment can be said to be also mistaken, but only in the sense a decision reached through logical or factual error can be said to be mistaken. It does not follow, indeed it is senseless to say, that the decision is *false*. A clear ex-

ample is a jury's judgment, based on false testimony or its own sloppy reasoning, that the defendant is the murderer. We call such judgments mistaken simply because in ordinary language and thought we have no clear recognition of the transcendental nature of the concepts of identity and reality. But if we think of their applications as decisions (which in fact we do in the case of a jury's judgment), then we can understand the judgments in question more easily, especially when we note that in ordinary language we do speak of mistaken, wrong decisions, even though we do not mean by this that they are *false* decisions.

The decision to impose the concept of reality (or of identity), like any other decision, may vary in degree of firmness. It may range from being almost automatic to being quite hesitant. But its degree of firmness, too, does not admit of genuine justification or explanation; there can be no question of its being reasonable or unreasonable. And even if made hesitantly the decision remains a decision. Hesitancy is a characteristic of how we come to make a decision, not of the decision itself. Just as there is no such thing as a false decision, there is no such thing as a half-decision.

There lies the untruth of skepticism. But there is also the truth of it, rooted in the fact that as with any other decisions we are not logically bound by our past or present applications of the concept of reality. If we were, they would not be genuine decisions. In the future we may change our applications of the concept, and therefore what we count as real now we may not count as real tomorrow. We may be determined now that we will not make a change, but we do not know now that we will not. Future applications of a concept are future decisions, and these, the skeptic would reasonably say, we cannot know. To that extent, and in that very special sense, the skeptic is right in holding that we cannot know of any perceived object that it is real. For any judgment about the reality of an object perceived now or in the past is hostage to the judgments directly or indirectly about it that may be made in the future. (Whether the oasis I see now is real depends in part on whether I shall see it also an hour from now.)

We can hardly object to the skeptic's claim, if so understood, without indulging in a search for suitably convenient accounts of knowledge and evidence, which we forswore at the very beginning. Moreover, skepticism with respect to future decisions enjoys considerable support from common sense, as well as from many philosophers who are not skeptics about the external world. It is also a direct consequence of what in chapter 3 I called the skeptic's general argument, according to which the only concepts of knowledge and evidence that seem both relevant and intelligible are the traditional, roughly Cartesian but also Humean ones, of knowledge as the unthinkability of mistake and of evidence as entailing that for which it is evidence. (That argument was a consequence of the dream-argument concerning the particular question, an argument in which I could find no fault.) Obviously, we have no such knowledge or evidence about our future decisions. To argue that we do (for example, through causal considerations) would require us to embark on a strategically misguided and probably

hopeless search for answers to skepticism about future decisions in order to find answers to skepticism about the external world. Have we in this way saved our knowledge of the external world only by destroying it? Our intention was not to save it but merely to acknowledge that there is untruth in skepticism. Nevertheless, a central thesis of this book is that there is also truth in it.

If what I have said so far here and earlier in chapter 5 is right, then there is a sense in which we make the world ourselves, and thus we may endorse Nelson Goodman's assertion that "even within what we perceive and remember, we dismiss as illusory or negligible what cannot be fitted into the architecture of the world we are building,"[1] as long as we bear in mind that we "make" the world ourselves only in virtue of the special character of the concepts of identity and existence. (Indeed, there are also what at the end of the previous chapter I called secondary transcendental concepts, but they presuppose the applications of the concepts of identity and existence, and thus the *worldliness* of the world, and serve the special role of making *thought* and *language* about the world possible.) We do not make the world by just "adopting" a certain language or theory or symbolic or conceptual scheme. Thus our view differs from the familiar forms of what may be called global conceptual irrealism (including Goodman's) by being orderly, hierarchical, uniquely focused, and enjoying an obvious rationale. It is committed to conceptual irrealism primarily with respect to identity. And this difference is due to the fundamental fact that, unlike those global irrealisms, it begins with an account of the concept of reality or existence (which is reducible to that of identity), a topic on which they remain surprisingly silent. One has no business being a realist or an irrealist without first providing and defending an account of the concept of reality. As to the secondary transcendental concepts, the rationale for them is that they are necessary for any thought and language about a world that is already "made."

Of course, I am fully aware that this view appears incredible. In the final section of this book I shall try to show that the appearance is deceptive. But something does need to be said about it here, at the very beginning, lest the reader decides to abandon us now! So let me urge that the view really depends on what at bottom are two tautologies. One is that if, in accordance with the thesis of chapter 1, by "ourselves" we understand a contentless consciousness directly confronted with objects, rather than some zoological species that happens to exist now in the world, then the only conception of ourselves we can form is in terms of the objects we perceptually and conceptually confront; there is nothing more to ourselves that is relevant, consciousness exhausts itself in its objects, it is the mere revelation of them. The second tautology is that the only world we conceive of and know is the world we do conceive of and know, the world we confront perceptually and conceptually, even though it is not self-contradictory to *say* that the world "in itself" is totally different. But how can a substantive view depend on tautologies? We don't *want* our view to be substantive. It

is intended to explicate certain concepts that have bedeviled our understanding of the relationship between ourselves and the world throughout the history of philosophy. And concepts are explicated only through tautologies, if the explication is adequate. In section 6 I shall say much more about these two tautologies.

2. The First Three Levels of the Skeptic's Question

Let us now get to some details. The skeptic may ask the particular *epistemic* question on several levels. On each of the initial three levels, discussed in this section, she would have an obvious objection to the answer I shall offer to her question on that level, an objection bound to occur to the reader. But I shall not even mention these objections because all of them will receive a general, though qualified, response in section 3. I hope the reader will keep this in mind when reading the next few pages.

On what presumably is the most fundamental level, that of identity judgments intended to confirm the reality of presently perceived visual and tactual objects (the fundamentality of this level is due to the previously noted fact that our conception of the world is almost entirely visual and tactual, and of course the present has an obvious epistemological priority), the skeptic may ask (with Berkeley), How do I know that the object I am touching now is the same as the object I see before me now? The answer, as I argued in the previous chapter, is that, in such a primary, noninferential case (I assume it is such, though in special circumstances it might not be), I just "see," immediately *conceive*, the objects as identical, as being one and the same object, thus establishing their reality in the way probably most familiar to us. (If I suspect that the seen object is hallucinatory I try to touch it, and if I suspect that the touched object is hallucinatory I try to see it.) I impose on them the concept of identity and thus the concept of reality. Once again, let me say that we must not think of identity as a mysterious dyadic relation the presence of which in any particular case renders the "two" things identical. This is especially evident in the example just given, since (as Berkeley was quick to note) there is nothing factual in it to ground the identity, not even similarity between the objects ("ideas") identified. Indeed, it is false to say of two entities that they are identical, and empty to say of one entity that it is identical with itself. Nevertheless, the standard application of the concept of identity is precisely to cases that appear to involve two entities. What "justifies" that application in the primary, noninferential cases, with which alone we are concerned here? Nothing. The concept of identity is imposed by us on the "two" objects of perception, and nothing in the world justifies this imposition, but also nothing in the world prohibits it.

We can now go further and argue that if we adopt a direct realist position with respect to memory, then we can reply to the skeptic's question on the second most fundamental level, that of the application of the concept

of identity and thus of the concept of reality to cases involving a presently perceived and a remembered object.

I shall not engage here in a detailed discussion of memory. It ought to be enough to point out that direct realism with regard to memory can be defended along lines quite similar to those of our defense of direct realism with regard to perception, since both are consequences of the general direct realist conception of consciousness, explained in chapter 1. Therefore, little needs to be said here in defense of direct realism with regard to memory. Corresponding to the mental-contents theory of perception would be the imagist or some other kind of representational theory of memory, namely, a theory holding that whatever else memory involves, when occurrent it involves awareness of a mental image or some other mental representation. That this view has no phenomenological plausibility even in the case of mere imagination was abundantly argued by Sartre in his two books on the imagination and little needs repeating here.[2] To imagine Peter is to be directly conscious of Peter, not of some mental simulacrum of Peter, though this consciousness is quite different from perception. And, we may now say, to remember Peter as he was perceived on a certain previous occasion is to be directly conscious of Peter as he was perceived then, not of a memory picture or representation of him. It is high time that we expelled this ghost from the machine! Of course, memory can be nonveridical, just as perception can, but this is a threat to direct realism with respect to memory no more than it is a threat to direct realism with respect to perception. Also analogously to perception, in veridical memory we expect that there is a causal connection between what is remembered and the remembering. But this is no more a reason for accepting a causal theory of memory than the analogous expectation in the case of perception was a reason for accepting a causal theory of perception. And, finally, of course the veridically remembered object or event is in the past, while the rememberer while remembering it is in the present. But such a temporal distance is no more paradoxical than the spatial distance between what is perceived and the perceiver.

If direct realism with respect to memory is granted, then our answer to the skeptic's question on the second level would be, mutatis mutandis, the same as our answer on the first level. In the primary, noninferential cases on the second level I impose the concept of identity and thus the concept of reality on the presently perceived and the remembered objects; I don't infer their identity from their perceived and remembered properties, nor of course do I perceive it. (Descartes's example of the piece of wax that is judged as he says by "the mind," not by the senses, to remain the same even through a virtually complete change in its observable properties illustrates the point, whatever Descartes's actual intentions may have been.) So it would seem that now we can be assured of the reality not only of some present, but also of some past objects, namely, all those we identify, through memory, with presently perceived objects. The person I now unexpectedly perceive is real (I am not hallucinating) because he is identical

with the person I remember seeing next door on numerous occasions. (The obvious objection will be addressed in section 3.) And thus we have, incidentally, a solution of the metaphysical problem of individual identity through time.

The third level on which the skeptic's question can be asked is that of public identifiability, for example, my identification of what I perceive with what you perceive, surely a crucial mode of confirming the reality of an object. Unfortunately, I cannot deal with it here in the detail it deserves. The reason is that to do so would require a full-scale ontological and phenomenological inquiry into the nature, indeed existence, of the self, or ego. Hume denied that he found any such entity, "to which our several impressions and ideas are suppos'd to have a reference." (This is the issue here, not that of personal identity through time.) When in *The Transcendence of the Ego* Sartre denied that consciousness has any inhabitants, he had in mind mainly an ego, a *subject* of consciousness (though he allowed that the ego can be an *object* of consciousness as external, transcendent, to consciousness). In "A Defense of Common Sense," Moore also expressed doubts about the existence of an ego. In the *Tractatus Logico-Philosophicus* Wittgenstein explicitly denied it. And so did Husserl in the *Logical Investigations*, though not in his later writings. If we were to accept their position, as I am inclined to do,[3] then the distinction between oneself and the other becomes extremely murky, as Derek Parfit has shown eloquently and at great length,[4] and so does the notion of public versus private identifiability. But what is not murky, and is sufficient for our purposes here, is that there cannot be a drastic divergence between my applications of the concepts of identity and reality, and another's applications. For the other is recognizable by me as someone whose judgments I must take into account only if she (generally) uses those concepts as I do. If she does not, not only would I not understand what she says and what she does, I would not regard the sounds she makes as applications of those concepts, indeed as genuine statements. This is why, though *irrealist* with respect to the concepts of identity and reality, our theory is not *relativist*. There is some similarity between what I have said and what Donald Davidson says, in a different way and with different motivation, in "The Very Idea of a Conceptual Scheme."[5]

3. The Fourth Level

The skeptic may now ask her question, indeed the question the reader has doubtless been ready to ask all along, on a fourth and for us much more difficult level: How do I know that the identifiability of the object, on any of the previous three levels, is indefinite, which is what the existence, the reality, of the object must consist in, according to your account? My provisional answer is that no sense can be given to the idea of an object's being genuinely (i.e., seriously and sincerely) identified on one occasion but not being so identifiable on any number of other occasions, whether by oneself

or by others. What could possibly prevent such identifications? Because of the very nature of the concept of identity there is nothing in the world or in logic to prevent us or others from making the additional identity judgments, when the occasion arises, since the application of the concept of identity is a matter of decision, though certainly not a whimsical or capricious one, a mere utterance of an identity sentence, but rather one exhibiting a conceptual habit.

For example, if the object seems nowhere to be found again, instead of judging that it was hallucinatory we may *rule* that it has ceased to exist, or for some reason has become permanently unavailable. If after the initial identification of a cube, on any of the first three levels, no further identification *seems* possible, if after identifying what I see now with what I saw earlier I no longer see before me anything that I would identify with it, nor does anyone else, I can *decide* that it has simply ceased to exist, or has moved to where it cannot be perceived. I have emphasized the words "rule" and "decide," because judgments of reality are ultimately judgments of identity and these cannot be expressive of discoveries, since there is nothing to discover; they are expressive of decisions. Which decision we make would depend on our general conception of the world, on how seriously we take our causal assumptions and what science tells us, on what perceptions we find ourselves having, but ultimately they depend on our habits of employing the concept of identity, for our conception of the world, our causal assumptions, our science, and our understanding of our perceptions all presuppose other judgments of reality and thus applications of the concept of identity.

The skeptic may argue that we do not know the reality of any present or past objects because we do not know that it will not be disconfirmed by our future perceivings. However, what matters is not the bare fact of our future perceivings but *what* they will be, and this is (as a matter of fact, not of logic) indistinguishable for us from *how* we shall conceptualize them, that is, what conceptual decisions we shall make about them, especially with respect to identity and difference between their objects and the objects of past and present perceivings, or between qualities of all those objects. For there is nothing to prevent us from identifying the object of *any* future perceiving with the object of any past or present perceiving. Of course, the occurrence of the future perceiving is an objective matter, it is not the result of conceptualization. But it is epistemically relevant only insofar as it is conceptualized. If it is not conceptualized, it neither confirms nor disconfirms anything. This is the point made familiar by opponents of the "given," from Wilfrid Sellars to Laurence BonJour and John McDowell. A conceptual irrealist, whether global or only with respect to the concept of identity, is not a peculiar sort of idealist who would regard the very occurrence of a perceiving as merely a conceptual matter. But neither would he regard it as epistemically relevant to anything if it is not conceptualized.

A present judgment of reality expresses also a determination to be willing to make identity judgments about the object on future suitable occa-

sions, since reality is indefinite identifiability. And now the skeptic may argue that we do not know that we will be willing to make the identity judgments we expected to be willing to make. But I have granted this. It is enough for our purposes that the skeptic may hold that we do not know what our future perceivings will be (and therefore whether the objects of our past and present perceivings are real), only on the grounds that we do not know what our conceptual decisions about them will be. As we have seen, presumably she would hold this because she holds in general that we do not know what our future decisions, of whatever kind, will be. But this would hardly be news. It would be either an epistemological claim about knowledge of future decisions, which would not be repugnant to common sense, or an existential claim about the human condition, one eloquently defended by Sartre and of course by many others, including nonphilosophers. At any rate, it would no longer be skepticism about the external world.

But suppose that originally I made the identity judgment regarding, say, the seen and the touched objects in what I now believe was a hallucination, and thus believe that the object is not indefinitely identifiable, whether by myself or by others. Clearly, I want to count the object as unreal and yet, equally clearly, when I originally perceived it I made a genuine identity judgment regarding it. Does it follow that identification on one occasion does not imply indefinite identifiability, and thus that either the concept of reality has to be understood in a way other than the one I have proposed or we must be willing to say that a genuine identity judgment can be wrong, thus allowing the skeptic to ask us how we can know with respect to any *identity* judgment that it is not wrong? No, there is another alternative. Just as there is nothing to prevent us from making an identity judgment, there is nothing to prevent us from *withdrawing, canceling,* a previously made identity judgment, not in the sense of counting it as false but in the sense of no longer subscribing to it, no longer taking it into account, exactly as we may no longer subscribe to or remain bound by a previous decision on any other matter, say, the pursuit of a certain course of action. And if the skeptic asks, How do I know on any particular occasion that the identity judgment I am making will not be withdrawn in the future, my reply would be the same as the one I gave earlier. We may not know what our future decisions, including cancelations of past decisions, will be, but for the general reasons I mentioned earlier, not for any reasons specific to skepticism about the external world.

5. The Dream-Argument Answered

Let us apply all this now to the skeptic's particular epistemic question examined in chapter 3: How do I know that I am not dreaming now? Even if I make identity judgments when dreaming, the skeptic would say, obviously the objects so identified would not be indefinitely identifiable, whether by others or by myself when I wake up, except perhaps when I am

dreaming of objects that happen to be real. But the cash-value of the question, How do I know that I am not dreaming now? lies in the possibility of my presently having the experience of what we call awakening from a dream and finding that what I had dreamt about is no longer identifiable by me or by others, at least not as it was perceived in the dream. What is this experience? For our purposes its only relevant feature is that it is the coming to accept the reality of the objects now perceived and to reject the previously accepted reality of the objects perceived in the dream. On what grounds would this be done? Ultimately, on none. We just find ourselves applying or being ready to apply the concept of identity to the newly perceived objects in certain ways, and we just find ourselves no longer applying or being willing to apply that concept to the previously (in the dream) perceived objects. Now, our view that reality is indefinite identifiability requires us to say that this would also involve our withdrawing the identity judgments we remember making in the dream, but this consequence is easily acceptable to common sense. Was the car I dreamt I drove the same as the car I dreamt purchasing? We may say in our dream report that it was, but we have no genuine motivation for *insisting* that it was. If the identity judgment is questioned, we may just shrug off the question by saying, Well what does it matter whether the car was or was not the same, that was just a dream after all! More complicated is the case in which we say we dreamt of an object that we now perceive when awake and regard as real (e.g., one dreamt of one's real car). One possible view is that there is no motivation for an answer to the question whether the object now perceived is the same as the dreamt object or merely resembles it in many respects. What is the cash-value of asking whether you dreamt of your real car or merely of a very similar car you believed was yours? Another answer is that the identity judgment would not be, need not be, withdrawn and thus the reality of the object rejected, because that in the dream which was unreal was not the object but the situation one dreamt the object to be in, for example, that one was driving it in Paris.

But, the skeptic will ask, How do you know that you will not presently have the experience of awakening from a dream and hence withdrawing the identity judgments you made in the dream and making very different ones? The answer is that nothing compels me to describe, to conceptualize, any experience I have as one of awakening from a dream. I could keep my present judgments and not make new, radically different, ones. I could regard the objects perceived in the dream as real and thus not as perceived in a dream, and I could regard the objects perceived later as unreal. I could conceptualize the experience as one of falling asleep and beginning to dream! Which I *shall* do is perhaps something I do not know now. But whatever I do, the resulting conceptual restructuring of my world is my work, and there is no room in it for false judgment, for mistake about reality, and thus lack of *knowledge*, there is room only for changing the decisions I make. There is nothing to which we can appeal in answering the question, How do I know that I am not dreaming now? for what is at issue

is reality, therefore, ultimately, identity, and identity is not a relation or anything else in the world the presence of which may justify our applications of the concept of identity. Neither our dreaming now nor our being awake now is a matter of fact. The experience of awakening, of course, is a matter of fact, but epistemically relevant only if conceptualized. This may be thought of as our final response to Descartes's dream-argument.

To reach this conclusion is not to accept skepticism. It is to deprive skepticism of its central presupposition: that the distinction between reality and unreality, which is rooted in the distinction between identity and nonidentity, is a distinction between matters of fact, matters about which it makes sense to speak of having knowledge or evidence. Ultimately, it is we who impose that distinction on the objects we confront. This is why, ordinarily, we take Descartes's dream-argument as a mere intellectual puzzle. We are the source of the reality of our world, and the possibility of our finding ourselves presently awakening from a dream is ordinarliy not regarded by us as a genuine possibility, or even just as an improbability. It is excluded as a genuine possibility, not because it involves contradiction or violates causal laws, but because it is alien to our *present* world, for the reality of which we alone are responsible. A fortiori, it is excluded also as just an improbability. That we are not aware of this fact is due only to our deeply ingrained habits of applying the concepts of identity and reality. Yet, the truth remains that, unless the skeptic's *general* argument in chapter 3, section 7, is met, we do not know or even have evidence now that we will not conceptualize an experience we shall presently have as one of awakening, that we will not make the relevant conceptual *decisions*. To this extent, and in this sense, the skeptic is right, is in the truth.

6. The Fifth Level: Qualitative Illusion

To be responsible for the reality of our world is not to have *created* it. The occurrence of our perceivings and experiences is not a function of the application of concepts, though what we perceive or experience something *as*, is. This is why nothing that I have said implies that there is no room for what we *call* objective error, which is most obvious with respect to the future, in cases of unfulfilled expectation with respect to what we shall perceive or experience. But even what we call objective error must be so understood that the "discovery" of it consists in our unexpectedly finding ourselves unwilling to make a certain application of the concept of identity; this unwillingness may be inseparable from the objective circumstances in which we find ourselves, but it is rendered neither justified nor unjustified by them.

What we call objective error is more common with respect to the qualities, not the reality, of the objects of perception. Seeing a cardboard object as a cube, even though we face only three sides, would be "erroneous" if what we saw turns out on inspection to be merely an ensemble of three square pieces of cardboard meeting in a single point at right angles. Of

course, nothing prevents us from identifying this three-sided object with the object earlier perceived as a cube; indeed ordinarily we would do so, we would not take ourselves to have been hallucinating. Nevertheless, we still would have made an "error" if we had judged that the three-sided object was a cube, and thus expected to be able to perceive six sides of it. It would be an "error" not regarding the reality of the object but regarding its nature, its qualities, properties.

The skeptic would now ask, on a *fifth* but not nearly as fundamental level as the first four, How do I know that what I shall perceive in the future will not show that I am wrong about the *qualities* of what I perceive now or of what I have perceived in the past? Such a question can be raised about shapes, colors, indeed about any perceived qualities of the object. They are not questions about the reality of the perceived object. The latter is guaranteed by our continued application of the concept of identity to *it*. The object perceived as a cube is identical with the object perceived as an ensemble of three cardboard squares, and just as real. Only it is not as it was perceived. So skepticism on the fifth level is only skepticism regarding the qualities of objects, not regarding their reality. It is relevant to the possibility of qualitative illusion, not of existential illusion.

It is with respect to this version of skepticism that our account of the concept of reality may seem to be impotent. But is it? We must recall the discussion of qualitative illusion in chapter 1. I appealed there to unreal perceptual expanses. And we can now say, as I did then, that the skeptic's question still concerns existence, reality, though not of material objects but of expanses that may but need not be identical with parts of the surfaces of material objects. Which shape of the perceived real object is its real shape? It is the shape of the perceived expanse that is identical with the object's surface and thus is indefinitely identifiable. And while whether it is or is not depends in part on our or others' *future* perceivings, the answer will ultimately rest on our decision to apply or not to apply the concept of identity to the expanses that are the objects of those perceivings. And in making that decision we also can rule that the case is not one of qualitative illusion but rather of qualitative change in the object. Whether we will do so would depend on our willingness to apply the concept of reality to both the newly perceived surface and the previously perceived surface of the object, in the context of our past experience, scientific judgments, and judgments about other presently perceived objects. The mention here of such a context does not at all signal even a partial commitment to a coherentist theory of justification. The context in question is relevant in the sense that it is part of the occasion that may trigger a genuine application of the concept of reality, not in the sense that, even in part, it determines the veridicality or justifiability of that application. The point is merely that we do not make genuine applications of the concept of reality, or indeed of any concept, in a vacuum!

So, skepticism with regard to the qualities of objects can be answered in the same way as we answered skepticism with regard to their reality. There

is no matter of fact that is responsible for what we call objective error about qualities. Objective error, whether about the reality or about the qualities of what we perceive, is our finding ourselves unwilling to make an application of the concept of reality which we had expected to be willing to make. It is *objective* in two ways: (1) we face a context, which is not our creation, in which we find ourselves unwilling to make the application, and (2) we expected to be willing to make the application but it turned out that we are unwilling. But it is an error only in the now familiar sense of our not having known and indeed having been mistaken about what future conceptual *decisions* we would make. This is why the skeptic cannot simply insist that we cannot know or even have evidence about what our future *perceivings* will be. There is a sense in which she is right. But there is a sense also in which she is wrong. As I pointed out earlier, our future perceivings are objective matters of fact, but they are *epistemically* relevant only if conceptualized. What we cannot know is how we shall conceptualize them, especially with respect to the identity or nonidentity of their objects with the objects of certain past and present perceivings. There is no independent sense in which we can or cannot know *what* they will be. Of course, this does not mean that perceivings are reducible to concepts or to applications of concepts. To hold that they are would be to adopt the peculiar sort of idealism I mentioned earlier. They are the *objective* contexts that trigger or fail to trigger applications of the concepts of identity and reality. But they do not render these applications true or false, right or wrong.

The skeptic may say that our judgments of the past and present reality of the qualities we perceive do presuppose that they will not be withdrawn, cancelled, in the future because of recalcitrant ("disconfirming") future perceivings, and if we cannot know that such perceivings will not occur then we cannot know of any past or present quality that it is real. But to say this would be once again to ignore the fact that future perceivings do not *as such* occasion withdrawals of judgments. They do so only if conceptualized in a certain way with respect to the identity or nonidentity of their objects with objects of past and present perceivings. Of course, we could deal with recalcitrant future perceivings, with unfulfilled expectation, by imposing our concepts of identity and reality in such a way that the perceivings would not be recalcitrant, the expectations would not be unfulfilled. If we expected to see a white cat and instead saw a black one, we could assert that black is white! But this would be whimsy, not a genuine judgment, it would not be a serious application of the concept of identity, it would not be an application that exhibits a habit, a way of life. What we cannot know is, not the qualities of the perceived objects, but what genuine decisions to apply the concept of identity we shall make in the future. So, once again, skepticism about the external world turns out to be skepticism about our future decisions.

Nevertheless, while our judgments of the reality of the objects we perceive usually consist in confident, responsible applications of the concept of identity, this is not quite so with our judgments of their qualities. Even

a casual acknowledgment of what science tells us seems to call for a certain skepticism. We have no difficulty in accepting the reality of a perceived table even if we agree that it is largely empty space containing some particles, for, despite what some philosophers have said, we have no difficulty in applying the concept of identity to the perceived table and the largely empty space. But doesn't the table have, say, color, while the space and the particles in it do not? Indeed, physics does not talk about the color of the latter since it does not need to talk about it in pursuing its own purposes. From this nothing follows about whether they do have color.[6] But under the influence of scientific or pseudoscientific considerations, we may decide that they do not. If so, we can still enforce the principle of the indiscernibility of identicals by denying that the colored perceptual expanse we call the surface of the table, which we do see, is real, yet asserting the identity of the table and the largely empty space. But we would have sacrificed our belief in the color of the table. What matters is not that color is a "secondary quality." A "primary quality," such as shape, is not an exception. Just consider what physics, especially on the quantum level, would say about the shape of our table!

This is why, to the extent to which we are influenced by science, we do not expect perception to be the arbiter of what qualities of the objects we perceive are real and what are not. We believe that is the business of science. But this is not skepticism; it is scientism. In fact, if she is to be at all consistent, the skeptic would immediately question the epistemic legitimacy of science, by questioning the sorts of nondemonstrative inferences with which it is rife. She would even receive some support from scientifically informed common sense, which tends to agree with Mark Twain that science is an endeavor in which "one gets such wholesome returns of conjecture out of such trifling investment of fact." Scientifically informed common sense takes science seriously enough to restrain itself from taking its own judgments about the perceived qualities of objects too seriously. But, like Mark Twain, it also would not be totally inimical to the skeptic's doubts about science. It may well be aware, for example, of the chaotic present state of astrophysics, the science of the nature of the universe as a whole.

The dialectical situation we face now is complex, confusing, but not unfamiliar. Science tells us that the world is qualitatively quite different from what we perceive it to be and thus supports skepticism about our knowledge of the qualities of perceived objects. On the other hand, consistent skepticism attacks the epistemic value of the scientific method, by questioning, in a way familiar to all of us, especially the epistemic value of induction and abduction. It thus undermines any skepticism about qualities that appeals to science. The moral to be drawn is that to be consistent with general skepticism about the external world, skepticism about the qualities of perceivable objects cannot appeal to what science tells us.

Of course, we should have expected this result. Science can hardly be granted any special authority in the appraisal of skepticism with regard to

the senses, for the familiar reason that to do so would beg the question against the skeptic, since ultimately what science tells us is necessarily, even if not wholly, based on what the senses tell *it*. But the deeper and not so familiar reason is that our concept of reality (or of identity) holds sway even over science, for we do not, cannot, accept scientific claims that conflict with it. We may perhaps accept an imaginary scientific account according to which the cardboard box we saw a moment ago and the drop of water we now see are really identical, that a peculiar transformation of the former into the latter has taken place. But we would not accept an imaginary scientist's claim that the cardboard box is really one of our political attitudes, just as most nonphilosophers and still some philosophers would not accept a materialist's claim that our headaches are nothing but electrical events in our brains. For the application of the concept of identity does take into account the qualities of the objects identified; it does not take place in a vacuum. It's just that its supposed correctness or incorrectness is not a logical or any other consequence of them, or of anything else. In fact, it is neither correct nor incorrect, if this means true or false; it is only a genuine manifestation of a habit, or an unserious, whimsical, mere utterance of an identity sentence.

Of course, it remains true that our decisions about the perceived qualities of objects are less confident than our decisions about their reality, either because of the influence of science or because of the accumulated wisdom of common sense, which is aware of such facts as perceptual relativity. But neither what science says nor the acknowledgment of perceptual relativity *justifies* this lesser confidence. They merely constitute contexts in which we make our conceptual decisions, they do not render them right or wrong, and nothing compels us to conceptualize them as even relevant. We just happen to do so.

6. The Sixth Level: Idealism? Irrealism?

The truth of skepticism with respect to what I have called the particular question is limited. It rests, with respect to the reality, as well as the qualities, of a perceived material object, not on the familiar worries about sense perception, but on considerations regarding the knowability of future decisions and perhaps regarding free will. Skepticism does not show that the judgments of identity and thus of reality we make now or have made in the past may be *false*, but it does show that we may withdraw them, cancel them. There is no room for error in such judgments, but there is plenty of room for change. We have seen that this applies also to the dream-problem. I do not know that I shall not presently have an experience I will conceptualize as one of awakening. I do not take this possibility seriously, it is just an intellectual game to speculate about it, but I have no argument against it. This is the truth of skepticism.

Yet there is also the untruth of skepticism. We can accept the reality and perhaps qualities of (some) material objects, even though we do not know

that the past and present judgments expressing this acceptance will not be withdrawn in the future. For we do know that they will not be shown to have been *false*, since there is nothing to make them false (or true). And we do know that we *can* always remain loyal to them because of our freedom in applying the concepts of identity and reality, though we do not know that in fact we *shall* remain loyal to them. The skeptic has not been given everything he wanted but, I believe, he has been given his due. Surely, in view of the history of the topic, nothing more and nothing less should have been expected. Skepticism with regard to the senses has become, in effect, skepticism with regard to our future decisions. It is to this extent and in this sense that skepticism with respect to the particular question is true. Yet our answer to the skeptic who asks whether we ever know in a particular perceptual situation that the perceived material object, or quality of it, is real remains that the question does not arise, since reality is an object not of knowledge but of decision. To this extent and in this sense, skepticism with respect to the particular question is untrue. If so, then skepticism with respect to the general question must also be untrue. Thus the conclusion in chapter 4 receives welcome additional support. But we must remember that, for the reasons I have explained in the present chapter, here untruth is not falsehood but the absence of truth. So we have no refutation of skepticism. But we do have an answer to it. As I warned in the introduction, this is the best that we should have expected.

Have we avoided skepticism only to accept idealism? Clearly, much depends on what is meant by "idealism." I certainly have not said that what we perceive is mental, or that it can exist only if perceived. On the contrary, one purpose of the first two chapters was precisely to deny this. Nor have I defended global conceptual irrealism (such as Nelson Goodman's). Insofar as it merely holds that how the world is *understood* (i.e., conceptualized) depends on the concepts we possess, it is a tautology, though a useful because an explicative one. But insofar as it holds that our conceptual scheme is not subject to revision by reference to, through comparison with, the extent and degrees to which it reflects the objective facts in the world, it is not at all a tautology and indeed I hold it to be false. Certainly, nothing that I have said leads to such global irrealism, especially when the latter is presented in a linguistically or culturally relativistic garb. Usually this would be done through a crass identification of concepts with words and of a conceptual scheme with a language, the latter perhaps glorified by being called a "form of life" or made to sound fashionably scientific by being called a "theory"; we even find the world itself sometimes described as a "text." Yet I have admitted to an irrealist core of my view, namely, that the fundamental concept, that of identity, corresponds to nothing in the world, and therefore that its application cannot be judged as right or wrong, except in the sense of being serious or whimsical, of fitting or not fitting our habits of its employment. (Would the medieval philosophers who accepted the doctrine of the transcendentals, and Aristotle, from whom they derived it, count as global irrealists, let alone idealists, just because they

recognized that the concept of being, which of course they regarded as essential to any thought and knowledge, corresponded to nothing that all beings share?)

Were all other concepts definable solely in terms of the concept of identity, our view would still differ from the familiar forms of global conceptual irrealism, as I pointed out earlier, by being orderly, hierarchical, uniquely focused, by reducing all "irrealism" to irrealism with respect to identity, and it would still be free from linguisticism, by which I mean the view Hilary Putnam once described as holding that "objects arise out of discourse, rather than being prior to discourse,"[7] a view that has marred much of twentieth-century philosophy. But they are not. Most concepts are derived ultimately from what we are aware of, whether perceptually or intellectually. One cannot have the concept of redness without having seen red things, at least not the concept of redness a normally sighted person has. To be sure, a concept is a principle of classification, as H. H. Price argued in his classic work on the subject, *Thinking and Experience*,[8] and thus its *use* in classification presupposes the concept of identity. But this does not mean that it is derived from the latter concept. Ordinarily, it is derived from awareness. The concept of redness is derived from *seeing* red things, not from a definition such as "x is red if and only if its color is identical with this [this being a paradigm of redness]," even if *saying* that A is red is true if and only if *saying* that its color is identical with this, is also true. As Roderick Chisholm has remarked in a different context, it is absurd to hold that "in order to believe, with respect to any particular thing x, that x has a certain property F, one must *compare* x with some other thing y and thus assert or believe of x that it has something in common with the other thing y."[9]

A concept must not be confused with the predicate expressing it. Not all concepts are expressed by words, and not all predicates express concepts. Most color shades I recognize I cannot name. And a grammatical predicate such as "grue," defined as applying to all things "examined before *t* just in case they are green but to other things just in case they are blue"[10] expresses before *t* no *applicable* principle of classification or concept that is different from that expressed by "green," and after *t* it expresses no *applicable* principle of classification or concept that is different from that expressed by "blue." This is why before *t* we *recognize* the greenness of green objects but not their grueness. Even if an object is in fact grue, we can no more properly say that in recognizing it as green we are recognizing it as grue than we can say that in recognizing a certain heavenly body as the evening star we are recognizing it as the morning star. The view that "grue" is not "projectible" only because it is not "entrenched" in our actual linguistic practices does indeed lead to conceptual relativism, but only by assuming the sort of extreme nominalism I have called linguisticism.

My rejection of global irrealism, linguisticism, and conceptual relativism is of course motivated by the sort of qualifiedly realist answer I wish to give to the skeptic about the external world. But it concerns directly only

realism with respect to the material objects we perceive, since their reality is what the skeptic with regard to the senses questions. It is not intended to imply an espousal of realism with respect to every domain that has been discussed in recent controversies between "realists" and "antirealists." For these domains are importantly different from each other, and one can be a realist with respect to some but not with respect to others.[11] To be a realist in ethics requires considerations quite different from those required by realism in the philosophy of science. Indeed, elsewhere I have defended the former,[12] but I would not defend the latter with respect to the more esoteric parts of physics. Similar remarks may be made with respect to theology, mathematics (I would be a realist with respect to parts but not all of it), aesthetics, and so on. I should be understood to be speaking of realism only with respect to the domain, the world, of perceivable material objects, for it is only the reality of these that the skeptic about the external world questions. Of course, to some extent irrealism about identity and reality ultimately affects all domains, but in most there are independent reasons for irrealism (realism) that are specific to them. I am an irrealist with respect to astrology, but hardly for any deep, ultimate conceptual reasons.

Once our concept of identity is fixed, that is, our habits for employing it are established, the general categorial structure of the world is also fixed, and the adequacy of our statements, theories, and thoughts to it can be determined, in principle, by a comparison with it. (Hence the realism in our view.) We can even describe this adequacy as truth, even truth as correspondence, in some sense of "correspondence." (*Which* sense that might be would depend, contrary to the prevalent opinion, not on semantic considerations or vague general concerns about realism vs. antirealism, but on what account we can give of the terms of the relation of correspondence, presumably judgments, on one hand, and states of affairs, on the other; I am uneasy about the latter and find little in the literature that is helpful.)[13] That what true judgments correspond to might be in part our work is irrelevant. An architect's judgments about the building he has designed or plans to design are not less true because he might have changed his mind, or because nothing in the world required that particular design. Moreover, there may be also the truth and falsehood of our judgments about the objects of our consciousness in abstraction from the imposition on them of the concept of reality. Such abstraction would correspond to Husserl's phenomenological reduction; our abstracting from the concept of reality would correspond to performing the *epoché*, the bracketing of the question of the reality of the world. In chapter 5 I referred to Plato's insistence in the *Theaetetus* that a Heraclitean world, in which everything is in flux, makes stable, lasting, genuine judgments impossible. The reason is that in such a world nothing is the same as anything else, nothing is recognizable. But the phenomenological reduction is not the affirmation of such a world. It is merely the abstention from affirming the reality of the world as seen from the natural standpoint. So our irrealism about identity has no special implications regarding even the truth of phenomenological judgments.

Yet, it may be said, the most important fact about the world is what is identical with what, and our view makes this fact merely one about our conceptual habits, even if, as we have seen, it does not imply conceptual relativism. Yes, but what are the alternatives? Those I argued against in chapter 5? Let the reader try to meet those arguments. If she cannot, perhaps she would see that her dissatisfaction stems not from a perception of cognitive failure on our part but from the cognitive illusion that Kant tried to dispel more than two centuries ago: the illusion that we make no contribution to our knowledge of the world, and therefore that our knowledge of it and *it* itself *qua* known are not partly a function of our cognitive endowment, whether perceptual or conceptual or logical. It is hardly idle science fiction to acknowledge that the world of beings (inhabiting perhaps another galaxy) with sense organs, concepts, and ways of reasoning completely different from ours would also be a world completely different from our world. (I am speaking here only metaphorically. There is only one world, but the point is that the aliens' perception and conception of it would be completely different from ours.) Of course, we could neither know nor conceive of that world. From this it does not follow that there cannot be such a world. What does follow is that the only world that is knowable and conceivable by us is *our* world. This, as I suggested earlier, is really a tautology, but a useful (because explicative) one. We can conceive of *there being* a completely alien world, but we cannot conceive of *that* world. Many contemporary "antirealists" seem insufficiently aware of this distinction.

The skeptic may surprise us now by ascending to a *sixth* level and asking, How do we know that such an alien world is not the real world, that our world is not completely illusory? It is here that we need the support of the argument against the skeptic in chapter 4 with respect to what I have called the general question. The skeptical reasoning on the sixth level cannot be taken by the skeptic as a serious, professional, philosophical reasoning. For, though the reality of the external world is not now in question, its nature is sufficiently in question as to raise doubt concerning the existence in it of anything describable as (human) philosophers, books, articles, lectures, including now also scientists and our sciences, especially astronomy and biology, the existence of some of which must be presupposed even to make sense of the skeptic's reasoning on this sixth level. After all, we are engaging in what is really *scientific* speculation! (Alien beings *where*? Alien in what *respects*? What is a *galaxy*?) To be able to take his own reasoning seriously on the sixth level, the skeptic must at least implicitly presuppose that there are scientists, that he has read some of their works, or at least listened to them, that there are such things as perceptual, conceptual, and reasoning capacities and that for scientific, not just philosophical, reasons we must assume that they can be very varied, yet also truth-conducive if the skeptical question on the sixth level is to have a point at all. To take his skepticism seriously the skeptic must presuppose precisely what he questions, namely, the existence of a universe more or

less as described by *our* science. Only then can he make sense of his hypothesis of there being totally different intelligent beings presumably on another planet, perhaps in another galaxy, who know the world while we do not! So, to give a full answer to the skeptic's particular question, to answer it on the sixth level, we must appeal to the answer to the skeptic's general question, which I gave in chapter 4, and therefore cannot appeal only to the earlier considerations in this chapter. We need both.

The reader's uneasiness, which I mentioned in section 1 of this chapter, will almost certainly have remained. It is really over my endorsement, even though in a highly qualified and restricted form, of the assertion (associated with Goodman) that "we make the world ourselves." And the source of uneasiness is to be found in the reference to "ourselves." If we have a purely naturalistic, zoological understanding of what we are, that is, that we are just animals of a certain species that came into existence a million or so years ago and perhaps will go out of existence a million or so years from now, then the assertion is not just puzzling but deserving of no attention at all. But this is not how we must understand "ourselves." The proper understanding was already suggested, though not developed, in chapter 1, where I argued for regarding consciousness as sui generis and as having no inhabitants, especially not a "self" or "ego." I pointed out also that it cannot be understood in terms of any scientific, in particular neurological, theories. We are therefore led to understanding the assertion that we make the world ourselves as meaning that *consciousness* does this, and that the conceptual decisions that accomplish it are events "in" consciousness, not in any egos or brains.

In chapter 1 I associated the general direct realist conception of consciousness with Wittgenstein, Moore, Heidegger, and Sartre but without mention of what they said or might have said about its "making the world." Moore, of course, would not have ascribed such a function to consciousness, but Wittgenstein, Heidegger, and Sartre did, though only Sartre explicitly referred to *consciousness* as constituting the world. But Heidegger did not hesitate to ascribe to Dasein a world-constituting function, and while Dasein is not mere consciousness, its Being-in-the-World can hardly be understood except in terms of "its" consciousness, its "understanding."[14] In his later philosophy Wittgenstein seemed to attribute this function to language, but, contrary to what he often implies, language can hardly serve it except as an embodiment of consciousness.

The truth is that none of the philosophers I have mentioned, nor any of their predecessors in the history of philosophy, developed adequately the conception of ourselves needed for understanding the assertion that we make the world ourselves. I have referred to them here only because they all emphasized the special nature of "ourselves" and thus at least the possibility of such a conception. Both Sartre and Heidegger explicitly took their investigations, respectively, of consciousness and Dasein to be investigations of "human reality," and in his earlier as well as his later philosophy Wittgenstein was obviously concerned with *human* language (we

don't know of any other). None of the three considered himself to be engaged in zoology, to be investigating just features of a certain zoological species, even though sometimes Wittgenstein wrote as if he did. If Heidegger and Wittgenstein avoided the word "consciousness," the reason surely was just their desire not to be associated with others who had used it.

If the account in chapter 1 of consciousness as translucent, as no-thing, and in particular as containing no inhabitants, such as an ego or self, is even approximately adequate, then we can be confident that we do have, however imperfectly, the conception of ourselves needed to understand the assertion that we make the world ourselves, not of course by creating it but by our applications of the concepts of identity and reality to what we confront perceptually and conceptually. We may put this by saying that we make the worldliness of the world, not the world itself. And while we do so with the concepts of identity and reality, there are also the secondary transcendental concepts mentioned at the end of chapter 5, such as those of relation and state of affairs, which seem to correspond to nothing given to us in consciousness but without which we cannot engage in any *thought* or *language* about the world, even though the *worldliness* of the world is due solely to the application of the primary transcendental concepts of identity and existence.

Indeed, there is a *sense* even in which consciousness first makes the world nonconceptually. It may be said to do so by providing the starting point of most empirical judgments, namely, the objects of perception, whether these exist or not. (The question whether they do belongs to the conceptual level, as I have argued in this and the previous chapter.) What our world is obviously depends on, though by no means is entailed or exhausted by, what we perceive. But, as argued in the first chapter, perceptual consciousness is not a thing, whether a substance or a relation. It does its part in making the world by being just the revelation, the lightening, of the objects that are conceptualized as a world, somewhat as the coming of dawn reveals, lightens, bushes and rocks after the darkness of night. What we must guard against in saying this, however, is the supposition that the revealed objects were there even before revealed. There would be no sense in this supposition *or in its negation,* since what is revealed may not exist and therefore, as I argued in chapter 5, neither mind-independence nor mind-dependence can be ascribed to it. Yet in conceptually structuring the world we must work with what perception has revealed to us.

All this suggests that our assertion that we make the world ourselves might become clearer if we now focused on the notion of "world," rather than on the notion of "ourselves." If by ourselves we mean a contentless consciousness directly confronted with objects but involving no *self*, then the only conception of ourselves we can form is in terms of the world, the objects we perceptually and then conceptually confront; there is nothing more to ourselves that is relevant. As Sartre said, consciousness exhausts itself in its objects because it is nothing but the revelation of them. In one of his last philosophical statements, he also said: "Consciousness is out-

side; there is no 'within' of consciousness."[15] Or, as Heidegger had earlier held, Dasein is essentially the unveiling of things.

But it was Wittgenstein, in his early philosophy, who was especially incisive in describing, though only in a few cryptic remarks, the very special nature of ourselves, of the world, and of our relationship to the world. In the *Tractatus Logico-Philosophicus*[16] he wrote: "There is no such thing as the subject that thinks or entertains ideas" (5.6321); "The subject does not belong in the world: rather, it is a limit of the world" (5.632); "Here it can be seen that solipsism, when its implications are followed out strictly, coincides with pure realism. The self of solipsism shrinks to a point without extension, and there remains the reality co-ordinated with it" (5.64). What Wittgenstein exactly meant is hardly evident, but obviously he held that when we ponder "our" relationship to the world we must avoid simple-minded conceptions of ourselves and the world.

We can follow up and also go far beyond Wittgenstein's tantalizing statements as follows. The word "I" is an indexical, not a name or definite description. It is closely related to the indexicals "here" and "now." But there is also a fourth indexical to which it is related, that designates the characteristically cognitive (perceptual and conceptual) side of oneself, though that indexical has no simple expression in ordinary language. It is the conjunction of the phrases "so perceived" and "thus understood," though neither requires the other. (They are indexical because "so" and "thus" are indexical.) We can now say that these four (or five) indexicals refer to oneself, directly or indirectly, and a way of putting this that is consonant with the direct realist conception of consciousness is to say that they refer to a certain perceptual and conceptual perspective upon the world defined by a certain "point," a *standpoint*. This point is fixed by the world viewed from it, and the world viewed from it is fixed by that point. The point is not a constituent of the world, though it can be described only as a point from which the world is perceived and understood. This is why, and it is in this sense that, there cannot be a sharp distinction between the world and ourselves. Each must be understood in terms of the other. The "point" to which the "self" shrinks thus determines the "limit" of anything that is recognizable as the world. But to say, instead, "recognizable by me," would be redundant, since we have no other basic understanding of "recognizable." This is a way of expressing a sort of solipsism. But I am not a mental substance or a physical thing or *anything else* in the world, *there* is just the world, and to say this is to express pure realism.

Returning to the nonsolipsistic mode of expression, we can bring all this together by saying that the world can only be our world, since no genuine distinction between it and ourselves can be made. The assertion that we make the world ourselves can be understood as amounting to denying any such distinction, though in order to make sense this must be understood in accordance with the direct realist conception of consciousness and the transcendental conception of identity and existence. We describe the world as "ours" in order to reflect its essentially perspectival character, its being

essentially "viewed" from a standpoint, whether spatiotemporal or perceptual or intellectual, its being organized by, or as Wittgenstein says, coordinated with, that standpoint, its being the limit set on things by the standpoint. But the point, the *self*, is nothing in itself. It is just a center of reference. It is like a geometrical point in space, which is extensionless, dimensionless, but defines a perspective on extended things, organizes them in relation to itself, and is indispensable to our orientation toward them. Traces of this seemingly extravagant thought can easily be found in common sense and also have been explored by some recent philosophers, especially by P. F. Strawson.[17]

It is commonplace, for example, to speak of the child's world, the adult's world, the soldier's world, the academic's world, and so forth. Such phrases are not intended to mark portions of the world. They serve to distinguish the world as viewed from the standpoint of the child, from that of the adult, and so on. And now we can ask ourselves what conception of the world can we have that is not one from what we carelessly call the *human* standpoint? I use the word "carelessly" because "human" can be taken in its zoological sense rather than the one suggested by what I said earlier about "ourselves." But if understood in the latter sense, then the answer to the question is that we can have no such conception, no conception of the world that is not from the human standpoint, an answer that is really a tautology. This I take to be the point of Putnam's rejection of what he calls "metaphysical realism."

It is also the point of Strawson's denial that in an apparent clash between at least some conceptual schemes (e.g., between those of common sense and physical science in regard to the colors we see and the textures we feel) there is genuine contradiction. Although my concern here is not with what Husserl might have called "regional standpoints," with Strawson's "relativity of 'really's," what Strawson says about the latter is useful. For it makes clear the inseparability of the world from ourselves (and of ourselves from the world), even though the world differs in accordance with the standpoint (what I also called a "perspective") we take upon it. I have suggested that such a standpoint is nothing but our perceptual and conceptual location, which determines a world and of course is itself determined, fixed by that world. Strawson implies no such Wittgensteinean gloss of what he says, indeed he may reject it, but despite its conceptual relativism the suggestiveness of what he does say remains useful for the thesis I am sketching here.

There is no genuine contradiction, for example, between science and common sense about the reality of colors, Strawson says, because these seemingly irreconcilable views can be seen as relative to different "standpoints," to different standards of "the real," and thus the "really"s typically occurring in them as themselves being relative; the concepts (or at least some of them) employed in one scheme are different from those employed in the other, and we cannot separate the concepts from the subject matter and judge independently which concepts are faithful to the subject mat-

ter.[18] The subject matter is permeated by the concepts. To question this "might be an invitation to step outside the conceptual scheme which we actually have—and then to justify it from some extraneous point of vantage. But there is nowhere to step; there is no such extraneous point of vantage."[19] There is no "metaphysically absolute standpoint from which we can judge between the two standpoints."[20] And, speaking of Wittgenstein's remarks on aspect-seeing, he writes: "the visual experience is *irradiated* by, or *infused* with, the concept; or it becomes *soaked with the concept.*"[21] The "picture of a *concept-free* access to facts, to reality" is "confused and ultimately self-contradictory." "[Y]ou can have no cognitive contact with, hence no knowledge of, Reality which does not involve the forming a belief, making a judgment, deploying concepts."[22]

Both Putnam and Strawson take themselves to be rejecting Kantian things-in-themselves (indeed, Putnam seems to define "metaphysical realism" in terms of that rejection), but this is neither necessary for their views, nor sufficiently understanding of Kant, nor conducive to our understanding of *them*. Something like the Kantian view serves at least as the background against which alone we can grasp the fact that though we do not *create* the world, we can have no conception of it except as "our" world.

So, we come back to what I said in section 1 of this chapter. The initially incredible claim that we make the world ourselves can be seen as a consequence of what really are two tautologies, though perhaps only two ways of stating the same tautology. The first is that "we" have the very special status of being the perceivers and conceivers of the world we perceive and conceive. This is why we cannot identify ourselves with a part of the world so perceived or conceived, whether mental (an ego) or material (a zoological species). We cannot coherently think of ourselves as being *any* part of the world. The second is that the only world we perceive and conceive is a world perceived and conceived by us, even though there is no contradiction in supposing that the world ("the thing-in-itself") is completely different from how we perceive or conceive it.

How can a substantive view depend on tautologies? I repeat the answer I gave in section 1. We do not *want* our view to be substantive. It is intended to explicate certain concepts needed for our understanding the relationship between ourselves and the world. And concepts are explicated through tautologies, though ordinarily tautologies hidden from us by various pictures we have inherited and become enslaved by. The pictures especially relevant to our present topic and also especially pernicious are that of ourselves as being essentially souls ("egos," "selves") inhabiting bodies and that offered by the contemporary zoologist of ourselves being essentially brains. This is why the explication provided by our tautologies can be revealing, illuminating, and liberating.

We can see now that the question whether our second answer to skepticism about the external world, the answer to the particular question, involves idealism or irrealism is simplistic. It is not inappropriate. But nei-

ther can it be answered by saying Yes or by saying No. It should be evident that the answer provided in the last few pages is neither a Yes nor a No.

And this fits my general conclusion about skepticism about the external world. There is both the untruth and the truth of skepticism. What was suggested in the introduction to this book should have prepared us for such a conclusion. Skepticism cannot be refuted in a simple, familiar, straightforward manner. At most it can be answered. And even the answer to it cannot be simple, familiar, and straightforward. Is this satisfactory? I believe that a similar verdict would be appropriate for every genuine philosophical issue. This is what is distinctive about philosophy. It is also what makes philosophy challenging and exciting.

NOTES

Introduction

1. See Richard H. Popkin, *The History of Skepticism*, rev. ed. (New York: Harper and Row, 1968). That, contrary to the usual opinion, German idealism was not an exception, is argued convincingly by Michael N. Foster in *Hegel and Skepticism* (Cambridge: Harvard University Press, 1989).

2. Michael Williams, *Unnatural Doubts* (Cambridge, Mass.: Blackwell, 1991), xx.

3. Thompson Clarke, "The Legacy of Skepticism," *Journal of Philosophy* 69 (1972); Barry Stroud, *The Significance of Philosophical Skepticism* (Oxford: Clarendon Press, 1984); P. F. Strawson, *Scepticism and Naturalism* (New York: Columbia University Press, 1985); Bernard Williams, *Descartes: The Project of Pure Inquiry* (Harmondsworth: Pelican, 1978); Thomas Nagel, *The View from Nowhere* (New York: Oxford University Press, 1986).

4. *The View from Nowhere*, 125.

5. Psychiatrists might call this a symptom of "obsessive-compulsive disorder." For reports of such cases, which according to her exemplify what she calls "skepticism gone wild," see Judith L. Rapoport, "The Biology of Obsessions and Compulsions," *Scientific American* 260, 3 (March 1989): 82–89, and *The Boy Who Couldn't Stop Washing: The Experience and Treatment of Obsessive-Compulsive Disorder* (New York: Dutton, 1989).

6. *Scepticism and Naturalism*, 13. Strawson (mistakenly, in my opinion) attributes this view to Hume.

7. G. E. Moore, *Principia Ethica* (Cambridge: Cambridge University Press, 1971, originally published in 1903), 20.

8. Paul Ziff, *Epistemic Analysis* (Dordrecht: Reidel, 1984), 188. See also William P. Alston, *Epistemic Justification* (Ithaca, N.Y.: Cornell University Press, 1989), chap. 5 et passim.

9. William P. Alston, "Internalism and Externalism in Epistemology," *Philosophical Topics* 14 (1986), 196.

10. Hilary Putnam, *Realism and Reason: Philosophical Papers*, vol. 3 (Cambridge: Cambridge University Press, 1983), 199–204, 299–303, et passim; Richard Foley, *The Theory of Epistemic Rationality* (Cambridge: Harvard University Press, 1987).

11. A detailed and highly critical discussion of this terminological and conceptual chaos in contemporary epistemology can be found in William P. Alston,

Epistemic Justification, and in Alvin Plantinga, *Warrant: The Current Debate* (New York: Oxford University Press, 1993).

12. Michael Dummett, *Truth and Other Enigmas* (Cambridge: Harvard University Press, 1978), 438. The essay from which I have quoted was originally published in 1975.

13. *Origins of Analytical Philosophy* (Cambridge: Harvard University Press, 1993), 4.

14. Keith S. Donnellan, "Belief and the Identity of Reference," *Midwest Studies in Philosophy* 14 (1989): 283. Kripke's puzzle (see his "A Puzzle about Belief," in *Meaning and Use*, ed. Avishai Margalit [Dordrecht: Reidel, 1979]) was that a Frenchman may say that Londres est jolie and continue to believe this, even though when later he actually visits London he may say that London is not pretty, if he happens to not know that he is speaking of the same city. In chapter 5 I shall suggest the metaphysical distinction needed to resolve the "paradox." Donnellan himself does not attempt to do so.

15. Michael Dummett, *The Logical Basis of Metaphysics* (London: Duckworth, 1991), 214–15.

16. C. I. Lewis, "The Given Element in Empirical Knowledge," *Philosophical Review* 61 (1952): 175.

17. Roderick M. Chisholm, "On the Nature of Empirical Evidence," in *Empirical Knowledge: Readings from Contemporary Sources*, ed. Roderick M. Chisholm and Robert J. Swartz (Englewood Cliffs, N.J.: Prentice-Hall, 1973), 232.

18. Henry E. Kyburg, Jr., "Convention, Confirmation, and Credibility," in *Knowledge and Skepticism*, ed. Marjorie Clay and Keith Lehrer (Boulder: Westview Press, 1989), 110.

19. An example of innovative work on skepticism is Stewart Umphrey's *Zetetic Skepticism* (Wakefield, N.H.: Longwood Academic, 1990). This impressive book shows we need to be innovative not only in answering skepticism but also in our understanding of it and of its varieties.

20. Richard Foley, "Skepticism and Rationality," in *Doubting: Contemporary Perspectives on Skepticism*, ed. Michael D. Roth and Glenn Ross (Dordrecht: Kluwer, 1990) and *Working Without a Net* (New York: Oxford University Press, 1993), especially chap. 2.

21. Saint Augustine, *Against the Academicians*, trans. Sister Mary Patricia Garvey (Milwaukee: Marquette University Press, 1957), 69.

Chapter 1. Direct Realism

1. Sextus Empiricus, *Selections from the Major Writings on Scepticism, Man and God*, ed. Philip P. Hallie, trans. Sanford G. Etheridge (Indianapolis: Hackett, 1985), 149.

2. It is encouraging to find recent works by distinguished American philosophers who seem to agree: William P. Alston, "Externalist Theories of Perception," *Philosophy and Phenomenological Research* 50, supp. (Fall 1990); Reinhardt Grossmann, *The Fourth Way: A Theory of Knowledge* (Bloomington: Indiana University Press, 1990); and Hilary Putnam, "The Dewey Lectures 1994," *Journal of Philosophy* 91, 9 (September 1994).

3. H. H. Price, *Perception* (London: Methuen, 1932), 26–27 and chap. 6.

4. Ibid., 24–25.

5. A. J. Ayer, *The Foundations of Empirical Knowledge* (London: Macmillan, 1953), 21.

6. This conception of direct realism is very much like what Hilary Putnam interprets William James's theory of perception to have been. See Putnam, *Realism with a Human Face* (Cambridge: Harvard University Press, 1990), chap. 17, and "The Dewey Lectures."

7. J. J. C. Smart, "Materialism," *Journal of Philosophy* 60, 22 (October, 1964): 651–52.

8. We find even as astute a writer on the topic of skepticism as Barry Stroud saying about Descartes:" [T]he epistemic priority of ideas or appearances or perceptions over external physical objects has fatal consequences." *The Significance of Philosophical Scepticism* (Oxford: Clarendon Press, 1984), 255. The fact is that, though a representationalist, Descartes was not led to his provisional skepticism by presupposing "the epistemic priority" Stroud mentions. If the evil demon could deceive him about three and two being five, why should the demon not be able to deceive him about his having the ideas, et cetera, he took for granted he had?

9. In *Sensations: A Defense of Type Materialism* (Cambridge: Cambridge University Press, 1991), Christopher S. Hill admits that we are not aware of visual sensations but argues that "the laws of folk psychology" make reference to them and that folk psychology is a well-confirmed theory (191). Hill and I must have attended different schools of folk psychology! He is a type materialist, identifying types of sensations with types of brain events and the qualities of the former with qualities of the latter. He defends these identifications largely on grounds of ontological simplicity, but appears to regard the virtues of ontological simplicity as only aesthetic (40).

10. It is significant that Ryle had extensive knowledge of phenomenology. See his *Collected Works*, vol. 1 (New York: Barnes and Noble, 1971), chaps. 10, 11, 12, and 13. For example, he explicitly endorses Sartre's rejection of the view that "imagining is witnessing things occurring or existing inside a private chamber" (193).

11. G. E. Moore, "A Defense of Common Sense," in his *Philosophical Papers* (London: Allen and Unwin, 1959), 48. See also his "The Subject-Matter of Psychology," *Proceedings of the Aristotelian Society*, n.s., 10 (1910), especially 51–52.

12. David Armstrong, *Perception and the Physical World* (London: Routledge and Kegan Paul, 1961) and *A Materialist Theory of the Mind* (London: Routledge and Kegan Paul, 1968); George Pitcher, *A Theory of Perception* (Princeton: Princeton University Press, 1971).

13. Paul Ziff, *Epistemic Analysis* (Dordrecht: Reidel, 1984), 92. His quotation is from W. V. Quine and J. S. Ullian, *The Web of Belief* (New York: Random House, 1970), 3.

14. David Hume, *A Treatise of Human Nature*, ed. L. A. Selby-Bigge (Oxford: Clarendon Press, 1888), 86.

15. Immanuel Kant, *Critique of Pure Reason*, trans. Norman Kemp Smith, (London: Macmillan, 1950), A822/B850.

16. William G. Lycan, *Judgment and Justification* (Cambridge: Cambridge University Press, 1988), 57, n. 4. But Lycan's general orientation is quite different from mine.

17. P. F. Strawson, "Perception and Its Objects," included in *Perceptual*

Knowledge, ed. Jonathan Dancy (Oxford: Oxford University Press, 1988), 104–105, originally published in *Perception and Identity*, ed. G. McDonald (Ithaca, N.Y.: Cornell University Press, 1979). For a recent criticism of the view, see Paul Snowdon, "The Objects of Perceptual Experience," *Proceedings of the Aristotelian Society*, supp. vol. 64 (1990).

18. Putnam, "The Dewey Lectures," 455.

19. "The Causal Theory of Perception," *Proceedings of the Aristotelian Society*, supp. vol. 35 (1961).

20. An example of a philosopher who supposes this is Georges Dicker, in *Perceptual Knowledge: An Analytical and Historical Study* (Dordrecht: Reidel, 1980). See also Robert Audi, *Belief, Justification, and Knowledge* (Belmont, Calif.: Wadsworth, 1988); John Pollock, *Knowledge and Justification* (Princeton: Princeton University Press, 1974) and *Contemporary Theories of Knowledge* (Totowa, N.J.: Rowman and Littlefield, 1986).

21. Roderick M. Chisholm, "Self-Profile," in *Roderick M. Chisholm*, ed. Radu J. Bogdan (Dordrecht: Reidel, 1986), 3–77.

22. Roderick M. Chisholm, *Theory of Knowledge*, 3d ed. (Englewood Cliffs, N.J.: Prentice-Hall, 1989), 67.

23. Alvin Plantinga, *Warrant and Proper Function* (New York: Oxford University Press, 1993), 98.

24. Georges Dicker *seems* to hold such a view, in his *Perceptual Knowledge*.

25. G. F. Stout, "The Nature of Universals and Propositions," *Proceedings of the British Academy* 10 (1921–1922); D. C. Williams, "On the Elements of Being," *Review of Metaphysics* 7 (1953): 3–18, 171–92, in his *Principles of Empirical Realism* (Springfield, Ill.: Thomas, 1966), 74–109; Keith Campbell, *Abstract Particulars* (Oxford: Blackwell, 1990).

26. J. M. Hinton, *Experiences* (Oxford: Clarendon Press, 1973); John McDowell, "Criteria, Defeasibility, and Knowledge," *Proceedings of the British Academy* (London: Oxford University Press, 1983) 68: 455–79, reprinted with omissions and revisions in Dancy, *Perceptual Knowledge*; Paul Snowdon, "Experience, Vision, and Causation," also in Dancy, *Perceptual Knowledge*. See Snowdon's related "The Objects of Perceptual Experience" and "How to Interpret 'Direct Perception?'" in *The Contents of Experience*, ed. Tim Crane (Cambridge: Cambridge University Press, 1992) and McDowell's also related "Singular Thought and the Extent of Inner Space," in *Subject, Thought, and Context*, ed. Philip Pettit and John McDowell (Oxford: Clarendon Press, 1986) and his recent *Mind and World* (Cambridge: Harvard University Press, 1994). Two very useful discussions of the view are John Hyman, "The Causal Theory of Perception" and William Child, "Vision and Experience: The Causal Theory and the Disjunctive Conception," both in *Philosophical Quarterly* 42, 168 (July 1992). But, not surprisingly, the view closest to our direct realism is Richard Routley's in *Exploring Meinong's Jungle* (Canberra: Australian National University, 1980), chap. 8, sec. 10.

27. *Experiences*, 140. Quotation from "Sensation," in *Contemporary British Philosophy*, ed. H. D. Lewis, Third Series (London: Allen and Unwin, 1956), 443–44.

28. John McDowell, *Mind and World*, 111–13.

29. Compare Frank Jackson, *Perception* (Cambridge: Cambridge University Press, 1976), 72–77.

30. The most detailed philosophical discussion, known to me, of the other

senses is in Moreland Perkins, *Sensing the World* (Indianapolis: Hackett, 1983). Unfortunately, Perkins is an *indirect* realist.

31. It is the failure to make this distinction that gives rise to J. J. Valberg's puzzle about experience. See his nonetheless quite important book *The Puzzle of Experience* (Oxford: Clarendon Press, 1992).

32. For an excellent account of these ways to physicalism, see Arthur W. Collins, *The Nature of Mental Things* (Notre Dame: University of Notre Dame Press, 1987), especially the preface and chap. 1.

33. J. L. Mackie, *Logic and Knowledge: Selected Papers,* vol. 1 (Oxford: Clarendon Press, 1985), 133–34.

34. Ibid., 141.

35. On this general topic, P. M. S. Hacker, *Appearance and Reality* (Oxford: Blackwell, 1987), is especially instructive.

36. Ludwig Wittgenstein, *Philosophical Invesgitations,* trans. G. E. M. Anscombe (Oxford: Blackwell, 1953), 207.

37. Ibid., §304.

38. G. E. Moore, "The Refutation of Idealism," *Mind,* n.s. 12 (1903), included in *Philosophical Studies* (London: Routledge and Kegan Paul, 1922), 29. See also Moore's "The Subject Matter of Psychology" and "A Defense of Common Sense," the latter included in *Philosophical Papers.*

39. See "Some Judgments of Perception," in *Philosophical Studies,* and "A Defense of Common Sense," in *Philosophical Papers.* The extent to which Moore was attracted by direct realism is especially evident in his "Reply to my Critics," in *The Philosophy of G. E. Moore,* ed. P. A. Schilpp (La Salle, Ill.: Open Court, 1942), 627–53.

40. Martin Heidegger, *The Basic Problems of Phenomenology,* trans. Albert Hofstadter (Bloomington: Indiana University Press, 1982), 63–65.

41. Jean-Paul Sartre, *The Transcendence of the Ego,* trans. Forrest Williams and Robert Kirkpatrick (New York: Noonday Press, 1951), 93. But what about, say, pains? Sartre does not discuss this topic there, but the natural view, which I shall adopt, is that they too are objects of consciousness, not acts of consciousness, and therefore not intentional, albeit we must regard them as mental if we are not materialists. If so, Sartre would need to allow for such inhabitants of the mind, but they would not be inhabitants of consciousness. Indeed, he explicitly distinguishes between consciousness and what he calls the psychic, e.g., the ego and its states, which is an object of, transcendent to, consciousness, even though in philosophical English it would be called mental. For a discussion of this general topic, see Edmund Husserl, *Logical Investigations,* trans. J. N. Findlay (New York: Humanities Press, 1970), 552–53, 598–600. See also Laird Addis, "Pains and Other Secondary Mental Entities," *Philosophy and Phenomenological Research* 47:59–74, and *Natural Signs* (Philadelphia: Temple University Press, 1989), passim.

42. Jean-Paul Sartre, *Being and Nothingness,* trans. Hazel E. Barnes (New York: Philosophical Library, 1956), 618.

43. Maurice Merleau-Ponty, *Phenomenology of Perception,* trans. Colin Smith (London: Routledge and Kegan Paul, 1962), 3.

44. Hilary Putnam, *Realism and Reason: Philosophical Papers,* vol. 3 (Cambridge: Cambridge University Press, 1983), 14. See also his *Reason, Truth and History* (Cambridge: Cambridge University Press, 1981), chap. 1.

45. *Realism and Reason,* 15. J. J. Valberg is one of the very few recent Anglo-

American philosophers acknowledging the mysterious nature of consciousness without embracing physicalism (see his already cited *Puzzle of Experience*), probably because of his acquaintance with the continental tradition. John McDowell, in the works cited earlier, is another such philosopher. His book *Mind and World* contains a number of references to Hans-Georg Gadamer, though none to Husserl, Heidegger, or Sartre.

46. *Realism and Reason*, 211.

47. Putnam, "The Dewey Lectures," 456.

48. Sartre discusses the issue in *Being and Nothingness*, 331–39. See also note 41.

49. Husserl, *Logical Investigations*, 596.

50. See Russell's *Introduction to Mathematical Philosophy* (London: Allen and Unwin, 1919), where he writes:

> The notion of "existence" has several forms . . . but the fundamental form is that which is derived immediately from the notion of "sometimes true." We say that an argument a "satisfies" a function ϕx if ϕa is true. . . . Now if ϕx is sometimes true, we may say there are x's for which it is true, or we may say "arguments satisfying ϕx *exist*." This is the fundamental meaning of the word "existence" (164).

51. I have discussed this topic in detail in *Being Qua Being: A Theory of Identity, Existence, and Predication* (Bloomington: Indiana University Press, 1979).

52. See my *Resemblance and Identity: An Examination of the Problem of Universals* (Bloomington: Indiana University Press, 1966), and *Being Qua Being*. The reason I find the issue whether properties are universals or particulars, "tropes," which I discussed in detail in those books, inappropriate for discussion here is that the problem of universals, contrary to recent rather simplistic opinions, is not a matter of evaluating arguments, but of subtle appreciation of the degree to which the analogies in terms of which it must be understood are illuminating. To develop these analogies here would require far more space than would be appropriate in a book on skepticism about the external world.

53. I explore this option in *The Concept of Knowledge* (Evanston: Northwestern University Press, 1970), pt. 3, by arguing that the notion of a pure perceptual expanse can be derived from ordinary notions by analogy. For an argument against the possibility of such an explanation, and an extensive discussion of the concept of a surface, see Avrum Stroll, *Surfaces* (Minneapolis: University of Minnesota Press, 1988). However, in my opinion, Stroll is excessively impressed by some of the quirks of ordinary usage, for example, that we (allegedly) don't speak of the surfaces of plants, animals, and people.

54. Price, *Perception*; Jackson, *Perception*.

55. Price, *Perception*, 106.

56. Thompson Clarke, "Seeing Surfaces and Physical Objects," in *Philosophy in America*, ed. Max Black (Ithaca, N.Y.: Cornell University Press, 1965).

57. The physicalist may wish to ponder Sartre's extensively developed view of the relationship between consciousness and the body in *Being and Nothingness*, pt. 3, chap. 2. There Sartre speaks of consciousness *existing* its body (329 et passim). He also writes: "I *am* my body to the extent that I *am*" (326).

And his most notable translator, Hazel E. Barnes, has written of Sartre's *materialism* ("Sartre as Materialist," in *The Philosophy of Jean-Paul Sartre*, ed. P. A. Schilpp (La Salle, Ill.: Open Court, 1981).

58. In fact, there seems to be a great deal of evidence that consciousness is a notion indispensable for our scientific understanding of a variety of phenomena. For a useful review of the scientific literature, see Drakon Nikolinakos, "General Anesthesia, Consciousness, and the Skeptical Challenge," *Journal of Philosophy* 16, 2 (February 1994). Needless to say, the scientists who recognize this take for granted that some sort of physiological account of consciousness may still be given.

Chapter **2.** The Adverbial Theory

1. The theory achieved its prominence chiefly through the efforts of Wilfrid Sellars and Roderick M. Chisholm; indeed, it is an essential part of their philosophical views. But there are important differences between their versions of the theory. Moreover, the most extended exposition and defense of it are to be found in the earlier writings of C. J. Ducasse. For textual references to these philosophers, see hereafter. Even earlier, the main principle of the theory was defended by G. Dawes Hicks in his contribution to a symposium, with G. E. Moore, W. E. Johnson, J. A. Smith, and James Ward, on "Are the Materials of Sense Affections of the Mind?" *Proceedings of the Aristotelian Society*, n.s., 17 (1917): 418–58.

2. J. L. Austin, *Sense and Sensibilia* (Oxford: Clarendon Press, 1962).

3. Gilbert Ryle, "Ordinary Language," *Philosophical Review* 62 (1953): 167–86.

4. See also my *Being Qua Being: A Theory of Identity, Existence, and Predication* (Bloomington: Indiana University Press, 1979).

5. The classic exposition of the sense-datum theory is H. H. Price's, in *Perception* (London: Methuen, 1932).

6. See also my *Concept of Knowledge* (Evanston: Northwestern University Press, 1970), pt. 3.

7. See, for example, Wilfrid Sellars, "Ontology and the Philosophy of Mind in Russell," in *Bertrand Russell's Philosophy*, ed. George Nakhnikian (New York: Barnes and Noble, 1974), 97–98; Roderick M. Chisholm, *Person and Object* (La Salle, Ill.: Open Court, 1976), 203, n. 55, but contrast the doctrine in "Thought and Its Reference," *American Philosophical Quarterly* 14 (1977): 167–72. Both Chisholm and Sellars have discussed the topic in many of their other works, some of which I shall consider later, but what I say in this chapter about these philosophers should not be regarded as an attempt at complete exegesis.

8. Cf. J. L. Austin on "linguistic phenomenology" in "A Plea for Excuses," *Collected Papers* (Oxford: Oxford University Press, 1961), 130.

9. Cf. Wilfried Sellars, *Science and Metaphysics* (London: Routledge and Kegan Paul, 1968), chap. 1. But Sellars does not argue that the explanatory role of the postulated sense impressions requires that they be understood adverbially. His theory of sense impressions must not be confused with the "theory of sensa," which he imagines science adopting in the future.

10. Roderick M. Chisholm, *Perceiving: A Philosophical Study* (Ithaca, N.Y.: Cornell University Press, 1957), 122.

11. Roderick M. Chisholm, *Theory of Knowledge*, 2d ed. (Englewood Cliffs, N.J.: Prentice-Hall, 1977), p. 30.

12. Roderick M. Chisholm, *Theory of Knowledge*, 3d ed. (Englewood Cliffs, N.J.: Prentice-Hall, 1989), 19 (Chisholm's italics).

13. Sellars, *Science and Metaphysics*, 168.

14. P. F. Strawson, "On Referring," *Mind* 59 (1950): 320–44.

15. Chisholm, *Person and Object*, 49.

16. C. J. Ducasse, *Nature, Mind, and Death* (La Salle, Ill.: Open Court, 1951), 259.

17. Ibid., 264–65.

18. Chisholm, *Perceiving*, 127.

19. Herbert Heidelberger, review of C. J. Ducasse, *Truth, Knowledge, and Causation*, in *Journal of Philosophy* 70 (1973): 755–59.

20. See, for example, *Science and Metaphysics*, chap. 1; *Science, Perception, and Reality* (London: Routledge and Kegan Paul, 1963), 91–95; "The Adverbial Theory of the Objects of Sensation," *Metaphilosophy* 6 (1975): 144–60. For an argument against such transcategorial analogies see Bruce Aune, "Comments," and for a defense of them see Sellars, "Rejoinder," both in *Intentionality, Minds, and Perception*, ed. Hector-Neri Castañeda (Detroit: Wayne University Press, 1967).

21. Frank Jackson, "On The Adverbial Analysis of Visual Experience," *Metaphilosophy* 6 (1975): 27–35; "The Existence of Mental Objects," *American Philosophical Quarterly* 13 (1976); *Perception* (Cambridge: Cambridge University Press, 1977). See also Albert Casullo's important articles "Adverbial Theories of Sensing and the Many-Property Problem," *Philosophical Studies* 44 (1983), 143–60, and "A Defense of Sense-Data" (*Philosophy and Phenomenological Research* 48 (1987), 45–61.

22. See Sellars's reply to Jackson in "The Adverbial Theory of the Objects of Sensation."

23. Chisholm, *Person and Object*, 50.

24. Michael Tye, "The Adverbial Approach to Visual Experience," *Philosophical Review* 93 (April 1984); the quotations are from, respectively, 204, 219, and 222. Following the first quotation, Tye abandons talk about events, but this is irrelevant to my point. For an acute critical discussion of this article and of the adverbial theory of sensing generally, see Albert Casullo, "A Defense of Sense-Data." See also Casullo's earlier article, "Adverbial Theories of Sensing and the Many-Property Problem."

25. Romane Clark, "Objects of Consciousness: The Nonrelational Theory of Sensing," *Philosophical Perspectives* 1 (1987): 491.

26. J. L. Mackie, *Logic and Knowledge: Selected Papers*, vol. 1 (Oxford: Clarendon Press, 1985), 111.

27. "Reply to My Critics," in *The Philosophy of G. E. Moore*, 3d ed., ed. Paul Arthur Schilpp (La Salle, Ill.: Open Court, 1968), 659. Ducasse's view is defended in his "Moore's Refutation of Idealism," in the same volume. This edition also includes letters that Ducasse and Moore exchanged on the topic.

28. Letter from Ducasse to Moore, in Schilpp, *The Philosophy of G. E. Moore*, 687b.

29. Letter from Moore to Ducasse, in Schilpp, *The Philosophy of G. E. Moore*, 687h.

30. Letter from Ducasse to Moore, in Schilpp, *The Philosophy of G. E.*

Moore, 687k–687m. Ducasse develops this view in "Objectivity, Objective Reference, and Perception," *Philosophy and Phenomenological Research* 2 (1941): 43–78. See also *Nature, Mind, and Death*, 282–86, 304–53.

31. Ducasse, *Nature, Mind, and Death*, 284.

32. Cf. "The Structure of Knowledge," in *Action, Knowledge, and Reality*, ed. Hector-Neri Castañeda (Indianapolis: Bobbs-Merrill, 1975), 312.

33. Sellars, *Science and Metaphysics*, 22.

34. Reinhardt Grossmann, review of James W. Cornman, *Perception, Common Sense, and Science*, in *International Studies in Philosophy* 8 (1976): 210–13.

35. Romane Clark, "The Sensuous Content of Perception," in Castañeda, *Action, Knowledge, and Reality*, 121.

36. Compare G. N. A. Vesey, *Perception* (London: Macmillan, 1971), 11.

37. Roderick M. Chisholm, *Theory of Knowledge*, 1st ed. (Englewood Cliffs, N.J.: Prentice-Hall, 1966), 98. Compare Sellars, *Science and Metaphysics*, 24–27.

38. James Cornman, *Perception, Common Sense, and Science* (New Haven: Yale University Press, 1975), 75. But I find Cornman's own formulation, "In some cases, the sensing in a wing-of-a-hen way is also a sensing in a hen-way," no improvement over Chisholm's. In virtue of *what* is one sensing included in both of certain two classes of sensings while another sensing is included in only one of these classes?

39. Maurice Merleau-Ponty, *Phenomenology of Perception*, trans. Colin Smith (London: Routledge and Kegan Paul, 1962), 13.

40. Aron Gurwitsch, *The Field of Consciousness* (Pittsburgh: Duquesne University Press, 1964), 4–5.

41. O. R. Jones, "After-Images," *American Philosophical Quarterly* 9 (1972): 151–52.

42. Edmund Husserl, *The Phenomenology of Internal Time Consciousness*, trans. James S. Churchill (Bloomington: Indiana University Press, 1964), 149.

43. Edmund Husserl, *Cartesian Meditations*, trans. Dorion Cairns (The Hague: Nijhoff, 1960), 44.

44. Chisholm, *Perceiving*, 149.

45. Ibid., 197.

46. Roderick M. Chisholm, "Thought and Its Reference," *American Philosophical Quarterly* 14 (1977): 167–72. All quotations from this article are from 167–68. Compare Ducasse, "Objectivity, Objective Reference, and Perception."

47. "I say that I am acquainted with an object when I have a direct cognitive relation to that object, i.e., when I am directly aware of the object itself. When I speak of a cognitive relation here, I do not mean the sort of relation which constitutes judgment, but the sort which constitutes presentation." *Mysticism and Logic* (New York: Longmans, Green, 1917), 209.

48. Cf. Keith Donnellan, "Reference and Definite Descriptions," *Philosophical Review* 75 (1966): 281–304.

49. Chisholm, *Person and Object*, 30.

50. Ibid., 24–30. Also "Thought and Its Reference," 169.

51. Cf. William P. Alston, "Externalist Theories of Perception," *Philosophy and Phenomenological Research* 50, supp. (Fall 1990), especially 94–97.

52. Compare Sartre: "[I]t is sensation which I give as the basis of my knowledge of the external world. This basis could not be the foundation of a *real* con-

tact with things; it does not allow us to conceive of an intentional structure of the mind." *Being and Nothingness*, trans. Hazel E. Barnes (New York: Philosophical Library, 1956), 314. James Cornman was sensitive to this difficulty of the adverbial theory: "Somehow . . . we must combine the adverbial sensing theory of sense experience with the perceptual presentation view of compatible common-sense realism." He admitted that the statement "Each event of a person immediately perceiving a physical object, *p*, occurs when and only when some event of the person sensing occurs as a result of stimulus from *p* appropriately affecting him" expresses neither logical equivalence nor causal connection, and suggests that it expresses "a criteriological equivalence, and about that I am only able to say that it is like the relationship between right-making characteristics and being right" (*Perception, Common Sense, and Science*, 340–42). He was also sensitive to the implausibility of supposing that in veridical perception perceiving and sensing are two events, and suggests that they are contingently identical (342–43).

53. See Gilbert Ryle, *The Concept of Mind* (London: Hutchinson, 1949), 200–201, 240–44; Ryle, "Sensation," in *Contemporary British Philosophy*, 3d series, ed. H. D. Lewis (London: Allen and Unwin, 1956). At the end of the latter he acknowledges that we need some term to describe the "affinity" of "having an after-image and seeing a misprint." I suggest that the term needed becomes evident if instead of the idiomatic expression "having an after-image" we use the no less ordinary expression "seeing an after-image." That term is simply "seeing an object," not "sensation."

54. Sartre, *Being and Nothingness*, 314.

55. Merleau-Ponty, *Phenomenology of Perception*, 3.

56. William James, *The Principles of Psychology* (New York, H. Holt, 1890), 2:1. According to James, sensation differs from perception "only in the extreme simplicity of its object or content" (2).

57. Compare Sartre's theory of emotional consciousness in *The Emotions: Outline of a Theory*, trans. Bernard Frechtman (New York: Philosophical Library, 1948).

58. Sartre, *Being and Nothingness*, lxi.

59. See Sartre, *The Transcendence of the Ego*, trans. Forrest Williams and Robert Kirkpatrick (New York: Noonday Press, 1951). Compare G. E. Moore's important but neglected article, "The Subject-Matter of Psychology," *Proceedings of the Aristotelian Society*, n.s., 10 (1910), especially 51–55, and "A Defense of Common Sense," *Philosophical Papers* (London: Allen and Unwin, 1959).

60. In *Being and Nothingness* Sartre says: "If sight is not the sum of visual sensations, can it not be the system of seen objects?" (316).

61. I discuss some of these considerations in appendix B of *Being Qua Being*. See also Daniel Barwick, *Intentional Implications* (Lanham, Md: University Press of America, 1994).

Chapter 3. The Skeptic's Argument

1. Cf. H. H. Price, *Perception* (London: Methuen, 1932), 24–27 and chap. 6.

2. See my *Skepticism in Ethics* (Bloomington: Indiana University Press, 1989).

3. William P. Alston has often expressed concern over such confusions. See, for example, his "Two Levels of Epistemic Justification," in *Epistemic Justification* (Ithaca, N.Y.: Cornell University Press, 1989).

4. Paul K. Moser, *Philosophy after Objectivity* (New York: Oxford University Press, 1993), 43, n. 24. Moser's point concerns Alston's well-known argument that even though no doxastic practice can be justified without circularity, this does not entail skepticism since it is compatible with many beliefs being in fact justified, indeed constituting knowledge. See Alston's "A 'Doxastic Practice' Approach to Epistemology," in *Knowledge and Skepticism*, ed. Marjorie Clay and Keith Lehrer (Boulder: Westview Press, 1989), *The Reliability of Sense Perception* (Ithaca, N.Y.: Cornell University Press, 1993), and especially *Perceiving God* (Ithaca, N.Y.: Cornell University Press, 1991).

5. Moser, *Philosophy after Objectivity*, 70.

6. *Descartes: Selected Philosophical Writings*, trans. J. Cottingham, R. Stoothoff, and D. Murdoch (New York: Cambridge University Press, 1988).

7. On this, see E. M. Curley, *Descartes against the Skeptics* (Cambridge: Harvard University Press, 1978): 52–53.

8. Hilary Putnam, "The Dewey Lectures, 1994" *Journal of Philosophy* 91, 9 (September 1994): 470–71.

9. Norman Malcolm, *Dreaming* (London: Routledge and Kegan Paul, 1959). For a useful collection of essays concerned with, or anticipating, Malcolm's view, see Charles E. M. Dunlop, *Philosophical Essays on Dreaming* (Ithaca, N.Y.: Cornell University Press, 1977).

10. Hilary Putnam, *Reason, Truth, and History* (Cambridge: Cambridge University Press, 1981), 7, 16.

11. Robert Nozick, *Philosophical Explanations* (Cambridge: Cambridge University Press, 1981), 168–69.

12. Daniel C. Dennett, *Consciousness Explained* (Boston: Little, Brown, 1991), 3–7. For a response, which requires a very difficult distinction between the brain's virtual "world" and the evil scientists' "world," the deception being *perhaps* physically possible only in the latter, see Ian Ravenscroft, "Dennett's Combinatorial Explosion Argument against Brains in Vats," *Australasian Journal of Philosophy* 72 (June 1994).

13. Dennett, *Consciousness Explained*, 5.

14. That this is desirable is argued vigorously by Marie McGinn in *Sense and Certainty: A Dissolution of Scepticism* (Oxford: Blackwell, 1989).

15. See Paul K. Moser, *Empirical Justification* (Dordrecht: Reidel, 1985), 8, 41, 55; see also his *Knowledge and Evidence* (Cambridge: Cambridge University Press, 1989), 43. But Moser appeals to the perspectival character of justification in order to contrast it with truth, not with evidence. He explicates the notion of evidence in terms of the notion of justification, and for this reason regards it as being also perspectival.

16. Alvin Plantinga, *Warrant and Proper Function* (New York: Oxford University Press, 1993), 86.

17. William P. Alston has argued this point repeatedly in the essays collected in his *Epistemic Justification*. He allows, of course, for voluntarism with respect to actions that can be expected to result in the beliefs in question.

18. In *Knowledge and Evidence* (chap. 1), Paul Moser argues convincingly that epistemology should not be encumbered with normative notions, on the grounds that they are superfluous.

19. Richard Foley, *The Theory of Epistemic Rationality* (Cambridge: Harvard University Press, 1987), 159. See also 73, section 3.2, et passim.

20. Ibid., 167. In *Working without a Net* (New York: Oxford University Press, 1993), Foley distinguishes throughout between what he calls "the epistemology of knowledge" (i.e., epistemology as it has been traditionally understood, in accordance with the etymology of the word) and his own "egocentric epistemology," freely admitting the irrelevance of knowledge for the latter. (See, for example, 54.)

21. See my *Skepticism in Ethics*, 191 and chap. 9 passim.

22. Cf. Bertrand Russell, *Human Knowledge* (New York: Simon and Schuster, 1967), 214.

23. On this, see Barry Stroud, "Understanding Human Knowledge in General," in Clay and Lehrer, *Knowledge and Skepticism*, 44–49.

24. Moser, *Philosophy after Objectivity,* 44 et passim.

25. Simon Blackburn, *Essays in Quasi-Realism* (New York: Oxford University Press, 1993), 45.

26. This is a familiar point, argued persuasively, for example, by John McDowell, in *Mind and World* (Cambridge: Harvard University Press, 1994). McDowell does not make the distinction between epistemic foundation and the given that I have made. See also Evan Fales, *In Defense of the Given* (Lanham, Md.: Rowman and Littlefield, 1997), which is the most important recent contribution to the topic mentioned in its title.

27. John McDowell writes: "We do not need to say that we have what mere animals have, non-conceptual content, and we have something else as well, since we can conceptualize that content and they cannot. Instead we can say that we have what mere animals have, perceptual sensitivity to features of our environment, but we have it in a special [conceptualized] form." *Mind and World*, 64. McDowell devotes pages 114–26 to developing this claim. Whether he is right does not affect the argument of this book, but one must wonder how philosophers can be so certain about the psychology of animals.

28. Michael Williams would disagree, but I have been unable to identify exactly what his grounds are. See his *Unnatural Doubts* (Cambridge, Mass.: Blackwell, 1991).

29. For a useful discussion of these terms, see Richard Fumerton, "The Internalism/Externalism Controversy," *Philosophical Perspectives* 2 (1988), and especially his *Metaepistemology and Skepticism* (Lanham, Md.: Rowman and Littlefield, 1995). Detailed discussions may be found also in Alston, *Epistemic Justification*, and Robert Audi, *The Structure of Justification* (Cambridge: Cambridge University Press, 1993). I should mention that all three books are also impressive comprehensive treatments of a number of epistemological topics unrelated to skepticism.

30. Cf. Tom Rockmore, *Hegel's Circular Epistemology* (Bloomington: Indiana University Press, 1986).

31. Bertrand Russell reports having frequently dreamed that he had waken up, "in fact once, after ether, [I] dreamed it a hundred times in the course of one dream." (*Human Knowledge*, 171–72).

32. Bertrand Russell, *The Problems of Philosophy* (New York: Oxford University Press, 1959; originally published in 1912), 122.

33. That this is the root of skepticism is vigorously argued by Michael Williams in *Unnatural Doubts*, but for the purpose of showing its illegitimacy.

Williams's reasons largely rest on his claim that knowledge of the external world is not a natural kind and therefore cannot be *generally* contrasted with knowledge of experience. I have found his reasoning unpersuasive, partly because of the insufficiently explained or defended notion of a natural kind, partly because of my doubts, explained in chapter 1, about the notion of "experience."

34. Nozick, *Philosophical Explanations*, 204–11. For discussions of Nozick's view, see the useful essays in Steven Luper-Foy, ed., *The Possibility of Knowledge* (Totowa, N.J.: Rowman and Littlefield, 1987); Laurence BonJour's and Richard Fumerton's are especially relevant. Judicious discussions of the general topic may be found in Robert Audi, *Belief, Justification, and Knowledge* (Belmont, Calif.: Wadsworth, 1988), 76–78, and "Justification, Deductive Closure and Reasons to Believe," *Dialogue* 30 (1991): 77–84.

35. Compare Barry Stroud, *The Significance of Philosophical Skepticism* (Oxford: Clarendon Press, 1984), 43.

36. Williams, *Unnatural Doubts*.

37. Stroud, 24 et passim.

38. Moser, *Knowledge and Evidence*. In his more recent book *Philosophy after Objectivity*, Moser changes his position (see 47 et passim) and adopts in effect a far-ranging skepticism (which he calls "agnosticism"). This book is of great importance, and has much appeal for a recovering skeptic like me, but I believe its agnosticism can be answered in the manner I shall attempt to answer standard skepticism. I shall refer several times to *Knowledge and Evidence*, even though its author no longer subscribes to its main thesis, because of its independent merits.

39. William G. Lycan, *Judgment and Justification* (Cambridge: Cambridge University Press, 1988).

40. Laurence BonJour, *The Structure of Empirical Knowledge* (Cambridge: Harvard University Press, 1985), 179–88. For an extended recent criticism of BonJour's view and coherentism in general, see Alvin Plantinga, *Warrant: The Current Debate* (New York: Oxford University Press, 1993), chaps. 4, 5, 6, and 7.

41. Ibid., 186.

42. Evan Fales, *Causation and Universals* (London: Routledge, 1990), 42–43.

43. David Armstrong, *What Is a Law of Nature?* (Cambridge: Cambridge University Press, 1983), 73.

44. Bertrand Russell, *The Problems of Philosophy*, 24–25.

45. J. L. Austin, *Sense and Sensibilia* (Oxford: Clarendon Press, 1962), 48–49.

46. All three articles are included in G. E. Moore, *Philosophical Papers* (London: Allen and Unwin, 1959).

47. This seems to be also Roderick M. Chisholm's general "response" to the skeptic, in *Theory of Knowledge*, 3d ed. (Englewood Cliffs, N. J.: Prentice-Hall, 1989).

48. Ludwig Wittgenstein, *On Certainty*, ed. G. E. M. Anscombe and G. H. von Wright, trans. Denis Paul and G. E. M. Anscombe (New York and Evanston: J. and J. Harper, 1969), §383.

49. Ibid., 34e, §260.

50. Compare G. E. Moore, *Philosophical Studies* (London: Routledge and Kegan Paul, 1958), 228.

51. Anthony Kenny, *Descartes: A Study of His Philosophy* (New York: Random House, 1968), 30. For a thoroughgoing criticism of Wittgensteinean attempts to show the reliability of sense perception, see Alston, *The Reliability of Sense Perception*, chap. 3.

52. Ludwig Wittgenstein, *Philosophical Investigations*, trans. G. E. M. Anscombe, 3d ed. (New York: Macmillan: 1972), §242.

53. David Hume, *A Treatise of Human Nature*, ed. L. A. Selby-Bigge (Oxford: Clarendon Press, 1888, originally published 1739), 181.

54. John Cook Wilson, *Statement and Inference* (Oxford: Clarendon Press, 1926), 1: 100 et passim.

55. Simon Blackburn appeals to the notion of "being unable to make anything out of" something in his explanation of some modalities in *Essays in Quasi-Realism* (Oxford: Oxford University Press, 1993), 65–66, 68–70. I suggest that the notion has equally appropriate application to some nonmodal cases, such as one's being in severe pain. It is not clear to me that Blackburn would disagree.

56. For example, Henry E. Kyburg makes the following reasonable suggestion: "The set of incorrigibilia here is quite straightforward: it is the set of sentences inscribed (say) by responsible scientists in their notebooks. No responsible scientist would ever withdraw (erase) such an inscription. But no one would ever take it as *evidence* without a consideration of the possibility of its being in error." "Convention, Confirmation, and Credibility," in Clay and Lehrer, *Knowledge and Skepticism*, 107.

57. See *Epistemic Justification*, 255–57.

58. There is extensive discussion of the uses of "certainty," "certain," "for certain," "makes certain," and other related expressions in Alan R. White, *The Nature of Knowledge* (Totowa, N. J.: Rowman and Littlefield, 1982), a book deserving far more attention than it has received.

59. William P. Alston, *A Realist Theory of Truth* (Ithaca, N.Y.: Cornell University Press, 1996).

60. See Alston, "A 'Doxastic Practice' Approach to Epistemology." Alston does not mention unthinkability of mistake when he argues against there being a privileged doxastic practice. See also his *Reliability of Sense Perception* and *Perceiving God* for sustained arguments that the familiar epistemic defenses of any doxastic practice are all infected with circularity.

61. See my *Concept of Knowledge* (Evanston: Northwestern University Press, 1970) and *Skepticism in Ethics*.

62. This is the view I defend in *Skepticism in Ethics*. But the intrinsic goods I acknowledge there are not Mill's.

Chapter **4**. A First Answer to the Skeptic

1. Cf. Martin Heidegger, *Being and Time*, trans. John Macquarie and Edward Robinson (San Francisco: Harper and Row, 1962), 246.

2. Jean-Paul Sartre, *The Psychology of Imagination* (Secaucus, N.J.: Citadel Press, 1972), 9.

3. Jean-Paul Sartre, *Being and Nothingness*, trans. Hazel E. Barnes (New York: Philosophical Library, 1956), introduction, part 1. The Phenomenon.

4. See "Interview," in *The Philosophy of Jean-Paul Sartre*, ed. P. A. Schilpp (La Salle, Ill.: Open Court), 10.

5. Sartre, *Psychology of Imagination*, 231–55.

6. Stanley Cavell, *The Claim of Reason* (Oxford: Clarendon Press, 1979), 224; see also 51, 56. But Cavell's distinction is not intended to play the role mine does, nor is his view about skepticism at all like mine.

7. Richard A. Fumerton, *Metaphysical and Epistemological Problems of Perception* (Lincoln: University of Nebraska Press, 1985), 31. Fumerton is not a direct realist, however.

8. For a criticism, though along lines somewhat different from mine, of abductive attempts to show the reliability of sense perception, see William P. Alston, *The Reliability of Sense Perception* (Ithaca: Cornell University Press, 1993), chap. 4.

9. G. E. Moore, "The Refutation of Idealism," in *Philosophical Studies* (London: Routledge and Kegan Paul, 1922), 27.

10. Robert J. Fogelin, "The Tendency of Hume's Skepticism," in *The Skeptical Tradition*, ed. Miles Burnyeat (Berkeley: University of California Press, 1983).

11. Crispin Wright, "Scepticism and Dreaming: Imploding the Demon," *Mind* 100, 398 (January 1991): 87–115. (There is much more in this rich article, however, than I have mentioned.) In *Descartes: The Project of Pure Inquiry* (New York: Penguin Books, 1978), Bernard Williams claims that in a dream one cannot rationally tell anything, including therefore that one is dreaming (312). But I have been unable to discover his grounds for making this astounding claim.

12. Barry Stroud, *The Significance of Philosophical Skepticism* (Oxford: Clarendon Press, 1984).

13. G. E. Moore, "A Defense of Common Sense," in *Philosophical Papers* (London: Allen and Unwin, 1959). See especially 39–41.

14. I am indebted here to Robert Howell.

15. Bertrand Russell, *Human Knowledge* (New York: Simon and Schuster, 1967), 180.

16. A somewhat similar view has been defended by Peter Klein in "Epistemic Compatibilism and Canonical Beliefs" and criticized by Richard Feldman in "Klein on Certainty and Canonical Beliefs," both in *Doubting: Contemporary Perspectives on Skepticism*, ed. Michael D. Roth and Glenn Ross (Dordrecht: Kluwer, 1990).

17. Ludwig Wittgenstein, *On Certainty*, ed. G. E. M. Anscombe and G. H. von Wright, trans. Denis Paul and G. E. M. Anscombe (New York: J. J. Harper, 1969), §55.

Chapter 5. Our Concept of Reality

1. The locus classicus for these views is Alexius Meinong, "Über Gegenstandstheorie," in *Alexius Meinong Gesamtausgabe*, vol. 2, Rudolf Haller and Rudolf Kindinger in collaboration with Roderick M. Chisholm (Graz: Akademische Druck- und Verlangsanstalt, 1971); translated in *Realism and the Background of Phenomenology*, 2d ed., ed. Roderick M. Chisholm (New York: Free Press, 1967) as "The Theory of Objects."

2. Bertrand Russell, *Introduction to Mathematical Philosophy* (London: Allen and Unwin, 1919), 169–70. In "The Philosophy of Logical Atomism" (in *Logic and Knowledge*, ed. Robert Charles Marsh [London: Allen and Unwin,

1956], 223), Russell writes of "a vivid instinct as to what is real" and adds: "I think Meinong is rather deficient in just that instinct for reality." But in "On Denoting" (also in Marsh, *Logic and Knowledge*, 41–56), where Russell first proposed his theory of definite descriptions, he merely claimed that his theory solves "puzzles" that Meinong's and Frege's fail to solve (47).

3. *Introduction to Mathematical Philosophy*, 164.

4. G. E. Moore, "Is Existence a Predicate?" *Proceedings of the Aristotelian Society, supp. vol. 15* (1936), 185.

5. It is to be found also in Russell's "On Denoting," *Principia Mathematica* (Cambridge: University Press, 1910–13), and "The Philosophy of Logical Atomism."

6. Incidentally, this is why Russell should not be interpreted as espousing a substitutional interpretation of quantification. See Ruth Barcan Marcus, "Interpreting Quantification," *Inquiry* 5 (1962): 252–59. W. V. Quine is right when he writes: "dogged reading of Whitehead and Russell supports the objectual interpretation." *The Roots of Reference* (La Salle, Ill.: Open Court, 1974), 99.

7. In "On Denoting" Russell says: "With our theory of denoting, we are able to hold that there are no unreal individuals" (55). More recently, Quine answered the question "What has being?" by saying, "Everything." *From a Logical Point of View*, 2d ed. (New York: Harper, 1961), 1.

8. Roderick M. Chisholm, *The First Person* (Minneapolis: University of Minnesota Press, 1981), 9–10.

9. Gustav Bergmann, *Realism: A Critique of Brentano and Meinong* (Madison: University of Wisconsin Press, 1966), 3.

10. Ibid., 352; also 214–18 et passim.

11. Gustav Bergmann, "Sketch of an Ontological Inventory," *Journal of the British Society for Phenomenology* 10, 1 (January, 1979), 4. See also his posthumously published *New Foundations of Ontology* (Madison: University of Wisconsin Press, 1992).

12. Reinhardt Grossmann, *The Categorical Structure of the World* (Bloomington: Indiana University Press, 1983), 406–11.

13. Rudolf Carnap, "Empiricism, Semantics, and Ontology," in *Meaning and Necessity* (Chicago: University of Chicago Press, 1956), 206.

14. Immanuel Kant, *Critique of Pure Reason*, trans. Norman Kemp Smith, (London: Macmillan, 1950) A598/B626–A601/B629. For an illuminating discussion of this aspect of Kant's philosophy, see Hans Seigfried, "Kant's 'Spanish Bank Account': *Realität* and *Wirklichkeit*," in *Interpreting Kant*, ed. Moltke S. Gram (Iowa City: University of Iowa Press, 1982).

15. Alexius Meinong, "Über die Stellung der Gegenstandstheorie im System der Wissenschaften," in *Gesamtausgabe*, 5: 16–17.

16. For some reasons against admitting states of affairs, see my "States of Affairs," in *Roderick M. Chisholm*, ed. Radu Bogdan (Dordrecht: Reidel, 1986).

17. Roderick M. Chisholm, "Beyond Being and Nonbeing," in *Jenseits von Sein und Nichtsein*, ed. Rudolf Haller (Graz: Akademische Druck- und Verlagsanstalt, 1972), 31–32.

18. Meinong, "The Theory of Objects," 83.

19. Gottlob Frege, "On Sense and Reference," in *Translations from the Philosophical Writings of Gottlob Frege*, ed. Peter Geach and Max Black, 2d ed. (Oxford: Blackwell, 1970), 62.

20. Ibid., 62–63.

21. See my *Being Qua Being: A Theory of Identity, Existence, and Predication* (Bloomington: Indiana University Press, 1979). Among other books defending or discussing roughly Meinongian theses, Richard Routley's impressive *Exploring Meinong's Jungle* (interim ed., monograph no. 3, Philosophy Department, Australian National University, Canberra, 1980) stands out as taking seriously and discussing in detail the question, which I have argued all Meinongian and anti-Meinongian theories must take seriously, indeed begin with, namely, "What is it for an object to exist?" Following Meinong, he writes: "There are certain sorts of questions about [nonentities] that lack determinate answers. . . . In the case of entities we can go on to detail . . . further features, to find out in principle at least by further investigation much more about their independently possessed properties: their features are detailable and refinable" (727). His view is not incompatible with mine. But mine attempts to answer the further question, "Why are there such differences between nonentities and entities?" The reason is that, unlike nonentities, entities are indefinitely identifiable through informative, genuine, identity judgments. To investigate an object and discover in it new properties, we must be able to identify it, again and again and again. Dennis Bradford, in *The Concept of Existence* (Lanham, Md.: University Press of America, 1980) also takes seriously the question, "What is it for something to exist?" and offers a view sympathetic to mine. Terence Parsons, in *Nonexistent Objects* (New Haven: Yale University Press, 1980), does not discuss our question, but what he says suggests that he might hold a position similar to Routley's. Karel Lambert, in *Meinong and the Principle of Independence* (Cambridge: Cambridge University Press, 1983) also does not discuss it and says nothing that suggests to me how he might answer it. Neither does Charles Crittenden in *Unreality* (Ithaca, N. Y.: Cornell University Press, 1991), which is chiefly concerned with fictional discourse.

22. See *Hegel's Logic*, trans. William Wallace (Oxford: Clarendon Press, 1975), §115.

23. Ludwig Wittgenstein, *Philosophical Investigations*, trans. G. E. M. Anscombe, 3d ed. (Oxford: Blackwell, 1958), §215. Cf. *Tractatus Logico-Philosophicus,* trans. D. F. Pears and B. F. McGuinness (London: Routledge and Kegan Paul), 5.5303. Meinong seems to endorse a somewhat similar view. See *Gesamtausgabe*, 2: 130–36.

24. David Lewis, *On the Plurality of Worlds* (New York: Blackwell, 1986), 202.

25. Immanuel Kant, *Prolegomena to any Future Metaphysics*, trans. L. W. Beck (New York: Liberal Arts Press, 1950), 65.

26. But if existence is indefinite identifiability, how should we understand our judgment that a given entity *began to exist* at t_1 and *ceased to exist* at t_n? Surely, it would have been in principle identifiable both before t_1, for example, through scientific prediction, and after t_n, e.g., through scientific inferences from presently existing objects? The answer is that through whatever property or properties the entity is identified (bare particulars are, by definition, not identifiable), it could be identified as possessing them only from t_1 to t_n even though the identifications themselves could take place both before t_1 and after t_n indefinitely.

27. Bertrand Russell, *My Philosophical Development* (London: Allen and Unwin, 1959), 172–73. See also my *Being Qua Being*, appendix A, and "States of Affairs."

28. However, Gustav Bergmann has argued that we do. See his *New Foundations of Ontology* (Madison: University of Wisconsin Press, 1992).

29. I develop this explanation in detail in *Being Qua Being.*

Chapter **6.** The Untruth and the Truth of Skepticism

1. Nelson Goodman, *Ways of Worldmaking* (Indianapolis: Hackett, 1978), 15.

2. See Jean-Paul Sartre, *Imagination*, trans. Forrest Williams (Ann Arbor: University of Michigan Press, 1972), and *The Psychology of the Imagination* (Secaucus, N.J.: Citadel Press, 1972).

3. See appendix B of my *Being Qua Being: A Theory of Identity, Existence, and Predication* (Bloomington: Indiana University Press, 1979).

4. Derek Parfit, *Reasons and Persons* (Oxford: Oxford University Press, 1986).

5. Donald Davidson, "The Very Idea of a Conceptual Scheme," *Proceedings and Addresses of the American Philosophical Association* 47 (1974), 5–20.

6. See Reinhardt Grossmann, *The Fourth Way* (Bloomington: Indiana University Press, 1990); also, though from a very different perspective, P. M. S. Hacker, *Appearance and Reality* (Oxford: Blackwell, 1987).

7. Hilary Putnam, *Realism and Reason. Philosophical Papers, vol. 3* (Cambridge: Cambridge University Press, 1983), xvi.

8. H. H. Price, *Thinking and Experience* (London: Hutchinson, 1954).

9. Roderick M. Chisholm, *Theory of Knowledge*, 3d ed. (Englewood Cliffs, N.J.: Prentice-Hall, 1989), 24.

10. See Nelson Goodman, *Fact, Fiction, and Forecast*, 2d ed. (Indianapolis: Bobbs-Merrill, 1965), 74 et passim. Goodman is by far the clearest representative of the sort of global irrealism I have in mind in this paragraph. I have been using the term "linguisticism" instead of the more common term "nominalism" because Goodman reserves the latter for any view that is not committed to the existence of classes, even if it is committed to the existence of universals. See *The Structure of Appearance*, 2d ed. (Indianapolis: Bobbs-Merrill, 1966), 142–45. Even the term "linguisticism" is applicable to Goodman's general philosophy only in a very general sense, since for many years he has held that what he calls "symbol systems" need not be linguistic, that they could be, for example, notational or pictorial. See his more recent work, coauthored with Catherine Z. Elgin, *Reconceptions in Philosophy* (Indianapolis: Hackett, 1988), especially vii, 9, 11, 126–29, and 155–56. But he also does deny that "there is a ready made world beyond discourse" (154 et passim). My objection to linguisticism narrowly understood would also apply to any broader view that regards human cognition as essentially employing symbols.

11. This is a familiar point. See, for example, the essays in the collection *Reality, Representation, and Projection,* ed. John Haldane and Crispin Wright (New York: Oxford University Press, 1993).

12. See my *Skepticism in Ethics* (Bloomington: Indiana University Press, 1989).

13. Regarding my misgivings about the notion of a state of affairs, see my "States of Affairs," in *Roderick M. Chisholm*, ed. Radu J. Bogdan (Dordrecht: Reidel, 1986).

14. Sartre writes: "Heidegger endows human reality with a self-understanding which he defines as an 'ekstatic pro-ject' of its own possibilities. . . .

But how could there be an understanding which would not in itself be the consciousness (of) being understanding?" *Being and Nothingness*, trans. Hazel E. Barnes (New York: Philosophical Library, 1956), 73.

15. Jean-Paul Sartre, "Interview," in *The Philosophy of Jean-Paul Sartre*, ed. Paul Arthur Schilpp (La Salle, Ill.: Open Court, 1981), 11.

16. Ludwig Wittgenstein, *Tractatus Logico-Philosophicus*, trans. D. F. Pears and B. F. McGuinness (London: Routledge and Kegan Paul, 1972).

17. In addition to P. F. Strawson, to whom some attention will be devoted shortly, see Thomas Nagel, *The View from Nowhere* (New York: Oxford University Press, 1986). But neither would subscribe to the view I have been developing.

18. P. F. Strawson, *Scepticism and Naturalism* (New York: Columbia University Press, 1985), 45.

19. P. F. Strawson, *Analysis and Metaphysics* (Oxford: Oxford University Press, 1992), 64.

20. *Scepticism and Naturalism*, 38.

21. P. F. Strawson, "Imagination and Perception," in *Freedom and Resentment and Other Essays* (London: Methuen, 1974), 57.

22. *Analysis and Metaphysics*, p. 86.

INDEX

DISC
LIBRARY

BGSU Libraries
A11320001479

Utopianism and Communitarianism

Lyman Tower Sargent and Gregory Claeys, *Series Editors*

This series offers historical and contemporary analyses of utopian literature, communal studies, utopian social theory, broad themes such as the treatment of women in these traditions, and new editions of fictional works of lasting value for both a general and scholarly audience.

Other titles in the series include:

The Concept of Utopia. Ruth Levitas

Low Living and High Thinking at Modern Times, New York. Roger Wunderlich

The Southern Land, Known. Gabriel de Foigny; David Fausett, trans. and ed.

The Unpredictable Adventure: A Comedy of Woman's Independence. Claire Myers Spotswood Owens; Miriam Kalman Harris, ed.

Unveiling a Parallel. Alice Ilgenfritz Jones and Ella Merchant; Carol Kolmerten, ed.

Women, Family, and Utopia: Communal Experiments of the Shakers, the Oneida Community, and the Mormons. Lawrence Foster

Women in Spiritual and Communitarian Societies in the United States. Wendy E. Chmielewski, Louis J. Kern, and Marlyn Klee-Hartzell, eds.

Writing the New World: Imaginary Voyages and Utopias of the Great Southern Land. David Fausett

Utopian Episodes

was composed in 10 on 12 Century Schoolbook
on Digital Compugraphic equipment
by Metricomp;
with display type in Chisel Expanded
by Dix Type Inc.;
printed by sheet-fed offset on 50-pound, acid-free Eggshell Cream
and Smyth-sewn and bound over binder's boards in ICG Arrestox B
by Maple-Vail Book Manufacturing Group, Inc.;
with dust jackets printed in 2 colors
by Johnson City Publishing, Co.;
and published by
Syracuse University Press
Syracuse, New York 13244-5160